GO MATH!

Volume 1

Made in the United States
Text printed on 100%
recycled paper

Houghton Mifflin Harcourt

2017 Edition

Printed in the U.S.A.

ISBN 978-0-544-71060-3

15   0928   23 22

4500842439   D E F G

GO MATH!

Authors

Juli K. Dixon, Ph.D.
Professor, Mathematics Education
University of Central Florida
Orlando, Florida

Edward B. Burger, Ph.D.
President, Southwestern University
Georgetown, Texas

Steven J. Leinwand
Principal Research Analyst
American Institutes for
    Research (AIR)
Washington, D.C.

Contributor

Rena Petrello
Professor, Mathematics
Moorpark College
Moorpark, CA

Matthew R. Larson, Ph.D.
K-12 Curriculum Specialist for
    Mathematics
Lincoln Public Schools
Lincoln, Nebraska

Martha E. Sandoval-Martinez
Math Instructor
El Camino College
Torrance, California

English Language Learners Consultant

Elizabeth Jiménez
CEO, GEMAS Consulting
Professional Expert on English
    Learner Education
Bilingual Education and
    Dual Language
Pomona, California

Dear Students and Families,

Welcome to **Go Math!**, Grade 4! In this exciting mathematics program, there are hands-on activities to do and real-world problems to solve. Best of all, you will write your ideas and answers right in your book. In **Go Math!**, writing and drawing on the pages helps you think deeply about what you are learning, and you will really understand math!

By the way, all of the pages in your **Go Math!** book are made using recycled paper. We wanted you to know that you can Go Green with **Go Math!**

Sincerely,

The Authors

Made in the United States
Text printed on 100% recycled paper

VOLUME 1
Place Value and Operations with Whole Numbers

Big Idea Develop a conceptual understanding of multi-digit multiplication, and division, including addition and subtraction to one million. Develop factors, multiples, and number patterns.

 Project Food in Space 2

Big Idea

GO DIGITAL

Go online! Your math lessons are interactive. Use *i*Tools, Animated Math Models, the Multimedia *e*Glossary, and more.

Chapter 1 Overview

In this chapter, you will explore and discover answers to the following **Essential Questions**:

- How can you use place value to compare, add, subtract, and estimate with whole numbers?

- How do you compare and order whole numbers?

- What are some strategies you can use to round whole numbers?

- How is adding and subtracting 5- and 6-digit numbers similar to adding and subtracting 3-digit numbers?

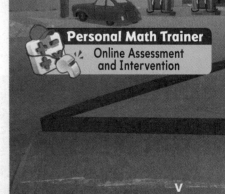

Personal Math Trainer
Online Assessment and Intervention

© Houghton Mifflin Harcourt Publishing Company

Divide by 1-Digit Numbers **195**

Chapter 4 Overview

In this chapter, you will explore and discover answers to the following **Essential Questions**:

• How can you divide by 1-digit numbers?
• How can you use remainders in division problems?
• How can you estimate quotients?
• How can you model division with a 1-digit divisor?

© Houghton Mifflin Harcourt Publishing Company

5 Factors, Multiples, and Patterns 277

VOLUME 2
Fractions and Decimals

Big Idea Develop a conceptual understanding of fraction equivalence and comparison. Use this understanding to add and subtract fractions with like denominators, to multiply fractions by whole numbers, and to relate fractions and decimals.

GO DIGITAL

Go online! Your math lessons are interactive. Use *i*Tools, Animated Math Models, the Multimedia *e*Glossary, and more.

Chapter 6 Overview

Essential Questions:
- What strategies can you use to compare fractions and write equivalent fractions?
- What models can help you compare and order fractions?
- How can you find equivalent fractions?
- How can you solve problems that involve fractions?

Chapter 7 Overview

Essential Questions:
- How do you add or subtract fractions that have the same denominator?
- Why do you add or subtract the numerators and not the denominators?
- Why do you rename mixed numbers when adding or subtracting fractions?
- How do you know that your sum or difference is reasonable?

Chapter 8 Overview

In this chapter, you will explore and discover answers to the following **Essential Questions**:

- How do you multiply fractions by whole numbers?
- How can you write a product of a whole number and a fraction as a product of a whole number and a unit fraction?

Practice and Homework

Lesson Check and Spiral Review in every lesson

Chapter 9 Overview

In this chapter, you will explore and discover answers to the following **Essential Questions**:

- How can you record decimal notation for fractions and compare decimal fractions?
- Why can you record tenths and hundredths as decimals and fractions?
- What are some different models you can use to find equivalent fractions?
- How can you compare decimal fractions?

Geometry, Measurement, and Data

Big Idea Develop a conceptual understanding that geometric figures can be analyzed and classified based on their properties, including angle measures. Develop relative sizes of measurement units and apply area and perimeter formulas for rectangles.

GO DIGITAL

Go online! Your math lessons are interactive. Use *i*Tools, Animated Math Models, the Multimedia *e*Glossary, and more.

Chapter 10 Overview

Essential Questions:
- How can you draw and identify lines and angles, and how can you classify shapes?
- What are the building blocks of geometry?
- How can you classify triangles and quadrilaterals?
- How do you recognize symmetry in a polygon?

Chapter 11 Overview

Essential Questions:
- How can you measure angles and solve problems involving angle measures?
- How can you use fractions and degrees to understand angle measures?
- How can you use a protractor to measure and classify angles?
- How can equations help you find the measurement of an angle?

Big Idea

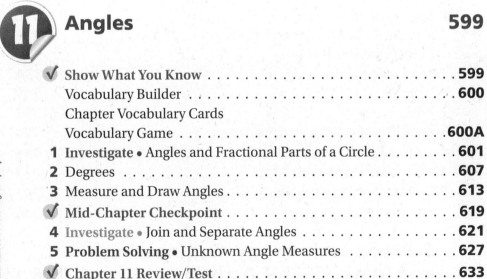

© Houghton Mifflin Harcourt Publishing Company

xii

Place Value and Operations with Whole Numbers

BIG IDEA Develop a conceptual understanding of multidigit multiplication and division, including addition and subtraction to one million. Develop factors, multiples, and number patterns.

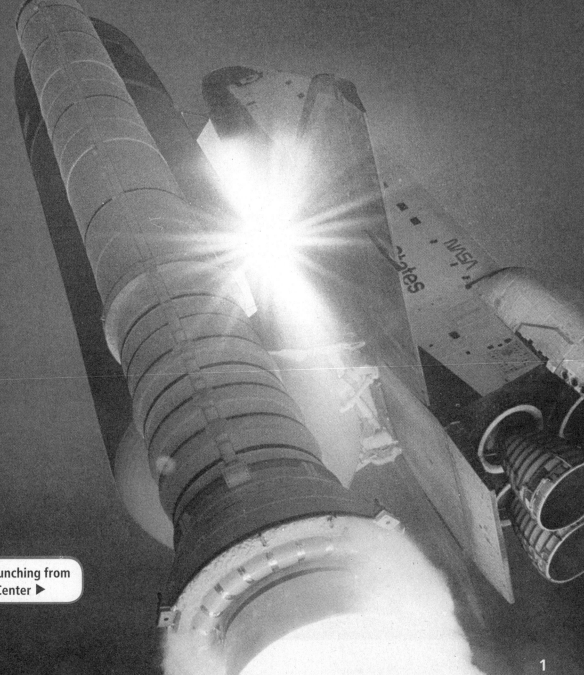

Space Shuttle launching from Kennedy Space Center ▶

Food in Space

The United States is planning a manned mission to Mars. The crew must take all of its food along on the journey, because there is no food available on Mars.

Get Started

Work with a partner. You are in charge of planning the amount of food needed for the Mars mission. Decide how much food will be needed for the entire trip. Use the Important Facts to help you plan. **Explain** your thinking.

Important Facts

- Length of trip to Mars: 6 months
- Length of stay on Mars: 6 months
- Length of return trip to Earth: 6 months
- Number of astronauts: 6
- 2 cups of water weigh 1 pound.
- 1 month = 30 days (on average).
- Each astronaut needs 10 cups of water and 4 pounds of food each day.

_____

_____

_____

_____

_____

_____

_____

_____

_____

_____

_____

Completed by _____

Chapter 1
Place Value, Addition, and Subtraction to One Million

 Show What You Know

 **Personal Math Trainer**
Online Assessment and Intervention

Check your understanding of important skills.

Name _____

▶ **Tens and Ones** Write the missing numbers.

1. 27 = _____ tens _____ ones

2. 93 = _____ tens _____ ones

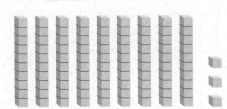

▶ **Regroup Hundreds as Tens** Regroup. Write the missing numbers.

3. 5 hundreds 4 tens = _____ tens

4. 8 hundreds 9 tens = _____ tens

▶ **Two-Digit Addition and Subtraction** Add or subtract.

5.   27
      + 34

6.   95
      + 46

7.   84
      − 27

 **Math in the Real World**

The home stadium of the Philadelphia Phillies is a large baseball park in Philadelphia, PA. Use the following clues to find the stadium's maximum capacity.

- The 5-digit number has a 4 in the greatest place-value position and a 1 in the least place-value position.
- The digit in the thousands place has a value of 3,000.
- The digit in the hundreds place is twice the digit in the thousands place.
- There is a 5 in the tens place.

Vocabulary Builder

▶ **Visualize It** •••••••••••••••••••••••••••••••••

Write the review words with a ✓ on the Word Line, from greatest to least place value.

Place Value

greatest
| _____

_____

_____

_____

least
| _____

▶ **Understand Vocabulary** •••••••••••••••••••••••••••••

Read the definition. Which word does it describe?

1. To replace a number with another number that tells about how

   many or how much _____

2. A way to write numbers by showing the value of each digit

   _____

3. A number close to an exact amount _____

4. Each group of three digits separated by commas in a

   multi-digit number _____

5. A way to write numbers by using the digits 0–9, with each digit

   having a place value _____

© Houghton Mifflin Harcourt Publishing Company

4

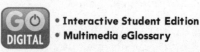

- **Interactive Student Edition**
- **Multimedia eGlossary**

Chapter 1 Vocabulary

estimate (*noun*)

estimación

31

expanded form

forma desarrollada

32

inverse operations

operaciones inversas

43

period

período

65

round

redondear

82

standard form

forma normal

87

thousands

miles

91

word form

en palabras

97

A way to write numbers by showing the value of each digit

Example: 253 = 200 + 50 + 3

A number that is close to an exact amount. An estimate tells about how much or about how many

Each group of three digits in a multi-digit number; periods are usually separated by commas or spaces

Example: 85,643,900 has three periods.

Period			Period		
hundred thousands	ten thousands	thousands	hundreds	tens	ones

Operations that undo each other, such as addition and subtraction or multiplication and division

Example: 6 × 8 = 48 and 48 ÷ 6 = 8

A way to write numbers by using the digits 0-9, with each digit having a place value

Example: 3,450 ⟵ standard form

To replace a number with another number that tells about how many or how much

A way to write numbers by using words

Example: Four hundred fifty-three thousand, two hundred twelve

The period after the ones period in the base-ten number system

Period			Period		
hundred thousands	ten thousands	thousands	hundreds	tens	ones

Going to Space

© Houghton Mifflin Harcourt Publishing Company • Image Credits: (bg) ©Datacraft Co Ltd/Getty Images; (b) ©Corbis

Word Box
- estimate
- expanded form
- inverse operations
- period
- round
- standard form
- thousands
- word form

For 2 players

Materials
- 1 red playing piece
- 1 blue playing piece
- Clue Cards
- 1 number cube

How to Play

1. Put your playing piece on START.
2. Toss the number cube, and move that many spaces.
3. If you land on one of these spaces:

   Blue Space Follow the directions.

   Red Space Take a Clue Card from the pile. Read the question. If you answer correctly, keep the card. If you do not, return the card to the bottom of the pile.
4. Collect at least 5 Clue Cards. Move around the track as many times as you need to.
5. When you have 5 Clue Cards, follow the closest center path to reach FINISH. You must reach FINISH by exact count.
6. The first player to reach FINISH wins.

TAKE A
CLUE CARD

Rockets have
turbo-boost!
Move ahead 1.

TAKE A
CLUE CARD

FINISH

Bad weather
delays launch.
Go back 1.

Engines need repair.
Go back 1.

TAKE A
CLUE CARD

FINISH

Launch is
a go!
Move ahead 1.

START ▶

TAKE A
CLUE CARD

The Write Way

Reflect

Choose one idea. Write about it in the space below.

- Describe how to write a three-digit number in three different ways.

- Is 44,000 a good estimate of 43,986? Explain how you know.

- Explain and illustrate two ways to round numbers.

Name _____

Model Place Value Relationships

Essential Question How can you describe the value of a digit?

Learning Objective You will model and describe the value of a digit using place value relationships.

🔑 Unlock the Problem

🔑 Activity Build numbers through 10,000.

Materials ■ base-ten blocks

1	10	100	1,000	10,000

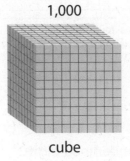

?

cube	long	flat	cube	_____
1	10 ones	_____ tens	_____ hundreds	_____ thousands

A small cube represents 1.

_____ small cubes make a long. The long represents _____.

_____ longs make a flat. The flat represents _____.

_____ flats make a large cube. The large cube represents _____.

---

1. Describe a pattern in the shapes of the models. What will be the shape of the model for 10,000?

   _____

   _____

   _____

Math Talk

Math Processes and Practices ⑤

Model What other type of base-ten block could you use to model 100,000?

2. Describe a pattern you see in the sizes of the models. How will the size of the model for 100,000 compare to the size of the model for 10,000?

   _____

   _____

   _____

Value of a Digit The value of a digit depends on its place-value position in the number. A place-value chart can help you understand the value of each digit in a number. The value of each place is 10 times the value of the place to the right.

 Write 894,613 in the chart. Find the value of the digit 9.

MILLIONS			THOUSANDS			ONES		
Hundreds	Tens	Ones	Hundreds	Tens	Ones	Hundreds	Tens	Ones
			8 hundred thousands	9 ten thousands	4 thousands	6 hundreds	1 ten	3 ones
			800,000	90,000	4,000	600	10	3

The value of the digit 9 is 9 ten thousands, or _____.

 Compare the values of the underlined digits.

2,<u>3</u>04   16,1<u>3</u>5

STEP 1 Find the value of 3 in 2,304.

Show 2,304 in a place-value chart.

THOUSANDS			ONES		
Hundreds	Tens	Ones	Hundreds	Tens	Ones

Think: The value of the digit 3 is _____.

Math Talk

Math Processes and Practices 6

Describe how you can compare the values of the digits without drawing a model.

Model the value of the digit 3.

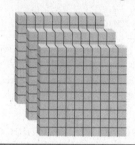

STEP 2 Find the value of 3 in 16,135.

Show 16,135 in a place-value chart.

THOUSANDS			ONES		
Hundreds	Tens	Ones	Hundreds	Tens	Ones

Think: The value of the digit 3 is _____.

Model the value of the digit 3.

Each hundred is 10 times as many as 10, so 3 hundreds is ten times as many as 3 tens.

So, the value of 3 in 2,304 is _____ times the value of 3 in 16,135.

Name _____

1. Complete the table below.

Number	1,000,000	100,000	10,000	1,000	100	10	1
Model	?	?	?				
Shape				cube	flat	long	cube
Group				10 hundreds	10 tens	10 ones	1 one

Find the value of the underlined digit.

2. 7̲03,890

3. 63,5̲40

4. 18̲2,034

✓ **5.** 345̲,890

_____ _____ _____ _____

Compare the values of the underlined digits.

6. 2̲,000 and 2̲00

The value of 2 in _____ is _____

times the value of 2 in _____ .

✓ **7.** 4̲0 and 4̲00

The value of 4 in _____ is _____

times the value of 4 in _____ .

Find the value of the underlined digit.

8. 2̲30,001

9. 80̲3,040

10. 46,84̲2

11. 9̲80,650

_____ _____ _____ _____

12. Greg has collected 4,385 pennies and Hannah has collected 3,899 pennies. How many times as great as the value of 3 in 4,385 is the value of 3 in 3,899?

_____

13. GO DEEPER Shawn wants to model the number 13,450 using base-ten blocks. How many large cubes, flats, and longs does he need to model the number?

_____

Problem Solving · Applications

Use the table for 14.

14. **GO DEEPER** What is the value of the digit 7 in the population of Memphis? What is the value of the digit 1 in the population of Denver? How many times as great as the value of the digit 1 in the population of Cleveland is this value?

_____

15. **THINK SMARTER** How many models of 100 do you need to model 3,200? Explain.

_____

_____

| City Populations ||
City	Population*
Cleveland	431,369
Denver	610,345
Memphis	676,640
*2009 U. S. Census Bureau Estimation	

16. **Math Processes and Practices ⑥** Sid wrote 541,309 on his paper. Using numbers and words, **explain** how the number would change if he exchanged the digits in the hundred thousands and tens places.

_____

_____

_____

_____

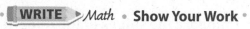

WRITE ▸ *Math* · **Show Your Work**

17. **THINK SMARTER** For numbers 17a–17e, select True or False for each statement.

17a. The value of 7 in 375,081 is 7,000.   ○ True   ○ False

17b. The value of 6 in 269,480 is 600,000.   ○ True   ○ False

17c. The value of 5 in 427,593 is 500.   ○ True   ○ False

17d. The value of 1 in 375,081 is 10.   ○ True   ○ False

17e. The value of 4 in 943,268 is 40,000.   ○ True   ○ False

Name _____

Model Place Value Relationships

Learning Objective You will model and describe the value of a digit using place value relationships.

Find the value of the underlined digit.

1. 6,0<u>3</u>5   **2.** 43,<u>7</u>82   **3.** 506,08<u>7</u>   **4.** 4<u>9</u>,254

_____   _____   _____   _____

5. 1<u>3</u>6,422   **6.** 673,<u>5</u>12   **7.** <u>8</u>14,295   **8.** 73<u>6</u>,144

_____   _____   _____   _____

Compare the values of the underlined digits.

9. 6,<u>3</u>00 and 5<u>3</u>0

The value of 3 in _____ is _____ times

the value of 3 in _____ .

10. <u>2</u>,783 and 7,<u>2</u>83

The value of 2 in _____ is _____ times

the value of 2 in _____ .

Problem Solving Real World

Use the table for 11–12.

11. What is the value of the digit 9 in the attendance at the Redskins vs. Titans game?

_____

12. The attendance at which game has a 7 in the ten thousands place?

_____

Football Game Attendance	
Game	**Attendance**
Redskins vs. Titans	69,143
Ravens vs. Panthers	73,021
Patriots vs. Colts	68,756

13. **WRITE** ▸ *Math* How does a digit in the ten thousands place compare to a digit in the thousands place?

_____

_____

_____

Lesson Check

1. During one season, a total of 453,193 people attended a baseball team's games. What is the value of the digit 5 in the number of people?

_____

_____

2. Hal forgot the number of people at the basketball game. He does remember that the number had four digits and a 3 in the tens place. Write a number that Hal could be thinking of.

_____

_____

Spiral Review

3. Hot dog buns come in packages of 8. For the school picnic, Mr. Spencer bought 30 packages of hot dog buns. How many hot dog buns did he buy?

_____

4. There are 8 students on the minibus. Five of the students are boys. What fraction of the students are boys?

_____

5. The clock below shows the time when Amber leaves home for school. At what time does Amber leave home?

6. Jeremy drew a polygon with four right angles and four sides with the same length.

_____

_____

FOR MORE PRACTICE
GO TO THE
Personal Math Trainer

Name _____

Read and Write Numbers

Essential Question How can you read and write numbers through hundred thousands?

Learning Objective You will read and write whole numbers through hundred thousands.

Unlock the Problem

The International Space Station uses 262,400 solar cells to change sunlight to electricity.

Write 262,400 in standard form, word form, and expanded form.

 Use a place-value chart.

Each group of three digits separated by a comma is called a **period**. Each period has hundreds, tens, and ones. The greatest place-value position in the thousands period is hundred thousands.

Write 262,400 in the place-value chart below.

PERIOD			PERIOD		
THOUSANDS			**ONES**		
Hundreds	Tens	Ones	Hundreds	Tens	Ones

The number 262,400 has two periods, thousands and ones.

Standard Form: 262,400

Word Form: two hundred sixty-two thousand, four hundred

Expanded Form: 200,000 + 60,000 + 2,000 + 400

Math Talk

Math Processes and Practices ⑦

Look for Structure How can you use a place value chart to find which digit in a number has the greatest value?

Try This! Use place value to read and write numbers.

Ⓐ Standard Form: _____

Word Form: ninety-two thousand, one hundred seventy

Expanded Form:

90,000 + 2,000 + _____ + 70

Ⓑ Standard Form: 200,007

Word Form:

two hundred _____, _____

Expanded Form:

_____ + 7

1. How can you use place value and period names to read and write 324,904 in word form?

_____

_____

_____

Read and write the number in two other forms.

2. four hundred eight thousand, seventeen

_____

_____

3. 65,058

_____

_____

Math Talk **Math Processes and Practices ②**

Symbols and Words
Explain how you can use the expanded form of a number to write the number in standard form.

On Your Own

Read and write the number in two other forms.

4. five hundred eight thousand

_____

5. forty thousand, six hundred nineteen

_____

6. 570,020

_____

_____

7. $400,000 + 60,000 + 5,000 + 100$

_____

_____

8. **THINK SMARTER** During the week of the county fair, fifteen thousand, six hundred nine entry tickets were sold. Is it correct to write the number as 15,069? Explain.

_____

_____

9. **GO DEEPER** There were 94,172 people at a football game on Saturday. On Monday, 1,000 fewer people were at a football game. In word form, how many people were at the football game on Monday?

_____

_____

10. Richard got 263,148 hits when he did an Internet search. What is the value of the digit 6 in this number? Explain.

_____

11. **THINK SMARTER** Yvonne wrote the numbers sixteen thousand, nine hundred eighteen and 64,704 on the board. Which of the numbers has a greater value in the thousands place?

_____

12. **GO DEEPER** Matthew found the sum of 3 thousands 4 hundreds 3 tens 1 one + 4 thousands 8 hundreds 3 tens 5 ones. Victoria found the sum of 5 thousands 7 hundreds 4 ones + 3 thousands 2 hundreds 3 tens 1 one. Who had the greater sum? What was the greater sum?

_____

Problem Solving • Applications

Use the table for 13–15.

13. **Math Processes and Practices ④** **Use Graphs** Which city has a population of two hundred fifty-five thousand, one hundred twenty-four?

_____

14. Write the population of Raleigh in expanded form and word form.

_____

_____

Major Cities in North Carolina	
City	Population*
Durham	229,171
Greensboro	255,124
Raleigh	405,612

*U.S. Census Bureau 2008 Estimated Population

15. **THINK SMARTER** **What's the Error?** Sophia said that the expanded form for 605,970 is 600,000 + 50,000 + 900 + 70. Describe Sophia's error and give the correct answer.

_____

_____

_____

Unlock the Problem

16. **GO DEEPER** Mark tossed six balls while playing a number game. Three balls landed in one section, and three balls landed in another section. His score is greater than one hundred thousand. What could his score be?

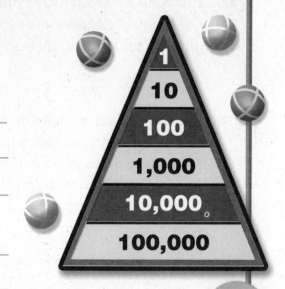

a. What do you know? _____

_____

_____

b. How can you use what you know about place value

to find what Mark's score could be? _____

_____

_____

_____

_____

_____

c. Draw a diagram to show one way to solve the problem.

d. Complete the sentences.

Three balls could have landed in the

_____ section.

Three balls could have landed in the

_____ section.

Mark's score could be _____

_____.

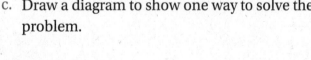

17. **THINK SMARTER** What is another way to write 615,004? Mark all that apply.

(A) six hundred fifteen thousand, four

(B) six hundred five thousand, fourteen

(C) 60,000 + 10,000 + 5,000 + 4

(D) 600,000 + 10,000 + 5,000 + 4

Read and Write Numbers

Learning Objective You will read and write whole numbers through hundred thousands.

Read and write the number in two other forms.

1. six hundred ninety-two thousand, four

standard form: 692,004;

expanded form: 600,000 +

90,000 + 2,000 + 4

_____

2. 314,207

_____

_____

_____

3. 600,000 +
80,000 + 10

_____

_____

_____

Use the number 913,256.

4. Write the name of the period that has the digits 913.

_____

5. Write the digit in the ten thousands place.

_____

6. Write the value of the digit 9.

_____

Problem Solving Real World

Use the table for 7 and 8.

Population in 2008

State	Population
Alaska	686,293
South Dakota	804,194
Wyoming	532,668

7. Which state had a population of eight hundred four thousand, one hundred ninety-four?

_____

8. What is the value of the digit 8 in Alaska's population?

_____

9. **WRITE** ▸*Math* Is *70 thousand* written in standard form or word form? Explain.

_____

_____

_____

Lesson Check

1. Based on a 2008 study, children 6–11 years old spend sixty-nine thousand, one hundred eight minutes a year watching television. What is this number written in standard form?

_____

2. What is the value of the digit 4 in the number 84,230?

_____

Spiral Review

3. An ant has 6 legs. How many legs do 8 ants have?

_____

4. Latricia's vacation is in 4 weeks. There are 7 days in a week. How many days is it until Latricia's vacation?

_____

5. Marta collected 363 cans. Diego collected 295 cans. How many cans did Marta and Diego collect?

_____

6. The city Tim lives in has 106,534 people. What is the value of the 6 in 106,534?

_____

FOR MORE PRACTICE
GO TO THE
Personal Math Trainer

Compare and Order Numbers

Essential Question How can you compare and order numbers?

Learning Objective You will compare and order whole numbers based on the values of the digits in each number using >, =, and < symbols.

Unlock the Problem

Grand Canyon National Park in Arizona had 651,028 visitors in July 2008 and 665,188 visitors in July 2009. In which year did the park have more visitors during the month of July?

- How many visitors were there in July 2008?

  _____

- How many visitors were there in July 2009?

  _____

Example 1 Use a place-value chart.

You can use a place-value chart to line up the digits by place value. Line up the ones with the ones, the tens with the tens, and so on. Compare 651,028 and 665,188.

Write 651,028 and 665,188 in the place-value chart below.

THOUSANDS			ONES		
Hundreds	Tens	Ones	Hundreds	Tens	Ones

Start at the left. Compare the digits in each place-value position until the digits differ.

STEP 1 Compare the hundred thousands.

651,028

665,188

6 hundred thousands ◯ 6 hundred thousands

⌐ Write <, >, or =.

The digits in the hundred thousands place are the same.

STEP 2 Compare the ten thousands.

651,028

665,188

5 ten thousands ◯ 6 ten thousands

⌐ Write <, >, or =.

5 ten thousands is less than 6 ten thousands so, 651,028 < 665,188.

Since 651,028 < 665,188, there were more visitors in July 2009 than in July 2008.

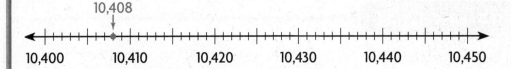

Example 2 Use a number line to order 10,408; 10,433; and 10,416 from least to greatest.

Locate and label each point on the number line. The first one is done for you.

10,408
↓

←┼┼┼┼┼┼┼◆┼┼→

10,400   10,410   10,420   10,430   10,440   10,450

Think: Numbers to the left are closer to 0.

So, the numbers from least to greatest are 10,408; 10,416; and 10,433.

$10,408 < 10,416 < 10,433$

Share and Show   MATH BOARD

1. Compare 15,327 and 15,341.
   Write $<$, $>$, or $=$. Use the number line to help.

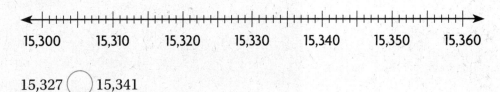

←┼┼→

15,300   15,310   15,320   15,330   15,340   15,350   15,360

15,327 ◯ 15,341

Compare. Write $<$, $>$, or $=$.

2. $631,328 ◯ $640,009

✓3. 56,991 ◯ 52,880

4. 708,561 ◯ 629,672

5. 143,062 ◯ 98,643

Order from greatest to least.

✓6. 20,650; 21,150; 20,890

_____

Math Talk

Math Processes and Practices ②

Use Reasoning Why do you not start with the ones digits when comparing three multi-digit numbers?

Name _____

On Your Own

Compare. Write <, >, or =.

7. $2,212 ◯ $2,600

8. 88,304 ◯ 88,304

9. $524,116 ◯ $61,090

10. 751,272 ◯ 851,001

Order from least to greatest.

11. 41,090; 41,190; 40,009

12. 910,763; 912,005; 95,408

_____

Math Processes and Practices 7 Identify Relationships **Algebra** Write all of the digits that can replace each ▪.

13. 567 < 5▪5 < 582

14. 464,545 > 4▪3,535 > 443,550

_____

15. **GO DEEPER** Leah's car has 156,261 miles on the odometer. Casey's car has 165,002 miles on the odometer. Mike's car has 145,834 miles on the odometer. Whose car has the most miles? Order the number of miles from least to greatest.

_____

16. **GO DEEPER** At Monica's Used Cars, the sales staff set a goal of $25,500 in sales each week. The sales for three weeks were $28,288; $25,369; and $25,876. Which total did not meet the goal?

_____

17. **THINK SMARTER** **What's the Error?** Max said that 36,594 is less than 5,980 because 3 is less than 5. **Describe** Max's error and give the correct answer.

_____

Problem Solving • Applications

Use the picture graph for 18–20.

18. **Math Processes and Practices ④ Use Graphs** In which month shown did Grand Canyon National Park have about 7,500 tent campers?

_____

19. **GO DEEPER** How many more campers were there in July and August than in June and September?

_____

20. What if during the month of October, the park had 22,500 tent campers? How many symbols would be placed on the picture graph for October?

_____

Grand Canyon National Park Tent Campers

Month (2008)	Estimated Number of Campers
June	🏕 🏕
July	🏕 🏕 🏕
August	🏕 🏕 🏕
September	🏕 🏕

Key: Each 🏕 = 5,000.

21. **THINK SMARTER** **What's the Question?** Compare: 643,251; 633,512; and 633,893. The answer is 633,512.

Math on the Spot

_____

_____

Personal Math Trainer

22. **THINK SMARTER +** Zachary's school set a goal of collecting 12,155 cans of food each day. In the first 3 days the school collected 12,250 cans; 10,505 cans; and 12,434 cans. Write each number in the box that tells whether or not the school met its goal.

| 12,250 | 10,505 | 12,434 |

Met the daily goal	Did not meet the daily goal

Compare and Order Numbers

Learning Objective You will compare and order whole numbers based on the values of the digits in each number using >, =, and < symbols.

Compare. Write <, >, or =.

1. 3,273 (<) 3,279

2. $1,323 ( ) $1,400

3. 52,692 ( ) 52,692

4. $413,005 ( ) $62,910

5. 382,144 ( ) 382,144

6. 157,932 ( ) 200,013

7. 401,322 ( ) 410,322

8. 989,063 ( ) 980,639

9. 258,766 ( ) 258,596

Order from least to greatest.

10. 23,710; 23,751; 23,715

11. 52,701; 54,025; 5,206

_____

_____

12. 465,321; 456,321; 456,231

13. $330,820; $329,854; $303,962

_____

_____

Problem Solving Real World

14. An online newspaper had 350,080 visitors in October, 350,489 visitors in November, and 305,939 visitors in December. What is the order of the months from greatest to least number of visitors?

_____

15. The total land area in square miles of each of three states is shown below.

Colorado: 103,718

New Mexico: 121,356

Arizona: 113,635

What is the order of the states from least to greatest total land area?

_____

16. **WRITE** ▸ *Math* Suppose the leftmost digits of two numbers are 8 and 3. Can you tell which number is greater? Explain.

_____

_____

_____

Lesson Check

1. At the yearly fund-raising drive, the nonprofit company's goal was to raise $55,500 each day. After three days, it had raised $55,053; $56,482; and $55,593. Which amount was less than the daily goal?

2. List these numbers in order from greatest to least: 90,048; 93,405; 90,543

Spiral Review

3. Write a fraction that is less than $\frac{5}{6}$ and has a denominator of 8.

4. What is the perimeter of the rectangle below?

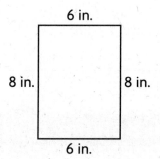

6 in.

8 in.   8 in.

6 in.

5. A website had 826,140 hits last month. What is the value of the 8 in 826,140?

6. Write 680,705 in expanded form.

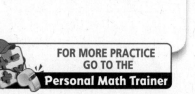

FOR MORE PRACTICE
GO TO THE
Personal Math Trainer

Name _____

Round Numbers

Essential Question How can you round numbers?

Learning Objective You will round whole numbers using place value understanding.

Unlock the Problem

During May 2008, the Mount Rushmore National Monument in South Dakota welcomed 138,202 visitors. A website reported that about 1 hundred thousand people visited the park during that month. Was the estimate reasonable?

- Underline what you are asked to find.
- Circle the information you will use.

An **estimate** tells you about how many or about how much. It is close to an exact amount. You can **round** a number to find an estimate.

One Way Use a number line.

To round a number to the nearest hundred thousand, find the hundred thousands it is between.

_____ < 138,202 < _____

Use a number line to see which hundred thousand 138,202 is closer to.

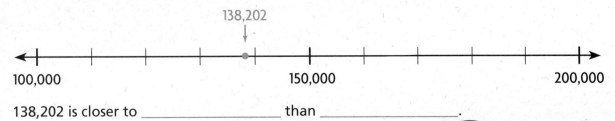

138,202 is closer to _____ than _____.

So, 1 hundred thousand is a reasonable estimate for 138,202.

Math Talk

Math Processes and Practices ④

Use Models How can you use a model to round numbers?

1. What number is halfway between 100,000 and 200,000?

_____

2. How does knowing where the halfway point is help you find which hundred thousand 138,202 is closer to? Explain.

_____

_____

_____

🔓 Another Way Use place value.

Mount Rushmore is located 5,725 feet above sea level. About how high is Mount Rushmore above sea level, to the nearest thousand feet?

To round a number to the nearest thousand, find the thousands it is between.

_____ < 5,725 < _____

Look at the digit in the place-value position to the right.

5,725
↑

Think: The digit in the hundreds place is 7.
So, 5,725 is closer to 6,000 than 5,000.

So, Mount Rushmore is about _____ feet above sea level.

Math Talk

Math Processes and Practices ⑥

Explain the difference in using a model and using place value when rounding numbers.

---

3. What number is halfway between 70,000 and 80,000?

_____

4. What is 75,000 rounded to the nearest ten thousand? Explain.

_____

_____

_____

Math Idea

When a number is exactly half way between two rounding numbers, round to the greater number.

Try This! Round to the place value of the underlined digit.

Ⓐ <u>6</u>4,999

_____

Ⓑ <u>8</u>50,000

_____

Ⓒ 30<u>1</u>,587

_____

Ⓓ 1<u>0</u>,832

_____

Name _____

 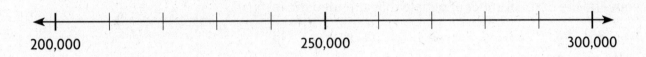
1. Suppose 255,113 people live in a city. Is it reasonable to say that about 300,000 people live in the city? Use the number line to help you solve the problem. Explain.

```
←—+——+——+——+——+——+——+——+——+——+——+→
200,000              250,000              300,000
```

_____

_____

Round to the place value of the underlined digit.

2. 934,567   ✓ 3. 641,267   4. 234,890   ✓ 5. 347,456

_____   _____   _____   _____

On Your Own

6. **GO DEEPER** To the nearest hundred, a factory produced 3,600 jars of applesauce on Thursday and 4,200 jars of applesauce on Friday. To the nearest thousand, how many jars of applesauce did they produce during the two days?

_____

Problem Solving • Applications

7. **THINK SMARTER** The number 2,▉00 is missing a digit. The number rounded to the nearest thousand is 3,000. List all of the possibilities for the missing digit. Explain your answer.

_____

_____

_____

_____

8. **GO DEEPER** A male elephant weighs 6,728 pounds. A female elephant weighs 5,843 pounds. To the nearest hundred, what is the total weight of the two elephants?

_____

9. **THINK SMARTER +** About 300,000 people attended a festival. For numbers 9a–9e choose Yes or No to show whether each number could be the exact number of people that attended the festival.

9a.   351,213   ○ Yes   ○ No

9b.   249,899   ○ Yes   ○ No

9c.   252,348   ○ Yes   ○ No

9d.   389,001   ○ Yes   ○ No

9e.   305,992   ○ Yes   ○ No

Connect to Science

Data Gathering

Some scientists count and measure groups of things. Benchmarks can be used to estimate the size of a group or a population. A *benchmark* is a known number of things that helps you understand the size or amount of a different number of things.

Use the benchmark to find a reasonable estimate for the number of coquina shells it would take to fill a jar.

It would take about 5 times the benchmark to fill the jar.
$100 + 100 + 100 + 100 + 100 = 500$

The most reasonable estimate for the number of coquina shells it would take to fill the jar is 500 shells.

Benchmark
100 shells

200; 500;
or 5,000

Math Processes and Practices ① **Evaluate Reasonableness** Use the benchmark to find a reasonable estimate. Circle the reasonable estimate.

10.

500 beads   1,500; 2,500; or 3,500

11.

10,000 blades of grass

1,000; 10,000; or 100,000

Name _____

Round Numbers

Learning Objective You will round whole numbers using place value understanding.

Round to the place value of the underlined digit.

1. 8<u>6</u>2,840

862,840   ___860,000___

↑
less than 5

- Look at the digit to the right.

- If the digit to the right is *less than* 5, the digit in the rounding place stays the same.

- If the digit to the right is *5 or greater,* the digit in the rounding place increases by one.

- Write zeros for the digits to the right of the rounding place.

2. 123,<u>4</u>99

_____

3. <u>5</u>52,945

_____

4. 3<u>8</u>9,422

_____

5. <u>2</u>09,767

_____

6. 19<u>1</u>,306

_____

7. <u>6</u>6,098

_____

Problem Solving Real World

Use the table for 8–9.

8. Find the height of Mt. Whitney in the table. Round the height to the nearest thousand feet.

_____ feet

9. What is the height of Mt. Bona rounded to the nearest ten thousand feet?

_____ feet

Mountain Heights		
Name	**State**	**Height (feet)**
Mt. Bona	Alaska	16,500
Mt. Whitney	California	14,494

10. **WRITE** ▸*Math* Jessie says to round 763,400 to the nearest ten thousand, he will round to 770,000. Is he right? Explain.

_____

_____

Lesson Check

1. What is 247,039 rounded to the nearest thousand?

_____

_____

2. To the nearest ten thousand, the population of Vermont was estimated to be about 620,000 in 2008. What might have been the exact population of Vermont in 2008?

_____

_____

Spiral Review

3. Write the symbol that makes the following number sentence true.

$546,322 \bigcirc $540,997

4. Pittsburgh International Airport had approximately 714,587 passengers in August 2009. Write a number that is greater than 714,587.

_____

_____

5. June made a design with 6 equal tiles. One tile is yellow, 2 tiles are blue, and 3 tiles are purple. What fraction of the tiles are yellow or purple?

_____

6. The fourth grade collected 40,583 cans and plastic bottles. Write this number in word form.

_____

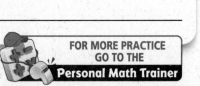

FOR MORE PRACTICE
GO TO THE
Personal Math Trainer

Name _____

Mid-Chapter Checkpoint

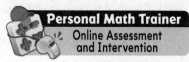

Vocabulary

Choose the best term from the box.

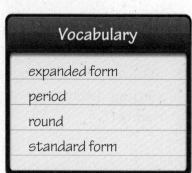

Vocabulary

expanded form

period

round

standard form

1. The _____ of 23,850 is 20,000 + 3,000 + 800 + 50. (p. 11)

2. You can _____ to find *about* how much or how many. (p. 23)

3. In 192,860 the digits 1, 9, and 2 are in the same

_____. (p. 11)

Concepts and Skills

Find the value of the underlined digit.

4. 3<u>8</u>0,671

5. 10,6<u>9</u>8

6. <u>6</u>50,234

_____

_____

_____

Write the number in two other forms.

7. 293,805

_____

_____

8. 300,000 + 5,000 + 20 + 6

_____

_____

Compare. Write <, >, or =.

9. 457,380 ◯ 458,590

10. 390,040 ◯ 39,040

11. 11,809 ◯ 11,980

Round to the place of the underlined digit.

12. <u>1</u>40,250

13. 10,<u>4</u>50

14. 12<u>6</u>,234

_____

_____

_____

© Houghton Mifflin Harcourt Publishing Company

15. Last year, three hundred twenty-three thousand people visited the museum. What is this number written in standard form?

_____

16. `GO DEEPER` Rachael rounded 16,473 to the nearest hundred. Then she rounded her answer to the nearest thousand. What is the final number?

_____

17. What is the highest volcano in the Cascade Range?

Cascade Range Volcanoes		
Name	**State**	**Height (ft)**
Lassen Peak	CA	10,457
Mt. Rainier	WA	14,410
Mt. Shasta	CA	14,161
Mt. St. Helens	WA	8,364

_____

18. Richard got 263,148 hits when he did an Internet search. What is the value of the digit 6 in this number?

_____

Name _____

Rename Numbers

Essential Question How can you rename a whole number?

Learning Objective You will represent an equivalent form of a whole number by using models and regrouping.

Investigate

Materials ■ base-ten blocks

You can regroup numbers to rename them.

A. Use large cubes and flats to model 1,200. Draw a quick picture to record your model.

The model shows _____ large cube and _____ flats.

Another name for 1,200 is _____ thousand _____ hundreds.

B. Use only flats to model 1,200.
Draw a quick picture to record your model.

The model shows _____ flats.

Another name for 1,200 is _____ hundreds.

Draw Conclusions

1. How is the number of large cubes and flats in the first model related to the number of flats in the second model?

_____

_____

2. Can you model 1,200 using only longs? Explain.

_____

_____

3. You renamed 1,200 as hundreds. How can you rename
1,200 as tens? Explain.

_____

_____

4. **THINK SMARTER** What would the models in Step A and Step B
look like for 5,200? How can you rename 5,200 as hundreds?

_____

_____

_____

Make Connections

You can also use a place-value chart to help rename numbers.

THOUSANDS			ONES		
Hundreds	Tens	Ones	Hundreds	Tens	Ones
5	0	0,	0	0	0

└─────────┘ 5 hundred thousands
└────────────────┘ 50 ten thousands
└───────────────────────┘ 500 thousands
└──────────────────────────────┘ 5,000 hundreds
└─────────────────────────────────────┘ 50,000 tens
└──┘ 500,000 ones

Write 32 hundreds on the place-value chart below. What is 32
hundreds written in standard form?

THOUSANDS			ONES		
Hundreds	Tens	Ones	Hundreds	Tens	Ones

└────────────────┘ 32 hundreds

32 hundreds written in standard form is _____ .

Math Processes and Practices ⑦

Look for Structure How can
a place-value chart help you
rename numbers?

Share and Show MATH BOARD

Rename the number. Draw a quick picture to help.

1. 150

_____ tens

2. 1,400

_____ hundreds

3. 2 thousands 3 hundreds

_____ hundreds

4. 13 hundreds

_____ thousand _____ hundreds

Rename the number. Use the place-value chart to help.

5. 18 thousands = _____

THOUSANDS			ONES		
Hundreds	Tens	Ones	Hundreds	Tens	Ones

6. 570,000 = 57 _____

THOUSANDS			ONES		
Hundreds	Tens	Ones	Hundreds	Tens	Ones

Rename the number.

7. 580 = _____ tens

8. 740,000 = _____ ten thousands

9. 8 hundreds 4 tens = 84 _____

10. 29 thousands = _____

 **Unlock the Problem** Real World

 Math on the Spot

11. **THINK SMARTER** A toy store is ordering 3,000 remote control cars. The store can order the cars in sets of 10. How many sets of 10 does the store need to order?

a. What information do you need to use?

_____

_____

b. What do you need to find?

_____

_____

c. How can renaming numbers help you solve this problem?

_____

_____

d. Describe a strategy you can use to solve the problem.

_____

_____

e. How many sets of 10 remote control cars does the store need to buy?

_____

12. **GO DEEPER** Ivan sold 53 boxes of oranges on Friday and 27 boxes on Saturday during a citrus sale. There were 10 oranges in each box. How many oranges did he sell in all?

_____

13. **Math Processes and Practices ②** **Use Reasoning** A store sold a total of 15,000 boxes of buttons last month, and 12,000 boxes this month. If the store sold 270,000 buttons, how many buttons were in each box?

_____

14. **THINK SMARTER** For numbers 14a–14d, select True or False for each statement.

14a. 9 hundreds 3 tens can be renamed as 39 tens. ○ True   ○ False

14b. 370,000 can be renamed as 37 ten thousands. ○ True   ○ False

14c. 780 can be renamed as 78 tens. ○ True   ○ False

14d. 42,000 can be renamed as 42 thousands. ○ True   ○ False

Rename Numbers

Learning Objective You will represent an equivalent form of a whole number by using models and regrouping.

Rename the number. Use the place-value chart to help.

1. 760 hundreds = ___76,000___

THOUSANDS			ONES		
Hundreds	Tens	Ones	Hundreds	Tens	Ones
	7	6,	0	0	0

2. 24 ten thousands = _____

THOUSANDS			ONES		
Hundreds	Tens	Ones	Hundreds	Tens	Ones

Rename the number.

3. 120,000 = _____
ten thousands

4. 4 thousands 7 hundreds = 47 _____

Problem Solving · Real World

5. For the fair, the organizers ordered 32 rolls of tickets. Each roll of tickets has 100 tickets. How many tickets were ordered in all?

_____

6. An apple orchard sells apples in bags of 10. The orchard sold a total of 2,430 apples one day. How many bags of apples was this?

_____

7. **WRITE** ▸*Math* Explain how you can rename 5,400 as hundreds. Include a quick picture or a place-value chart in your explanation.

_____

Lesson Check

1. A dime has the same value as 10 pennies. Marley brought 290 pennies to the bank. How many dimes did Marley get?

   _____

2. A citrus grower ships grapefruit in boxes of 10. One season, the grower shipped 20,400 boxes of grapefruit. How many grapefruit were shipped?

   _____

Spiral Review

3. There were 2,605 people at the basketball game. A reporter rounded this number to the nearest hundred for a newspaper article. What number did the reporter use?

   _____

4. To get to Level 3 in a game, a player must score 14,175 points. Ann scores 14,205 points, Ben scores 14,089 points, and Chuck scores 10,463 points. Which score is greater than the Level 3 score?

   _____

5. Henry counted 350 lockers in his school. Hayley counted 403 lockers in her school. How does the 3 in 350 compare to the 3 in 403?

   _____

   _____

6. There are 4 muffins on each plate. There are 0 plates of lemon muffins. How many lemon muffins are there?

   _____

   _____

© Houghton Mifflin Harcourt Publishing Company

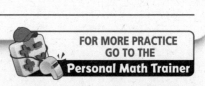
FOR MORE PRACTICE
GO TO THE
Personal Math Trainer

Name _____

Add Whole Numbers

Essential Question How can you add whole numbers?

Learning Objective You will add multi-digit whole numbers and determine whether solutions are reasonable.

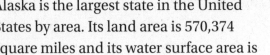 **Unlock the Problem** (Real World)

Alaska is the largest state in the United States by area. Its land area is 570,374 square miles and its water surface area is 86,051 square miles. Find the total area of Alaska.

 Find the sum.

Add. 570,374 + 86,051

Think: It is important to line up the addends by place value when adding two numbers.

- Underline what you are asked to find.
- Circle the information you will use.

▲ The area of Alaska is outlined in the photo above.

STEP 1 Add the ones.

Add the tens. Regroup.

12 tens = 1 hundred _____ tens

$$\begin{array}{r} \overset{1}{5}70,374 \\ +\ 86,051 \\ \hline \end{array}$$

STEP 2 Add the hundreds.

Add the thousands.

$$\begin{array}{r} \overset{1}{5}70,374 \\ +\ 86,051 \\ \hline 25 \end{array}$$

STEP 3 Add the ten thousands.

Regroup.

15 ten thousands =

1 hundred thousand _____ ten thousands

$$\begin{array}{r} \overset{1}{5}7\overset{1}{0},374 \\ +\ 86,051 \\ \hline 6,425 \end{array}$$

Math Talk

Math Processes and Practices ⑧

Draw Conclusions How do you know when to regroup when adding?

STEP 4 Add the hundred thousands.

$$\begin{array}{r} \overset{1}{5}7\overset{1}{0},374 \\ +\ 86,051 \\ \hline 56,425 \end{array}$$

So, the total area of Alaska is _____ square miles.

© Houghton Mifflin Harcourt Publishing Company • Image Credits: (t) ©Stocktrek Images/Getty Images

Estimate You can estimate to tell whether an answer is reasonable.
To estimate a sum, round each addend before you add.

🔒 **Example** Estimate. Then find the sum.

Juneau has an area of 2,717 square miles. Valdez has an area of
222 square miles. What is their combined area?

Ⓐ Estimate. Use the grid to help you align the addends by place value.

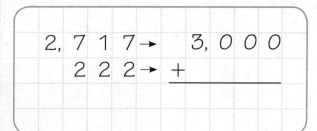

Round to the nearest thousand.

Round to the nearest hundred.

So, the combined area of Juneau and Valdez is about _____
square miles.

Ⓑ Find the sum.

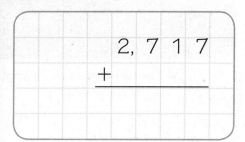

Think: Begin by adding the ones.

⚠️ **ERROR Alert**
Remember to align the addends by place value.

So, the combined area of Juneau and Valdez is _____
square miles.

• Is the sum reasonable? Explain.

_____

Share and Show

1. Use the grid to find 738,901 + 162,389.

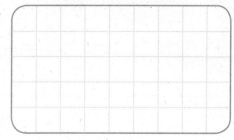

Use the grid to align the addends by place value.

Name _____

Estimate. Then find the sum.

2. Estimate: _____

$$\begin{array}{r} 72{,}931 \\ +18{,}563 \\ \hline \end{array}$$

3. Estimate: _____

$$\begin{array}{r} 432{,}068 \\ +239{,}576 \\ \hline \end{array}$$

4. Estimate: _____

$$\begin{array}{r} 64{,}505 \\ +38{,}972 \\ \hline \end{array}$$

Math Talk Math Processes and Practices ⑥

Explain how estimating helps you know if your answer is reasonable.

On Your Own

Estimate. Then find the sum.

5. Estimate: _____

$$\begin{array}{r} 839{,}136 \\ +120{,}193 \\ \hline \end{array}$$

6. Estimate: _____

$$\begin{array}{r} 186{,}231 \\ +\ 88{,}941 \\ \hline \end{array}$$

7. Estimate: _____

$$\begin{array}{r} 744{,}201 \\ +168{,}900 \\ \hline \end{array}$$

8. **GO DEEPER** For the first football game of the season, 62,732 fans attended. The number of fans at the second game was 469 more than at the first game. What is the total number of fans that attended the first two games?

_____

9. **GO DEEPER** Daisy's Flower Shop sold 135,649 flowers during its first year. The second year, the shop sold 9,754 more flowers than it did its first year. The third year, it sold 1,343 more flowers than it did in the second year. How many flowers did the shop sell during the three years?

_____

Math Processes and Practices ② **Reason Abstractly** **Algebra** Find the missing number and name the property you used to find it. Write *Commutative* or *Associative*.

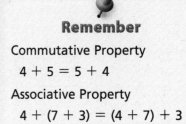

Remember

Commutative Property
$4 + 5 = 5 + 4$

Associative Property
$4 + (7 + 3) = (4 + 7) + 3$

10. $(4{,}580 + 5{,}008) + 2{,}351 = 4{,}580 + ($ _____ $+ 2{,}351)$

_____

11. $7{,}801 +$ _____ $= 4{,}890 + 7{,}801$ _____

12. $2{,}592 + 3{,}385 = 3{,}385 +$ _____ _____

Problem Solving • Applications

Use the table for 13–14.

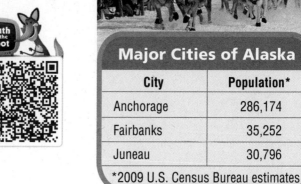

13. **THINKSMARTER** What is the combined population of the three major Alaskan cities? Estimate to verify your answer.

_____

14. **Math Processes and Practices ⑥** The digit 5 occurs two times in the population of Fairbanks. What is the value of each 5? **Explain** your answer.

_____

_____

_____

Major Cities of Alaska	
City	**Population***
Anchorage	286,174
Fairbanks	35,252
Juneau	30,796

*2009 U.S. Census Bureau estimates

15. **GO DEEPER** Kaylie has 164 stamps in her collection. Her friend Nellie has 229 more stamps than Kaylie. How many stamps do Kaylie and Nellie have?

_____

WRITE ▸ *Math* · **Show Your Work**

16. **THINKSMARTER** Alaska's Glacier Bay National Park had 431,986 visitors one year. The next year, the park had 22,351 more visitors than the year before. How many people visited during the two years? Show your work and explain how you found your answer.

_____

_____

_____

_____

Add Whole Numbers

Learning Objective You will add multi-digit whole numbers and determine whether solutions are reasonable.

Estimate. Then find the sum.

1. Estimate: ___90,000___

    1 1
    63,824 → 60,000
    + 29,452 →+ 30,000
    _____ _____
    93,276   90,000

2. Estimate: _____

    73,404
    + 27,865

3. Estimate: _____

    403,446
    + 396,755

4. Estimate: _____

    137,638
    + 52,091

5. Estimate: _____

    200,629
    + 28,542

6. Estimate: _____

    212,514
    + 396,705

Problem Solving Real World

Use the table for 7–9.

7. Beth and Cade were on one team. What was their total score?

    _____

8. Dillan and Elaine were on the other team. What was their total score?

    _____

9. Which team scored the most points?

    _____

Individual Game Scores	
Student	**Score**
Beth	251,567
Cade	155,935
Dillan	188,983
Elaine	220,945

10. **WRITE** ▸ *Math* Write a story problem that can be solved by finding the sum of 506,211 and 424,809. Then solve the problem.

    _____

    _____

Lesson Check

1. The coastline of the United States is 12,383 miles long. Canada's coastline is 113,211 miles longer than the coastline of the United States. How long is the coastline of Canada?

   _____

2. Germany is the seventh largest European country and is slightly smaller by area than Montana. Germany has a land area of 134,835 square miles and a water area of 3,011 square miles. What is the total area of Germany?

   _____

Spiral Review

3. In an election, about 500,000 people voted in all. What could be the exact number of people who voted in the election?

   _____

4. In 2007, Pennsylvania had approximately 121,580 miles of public roads. What is 121,580 rounded to the nearest thousand?

   _____

5. Order these numbers from least to greatest: 749,340; 740,999; 740,256

   _____

6. Which symbol makes the following statement true?

   $413,115 ◯ $431,511

FOR MORE PRACTICE
GO TO THE
Personal Math Trainer

Name _____

Subtract Whole Numbers

Essential Question How can you subtract whole numbers?

Learning Objective You will subtract multi-digit whole numbers and determine whether solutions are reasonable.

Unlock the Problem

Mt. Bear and Mt. Bona are two mountains in Alaska. Mt. Bear is 14,831 feet tall and Mt. Bona is 16,421 feet tall. How much taller is Mt. Bona than Mt. Bear?

Estimate. $16,000 - 15,000 =$ _____

Subtract. $16,421 - 14,831$

▲ Mt. Bear and Mt. Bona are in the St. Elias Mountain Range located in the Wrangell-St. Elias National Park and Preserve in Alaska.

STEP 1 Subtract the ones.

Regroup to subtract the tens.

4 hundreds 2 tens =

3 hundreds _____ tens

$$\begin{array}{r} \overset{\scriptstyle 3\,12}{16,\cancel{4}21} \\ -14,831 \\ \hline \end{array}$$

STEP 2 Regroup to subtract the hundreds.

6 thousands 3 hundreds =

5 thousands _____ hundreds

$$\begin{array}{r} \overset{\scriptstyle 5\ \ \ 13}{\overset{}{16,\cancel{4}21}} \\ -14,831 \\ \hline 90 \end{array}$$

STEP 3 Subtract the thousands.

Subtract the ten thousands.

$$\begin{array}{r} \overset{\scriptstyle 5\ \ \ 13}{\overset{}{16,\cancel{4}21}} \\ -14,831 \\ \hline ,590 \end{array}$$

So, Mt. Bona is _____ feet taller than Mt. Bear. Since _____ is

close to the estimate of _____, the answer is reasonable.

Try This! Use addition to check your answer.

$$\begin{array}{r} \overset{13}{\cancel{1}}\overset{\cancel{5}\;\cancel{3}12}{6,4\cancel{2}1} \\ -14,831 \\ \hline 1,590 \end{array}$$

$$\begin{array}{r} \overset{1\;\;1}{\;\;\;1,590} \\ +14,831 \\ \hline \end{array}$$

So, the answer checks.

Share and Show MATH BOARD

1. Subtract. Use the grid to record the problem.

   637,350 − 43,832

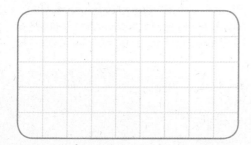

Math Talk Math Processes and Practices ⑧

Draw Conclusions How do you know which places to regroup to subtract?

Estimate. Then find the difference.

2. Estimate: _____	3. Estimate: _____	4. Estimate: _____
$\begin{array}{r}14,659\\-11,584\\\hline\end{array}$	$\begin{array}{r}456,912\\-\;37,800\\\hline\end{array}$	$\begin{array}{r}407,001\\-184,652\\\hline\end{array}$

On Your Own

Estimate. Then find the difference.

5. Estimate: _____	6. Estimate: _____	7. Estimate: _____
$\begin{array}{r}942,385\\-461,803\\\hline\end{array}$	$\begin{array}{r}798,300\\-348,659\\\hline\end{array}$	$\begin{array}{r}300,980\\-159,000\\\hline\end{array}$

Name _____

Practice: Copy and Solve Subtract. Add to check.

8. 653,809 − 256,034

9. 258,197 − 64,500

10. 496,004 − 398,450

11. 500,000 − 145,609

 Reason Abstractly Algebra Find the missing digit.

12.
```
  6,532
− 4,1_5
─────────
  2,407
```

13.
```
 _08,665
−659,420
─────────
 149,245
```

14.
```
 697,320
−432,_08
─────────
 264,712
```

Problem Solving • Applications

Use the table for 15–16.

15. **Math Processes and Practices ①** **Estimate Reasonableness** How many more acres were grown in 1996 than in 1986? Estimate to check the reasonableness of your answer.

_____

_____

16. What is the difference between the greatest number of acres and the least number of acres used for growing oranges?

_____

Orange Groves in Florida

Year	Acres
1966	673,086
1976	628,657
1986	466,256
1996	656,598

17. **GO DEEPER** Workers at a paper company count the number of boxes of paper in the warehouse each month. In January, there were 106,341 boxes of paper. In February, there were 32,798 fewer boxes than there were in January. In March, there were 25,762 fewer boxes than there were in February. How many boxes were in the warehouse in March?

18. **THINK SMARTER** There are 135,663 kilometers of U.S. coastline that border the Pacific Ocean. There are 111,866 kilometers of U.S. coastline that border the Atlantic Ocean. How many more kilometers of U.S. coastline border the Pacific Ocean than the Atlantic Ocean? Solve the problem and show how to check your answer.

_____

19. **THINK SMARTER** **What's the Error?** Maryland has an area of 12,407 square miles. Texas has an area of 268,601 square miles. How much larger is Texas than Maryland?

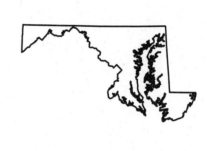

Read how Janice solved the problem.
Find her error.

Solve the problem and correct her error.

Texas: 268,601 square miles
Maryland: 12,407 square miles
I can subtract to find the difference.

$$\begin{array}{r} 268{,}601 \\ -\ 12{,}407 \\ \hline 144{,}531 \end{array}$$

So, Texas is _____ square miles larger than Maryland.

• **Math Processes and Practices 3** **Verify Reasoning of Others** Describe Janice's error.

_____

_____

Subtract Whole Numbers

Learning Objective You will subtract multi-digit whole numbers and determine whether solutions are reasonable.

Estimate. Then find the difference.

1. Estimate: ___600,000___

$$
\begin{array}{r}
{\scriptstyle 9} \\
{\scriptstyle 7\ 10\ 15\ 6\ 13} \\
7\,8\,0\text{,}5\,7\,3 \\
-\ 2\,2\,9\text{,}6\,1\,5 \\
\hline
5\,5\,0\text{,}9\,5\,8
\end{array}
$$

Think: 780,573 rounds to 800,000.
229,615 rounds to 200,000.
So an estimate is 800,000 − 200,000 = 600,000.

2. Estimate: _____

$$
\begin{array}{r}
428\text{,}731 \\
-\ 175\text{,}842 \\
\hline
\end{array}
$$

3. Estimate: _____

$$
\begin{array}{r}
920\text{,}026 \\
-\ 535\text{,}722 \\
\hline
\end{array}
$$

4. Estimate: _____

$$
\begin{array}{r}
253\text{,}495 \\
-\ 48\text{,}617 \\
\hline
\end{array}
$$

Problem Solving • Real World

Use the table for 5 and 6.

5. How many more people attended the Magic's games than attended the Pacers' games?

_____

6. How many fewer people attended the Pacers' games than attended the Clippers' games?

_____

Season Attendance for Three NBA Teams	
Team	**Attendance**
Indiana Pacers	582,295
Orlando Magic	715,901
Los Angeles Clippers	670,063

7. **WRITE** ▸*Math* Write a story problem that can be solved by finding the difference of 432,906 and 61,827. Then solve the problem.

_____

_____

_____

Lesson Check

1. This year, a farm planted 400,000 corn stalks. Last year, the farm planted 275,650 corn stalks. How many more corn stalks did the farm plant this year than last year?

2. One machine can make 138,800 small paper clips in one day. Another machine can make 84,250 large paper clips in one day. How many more small paper clips than large paper clips are made by the two machines in one day?

Spiral Review

3. In three baseball games over a weekend, 125,429 people came to watch. The next weekend, 86,353 people came to watch the games. How many people total watched the six baseball games?

4. Kevin read the number "two hundred seven thousand, forty-eight" in a book. What is this number in standard form?

5. A museum had 275,608 visitors last year. What is this number rounded to the nearest thousand?

6. At the Millville Theater, a play ran for several weeks. In all, 28,175 people saw the play. What is the value of the digit 8 in 28,175?

© Houghton Mifflin Harcourt Publishing Company

FOR MORE PRACTICE
GO TO THE
Personal Math Trainer

Name _____

Problem Solving • Comparison Problems with Addition and Subtraction

Essential Question How can you use the strategy *draw a diagram* to solve comparison problems with addition and subtraction?

Learning Objective You will use the strategy *draw a diagram* to solve comparison problems with addition and subtraction.

¶ Unlock the Problem

Hot air balloon festivals draw large crowds of people. The attendance on the first day of one festival was 17,350. On the second day the attendance was 18,925. How many more people attended the hot air balloon festival on the second day?

Use the graphic organizer to help you solve the problem.

Read the Problem

What do I need to find?	**What information do I need to use?**	**How will I use the information?**
Write what you need to find.	_____ people attended on the first day,	What strategy can you use?
_____	_____ people attended on the second day.	_____
_____		_____
_____		_____

Solve the Problem

I can draw a bar model and write an equation to represent the problem.

18,925

17,350

$18,925 - 17,350 =$ _____

So, _____ more people attended the festival on the second day.

🔓 Try Another Problem

During an event, a hot air balloon traveled a distance of 5,110 feet during the first trip and 850 feet more during the second trip. How far did it travel during the second trip?

Read the Problem

What do I need to find?	What information do I need to use?	How will I use the information?

Solve the Problem

- Is your answer reasonable? Explain how you know.

_____

_____

Math Talk

Math Processes and Practices 8

Generalize How can inverse operations be used to check your answer?

© Houghton Mifflin Harcourt Publishing Company • Image Credits: (t) ©PhotoDisc/Getty Images

Name _____

Share and Show

1. Hot air balloons are able to fly at very high altitudes. A world record height of 64,997 feet was set in 1988. In 2005, a new record of 68,986 feet was set. How many feet higher was the 2005 record than the 1988 record?

   First, draw a diagram to show the parts of the problem.

   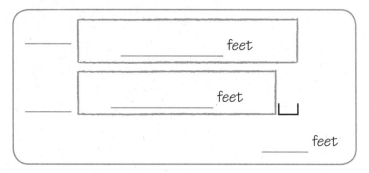

   _____ _____ feet

   _____ _____ feet

   _____ feet

   Next, write the problem you need to solve.

   _____

   Last, solve the problem to find how many feet higher the 2005 record was than the 1988 record.

   So, the 2005 record was _____ feet higher.

2. What if a new world altitude record of 70,000 feet was set? How many feet higher would the new record be than the 2005 record?

   _____

☑ 3. Last year, the ticket sales for a commercial hot air balloon ride were $109,076. This year, the ticket sales were $125,805. How much more were the ticket sales this year?

   _____

☑ 4. A musician's first album sells 234,499 copies the first week it was released. During the second week, another 432,112 albums were sold. How many more albums were sold during the second week than the first week?

   _____

Unlock the Problem

√ Use the Problem Solving MathBoard
√ Underline important facts.
√ Choose a strategy you know.

▲ Dr. Vijaypat Singhania flew the world's largest hot-air balloon when he made his record-breaking flight. The balloon he flew was over 20 stories tall.

© Houghton Mifflin Harcourt Publishing Company • Image Credits: (t) ©AFP/Getty Images

On Your Own

Use the information in the table for 5–6.

5. **Math Processes and Practices ④** **Use Models** Steve Fossett attempted to fly around the world in a balloon several times before he succeeded in 2002. How many more miles did he fly during the 2002 flight than during the August 1998 flight?

Steve Fossett's Balloon Flights	
Year	**Distance in Miles**
1996	2,200
1997	10,360
1998 (January)	5,803
1998 (August)	14,235
2001	3,187
2002	20,482

6. **GO DEEPER** Is the combined distance for the 1998 flights more or less than the distance for the 2002 flight? By how much? Explain.

7. **THINK SMARTER** There were 665 hot air balloon pilots at a hot air balloon race. There were 1,550 more ground crew members than there were pilots. How many pilots and ground crew members were there all together?

Personal Math Trainer

8. **THINK SMARTER +** The first year Becky owned her car she drove it 14,378 miles. The second year she drove it 422 fewer miles than the first year. She bought the car with 16 miles on it. How many miles were on the car at the end of the second year? Show your work.

Name _____

Problem Solving • Comparison Problems with Addition and Subtraction

Learning Objective You will use the strategy *draw a diagram* to solve comparison problems with addition and subtraction.

Use the information in the table for 1–3.

Surface Area of the Great Lakes	
Lake	**Surface Area (in square miles)**
Lake Superior	31,700
Lake Michigan	22,278
Lake Huron	22,973
Lake Erie	9,906
Lake Ontario	7,340

1. How many square miles larger is the surface area of Lake Huron than the surface area of Lake Erie?

   Think: How can a bar model help represent the problem? What equation can be written?

   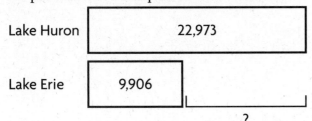

   Lake Huron 22,973

   Lake Erie 9,906 ?

   $22,973 - 9,906 =$ __13,067__ square miles

   _____13,067 square miles_____

2. Which lake has a surface area that is 14,938 square miles greater than the surface area of Lake Ontario? Draw a model and write a number sentence to solve the problem.

   _____

3. Lake Victoria has the largest surface area of all lakes in Africa. Its surface area is 26,828 square miles. How much larger is the surface area of Lake Superior than that of Lake Victoria?

   _____

4. **WRITE** ▸*Math* Write a comparison problem you can solve using addition or subtraction. Draw a bar model to represent the situation. Describe how the information in the bar model is related to the problem.

   _____

Lesson Check

1. The Mariana Trench in the Pacific Ocean is about 36,201 feet deep. The Puerto Rico Trench in the Atlantic Ocean is about 27,493 feet deep. Draw a bar model to find how many feet deeper the Mariana Trench is than the Puerto Rico Trench.

2. At 1,932 feet, Crater Lake in Oregon, is the deepest lake in the United States. The world's deepest lake, Lake Baykal in Russia, is 3,383 feet deeper. Draw a bar model to find how deep Lake Baykal is.

Spiral Review

3. Write a number that is greater than 832,458, but less than 832,500.

4. A stadium in Pennsylvania seats 107,282 people. A stadium in Arizona seats 71,706 people. Based on these facts, how many more people does the stadium in Pennsylvania seat than the stadium in Arizona?

5. What is 399,713 rounded to the place value of the underlined digit?

6. About 400,000 people visited an art museum in December. What could be the exact number of people who visited the art museum?

FOR MORE PRACTICE
GO TO THE
Personal Math Trainer

Name _____

1. Select a number for ■ that will make a true comparison. Mark all that apply.

$$703,209 > ■$$

(A) 702,309   (C) 703,209   (E) 730,029

(B) 703,029   (D) 703,290   (F) 730,209

2.   Nancy wrote the greatest number that can be made using each of these digits exactly once.

| 5 | 3 | 4 | 9 | 8 | 1 |

Part A

What was Nancy's number? How do you know this is the greatest possible number for these digits?

Part B

What is the least number that can be made using each digit exactly once? Explain why the value of the 4 is greater than the value of the 5.

GO DIGITAL Assessment Options
Chapter Test

For 3–4, use the table.

U.S. Mountain Peaks					
Name	State	Height (ft)	Name	State	Height (ft)
Blanca Peak	CO	14,345	Mount Whitney	CA	14,494
Crestone Peak	CO	14,294	University Peak	AK	14,470
Humboldt Peak	CO	14,064	White Mountain	CA	14,246

3. Write the name of each mountain peak in the box that describes its height, in feet.

Between 14,000 feet and 14,300 feet	Between 14,301 feet and 14,500 feet

4. Circle the name of the tallest peak. Explain how you know which of the mountain peaks is the tallest.

5. Mr. Rodriguez bought 420 pencils for the school. If there are 10 pencils in a box, how many boxes did he buy?

    (A)   42

    (B)   420

    (C)   430

    (D) 4,200

6. Bobby and Cheryl each rounded 745,829 to the nearest ten thousand. Bobby wrote 750,000 and Cheryl wrote 740,000. Who is correct? Explain the error that was made.

Name _____

7. The total season attendance for a college team's home games, rounded to the nearest ten thousand, was 270,000. For numbers 7a–7d, select Yes or No to tell whether the number could be the exact attendance.

7a.	265,888	○ Yes	○ No
7b.	260,987	○ Yes	○ No
7c.	274,499	○ Yes	○ No
7d.	206,636	○ Yes	○ No

For 8–10, use the table.

The table shows recent population data for Sacramento, California.

Population of Sacramento, CA			
Age in years	Population	Age in years	Population
Under 5	35,010	20 to 34	115,279
5 to 9	31,406	35 to 49	92,630
10 to 14	30,253	50 to 64	79,271
15 to 19	34,219	65 and over	49,420

8. How many children are under 10 years old? Show your work.

9. How many people are between the ages of 20 and 49? Show your work.

10. How many more children are under the age of 5 than between the ages of 10 and 14? Show your work.

11. For numbers 11a–11d, select True or False for each sentence.

11a. The value of 7 in 375,092
is 7,000.   ○ True   ○ False

11b. The value of 5 in 427,593
is 500.   ○ True   ○ False

11c. The value of 2 in 749,021
is 200.   ○ True   ○ False

11d. The value of 4 in 842,063
is 40,000.   ○ True   ○ False

12. Select another way to show 403,871. Mark all that apply.

Ⓐ four hundred three thousand, eight hundred one

Ⓑ four hundred three thousand, seventy-one

Ⓒ four hundred three thousand, eight hundred seventy-one

Ⓓ 400,000 + 38,000 + 800 + 70 + 1

Ⓔ 400,000 + 3,000 + 800 + 70 + 1

Ⓕ 4 hundred thousands + 3 thousands + 8 hundreds +
7 tens + 1 one

13. **THINK SMARTER +**  Lexi, Susie, and Rial are playing an online word game. Rial scores 100,034 points. Lexi scores 9,348 fewer points than Rial and Susie scores 9,749 more points than Lexi. What is Susie's score? Show your work.

14. There were 13,501 visitors to a museum in June. What is this number rounded to the nearest ten thousand? Explain how you rounded.

_____

_____

15. New Mexico has an area of 121,298 square miles. California has
an area of 155,779 square miles. How much greater is the area, in
square miles, of California than the area of New Mexico? Show
your work and explain how you know the answer is reasonable.

16. Circle the choice that completes the statement.

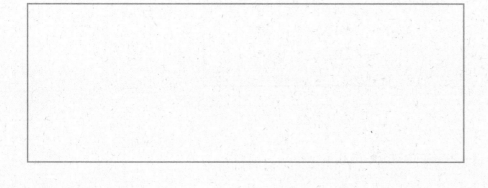

10,000 less than 24,576 is | equal to / greater than / less than | 1,000 less than 14,576

17. Match the number to the value of its 5.

45,678 •   • 500

757,234 •   • 50

13,564 •   • 50,000

3,450 •   • 5,000

18. During September and October, a total of 825,150 visitors went to Grand Canyon National Park. If 448,925 visitors went to the park in September, how many visitors went to the park in October? Show your work.

19. A college baseball team had 3 games in April. Game one had an attendance of 14,753 people. Game two had an attendance of 20,320 people. Game three had an attendance of 14,505 people. Write the games in order from the least attendance to the greatest attendance. Use pictures, words, or numbers to show how you know.

20. Caden made a four-digit number with a 5 in the thousands place, a 5 in the ones place, a 6 in the tens place, and a 4 in the hundreds place. What was the number?

_____

Chapter 2
Multiply by 1-Digit Numbers

Show What You Know

 **Personal Math Trainer** Online Assessment and Intervention

Check your understanding of important skills.

Name _____

▶ **Arrays** Write a multiplication sentence for the array.

1.

2.

_____   _____   _____   _____

▶ **Multiplication Facts** Find the product.

3. _____ = 9 × 6   4. _____ = 7 × 8   5. 8 × 4 = _____

▶ **Regroup Through Thousands**
Regroup. Write the missing numbers.

6. 9 tens 10 ones = _____ hundred

7. 60 hundreds = _____ thousands

8. 25 tens = _____ hundreds 5 tens

9. 14 ones = _____ ten _____ ones

10. 3 tens 12 ones = _____ tens 2 ones

The Arctic Lion's Mane Jellyfish is one of the largest known animals. Its tentacles can be as long as 120 feet. Find how this length compares to your height. Round your height to the nearest foot. 120 feet is _____ times as long as _____ feet.

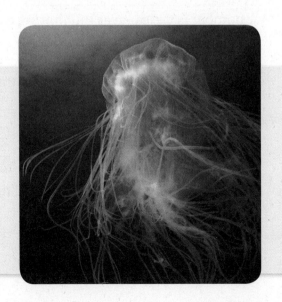

Vocabulary Builder

▶ Visualize It ●

Complete the flow map, using the words with a ✓.

Multiplying

What can you do?	What can you use?	What are some examples?
_____ products.	Use _____ and mental math.	3 × 48 = ▪ ↓ ↓ 3 × 50 = 150
_____ ones as tens.	Use _____ .	12 ones = 1 ten 2 ones

▶ Understand Vocabulary ● ● ● ● ● ● ● ● ● ● ● ● ● ● ● ● ● ● ●

Complete the sentences.

1. The _____ states that multiplying a sum by a
   number is the same as multiplying each addend by the number and then
   adding the products.

2. A number that is multiplied by another number to find a product

   is called a _____ .

3. A method of multiplying in which the ones, tens, hundreds, and

   so on are multiplied separately and then the products are added together is

   called the _____ method.

GO DIGITAL
• Interactive Student Edition
• Multimedia eGlossary

Chapter 2 Vocabulary

Distributive Property

propiedad distributiva

23

estimate (*verb*)

estimar

30

factor

factor

33

partial product

producto parcial

61

place value

valor posicional

68

product

producto

72

regroup

reagrupar

78

round

redondear

82

To find an answer that is close to the exact amount

The property that states that multiplying a sum by a number is the same as multiplying each addend by the number and then adding the products

Example: $5 \times (10 + 6) = (5 \times 10) + (5 \times 6)$

A method of multiplying in which the ones, tens, hundreds, and so on are multiplied separately and then the products are added together

$$
\begin{array}{r}
182 \\
\times\ \ \ 6 \\
\hline
600 \\
480 \\
+\ \ \ 12 \\
\hline
1{,}092
\end{array}
$$

← Partial products

A number that is multiplied by another number to find a product

Example: $4 \times 5 = 20$

factor   factor

The answer to a multiplication problem

Example: $4 \times 5 = 20$

product

The value of a digit in a number, based on the location of the digit

---

To replace a number with another number that tells about how many or how much

To exchange amounts of equal value to rename a number

Example: $5 + 8 = 13$ ones or 1 ten 3 ones

Game

Picture It

For 3 to 4 players

Materials

- timer
- sketch pad

How to Play

1. Take turns to play.

2. To take a turn, choose a word from the Word Box, but do not tell the word to the other players.

3. Set the timer for 1 minute.

4. Draw pictures and numbers to give clues about the word.

5. The first player to guess the word before time runs out gets 1 point. If that player can use the word in a sentence, he or she gets 1 more point. Then that player gets a turn choosing a word.

6. The first player to score 10 points wins.

Word Box
Distributive Property
estimate
factor
partial product
place value
product
regroup
round

The Write Way

Reflect

Choose one idea. Write about it.

- Explain the Distributive Property so that a younger child could understand it.
- Write two questions you have about regrouping.
- Describe the steps you would take find the product of 354 and 6.

Name _____

Multiplication Comparisons

Essential Question How can you model multiplication comparisons?

Learning Objective You will use models to interpret a multiplication equation as a comparison and write a comparison sentence.

You can use multiplication to compare amounts. For example, you can think of $15 = 3 \times 5$ as a comparison in two ways:

Remember

The Commutative Property states that you can multiply two factors in any order and get the same product.

15 is 3 times as many as 5.

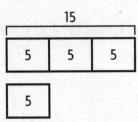

15 is 5 times as many as 3.

15
3 3 3 3 3

3

Unlock the Problem

Carly has 9 pennies. Jack has 4 times as many pennies as Carly. How many pennies does Jack have?

 Draw a model and write an equation to solve.

- **What do you need to compare?**

_____

_____

MODEL

Carly [ ]

Jack [| | |]

RECORD

Use the model to write an equation and solve.

$n = \underline{\hspace{1cm}} \times \underline{\hspace{1cm}}$

$n = \underline{\hspace{1cm}}$

The value of n is 36.

Think: n is how many pennies Jack has.

So, Jack has _____ pennies.

 Math Talk

Math Processes and Practices ①

Describe what is being compared and explain how the comparison model relates to the equation.

- **THINK SMARTER** Explain how the equation for *4 is 2 more than 2* is different from the equation for *4 is 2 times as many as 2.*

_____

_____

🔒 Example Draw a model and write an equation to solve.

Miguel has 3 times as many rabbits as Sara. Miguel has 6 rabbits. How many rabbits does Sara have?

- How many rabbits does Miguel have? _____
- How many rabbits does Sara have?

_____

_____

MODEL

Think: You don't know how many rabbits Sara has. Use n for Sara's rabbits.

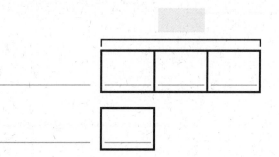

RECORD

Use the model to write an equation and solve.

$6 = \underline{\quad} \times \underline{\quad}$

$6 = 3 \times \underline{\quad}$ **Think:** 3 times what number equals 6?

The value of n is 2.

Think: n is how many rabbits Sara has.

So, Sara has 2 rabbits.

Try This! Write an equation or a comparison sentence.

Ⓐ Write an equation.

21 is 7 times as many as 3.

$\underline{\quad} = \underline{\quad} \times \underline{\quad}$

Ⓑ Write a comparison sentence.

$8 \times 5 = 40$

$\underline{\quad}$ times as many as $\underline{\quad}$ is $\underline{\quad}$.

Share and Show MATH BOARD

1. There are 8 students in the art club. There are 3 times as many students in chorus. How many students are in chorus?

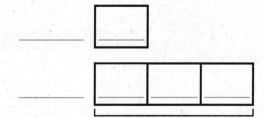

Write an equation and solve.

$n = \underline{\quad} \times \underline{\quad}$

$n = \underline{\quad}$

The value of n is $\underline{\quad}$.

So, there are _____ students in chorus.

Math Talk

Math Processes and Practices ⑥

Explain how you could write the equation a different way.

Draw a model and write an equation.

2. 6 times as many as 2 is 12.

☑ **3.** 20 is 4 times as many as 5.

_____

_____

Write a comparison sentence.

4. $18 = 9 \times 2$

_____ is _____ times as many as _____ .

☑ **5.** $8 \times 4 = 32$

_____ times as many as _____ is _____ .

On Your Own

Write a comparison sentence.

6. $5 \times 7 = 35$

_____ times as many as _____ is _____ .

7. $54 = 6 \times 9$

_____ is _____ times as many as _____ .

8. GO DEEPER One week, Jake and Sally collected canned goods for a food drive. On Monday, Jake collected 4 boxes and Sally collected 2 boxes. At the end of the week, Jake had 3 times as many boxes as he had on Monday. Sally had 4 times as many boxes as she had on Monday. Together, how many boxes of canned goods did they have at the end of the week?

_____

9. GO DEEPER Nando has 4 goldfish. Jill has 3 goldfish. Cooper has 2 times as many goldfish as Nando and Jill combined. Write an equation that compares the number of goldfish Cooper has with the number of goldfish that Nando and Jill have.

_____

10. Math Processes and Practices ② **Represent a Problem** Write a comparison sentence about pet food that could be represented using the equation $12 = 4 \times 3$.

_____

_____

_____

🔑 Unlock the Problem (Real World)

11. *THINK SMARTER* Luca has 72 baseball cards.
This is 8 times as many cards as Han has.
How many baseball cards does Han have?

a. What do you need to find? _____

_____

b. How can you use a model to find the number of cards Han has?

_____

c. Draw the model.

d. Write an equation and solve.

_____ = _____ × _____

_____ = _____

So, Han has _____ baseball cards.

12. *THINK SMARTER* Complete the statements to describe each model.

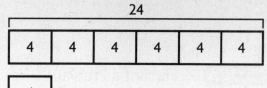

| 24 |
| 4 | 4 | 4 | 4 | 4 | 4 |

4

| 24 |
| 6 | 6 | 6 | 6 |

6

24 is [ ] times as many as [ ].   24 is [ ] times as many as [ ].

Name _____

Multiplication Comparisons

Learning Objective You will use models to interpret a multiplication equation as a comparison and write a comparison sentence.

Write a comparison sentence.

1. $6 \times 3 = 18$

____6____ times as many as __3__ is __18__.

2. $63 = 7 \times 9$

_____ is _____ times as many as _____.

3. $5 \times 4 = 20$

_____ times as many as _____ is _____.

4. $48 = 8 \times 6$

_____ is _____ times as many as _____.

Write an equation.

5. 2 times as many as 8 is 16.

_____

6. 42 is 6 times as many as 7.

_____

7. 3 times as many as 5 is 15.

_____

8. 36 is 9 times as many as 4.

_____

Problem Solving Real World

9. Alan is 14 years old. This is twice as old as his brother James is. How old is James?

_____

10. There are 27 campers. This is nine times as many as the number of counselors. How many counselors are there?

_____

11. **WRITE** ▸*Math* Draw a model, and write an equation to represent "4 times as many as 3 is 12." Explain your work.

_____

_____

Lesson Check

1. Write an equation that represents this comparison sentence.

   24 is 4 times as many as 6.

   _____

   _____

2. Write a comparison sentence that represents this equation.

   $5 \times 9 = 45$

   _____

   _____

Spiral Review

3. Which symbol makes the following statement true?

   547,098 $\bigcirc$ 574,908

4. What is the standard form for $200,000 + 80,000 + 700 + 6$?

   _____

5. Sean and Leah are playing a computer game. Sean scored 72,491 points. Leah scored 19,326 points more than Sean. How many points did Leah score?

6. A baseball stadium has 38,496 seats. Rounded to the nearest thousand, how many seats is this?

   _____

FOR MORE PRACTICE GO TO THE Personal Math Trainer

Name _____

Comparison Problems

Essential Question How does a model help you solve a comparison problem?

Learning Objective You will solve real-world problems with whole numbers involving multiplicative comparison using drawings and equations.

 Unlock the Problem

Evan's dog weighs 7 times as much as Oxana's dog. Together, the dogs weigh 72 pounds. How much does Evan's dog weigh?

Example 1 Use a multiplication model.

STEP 1 Draw a model. Let n represent the unknown.

> **Think:** Let n represent how much Oxana's dog weighs. Together, the dogs weigh 72 pounds.

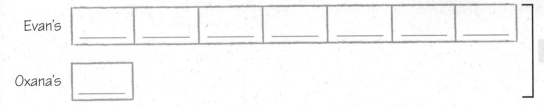

Evan's

Oxana's

STEP 2 Use the model to write an equation. Find the value of n.

_____ $\times n =$ _____   **Think:** There are 8 parts. The parts together equal 72.

$8 \times$ _____ $= 72$ **Think:** What times 8 equals 72?

The value of n is 9.

n is how much _____ weighs.

STEP 3 Find how much Evan's dog weighs.

> **Think:** Evan's dog weighs 7 times as much as Oxana's dog.

Evan's dog = _____ $\times$ _____   Multiply.

= _____

So, Evan's dog weighs 63 pounds.

 Math Talk

Math Processes and Practices ⑥

Attend to Precision How can you tell if you found the correct weight of Evan's dog?

To find how many times as much, use a multiplication model. To find how many more or fewer, model the addition or subtraction.

Evan's dog weighs 63 pounds. Oxana's dog weighs 9 pounds. How much more does Evan's dog weigh than Oxana's dog?

🔒 Example 2 Use an addition or subtraction model.

STEP 1 Draw a model. Let n represent the unknown.

Think: Let n represent the difference.

_____ ┌────────────────────────────────┐
                 │   _____   │
                 └────────────────────────────────┘
_____ ┌────────┐
                 │   │ └──────────────────────────────┐
                 └────────┘   │
                                                            │
                        ▭   │
_____

STEP 2 Use the model to write an equation. Find the value of n.

_____ – _____ = n   Think: The model shows a difference.

   63 – 9 = _____   Subtract.

The value of n is _____.

n is _____.

So, Evan's dog weighs 54 pounds more than Oxana's dog.

Share and Show 🖊 MATH BOARD

Math Talk

Math Processes and Practices ④

Use Models How do you know which model to use to solve a comparison problem?

1. Maria's dog weighs 6 times as much as her rabbit. Together the pets weigh 56 pounds. What does Maria's dog weigh?

Draw a model. Let n represent the unknown.

_____ ┌──────┬──────┬──────┬──────┬──────┬──────┐
        │   │   │   │   │   │   │ ┐
        └──────┴──────┴──────┴──────┴──────┴──────┘ │
_____ ┌──────┐   │
        │   │   │ ▭
        └──────┘   ┘

Write an equation to find the value of n. $7 \times n =$ _____. n is _____ pounds.

Multiply to find how much Maria's dog weighs. $8 \times 6 =$ _____

So, Maria's dog weighs _____ pounds.

70

Draw a model. Write an equation and solve.

2. Last month Kim trained 3 times as many dogs as cats. If the total number of cats and dogs she trained last month is 28, how many cats did Kim train?

Draw a model.   Write an equation and solve.

_____

_____

_____

3. How many more dogs than cats did Kim train?

Draw a model.   Write an equation and solve.

_____

_____

_____

On Your Own

Practice: Copy and Solve Draw a model.

Write an equation and solve.

4. At the dog show, there are 4 times as many boxers as spaniels. If there are a total of 30 dogs, how many dogs are spaniels?

5. There are 5 times as many yellow labs as terriers in the dog park. If there are a total of 18 dogs, how many dogs are terriers?

6. Ben has 3 times as many guppies as goldfish. If he has a total of 20 fish, how many guppies does he have?

7. GO DEEPER Carlita saw 5 times as many robins as cardinals while bird watching. She saw a total of 24 birds. How many more robins did she see than cardinals?

Problem Solving · Applications

8. **GO DEEPER** To get to a dog show, Mr. Luna first drives
7 miles west from his home and then 3 miles north. Next,
he turns east and drives 11 miles. Finally, he turns north
and drives 4 miles to the dog show. How far north of
Mr. Luna's home is the dog show?

To solve the problem, Dara and Cliff drew diagrams.
Which diagram is correct? Explain.

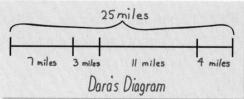

_____

_____

_____

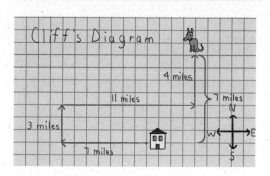

9. **Math Processes and Practices ②** **Use Reasoning** Valerie and Bret have a total
of 24 dog show ribbons. Bret has twice as many ribbons as
Valerie. How many ribbons does each have?

_____

_____

WRITE ▸ Math
Show Your Work

10. **THINK SMARTER** Noah built a fenced dog
run that is 8 yards long and 6 yards wide.
He placed posts at every corner and every
yard along the length and width of the run.
How many posts did he use?

11. **THINK SMARTER** Last weekend, Mandy collected 4 times as many shells as
Cameron. Together, they collected 40 shells. How many shells did Mandy
collect? Complete the bar model. Then, write an equation and solve.

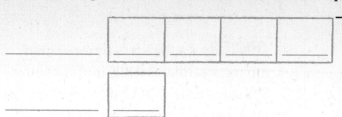

Comparison Problems

Learning Objective You will solve real-world problems with whole numbers involving multiplicative comparison using drawings and equations.

Draw a model. Write an equation and solve.

1. Stacey made a necklace using 4 times as many blue beads as red beads. She used a total of 40 beads. How many blue beads did Stacey use?

   Think: Stacey used a total of 40 beads. Let n represent the number of red beads.

   blue $\boxed{n}\ \boxed{n}\ \boxed{n}\ \boxed{n}$ ⎤
   red $\boxed{n}$ ⎦ 40

   $5 \times n = 40; 5 \times 8 = 40;$
   _____

   $4 \times 8 = 32$ blue beads
   _____

2. At the zoo, there were 3 times as many monkeys as lions. Tom counted a total of 24 monkeys and lions. How many monkeys were there?

   _____

   _____

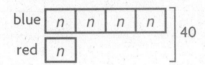

3. Rafael counted a total of 40 white cars and yellow cars. There were 9 times as many white cars as yellow cars. How many white cars did Rafael count?

   _____

4. Sue scored a total of 35 points in two games. She scored 6 times as many points in the second game as in the first. How many more points did she score in the second game?

   _____

5. **WRITE** ▸*Math* Write a problem involving *how much more than* and solve it. Explain how drawing a diagram helped you solve the problem.

   _____

   _____

Lesson Check

1. Sari has 3 times as many pencil erasers as Sam. Together, they have 28 erasers. How many erasers does Sari have?

2. In Sean's fish tank, there are 6 times as many goldfish as guppies. There are a total of 21 fish in the tank. How many more goldfish are there than guppies?

Spiral Review

3. Barbara has 9 stuffed animals. Trish has 3 times as many stuffed animals as Barbara. How many stuffed animals does Trish have?

4. There are 104 students in the fourth grade at Allison's school. One day, 15 fourth-graders were absent. How many fourth-graders were at school that day?

5. Joshua has 112 rocks. Jose has 98 rocks. Albert has 107 rocks. Write the boy's names in order from the least to the greatest number of rocks owned.

6. Alicia has 32 stickers. This is 4 times as many stickers as Benita has. How many stickers does Benita have?

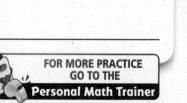

FOR MORE PRACTICE
GO TO THE
Personal Math Trainer

Name _____

Multiply Tens, Hundreds, and Thousands

Essential Question How does understanding place value help you multiply tens, hundreds, and thousands?

Learning Objective You will use place value to multiply tens, hundreds, and thousands.

 Unlock the Problem Real World

Each car on a train has 200 seats. How many seats are on a train with 8 cars?

Find 8 × 200.

One Way Draw a quick picture.

⟶ | T |

Think: 10 hundreds = 1,000

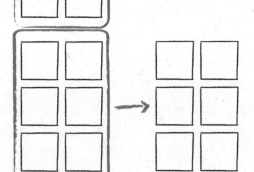

⟶

Think: 6 hundreds = 600

1,000 + 600 = _____

Another Way Use place value.

8 × 200 = 8 × _____ hundreds

= _____ hundreds

= _____ **Think:** 16 hundreds is 1 thousand, 6 hundreds.

So, there are _____ seats on a train with 8 cars.

 Math Talk

Math Processes and Practices 7

Look for a Pattern How can finding 8 × 2 help you find 8 × 200?

© Houghton Mifflin Harcourt Publishing Company • Image Credits: (t) ©Corbis

❶ Other Ways

Ⓐ Use a number line.

Bob's Sled Shop rents 4,000 sleds each month.
How many sleds does the store rent in 6 months?

Find 6 × 4,000.

Multiplication can be thought of as repeated addition.
Draw jumps to show the product.

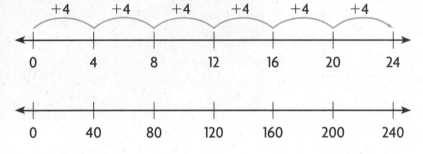

+4 +4 +4 +4 +4 +4

0   4   8   12   16   20   24

$6 \times 4 = 24$ ← basic fact

0   40   80   120   160   200   240

$6 \times 40 = 240$

0   400   800   1,200   1,600   2,000   2,400

$6 \times 400 = 2,400$

0   4,000   8,000   12,000   16,000   20,000   24,000

$6 \times 4,000 = 24,000$

So, Bob's Sled Shop rents _____ sleds in 6 months.

Ⓑ Use patterns.

Basic fact:

$3 \times 7 = 21$ ← basic fact

$3 \times 70 = 210$

$3 \times 700 =$ _____

$3 \times 7,000 =$ _____

Basic fact with a zero:

$8 \times 5 = 40$ ← basic fact

$8 \times 50 = 400$

$8 \times 500 =$ _____

$8 \times 5,000 =$ _____

- How does the number of zeros in the product of 8 and 5,000
  compare to the number of zeros in the factors? Explain.

_____

_____

Math Talk

Math Processes and Practices ⑤

Use Patterns to tell how the number of zeros in the factors and products changes in Example B.

Name _____

 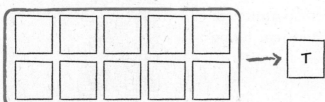

1. Use the drawing to find 2×500.

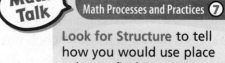

Math Talk — Math Processes and Practices ⑦

Look for Structure to tell how you would use place value to find 2×500.

$2 \times 500 =$ _____

Complete the pattern.

2. $3 \times 8 = 24$

$3 \times 80 =$ _____

$3 \times 800 =$ _____

$3 \times 8{,}000 =$ _____

3. $6 \times 2 = 12$

$6 \times 20 =$ _____

$6 \times 200 =$ _____

$6 \times 2{,}000 =$ _____

✓ **4.** $4 \times 5 =$ _____

$4 \times 50 =$ _____

$4 \times 500 =$ _____

$4 \times 5{,}000 =$ _____

Find the product.

✓ **5.** $6 \times 500 = 6 \times$ _____ hundreds

= _____ hundreds

= _____

6. $9 \times 5{,}000 = 9 \times$ _____ thousands

= _____ thousands

= _____

On Your Own

Find the product.

7. $7 \times 6{,}000 =$ _____

8. $4 \times 80 =$ _____

9. $3 \times 500 =$ _____

Math Processes and Practices ② Use Reasoning **Algebra** Find the missing factor.

10. _____ $\times 9{,}000 = 63{,}000$

11. $7 \times$ _____ $= 56{,}000$

12. $8 \times$ _____ $= 3{,}200$

13. **Math Processes and Practices ⑤** Communicate How does the number of zeros in the product of 8 and 5,000 compare to the number of zeros in the factors? Explain.

_____

_____

Unlock the Problem

14. **THINK SMARTER** Joe's Fun and Sun rents beach chairs. The store rented 300 beach chairs each month in April and in May. The store rented 600 beach chairs each month from June through September. How many beach chairs did the store rent during the 6 months?

a. What do you need to know? _____

_____

b. How will you find the number of beach chairs? _____

_____

c. Show the steps you use to solve the problem.

d. Complete the sentences.

For April and May, a total of _____ beach chairs were rented.

For June through September, a total of

_____ beach chairs were rented.

Joe's Fun and Sun rented _____ beach chairs during the 6 months.

15. **GO DEEPER** Mariah makes bead necklaces. Beads are packaged in bags of 50 and bags of 200. Mariah bought 4 bags of 50 beads and 3 bags of 200 beads. How many

beads did Mariah buy? _____

16. **THINK SMARTER** Carmen has three books of 20 stamps and five books of 10 stamps. How many stamps does Carmen have? Complete the equation using the numbers on the tiles.

_____ × 20 + _____ × 10 = _____

3	5
110	50
60	100

Multiply Tens, Hundreds, and Thousands

Learning Objective You will use place value to multiply tens, hundreds, and thousands.

Find the product.

1. $4 \times 7{,}000 =$ ___**28,000**___

   Think: $4 \times 7 = 28$
   So, $4 \times 7{,}000 = 28{,}000$

2. $9 \times 60 =$ _____

3. $8 \times 200 =$ _____

4. $5 \times 6{,}000 =$ _____

5. $7 \times 800 =$ _____

6. $8 \times 90 =$ _____

7. $6 \times 3{,}000 =$ _____

8. $3 \times 8{,}000 =$ _____

9. $5 \times 500 =$ _____

10. $9 \times 4{,}000 =$ _____

Problem Solving · Real World

11. A bank teller has 7 rolls of coins. Each roll has 40 coins. How many coins does the bank teller have?

    _____

12. Theo buys 5 packages of paper. There are 500 sheets of paper in each package. How many sheets of paper does Theo buy?

    _____

13. **WRITE** ▸*Math* Explain how finding 7×20 is similar to finding $7 \times 2{,}000$. Then find each product.

    _____

    _____

Lesson Check

1. A plane is traveling at a speed of 400 miles per hour. How far will the plane travel in 5 hours?

   _____

2. One week, a clothing factory made 2,000 shirts in each of 6 different colors. How many shirts did the factory make in all?

   _____

Spiral Review

3. Write a comparison sentence to represent this equation.

   $$6 \times 7 = 42$$

   _____

   _____

4. The population of Middleton is six thousand, fifty-four people. Write this number in standard form.

   _____

   _____

5. In an election for mayor, 85,034 people voted for Carl Green and 67,952 people voted for Maria Lewis. By how many votes did Carl Green win the election?

   _____

6. Meredith picked 4 times as many green peppers as red peppers. If she picked a total of 20 peppers, how many green peppers did she pick?

   _____

**FOR MORE PRACTICE
GO TO THE
Personal Math Trainer**

Name _____

Estimate Products

Essential Question How can you estimate products by rounding and determine if exact answers are reasonable?

Learning Objective You will estimate products using place value understanding to round multi-digit whole numbers to given place values and determine if exact answers are reasonable.

 Unlock the Problem Real World

An elephant can reach as high as 23 feet with its trunk. It uses its trunk to pick up objects that weigh up to 3 times as much as a 165-pound person. About how much weight can an African elephant pick up with its trunk?

- Cross out the information you will not use.
- Circle the numbers you will use.
- How will you use the numbers to solve the problem?

_____

One Way Estimate by rounding.

STEP 1 Round the greater factor to the nearest hundred.

3×165

↓

3×200

STEP 2 Use mental math.

Think: $3 \times 200 = 3 \times 2$ hundreds

= 6 hundreds

= _____

So, an African elephant can pick up about 600 pounds with its trunk.

Another Way Estimate by finding two numbers the exact answer is between.

3×165 3×165

↓   ↓

$3 \times 100 =$ _____ $3 \times 200 =$ _____

Think: 165 is between 100 and 200. Use those numbers to estimate.

An African elephant is the largest living land mammal.

So, the African elephant can pick up between 300 and 600 pounds.

1. Is 200 less than or greater than 165? _____

2. So, would the product of 3 and 165 be less than or

   greater than 600? _____

 Math Talk

Math Processes and Practices 6

Compare Is the exact answer closer to 300 or 600? Why?

Describe Reasonableness You can estimate a product to find whether an exact answer is reasonable.

🔑 **Tell whether an exact answer is reasonable.**

Eva's horse eats 86 pounds each week. Eva solved the equation below to find how much feed she needs for 4 weeks.

$4 \times 86 = $ ■

Eva says she needs 344 pounds of feed.
Is her answer reasonable?

🔑 **One Way** Estimate.

  4×86
         ↓ **Think:** Round to the nearest ten.
_____ × _____ = _____

344 is close to 360.

🔑 **Another Way** Find two numbers the exact answer is between.

  4×86 4×86
         ↓   ↓
_____ × _____ = _____   _____ × _____ = _____

_____ is between _____ and _____.

So, 344 pounds of feed is reasonable.

Share and Show

1. Estimate the product by rounding.

   $5 \times 2{,}213$
          ↓
   _____ × _____ = _____

2. Estimate the product by finding two numbers the exact answer is between.

   $5 \times 2{,}213$ $5 \times 2{,}213$

   _____ × _____ = _____   _____ × _____ = _____

Math Talk Math Processes and Practices ⑥
How do you know that an exact answer of 11,065 is reasonable? **Explain.**

Name _____

Tell whether the exact answer is reasonable.

✓ 3. Kira needs to make color copies of a horse show flyer. The printer can make 24 copies in 1 minute. Kira says the printer makes 114 copies in 6 minutes.

_____

_____

_____

✓ 4. Jones Elementary is having a car wash to raise money for a community horse trail. Each car wash ticket costs $8. Tiara says the school will receive $1,000 if 125 tickets are sold.

_____

_____

_____

On Your Own

Tell whether the exact answer is reasonable.

5. **Math Processes and Practices 1** Evaluate Reasonableness
Mrs. Hense sells a roll of coastal Bermuda horse hay for $58. She says she will make $174 if she sells 3 rolls.

_____

_____

_____

6. Mr. Brown sells horse supplies. A pair of riding gloves sells for $16. He says he will make $144 if he sells 9 pairs.

_____

_____

_____

7. **GO DEEPER** Path A and Path B are walking paths used for horses. Path A is 118 feet long. Path B is 180 feet long. Carlos walks his horse down each path 3 times. Which path did Carlos use to walk his horse about 500 feet? Explain.

_____

_____

_____

_____

8. **THINK SMARTER** Students in the third grade sell 265 tickets to the school play. Students in the fourth grade sell 3 times as many tickets as the third grade students. Estimate the number of tickets the fourth grade students sold by finding the two numbers the exact answer is between.

The students sold between

0		300	
300	and	600	tickets.
600		900	
800		1,200	

Connect to Reading

Make Predictions

As you read a story, you make predictions about what might happen next or about how the story will end.

When you solve a math problem, you make predictions about what your answer might be.

An *estimate* is a prediction because it helps you to determine whether your answer is correct. For some problems, it is helpful to make two estimates—one that is less than the exact answer and one that is greater.

Predict whether the exact answer will be *less than* or *greater than* the estimate. Explain your answer.

9. **THINK SMARTER** The food stand at the zoo sold 2,514 pounds of hamburger last month. The average cost of a pound of hamburger is $2. Jeremy estimates that about $6,000 worth of hamburger was sold last month.

_____

_____

_____

_____

10. **GO DEEPER** A zoo bought 2,240 pounds of fresh food for the bears this month. The average cost of a pound of food is $4. Jeremy estimates that about $8,000 was spent on fresh food for the bears this month.

_____

_____

_____

_____

© Houghton Mifflin Harcourt Publishing Company • Image Credits: (t) ©Ross Armstrong/Alamy; (bc) ©Hogne Haug/Alamy; (tc) ©Wim van den Heever/Getty Images; (b) ©Comstock/Getty Images

Name _____

Estimate Products

Learning Objective You will estimate products using place value understanding to round multi-digit whole numbers to given place values and determine if exact answers are reasonable.

Estimate the product by rounding.

1. 4 × 472

   4 × 472

   ↓

   4 × **500**

   _____2,000_____

2. 2 × 6,254

3. 9 × 54

4. 5 × 5,503

Find two numbers the exact answer is between.

5. 3 × 567

6. 6 × 7,381

7. 4 × 94

8. 8 × 684

Problem Solving (Real World)

9. Isaac drinks 8 glasses of water each day. He says he will drink 2,920 glasses of water in a year that has 365 days. Is the exact answer reasonable? **Explain.**

10. Most Americans throw away about 1,365 pounds of trash each year. Is it reasonable to estimate that Americans throw away over 10,000 pounds of trash in 5 years? **Explain.**

11. **WRITE** ▸Math Describe a real-life multiplication situation for which an estimate makes sense.

Lesson Check

1. A theater has 4,650 seats. If the theater sells all the tickets for each of its 5 shows, about how many tickets will the theater sell?

   _____

2. Washington Elementary has 4,358 students. Jefferson High School has 3 times as many students as Washington Elementary. About how many students does Jefferson High School have?

   _____

Spiral Review

3. Diego has 4 times as many autographed baseballs as Melanie has. Diego has 24 autographed baseballs. How many autographed baseballs does Melanie have?

   _____

4. Mr. Turkowski bought 4 boxes of envelopes at the office supply store. Each box has 500 envelopes. How many envelopes did Mr. Turkowski buy?

   _____

5. Pennsylvania has a land area of 44,816 square miles. What is the land area of Pennsylvania rounded to the nearest hundred?

   _____

6. The table shows the types of DVDs customers rented from Sunshine Movie Rentals last year.

Movie Rentals	
Type	Number Rented
Comedy	6,720
Drama	4,032
Action	5,540

   How many comedy and action movies were rented last year?

   _____

FOR MORE PRACTICE GO TO THE
Personal Math Trainer

Name _____

Multiply Using the Distributive Property

Essential Question How can you use the Distributive Property to multiply a 2-digit number by a 1-digit number?

Learning Objective You will use the Distributive Property to multiply a 2-digit number by a 1-digit number.

Investigate

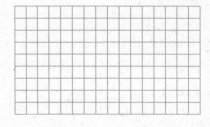

Materials ■ color pencils, grid paper

You can use the Distributive Property to break apart numbers to make them easier to multiply.

The **Distributive Property** states that multiplying a sum by a number is the same as multiplying each addend by the number and then adding the products.

A. Outline a rectangle on the grid to model 6 × 13.

B. Think of 13 as 5 + 8. Break apart the model to show 6 × (5 + 8). Label and shade the smaller rectangles. Use two different colors.

Use the Distributive Property. Find the product each smaller rectangle represents. Then find the sum of the products. Record your answers.

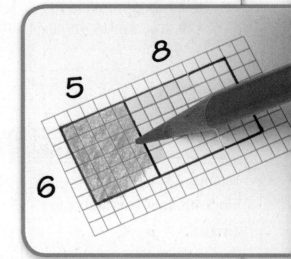

_____ × _____ = _____

_____ × _____ = _____

_____ + _____ = _____

C. Model 6 × 13 again. Think of 13 as a different sum. Break apart the model to show 6 × (_____ + _____). Find the product each smaller rectangle represents. Then find the sum of the products. Record your answers.

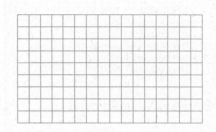

_____ × _____ = _____

_____ × _____ = _____

_____ + _____ = _____

Draw Conclusions

1. Explain how you found the total number of squares in each model in Steps B and C.

   _____

   _____

   _____

2. Compare the sums of the products in Steps B and C with those of your classmates. What can you conclude?

   _____

   _____

3. **THINK SMARTER** To find 7 × 23, is it easier to break apart the factor, 23, as 20 + 3 or 15 + 8? Explain.

   _____

   _____

Make Connections

Hands On

Another way to model the problem is to use base-ten blocks to show tens and ones.

STEP 1	STEP 2	STEP 3
Use base-ten blocks to model 6 × 13.	Break the model into tens and ones.	Add the tens and the ones to find the product.
6 rows of 1 ten 3 ones	(6 × 1 ten) (6 × 3 ones)	(6 × 10) + (6 × 3)
	(6 × 10) (6 × 3)	60 + 18
	_____ _____	_____

So, 6 × 13 = 78.

In Step 2, the model is broken into two parts. Each part shows a **partial product**. The partial products are 60 and 18.

Math Talk

Math Processes and Practices 4

Model Mathematics Why is this a good model for the problem?

Name _____

Share and Show MATH BOARD

Model the product on the grid. Record the product.

1. $3 \times 13 =$ _____

2. $5 \times 14 =$ _____

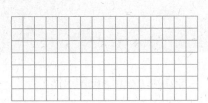 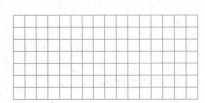

Find the product.

3. $6 \times 14 =$ _____

4. $5 \times 18 =$ _____

5. $4 \times 16 =$ _____

Use grid paper or base-ten blocks to model the product. Then record the product.

6. $7 \times 12 =$ _____

7. $5 \times 16 =$ _____

8. $9 \times 13 =$ _____

Problem Solving • Applications Real World

9. **Math Processes and Practices ⑥** **Explain** how modeling partial products can be used to find the products of greater numbers.

_____

_____

_____

10. **THINK SMARTER** Use the Distributive Property to model the product on the grid. Record the product.

$4 \times 14 =$ _____

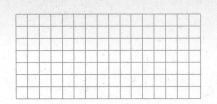

11. **THINK SMARTER** Kyle went to a fruit market. The market sells a wide variety of fruits and vegetables. The picture at the right shows a display of oranges.

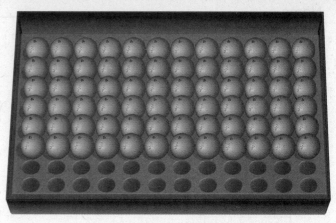

Write a problem that can be solved using the picture.

Pose a problem.

_____

_____

_____

_____

_____

_____

Solve your problem.

_____

_____

_____

_____

_____

_____

- **GO DEEPER** Describe how you could change the problem by changing the number of rows of oranges and the number of empty spaces in the picture. Then solve the problem.

_____

_____

_____

_____

Multiply Using the Distributive Property

Learning Objective You will use the Distributive Property to multiply a 2-digit number by a 1-digit number.

Model the product on the grid. Record the product.

1. $4 \times 19 =$ __76__

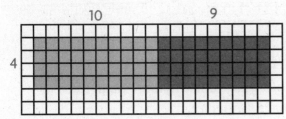

$4 \times 10 = 40$ and $4 \times 9 = 36$

$40 + 36 = 76$

2. $5 \times 13 =$ _____

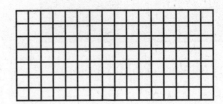

Find the product.

3. $4 \times 14 =$ _____

4. $3 \times 17 =$ _____

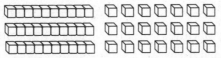

5. $6 \times 15 =$ _____

Problem Solving Real World

6. Michael arranged his pennies in the following display.

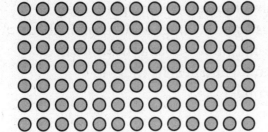

How many pennies does Michael have in all?

_____

7. WRITE ▸*Math* Explain how you can use a model to find 6×17.

_____

_____

_____

_____

Lesson Check

1. The model shows how Maya planted flowers in her garden.

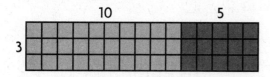

How many flowers did Maya plant?

_____

2. The model below represents the expression 5 × 18.

How many tens will there be in the final product?

_____

Spiral Review

3. Center City has a population of twenty-one thousand, seventy people. Write the population in standard form.

_____

4. Central School collected 12,516 pounds of newspaper to recycle. Eastland School collected 12,615 pounds of newspapers. How many more pounds of newspaper did Eastland School collect than Central School?

_____

5. Allison has 5 times as many baseball cards as football cards. In all, she has 120 baseball and football cards. How many baseball cards does Allison have?

_____

6. A ruby-throated hummingbird beats its wings about 53 times each second. About how many times does a ruby-throated hummingbird beat its wings in 5 seconds?

_____

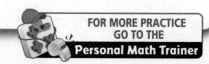

FOR MORE PRACTICE
GO TO THE
Personal Math Trainer

Name _____

Multiply Using Expanded Form

Essential Question How can you use expanded form to multiply a multidigit number by a 1-digit number?

Learning Objective You will use expanded form to multiply by a 1-digit number.

 Unlock the Problem *Real World*

🔑 **Example 1** Use expanded form.

Multiply. 5 × 143

$5 \times 143 = 5 \times ($ _____ + _____ + _____ $)$ Write 143 in expanded form.

$\qquad = (5 \times 100) + ($ _____ × _____ $) + ($ _____ × _____ $)$ Use the Distributive Property.

SHADE THE MODEL	THINK AND RECORD
STEP 1 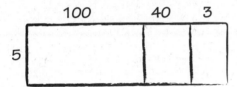	Multiply the hundreds. $(5 \times 100) + (5 \times 40) + (5 \times 3)$ _____ $+ (5 \times 40) + (5 \times 3)$
STEP 2 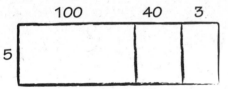	Multiply the tens. $(5 \times 100) + (5 \times 40) + (5 \times 3)$ $500 \quad + $ _____ $+ (5 \times 3)$
STEP 3 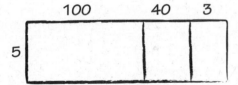	Multiply the ones. $(5 \times 100) + (5 \times 40) + (5 \times 3)$ $500 \quad + \quad 200 \quad + $ _____
STEP 4 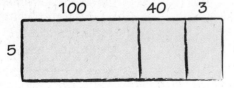	Add the partial products. $\begin{array}{r} 500 \\ 200 \\ +\ 15 \\ \hline \end{array}$

So, 5 × 143 = _____ .

 Math Talk

Math Processes and Practices ❶

Evaluate Reasonableness How do you know your answer is reasonable?

🔒 Example 2 Use expanded form.

The gift shop at the animal park orders 3 boxes of toy animals. Each box has 1,250 toy animals. How many toy animals does the shop order?

Multiply. 3 × 1,250

STEP 1

Write 1,250 in expanded form. Use the Distributive Property.

3 × 1,250 = 3 × (_____ + _____ + _____)

= (3 × 1,000) + (_____ × _____) + (_____ × _____)

STEP 2

Add the partial products.

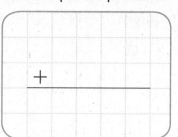

So, the shop ordered _____ animals.

Share and Show MATH BOARD

1. Find 4 × 213. Use expanded form.

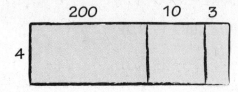

4 × 213 = _____ × (_____ + _____ + _____)

= (_____ × _____) + (_____ × _____) + (_____ × _____)   Use the Distributive Property.

= _____ + _____ + _____

= _____

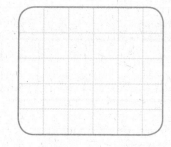

Record the product. Use expanded form to help.

✓ 2. 4 × 59 = _____

✓ 3. 3 × 288 = _____

Math Talk

Math Processes and Practices ②

Represent a Problem How did using the Distributive Property make finding the product easier?

Name _____

Record the product. Use expanded form to help.

4. $4 \times 21 =$ _____

5. $6 \times 35 =$ _____

6. `GO DEEPER` A hotel has 128 rooms on each floor. There are 4 floors in all. If 334 of the rooms in the hotel have been cleaned, how many rooms still need to be cleaned?

_____

7. `GO DEEPER` Ben wants to buy 2 blue sweaters for $119 each and 3 brown sweaters for $44 each. How much will Ben spend on the five sweaters?

_____

WRITE ▸ *Math*
Show Your Work

8. `GO DEEPER` A jeweler has 36 inches of silver chain. She needs 5 times that much to make some necklaces and 3 times that amount to make some bracelets. How much silver chain does the jeweler need to make her necklaces and bracelets?

_____

9. `GO DEEPER` Gretchen walks her dog 3 times a day. Each time she walks the dog, she walks 1,760 yards. How many yards does she walk her dog in 3 days?

_____

10. `Math Processes and Practices 4` **Write an Expression** Which expression could you write to show how to multiply 9×856 using place value and expanded form?

_____

11. `GO DEEPER` Jennifer bought 4 packages of tacks. There are 48 tacks in a package. She used 160 of the tacks to put up posters. How many tacks does she have left? Explain.

_____

_____

_____

_____

Problem Solving • Applications

Use the table for 12–13.

Sacco Nursery Plant Sale Prices per Tree		
Tree	Regular Price	Discounted Price (4 or more)
Flowering Cherry	$59	$51
Italian Cypress	$79	$67
Muskogee Crape Myrtle	$39	$34
Royal Empress	$29	$25

12. What is the total cost of 3 Italian cypress trees?

_____

13. **THINK SMARTER** **What's the Error?**
Tanya says that the difference in the
cost of 4 flowering cherry trees and
4 Muskogee crape myrtles is $80.
Is she correct? Explain.

_____

_____

_____

WRITE ▸*Math* • **Show Your Work** • • • • • • • • •

14. **WRITE** ▸*Math*   What is the greatest possible product
of a 2-digit number and a 1-digit number? Explain
how you know.

_____

_____

_____

15. **THINK SMARTER** Multiply 5 × 381 using place value and expanded form.
Select a number from each box to complete the expression.

$$(5 \times \boxed{\begin{array}{c}30\\300\end{array}}) + (5 \times \boxed{\begin{array}{c}8\\80\end{array}}) + (5 \times \boxed{\begin{array}{c}1\\10\end{array}})$$

Multiply Using Expanded Form

Learning Objective You will use expanded form to multiply by a 1-digit number.

Record the product. Use expanded form to help.

1. $7 \times 14 =$ _____ 98 _____

$7 \times 14 = 7 \times (10 + 4)$

$\qquad = (7 \times 10) + (7 \times 4)$

$\qquad = 70 + 28$

$\qquad = 98$

2. $8 \times 43 =$ _____

3. $6 \times 532 =$ _____

4. $5 \times 923 =$ _____

Problem Solving Real World

5. The fourth-grade students at Riverside School are going on a field trip. There are 68 students on each of the 4 buses. How many students are going on the field trip?

_____

6. There are 5,280 feet in one mile. Hannah likes to walk 5 miles each week for exercise. How many feet does Hannah walk each week?

_____

7. **WRITE** ▸ *Math* Explain how you can find 3×584 using expanded form.

_____

_____

_____

Lesson Check

1. Write an expression that shows how to multiply 7 × 256 using expanded form and the Distributive Property.

_____

_____

2. Sue uses the expression (8 × 3,000) + (8 × 200) + (8 × 9) to help solve a multiplication problem. What is Sue's multiplication problem?

_____

_____

Spiral Review

3. What is another way to write 9 × 200?

_____

_____

4. What is the value of the digit 4 in 46,000?

_____

_____

5. Chris bought 6 packages of napkins for his restaurant. There were 200 napkins in each package. How many napkins did Chris buy?

6. List these numbers in order from **least** to **greatest**.

8,251; 8,125; 8,512

_____

_____

**FOR MORE PRACTICE
GO TO THE**
Personal Math Trainer

Name _____

Multiply Using Partial Products

Essential Question How can you use place value and partial products to multiply by a 1-digit number?

Learning Objective You will use place value understanding and partial products to multiple a whole number of up to 4-digits by a 1-digit whole number.

 Unlock the Problem

CONNECT How can you use what you know about the Distributive Property to break apart numbers to find products of 3-digit and 1-digit numbers?

 Use place value and partial products.

• How can you write 182 as a sum of hundreds, tens, and ones?

_____

Multiply. 6 × 182   **Estimate.** 6 × 200 = _____

SHADE THE MODEL	THINK AND RECORD

STEP 1

182
× 6

← Multiply the hundreds.
6 × 1 hundred = 6 hundreds

STEP 2

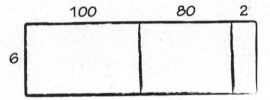

182
× 6
600

← Multiply the tens.
6 × 8 tens = 48 tens

STEP 3

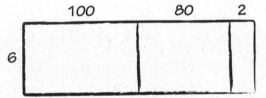

182
× 6
600
480

← Multiply the ones.
6 × 2 ones = 12 ones

STEP 4

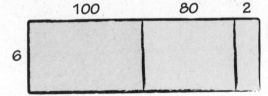

182
× 6
600
480
+ 12

← Add the partial products.

So, 6 × 182 = 1,092. Since 1,092 is close to the estimate of 1,200, it is reasonable.

Math Talk Math Processes and Practices ②

Use Reasoning How can you use the Distributive Property to find 4 × 257?

Example

Use place value and partial products.

Multiply. 2 × 4,572   **Estimate.** 2 × 5,000 = _____

$$\begin{array}{r} 4{,}572 \\ \times \quad 2 \\ \hline \end{array}$$

← 2 × 4 thousands = 8 thousands

← 2 × 5 hundreds = 1 thousand

← 2 × 7 tens = 1 hundred, 4 tens

← 2 × 2 ones = 4 ones

← Add the partial products.

Share and Show

 MATH BOARD

1. Use the model to find 2 × 137.

	100	30	7
2			

$$\begin{array}{r} 137 \\ \times \quad 2 \\ \hline \\ \\ + \\ \hline \end{array}$$

Estimate. Then record the product.

2. Estimate: _____

$$\begin{array}{r} 190 \\ \times \quad 3 \\ \hline \\ \\ + \\ \hline \end{array}$$

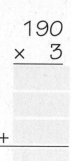 3. Estimate: _____

$$\begin{array}{r} 471 \\ \times \quad 4 \\ \hline \\ \\ + \\ \hline \end{array}$$

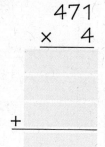 4. Estimate: _____

$$\begin{array}{r} \$3{,}439 \\ \times \quad 7 \\ \hline \\ \\ \\ + \\ \hline \end{array}$$

Math Talk

Math Processes and Practices ⑥

Explain how using place value and expanded form makes it easier to find products.

Name _____

On Your Own

Estimate. Then record the product.

5. Estimate: _____

$$\begin{array}{r} \$53 \\ \times \quad 4 \\ \hline \\ + \\ \hline \end{array}$$

6. Estimate: _____

$$\begin{array}{r} \$473 \\ \times \quad 9 \\ \hline \\ \\ + \\ \hline \end{array}$$

7. Estimate: _____

$$\begin{array}{r} 608 \\ \times \quad 6 \\ \hline \\ \\ + \\ \hline \end{array}$$

Practice: Copy and Solve Estimate. Then record the product.

8. 2×78

9. $2 \times \$210$

10. $9 \times \$682$

11. $8 \times 8{,}145$

Math Processes and Practices ② Use Reasoning **Algebra** Find the missing digit.

12.
$$\begin{array}{r} \boxed{}5 \\ \times \quad 7 \\ \hline 455 \end{array}$$

13.
$$\begin{array}{r} 248 \\ \times \quad 3 \\ \hline \boxed{}44 \end{array}$$

14.
$$\begin{array}{r} \$395 \\ \times \quad \boxed{} \\ \hline \$2{,}370 \end{array}$$

15.
$$\begin{array}{r} 3{,}748 \\ \times \quad 4 \\ \hline 1\boxed{}{,}992 \end{array}$$

16. GO DEEPER A store bought 9 cases of light bulbs in May and 8 cases in June. There are 48 light bulbs in a case. How many light bulbs did the store buy in May and June?

_____

17. GO DEEPER Mr. Wilson saved $2,500 to buy airline tickets for his family. He bought 6 airline tickets for $372 each. How much of his savings does Mr. Wilson have after he buys the tickets?

_____

18. GO DEEPER Coach Ramirez bought 8 cases of bottled water for a road race. There are 24 bottles in each case. After the race, 34 bottles of water were left. How many bottles were used at the race? Explain.

_____

_____

_____

Problem Solving • Applications Real World

19. **Math Processes and Practices 4 Use Diagrams** Look at the picture. Kylie has 832 songs on her portable media player. Lance has 3 times as many songs. How many fewer songs can Lance add to his player than Kylie can add to hers?

Up To 9,000 Songs
Battery Life For
Audio: 22 Hours

20. **GO DEEPER** James wants to buy the new portable media player shown. He has 5 times as many songs as Susan. Susan has 1,146 songs. Will all of his songs fit on the portable media player? How many songs does James have?

WRITE *Math* · **Show Your Work**

21. **THINK SMARTER** The sum of a 3-digit number and a 1-digit number is 217. The product of the numbers is 642. If one number is between 200 and 225, what are the numbers?

22. **THINK SMARTER** Mrs. Jackson bought 6 gallons of juice for a party. Each gallon has 16 cups. After the party, 3 cups of juice were left over. At the party, how many cups did people drink? Show your work and explain how you found your answer.

Multiply Using Partial Products

Learning Objective You will use place value understanding and partial products to multiple a whole number of up to 4-digits by a 1-digit whole number.

Estimate. Then record the product.

1. Estimate: 1,200

```
    243
×     6
  1,200
    240
+    18
  1,458
```

2. Estimate: _____

```
  640
×   3
```

3. Estimate: _____

```
  $149
×     5
```

4. Estimate: _____

```
  721
×   8
```

5. Estimate: _____

```
  293
×   4
```

6. Estimate: _____

```
  $416
×    6
```

7. Estimate: _____

```
  961
×   2
```

8. Estimate: _____

```
  837
×   9
```

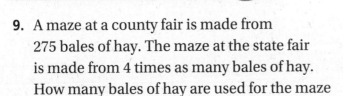

Problem Solving Real World

9. A maze at a county fair is made from 275 bales of hay. The maze at the state fair is made from 4 times as many bales of hay. How many bales of hay are used for the maze at the state fair?

_____

10. Pedro gets 8 hours of sleep each night. How many hours does Pedro sleep in a year with 365 days?

_____

11. **WRITE** Math Explain how you can find 4×754 using two different methods.

_____

_____

Lesson Check

1. A passenger jet flies at an average speed of 548 miles per hour. At that speed, how many miles does the plane travel in 4 hours?

2. Use the model to find 3×157.

	100	50	7
3			

Spiral Review

3. The school fun fair made $1,768 on games and $978 on food sales. How much money did the fun fair make on games and food sales?

4. Use the table below.

State	Population
North Dakota	646,844
Alaska	698,473
Vermont	621,760

List the states from least to greatest population.

5. A National Park covers 218,375 acres. What is this number written in expanded form?

6. Last year a business had profits of $8,000. This year its profits are 5 times as great. What are this year's profits?

FOR MORE PRACTICE
GO TO THE
Personal Math Trainer

Name _____

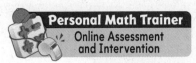

Vocabulary

Choose the best term from the box to complete the sentence.

1. To find the product of a two-digit number and a 1-digit number, you can multiply the tens, multiply the ones, and find

   the sum of each _____. (p. 88)

2. The _____ states that multiplying a sum by a number is the same as multiplying each addend by the number and then adding the products. (p. 87)

Concepts and Skills

Write a comparison sentence.

3. $5 \times 9 = 45$

   _____ times as many as _____ is _____.

4. $24 = 6 \times 4$

   _____ is _____ times as many as _____.

5. $54 = 6 \times 9$

   _____ is _____ times as many as _____.

6. $8 \times 6 = 48$

   _____ times as many as _____ is _____.

Estimate. Then record the product.

7. Estimate: _____

   $$\begin{array}{r} 75 \\ \times\ 5 \\ \hline \end{array}$$

8. Estimate: _____

   $$\begin{array}{r} 12 \\ \times\ 6 \\ \hline \end{array}$$

9. Estimate: _____

   $$\begin{array}{r} 28 \\ \times\ 3 \\ \hline \end{array}$$

10. Estimate: _____

    $$\begin{array}{r} \$43 \\ \times\ \ 6 \\ \hline \end{array}$$

Record the product. Use expanded form to help.

11. $5 \times 64 =$ _____

12. $3 \times 272 =$ _____

13. There are 6 times as many dogs as cats. If the total number of dogs and cats is 21, how many dogs are there?

_____

14. The table below shows the number of calories in 1 cup of different kinds of berries. How many calories are in 4 cups of blackberries?

Berry Nutrition	
Berry	Number of Calories in 1 Cup
Blackberries	62
Blueberries	83
Raspberries	64
Strawberries	46

_____

15. GO DEEPER The skating rink rented 218 pairs of skates during the month of April and 3 times that many in May. How many pairs of skates did the skating rink rent during April and May?

_____

Multiply Using Mental Math

Essential Question How can you use mental math and properties to help you multiply numbers?

Learning Objective You will use mental math and properties of operations to multiply a whole number of up to 4-digits by a 1-digit whole number.

Unlock the Problem

Properties of Multiplication can make multiplication easier.

There are 4 sections of seats in the Playhouse Theater. Each section has 7 groups of seats. Each group has 25 seats. How many seats are there in the theater?

🔑 **Find 4 × 7 × 25.**

$4 \times 7 \times 25 = 4 \times 25 \times 7$ Commutative Property

         = _____ × 7   **Think:** 4 × 25 = 100

         = _____   **Think:** 100 × 7 = 700

So, there are 700 seats in the theater.

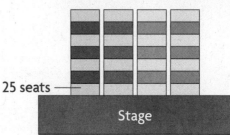

25 seats ———

Stage

Math Talk   Math Processes and Practices ⑧

Draw Conclusions What do you know about 4 × 25 that will help you find 6 × 25?

Try This! Use mental math and properties.

Ⓐ **Find (6 × 10) × 10.**

   $(6 \times 10) \times 10 = 6 \times (10 \times 10)$ Associative Property

           = 6 × _____

           = _____

Ⓑ **Find (4 × 9) × 250.**

   $(4 \times 9) \times 250 = 250 \times (4 \times 9)$ Commutative Property

           $= (250 \times 4) \times 9$ Associative Property

           = _____ × 9

           = _____

Remember

The Associative Property states that you can group factors in different ways and get the same product. Use parentheses to group the factors you multiply first.

More Strategies Choose the strategy that works best with the numbers in the problems.

🔑 Examples

A Use friendly numbers.

Multiply. 24 × 250

Think: 24 = 6 × 4 and 4 × 250 = 1,000

24 × 250 = 6 × 4 × 250

= 6 × _____

= _____

B Use halving and doubling.

Multiply. 16 × 50

Think: 16 can be divided evenly by 2.

16 ÷ 2 = 8   Find half of 16.

8 × 50 = _____   Multiply.

2 × 400 = _____   Double 400.

C Use addition.

Multiply. 4 × 625

Think: 625 is 600 plus 25.

4 × 625 = 4 × (600 + 25)

= (4 × 600) + (4 × 25)

= _____ + _____

= _____

D Use subtraction.

Multiply. 5 × 398

Think: 398 is 2 less than 400.

5 × 398 = 5 × (400 − 2)

= (5 × _____) − (5 × 2)

= 2,000 − _____

= _____

- What property is being used in Examples C and D? _____

Share and Show

1. Break apart the factor 112 to find 7 × 112 by using mental math and addition.

7 × 112 = 7 × (_____ + 12)

= _____

= _____

= _____

Name _____

Find the product. Tell which strategy you used.

2. $4 \times 6 \times 50$ ✓**3.** 5×420 ✓**4.** 6×298

_____   _____   _____

_____   _____   _____

On Your Own

Math Talk

Math Processes and Practices ⑦

Identify Relationships
How is using an addition strategy related to using a subtraction strategy?

Find the product. Tell which strategy you used.

5. 14×50 **6.** 32×25 **7.** $8 \times 25 \times 23$

_____   _____   _____

_____   _____   _____

Practice: Copy and Solve Use a strategy to find the product.

8. 16×400 **9.** $3 \times 31 \times 10$ **10.** 3×199 **11.** $3 \times 1,021$

Math Processes and Practices ⑦ **Identify Relationships** **Algebra** Use mental math to find the unknown number.

12. $21 \times 40 = 840$, so $21 \times 42 =$ _____ .

13. $9 \times 60 = 540$, so $18 \times 30 =$ _____ .

14. _GO DEEPER_ The science museum sells dinosaur models to schools and libraries for $107 each. The town library buys 3 models. The town elementary school buys 5 models. What is the total cost of the models the town buys?

15. _GO DEEPER_ Kyle and Karen each bought 6 books of ride tickets at the fair. Each book has 15 tickets. How many tickets did they buy altogether?

_____   _____

Problem Solving · Applications

Use the table for 16–18.

16. **GO DEEPER** Three thousand, forty-three people buy tickets at the gate for Section N and one hundred people buy tickets at the gate for Section L. How much money is collected for Section N and Section L at the gate?

_____

17. **Math Processes and Practices ①** **Use Diagrams** Tina and 3 of her friends buy the full season plan for Section M. If there are 45 games in the full season, how much money do they spend?

_____

18. **THINK SMARTER** When the full season tickets first went on sale, 2,000 Full Season tickets sold for Section N. Two weeks after the tickets first went on sale, another 1,500 full season tickets were sold for Section N. How much money was spent on full season tickets for Section N in total? How much more money was spent when the tickets first went on sale than after the first two weeks?

_____

Arena Ticket Prices Per Game

Section	Full Season	15-Game Plan	Gate Price
K	$44	$46	$48
L	$30	$32	$35
M	$25	$27	$30
N	$20	$22	$25

WRITE *Math* · **Show Your Work**

Personal Math Trainer

19. **THINK SMARTER +** Find 6 × 407. Show your work and explain why the strategy you chose works best with the factors.

_____

_____

_____

Multiply Using Mental Math

Learning Objective You will use mental math and properties of operations to multiply a whole number of up to 4-digits by a 1-digit whole number.

Find the product. Tell which strategy you used.

1. 6 × 297   **Think:** 297 = 300 − 3
$$6 × 297 = 6 × (300 − 3)$$
$$= (6 × 300) − (6 × 3)$$
$$= 1,800 − 18$$
$$= 1,782$$

1,782;

use subtraction

2. 14 × 25 × 4   **3.** 8 × 604   **4.** 50 × 28

_____   _____   _____

_____   _____   _____

Problem Solving Real World

5. Section J in an arena has 20 rows. Each row has 15 seats. All tickets cost $18 each. If all the seats are sold, how much money will the arena collect for Section J?

6. At a high-school gym, the bleachers are divided into 6 equal sections. Each section can seat 395 people. How many people can be seated in the gym?

_____   _____

7. **WRITE** ▸*Math* Show how to multiply 6 × 298 using friendly numbers and then using properties and mental math. Write about which method you like better and why.

_____
_____
_____
_____

Lesson Check

1. Pencils come in cartons of 24 boxes. A school bought 50 cartons of pencils for the start of school. Each box of pencils cost $2. How much did the school spend on pencils?

   _____

2. The school also bought 195 packages of markers. There are 6 markers in a package. How many markers did the school buy?

   _____

Spiral Review

3. Alex has 175 baseball cards. Rodney has 3 times as many baseball cards as Alex. How many fewer cards does Alex have than Rodney?

   _____

   _____

4. A theater seats 1,860 people. The last 6 shows have been sold out. Estimate the total number of people attending the last 6 shows.

   _____

   _____

5. At one basketball game, there were 1,207 people. At the next game, there were 958 people. How many people were at the two games?

   _____

6. Bill bought 4 jigsaw puzzles. Each puzzle has 500 pieces. How many pieces are in all the puzzles?

   _____

© Houghton Mifflin Harcourt Publishing Company

FOR MORE PRACTICE
GO TO THE
Personal Math Trainer

Name _____

Problem Solving • Multistep Multiplication Problems

Essential Question When can you use the *draw a diagram* strategy to solve a multistep multiplication problem?

Learning Objective You will use the strategy *draw a diagram* to solve multistep multiplication problems.

Unlock the Problem

At the sea park, one section in the stadium has 9 rows with 18 seats in each row. In the center of each of the first 6 rows, 8 seats are in the splash zone. How many seats are not in the splash zone?

Use the graphic organizer to help you solve the problem.

Read the Problem	Solve the Problem
What do I need to find? I need to find the number of seats that _____ in the splash zone.	I drew a diagram of the section to show 9 rows of 18 seats. In the center, I outlined a section to show the 6 rows of 8 seats in the splash zone. 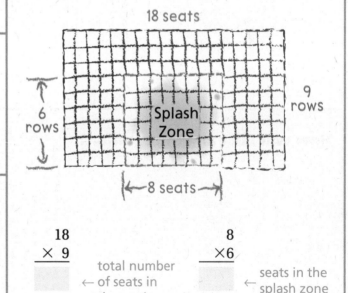
What information do I need to use? There are 9 rows with _____ seats in each row of the section. There are 6 rows with _____ seats in each row of the splash zone.	
How will I use the information? I can _____ to find both the number of seats in the section and the number of seats in the splash zone.	18 × 9 _____ ← total number of seats in the section 8 ×6 _____ ← seats in the splash zone

1. What else do you need to do to solve the problem?

_____

_____

🔑 Try Another Problem

At the sea park, one section of the shark theater has 8 rows with 14 seats in each row. In the middle of the section, 4 rows of 6 seats are reserved. How many seats are not reserved?

Read the Problem	Solve the Problem
What do I need to find?	
What information do I need to use?	
How will I use the information?	

2. How did your diagram help you solve the problem?

_____

_____

Math Processes and Practices ②

Reason Abstractly How do you know your answer is correct?

Name _____

Unlock the Problem
√ Use the Problem Solving MathBoard
√ Underline important facts.
√ Choose a strategy you know.

Share and Show | MATH BOARD

1. The seats in Sections A and B of the stadium are all taken for the last show. Section A has 8 rows of 14 seats each. Section B has 6 rows of 16 seats each. How many people are seated in Sections A and B for the last show?

   First, draw and label a diagram. **Next**, find the number of seats in each section.

   Section A   Section B

   Last, find the total number of seats. _____ + _____ = _____

   There are _____ people seated in Sections A and B for the last show.

WRITE ▸ *Math*
Show Your Work

2. What if Sections A and B each had 7 rows? How many people would have been seated in Sections A and B?

   _____

3. Brenda's vegetable garden has 13 rows with 8 plants in each row. Brenda plans to plant peppers in the first 2 rows and the last 2 rows of the garden. The rest of the rows will be tomatoes. How many tomato plants will Brenda plant?

   _____

4. **GO DEEPER** There are 8 rows of 22 chairs set up for an awards ceremony at the school. In each row, the 2 chairs on each end are reserved for students receiving awards. The rest of the chairs are for guests. How many chairs are there for guests?

   _____

On Your Own

Use the graph for 5–6.

5. 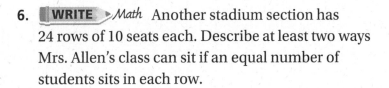 Mr. Torres took his students to the dolphin show. Each row in the stadium had 11 seats. One adult sat at each end of a row, and each group of 4 students was seated between 2 adults. Mr. Torres sat by himself. How many adults were there?

_____

6. **WRITE** ▸*Math* Another stadium section has 24 rows of 10 seats each. Describe at least two ways Mrs. Allen's class can sit if an equal number of students sits in each row.

_____

_____

_____

7. **THINK SMARTER** Carol, Ann, and Liz each bought a toy fish. Carol's fish is 10 inches longer than Ann's fish. Liz's fish is 2 inches longer than twice the length of Ann's fish. Ann's fish is 12 inches long. Find the length of each toy fish.

_____

8. **Math Processes and Practices ❶ Evaluate Relationships** Nell made a secret code. Each code word has 2 letters. Each word begins with a consonant and ends with a vowel. How many code words can Nell make with 3 consonants and 2 vowels?

_____

9. **THINK SMARTER** Allie is building a patio. The patio will have 8 tiles in each of 13 rows. She has already built the center section with 4 tiles in each of 7 rows. How many more tiles are needed to complete the patio? Show your work.

_____

_____

Sea Park Field Trips

Teacher	Number of Students
Ms. Bird	
Mr. Torres	
Mrs. Allen	

0   6   12   18   24   30   36   42

Number of Students

WRITE ▸*Math* • **Show Your Work** • • • • • •

Name _____

Problem Solving • Multistep Multiplication Problems

Learning Objective You will use the strategy *draw a diagram* to solve multistep multiplication problems.

Solve each problem.

1. A community park has 6 tables with a chessboard painted on top. Each board has 8 rows of 8 squares. When a game is set up, 4 rows of 8 squares on each board are covered with chess pieces. If a game is set up on each table, how many total squares are NOT covered by chess pieces?

   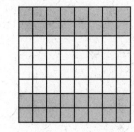

   $4 \times 8 = 32$
   $32 \times 6 = \blacksquare$

   _____**192 squares**_____

2. Jonah and his friends go apple picking. Jonah fills 5 baskets. Each basket holds 15 apples. If 4 of Jonah's friends pick the same amount as Jonah, how many apples do Jonah and his friends pick in all? Draw a diagram to solve the problem.

   _____

3. **WRITE** ▸*Math* Write a word problem that can be solved using multiplication of two-digit numbers. Solve your word problem and explain the solution.

   _____

   _____

   _____

   _____

Lesson Check

1. At a tree farm, there are 9 rows of 36 spruce trees. In each row, 14 of the spruce trees are blue spruce. How many spruce trees are NOT blue spruce?

2. Ron is tiling a countertop. He needs to place 54 square tiles in each of 8 rows to cover the counter. He wants to randomly place 8 groups of 4 blue tiles each and have the rest of the tiles be white. How many white tiles will Ron need?

Spiral Review

3. Juan reads a book with 368 pages. Savannah reads a book with 172 fewer pages than Juan's book. How many pages are in the book Savannah reads?

4. Hailey has bottles that hold 678 pennies each. About how many pennies does she have if she has 6 bottles filled with pennies?

5. Terrence plants a garden that has 8 rows of flowers, with 28 flowers in each row. How many flowers did Terrence plant?

6. Kevin has 5 fish in his fish tank. Jasmine has 4 times as many fish as Kevin has. How many fish does Jasmine have?

FOR MORE PRACTICE
GO TO THE
Personal Math Trainer

Name _____

Multiply 2-Digit Numbers with Regrouping

Essential Question How can you use regrouping to multiply a 2-digit number by a 1-digit number?

Learning Objective You will use regrouping to multiply a 2-digit number by a 1-digit number.

🔑 Unlock the Problem

A Thoroughbred racehorse can run at speeds of up to 60 feet per second. During practice, Celia's horse runs at a speed of 36 feet per second. How far does her horse run in 3 seconds?

- Underline important information.
- Is there information you will not use? If so, cross out the information.

🔓 Example 1

Multiply. 3×36 **Estimate.** $3 \times 40 =$ _____

MODEL	THINK	RECORD

STEP 1

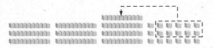

Multiply the ones.
3×6 ones = 18 ones
Regroup the 18 ones.

$$\begin{array}{r} \overset{1}{3}6 \\ \times\ 3 \\ \hline 8 \end{array}$$

Regroup 18 ones as 1 ten 8 ones.

STEP 2

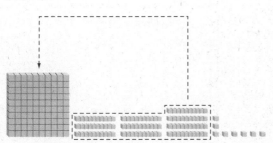

Multiply the tens.
3×3 tens = 9 tens
Add the regrouped ten.
9 tens + 1 ten = 10 tens

$$\begin{array}{r} \overset{1}{3}6 \\ \times\ 3 \\ \hline 108 \end{array}$$

10 tens is the same as 1 hundred 0 tens.

So, Celia's racehorse runs _____ feet in 3 seconds.

Since _____ is close to the estimate of _____, the answer is reasonable.

Math Talk

Math Processes and Practices ❸

Apply Look at Step 1. How does the model support your work?

Chapter 2   **119**

🔒 Example 2

Multiply. 8 × 22   **Estimate.** 8 × 20 = _____

MODEL	THINK	RECORD

STEP 1

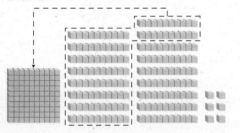

Multiply the ones.
8 × 2 ones = 16 ones

Regroup the 16 ones.

$$\begin{array}{r} \overset{1}{2}2 \\ \times\ 8 \\ \hline 6 \end{array}$$

Regroup
16 ones as
1 ten 6 ones.

STEP 2

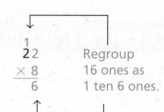

Multiply the tens.
8 × 2 tens = 16 tens

Add the regrouped ten.
16 tens + 1 ten = 17 tens

$$\begin{array}{r} \overset{1}{2}2 \\ \times\ 8 \\ \hline 176 \end{array}$$

17 tens is
the same as 1
hundred 7 tens.

So, 8 × 22 = _____. Since _____ is close to the estimate

of _____, it is reasonable.

Try This! **Multiply.** 7 × $68

Estimate. 7 × $68	Use partial products.	Use regrouping.
	$\begin{array}{r} \$\ 6\ 8 \\ \times\ \ \ \ \ 7 \\ \hline \end{array}$	$\begin{array}{r} \$\ 6\ 8 \\ \times\ \ \ \ \ 7 \\ \hline \end{array}$

- **Math Processes and Practices ⑦** **Identify Relationships** Look at the partial products and regrouping
methods above. How are the partial products 420 and 56 related to 476?

Name _____

1. Use the model to find the product.

$$2 \times 36 = \underline{\hspace{2cm}}$$

Estimate. Then record the product.

2. Estimate: _____

$$\begin{array}{r} 42 \\ \times\ 4 \\ \hline \end{array}$$

3. Estimate: _____

$$\begin{array}{r} 32 \\ \times\ 2 \\ \hline \end{array}$$

✓ 4. Estimate: _____

$$\begin{array}{r} 81 \\ \times\ 5 \\ \hline \end{array}$$

✓ 5. Estimate: _____

$$\begin{array}{r} \$63 \\ \times\ \ 7 \\ \hline \end{array}$$

Math Talk

Math Processes and Practices ⑦

Look for Structure What are the steps for using place value and regrouping to find 3×78?

On Your Own

Estimate. Then record the product.

6. Estimate: _____

$$\begin{array}{r} 33 \\ \times\ 2 \\ \hline \end{array}$$

7. Estimate: _____

$$\begin{array}{r} \$25 \\ \times\ \ 3 \\ \hline \end{array}$$

8. Estimate: _____

$$\begin{array}{r} 36 \\ \times\ 8 \\ \hline \end{array}$$

9. Estimate: _____

$$\begin{array}{r} \$94 \\ \times\ \ 5 \\ \hline \end{array}$$

Practice: Copy and Solve **Estimate. Then record the product.**

10. 3×82 11. 9×41 12. 6×75 13. $7 \times \$23$ 14. $8 \times \$54$

Math Processes and Practices ⑦ **Identify Relationships** **Algebra** Write a rule. Find the unknown numbers.

15.

Carton		1	2	3	4	5
Eggs		12	24		48	

16.

Row		2	3	4	5	6
Seats		32	48	64		

17. **GO DEEPER** It will cost $73 per hour to rent a sailboat and $88 per hour to rent a ski boat. How much more will it cost to rent a ski boat than a sailboat for 4 hours?

_____

© Houghton Mifflin Harcourt Publishing Company

Problem Solving • Applications

Use the table for 18–19.

18. **GO DEEPER** At the speeds shown, how much farther could a black-tailed jackrabbit run than a desert cottontail in 7 seconds?

    _____

19. A black-tailed jackrabbit hops about 7 feet in a single hop. How far can it hop in 5 seconds?

    _____

Running Speeds	
Animal	Speed (feet per second)
Black-tailed Jackrabbit	51
Desert Cottontail	22

▲ **Desert Cottontail**

20. **GO DEEPER** Mr. Wright bought a 3-pound bag of cat food and a 5-pound bag of dog food. There are 16 ounces in each pound. How many ounces of pet food did Mr. Wright buy?

    _____

21. **THINK SMARTER** The sum of two numbers is 31. The product of the two numbers is 150. What are the numbers?

    _____

22. **Math Processes and Practices ② Use Reasoning** 6 × 87 is greater than 5 × 87. How much greater? Explain how you know without multiplying.

    _____

    _____

WRITE ▸ *Math*
Show Your Work

23. **THINK SMARTER** Multiply 6 × 73. For 23a–23d, select True or False for each statement.

    23a. A reasonable estimate of the product is $420.   ○ True   ○ False

    23b. Using partial products, the products are 42 and 180.   ○ True   ○ False

    23c. Using regrouping, 18 ones are regrouped as 8 tens and 1 one.   ○ True   ○ False

    23d. The product is 438.   ○ True   ○ False

Multiply 2-Digit Numbers with Regrouping

Learning Objective You will use regrouping to multiply a 2-digit number by a 1-digit number.

Estimate. Then record the product.

1. Estimate: __150__

   ¹
   46
   × 3
   ———
   138

2. Estimate: _____

   32
   × 8

3. Estimate: _____

   $55
   × 2

4. Estimate: _____

   61
   × 8

5. Estimate: _____

   37
   × 9

6. Estimate: _____

   $18
   × 7

7. Estimate: _____

   83
   × 5

8. Estimate: _____

   95
   × 8

Problem Solving · Real World

9. Sharon is 54 inches tall. A tree in her backyard is 5 times as tall as she is. The floor of her treehouse is at a height that is twice as tall as she is. What is the difference, in inches, between the top of the tree and the floor of the treehouse?

   _____

10. Mr. Diaz's class is taking a field trip to the science museum. There are 23 students in the class, and a student admission ticket is $8. How much will the student tickets cost?

    _____

11. **WRITE** ▸Math Compare partial products and regrouping. Describe how the methods are alike and different.

    _____

    _____

    _____

    _____

Lesson Check

1. A ferryboat makes four trips to an island each day. The ferry can hold 88 people. If the ferry is full on each trip, how many passengers are carried by the ferry each day?

2. Julian counted the number of times he drove across the Seven Mile Bridge while vacationing in the Florida Keys. He crossed the bridge 34 times. How many miles in all did Julian drive crossing the bridge?

Spiral Review

3. Sebastian wrote the population of his city as $300,000 + 40,000 + 60 + 7$. Write the population of Sebastian's city in standard form.

4. A plane flew 2,190 kilometers from Chicago to Flagstaff. Another plane flew 2,910 kilometers from Chicago to Oakland. How much farther did the plane that flew to Oakland fly than the plane that flew to Flagstaff?

5. Tori buys 27 packages of miniature racing cars. Each package contains 5 cars. About how many miniature racing cars does Tori buy?

6. Use the Distributive Property to write an expression equivalent to $5 \times (3 + 4)$.

FOR MORE PRACTICE
GO TO THE
Personal Math Trainer

Name _____

Multiply 3-Digit and 4-Digit Numbers with Regrouping

Learning Objective You will use regrouping to multiply a 3- and 4-digit number by a 1-digit number.

Essential Question How can you use regrouping to multiply?

🔑 Unlock the Problem

Alley Spring, in Missouri, produces an average of 567 million gallons of water per week. How many million gallons of water do the springs produce in 3 weeks?

Multiply. 3×567

Estimate. $3 \times$ _____ = _____

THINK	RECORD

STEP 1

Multiply the ones.

3×7 ones = _____ ones
Regroup the 21 ones.

$$\begin{array}{r} {\scriptstyle 2} \\ 56\underline{7} \\ \times\quad 3 \\ \hline 1 \end{array}$$

Regroup the 21 ones as 2 tens and 1 one.

STEP 2

Multiply the tens.

3×6 tens = _____ tens
Add the regrouped tens.
18 tens + 2 tens = 20 tens
Regroup the 20 tens.

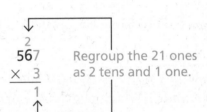

$$\begin{array}{r} {\scriptstyle 2\,2} \\ 5\underline{6}7 \\ \times\quad 3 \\ \hline 01 \end{array}$$

Regroup 20 tens as 2 hundreds 0 tens.

STEP 3

Multiply the hundreds.

3×5 hundreds = _____ hundreds
Add the regrouped hundreds.
15 hundreds + 2 hundreds = 17 hundreds

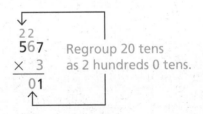

$$\begin{array}{r} {\scriptstyle 2\,2} \\ 567 \\ \times\quad 3 \\ \hline 1{,}701 \end{array}$$

17 hundreds is the same as 1 thousand 7 hundreds.

So, Alley Spring produces _____ million gallons of water in 3 weeks.

🔑 Example

Use an estimate or an exact answer.

The table shows the prices of three vacation packages. Jake, his parents, and his sister want to choose a package.

Lakefront Vacations	Adult	Child
Package A	$1,299	$619
Package B	$849	$699
Package C	$699	$484

A About how much would Package C cost Jake's family?

STEP 1

Estimate the cost for 2 adults.

2 × $699

↓

2 × $700 = _____

STEP 2

Estimate the cost for 2 children.

2 × $484

↓

2 × $500 = _____

STEP 3

Add to estimate the total cost.

```
    _____
  +
    _____
```

So, Package C would cost Jake's family about $2,400.

B Jake's family wants to compare the total costs of Packages A and C. Which plan costs more? How much more does it cost?

Math Talk Math Processes and Practices ❶

Analyze How did you use the information to know that you needed an estimate?

Package A

Adults	Children	Total Cost
$1,299	$619	
× 2	× 2	+

Package C

Adults	Children	Total Cost
$699	$484	
× 2	× 2	+

Subtract to compare the total costs of the packages.

```
  $3,836
− $2,366
_____
```

Math Talk Math Processes and Practices ❶

Make Sense of Problems How did you use the information to know that you needed an exact answer?

So, Package _____ would cost _____ more than Package _____.

Name _____

Share and Show MATH BOARD

1. Tell what is happening in Step 1 of the problem.

_____

_____

STEP 1	STEP 2	STEP 3	STEP 4
2	4 2	1 4 2	1 4 2
1,274	1,274	1,274	1,274
× 6	× 6	× 6	× 6
4	44	644	7,644

Estimate. Then find the product.

2. Estimate: _____

603
× 4

3. Estimate: _____

1,935
× 7

4. Estimate: _____

$8,326
× 5

Math Talk — Math Processes and Practices 6

Explain how you can use estimation to find how many digits the product 4 × 1,861 will have.

On Your Own

Estimate. Then find the product.

5. Estimate: _____

$3,316
× 8

6. Estimate: _____

$2,900
× 7

7. Estimate: _____

$4,123
× 6

8. GO DEEPER Mr. Jackson has $5,400 to buy supplies for the school computer lab. He buys 8 boxes of printer ink that cost $149 each and 3 printers that cost $1,017 each. How much money will Mr. Jackson have left after he buys the printer ink and printers?

_____

Practice: Copy and Solve Compare. Write <, >, or = .

9. 5 × 352 ◯ 4 × 440

10. 6 × 8,167 ◯ 9,834 × 5

11. 3,956 × 4 ◯ 5 × 7,692

12. 740 × 7 ◯ 8 × 658

13. 4 × 3,645 ◯ 5 × 2,834

14. 6,573 × 2 ◯ 4,365 × 3

Problem Solving • Applications

15. **GO DEEPER** Airplane tickets to Fairbanks, Alaska, will cost $958 each. Airplane tickets to Vancouver, Canada, will cost $734. How much can the four members of the Harrison family save on airfare by vacationing in Vancouver?

_____

16. **THINK SMARTER** Philadelphia, Pennsylvania, is 2,147 miles from Salt Lake City, Utah, and 2,868 miles from Portland, Oregon. What is the difference in the round-trip distances between Philadelphia and each of the other two cities? Explain whether you need an estimate or an exact answer.

_____

_____

17. **Math Processes and Practices ❸** Verify the Reasoning of Others
Joe says that the product of a 4-digit number and a 1-digit number is always a 4-digit number. Does Joe's statement make sense? Explain.

_____

_____

_____

18. **THINK SMARTER** What number is 150 more than the product of 5 and 4,892? Explain how you found the answer.

_____

_____

_____

Name _____

Multiply 3-Digit and 4-Digit Numbers with Regrouping

Learning Objective You will use regrouping to multiply a 3- and 4-digit number by a 1-digit number.

Estimate. Then find the product.

1. Estimate: __4,000__

$$
\begin{array}{r}
1\ 2\ 2 \\
1,467 \\
\times\qquad 4 \\
\hline
5,868
\end{array}
$$

2. Estimate: _____

$$
\begin{array}{r}
5,339 \\
\times\qquad 6 \\
\hline
\end{array}
$$

3. Estimate: _____

$$
\begin{array}{r}
\$879 \\
\times\qquad 8 \\
\hline
\end{array}
$$

4. Estimate: _____

$$
\begin{array}{r}
3,182 \\
\times\qquad 5 \\
\hline
\end{array}
$$

5. Estimate: _____

$$
\begin{array}{r}
4,616 \\
\times\qquad 3 \\
\hline
\end{array}
$$

6. Estimate: _____

$$
\begin{array}{r}
\$2,854 \\
\times\qquad 9 \\
\hline
\end{array}
$$

7. Estimate: _____

$$
\begin{array}{r}
7,500 \\
\times\qquad 2 \\
\hline
\end{array}
$$

8. Estimate: _____

$$
\begin{array}{r}
948 \\
\times\qquad 7 \\
\hline
\end{array}
$$

Problem Solving Real World

9. Lafayette County has a population of 7,022 people. Columbia County's population is 8 times as great as Lafayette County's population. What is the population of Columbia County?

10. A seafood company sold 9,125 pounds of fish last month. If 6 seafood companies sold the same amount of fish, how much fish did the 6 companies sell last month in all?

_____

_____

11. **WRITE** ▸*Math* Explain how finding 4×384 can help you find $4 \times 5,384$. Then find both products.

_____

_____

_____

Lesson Check

1. By recycling 1 ton of paper, 6,953 gallons of water are saved. How many gallons of water are saved by recycling 4 tons of paper?

   _____

2. Esteban counted the number of steps it took him to walk to school. He counted 1,138 steps. How many steps does he take walking to and from school each day?

   _____

Spiral Review

3. A website has 13,406 people registered. What is the word form of this number?

   _____

   _____

4. In one year, the McAlister family drove their car 15,680 miles. To the nearest thousand, how many miles did they drive their car that year?

   _____

   _____

5. Connor scored 14,370 points in a game. Amy scored 1,089 fewer points than Connor. How many points did Amy score?

   _____

6. Lea buys 6 model cars that each cost $15. She also buys 4 bottles of paint that each cost $11. How much does Lea spend on model cars and paint?

   _____

**FOR MORE PRACTICE
GO TO THE**
Personal Math Trainer

Solve Multistep Problems Using Equations

Essential Question How can you represent and solve multistep problems using equations?

Learning Objective You will model and solve multistep problems using equations.

Unlock the Problem

Crismari's computer has 3 hard drives with 64 gigabytes of space each and 2 hard drives with 16 gigabytes of space each. The files on her computer use 78 gigabytes of space. How much hard drive space does her computer have left?

• Underline the important information.

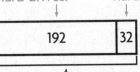

One Way Use multiple single-step equations.

STEP 1 Find how much hard drive space is on 3 hard drives with 64 gigabytes of space each.

| 64 | 64 | 64 |

← 3 hard drives with 64 gigabytes.

n ← Total space on 3 hard drives with 64 gigabytes.

$3 \times 64 = n$

$\_\_\_\_\_ = n$

STEP 2 Find how much hard drive space is on 2 hard drives with 16 gigabytes of space.

| 16 | 16 |

← 2 hard drives with 16 gigabytes.

p ← Total space on 2 hard drives with 16 gigabytes.

$2 \times 16 = p$

$\_\_\_\_\_ = p$

STEP 3 Find the total hard drive space on the computer.

Total space on 64-gigabyte hard drives.   Total space on 16-gigabyte hard drives.

| 192 | 32 |

A ← Total space on computer.

$192 + 32 = A$

$\_\_\_\_\_ = A$

STEP 4 The files use 78 gigabytes of space. Find how much hard drive space the computer has left.

space left   space used

| y | 78 |

224 ← Total hard drive space on the computer.

$224 - 78 = y$

$\_\_\_\_\_ = y$

So, Crismari has _____ gigabytes of hard drive space left on her computer.

Order of Operations The Order of Operations is a special set of rules that gives the order in which calculations are done in an expression. First, multiply and divide from left to right. Then, add and subtract from left to right.

 **Another Way** Use one multistep equation.

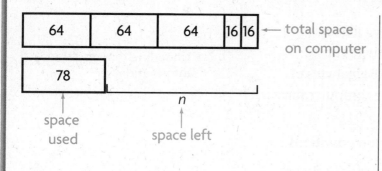

$3 \times 64 + 2 \times 16 - 78 = n$

_____ + _____ × _____ − _____ = n

_____ + _____ − _____ = n

_____ − _____ = n

_____ = n

Share and Show MATH BOARD

1. Use the order of operations to find the value of n.

$5 \times 17 + 5 \times 20 - 32 = n$

_____ + _____ × _____ − _____ = n ← First, multiply 5×17.

_____ + _____ − _____ = n ← Next, multiply 5×20.

_____ − _____ = n ← Then, add the two products.

_____ = n ← Finally, subtract to find n.

Find the value of n.

2. $3 \times 22 + 7 \times 41 - 24 = n$

_____ = n

3. $4 \times 34 + 6 \times 40 - 66 = n$

_____ = n

4. $2 \times 62 + 8 \times 22 - 53 = n$

_____ = n

5. $6 \times 13 + 9 \times 34 - 22 = n$

_____ = n

Math Talk

Math Processes and Practices ②

Use Reasoning If you solve $6 \times 3 + 2$ by adding before multiplying, will you get the same answer? Explain.

Name _____

Find the value of _n_.

6. $8 \times 42 + 3 \times 59 - 62 = n$

7. $6 \times 27 + 2 \times 47 - 83 = n$

_____ $= n$

_____ $= n$

Problem Solving • Applications

8. GO DEEPER   Maggie has 3 binders with 25 stamps in each binder. She has 5 binders with 24 baseball cards in each binder. If she gives 35 stamps to a friend, how many stamps and cards does she have left?

WRITE ▸ Math
Show Your Work

_____

9. Math Processes and Practices ❶ **Evaluate** Maddox has 4 boxes with 32 marbles in each box. He has 7 boxes with 18 shells in each box. If he gets 20 marbles from a friend, how many marbles and shells does he have?

_____

Personal Math Trainer

10. THINK SMARTER +   The soccer team sells 54 bagels with cream cheese for $2 each and 36 muffins for $1 each during a bake sale. The coach uses the money to buy socks for the 14 players. The socks cost $6 per pair. How much money does the coach have left? Explain how you found your answer.

_____

_____

_____

_____

_____

11. **THINK SMARTER** **What's the Error?** Dominic has 5 books with 12 postcards in each book. He has 4 boxes with 20 coins in each box. If he gives 15 post cards to a friend, how many postcards and coins does he have?

Dominic drew this model.

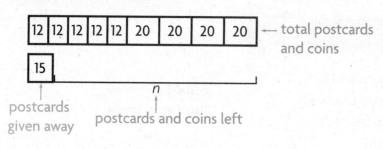

| 12 | 12 | 12 | 12 | 12 | 20 | 20 | 20 | 20 | ← total postcards and coins

| 15 |

↑ postcards given away

n
postcards and coins left

Dominic used these steps to solve.

$5 \times 12 + 4 \times 20 - 15 = n$

$60 + 4 \times 20 - 15 = n$

$64 \times 20 - 15 = n$

$1{,}280 - 15 = n$

$1{,}265 = n$

Look at the steps Dominic used to solve this problem. Find and describe his error.

_____

_____

Use the correct steps to solve the problem.

_____

_____

_____

_____

_____

So, there are _____ postcards and coins left.

Solve Multistep Problems Using Equations

Learning Objective You will model and solve multistep problems using equations.

Find the value of n.

1. $4 \times 27 + 5 \times 34 - 94 = n$

   $108 + 5 \times 34 - 94 = n$

   $108 + 170 - 94 = n$

   $278 - 94 = n$

   $184 = n$

2. $7 \times 38 + 3 \times 45 - 56 = n$

   _____ $= n$

3. $6 \times 21 + 7 \times 29 - 83 = n$

   _____ $= n$

4. $9 \times 19 + 2 \times 57 - 75 = n$

   _____ $= n$

Problem Solving (Real World)

5. A bakery has 4 trays with 16 muffins on each tray. The bakery has 3 trays of cupcakes with 24 cupcakes on each tray. If 15 cupcakes are sold, how many muffins and cupcakes are left?

6. Katy bought 5 packages of stickers with 25 stickers in each package. She also bought 3 boxes of markers with 12 markers in each box. If she receives 8 stickers from a friend, how many stickers and markers does Katy have now?

_____

_____

7. **WRITE** ▸ *Math* Write a word problem that could be solved by writing and solving a multistep equation. Then solve your problem.

_____

_____

_____

Lesson Check

1. What is the value of *n*?

$$9 \times 23 + 3 \times 39 - 28 = n$$

_____

2. What is the value of *n*?

$$4 \times 28 + 6 \times 17 - 15 = n$$

_____

Spiral Review

3. Write an expression that shows how you can multiply 9×475 using expanded form and the Distributive Property.

_____

4. Write an equation that represents this comparison sentence.

32 is 8 times as many as 4

_____

5. Between which pair of numbers is the exact product of 379 and 8?

_____

6. Write an expression that shows how to use the halving and doubling strategy to find 28×50.

_____

© Houghton Mifflin Harcourt Publishing Company

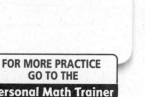

FOR MORE PRACTICE
GO TO THE
Personal Math Trainer

☑ Chapter 2 Review/Test

For 1–3, use the table.

Prices for Trees					
Tree	Regular Price	Price for 3 or more	Tree	Regular Price	Price for 3 or more
Ivory Silk Lilac	$25	$22	Hazelnut	$9	$8
White Pine	$40	$37	Red Maple	$9	$8
Bur Oak	$35	$32	Birch	$9	$8

1. What is the cost of 3 Bur Oak trees? Show your work.

2. Mr. Tan buys 4 White Pine trees and 5 Birch trees. What is the cost of the trees? Show your work and explain how you found the answer.

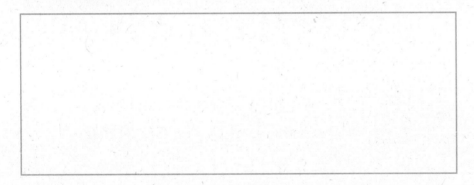

3. Rudy will buy 3 Ivory Silk Lilac trees or 2 Bur Oak trees. He wants to buy the trees that cost less. What trees will he buy? How much will he save? Show your work.

4. For numbers 4a–4d, select True or False for each equation.

4a. $7 \times 194 = 1{,}338$ ○ True   ○ False

4b. $5 \times 5{,}126 = 25{,}630$ ○ True   ○ False

4c. $8 \times 367 = 2{,}926$ ○ True   ○ False

4d. $4 \times 3{,}952 = 15{,}808$ ○ True   ○ False

5. Part A

Draw a line to match each section in the model to the partial product it represents.

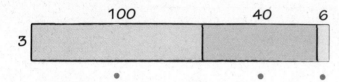

•   •   •

3×6 3×100 3×40

Part B

Then find 3×146. Show your work and explain.

Name _____

6. For numbers 6a–6c, write an equation or a comparison sentence using the numbers on the tiles.

6a.

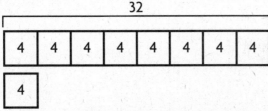

| | times as many as | | is | | .

6b.

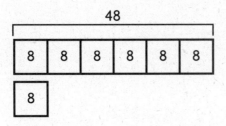

| | × | | = | |

6c. $9 \times 3 = 27$

| | times as many as | | is | | .

7. Multiply 7×43. For 7a–7d, select True or False for each statement.

7a. A reasonable estimate of the product is 280. ○ True ○ False

7b. Using partial products, the products are 21 and 28. ○ True ○ False

7c. Using regrouping, 21 ones are regrouped as 1 ten and 2 ones. ○ True ○ False

7d. The product is 301. ○ True ○ False

8. It costs 9,328 points to build each apartment building in the computer game *Big City Building*. What is the cost to build 5 apartment buildings? Show your work.

9. Multiply 7 × 462 using place value and expanded form.
   Choose the number from the box to complete the expression.

$$(7 \times \boxed{\begin{array}{c} 4 \\ 40 \\ 400 \end{array}}) + (7 \times \boxed{\begin{array}{c} 600 \\ 60 \\ 6 \end{array}}) + (7 \times \boxed{\begin{array}{c} 2 \\ 20 \\ 200 \end{array}})$$

10. For numbers 10a–10b, use place value to find the product.

   10a. $3 \times 600 = 3 \times \boxed{}$ hundreds

         $= \boxed{}$ hundreds

         $= \boxed{}$

   10b. $5 \times 400 = 5 \times \boxed{}$ hundreds

         $= \boxed{}$ hundreds

         $= \boxed{}$

11. **GO DEEPER** Liam has 3 boxes of baseball cards with 50 cards in
    each box. He also has 5 boxes with 40 basketball cards in each box.
    If Liam goes to the store and buys 50 more baseball cards, how
    many baseball and basketball cards does Liam have? Show your
    work.

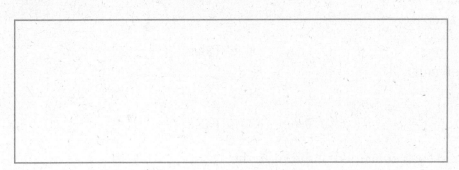

140

12. There is a book sale at the library. The price for each book is $4. Which expression can be used to show how much money the library will make if it sells 289 books? Use the numbers on the tiles to complete your answer.

2	4	8	9

80	90	200

(4 × _____) + (4 × _____) + (4 × _____)

13. **THINK SMARTER +** Find 8 × 397. Show your work and explain why the strategy you chose works best with the factors.

14. A clown bought 6 bags of round balloons with 24 balloons in each bag. The clown also bought 3 bags of long balloons with 36 balloons in each bag.

Part A

How many more round balloons than long balloons did the clown buy? Show your work.

Part B

The clown also bought 5 bags of heart-shaped balloons with 14 balloons in each bag. When the clown blew up all of the round, long, and heart-shaped balloons, 23 balloons burst. How many blown-up balloons were left? Explain your answer.

15. Hector planted 185 flowers in 2 days. There were 5 volunteers, including Hector, who each planted about the same number of flowers. About how many flowers did they plant?

185

400

500

1,000

16. Jay and Blair went fishing. Together, they caught 27 fish. Jay caught 2 times as many fish as Blair. How many fish did Jay and Blair each catch? Write an equation and solve. Explain your work.

17. At the pet fair, Darlene's dog weighed 5 times as much as Leah's dog. Together, the dogs weighed 84 pounds. How much did each dog weigh? Complete the bar model. Write an equation and solve.

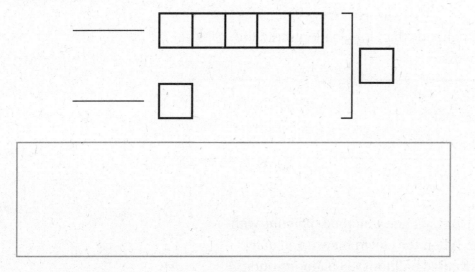

18. Use the Distributive Property to model the product on the grid. Record the product.

$4 \times 12 =$ _____

© Houghton Mifflin Harcourt Publishing Company

Chapter 3 Multiply 2-Digit Numbers

✓ Show What You Know

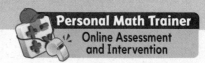

Check your understanding of important skills.

Name _____

▶ **Practice Multiplication Facts** Find the product.

1. $8 \times 7 =$ _____

$7 \times 8 =$ _____

2. $3 \times (2 \times 4) =$ _____

$(3 \times 2) \times 4 =$ _____

▶ **2-Digit by 1-Digit Multiplication** Find the product.

3. $\begin{array}{r} 28 \\ \times\ 3 \\ \hline \end{array}$

4. $\begin{array}{r} 56 \\ \times\ 6 \\ \hline \end{array}$

5. $\begin{array}{r} 71 \\ \times\ 5 \\ \hline \end{array}$

6. $\begin{array}{r} 69 \\ \times\ 8 \\ \hline \end{array}$

7. $\begin{array}{r} 36 \\ \times\ 4 \\ \hline \end{array}$

▶ **Multiply by 1-Digit Numbers** Find the product.

8. $\begin{array}{r} 72 \\ \times\ 4 \\ \hline \end{array}$

9. $\begin{array}{r} 456 \\ \times\ 5 \\ \hline \end{array}$

10. $\begin{array}{r} 804 \\ \times\ 7 \\ \hline \end{array}$

11. $\begin{array}{r} 1,341 \\ \times\ 9 \\ \hline \end{array}$

12. $\begin{array}{r} 65 \\ \times\ 6 \\ \hline \end{array}$

13. $\begin{array}{r} 392 \\ \times\ 8 \\ \hline \end{array}$

14. $\begin{array}{r} 1,478 \\ \times\ 3 \\ \hline \end{array}$

15. $\begin{array}{r} \$1,627 \\ \times\ 2 \\ \hline \end{array}$

16. $\begin{array}{r} 584 \\ \times\ 7 \\ \hline \end{array}$

17. $\begin{array}{r} 2,837 \\ \times\ 4 \\ \hline \end{array}$

Math in the Real World

Yellowstone National Park, which is located in Wyoming, Montana, and Idaho, was America's first National Park. The park has over 500 geysers. Grand Geyser erupts about every 8 hours.

Based on this estimate, how many times would you see this geyser erupt if you could watch it for 1 year? There are 24 hours in a day and 365 days in a year.

Vocabulary Builder

▶ Visualize It

Complete the H-diagram using the words with a ✓.

Multiplication Words		Estimation Words

▶ Understand Vocabulary

Draw a line to match each word or phrase with its definition.

Word

1. Commutative Property of Multiplication

2. estimate

3. compatible numbers

4. factor

5. regroup

Definition

• A number that is multiplied by another number to find a product

• To exchange amounts of equal value to rename a number

• To find an answer that is close to the exact amount

• Numbers that are easy to compute mentally

• The property that states when the order of two factors is changed, the product is the same.

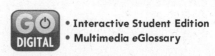

• Interactive Student Edition
• Multimedia eGlossary

Chapter 3 Vocabulary

Associative Property of Multiplication

propiedad asociativa de la multiplicación 4

Commutative Property of Multiplication

Propiedad conmutativa de la multiplicación 13

compatible numbers

números compatibles 15

estimate (*verb*)

estimar 30

factor

factor 33

partial product

producto parcial 61

place value

valor posicional 68

regroup

reagrupar 78

The property that states that when the order of two factors is changed, the product is the same

Example: $3 \times 5 = 5 \times 3$

The property that states that you can group factors in different ways and still get the same product

Example: $3 \times (4 \times 2) = (3 \times 4) \times 2$

To find an answer that is close to the exact amount

Numbers that are easy to compute mentally

Example: Estimate. $176 \div 8$

160 divides easily by 8

↑

compatible number

A method of multiplying in which the ones, tens, hundreds, and so on are multiplied separately and then the products are added together

$$
\begin{array}{r}
182 \\
\times\ \ 6 \\
\hline
600 \\
480 \quad \leftarrow \text{Partial products} \\
+\ \ \ 12 \\
\hline
1{,}092
\end{array}
$$

A number that is multiplied by another number to find a product

Example: $4 \times 5 = 20$

factor   factor

To exchange amounts of equal value to rename a number

Example: $5 + 8 = 13$ ones or 1 ten 3 ones

The value of a digit in a number, based on the location of the digit

Matchup

For 3 to 4 players

Materials

- 1 set of word cards

How to Play

1. Put the cards face-down in rows. Take turns to play.
2. Choose two cards and turn them face-up.
   - If the cards show a word and its meaning, it's a match. Keep the pair and take another turn.
   - If the cards do not match, turn them back over.
3. The game is over when all cards have been matched. The players count their pairs. The player with the most pairs wins.

Word Box

Associative
   Property of
   Multiplication
Commutative
   Property of
   Multiplication
compatible
   numbers
estimate
factor
partial product
place value
regroup

The Write Way

Reflect

Choose one idea. Write about it.

- Do 36 × 29 and 29 × 36 represent the same product? Explain why or why not.

- Explain in your words what the Associative Property of Multiplication means.

- A reader of your math advice column writes, "I can't remember what compatible numbers are or how to use them." Write a letter that helps your reader with this problem.

Name _____

Multiply by Tens

Essential Question What strategies can you use to multiply by tens?

Learning Objective You will use the Associative Property of Multiplication and place value understanding to multiply by tens.

 Unlock the Problem

Animation for a computer-drawn cartoon requires about 20 frames per second. How many frames would need to be drawn for a 30-second cartoon?

- The phrase "20 frames per second" means 20 frames are needed for each second of animation. How does this help you know what operation to use?

_____

_____

One Way Use place value.

Multiply. 30 × 20

You can think of 20 as 2 tens.

30 × 20 = 30 × _____ tens

      = _____ tens

      = 600

Remember

The Associative Property states that you can group factors in different ways and get the same product. Use parentheses to group the factors you multiply first.

Another Way Use the Associative Property.

You can think of 20 as 2 × 10.

30 × 20 = 30 × (2 × 10)

      = (30 × 2) × 10

      = _____ × _____

      = _____

So, _____ frames would need to be drawn.

 Math Talk Math Processes and Practices ⑦

Look for Structure How can you use place value to tell why 60 × 10 = 600?

- Compare the number of zeros in each factor to the number of zeros in the product. What do you notice?

_____

_____

❶ Other Ways

A Use a number line and a pattern to multiply 15 × 20.

Draw jumps to show the product.

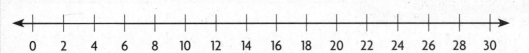

0 2 4 6 8 10 12 14 16 18 20 22 24 26 28 30

15 × 2 = _____

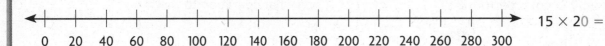

0 20 40 60 80 100 120 140 160 180 200 220 240 260 280 300

15 × 20 = _____

B Use mental math to find 14 × 30.

Use the halving-and-doubling strategy.

STEP 1 Find half of 14 to make the problem simpler.	**STEP 2** Multiply.	**STEP 3** Double 210.
Think: To find half of a number, divide by 2.		**Think:** To double a number, multiply by 2.
14 ÷ 2 = _____	7 × 30 = _____	2 × 210 = _____

So, 14 × 30 = 420.

Try This! Multiply.

Use mental math to find 12 × 40.	Use place value to find 12 × 40.

Share and Show

1. Find 20 × 27. Tell which method you chose. Explain what happens in each step.

_____

_____

Name _____

Choose a method. Then find the product.

2. 10×12

3. 20×20

☑**4.** 40×24

☑**5.** 11×60

Math Talk Math Processes and Practices **7**

Identify Relationships
How can you use
$30 \times 10 = 300$ to
find 30×12?

On Your Own

Choose a method. Then find the product.

6. 70×55

7. 17×30

8. 30×60

9. 12×90

Math Processes and Practices **2** **Reason Quantitatively Algebra Find the unknown digit in the number.**

10. $64 \times 40 = 2,56$■

11. $29 \times 50 = 1,$⬠50

12. 3◆$\times 47 = 1,410$

■ = _____

⬠ = _____

◆ = _____

13. GO DEEPER Caroline packs 12 jars of jam in a box. She has 40 boxes. She has 542 jars of jam. How many jars of jam will she have left when all the boxes are full?

14. GO DEEPER Alison is preparing for a math contest. Each day, she works on multiplication problems for 20 minutes and division problems for 10 minutes. How many minutes does Alison practice multiplication and division problems in 15 days?

Problem Solving • Applications

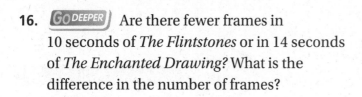

Use the table for 15–16.

15. **Math Processes and Practices ④ Use Graphs** How many frames did it take to produce 50 seconds of *Pinocchio*?

_____

16. **GO DEEPER** Are there fewer frames in 10 seconds of *The Flintstones* or in 14 seconds of *The Enchanted Drawing*? What is the difference in the number of frames?

_____

17. **THINK SMARTER** The product of my number and twice my number is 128. What is half my number? Explain how you solved the problem.

_____

_____

_____

18. **THINK SMARTER** Tanya says that the product of a multiple of ten and a multiple of ten will always have only one zero. Is she correct? Explain.

_____

_____

Animated Productions

Title	Date Released	Frames per Second
The Enchanted Drawing©	1900	20
Little Nemo©	1911	16
Snow White and the Seven Dwarfs©	1937	24
Pinocchio©	1940	19
The Flintstones™	1960–1966	24

WRITE *Math* • Show Your Work

19. **THINK SMARTER** For numbers 19a–19e, select Yes or No to tell whether the answer is correct.

19a. $28 \times 10 = 280$ ⭘ Yes ⭘ No

19b. $15 \times 20 = 300$ ⭘ Yes ⭘ No

19c. $17 \times 10 = 17$ ⭘ Yes ⭘ No

19d. $80 \times 10 = 800$ ⭘ Yes ⭘ No

19e. $16 \times 30 = 1{,}800$ ⭘ Yes ⭘ No

Multiply by Tens

Learning Objective You will use the Associative Property of Multiplication and place value understanding to multiply by tens.

Choose a method. Then find the product.

1. 16×60

Use the halving-and-doubling strategy.

Find half of 16: $16 \div 2 = 8$.

Multiply 60 by this number: $8 \times 60 = 480$

Double this result: $2 \times 480 = 960$

_____960_____

2. 80×22　　　　　**3.** 30×52　　　　　**4.** 60×20

_____　　　_____　　　_____

Problem Solving Real World

5. Kenny bought 20 packs of baseball cards. There are 12 cards in each pack. How many cards did Kenny buy?

_____

6. The Hart family drove 10 hours to their vacation spot. They drove an average of 48 miles each hour. How many miles did they drive?

_____

7. **WRITE** ▸*Math* Write the steps for how to use a number line to multiply a 2-digit number by 20. Give an example.

_____

_____

_____

_____

Lesson Check

1. For the school play, 40 rows of chairs are set up. There are 22 chairs in each row. How many chairs are there?

2. At West School, there are 20 classrooms. Each classroom has 20 students. How many students are at West School?

Spiral Review

3. Alex has 48 stickers. This is 6 times the number of stickers Max has. How many stickers does Max have?

4. Ali's dog weighs 8 times as much as her cat. Together, the two pets weigh 54 pounds. How much does Ali's dog weigh?

5. Allison has 3 containers with 25 crayons in each. She also has 4 boxes of markers with 12 markers in each box. She gives 10 crayons to a friend. How many crayons and markers does Allison have now?

6. The state of Utah covers 82,144 square miles. The state of Montana covers 145,552 square miles. What is the total area of the two states?

FOR MORE PRACTICE
GO TO THE
Personal Math Trainer

Name _____

Estimate Products

Essential Question What strategies can you use to estimate products?

Learning Objective You will use compatible numbers and rounding to estimate products.

🔑 Unlock the Problem (Real World)

On average, the Smith family opens the door of their refrigerator 32 times each day. There are 31 days in May. About how many times is the refrigerator door opened in May?

• Underline any information you will need.

🔒 One Way Use rounding and mental math.

Estimate. 31 × 32

STEP 1 Round each factor.

31 × 32

↓   ↓

30 × 30

STEP 2 Use mental math.

3 × 3 = 9 ← basic fact

30 × 30 = _____

Math Talk

Math Processes and Practices 6

Compare Is the exact product greater than or less than 900? Explain.

So, the Smith family opens the refrigerator door about 900 times during the month of May.

---

1. On average, a refrigerator door is opened 38 times each day. About how many fewer times in May is the Smith family's refrigerator door opened than the average refrigerator door?

 Show your work.

All 24 light bulbs in the Park family's home are CFL light bulbs. Each CFL light bulb uses 28 watts to produce light. About how many watts will the light bulbs use when turned on all at the same time?

🔑 Another Way Use mental math and compatible numbers.

Compatible numbers are numbers that are easy to compute mentally.

Estimate. 24 × 28

STEP 1 Use compatible numbers.

24 × 28
↓   ↓
25 × 30   Think: 25 × 3 = 75

So, about 750 watts are used.

STEP 2 Use mental math.

25 × 3 = 75

25 × 30 = _____

Try This! Estimate 26 × $79.

Ⓐ Round to the nearest ten

26   × $79
↓   ↓

_____ × _____ = _____

26 × $79 is about _____ .

Ⓑ Compatible numbers

26   × $79   Think: How can you use
↓   ↓   25 × 4 = 100 to
                       help find 25 × 8?

25   × $80 = _____

26 × $79 is about _____ .

2. Explain why $2,400 and $2,000 are both reasonable estimates.

_____

_____

3. In what situation might you choose to find an estimate rather than an exact answer?

_____

_____

Share and Show

1. To estimate the product of 62 and 28 by rounding, how would you round the factors? What would the estimated product be?

_____

© Houghton Mifflin Harcourt Publishing Company • Image Credits: (tr) ©Bob Elam/Alamy

Name _____

Estimate the product. Choose a method.

2. 96×34

✓ 3. $47 \times \$39$

✓ 4. 78×72

Math Talk

Math Processes and Practices ➊

Describe how you know if an estimated product will be greater than or less than the exact answer.

On Your Own

Estimate the product. Choose a method.

5. 41×78

6. 51×73

7. 34×80

Practice: Copy and Solve **Estimate the product. Choose a method.**

8. 61×31

9. 52×68

10. 26×44

11. $57 \times \$69$

THINK SMARTER **Find two possible factors for the estimated product.**

12. 2,800

13. 8,100

14. 5,600

15. 2,400

16. **GO DEEPER** Mr. Parker jogs for 35 minutes each day. He jogs 5 days in week 1, 6 days in week 2, and 7 days in week 3. About how many minutes does he jog?

17. **GO DEEPER** There are 48 beads in a package. Candice bought 4 packages of blue, 9 packages of gold, 6 packages of red, and 2 packages of silver beads. About how many beads did Candice buy?

Problem Solving • Applications

18. **GO DEEPER** On average, a refrigerator door is opened 38 times each day. Len has two refrigerators in his house. Based on this average, about how many times in a 3-week period are the refrigerator doors opened?

_____

19. The cost to run a refrigerator is about $57 each year. About how much will it have cost to run by the time it is 15 years old?

_____

20. **THINK SMARTER** If Mel opens his refrigerator door 36 times every day, about how many times will it be opened in April? Will the exact answer be more than or less than the estimate? Explain.

_____

_____

_____

_____

21. **Math Processes and Practices ②** **Represent a Problem** What question could you write for this answer? The estimated product of two numbers, that are not multiples of ten, is 2,800.

| WRITE ▸ *Math* · **Show Your Work**

_____

_____

22. **THINK SMARTER** Which is a reasonable estimate for the product? Write the estimate. An estimate may be used more than once.

| 30 × 20 | 25 × 50 | 20 × 20 |

26 × 48 [＿＿＿]   28 × 21 [＿＿＿]

21 × 22 [＿＿＿]   51 × 26 [＿＿＿]

Estimate Products

Learning Objective You will use compatible numbers and rounding to estimate products.

Estimate the product. Choose a method.

1. 38 × 21

38 × 21
↓   ↓
40 × 20

_____800_____

2. 63 × 19

_____

3. 27 × $42

_____

4. 73 × 67

_____

5. 37 × $44

_____

6. 45 × 22

_____

 Problem Solving *Real World*

7. A dime has a diameter of about 18 millimeters. About how many millimeters long would a row of 34 dimes be?

_____

8. A half-dollar has a diameter of about 31 millimeters. About how many millimeters long would a row of 56 half-dollars be?

_____

9. **WRITE** ▸*Math* Describe a real-life multiplication situation for which an estimate makes sense. Explain why it makes sense.

_____

_____

Lesson Check

1. What is a reasonable estimate for the product of 43 × 68?

   _____

   _____

2. Marissa burns 93 calories each time she plays fetch with her dog. She plays fetch with her dog once a day. About how many calories will Marissa burn playing fetch with her dog in 28 days?

   _____

   _____

Spiral Review

3. Use the model to find 3 × 126.

   ```
           100        20  6
       ┌──────────────┬──┬─┐
     3 │              │  │ │
       └──────────────┴──┴─┘
   ```

   _____

4. A store sold a certain brand of jeans for $38. One day, the store sold 6 pairs of jeans of that brand. How much did the 6 pairs of jeans cost?

   _____

5. The Gateway Arch in St. Louis, Missouri, weighs about 20,000 tons. Write an amount that could be the exact number of tons the Arch weighs.

   _____

   _____

6. What is another name for 23 ten thousands?

   _____

   _____

FOR MORE PRACTICE
GO TO THE
Personal Math Trainer

Name _____

Area Models and Partial Products

Essential Question How can you use area models and partial products to multiply 2-digit numbers?

Investigate

Materials ■ color pencils

How can you use a model to break apart factors and make them easier to multiply?

A. Outline a rectangle on the grid to model 13 × 18. Break apart the model into smaller rectangles to show factors broken into tens and ones. Label and shade the smaller rectangles. Use the colors below.

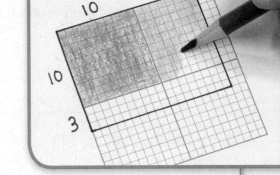

B. Find the product of each smaller rectangle. Then, find the sum of the partial products. Record your answers.

▢ = 10 × 10

▢ = 10 × 8

▢ = 3 × 10

▢ = 3 × 8

100 + ▢ + ▢ + ▢ = _____

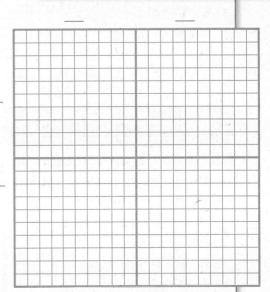

C. Draw the model again. Break apart the whole model to show factors different from those shown the first time. Label and shade the four smaller rectangles and find their products. Record the sum of the partial products to represent the product of the whole model.

_____ + _____ + _____ + _____ = _____

Draw Conclusions

1. Explain how you found the total number of squares in the whole model.

   _____

   _____

2. Compare the two models and their products. What can you conclude? Explain.

   _____

   _____

3. To find the product of 10 and 33, which is the easier computation, $(10 \times 11) + (10 \times 11) + (10 \times 11)$ or $(10 \times 30) + (10 \times 3)$? Explain.

   _____

   _____

Make Connections

You can draw a simple diagram to model and break apart factors to find a product. Find 15×24.

Remember

24 is 2 tens 4 ones.

STEP 1 Draw a model to show 15×24. Break apart the factors into tens and ones to show the partial products.

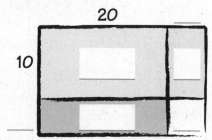

STEP 2 Write the product for each of the smaller rectangles.

(10 × 2 tens)	(10 × 4 ones)	(5 × 2 tens)	(5 × 4 ones)
(10 × 20)	(10 × 4)	(5 × 20)	(5 × 4)

STEP 3 Add to find the product for the whole model.

So, $15 \times 24 = 360$.

The model shows four parts. Each part represents a partial product. The partial products are 200, 40, 100, and 20.

Math Talk

Math Processes and Practices ②

Use Reasoning How does breaking apart the factors into tens and ones make finding the product easier?

Name _____

Find the product.

1. 16 × 19 = _____

10   9
| 10 | 100 | 90 |
| 6 | 60 | 54 |

2. 18 × 26 = _____

20   6
| 10 | | |
| 8 | | |

✓ 3. 27 × 39 = _____

30   9
| 20 | | |
| 7 | | |

Draw a model to represent the product.
Then record the product.

4. 14 × 16 = _____

✓ 5. 23 × 25 = _____

Problem Solving • Applications Real World

6. **Math Processes and Practices 6** **Explain** how modeling partial products can be used to find the products of greater numbers.

_____

_____

7. **GO DEEPER** Emma bought 16 packages of rolls for a party. There were 12 rolls in a package. After the party there were 8 rolls left over. How many rolls were eaten? Explain.

_____

_____

Sense or Nonsense?

8. **THINK SMARTER** Jamal and Kim used different ways to solve
12 × 15 by using partial products. Whose answer makes sense?
Whose answer is nonsense? Explain your reasoning.

Jamal's Work

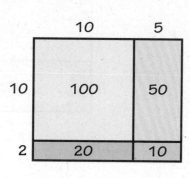

$$100 + 20 + 10 = 130$$

Kim's Work

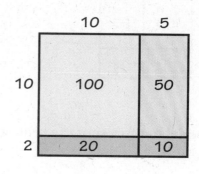

$$120 \quad + 60 = 180$$

a. For the answer that is nonsense, write an answer that makes sense.

b. Look at Kim's method. Can you think of another way Kim
could use the model to find the product? Explain.

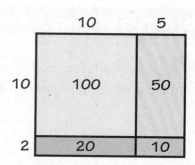

9. **THINK SMARTER** Look at the model in 8b. How would the partial
products change if the product was 22 × 15? Explain why you think the
products changed.

160

Area Models and Partial Products

Learning Objective You will use area models and partial products to multiply two 2-digit numbers.

Draw a model to represent the product.
Then record the product.

1. 13 × 42

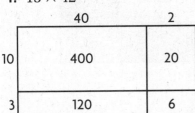

	40	2
10	400	20
3	120	6

400 + 20 + 120 + 6 = <u>546</u>

2. 18 × 34

_____

3. 22 × 26

_____

Problem Solving · Real World

4. Sebastian made the following model to find the product 17 × 24.

	20	4
10	200	40
7	14	28

200 + 40 + 14 + 28 = 282

Is his model correct? **Explain**.

_____

_____

5. Each student in Ms. Sike's kindergarten class has a box of crayons. Each box has 36 crayons. If there are 18 students in Ms. Sike's class, how many crayons are there?

_____

6. **WRITE** ▸*Math* Describe how to model 2-digit by 2-digit multiplication using an area model.

_____

_____

Lesson Check

1. What product does the model below represent?

	20	3
10	200	30
7	140	21

_____

2. What product does the model below represent?

	13	2
10	130	20
5	65	10

_____

Spiral Review

3. Mariah builds a tabletop using square tiles. There are 12 rows of tiles and 30 tiles in each row. How many tiles does Mariah use?

_____

4. Trevor bakes 8 batches of biscuits, with 14 biscuits in each batch. He sets aside 4 biscuits from each batch for a bake sale and puts the rest in a container. How many biscuits does Trevor put in the container?

_____

5. Li feeds her dog 3 cups of food each day. About how many cups of food does her dog eat in 28 days?

_____

_____

6. Find the product of $20 \times 9 \times 5$. Tell which property you used.

_____

_____

FOR MORE PRACTICE
GO TO THE
Personal Math Trainer

Name _____

Multiply Using Partial Products

Essential Question How can you use place value and partial products to multiply 2-digit numbers?

Learning Objective You will use partial products and place value understanding to multiply two 2-digit numbers.

🔑 Unlock the Problem

CONNECT You know how to break apart a model to find partial products. How can you use what you know to find and record a product?

 Multiply. 34 × 57   **Estimate.** 30 × 60 = _____

SHADE THE MODEL	THINK AND RECORD

STEP 1

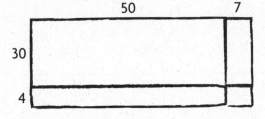

57
× 34
_____
← Multiply the tens by the tens.
   30 × 5 tens = 150 tens

STEP 2

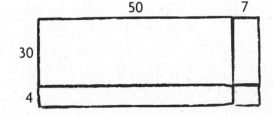

57
×34
_____
1,500
← Multiply the ones by the tens.
   30 × 7 ones = 210 ones

STEP 3

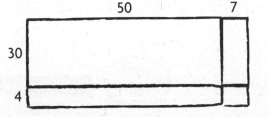

57
×34
_____
1,500
210
← Multiply the tens by the ones.
   4 × 5 tens = 20 tens

STEP 4

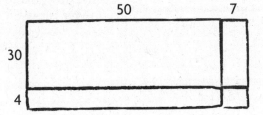

57
×34
_____
1,500
210
200
+ _____
← Multiply the ones by the ones.
   4 × 7 ones = 28 ones
← Add the partial products.

So, 34 × 57 = 1,938. Since 1,938 is close to the estimate of 1,800, it is reasonable.

Math Talk

Math Processes and Practices ⑧

Use Repeated Reasoning You can write 10 × 4 ones = 40 ones as 10 × 4 = 40. What is another way to write 10 × 3 tens = 30 tens?

🔑 Example

The apples from each tree in an orchard can fill 23 bushel baskets. If 1 row of the orchard has 48 trees, how many baskets of apples can be filled?

Multiply. 48 × 23   **Estimate. 50 × 20 = _____**

THINK	RECORD

STEP 1

Multiply the tens by the tens.

$$\begin{array}{r} 23 \\ \times\ 48 \\ \hline \end{array}$$

← 40 × _____ tens = _____ tens

STEP 2

Multiply the ones by the tens.

$$\begin{array}{r} 23 \\ \times\ 48 \\ \hline 800 \\ \end{array}$$

← 40 × _____ ones = _____ ones

STEP 3

Multiply the tens by the ones.

$$\begin{array}{r} 23 \\ \times\ 48 \\ \hline 800 \\ 120 \\ \end{array}$$

← 8 × _____ tens = _____ tens

STEP 4

Multiply the ones by the ones. Then add the partial products.

$$\begin{array}{r} 23 \\ \times\ 48 \\ \hline 800 \\ 120 \\ 160 \\ + \\ \hline \end{array}$$

← 8 × _____ ones = _____ ones

So, 1,104 baskets can be filled.

Math Talk

Math Processes and Practices ❶

Evaluate Reasonableness
How do you know your answer is reasonable?

Share and Show

1. Find 24 × 34.

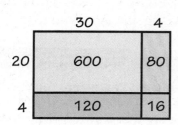

	30	4
20	600	80
4	120	16

$$\begin{array}{r} 3\ 4 \\ \times\ 2\ 4 \\ \hline \end{array}$$

Name _____

Record the product.

2.
  12
× 12

3.
  31
× 24

 4.
  25
× 43

 5.
  37
× 26

Math Talk Math Processes and Practices ④

Model Mathematics How would you model and record 74 × 25?

On Your Own

Record the product.

6.
  54
× 15

7.
  87
× 16

8.
  62
× 56

9.
  49
× 63

Practice: Copy and Solve Record the product.

10. 38 × 47

11. 46 × 27

12. 72 × 53

13. 98 × 69

14. 53 × 68

15. 76 × 84

16. 92 × 48

17. 37 × 79

Math Processes and Practices ② **Reason Abstractly** **Algebra** Find the unknown digits. Complete the problem.

18.
    6
×   4
‾‾‾‾‾‾
1,400
  120
  280
+ 24
‾‾‾‾‾‾

19.
    2
×   7
‾‾‾‾‾‾
7,200
  180
  560
+ 14
‾‾‾‾‾‾

20.
    6
× 5
‾‾‾‾‾‾
1,500
  300
   90
+ 18
‾‾‾‾‾‾

21.
  3
×   8
‾‾‾‾‾‾
600
 80
240
+ 32
‾‾‾‾‾‾

Problem Solving • Applications

Use the picture graph for 22–24.

22. 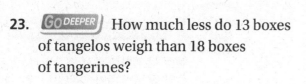 **Use Graphs** A fruit-packing warehouse is shipping 15 boxes of grapefruit to a store in Santa Rosa, California. What is the total weight of the shipment?

_____

Pounds of Citrus Fruit per Box	
Citrus Fruit	**Weight per Box (in pounds)**
Grapefruit	◐◐◐◐◐◐◐◗
Orange	◐◐◐◐◐◐◐◐
Tangelo	◐◐◐◐◐◐◐◐
Tangerine	◐◐◐◐◐◐◐◐◗

Key: Each ◐ = 10 pounds.

23. 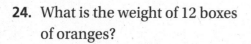 How much less do 13 boxes of tangelos weigh than 18 boxes of tangerines?

_____

24. What is the weight of 12 boxes of oranges?

_____

WRITE *Math* • **Show Your Work**

25. **THINK SMARTER** Each person in the United States eats about 65 fresh apples each year. Based on this estimate, how many apples do 3 families of 4 eat each year?

_____

26. **GO DEEPER** The product 26 × 93 is greater than 25 × 93. How much greater? Explain how you know without multiplying.

_____

_____

_____

27. 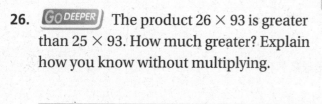 Margot wants to use partial products to find 22 × 17. Write the numbers in the boxes to show 22 × 17.

$$\left(\boxed{} \times \boxed{}\right) + \left(\boxed{} \times \boxed{}\right) + \left(\boxed{} \times \boxed{}\right) + \left(\boxed{} \times \boxed{}\right)$$

Multiply Using Partial Products

Learning Objective You will use partial products and place value understanding to multiply two 2-digit numbers.

Record the product.

1.
```
    23
×   79
 1,400
   210
   180
+   27
 1,817
```

2.
```
    56
×   32
```

3.
```
    87
×   64
```

4.
```
    33
×   25
```

5.
```
    94
×   12
```

6.
```
    51
×   77
```

7.
```
    69
×   49
```

 Problem Solving Real World

8. Evelyn drinks 8 glasses of water a day, which is 56 glasses of water a week. How many glasses of water does she drink in a year? (1 year = 52 weeks)

_____

9. Joe wants to use the Hiking Club's funds to purchase new walking sticks for each of its 19 members. The sticks cost $26 each. The club has $480. Is this enough money to buy each member a new walking stick? If not, how much more money is needed?

_____

10. **WRITE** ▸*Math* Explain why it works to break apart a number by place values to multiply.

_____

_____

_____

_____

Lesson Check

1. A carnival snack booth made $76 selling popcorn in one day. It made 22 times as much selling cotton candy. How much money did the snack booth make selling cotton candy?

   _____

2. List the partial products of 42 × 28.

   _____

Spiral Review

3. Last year, the city library collected 117 used books for its shelves. This year, it collected 3 times as many books. How many books did it collect this year?

   _____

4. Washington Elementary has 232 students. Washington High has 6 times as many students. How many students does Washington High have?

   _____

5. List the partial products of 35 × 7.

   _____

6. Shelby has ten $5 bills and thirteen $10 bills. How much money does Shelby have in all?

   _____

FOR MORE PRACTICE
GO TO THE
Personal Math Trainer

Name _____

✓ Mid-Chapter Checkpoint

Personal Math Trainer
Online Assessment
and Intervention

Concepts and Skills

1. Explain how to find 40 × 50 using mental math.

   _____

   _____

2. What is the first step in estimating 56 × 27?

   _____

Choose a method. Then find the product.

3. 35 × 10 _____   4. 19 × 20 _____   5. 12 × 80 _____

6. 70 × 50 _____   7. 58 × 40 _____   8. 30 × 40 _____

9. 14 × 60 _____   10. 20 × 30 _____   11. 16 × 90 _____

Estimate the product. Choose a method.

12. 81 × 38 _____   13. 16 × $59 _____   14. 43 × 25 _____

15. 76 × 45 _____   16. 65 × $79 _____   17. 92 × 38 _____

18. 37 × 31 _____   19. 26 × $59 _____   20. 54 × 26 _____

21. 52 × 87 _____   22. 39 × 27 _____   23. 63 × 58 _____

24. Ms. Traynor's class is taking a field trip to the zoo. The trip will cost $26 for each student. There are 22 students in her class. What is a good estimate for the cost of the students' field trip?

_____

25. Tito wrote the following on the board. What is the unknown number?

$$50 \times 80 = 50 \times (8 \times 10)$$
$$= (50 \times 8) \times 10$$
$$= ? \times 10$$
$$= 4{,}000$$

_____

26. What are the partial products that result from multiplying 15×32?

_____

27. GO DEEPER A city bus company sold 39 one-way tickets and 20 round-trip tickets from West Elmwood to East Elmwood. One-way tickets cost $14. Round trip tickets cost $25. How much money did the bus company collect?

_____

Multiply with Regrouping

Essential Question How can you use regrouping to multiply 2-digit numbers?

Learning Objective You will use place value understanding and regrouping to multiply two 2-digit numbers.

 Unlock the Problem

By 1914, Henry Ford had streamlined his assembly line to make a Model T Ford car in 93 minutes. How many minutes did it take to make 25 Model Ts?

▲ The first production Model T Ford was assembled on October 1, 1908.

Use place value and regrouping.

Multiply. 93×25 **Estimate.** $90 \times 30 = $ _____

THINK	RECORD
STEP 1 • Think of 93 as 9 tens and 3 ones. • Multiply 25 by 3 ones.	$\begin{array}{r} 1 \\ 25 \\ \times\,93 \\ \hline \end{array}$ ← 3×25
STEP 2 • Multiply 25 by 9 tens.	$\begin{array}{r} 4 \\ \cancel{1} \\ 25 \\ \times\,93 \\ \hline 75 \\ \end{array}$ ← 90×25
STEP 3 • Add the partial products.	$\begin{array}{r} 4 \\ \cancel{1} \\ 25 \\ \times\,93 \\ \hline 75 \\ 2{,}250 \\ \hline \end{array}$

So, 93×25 is 2,325. Since _____ is close

to the estimate of _____, the answer is reasonable.

Math Talk

Math Processes and Practices ⑧

Use Repeated Reasoning Why do you get the same answer whether you multiply 93×25 or 25×93?

Different Ways to Multiply You can use different ways to multiply and still get the correct answer. Shawn and Patty both solved 67 × 40 correctly, but they used different ways.

Look at Shawn's paper.

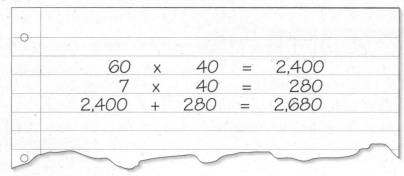

60	×	40	=	2,400
7	×	40	=	280
2,400	+	280	=	2,680

So, Shawn's answer is 67 × 40 = 2,680.

Look at Patty's paper.

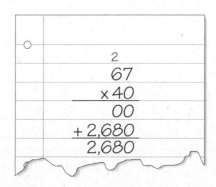

```
    2
   67
  × 40
   00
+2,680
 2,680
```

So, Patty also found 67 × 40 = 2,680.

1. What method did Shawn use to solve the problem?

_____

2. What method did Patty use to solve the problem?

_____

Share and Show

1. Look at the problem. Complete the sentences.

Multiply _____ and _____ to get 0.

Multiply _____ and _____ to get 1,620.

Add the partial products.

0 + 1,620 = _____

$$\begin{array}{r} 4 \\ 27 \\ \times 60 \\ \hline 0 \\ +1{,}620 \\ \hline \end{array}$$

Name _____

Estimate. Then find the product.

2. Estimate: _____

$$\begin{array}{r} 68 \\ \times\ 53 \\ \hline \end{array}$$

3. Estimate: _____

$$\begin{array}{r} 61 \\ \times\ 54 \\ \hline \end{array}$$

4. Estimate: _____

$$\begin{array}{r} 90 \\ \times\ 27 \\ \hline \end{array}$$

Math Talk Math Processes and Practices **8**

Generalize Why can you omit zeros of the first partial product when you multiply 20×34?

On Your Own

Estimate. Then find the product.

5. Estimate: _____

$$\begin{array}{r} 30 \\ \times\ 47 \\ \hline \end{array}$$

6. Estimate: _____

$$\begin{array}{r} 78 \\ \times\ 56 \\ \hline \end{array}$$

7. Estimate: _____

$$\begin{array}{r} 27 \\ \times\ 25 \\ \hline \end{array}$$

Practice: Copy and Solve **Estimate. Then find the product.**

8. 34×65 **9.** $42 \times \$13$ **10.** 60×17 **11.** 62×45 **12.** $57 \times \$98$

Math Processes and Practices 7 **Look for a Pattern** **Algebra** **Write a rule for the pattern.**
Use your rule to find the unknown numbers.

13.

Hours	h	5	10	15	20	25
Minutes	m	300	600	900		

Rule: _____

14. **GO DEEPER** Owners of a summer camp are buying new cots for their cabins. There are 16 cabins. Each cabin needs 6 cots. Each cot costs $92. How much will the new cots cost?

_____

15. **GO DEEPER** A theater has 28 rows of 38 seats downstairs and 14 rows of 26 seats upstairs. How many seats does the theater have?

_____

© Houghton Mifflin Harcourt Publishing Company

Unlock the Problem

16. **THINK SMARTER** Machine A can label 11 bottles in 1 minute. Machine B can label 12 bottles in 1 minute. How many bottles can both machines label in 15 minutes?

a. What do you need to know? _____

_____

b. What numbers will you use? _____

c. Tell why you might use more than one operation to solve the problem.

_____

_____

_____

d. Solve the problem.

So, both machines can label _____ bottles

in _____ minutes.

17. **Math Processes and Practices ①** **Make Sense of Problems**
A toy company makes wooden blocks. A carton holds 85 blocks. How many blocks can 19 cartons hold?

_____

18. **GO DEEPER** A company is packing cartons of candles. Each carton can hold 75 candles. So far, 50 cartons have been packed, but only 30 cartons have been loaded on a truck. How many more candles are left to load on the truck?

_____

Personal Math Trainer

19. **THINK SMARTER +** Mr. Garcia's class raised money for a field trip to the zoo. There are 23 students in his class. The cost of the trip will be $17 for each student. What is the cost for all the students? Explain how you found your answer.

_____

_____

Multiply with Regrouping

Learning Objective You will use place value understanding and regrouping to multiply two 2-digit numbers.

Estimate. Then find the product.

1. Estimate: _____2,700_____

Think: 87 is close to 90 and 32 is close to 30.

$$90 \times 30 = 2,700$$

$$
\begin{array}{r}
\overset{2}{\underset{1}{}} \\
87 \\
\times\ \ 32 \\
\hline
174 \\
+\ 2,610 \\
\hline
2,784
\end{array}
$$

2. Estimate: _____

$$
\begin{array}{r}
73 \\
\times\ \ 28 \\
\hline
\end{array}
$$

3. Estimate: _____

$$
\begin{array}{r}
48 \\
\times\ \ 38 \\
\hline
\end{array}
$$

4. Estimate: _____

$$
\begin{array}{r}
59 \\
\times\ \ 52 \\
\hline
\end{array}
$$

Problem Solving · Real World

5. Baseballs come in cartons of 84 baseballs. A team orders 18 cartons of baseballs. How many baseballs does the team order?

6. There are 16 tables in the school lunch room. Each table can seat 22 students. How many students can be seated at lunch at one time?

_____   _____

7. **WRITE** ▸*Math* Write about which method you prefer to use to multiply two 2-digit numbers—regrouping, partial products, or breaking apart a model. Explain why.

_____

_____

_____

_____

Lesson Check

1. The art teacher has 48 boxes of crayons. There are 64 crayons in each box. How many crayons does the teacher have?

2. A basketball team scored an average of 52 points in each of 15 games. Based on the average, how many points did the team score in all?

Spiral Review

3. One Saturday, an orchard sold 83 bags of apples. There are 27 apples in each bag. How many apples were sold?

4. Hannah has a grid of squares that has 12 rows with 15 squares in each row. She colors 5 rows of 8 squares in the middle of the grid blue. She colors the rest of the squares red. How many squares does Hannah color red?

5. Gabriella has 4 times as many erasers as Leona. Leona has 8 erasers. How many erasers does Gabriella have?

6. Phil has 3 times as many rocks as Peter. Together, they have 48 rocks. How many more rocks does Phil have than Peter?

FOR MORE PRACTICE
GO TO THE
Personal Math Trainer

Choose a Multiplication Method

Essential Question How can you find and record products of two 2-digit numbers?

Learning Objective You will choose a method to find and record products of two 2-digit numbers.

Unlock the Problem

Did you know using math can help prevent you from getting a sunburn?

The time it takes to burn without sunscreen multiplied by the SPF, or sun protection factor, is the time you can stay in the sun safely with sunscreen.

If today's UV index is 8, Erin will burn in 15 minutes without sunscreen. If Erin puts on lotion with an SPF of 25, how long will she be protected?

- Underline the sentence that tells you how to find the answer.
- Circle the numbers you need to use. What operation will you use?

_____

One Way Use partial products to find 15 × 25.

```
     25
   × 15
  _____
  ☐☐☐☐   ← 10 × 2 tens  =  20 tens
  ☐☐☐☐   ← 10 × 5 ones  =  50 ones
  ☐☐☐☐   ←  5 × 2 tens  =  10 tens
+ ☐☐☐☐   ←  5 × 5 ones  =  25 ones
  _____
  ☐☐☐☐   ← Add.
```

▲ Sunscreen helps to prevent sunburn.

Draw a picture to check your work.

So, if Erin puts on lotion with an SPF of 25, she will be protected for 375 minutes.

Math Talk

Math Processes and Practices 6

Explain how it was easier to find the product using partial products.

🔑 **Another Way** Use regrouping to find 15 × 25.

Estimate. 20 × 20 = _____

STEP 1	**STEP 2**	**STEP 3**
Think of 15 as 1 ten 5 ones. Multiply 25 by 5 ones, or 5.	Multiply 25 by 1 ten, or 10.	Add the partial products.

STEP 1

$$\begin{array}{r} \overset{2}{2}5 \\ \times\ 15 \\ \hline \end{array}$$
← 5 × 25

STEP 2

$$\begin{array}{r} \overset{2}{2}5 \\ \times\ 15 \\ \hline 125 \end{array}$$
← 10 × 25

STEP 3

$$\begin{array}{r} \overset{2}{2}5 \\ \times\ 15 \\ \hline 125 \\ +\ 250 \\ \hline \end{array}$$

Try This! Multiply. 57 × $43

Estimate. 57 × $43

Use partial products.

$$\begin{array}{r} \$\ 4\ 3 \\ \times\ \ \ 5\ 7 \end{array}$$

Use regrouping.

$$\begin{array}{r} \$\ 4\ 3 \\ \times\ \ \ 5\ 7 \end{array}$$

1. How do you know your answer is reasonable?

_____

_____

2. Look at the partial products and regrouping methods above. How are the partial products 2,000 and 150 related to 2,150?

_____

How are the partial products 280 and 21 related to 301?

_____

Name _____

1. Find the product.

$$
\begin{array}{r}
5\ 4 \\
\times\ 2\ 9 \\
\hline
\end{array}
$$

Math Talk Math Processes and Practices **8**

Draw Conclusions Why do you begin with the ones place when you use the regrouping method to multiply?

Estimate. Then choose a method to find the product.

2. Estimate: _____

$$
\begin{array}{r}
36 \\
\times\ 14 \\
\hline
\end{array}
$$

3. Estimate: _____

$$
\begin{array}{r}
63 \\
\times\ 42 \\
\hline
\end{array}
$$

✓**4.** Estimate: _____

$$
\begin{array}{r}
84 \\
\times\ 53 \\
\hline
\end{array}
$$

✓**5.** Estimate: _____

$$
\begin{array}{r}
71 \\
\times\ 13 \\
\hline
\end{array}
$$

On Your Own

Practice: Copy and Solve **Estimate. Find the product.**

6. $29 \times \$82$

7. 57×79

8. 80×27

9. $32 \times \$75$

10. 55×48

11. $19 \times \$82$

12. $25 \times \$25$

13. 41×98

Math Processes and Practices 7 **Identify Relationships** **Algebra** Use mental math to find the number.

14. $30 \times 14 = 420$, so $30 \times 15 =$ _____.

15. $25 \times 12 = 300$, so $25 \times$ _____ $= 350$.

16. **Math Processes and Practices 6** The town conservation manager bought 16 maple trees for $26 each. She paid with five $100 bills. How much change will the manager receive? **Explain**.

_____

_____

17. **GO DEEPER** Each of 25 students in Group A read for 45 minutes. Each of 21 students in Group B read for 48 minutes. Which group read for more minutes? Explain.

_____

Unlock the Problem

18. **THINK SMARTER** Martin collects stamps. He counted 48 pages in his collector's album. The first 20 pages each have 35 stamps in 5 rows. The rest of the pages each have 54 stamps. How many stamps does Martin have in his album?

a. What do you need to know? _____

_____

b. How will you use multiplication to find the number of stamps? _____

_____

c. Tell why you might use addition and subtraction to help solve the problem.

_____

_____

d. Show the steps to solve the problem.

e. Complete the sentences.

Martin has a total of _____ stamps on the first 20 pages.

There are _____ more pages after the first 20 pages in Martin's album.

There are _____ stamps on the rest of the pages.

There are _____ stamps in the album.

---

19. **THINK SMARTER** Select the expressions that have the same product as 35×17. Mark all that apply.

- ◯ $(30 \times 10) + (30 \times 7) + (5 \times 10) + (5 \times 7)$
- ◯ $(30 \times 17) + (5 \times 17)$
- ◯ $(35 \times 30) + (35 \times 5) + (35 \times 10) + (35 \times 7)$
- ◯ $(35 \times 10) + (35 \times 7)$
- ◯ $(35 \times 10) + (30 \times 10) + (5 \times 10) + (5 \times 7)$
- ◯ $(35 \times 30) + (35 \times 5)$

Choose a Multiplication Method

Learning Objective You will choose a method to find and record products of two 2-digit numbers.

Estimate. Then choose a method to find the product.

1. Estimate: _1,200_

$$\begin{array}{r} 31 \\ \times\ 43 \\ \hline 93 \\ +\ 1,240 \\ \hline 1,333 \end{array}$$

2. Estimate: _____

$$\begin{array}{r} 67 \\ \times\ 85 \\ \hline \end{array}$$

3. Estimate: _____

$$\begin{array}{r} 68 \\ \times\ 38 \\ \hline \end{array}$$

4. Estimate: _____

$$\begin{array}{r} 95 \\ \times\ 17 \\ \hline \end{array}$$

5. Estimate: _____

$$\begin{array}{r} 49 \\ \times\ 54 \\ \hline \end{array}$$

6. Estimate: _____

$$\begin{array}{r} 91 \\ \times\ 26 \\ \hline \end{array}$$

7. Estimate: _____

$$\begin{array}{r} 82 \\ \times\ 19 \\ \hline \end{array}$$

Problem Solving Real World

8. A movie theatre has 26 rows of seats. There are 18 seats in each row. How many seats are there?

_____

9. Each class at Briarwood Elementary collected at least 54 cans of food during the food drive. If there are 29 classes in the school, what was the least number of cans collected?

_____

10. **WRITE** ▸Math How is multiplication using partial products different from multiplication using regrouping? How are they similar?

_____

_____

_____

Lesson Check

1. A choir needs new robes for each of its 46 singers. Each robe costs $32. What will be the total cost for all 46 robes?

   _____

2. A wall on the side of a building is made up of 52 rows of bricks with 44 bricks in each row. How many bricks make up the wall?

   _____

Spiral Review

3. Write an expression that shows how to multiply 4 × 362 using place value and expanded form.

   _____

   _____

4. Use the model below. What is the product 4 × 492?

   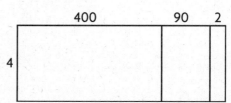

   _____

   _____

5. What is the sum 13,094 + 259,728?

6. During the 2008–2009 season, there were 801,372 people who attended the home hockey games in Philadelphia. There were 609,907 people who attended the home hockey games in Phoenix. How much greater was the home attendance in Philadelphia than in Phoenix that season?

   _____   _____

FOR MORE PRACTICE
GO TO THE
Personal Math Trainer

Name _____

Problem Solving • Multiply 2-Digit Numbers

Essential Question How can you use the strategy *draw a diagram* to solve multistep multiplication problems?

Learning Objective You will use the strategy *draw a diagram* to solve multistep multiplication problems.

Unlock the Problem

During the 2010 Great Backyard Bird Count, an average of 42 bald eagles were counted in each of 20 locations throughout Alaska. In 2009, an average of 32 bald eagles were counted in each of 26 locations throughout Alaska. Based on this data, how many more bald eagles were counted in 2010 than in 2009?

Use the graphic organizer to help you solve the problem.

Read the Problem	Solve the Problem
What do I need to find?	• First, find the total number of bald eagles counted in 2010.
I need to find _____ bald eagles were counted in 2010 than in 2009.	_____ × _____
	= _____ bald eagles counted in 2010
What information do I need to use?	• Next, find the total number of bald eagles counted in 2009.
In 2010, _____ locations counted an average of _____ bald eagles each.	= _____ × _____
In 2009 _____ locations counted an average of _____ bald eagles each.	= _____ bald eagles counted in 2009
How will I use the information?	• Last, draw a bar model. I need to subtract.
I can solve simpler problems.	
Find the number of bald eagles counted in _____.	*840 bald eagles in 2010*
Find the number of bald eagles counted in _____.	*832 bald eagles in 2009* ?
Then draw a bar model to compare the _____ count to the _____ count.	$840 - 832 =$ _____
	So, there were _____ more bald eagles counted in 2010 than in 2009.

🔒 Try Another Problem

Prescott Valley, Arizona, reported a total of 29 mourning doves in the Great Backyard Bird Count. Mesa, Arizona, reported 20 times as many mourning doves as Prescott Valley. If Chandler reported a total of 760 mourning doves, how many more mourning doves were reported in Chandler than in Mesa?

Mourning dove ▲

Read the Problem	Solve the Problem
What do I need to find?	
What information do I need to use?	
How will I use the information?	760 mourning doves in Chandler
	580 mourning doves in Mesa
	?

• Is your answer reasonable? Explain. _____

_____

_____

Math Talk

© Houghton Mifflin Harcourt Publishing Company • (t) ©William Leaman/Alamy Images

Math Processes and Practices ②

Reason Abstractly What is another way you could solve this problem?

Name _____

Share and Show

Unlock the Problem

✓ Underline important facts.
✓ Choose a strategy.
✓ Use the Problem Solving MathBoard.

✓ **1.** An average of 74 reports with bird counts were turned in each day in June. An average of 89 were turned in each day in July. How many reports were turned in for both months? (Hint: There are 30 days in June and 31 days in July.)

First, write the problem for June.

_____

Next, write the problem for July.

_____

Last, find and add the two products.

_____ reports were turned in for both months.

✓ **2.** What if an average of 98 reports were turned in each day for the month of June? How many reports were turned in for June? Describe how your answer for June would be different.

_____

_____

_____

3. GO DEEPER There are 48 crayons in a box. There are 12 boxes in a carton. Mr. Johnson ordered 6 cartons of crayons for the school. How many crayons did he get?

_____

4. Math Processes and Practices ① **Make Sense of Problems** Each of 5 bird-watchers reported seeing 15 roseate spoonbills in a day. If they each reported seeing the same number of roseate spoonbills over 14 days, how many would be reported?

_____

WRITE ▸ Math · **Show Your Work**

On Your Own

5. **THINK SMARTER** On each of Maggie's bird-watching trips, she has seen at least 24 birds. If she has taken 4 of these trips each year over the past 16 years, at least how many birds has Maggie seen?

_____

6. **Math Processes and Practices 1** Make Sense of Problems
There are 12 inches in a foot. In September, Mrs. Harris orders 32 feet of ribbon for the Crafts Club. In January, she orders 9 feet less. How many inches of ribbon does Mrs. Harris order? Explain how you found your answer.

_____

_____

_____

7. **GO DEEPER** Lydia is having a party on Saturday. She decides to write a riddle on her invitations to describe her house number on Cypress Street. Use the clues to find Lydia's address.

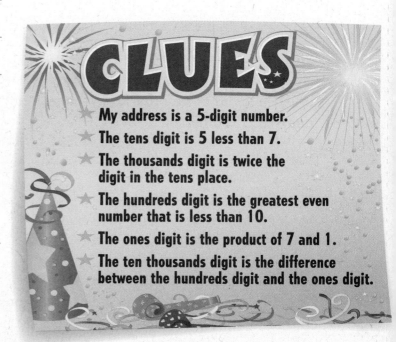

CLUES

★ My address is a 5-digit number.
★ The tens digit is 5 less than 7.
★ The thousands digit is twice the digit in the tens place.
★ The hundreds digit is the greatest even number that is less than 10.
★ The ones digit is the product of 7 and 1.
★ The ten thousands digit is the difference between the hundreds digit and the ones digit.

_____

Personal Math Trainer

8. **THINK SMARTER+** A school is adding 4 rows of seats to the auditorium. There are 7 seats in each row. Each new seat costs $99. What is the total cost for the new seats? Show your work.

_____

Problem Solving • Multiply 2-Digit Numbers

Learning Objective You will use the strategy *draw a diagram* to solve multistep multiplication problems.

Solve each problem. Use a bar model to help.

1. Mason counted an average of 18 birds at his bird feeder each day for 20 days. Gloria counted an average of 21 birds at her bird feeder each day for 16 days. How many more birds did Mason count at his feeder than Gloria counted at hers?

   Birds counted by Mason: **18 × 20 = 360**

   Birds counted by Gloria: **21 × 16 = 336**

   Draw a bar model to compare.

   Subtract. **360 − 336 = 24**

360 birds counted by Mason

336 birds counted by Gloria
   ?

   So, Mason counted __24__ more birds.

2. The 24 students in Ms. Lee's class each collected an average of 18 cans for recycling. The 21 students in Mr. Galvez's class each collected an average of 25 cans for recycling. How many more cans were collected by Mr. Galvez's class than Ms. Lee's class?

   _____

3. At East School, each of the 45 classrooms has an average of 22 students. At West School, each of the 42 classrooms has an average of 23 students. How many more students are at East School than at West School?

   _____

4. **WRITE** ▸ *Math* Draw a bar model that shows how the number of hours in March compares with the number of hours in February of this year.

Lesson Check

1. Ace Manufacturing ordered 17 boxes with 85 ball bearings each. They also ordered 15 boxes with 90 springs each. How many more ball bearings than springs did they order?

_____

2. Elton hiked 16 miles each day on a 12-day hiking trip. Lola hiked 14 miles each day on her 16-day hiking trip. In all, how many more miles did Lola hike than Elton hiked?

_____

Spiral Review

3. An orchard has 24 rows of apple trees. There are 35 apple trees in each row. How many apple trees are in the orchard?

_____

4. An amusement park reported 354,605 visitors last summer. What is this number rounded to the nearest thousand?

_____

5. Attendance at the football game was 102,653. What is the value of the digit 6?

_____

6. Jill's fish weighs 8 times as much as her parakeet. Together, the pets weigh 63 ounces. How much does the fish weigh?

_____

FOR MORE PRACTICE
GO TO THE
Personal Math Trainer

✓ Chapter 3 Review/Test

1. Explain how to find 40 × 50 using mental math.

```

```

2. Mrs. Traynor's class is taking a field trip to the zoo. The trip will cost $26 for each student. There are 22 students in her class.

Part A

Round each factor to estimate the total cost of the students' field trip.

```

```

Part B

Use compatible numbers to estimate the total cost of the field trip.

```

```

Part C

Which do you think is the better estimate? Explain.

```

```

3. For numbers 3a–3e, select Yes or No to show if the answer is correct.

3a. $35 \times 10 = 350$ ○ Yes   ○ No

3b. $19 \times 20 = 380$ ○ Yes   ○ No

3c. $12 \times 100 = 120$ ○ Yes   ○ No

3d. $70 \times 100 = 7{,}000$ ○ Yes   ○ No

3e. $28 \times 30 = 2{,}100$ ○ Yes   ○ No

4. There are 23 boxes of pencils in Mr. Shaw's supply cabinet. Each box contains 100 pencils. How many pencils are in the supply cabinet?

_____ pencils

5. Which would provide a reasonable estimate for each product? Write the estimate beside the product. An estimate may be used more than once.

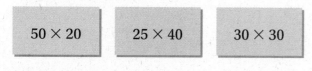

| 50 × 20 | 25 × 40 | 30 × 30 |

23×38 [_____] 46×18 [_____]

31×32 [_____] 39×21 [_____]

6. There are 26 baseball teams in the league. Each team has 18 players. Write a number sentence that will provide a reasonable estimate for the number of players in the league. Explain how you found your estimate.

7. The model shows 48×37. Write the partial products.

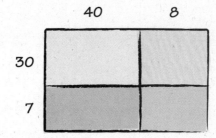

190

8. Jess made this model to find the product 32 × 17. Her model is incorrect.

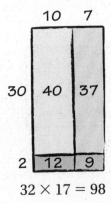

$$32 \times 17 = 98$$

Part A

What did Jess do wrong?

Part B

Redraw the model so that it is correct.

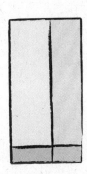

Part C

What is the actual product 32 × 17?

_____

9. Tatum wants to use partial products to find 15 × 32. Write the numbers in the boxes to show 15 × 32.

$$\left(\boxed{} \times \boxed{} \right) + \left(\boxed{} \times \boxed{} \right) + \left(\boxed{} \times \boxed{} \right) + \left(\boxed{} \times \boxed{} \right)$$

10. Which product is shown by the model? Write the letter of the product on the line below the model.

(A) 17 × 36   (B) 24 × 14   (C) 13 × 13

	10	3
10	100	30
3	30	9

	30	6
10	300	60
7	210	42

	10	4
20	200	80
4	40	16

_____   _____   _____

11. 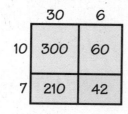 Mrs. Jones places 3 orders for school T-shirts. Each order has 16 boxes of shirts and each box holds 17 shirts. How many T-shirts does Mrs. Jones order? Use partial products to help you.

12. Write the unknown digits. Use each digit exactly once.

```
      46
    × 93
   ─────
  3, ▢ 00
    5 ▢ 0
      ▢ 20
  + 1 ▢
   ─────
  4, ▢ 78
```

| 1 | 2 | 4 | 6 | 8 |

13. Mike has 16 baseball cards. Niko has 17 times as many baseball cards as Mike does. How many baseball cards does Niko have?

_____ baseball cards

14. Multiply.

    36 × 28 = _____

Name _____

15. A farmer planted 42 rows of tomatoes with 13 plants in each row. How many tomato plants did the farmer grow?

42 × 13 = _____ tomato plants

16. Select another way to show 25 × 18. Mark all that apply.

○ (20 × 10) + (20 × 8) + (5 × 10) + (5 × 8)

○ (25 × 20) + (25 × 5) + (25 × 10) + (25 × 8)

○ (20 × 18) + (5 × 10) + (5 × 8)

○ (25 × 10) + (25 × 8)

○ (25 × 20) + (25 × 5)

17. Terrell runs 15 sprints. Each sprint is 65 meters. How many meters does Terrell run? Show your work.

18. THINK SMARTER + There are 3 new seats in each row in a school auditorium. There are 15 rows in the auditorium. Each new seat cost $74. What is the cost for the new seats? Explain how you found your answer.

Personal Math Trainer

19. Ray and Ella helped move their school library to a new building. Ray packed 27 boxes with 25 books in each box. Ella packed 23 boxes with 30 books in each box. How many more books did Ella pack? Show your work.

20. Julius and Walt are finding the product of 25 and 16.

	Julius	Walt
	25	25
	× 16	× 16
	150	200
	+ 250	50
	500	120
		+ 300
		670

Part A

Julius' answer is incorrect. What did Julius do wrong?

Part B

What did Walt do wrong?

Part C

What is the correct product?

21. A clothing store sells 26 shirts and 22 pairs of jeans. Each item of clothing costs $32.

Part A

What is a reasonable estimate for the total cost of the clothing? Show or explain how you found your answer.

Part B

What is the exact answer for the total cost of the clothing? Show or explain how you found your answer.

✓ Show What You Know

Personal Math Trainer
Online Assessment and Intervention

Check your understanding of important skills.

Name _____

▶ **Use Arrays to Divide** Draw to complete each array.
Then complete the number sentence.

1.

    8 ÷ 4 = _____

2.

    21 ÷ 3 = _____

▶ **Multiples** Write the first six multiples of the number.

3. 4: _____

4. 10: _____

▶ **Subtract Through 4-Digit Numbers** Find the difference.

5.	6.	7.	8.
626 − 8	744 − 36	5,413 −2,037	8,681 − 422

 **Math in the Real World**

Each digit in the division example has been replaced with the same letter throughout. (r stands for remainder.) The digits used were 1, 2, 3, 4, 5, 7, and 9. Find the numbers. Clue: U is 5.

```
    SU rE
U)CAN
 −CU
  IN
 −IU
   E
```

Vocabulary Builder

▶ **Visualize It** •

Sort the words into the Venn diagram.

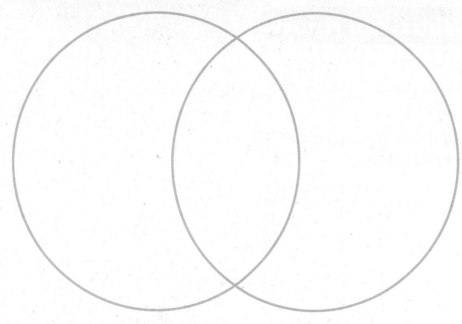

Multiplication Words   Division Words

Review Words

Distributive Property

divide

dividend

division

divisor

factor

multiplication

product

quotient

Preview Words

compatible numbers

multiple

partial quotient

remainder

▶ **Understand Vocabulary** •

Write the word that answers the riddle.

1. I am the method of dividing in which multiples of the divisor are subtracted from the dividend and then the quotients are added together.

   _____

2. I am the number that is to be divided in a division problem.

   _____

3. I am the amount left over when a number cannot be

   divided equally. _____

4. I am the number that divided the dividend.

   _____

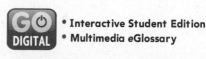

• **Interactive Student Edition**
• **Multimedia eGlossary**

compatible numbers

números compatibles

15

Distributive Property

propiedad distributiva

23

dividend

dividendo

24

divisor

divisor

26

multiple

múltiplo

55

partial quotient

cociente parcial

62

quotient

cociente

75

remainder

residuo

79

The property that states that multiplying a sum by a number is the same as multiplying each addend by the number and then adding the products

Example: $5 \times (10 + 6) = (5 \times 10) + (5 \times 6)$

Numbers that are easy to compute mentally

Example: Estimate. $176 \div 8$

160 divides easily by 8

↑
compatible number

The number that divides the dividend

Example: $15 \div 3 = 5$

↑
divisor

The number that is to be divided in a division problem

Example: $36 \div 6 = 6$

↑
dividend

A method of dividing in which multiples of the divisor are subtracted from the dividend and then the quotients are added together

Example:

$$
\begin{array}{r}
5\overline{)125} \quad \text{Partial Quotients}\\
-50 \quad 10 \times 5 \quad 10\\
\hline
75\\
-50 \quad 10 \times 5 \quad 10\\
\hline
25\\
-25 \quad 5 \times 5 \quad +5\\
\hline
0 \quad\quad\quad\quad 25
\end{array}
$$

The product of a number and a counting number is called a multiple of the number

Example:

$$
\begin{array}{cccc}
3 & 3 & 3 & 3\\
\times 1 & \times 2 & \times 3 & \times 4\\
\hline
3 & 6 & 9 & 12
\end{array}
$$

← counting numbers
← multiples of 3

The amount left over when a number cannot be divided equally

Example:
$$3\overline{)14} \quad 4\text{ R}2$$

↑
remainder

The number, not including the remainder, that results from dividing

Example: $35 \div 7 = 5$

↑
quotient

Pick It

For 3 to 4 players

Materials

- 4 sets of word cards.

How to Play

1. Each player is dealt 5 cards. The remaining cards are a draw pile.
2. To take a turn, ask any player if he or she has a word that matches one of your word cards.
3. If the player has the word, he or she gives the card to you, and you must define the word.
   - If you are correct, keep the card and put the matching pair in front of you. Take another turn.
   - If you are wrong, return the card. Your turn is over.
4. If the player does not have the word, he or she answers, "Pick it." Then you take a card from the draw pile.
5. If the card you draw matches one of your word cards, follow the directions for Step 3 above. If it does not, your turn is over.
6. The game is over when one player has no cards left. The player with the most pairs wins.

Word Box
compatible numbers
Distributive Property
dividend
divisor
multiple
partial quotient
quotient
remainder

The Write Way

Reflect

Choose one idea. Write about it.

- Write a paragraph that uses at least three of these words.

  dividend   divisor   multiple   quotient   remainder

- Explain how you know that the quotient of 143 ÷ 5 has a remainder.

- Think about what you learned about division in math class today. Complete one of these sentences.

  I learned that _____.

  I was surprised that _____.

  I noticed that _____.

  I discovered that _____.

Name _____

Estimate Quotients Using Multiples

Essential Question How can you use multiples to estimate quotients?

Learning Objective You will use multiples to estimate quotients.

Unlock the Problem

The bakery made 110 pumpkin muffins. They will be packed in boxes with 8 muffins in each box. About how many boxes will there be?

You can use multiples to estimate.

A **multiple** of a number is the product of a number and a counting number. 1, 2, 3, 4, and so on, are counting numbers.

 Estimate. 110 ÷ 8

Think: What number multiplied by 8 is about 110?

STEP 1 List the multiples of 8 until you reach 110 or greater.

Counting number	1	2	3	4	5	6	7	8	9	10	11	12	13	14
Multiple of 8	8	16	24	32			56	64				96		112

STEP 2 Find the multiples of 8 that 110 is between.

13 × 8 = _____

14 × 8 = _____

110 is between _____ and _____ , so 110 ÷ 8 is between 13 and 14.

110 is closest to _____ , so 110 ÷ 8 is about _____ .

So, there will be about _____ boxes.

 Math Talk **Math Processes and Practices 7**

Identify Relationships When estimating a quotient, how do you know which two numbers it is between?

Try This!

List the next 8 multiples of 10.

10, 20, _____

List the next 7 multiples of 100.

100, 200, _____

© Houghton Mifflin Harcourt Publishing Company • Image Credits: (t) ©Matthew Antonino/Alamy Images

🔑 Example Estimate. 196 ÷ 4

Think: What number times 4 is about 196?

STEP 1 List the next 6 multiples of 4.

4, 8, 12, 16, _____

Are any multiples close to 196? _____
_____

Think: If I multiply by multiples of 10, the products will be greater. Using multiples of 10 will get me to 196 faster.

STEP 2 Multiply 4 by multiples of 10.

$10 \times 4 = 40$

$20 \times 4 = 80$

$30 \times 4 =$ _____

$40 \times 4 =$ _____

$50 \times 4 =$ _____

The quotient is between 40 and 50.

_____ $\times$ 4 is closest to _____, so 196 ÷ 4 is about _____.

Share and Show

1. A restaurant has 68 chairs. There are six chairs at each table. About how many tables are in the restaurant?

   Estimate. 68 ÷ 6

   Think: What number times 6 is about 68?

   $10 \times 6 =$ _____

   $11 \times 6 =$ _____

   $12 \times 6 =$ _____

   68 is closest to _____, so the best estimate is

   about _____ tables are in the restaurant.

Math Talk

Math Processes and Practices ⑤

Communicate When do you multiply the divisor by multiples of 10 to estimate a quotient? Explain.

© Houghton Mifflin Harcourt Publishing Company

Name _____

Find two numbers the quotient is between. Then estimate the quotient.

✓ **2.** 41 ÷ 3

_____

_____

✓ **3.** 192 ÷ 5

_____

_____

On Your Own

Find two numbers the quotient is between. Then estimate the quotient.

4. 90 ÷ 7

_____

_____

5. 67 ÷ 4

_____

_____

6. 281 ÷ 9

_____

_____

7. 102 ÷ 7

_____

_____

8. 85 ÷ 6

_____

_____

9. 220 ÷ 8

_____

_____

Decide whether the actual quotient is greater than or less than the estimate given. Write < or >.

10. 83 ÷ 8 ◯ 10

11. 155 ÷ 4 ◯ 40

12. 70 ÷ 6 ◯ 11

13. What's the Question? A dolphin's heart beats 688 times in 6 minutes. Answer: about 100 times.

_____

_____

14. **Math Processes and Practices ①** **Analyze** A mother bottlenose dolphin ate about 278 pounds of food in one week. About how much food did she eat in a day?

_____

_____

15. **GO DEEPER** Tanya has $42 to spend at the Dolphin Island store. T-shirts sell for $7 each and a pair of sunglasses sells for $6. Tanya buys 3 T-shirts. How many pairs of sunglasses can she buy with the amount of money she has left?

_____

Problem Solving • Applications

16. **THINK SMARTER** If a bottlenose dolphin can eat 175 pounds of fish, squid, and shrimp in a week, about how many pounds of food does it eat in a day? Milo says the answer is about 20 pounds. Leah says the answer is about 30 pounds. Who is correct? Explain.

_____

_____

_____

_____

17. **GO DEEPER** Four families went out for lunch. The total food bill came to $167. The families also left a $30 tip for the waitress. If each family spent the same amount, about how much did each family spend on dinner? Explain how you found your answer.

_____

_____

_____

_____

WRITE *Math*
Show Your Work

18. **THINK SMARTER** There are 6 showings of a film about Van Gogh at the Art Museum. A total of 459 people saw the film. The same number of people were at each showing. About how many people were at each showing? Circle the numbers the quotient is between. Then explain how you found your answer.

    40   50   60   70   80

_____

_____

Estimate Quotients Using Multiples

Learning Objective You will use multiples to estimate quotients.

Find two numbers the quotient is between. Then estimate the quotient.

1. $175 \div 6$

between 20 and
_____
30 about 30

Think: $6 \times 20 = 120$ and $6 \times 30 = 180$.
So, $175 \div 6$ is between 20 and 30. Since 175 is closer to 180 than to 120, the quotient is about 30.

2. $53 \div 3$

_____

_____

3. $75 \div 4$

_____

_____

4. $215 \div 9$

_____

_____

5. $284 \div 5$

_____

_____

6. $191 \div 3$

_____

_____

7. $100 \div 7$

_____

_____

Problem Solving Real World

8. Joy collected 287 aluminum cans in 6 hours. About how many cans did she collect per hour?

_____

9. Paul sold 162 cups of lemonade in 5 hours. About how many cups of lemonade did he sell each hour?

_____

10. **WRITE** ▸ *Math* Write a word problem that you can solve using multiples to estimate the quotient. Include a solution.

_____

_____

_____

Lesson Check

1. Abby did 121 sit-ups in 8 minutes. Estimate the number of sit-ups she did in 1 minute.

   _____

   _____

2. The Garibaldi family drove 400 miles in 7 hours. Estimate the number of miles they drove in 1 hour.

   _____

   _____

Spiral Review

3. Twelve boys collected 16 aluminum cans each. Fifteen girls collected 14 aluminum cans each. How many more cans did the girls collect than the boys?

   _____

4. George bought 30 packs of football cards. There were 14 cards in each pack. How many cards did George buy?

   _____

5. Sarah made a necklace using 5 times as many blue beads as white beads. She used a total of 30 beads. How many blue beads did Sarah use?

   _____

6. This year, Ms. Webster flew 145,000 miles on business. Last year, she flew 83,125 miles on business. How many more miles did Ms. Webster fly on business this year?

   _____

FOR MORE PRACTICE
GO TO THE
Personal Math Trainer

Name _____

Remainders

Essential Question How can you use models to divide whole numbers that do not divide evenly?

Learning Objective You will use models to find whole-number quotients and remainders with up to 2-digit dividends and 1-digit divisors.

Investigate

Materials ■ counters

Andrea and 2 friends are playing a game of dominoes. There are 28 dominoes in the set. Andrea wants each player to receive the same number of dominoes. Can she divide them equally among the 3 players? Why or why not?

You can use division to find the number of dominoes each player will receive.

A. Use 28 counters to represent the 28 dominoes. Then draw 3 circles to represent the 3 players.

B. Share the counters equally among the 3 groups by placing them in the circles.

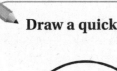
Draw a quick picture to show your work.

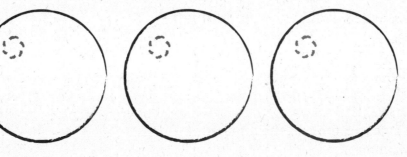

C. Find the number of counters in each group and the number of counters left over. Record your answer.

_____ counters in each group

_____ counter left over

Draw Conclusions

1. How many dominoes does each player receive? _____

   How many dominoes are left over? _____

2. Explain how the model helped you find the number of dominoes each player receives. Why is 1 counter left outside the equal groups?

   _____

   _____

   _____

3. Use counters to represent a set of 28 dominoes. How many players can play dominoes if each player receives 9 dominoes? Will any dominoes be left over? Explain.

   _____

   _____

Make Connections

Hands On

When a number cannot be divided evenly, the amount left over is called the **remainder**.

Use counters to find 39 ÷ 5.

• Use 39 counters.

• Share the counters equally among 5 groups. The number of counters left over is the remainder.

Draw a quick picture to show your work.

For 39 ÷ 5, the quotient is _____ and the remainder

is _____, or 7 r4.

Math Talk

Math Processes and Practices 8

Generalize How do you know when there will be a remainder in a division problem?

204

Name _____

Share and Show MATH BOARD

Use counters to find the quotient and remainder.

1. $10 \div 3$

2. $28 \div 5$

3. $15 \div 6$

4. $11 \div 3$

_____

5. $29 \div 4$

6. $34 \div 5$

7. $25 \div 3$

✓8. $7\overline{)20}$

_____

Divide. Draw a quick picture to help.

9. $4\overline{)35}$

✓10. $23 \div 8$

_____

Problem Solving • Applications Real World

11. **Math Processes and Practices 6** **Explain** how you use a quick picture to find the quotient and remainder.

_____

_____

_____

_____

12. **GO DEEPER** Alyson has 46 beads to make bracelets. Each bracelet has 5 beads. How many more beads does Alyson need so that all the beads she has are used? Explain.

_____

_____

13. **THINK SMARTER** For 13a–13d, choose Yes or No to tell whether the division expression has a remainder.

13a. $36 \div 9$ ○ Yes ○ No

13b. $23 \div 3$ ○ Yes ○ No

13c. $82 \div 9$ ○ Yes ○ No

13d. $28 \div 7$ ○ Yes ○ No

What's the Error?

14. **THINK SMARTER** Macy, Kayley, Maddie, and Rachel collected
13 marbles. They want to share the marbles equally. How many
marbles will each of the 4 girls get? How many marbles will be
left over?

Oscar used a model to solve this problem. He says his
model represents $4\overline{)13}$. What is his error?

Look at the way Oscar solved this problem. Find and describe his error.	**Draw a correct model and solve the problem.**
_____	
	So, each of the 4 girls will get _____ marbles and _____ marble will be left over.

Name _____

Remainders

Learning Objective You will use models to find whole-number quotients and remainders with up to 2-digit dividends and 1-digit divisors.

Use counters to find the quotient and remainder.

1. $13 \div 4$

_____3 r1_____

2. $24 \div 7$

_____

3. $39 \div 5$

_____

4. $36 \div 8$

_____

5. $6\overline{)27}$

_____

6. $25 \div 9$

_____

7. $3\overline{)17}$

_____

8. $26 \div 4$

_____

Divide. Draw a quick picture to help.

9. $14 \div 3$

10. $5\overline{)29}$

_____   _____

Problem Solving · Real World

11. Mark drew the following model and said it represented the problem $21 \div 4$. Is Mark's model correct? If so, what is the quotient and remainder? If not, what is the correct quotient and remainder?

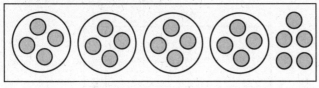

_____

_____

12. **WRITE** *Math* Describe a real-life situation where you would have a remainder.

_____

_____

_____

Lesson Check

1. What is the quotient and remainder for 32 ÷ 6?

2. What is the remainder in the division problem modeled below?

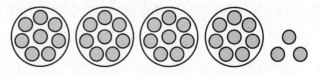

Spiral Review

3. Each kit to build a castle contains 235 parts. How many parts are in 4 of the kits?

4. In 2010, the population of Alaska was about 710,200. What is this number written in word form?

5. At the theater, one section of seats has 8 rows with 12 seats in each row. In the center of each of the first 3 rows are 4 broken seats that cannot be used. How many seats can be used in the section?

6. What partial products are shown by the model below?

	30	4
10		
6		

FOR MORE PRACTICE
GO TO THE
Personal Math Trainer

Name _____

Interpret the Remainder

Essential Question How can you use remainders in division problems?

Unlock the Problem

Magda has some leftover wallpaper 73 inches long. She wants to cut it into 8 pieces to use around the photos in her scrapbook. Each piece will have equal length. How long will each piece be?

When you solve a division problem with a remainder, the way you interpret the remainder depends on the situation and the question.

One Way Write the remainder as a fraction.

The divisor is _____ pieces.

The _____ is 73 inches.

Divide to find the quotient and remainder. $8\overline{)73}$ $\overset{9}{}$ r1

The remainder represents 1 inch left over, which can also be divided into 8 equal parts and written as a fraction.

Remember
You can use multiples, counters, or draw a quick picture to divide.

$$\frac{\text{remainder}}{\text{divisor}} = \underline{\hspace{1.5cm}}$$

Write the quotient with the remainder written as a fraction. _____

So, each piece will be _____ inches long.

Try This!

Daniel made 32 ounces of soup for 5 people. How many ounces will each person get? Complete the division.

$5\overline{)32}$ _____

Each person gets _____ ounces.

Math Talk

Math Processes and Practices 7

Explain what the 2 in the answer represents.

Chapter 4   **209**

Other Ways

A Use only the quotient.

Ben is a tour guide at a glass-blowing studio. He can take no more than 7 people at a time on a tour. If 80 people want to see the glass-blowing demonstration, how many groups of 7 people will Ben show around?

First, divide to find the quotient and remainder.
Then, decide how to use the quotient and remainder.

The quotient is _____ .

$$\begin{array}{r} 11 \text{ r} \\ 7\overline{)80} \end{array}$$

The remainder is _____ .

Ben can give tours to 7 people at a time. The quotient is the number of tour groups of exactly 7 people he can show around.

So, Ben gives tours to _____ groups of 7 people.

B Add 1 to the quotient.

If Ben gives tours to all 80 people, how many tours will he give? A tour can have no more than 7 people. To show all 80 people around, Ben will have to give 1 more tour.

So, Ben will give _____ tours in all for 80 people.

C Use only the remainder.

Ben gives tours to all 80 people. After he completes the tours for groups of 7 people, how many people are in his last tour?

The remainder is 3.

So, Ben's last tour will have _____ people.

Math Talk

Math Processes and Practices 8

Use Repeated Reasoning
Why would you not write the remainder as a fraction when you found the number of vans needed?

Try This!

Students are driven to soccer games in vans. Each van holds 9 students. How many vans are needed for 31 students?

Divide. $31 \div 9$ _____

Since there are _____ students left over, _____ vans are needed to carry 31 students.

Name _____

Share and Show MATH BOARD

1. Olivia baked 53 mini-loaves of banana bread to be sliced for snacks at a craft fair. She will place an equal number of loaves in 6 different locations. How many loaves will be at each location?

   a. Divide to find the quotient and remainder.

   b. Decide how to use the quotient and remainder to answer the question.

   $6\overline{)53}$ r

   _____

Interpret the remainder to solve.

2. What if Olivia wants to put only whole loaves at each location? How many loaves will be at each location?

   _____

3. Ed carves 22 small wooden animals to sell at the craft fair. He displays them in rows with 4 animals in a row. How many animals will not be in equal rows?

   _____

On Your Own

Interpret the remainder to solve.

4. Myra has a 17-foot roll of crepe paper to make 8 streamers to decorate for a party. How long will each streamer be if she cuts the roll into equal pieces?

   _____

5. **THINK SMARTER** Juan has a piano recital next month. Last week he practiced for 8 hours in the morning and 7 hours in the afternoon. Each practice session is 2 hours long. How many full practice sessions did Juan complete?

   _____

6. **GO DEEPER** A total of 25 students sign up to be hosts on Parent's Night. Teams of 3 students greet parents. How many students cannot be on a team? Explain.

   _____

   _____

   _____

Problem Solving · Applications

Use the picture for 7–9.

7. Teresa is making sock puppets just like the one in the picture. If she has 53 buttons, how many puppets can she make?

_____

8. **THINK SMARTER** Write a question about Teresa and the sock puppets for which the answer is 3. Explain the answer.

_____
_____
_____
_____

9. **Math Processes and Practices 3** Interpret a Result How many more buttons will Teresa need if she wants to make 12 puppets? Explain.

_____
_____
_____
_____

WRITE Math
Show Your Work

10. **GO DEEPER** A total of 56 students signed up to play in a flag football league. If each team has 10 students, how many more students will need to sign up so all of the students can be on a team?

_____

Personal Math Trainer

11. **THINK SMARTER +** A teacher plans for groups of her students to eat lunch at tables. She has 34 students in her class. Each group will have 7 students. How many tables will she need? Explain how to use the quotient and remainder to answer the question.

_____
_____

Interpret the Remainder

Learning Objective You will interpret the
remainder to solve division problems.

Interpret the remainder to solve.

1. Hakeem has 100 tomato plants. He wants
   to plant them in rows of 8. How many full
   rows will he have?

   _____ **12 full rows** _____

Think: $100 \div 8$ is 12 with a remainder of 4.
The question asks "how many full rows," so
use only the quotient.

2. A teacher has 27 students in her class.
   She asks the students to form as many
   groups of 4 as possible. How many
   students will not be in a group?

   _____

3. A sporting goods company can ship
   6 footballs in each carton. How many
   cartons are needed to ship 75 footballs?

   _____

Problem Solving Real World

4. Joanna has 70 beads. She uses 8 beads
   for each bracelet. She makes as many
   bracelets as possible. How many beads
   will Joanna have left over?

   _____

5. A teacher wants to give 3 markers to each of
   her 25 students. Markers come in packages
   of 8. How many packages of markers will the
   teacher need?

   _____

6. **WRITE** ▸*Math* Write word problems that represent each way
   you can use a remainder in a division problem. Include solutions.

   _____

   _____

Lesson Check

1. Marcus sorts his 85 baseball cards into stacks of 9 cards each. How many stacks of 9 cards can Marcus make?

2. A minivan can hold up to 7 people. How many minivans are needed to take 45 people to a basketball game?

Spiral Review

3. Mrs. Wilkerson cut some oranges into 20 equal pieces to be shared by 6 friends. How many pieces did each person get and how many pieces were left over?

4. A school bought 32 new desks. Each desk cost $24. Estimate how much the school spent on the new desks.

5. Kris has a box of 8 crayons. Sylvia's box has 6 times as many crayons as Kris's box. How many crayons are in Sylvia's box?

6. Yesterday, 1,743 people visited the fair. Today, there are 576 more people at the fair than yesterday. How many people are at the fair today?

© Houghton Mifflin Harcourt Publishing Company

FOR MORE PRACTICE
GO TO THE
Personal Math Trainer

Name _____

Divide Tens, Hundreds, and Thousands

Essential Question How can you divide numbers through thousands by whole numbers to 10?

Learning Objective You will use place value to divide tens, hundreds, and thousands.

 Unlock the Problem Real World

Dustin is packing apples in gift boxes. Each gift box holds 4 apples. How many boxes can Dustin pack with 120 apples?

You can divide using basic facts and place value.

Example 1 Divide. $120 \div 4$

STEP 1 Identify the basic fact. $12 \div 4$

STEP 2 Use place value. $120 = $ _____ tens

STEP 3 Divide.   12 tens $\div$ 4 = _____ tens   ← Think: 4×3 tens = 12 tens

$\qquad\qquad\qquad\qquad\qquad = $ _____

$\qquad\qquad\qquad\qquad 120 \div 4 = 30$

So, Dustin can pack _____ boxes.

Example 2 Divide. $1{,}200 \div 4$

STEP 1 Identify the basic fact. $12 \div 4$

STEP 2 Use place value. $1{,}200 = $ _____ hundreds

STEP 3 Divide.   12 hundreds $\div$ 4 = _____ hundreds   ← Think: 4×3 hundreds = 12 hundreds

$\qquad\qquad\qquad\qquad\qquad = $ _____

$\qquad\qquad\qquad\qquad 1{,}200 \div 4 = 300$

 Math Talk   Math Processes and Practices ⑦

Look for a Pattern What pattern do you notice in the place value of the dividends and quotients?

- **Math Processes and Practices ⑥** **Explain** how to use a basic fact and place value to divide $4{,}000 \div 5$.

_____

_____

Chapter 4   **215**

Share and Show MATH BOARD

Math Talk Math Processes and Practices ⑥

Compare How are Exercises 1 and 2 alike and how are they different?

1. Divide. 2,800 ÷ 7

   What basic fact can you use? _____

   2,800 = 28 _____

   28 hundreds ÷ 7 = _____

   2,800 ÷ 7 = _____

2. Divide. 280 ÷ 7

   What basic fact can you use? _____

   280 = 28 _____

   28 tens ÷ _____ = 4 _____

   280 ÷ 7 = _____

Use basic facts and place value to find the quotient.

✓ 3. 360 ÷ 6 = _____

4. 2,000 ÷ 5 = _____

✓ 5. 4,500 ÷ 9 = _____

On Your Own

Use basic facts and place value to find the quotient.

6. 560 ÷ 8 = _____

7. 6,400 ÷ 8 = _____

8. 3,500 ÷ 7 = _____

Math Processes and Practices ⑤ Use Patterns **Algebra** **Find the unknown number.**

9. 420 ÷ ■ = 60 _____

10. ■ ÷ 4 = 30 _____

11. 810 ÷ ■ = 90 _____

12. *THINK SMARTER* Divide 400 ÷ 40. Explain how patterns and place value can help.

   _____

   _____

13. *GO DEEPER* Eileen collected 98 empty cans to recycle, and Carl collected 82 cans. They packed an equal number of cans into each of three boxes to take to the recycling center. How many cans were in each box?

   _____

14. *GO DEEPER* It costs a baker $18 to make a small cake. He sells 8 small cakes for $240. How much more is the selling price of each cake than the cost?

   _____

Problem Solving • Applications

15. Jamal put 600 pennies into 6 equal rolls. How many pennies were in each roll?

_____

16. Sela has 6 times as many coins now as she had 4 months ago. If Sela has 240 coins now, how many coins did she have 4 months ago?

_____

17. **THINK SMARTER** Chip collected 2,090 dimes. Sue collected 1,910 dimes. They divided all their dimes into 8 equal stacks. How many dimes are in each stack?

_____

18. **Math Processes and Practices ⑤** **Communicate** Mr. Roberts sees a rare 1937 penny. The cost of the penny is $210. If he saves $3 each week, will Mr. Roberts have enough money to buy the penny in one year? Explain.

WRITE *Math* • **Show Your Work** · · · · ·

_____

_____

_____

19. **GO DEEPER** Mrs. Fletcher bought 5 coins for $32 each. Later, she sold all the coins for $300. How much more did Mrs. Fletcher receive for each coin than she paid? Explain.

_____

_____

_____

20. **THINK SMARTER** Which quotients are equal to 20? Mark all that apply.

(A) $600 \div 2$

(B) $1,200 \div 6$

(C) $180 \div 9$

(D) $140 \div 7$

(E) $500 \div 5$

Connect to Science

Insect Flight

True flight is shared only by insects, bats, and birds. Flight in insects varies from the clumsy flight of some beetles to the acrobatic moves of dragonflies.

The wings of insects are not moved by muscles attached to the wings. Muscles in the middle part of the body, or thorax, move the wings. The thorax changes shape as the wings move.

Insect Wing Beats in 3 Minutes	
Insect	Approximate Number of Wing Beats
Aeschnid Dragonfly	6,900
Damselfly	2,700
Large White Butterfly	2,100
Scorpion Fly	5,000

21. About how many times does a damselfly's wings beat in 1 minute?

_____

22. About how many times do a scorpion fly's wings beat in 6 minutes?

_____

23. **THINK SMARTER** In one minute, about how many more times do a damselfly's wings beat than a large white butterfly's wings?

_____

24. **What's the Question?** The answer is about 2,300 times.

_____

_____

Divide Tens, Hundreds, and Thousands

Learning Objective You will use place value to divide tens, hundreds, and thousands.

Use basic facts and place value to find the quotient.

1. $3,600 \div 4 = $ ___900___

   Think: 3,600 is 36 hundreds.

   Use the basic fact $36 \div 4 = 9$.

   So, 36 hundreds $\div$ 4 = 9 hundreds, or 900.

2. $240 \div 6 = $ _____

3. $5,400 \div 9 = $ _____

4. $300 \div 5 = $ _____

5. $4,800 \div 6 = $ _____

6. $420 \div 7 = $ _____

7. $150 \div 3 = $ _____

8. $6,300 \div 7 = $ _____

9. $1,200 \div 4 = $ _____

10. $360 \div 6 = $ _____

Problem Solving Real World

11. At an assembly, 180 students sit in 9 equal rows. How many students sit in each row?

   _____

12. Hilary can read 560 words in 7 minutes. How many words can Hilary read in 1 minute?

   _____

13. A company produces 7,200 gallons of bottled water each day. The company puts 8 one-gallon bottles in each carton. How many cartons are needed to hold all the one-gallon bottles produced in one day?

   _____

14. An airplane flew 2,400 miles in 4 hours. If the plane flew the same number of miles each hour, how many miles did it fly in 1 hour?

   _____

15. **WRITE** ▸ *Math* Explain how your knowledge of place value helps you divide a number in the thousands by whole numbers to 10. Give an example to support your explanation.

   _____

   _____

Lesson Check

1. A baseball player hits a ball 360 feet to the outfield. It takes the ball 4 seconds to travel this distance. How many feet does the ball travel in 1 second?

   _____

2. Sebastian rides his bike 2,000 meters in 5 minutes. How many meters does he bike in 1 minute?

   _____

Spiral Review

3. A full container of juice holds 64 fluid ounces. How many 7-fluid ounce servings of juice are in a full container?

   _____

4. Paolo pays $244 for 5 identical calculators. About how much does Paolo pay for one calculator?

   _____

5. A football team paid $28 per jersey. They bought 16 jerseys. How much money did the team spend on jerseys?

   _____

6. Suzanne bought 50 apples at the apple orchard. She bought 4 times as many red apples as green apples. How many more red apples than green apples did Suzanne buy?

   _____

FOR MORE PRACTICE
GO TO THE
Personal Math Trainer

Name _____

Estimate Quotients Using Compatible Numbers

Essential Question How can you use compatible numbers to estimate quotients?

Learning Objective You will use compatible numbers to estimate quotients.

 Unlock the Problem Real World

A horse's heart beats 132 times in 3 minutes. About how many times does it beat in 1 minute?

You can use compatible numbers to estimate quotients.

Compatible numbers are numbers that are easy to compute mentally.

- Will a horse's heart beat more or fewer than 132 times in 1 minute?

  _____

- What operation will you use to solve the problem?

  _____

🔒 Example 1 Estimate. 132 ÷ 3

STEP 1 Find a number close to 132 that divides easily by 3. Use basic facts.

12 ÷ 3 is a basic fact. 120 divides easily by 3.

15 ÷ 3 is a basic fact. 150 divides easily by 3.

Think: Choose 120 because it is closer to 132.

STEP 2 Use place value.

120 = _____ tens

12 ÷ 3 = _____

12 tens ÷ 3 = _____ tens

120 ÷ 3 = _____

So, a horse's heart beats about _____ times a minute.

🔒 Example 2 Use compatible numbers to find two estimates that the quotient is between. 1,382 ÷ 5

STEP 1 Find two numbers close to 1,382 that divide easily by 5.

_____ ÷ 5 is a basic fact. 1,000 divides easily by 5.

_____ ÷ 5 is a basic fact. 1,500 divides easily by 5.

1,382 is between _____ and _____.

So, 1,382 ÷ 5 is between _____ and _____.

STEP 2 Divide each number by 5. Use place value.

1,000 ÷ 5

_____ hundreds ÷ 5 = _____ hundreds, or _____

1,500 ÷ 5

_____ hundreds ÷ 5 = _____ hundreds, or _____

 Math Talk

Math Processes and Practices ❻

Explain which estimate you think is more reasonable.

Share and Show

1. Estimate. 1,718 ÷ 4   **Think:** What number close to 1,718 is easy to divide by 4?

_____ is close to 1,718.   What basic fact can you use? _____ ÷ 4

_____ is close to 1,718.   What basic fact can you use? _____ ÷ 4

Choose 1,600 because _____ _____.

16 ÷ 4 = _____

1,600 ÷ _____ = _____

1,718 ÷ 4 is about _____

> **Math Talk**
>
> **Math Processes and Practices ❸**
>
> **Apply** How might your estimate change if the problem were 1,918 ÷ 4?

Use compatible numbers to estimate the quotient.

2. 455 ÷ 9

3. 1,509 ÷ 3

✅ **4.** 176 ÷ 8

✅ **5.** 2,795 ÷ 7

On Your Own

Use compatible numbers to find two estimates that the quotient is between.

6. 5,321 ÷ 6

7. 1,765 ÷ 6

8. 1,189 ÷ 3

9. 2,110 ÷ 4

Math Processes and Practices ❷ Reason Abstractly Algebra Estimate to compare. Write <, >, or =.

10. 613 ÷ 3 ◯ 581 ÷ 2

11. 364 ÷ 4 ◯ 117 ÷ 6

12. 2,718 ÷ 8 ◯ 963 ÷ 2

_____   _____   _____   _____   _____   _____
estimate   estimate   estimate   estimate   estimate   estimate

13. **GO DEEPER** If Cade shoots 275 free throw baskets in 2 hours, about how many can he shoot in 5 hours?

14. **GO DEEPER** A carpenter has 166 doorknobs in his workshop. Of those doorknobs, 98 are round and the rest are square. If he wants to place 7 square doorknobs in each bin, about how many bins would he need?

Name _____

Problem Solving • Applications

Use the table for 15–17.

Animal Heartbeats in 5 Minutes	
Animal	**Number of Heartbeats**
Whale	31
Cow	325
Pig	430
Dog	520
Chicken	1,375

15. About how many times does a chicken's heart beat in 1 minute?

_____

16. **GO DEEPER** About how many times does a cow's heart beat in 2 minutes?

_____

17. **Math Processes and Practices ②** **Use Reasoning** About how many times faster does a cow's heart beat than a whale's?

_____

WRITE ▸*Math* • **Show Your Work** • • • •

18. **THINK SMARTER** Martha had 154 stamps and her sister had 248 stamps. They combined their collections and put the stamps in an album. If they want to put 8 stamps on each page, about how many pages would they need?

_____

19. Jamie and his two brothers divided a package of 125 toy cars equally. About how many cars did each of them receive?

_____

20. **THINK SMARTER** Harold and his brother collected 2,019 cans over a 1-year period. Each boy collected the same number of cans. About how many cans did each boy collect? Explain how you found your answer.

_____

_____

_____

Connect to Reading

Cause and Effect

The reading skill *cause and effect* can help you understand how one detail in a problem is related to another detail.

Chet wants to buy a new bike that costs $276. Chet mows his neighbor's lawn for $15 each week. Since Chet does not have money saved, he needs to decide which layaway plan he can afford to buy the new bike.

Bike Shop Layaway Plans	
Plan A	3 months (3 equal payments)
Plan B	6 months (6 equal payments)

Cause:		Effect:
Chet does not have money saved to purchase the bike.	$\rightarrow$	Chet will have to decide which layaway plan he can afford to purchase the bike.

Which plan should Chet choose?

3-month layaway:

$276 ÷ 3

Estimate.

$270 ÷ 3 _____

6-month layaway:

$276 ÷ 6

Estimate.

$300 ÷ 6 _____

Chet earns $15 each week. Since there are usually 4 weeks in a month, multiply to see which payment he can afford.

$15 × 4 = _____

So, Chet can afford the _____ layaway plan.

Use estimation to solve.

21. Sofia wants to buy a new bike that costs $214. Sofia helps her grandmother with chores each week for $18. Estimate to find which layaway plan Sofia should choose and why.

_____

_____

_____

_____

22. **WRITE** ▸*Math* Describe a situation when you have used cause and effect to help you solve a math problem.

_____

_____

_____

_____

_____

Estimate Quotients Using Compatible Numbers

Learning Objective You will use compatible numbers to estimate quotients.

Use compatible numbers to estimate the quotient.

1. $389 \div 4$

$\underline{400 \div 4 = 100}$

2. $358 \div 3$

3. $784 \div 8$

4. $179 \div 9$

5. $315 \div 8$

6. $2{,}116 \div 7$

7. $4{,}156 \div 7$

8. $474 \div 9$

Use compatible numbers to find two estimates that the quotient is between.

9. $1{,}624 \div 3$

10. $2{,}593 \div 6$

11. $1{,}045 \div 2$

12. $1{,}754 \div 9$

Problem Solving · Real World

13. A CD store sold 3,467 CDs in 7 days. About the same number of CDs were sold each day. About how many CDs did the store sell each day?

14. Marcus has 731 books. He puts about the same number of books on each of 9 shelves in his bookcase. About how many books are on each shelf?

15. **WRITE** ▸ *Math* How can you estimate $1{,}506 \div 2$ so that it is close to the actual answer of 753?

_____

_____

_____

Lesson Check

1. Jamal is planting seeds for a garden nursery. He plants 9 seeds in each container. If Jamal has 296 seeds to plant, about how many containers will he use?

   _____

2. Winona purchased a set of vintage beads. There are 2,140 beads in the set. If she uses the beads to make bracelets that have 7 beads each, about how many bracelets can she make?

   _____

Spiral Review

3. A train traveled 360 miles in 6 hours. How many miles per hour did the train travel?

   _____

4. An orchard has 12 rows of pear trees. Each row has 15 pear trees. How many pear trees are there in the orchard?

   _____

5. Megan rounded 366,458 to 370,000. To which place did Megan round the number?

   _____

6. Mr. Jessup, an airline pilot, flies 1,350 miles a day. How many miles will he fly in 8 days?

   _____

FOR MORE PRACTICE
GO TO THE
Personal Math Trainer

Name _____

Division and the Distributive Property

Essential Question How can you use the Distributive Property to find quotients?

Investigate

Materials ■ color pencils ■ grid paper

You can use a model and the Distributive Property to break apart numbers to make them easier to divide.

To use the Distributive Property with division, find the quotient each smaller rectangle represents. Then find the sum of the quotients.

A. Outline a rectangle on a grid to model $69 \div 3$.

Shade columns of 3 until you have 69 squares.

How many groups of 3 can you make? _____

B. Think of 69 as $60 + 9$. Break apart the model into two rectangles to show $(60 + 9) \div 3$. Label and shade the smaller rectangles. Use two different colors.

C. Each rectangle models a division.

$$69 \div 3 = (\underline{\hspace{1cm}} \div 3) + (\underline{\hspace{1cm}} \div 3)$$

$$= \underline{\hspace{1cm}} + \underline{\hspace{1cm}}$$

$$= \underline{\hspace{1cm}}$$

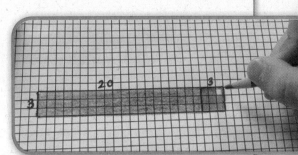

D. Outline another model to show $68 \div 4$.

How many groups of 4 can you make? _____

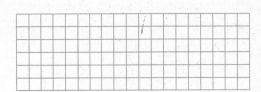

E. Think of 68 as $40 + 28$. Break apart the model, label, and shade to show two divisions.

$$68 \div 4 = (\underline{\hspace{1cm}} \div 4) + (\underline{\hspace{1cm}} \div 4)$$

$$= \underline{\hspace{1cm}} + \underline{\hspace{1cm}}$$

$$= \underline{\hspace{1cm}}$$

Draw Conclusions

1. Explain how each small rectangle models a quotient and a product in Step C.

_____

_____

_____

2. Compare your answer in Step A to the final quotient in Step C. What can you conclude?

_____

_____

3. **THINK SMARTER** To find the quotient 91 ÷ 7, would you break up the dividend into 90 + 1 or 70 + 21? Explain.

_____

_____

Make Connections

Hands On

Math Talk

Math Processes and Practices ❼

Look for Structure Describe another way you could use the Distributive Property to solve 68 ÷ 4.

You can also model 68 ÷ 4 using base-ten blocks.

STEP 1 Model 68.

68 = _____ + _____

STEP 2 Share the tens equally among 4 groups with 2 tens left. Regroup 2 tens as 20 ones. Share them equally among the 4 groups.

60 ÷ 4 = _____

STEP 3 Share the 8 ones equally among the 4 equal groups.

8 ÷ 4 = _____

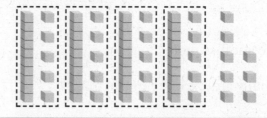

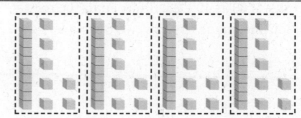

So, 68 ÷ 4 = (60 ÷ 4) + (8 ÷ 4) = _____ + _____ = _____

228

© Houghton Mifflin Harcourt Publishing Company

Name _____

Model the division on the grid.

1. $26 \div 2 = ($ _____ $\div 2) + ($ _____ $\div 2)$

    $= $ _____ $+$ _____

    $= $ _____

2. $45 \div 3 = ($ _____ $\div 3) + ($ _____ $\div 3)$

    $= $ _____ $+$ _____

    $= $ _____

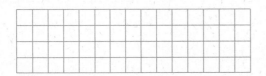

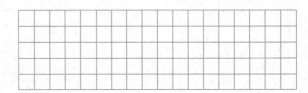

Find the quotient.

3. $86 \div 2$

    $= ($ _____ $\div 2) + ($ _____ $\div 2)$

    $= $ _____ $+$ _____

    $= $ _____

4. $208 \div 4$

    $= ($ _____ $\div 4) + ($ _____ $\div 4)$

    $= $ _____ $+$ _____

    $= $ _____

Use base-ten blocks to model the quotient.
Then record the quotient.

5. $88 \div 4 = $ _____

6. $36 \div 3 = $ _____

7. $186 \div 6 = $ _____

8. **WRITE** ▸Math Explain how you can model finding quotients using the Distributive Property.

    _____

    _____

    _____

    _____

    _____

9.   Justin earned $50 mowing lawns and $34 washing cars. He wants to divide his money into 3 equal accounts. How much will he put in each account? Explain.

    _____

    _____

    _____

    _____

    _____

Pose a Problem

10. **THINK SMARTER** Christelle went to a gift shop. The shop sells candles in a variety of sizes and colors. The picture shows a display of candles.

Write a problem that can be solved using the picture.

Pose a problem.

Solve your problem.

• **Math Processes and Practices ①** **Describe** how you could change the problem by changing the number of rows of candles. Then solve the problem.

_____

_____

_____

_____

11. **THINK SMARTER** For 11a–11d, choose Yes or No to indicate if the expression shows a way to break apart the dividend to find the quotient $147 \div 7$.

11a. $(135 \div 7) + (10 \div 7)$ ○ Yes ○ No

11b. $(147 \div 3) + (147 \div 4)$ ○ Yes ○ No

11c. $(140 \div 7) + (7 \div 7)$ ○ Yes ○ No

11d. $(70 \div 7) + (77 \div 7)$ ○ Yes ○ No

Name _____

Division and the Distributive Property

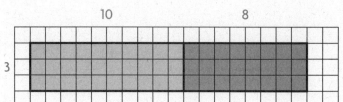

Learning Objective You will use a model and the Distributive Property to find whole number quotients with up to 3-digit dividends and 1-digit divisors.

Find the quotient.

1. $54 \div 3 = ($ ___30___ $\div 3) + ($ ___24___ $\div 3)$

   $= $ ___10___ $+$ ___8___

   $= $ ___18___

2. $81 \div 3 =$ _____

3. $232 \div 4 =$ _____

4. $305 \div 5 =$ _____

5. $246 \div 6 =$ _____

6. $69 \div 3 =$ _____

7. $477 \div 9 =$ _____

Problem Solving Real World

8. Cecily picked 219 apples. She divided the apples equally into 3 baskets. How many apples are in each basket?

   _____

9. Jordan has 260 basketball cards. He divides them into 4 equal groups. How many cards are in each group?

   _____

10. The Wilsons drove 324 miles in 6 hours. If they drove the same number of miles each hour, how many miles did they drive in 1 hour?

    _____

11. Phil has 189 stamps to put into his stamp album. He puts the same number of stamps on each of 9 pages. How many stamps does Phil put on each page?

    _____

12. **WRITE** ▸*Math* Explain how to use the Distributive Property to solve $48 \div 3$. Include a model to support your explanation.

    _____

    _____

Lesson Check

1. A landscaping company planted 176 trees in 8 equal rows in the new park. How many trees did the company plant in each row?

_____

2. Arnold can do 65 push-ups in 5 minutes. How many push-ups can he do in 1 minute?

_____

Spiral Review

3. Last Saturday, there were 1,486 people at the Cineplex. There were about the same number of people in each of the 6 theaters. Between which two numbers does the number of people in each theater fall?

_____

_____

4. Nancy walked 50 minutes each day for 4 days last week. Gillian walked 35 minutes each day for 6 days last week. How does the total number of minutes that Gillian walked compare to the total number of minutes that Nancy walked?

_____

_____

5. Three boys share 28 toy cars equally. How many cars did each boy get and how many were left over?

_____

6. An airplane flies at a speed of 474 miles per hour. How many miles does the plane fly in 5 hours?

_____

FOR MORE PRACTICE GO TO THE
Personal Math Trainer

Name _____

 **✓ Mid-Chapter Checkpoint**

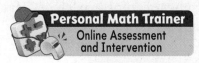
Personal Math Trainer
Online Assessment
and Intervention

Vocabulary

Choose the best term from the box to complete the sentence.

Vocabulary
counting numbers
compatible numbers
multiple
remainder

1. A number that is the product of a number and a counting

   number is called a _____ . (p. 197)

2. Numbers that are easy to compute mentally are called

   _____ . (p. 221)

3. When a number cannot be divided evenly, the amount

   left over is called the _____ . (p. 204)

Concepts and Skills

Divide. Draw a quick picture to help.

4. 26 ÷ 3 _____

5. 19 ÷ 4 _____

Use basic facts and place value to find the quotient.

6. 810 ÷ 9 = _____

7. 210 ÷ 7 = _____

8. 3,000 ÷ 6 = _____

Use compatible numbers to estimate the quotient.

9. 635 ÷ 9

   _____

10. 412 ÷ 5

    _____

11. 490 ÷ 8

    _____

Use grid paper or base-ten blocks to model the quotient.
Then record the quotient.

12. 63 ÷ 3 = _____

13. 85 ÷ 5 = _____

14. 168 ÷ 8 = _____

© Houghton Mifflin Harcourt Publishing Company

15. Ana has 296 coins in her coin collection. She put the same number of coins in each of 7 jars. About how many coins are in each jar?

_____

16. Which two estimates is the quotient 345 ÷ 8 between?

_____

17. GO DEEPER A total of 8,644 people went to the football game. Of those people, 5,100 sat on the home side and the rest sat on the visitor's side. If the people sitting on the visitor's side filled 8 equal-sized sections, about how many people sat in each of the sections?

_____

18. There are 4 students on a team for a relay race. How many teams can be made from 27 students?

_____

19. Eight teams of high school students helped clean up trash in the community. Afterwards, they shared 23 pizzas equally. How many pizzas did each team get?

_____

234

Divide Using Repeated Subtraction

Essential Question How can you use repeated subtraction and multiples to find quotients?

Learning Objective You will use repeated subtraction and multiples to find quotients.

Investigate

Materials ■ counters ■ grid paper

John is building a backyard pizza oven with an arch opening. He has 72 bricks. He will place 6 bricks at a time as he builds the oven. If he arranges the bricks in piles of 6, how many piles will he have?

You can use repeated subtraction to divide $72 \div 6$.

A. Begin with 72 counters. Subtract 6 counters.

   How many are left? _____

B. Record the subtraction on grid paper as shown. Record the number of counters left and the number of times you subtracted.

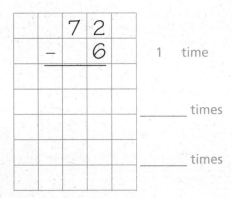

C. Can you reach zero evenly? Explain.

   _____

   _____

D. Count the number of times you subtracted 6 counters. _____

   So, there are _____ piles of 6 bricks.

© Houghton Mifflin Harcourt Publishing Company • Image Credits: (t) ©Houghton Mifflin Harcourt

Draw Conclusions

1. Explain the relationship between the divisor, the dividend, the quotient, and the number of times you subtracted the divisor from the dividend.

   _____

   _____

2. What happens if you subtract multiples of 6? Complete the example at the right.

   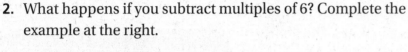

   - What multiples of 6 did you use? How did you use them?

     _____

   - What numbers did you add? Why?

     _____

     _____

   - How did using multiples of the divisor help you?

     _____

     _____

3. *THINK SMARTER* Why should you subtract 10 × 6 and not 9 × 6 or 20 × 6?

   _____

   _____

   _____

Math Talk — Math Processes and Practices ④

Use Models How does subtracting counters and counting back on a number line help you divide?

Make Connections

Another way to divide by repeated subtraction is to use a number line. Count back by 4s from 52 to find 52 ÷ 4.

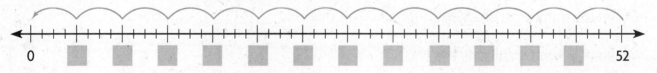

How many equal groups of 4 did you subtract? _____

So, 52 ÷ 4 = _____.

236

Name _____

Use repeated subtraction to divide.

✓ **1.** 84 ÷ 7 _____

✓ **2.** 60 ÷ 4 _____

3. 91 ÷ 8 _____

Draw a number line to divide.

4. 65 ÷ 5 = _____

Problem Solving • Applications Real World

5. Math Processes and Practices ⑤ **Use Appropriate Tools** Can you divide 32 by 3 evenly? Use the number line to explain your answer.

0   32

_____

_____

_____

6. GO DEEPER John has $40 to spend at the yard sale. He buys 6 books for $2 each. He would like to spend the rest of his money on model cars for his collection. If the cars cost $7 each, how many can he buy? Explain.

_____

_____

_____

Unlock the Problem

7. **THINK SMARTER** A new playground will be 108 feet long. Builders need to allow 9 feet of space for each piece of climbing equipment. They want to put as many climbers along the length of the playground as possible. How many climbers can they place?

a. What are you asked to find?

_____

b. How can you use repeated subtraction to solve the problem?

_____

_____

c. Tell why you might use multiples of the divisor to solve the problem.

_____

_____

d. Show steps to solve the problem.

e. Complete the sentences.

There are _____ equal parts of the

playground, each _____ feet long.

So, _____ climbers can fit along the length of the playground.

8. **THINK SMARTER** Which model matches each expression? Write the letter on the line next to the model.

Ⓐ   36 ÷ 3

0   36

Ⓑ   36 ÷ 2

0   36

Divide Using Repeated Subtraction

Use repeated subtraction to divide.

1. $42 \div 3 = $ _____14_____   **2.** $72 \div 4 = $ _____   **3.** $93 \div 3 = $ _____

```
  3)42
  −30   ←10 × 3   10
   12
  −12   ← 4 × 3   +4
    0              14
```

4. $35 \div 4$ _____   **5.** $93 \div 10$ _____   **6.** $86 \div 9$ _____

Draw a number line to divide.

7. $70 \div 5 = $ _____

Problem Solving Real World

8. Gretchen has 48 small shells. She uses 2 shells to make one pair of earrings. How many pairs of earrings can she make?

9. WRITE ▸ *Math* Show how you can use repeated subtraction to find $84 \div 6$.

_____   _____

Lesson Check

1. Randall collects postcards that his friends send him when they travel. He can put 6 cards on one scrapbook page. How many pages does Randall need to fit 42 postcards?

   _____

2. Ari stocks shelves at a grocery store. He puts 35 cans of juice in each display case. The case has 4 shelves with an equal number of cans, and one shelf with only 3 cans. How many cans are on each of the equal shelves?

   _____

Spiral Review

3. Fiona sorted her CDs into separate bins. She placed 4 CDs in each bin. If she has 160 CDs, how many bins did she fill?

   _____

4. Eamon is arranging 39 books on 3 shelves. If he puts the same number of books on each shelf, how many books will there be on each shelf?

   _____

5. A newborn boa constrictor measures 18 inches long. An adult boa constrictor measures 9 times the length of the newborn plus 2 inches. How long is the adult?

   _____

6. Madison has 6 rolls of coins. Each roll has 20 coins. How many coins does Madison have?

   _____

FOR MORE PRACTICE
GO TO THE
Personal Math Trainer

Name _____

Divide Using Partial Quotients

Essential Question How can you use partial quotients to divide by 1-digit divisors?

Learning Objective You will use partial quotients to divide by 1-digit divisors.

🔑 Unlock the Problem

At camp, there are 5 players on each lacrosse team. If there are 125 people on lacrosse teams, how many teams are there?

- Underline what you are asked to find.
- Circle what you need to use.
- What operation can you use to find the number of teams?

_____

🔒 One Way Use partial quotients.

In the **partial quotient** method of dividing, multiples of the divisor are subtracted from the dividend and then the partial quotients are added together.

Divide. $125 \div 5$ **Write.** $5\overline{)125}$

STEP 1

Start by subtracting a greater multiple, such as 10 times the divisor. For example, you know that you can make at least 10 teams of 5 players.

Continue subtracting until the remaining number is less than the multiple, 50.

STEP 2

Subtract smaller multiples, such as 5, 2, or 1 times the divisor until the remaining number is less than the divisor. In other words, keep subtracting multiples until you no longer have enough players to make a team.

Then add the partial quotients to find the quotient.

So, there are _____ lacrosse teams.

Partial Quotients

$$5\overline{)125} \quad \downarrow$$
$$- \underline{\hspace{1.2cm}} \quad 10 \times \underline{\hspace{1cm}} \quad 10$$
$$- \underline{\hspace{1.2cm}} \quad 10 \times \underline{\hspace{1cm}} \quad 10$$
$$- \underline{\hspace{1.2cm}} \quad 5 \times \underline{\hspace{1cm}} \quad +5$$

Math Talk

Math Processes and Practices ⑧

Use Repeated Reasoning How did you use partial quotients to solve the problem?

🔑 Another Way Use rectangular models to record the partial quotients.

Jarod and Ana also found the number of teams using partial quotients. They recorded the partial quotients using rectangular models. They each still had 25 as the quotient.

Jarod

```
    ┌──────────────────────┐
5   │        125           │
    └──────────────────────┘

      10
    ┌──────┬───────────────┐          125
5   │  50  │      75       │        -
    └──────┴───────────────┘          75

      10      10
    ┌──────┬──────┬────────┐           75
5   │  50  │  50  │   25   │         -
    └──────┴──────┴────────┘           25

      10      10     5
    ┌──────┬──────┬──────┐             25
5   │  50  │  50  │  25  │           -
    └──────┴──────┴──────┘             0
```

10 + 10 + 5 = _____

Ana

```
    ┌──────────────────────┐
5   │        125           │
    └──────────────────────┘

         20
    ┌─────────────┬────────┐          125
5   │    100      │   25   │        -
    └─────────────┴────────┘           25

         20           5
    ┌─────────────┬────────┐           25
5   │    100      │   25   │         -
    └─────────────┴────────┘           0
```

20 + 5 = _____

Math Talk

Math Processes and Practices ②

Reason Abstractly Why might you prefer to use one method rather than the other?

Share and Show MATH BOARD

1. Lacrosse is played on a field 330 ft long. How many yards long is a lacrosse field? (3 feet = 1 yard)

Divide. Use partial quotients.

$$3\overline{)330}$$

$-$ _____   100 × ☐   100

_____

_____   10 × ☐   + 10

_____

So, the lacrosse field is _____ yards long.

Divide. Use partial quotients.

✓ **2.** 3)225

Divide. Use rectangular models to record the partial quotients.

✓ **3.** 428 ÷ 4 = _____

On Your Own

Divide. Use partial quotients.

Math Talk

Math Processes and Practices **6**

Make Connections How could you solve Problems 2 and 3 a different way?

4. 7)224

5. 7)259

6. 8)864

7. 6)738

Divide. Use rectangular models to record the partial quotients.

8. 328 ÷ 2 = _____

9. 475 ÷ 5 = _____

10. 219 ÷ 3 = _____

11. 488 ÷ 4 = _____

12. **Math Processes and Practices ②** **Use Reasoning** What is the least number you can divide by 5 to get a three-digit quotient? Explain how you found your answer.

_____

_____

_____

Problem Solving • Applications

Use the table for 13–15.

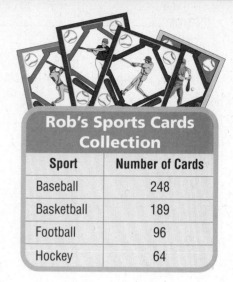

Rob's Sports Cards Collection

Sport	Number of Cards
Baseball	248
Basketball	189
Football	96
Hockey	64

13. Rob wants to put 8 baseball cards on each page in an album. How many pages will he fill?

14. **GO DEEPER** Rob filled 5 plastic boxes with hockey cards. There were the same number of cards in each box. How many cards did he put in each box? How many cards were left over?

15. **THINK SMARTER** Rob filled 3 fewer plastic boxes with football cards than basketball cards. He filled 9 boxes with basketball cards. How many boxes did he fill with football cards? How many football cards were in each box?

• • • **WRITE** *Math* • **Show Your Work** • • • •

16. **GO DEEPER** Marshall can buy 5 T-shirts for $60. If each shirt costs the same amount, what is the cost of 4 T-shirts?

17. **THINK SMARTER** Use partial quotients. Fill in the blanks.

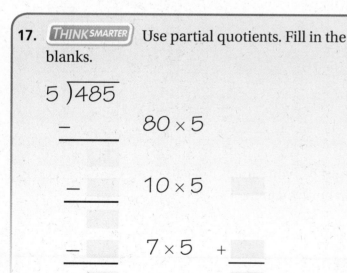

$$5\overline{)485}$$

$$-\underline{\quad\quad}\quad 80\times5$$

$$-\underline{\quad\quad}\quad 10\times5 \quad\underline{\quad}$$

$$-\underline{\quad\quad}\quad 7\times5 \quad+\underline{\quad}$$

244

Divide Using Partial Quotients

Learning Objective You will use partial quotients to divide by 1-digit divisors.

Divide. Use partial quotients.

1. 8)184
       −80   10 × 8   10
       ‾‾‾‾
       104
       −80   10 × 8   10
       ‾‾‾‾
        24
       −24   3 × 8   +3
       ‾‾‾‾   ‾‾‾‾
         0   23

2. 6)258

3. 5)630

Divide. Use rectangular models to record the partial quotients.

4. $246 \div 3 =$ _____

5. $126 \div 2 =$ _____

6. $605 \div 5 =$ _____

Divide. Use either way to record the partial quotients.

7. $492 \div 3 =$ _____

8. $198 \div 9 =$ _____

9. $692 \div 4 =$ _____

Problem Solving Real World

10. Allison took 112 photos on vacation. She wants to put them in a photo album that holds 4 photos on each page. How many pages can she fill?

    _____

11. **WRITE** ▸*Math* Explain how to use partial quotients to divide 235 by 5.

    _____

    _____

    _____

Lesson Check

1. Annaka used partial quotients to divide 145 ÷ 5. What could be the partial quotients Annaka used?

_____

_____

2. Mel used partial quotients to find the quotient of 378 ÷ 3. What could be the partial quotients that Mel found?

_____

_____

Spiral Review

3. What are the partial products of 42 × 5?

_____

4. Mr. Watson buys 4 gallons of paint that cost $34 per gallon. How much does Mr. Watson spend on paint?

_____

5. Use the area model to find the product of 28 × 32.

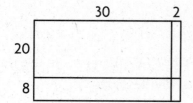

6. An adult male lion eats about 108 pounds of meat per week. About how much meat does an adult male lion eat in one day?

_____

FOR MORE PRACTICE
GO TO THE
Personal Math Trainer

Name _____

Model Division with Regrouping

Essential Question How can you use base-ten blocks to model division with regrouping?

Learning Objective You will use base-ten blocks and draw quick pictures to model division with regrouping.

Investigate

Materials ■ base-ten blocks

The librarian wants to share 54 books equally among 3 classes. How many books will she give to each class?

A. Draw 3 circles to represent the classes. Then use base-ten blocks to model 54. Show 54 as 5 tens 4 ones.

B. Share the tens equally among the 3 groups.

C. If there are any tens left, regroup them as ones. Share the ones equally among the 3 groups.

D. There are _____ ten(s) and _____ one(s) in each group.

So, the librarian will give _____ books to each class.

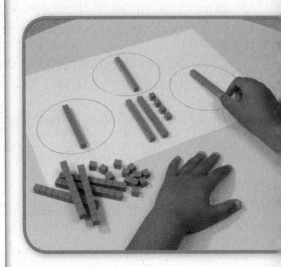

Draw Conclusions

1. **THINK SMARTER** Explain why you needed to regroup in Step C.

_____

_____

2. How you can use base-ten blocks to find the quotient of 92 ÷ 4?

_____

_____

_____

_____

Make Connections

Use the quick picture at the bottom of the page to help you divide.
Record each step.

Find 76 ÷ 3.

STEP 1
Model 76 as 7 tens 6 ones.
Draw three circles to represent equal groups.

$$3\overline{)76}$$

STEP 2
Share the 7 tens equally among the 3 groups.
Cross out the tens you use.

There are _____ tens in each group.

_____ tens were used. There is _____ ten left over.

← tens in each group

$$3\overline{)76}$$

$$-$$

← tens used

← ten left over

STEP 3
One ten cannot be shared among 3 groups
without regrouping.
Regroup 1 ten by drawing 10 ones.

There are now _____ ones to share.

$$\begin{array}{r} 2 \\ 3\overline{)76} \\ -6 \end{array}$$

← ones to share

STEP 4
Share the ones equally among the 3 groups.
Cross out the ones you use.

There are _____ ones in each group.

_____ ones were used. There is _____ one left over.

← ones in each group

$$\begin{array}{r} 2 \\ 3\overline{)76} \\ -6 \\ \hline 16 \end{array}$$

$$-$$

← ones used

← one left over

There are 3 groups of _____ and _____ left over.

So, for 76 ÷ 3, the quotient is _____ and the remainder is _____.

This can be written as _____.

 Math Talk

Math Processes and Practices ④

Interpret a Result Why do you share tens equally among groups before sharing ones?

248

© Houghton Mifflin Harcourt Publishing Company

Name _____

Divide. Use base-ten blocks.

1. 48 ÷ 3 _____

2. 84 ÷ 4 _____

3. 72 ÷ 5 _____

4. Divide. Draw a quick picture. Record the steps.

84 ÷ 3 _____

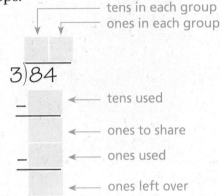

tens in each group
ones in each group

3)84

← tens used

← ones to share

← ones used

← ones left over

Problem Solving • Applications

5. WRITE ▸*Math* Explain why you did not need to regroup in Exercise 2.

_____

6. GO DEEPER Mindy is preparing fruit boxes for gifts. She divides 36 apples evenly into 6 boxes. Then she divided 54 bananas evenly into the same 6 boxes. How many pieces of fruit are in each of Mindy's boxes?

_____

7. THINK SMARTER Ami needs to divide these base-ten blocks among 4 equal groups.

Describe a model that would show how many are in each group.

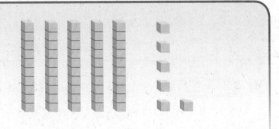

Sense or Nonsense?

8. **THINK SMARTER** Angela and Zach drew quick pictures to find 68 ÷ 4. Whose quick picture makes sense? Whose quick picture is nonsense? Explain your reasoning.

I drew 1 ten and 2 ones in each group.

I drew 1 ten and 7 ones in each group.

Angela's Quick Picture

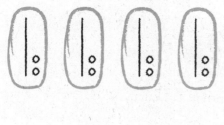

_____

_____

_____

_____

_____

Zach's Quick Picture

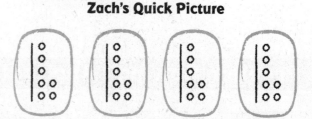

_____

_____

_____

_____

_____

9. **Math Processes and Practices 1** **Analyze** What did Angela forget to do after she shared the tens equally among the 4 groups?

_____

_____

Model Division with Regrouping

Learning Objective You will use base-ten blocks and draw quick pictures to model division with regrouping.

Divide. Use base-ten blocks.

1. 63 ÷ 4 ___15 r3___

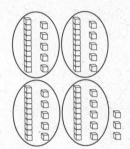

2. 83 ÷ 3 _____

Divide. Draw quick pictures. Record the steps.

3. 85 ÷ 5 _____

4. 97 ÷ 4 _____

Problem Solving Real World

5. Tamara sold 92 cold drinks during her 2-hour shift at a festival food stand. If she sold the same number of drinks each hour, how many cold drinks did she sell each hour?

6. **WRITE** ▸Math Write a division problem that has a 2-digit dividend and a 1-digit divisor. Show how to solve it by drawing a quick picture.

Lesson Check

1. Gail bought 80 buttons to put on the shirts she makes. She uses 5 buttons for each shirt. How many shirts can Gail make with the buttons she bought?

2. Marty counted how many breaths he took in 3 minutes. In that time, he took 51 breaths. He took the same number of breaths each minute. How many breaths did Marty take in one minute?

Spiral Review

3. Kate is solving brain teasers. She solved 6 brain teasers in 72 minutes. How long did she spend on each brain teaser?

4. Jenny works at a package delivery store. She puts mailing stickers on packages. Each package needs 5 stickers. How many stickers will Jenny use if she is mailing 105 packages?

5. The Puzzle Company packs standard-sized puzzles into boxes that hold 8 puzzles. How many boxes would it take to pack up 192 standard-sized puzzles?

6. Mt. Whitney in California is 14,494 feet tall. Denali in Alaska is 5,826 feet taller than Mt. Whitney. How tall is Denali?

FOR MORE PRACTICE
GO TO THE
Personal Math Trainer

Place the First Digit

Essential Question How can you use place value to know where to place the first digit in the quotient?

Learning Objective You will use place value to determine where to place the first digit in the quotient.

Unlock the Problem Real World

Victor took 144 photos on a digital camera.
The photos are to be placed equally in 6 photo albums.
How many photos will be in each album?

- Underline what you are asked to find.
- Circle what you need to use.

 **Example 1** Divide. 144 ÷ 6

STEP 1 Use place value to place the first digit.
Look at the hundreds in 144.
1 hundred cannot be shared among 6 groups
without regrouping.
Regroup 1 hundred as 10 tens.

Now there are _____ tens to share among 6 groups.

The first digit of the quotient will be in the _____ place.

144

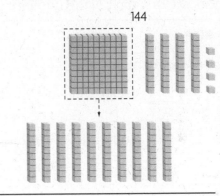

STEP 2 Divide the tens.

$$6\overline{)144} \quad \begin{array}{c} 2 \end{array}$$
−

Divide. 14 tens ÷ 6

Multiply. 6 × 2 tens

Subtract. 14 tens − 12 tens
Check. 2 tens cannot be shared among
6 groups without regrouping.

STEP 3 Divide the ones.
Regroup 2 tens as 20 ones.

Now there are _____ ones to share among 6 groups.

$$\begin{array}{r} 24 \\ 6\overline{)144} \\ -12\downarrow \\ \hline 24 \\ - \\ \hline \end{array}$$

Divide. _____ ones ÷ _____

Multiply. _____ × _____ ones

Subtract. _____ ones − _____ ones
Check. 0 ones cannot be shared among 6 groups.

Math Idea
After you divide each place, the remainder should be less than the divisor.

Math Talk Math Processes and Practices ③

Apply How would the answer change if Victor had 146 photos?

So, there will be _____ photos in each album.

Example 2 Divide. 287 ÷ 2

Omar has 287 photographs of animals. If he wants to put the photos into 2 groups of the same size, how many photos will be in each group?

STEP 1

Use place value to place the first digit.
Look at the hundreds in 287.
2 hundreds can be shared between 2 groups.

So, the first digit of the quotient will be in the _____ place.

STEP 2

Divide the hundreds.

```
   1
2)287
 ─
```

Divide. 2 hundreds ÷ 2

Multiply. 2 × 1 hundred

Subtract. 2 hundreds − 2 hundreds.

0 hundreds are left.

STEP 3

Divide the tens.

```
   14
2)287
 -2↓
   0
 ─
```

Divide. _____ tens ÷ _____

Multiply. _____ × _____ tens

Subtract. _____ tens − _____ tens 0 tens are left.

STEP 4

Divide the ones.

```
   143 r1
2)287
 -2│
   08│
  -8↓
   07
 ─
```

Divide. _____ ones ÷ _____

Multiply. _____ × _____ ones

Subtract. _____ ones − _____ ones
1 one cannot be equally shared between 2 groups.

So, there will be _____ photos in each group with 1 photo left.

254

© Houghton Mifflin Harcourt Publishing Company • Image Credits: (cl) ©Dennis MacDonald/Alamy, (cr) ©david sanger photography/Alamy (t) Houghton Mifflin Harcourt

Name _____

1. There are 452 pictures of dogs in 4 equal groups.
   How many pictures are in each group? Explain
   how you can use place value to place the first digit
   in the quotient.

$$4\overline{)452}$$

_____

_____

Divide.

2. $4\overline{)166}$ 3. $5\overline{)775}$

Math Talk

Math Processes and Practices 7

Look for Structure How
did you know where to
place the first digit of the
quotient in Exercise 2?

On Your Own

Divide.

4. $4\overline{)284}$ 5. $5\overline{)394}$ 6. $3\overline{)465}$ 7. $8\overline{)272}$

Practice: Copy and Solve **Divide.**

8. $516 \div 2$ 9. $516 \div 3$ 10. $516 \div 4$ 11. $516 \div 5$

12. **Math Processes and Practices 6** Look back at your answers to Exercises 8–11. What
    happens to the quotient when the divisor increases? **Explain.**

_____

13. **GO DEEPER** Reggie has 192 pictures of
    animals. He wants to keep half and then
    divide the rest equally among three friends.
    How many pictures will each friend get?

14. **GO DEEPER** There are 146 students,
    5 teachers, and 8 chaperones going to the
    theater. To reserve their seats, they need to
    reserve entire rows. Each row has 8 seats.
    How many rows must they reserve?

_____

🔑 Unlock the Problem

15. THINK SMARTER Nan wants to put 234 pictures in an album with a blue cover. How many full pages will she have in her album?

a. What do you need to find?

_____

b. How will you use division to find the number of full pages?

_____

_____

_____

Photo Albums	
Color of cover	Pictures per page
Blue	4
Green	6
Red	8

c. Show the steps you will use to solve the problem.

d. Complete the following sentences.

Nan has _____ pictures.

She wants to put the pictures in an album

with pages that each hold _____ pictures.

She will have an album with _____ full

pages and _____ pictures on another page.

---

16. GO DEEPER Mr. Parsons bought 293 apples to make pies for his shop. Six apples are needed for each pie. If Mr. Parsons makes the greatest number of apple pies possible, how many apples will be left?

_____

17. THINK SMARTER Carol needs to divide 320 stickers equally among 4 classes. In which place is the first digit of the quotient? Choose the word that completes the sentence.

The first digit of the quotient is in

the | ones / tens / hundreds / thousands | place.

© Houghton Mifflin Harcourt Publishing Company • Image Credits: (t) ©Stockdisk/Getty Images

Place the First Digit

Learning Objective You will use place value to determine where to place the first digit in the quotient.

Divide.

1.
```
     62
 3)186
  -18↓
    06
    -6
     0
```

2. $4\overline{)298}$

3. $3\overline{)461}$

4. $9\overline{)315}$

5. $2\overline{)988}$

6. $4\overline{)604}$

7. $6\overline{)796}$

8. $5\overline{)449}$

Problem Solving · Real World

9. There are 132 projects in the science fair. If 8 projects can fit in a row, how many full rows of projects can be made? How many projects are in the row that is not full?

10. There are 798 calories in six 10-ounce bottles of apple juice. How many calories are there in one 10-ounce bottle of apple juice?

_____

_____

11. **WRITE** ▸*Math* Write a division problem that will have a 2-digit quotient and another division problem that will have a 3-digit quotient. Explain how you chose the divisors and dividends.

_____

_____

_____

Lesson Check

1. To divide 572 ÷ 4, Stanley estimated to place the first digit of the quotient. In which place is the first digit of the quotient?

_____

2. Onetta biked 325 miles in 5 days. If she biked the same number of miles each day, how far did she bike each day?

_____

Spiral Review

3. Mort makes beaded necklaces that he sells for $32 each. About how much will Mort make if he sells 36 necklaces at the local art fair?

_____

4. Estimate the product of 54 × 68.

_____

5. Ms. Eisner pays $888 for 6 nights in a hotel. How much does Ms. Eisner pay per night?

_____

6. What division problem does the model show?

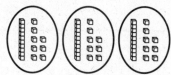

_____

**FOR MORE PRACTICE
GO TO THE
Personal Math Trainer**

Name _____

Divide by 1-Digit Numbers

Essential Question How can you divide multidigit numbers and check your answers?

Learning Objective You will find whole-number quotients and remainders with up to 4-digit dividends and 1-digit divisors.

Unlock the Problem

Students in the third, fourth, and fifth grades made 525 origami animals to display in the library. Each grade made the same number of animals. How many animals did each grade make?

Example 1 Divide. 525 ÷ 3

STEP 1 Use place value to place the first digit. Look at the hundreds in 525. 5 hundreds can be shared among 3 groups without regrouping. The first digit of the quotient will be in the _____ place.

 Math Talk

Math Processes and Practices ⑧

Use Repeated Reasoning At the checking step, what would you do if the number is greater than the divisor?

STEP 2 Divide the hundreds.

$$3\overline{)525}$$ with quotient 1

Divide. Share _____ hundreds equally among _____ groups.

Multiply. _____ × _____

Subtract. _____ − _____.

Check. _____ hundreds cannot be shared among 3 groups without regrouping.

STEP 3 Divide the tens.

$$3\overline{)525}$$
$$-3\downarrow$$
$$22$$
quotient 17

Divide. Share _____ equally among _____ groups.

Multiply. _____

Subtract. _____ − _____

Check. _____

_____

STEP 4 Divide the ones.

$$3\overline{)525}$$
$$-3\downarrow$$
$$22\downarrow$$
$$-21\downarrow$$
$$15$$
quotient 175

Divide. Share _____ equally among _____ groups.

Multiply. _____

Subtract. _____ − _____

Check. _____ are left.

So, each class made _____ origami animals.

There are 8,523 sheets of origami paper to be divided equally among 8 schools. How many sheets of origami paper will each school get?

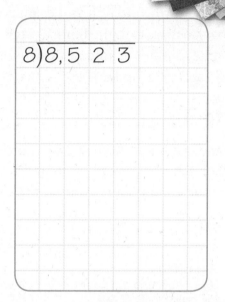

Example 2 Divide. 8,523 ÷ 8

STEP 1 Use place value to place the first digit.

Look at the thousands in 8,523. 8 thousands can be shared among 8 groups without regrouping.

The first digit of the quotient will be

in the _____ place.
_____

STEP 2 Divide the thousands.
_____

STEP 3 Divide the hundreds.
_____

STEP 4 Divide the tens.
_____

STEP 5 Divide the ones.

So, each school will get _____ sheets of origami paper.

There will be _____ sheets left.

$$8 \overline{)8{,}5\ 2\ 3}$$

! ERROR Alert

Place a zero in the quotient when a place in the dividend cannot be divided by the divisor.

CONNECT Division and multiplication are inverse operations. You can use multiplication to check your answer to a division problem.

Multiply the quotient by the divisor. If there is a remainder, add it to the product. The result should equal the dividend.

Divide.

quotient →   1,065 r3   ← remainder
divisor → 8$\overline{)8{,}523}$ ← dividend

Check.

```
      1,065   ← quotient
    ×     8   ← divisor
      8,520
    +     3   ← remainder
      8,523   ← dividend
```

The check shows that the division is correct.

Name _____

1. Ollie used 852 beads to make 4 bracelets. He put the same number of beads on each bracelet. How many beads does each bracelet have? Check your answer.

Divide.

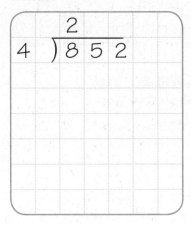

Check.

> **Math Talk**
>
> Math Processes and Practices ⑦
>
> **Identify Relationships**
> How could you check to see if your quotient is correct?

So, each bracelet has _____ beads.

Divide and check.

2. 2) 394

✓ 3. 2) 803

✓ 4. 4) 3,448

On Your Own

Divide and check.

5. 2) 816

6. 4) 709

7. 3) 267

8. *GO DEEPER* The flower shop received a shipment of 248 pink roses and 256 red roses. The shop owner uses 6 roses to make one arrangement. How many arrangements can the shop owner make if he uses all the roses?

_____

Problem Solving · Applications

Use the table for 9–11.

9. **THINK SMARTER** Four teachers bought 10 origami books and 100 packs of origami paper for their classrooms. They will share the cost of the items equally. How much should each teacher pay?

The Craft Store	
Item	**Price**
Origami Book	$24 each
Origami Paper	$6 per pack
Origami Kit	$8 each

_____

10. **Math Processes and Practices ⑤ Communicate** Six students shared equally the cost of 18 of one of the items in the chart. Each student paid $24. What item did they buy? Explain how you found your answer.

WRITE ▸ *Math*
Show Your Work

_____

_____

_____

_____

11. Ms. Alvarez has $1,482 to spend on origami paper. How many packs can she buy?

_____

12. **GO DEEPER** Evan made origami cranes with red, blue, and yellow paper. The number of cranes in each color is the same. If there are 342 cranes, how many of them are blue or yellow?

_____

13. **THINK SMARTER** On Monday 336 fourth graders went on a field trip to a local park. The teachers divided the students into 8 groups.

Use a basic fact. Estimate the number of students in each group. Show your work.

_____

_____

Divide by 1-Digit Numbers

Learning Objective You will find whole-number quotients and remainders with up to 4-digit dividends and 1-digit divisors.

Divide and check.

1.
```
      318
   2)636
    −6↓
     03
     −2↓
      16
     −16
       0
```

```
   318
 ×   2
   636
```

2. 4)631

3. 8)906

Problem Solving · Real World

Use the table for 4 and 5.

4. The Briggs rented a car for 5 weeks. What was the cost of their rental car per week?

_____

5. The Lees rented a car for 4 weeks. The Santos rented a car for 2 weeks. Whose weekly rental cost was lower? **Explain**.

Rental Car Costs	
Family	**Total Cost**
Lee	$632
Brigg	$985
Santo	$328

_____

_____

6. **WRITE** ▸*Math* Josey got an answer of 167 r4 for 3)505. Explain and correct Josey's error.

_____

_____

_____

_____

_____

Lesson Check

1. Write an expression that can be used to check the quotient of 646 ÷ 3.

_____

_____

2. There are 8 volunteers at the telethon. The goal for the evening is to raise $952. If each volunteer raises the same amount, what is the minimum amount each needs to raise to meet the goal?

_____

Spiral Review

3. What product is shown by the model?

_____

4. The computer lab at a high school ordered 26 packages of CDs. There were 50 CDs in each package. How many CDs did the computer lab order?

_____

5. Write a division problem whose quotient has its first digit in the hundreds place.

_____

_____

6. Sharon has 64 fluid ounces of juice. She is going to use the juice to fill as many 6-ounce glasses as possible. She will drink the leftover juice. How much juice will Sharon drink?

_____

_____

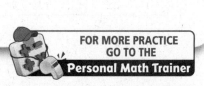

**FOR MORE PRACTICE
GO TO THE
Personal Math Trainer**

Name _____

Problem Solving • Multistep Division Problems

Essential Question How can you use the strategy *draw a diagram* to solve multistep division problems?

Learning Objective You will use the strategy *draw a diagram* to solve multistep division problems.

Unlock the Problem

Lucia picked 3 times as much corn as Eli. Together, they picked 96 ears of corn. Eli wants to divide the number of ears he picked equally among 8 bags. How many ears of corn will Eli put in each of the 8 bags?

Read the Problem	Solve the Problem
What do I need to find? I need to find the number of _____ that will go in each bag.	I can draw bar models to visualize the information given. First, I will model and compare to find the number of ears of corn that Eli picked.
What information do I need to use? Lucia picked _____ times as much corn as Eli. Together they picked _____ ears of corn. The number of ears Eli picked are divided equally among _____ bags.	Lucia's ▭▭▭ } 96 Eli's ▭ $96 \div 4 =$ _____ ↑ number of parts
How will I use the information? I will make a bar model for each step to visualize the information. Then I will _____ to find the number of ears Eli picked and _____ to find the number for each bag.	Then I will model and divide to find how many ears of corn Eli will put in each bag. ▭▭▭▭▭▭▭▭ 24

1. How many ears of corn will Eli put in each bag? _____

2. How can you check your answers? _____

_____

Chapter 4   265

🔓 Try Another Problem

There are 8 dinner rolls in a package. How many packages will be needed to feed 64 people if each person has 2 dinner rolls?

Read the Problem	Solve the Problem
What do I need to find?	
What information do I need to use?	
How will I use the information?	

3. How many packages of rolls will be needed? _____

4. How did drawing a bar model help you solve the problem?

_____

_____

_____

Math Talk

Math Processes and Practices 1

Analyze What other method could you have used to solve the problem?

266

Name _____

Share and Show

Unlock the Problem

✓ Use the Problem Solving MathBoard.
✓ Underline important facts.
✓ Choose a strategy you know.

1. A firehouse pantry has 52 cans of vegetables and 74 cans of soup. Each shelf holds 9 cans. What is the least number of shelves needed for all the cans?

   First, draw a bar model for the total number of cans.

   Next, add to find the total number of cans.

   Then, draw a bar model to show the number of shelves needed.

   Finally, divide to find the number of shelves needed.

Math Talk

Math Processes and Practices ❶

Evaluate How could you check to see that your answer is correct?

WRITE ▸ *Math*
Show Your Work

So, _____ shelves are needed to hold all of the cans.

2. **THINK SMARTER** What if 18 cans fit on a shelf? What is the least number of shelves needed? Describe how your answer would be different.

   _____

   _____

   _____

3. Julio's dad bought 10 dozen potatoes. The potatoes were equally divided into 6 bags. How many potatoes are in each bag?

   _____

4. At the garden shop, each small tree costs $125 and each large tree costs $225. How much will 3 small trees and 1 large tree cost?

   _____

On Your Own

5. *THINK SMARTER*   Ms. Johnson bought 6 bags of balloons. Each bag has 25 balloons. She fills all the balloons and puts 5 balloons in each bunch. How many bunches can she make?

_____

6. *THINK SMARTER*   An adult's dinner costs $8. A family of 2 adults and 2 children pays $26 for their dinners. How much does a child's dinner cost? Explain.

_____

_____

_____

_____

7. *Math Processes and Practices 5* **Communicate**   Use the table at the right. Maria bought 80 ounces of apples. She needs 10 apples to make a pie. How many apples will be left over? Explain.

_____

_____

_____

_____

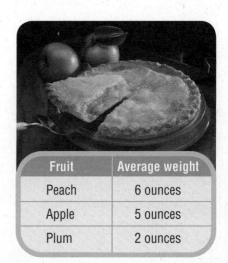

Fruit	Average weight
Peach	6 ounces
Apple	5 ounces
Plum	2 ounces

8. *GO DEEPER*   Taylor has 16 tacks. She buys 2 packages of 36 tacks each. How many garage sale posters can she put up if she uses 4 tacks for each poster?

_____

Personal Math Trainer

9. *THINK SMARTER +*   Ryan bought 8 dozen bandages for the track team first-aid kit. The bandages were divided equally into 4 boxes.

How many bandages are in each box?

_____

Name _____

Problem Solving • Multistep Division Problems

Learning Objective You will use the strategy *draw a diagram* to solve multistep division problems.

Solve. Draw a diagram to help you.

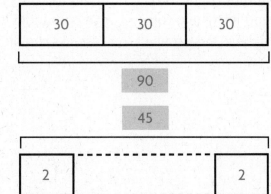

1. There are 3 trays of eggs. Each tray holds 30 eggs. How many people can be served if each person eats 2 eggs?

   Multiply to find the total number of eggs.

   Think: What do I need to find? How can I draw a diagram to help?

   Divide to find how many people can be served 2 eggs.

   <u>45 people can be served.</u>

2. There are 8 pencils in a package. How many packages will be needed for 28 children if each child gets 4 pencils?

   _____

3. There are 3 boxes of tangerines. Each box has 93 tangerines. The tangerines will be divided equally among 9 classrooms. How many tangerines will each classroom get?

   _____

4. **WRITE** ▸*Math* Write a two-step problem that you can solve using the strategy *draw a diagram*. Explain how you can use the strategy to find the solution.

   _____

   _____

© Houghton Mifflin Harcourt Publishing Company

Lesson Check

1. Gavin buys 89 blue pansies and 86 yellow pansies. He will plant the flowers in 5 rows with an equal number of plants in each row. Draw a bar model to help you find how many plants will be in each row.

2. A pet store receives 7 boxes of cat food. Each box has 48 cans. The store wants to put the cans in equal stacks of 8 cans. Draw a bar model to help you find how many stacks can be formed.

Spiral Review

3. What product does the model show?

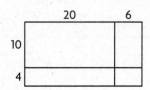

4. Mr. Hatch bought 4 round-trip airplane tickets for $417 each. He also paid $50 in baggage fees. How much did Mr. Hatch spend?

5. Mae read 976 pages in 8 weeks. She read the same number of pages each week. How many pages did she read each week?

6. Yolanda and her 3 brothers shared a box of 156 toy dinosaurs. About how many dinosaurs did each child get?

FOR MORE PRACTICE
GO TO THE
Personal Math Trainer

✓ Chapter 4 Review/Test

Personal Math Trainer
Online Assessment
and Intervention

1. There are 9 showings of a film about endangered species at the science museum. A total of 459 people saw the film. The same number of people were at each showing. About how many people were at each showing? Select the numbers the quotient is between.

   (A) 40   (B) 50   (C) 60   (D) 70   (E) 80

2. Between which two numbers is the quotient of $87 \div 5$? Write the numbers in the boxes.

   5   10   15   20   25

   The quotient is between ☐ and ☐.

3. Look at the model. What division does it show?

   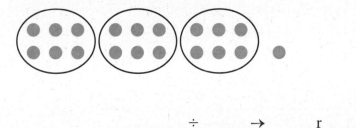

   _____ ÷ _____ → _____ r _____

4. For 4a–4d, choose Yes or No to tell whether the division expression has a remainder.

		Yes	No
4a.	$28 \div 4$	○ Yes	○ No
4b.	$35 \div 2$	○ Yes	○ No
4c.	$40 \div 9$	○ Yes	○ No
4d.	$45 \div 5$	○ Yes	○ No

5. A park guide plans the swan boat rides for 40 people. Each boat can carry 6 people at a time. What is the best way to interpret the remainder in this situation so that everyone gets a ride?

_____

6. Nolan divides his 88 toy cars into boxes. Each box holds 9 cars. How many boxes does Nolan need to store all of his cars?

_____ boxes

7. A group of 140 tourists are going on a tour. The tour guide rents 15 vans. Each van holds 9 tourists.

Part A

Write a division problem that can be used to find the number of vans needed to carry the tourists. Then solve.

Part B

What does the remainder mean in the context of the problem?

Part C

How can you use your answer to determine if the tour guide rented enough vans? Explain.

8. Solve.

$3{,}200 \div 8 =$ _____

9. Which quotients are equal to 300? Mark all that apply.

(A) 1,200 ÷ 4   (C) 2,400 ÷ 8   (E) 90 ÷ 3

(B) 180 ÷ 9   (D) 2,100 ÷ 7   (F) 3,000 ÷ 3

10. Margo estimated 188 ÷ 5 to be between 30 and 40. Which basic facts did she use to help her estimate? Mark all that apply.

(A) 10 ÷ 5   (B) 15 ÷ 5   (C) 20 ÷ 5   (D) 25 ÷ 5

11. Mathias and his brother divided 2,029 marbles equally. About how many marbles did each of them receive?

12. For 12a–12d, choose Yes or No to show how to use the Distributive Property to break apart the dividend to find the quotient 132 ÷ 6.

		Yes	No
12a.	(115 ÷ 6) + (17 ÷ 6)	○ Yes	○ No
12b.	(100 ÷ 6) + (32 ÷ 6)	○ Yes	○ No
12c.	(90 ÷ 6) + (42 ÷ 6)	○ Yes	○ No
12d.	(72 ÷ 6) + (60 ÷ 6)	○ Yes	○ No

13. There are 136 people waiting for a river raft ride. Each raft holds 8 people. Silvia used the work below to find the number of rafts needed. Explain how Silvia's work can be used to find the number of rafts needed.

```
8)136
  −80
   56
  −56
    0
```

14. A traveling circus brings along everything it needs for a show in big trucks.

Part A

The circus sets up chairs in rows with 9 seats in each row. How many rows will need to be set up if 513 people are expected to attend the show?

_____ rows

Part B

Can the rows be divided into a number of equal sections? Explain how you found your answer.

Part C

Circus horses eat about 250 pounds of horse food per week. About how many pounds of food does a circus horse eat each day? Explain.

15. Hilda wants to save 825 digital photographs in an online album. Each folder of the album can save 6 photographs. She uses division to find out how may full folders she will have. In what place is the first digit of the quotient?

_____

© Houghton Mifflin Harcourt Publishing Company

16. Which model matches each expression? Write the letter in the box next to the model.

 A $60 \div 5$ **B** $72 \div 4$ **C** $60 \div 4$ **D** $72 \div 6$

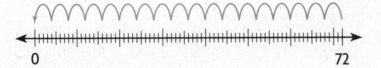

0   72

[ ]

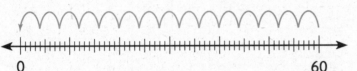

0   60

[ ]

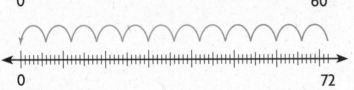

0   72

[ ]

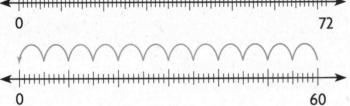

0   60

[ ]

17. Popcorn was donated for the school fair by 3 different popcorn vendors. They donated a total of 636 bags of popcorn. Each vendor donated the same number of bags. How many bags of popcorn did each vendor donate?

_____ bags

18. Use partial quotients. Fill in the blanks.

$8\overline{)832}$

−_____ 100×8 _____

_____

−_____ 4×8 _____

_____

19. Zack needs to divide these base-ten blocks into 3 equal groups.

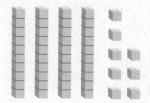

Draw or describe a model to show how many are in each group.

20. Jim needs to divide 750 coupon books equally among 9 stores. In which place is the first digit of the quotient? Choose the word that makes the sentence true.

The first digit of the quotient is in the | ones / tens / hundreds / thousands | place.

21. *THINK SMARTER +* Ursula bought 9 dozen rolls of first aid tape for the health office. The rolls were divided equally into 4 boxes. How many rolls are in each box?

_____ rolls

22. *GO DEEPER* There are 112 seats in the school auditorium. There are 7 seats in each row. There are 70 people seated, filling up full rows of seats. How many rows are empty?

_____ rows

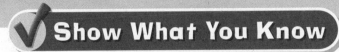

✓ Show What You Know

Check your understanding of important skills.

Name _____

▶ **Skip-Count** Skip-count to find the unknown numbers.

1. Skip count by 3s.

   ___3___ , _____ , _____ , _____

2. Skip count by 5s.

   ___5___ , _____ , _____ , _____

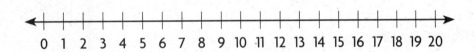

0 1 2 3 4 5 6 7 8 9 10 11 12 13 14 15 16 17 18 19 20

▶ **Arrays** Use the array to find the product.

3.

   _____ rows of _____ = _____

4.

   _____ rows of _____ = _____

▶ **Multiplication Facts** Find the product.

5. $4 \times 5 =$ _____

6. $9 \times 4 =$ _____

7. $6 \times 7 =$ _____

Recycled plastic helps keep people warm. Some factories use recycled plastic, combined with other fabrics, to make winter jackets. A warehouse has 46 truckloads of recycled plastic. They use 8 truckloads each day. When there are fewer than 16 truckloads, more needs to be ordered. Figure out how many truckloads will be left after 2 days. After 3 days. When will more need to be ordered?

Vocabulary Builder

▶ **Visualize It** •

Complete the flow map by using the words with a ✓.

Multiplying

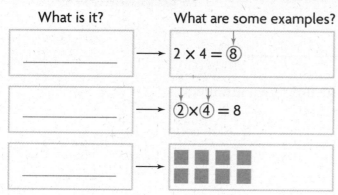

What is it?   What are some examples?

_____ ⟶ $2 \times 4 = ⑧$

_____ ⟶ $②\times④ = 8$

_____ ⟶ ▦

▶ **Understand Vocabulary** •

Complete the sentences by using preview words.

1. A number that is a factor of two or more numbers is a

   _____.

2. A number that is a multiple of two or more numbers is a

   _____.

3. A number that has exactly two factors, 1 and itself, is a

   _____.

4. A number that has more than two factors is a

   _____.

5. A number is _____ by another number if the
   quotient is a counting number and the remainder is 0.

6. An ordered set of numbers or objects is a _____.

7. Each number in a pattern is called a _____.

GO DIGITAL • Interactive Student Edition
              • Multimedia *eGlossary*

Chapter 5 Vocabulary

common factor

factor común

10

common multiple

múltiplo común

11

composite number

número compuesto

16

divisible

divisible

25

factor

factor

33

pattern

patrón

63

prime number

número primo

71

term

término

90

A number that is a multiple of two or more numbers

A number that is a factor of two or more numbers

8   factors   6

$2 \times 2 \times (2)$ ← common factor → $(2) \times 3$

A number is divisible by another number if the quotient is a counting number and the remainder is zero

Example: 18 is divisible by 3.

A number having more than two factors

Example: 6 is a composite number. Its factors are 1, 2, 3, and 6.

An ordered set of numbers or objects; the order helps you predict what will come next

Examples: 2, 4, 6, 8, 10

A number that is multiplied by another number to find a product

Example: $4 \times 5 = 20$

factor   factor

A number or object in a pattern

A number that has exactly two factors: 1 and itself

Examples: 2, 3, 5, 7, 11, 13, 17, and 19 are prime numbers. 1 is not a prime number.

Guess the Word

Word Box

common factor
common multiple
composite number
divisible
factor
prime number
pattern
term

For 3 to 4 players

Materials

• timer

How to Play

1. Take turns to play.

2. Choose a math term, but do not say it aloud.

3. Set the timer for 1 minute.

4. Give a one-word clue about your term. Give each player one chance to guess the term.

5. If nobody guesses correctly, repeat Step 4 with a different clue. Repeat until a player guesses the term or time runs out.

6. The player who guesses your term gets 1 point. If the player can use the word in a sentence, he or she gets 1 more point. Then that player gets a turn.

7. The first player to score 10 points wins.

© Houghton Mifflin Harcourt Publishing Company • ©Dmitriy Pichugin/Fotolia

The Write Way

Reflect

Choose one idea. Write about it.

- Which solution to finding the common factors of 6 and 8 is correct? Explain how you know.

  Eli's solution: 1 and 2

  Fiona's solution: 1, 2, 3, 4, 6, and 8

- Summarize the differences between prime numbers and composite numbers.

- Write about a time you were confused learning the ideas in this chapter. What did you do to get help? How did you figure out what was confusing to you?

Name _____

Model Factors

Essential Question How can you use models to find factors?

Learning Objective You will make arrays using square tiles to find and record all the factors of a whole number.

 Unlock the Problem *Real World*

A **factor** is a number multiplied by another number to find a product. Every whole number greater than 1 has at least two factors, that number and 1.

$$18 = 1 \times 18 \qquad 7 = 7 \times 1 \qquad 342 = 1 \times 342$$
$$\quad\;\uparrow\quad\;\;\uparrow$$
$$\text{factor}\;\;\text{factor}$$

Many numbers can be broken into factors in different ways.

$$16 = 1 \times 16 \qquad 16 = 4 \times 4 \qquad 16 = 2 \times 8$$

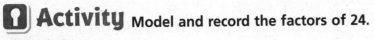 **Activity** Model and record the factors of 24.

Materials ■ square tiles

Use all 24 tiles to make as many different arrays as you can. Record the arrays in the grid, and write the factors modeled.

Math Idea
When you are asked to find factors of a whole number, only list factors that are also whole numbers.

$$2 \times 12 = 24$$

Factors: _____, _____

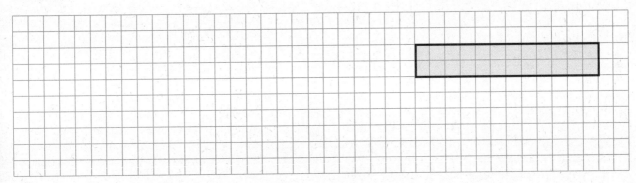

_____ × _____ = 24   _____ × _____ = 24   _____ × _____ = 24

Factors: ____, ____   Factors: ____, ____   Factors: ____, ____

The factors of 24, from least to greatest, are

_____, _____, _____, _____, _____, _____, _____, and _____.

Two factors that make a product are sometimes called a factor pair. How many factor pairs does 24 have? Explain.

_____

 Math Talk **Math Processes and Practices** ❷

Reason Abstractly Can you arrange the tiles in each array another way and show the same factors? Explain.

Chapter 5   **279**

1. Use the arrays to name the factors of 12.

 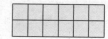

_____ × _____ = 12   _____ × _____ = 12   _____ × _____ = 12

The factors of 12 are 1, _____, 3, _____, 6, and _____.

Math Talk

Use Math Vocabulary
Explain how the numbers 3 and 12 are related. Use the word *factor* in your explanation.

Use tiles to find all the factors of the product. Record the arrays and write the factors shown.

2. 5: _____

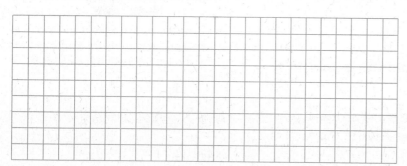

3. 20: _____

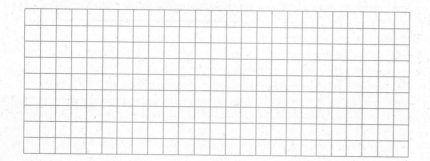

4. 25: _____

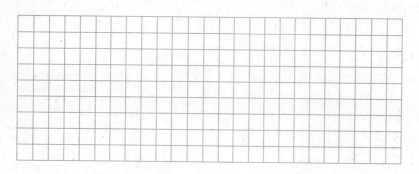

Name _____

Practice: Copy and Solve Use tiles to find all the factors of the product. Record the arrays on grid paper and write the factors shown.

5. 9   **6.** 21   **7.** 17   **8.** 18

Problem Solving • Applications

Use the diagram for 9–10.

9. **Math Processes and Practices 6** Pablo is using 36 tiles to make a patio. Can he arrange the tiles in another way and show the same factors? Draw a quick picture and **explain**.

Pablo's Tiles

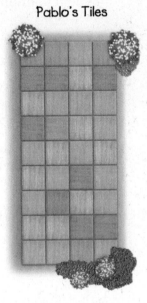

_____

_____

_____

10. **THINK SMARTER** How many different rectangular arrays can Pablo make with all 36 tiles, so none of the arrays show the same factors?

_____

11. If 6 is a factor of a number, what other numbers must be factors of the number?

_____

12. **GO DEEPER** Jean spent $16 on new T-shirts. If each shirt cost the same whole-dollar amount, how many could she have bought?

_____

Unlock the Problem

13. **GO DEEPER** Carmen has 18 connecting cubes. She wants to model a house shaped like a rectangle. If the model has a height of one connecting cube, how many different ways can Carmen model the house using all 18 connecting cubes and none of the models show the same side lengths?

a. What do you need to know? _____

_____

b. How is finding the number of ways to model a rectangular house

related to finding factor pairs? _____

_____

_____

c. Why is finding the factor pairs only the first step in solving the problem? _____

_____

_____

d. Show the steps you used to solve the problem.

_____

_____

_____

_____

e. Complete the sentences. Factor pairs for

18 are _____

_____

There are _____ different ways Carmen can arrange the cubes to model the house.

14. **THINK SMARTER** Sarah was organizing vocabulary words using index cards. She arranged 40 index cards in the shape of a rectangle on a poster. For 14a–14e, choose Yes or No to tell whether a possible arrangement of cards is shown.

14a. 4 rows of 10 cards   ○ Yes ○ No   14d. 40 rows of 1 card   ○ Yes ○ No

14b. 6 rows of 8 cards   ○ Yes ○ No   14e. 35 rows of 5 cards   ○ Yes ○ No

14c. 20 rows of 2 cards   ○ Yes ○ No

Model Factors

Learning Objective You will make arrays using square tiles to find and record all the factors of a whole number.

Use tiles to find all the factors of the product.
Record the arrays on grid paper and write the factors shown.

1. 15

$1 \times 15 = 15$
_____
$3 \times 5 = 15$
1, 3, 5, 15

2. 30

_____
_____

3. 45

_____
_____

4. 19

_____
_____

5. 40

_____
_____
_____

6. 36

_____
_____
_____

7. 22

_____
_____
_____

8. 4

_____
_____
_____

Problem Solving Real World

9. Brooke has to set up 70 chairs in equal rows for the class talent show. But, there is not room for more than 20 rows. What are the possible number of rows that Brooke could set up?

_____

10. Eduardo thinks of a number between 1 and 20 that has exactly 5 factors. What number is he thinking of?

_____

11. **WRITE** ▸ *Math* Have students write the answer to the Essential Question and draw examples to explain their answer.

_____

_____

_____

_____

Lesson Check

1. List all the factors of 24.

_____

_____

2. Natalia has 48 tiles. Write a factor pair for the number 48.

_____

_____

Spiral Review

3. The Pumpkin Patch is open every day. If it sells 2,750 pounds of pumpkins each day, about how many pounds does it sell in 7 days?

_____

_____

4. What is the remainder in the division problem modeled below?

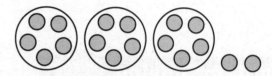

_____

_____

5. Represent the model shown below using a multiplication equation.

_____

_____

6. Channing jogs 10 miles a week. How many miles will she jog in 52 weeks?

_____

_____

FOR MORE PRACTICE
GO TO THE
Personal Math Trainer

Name _____

Factors and Divisibility

Essential Question How can you tell whether one number is a factor of another number?

Learning Objective You will use a list of factor pairs and divisibility rules to tell whether one number is a factor of another number for whole numbers in the range 1–100.

🔑 Unlock the Problem

Students in Carlo's art class painted 32 square tiles for a mosaic. They will arrange the tiles to make a rectangle. Can the rectangle have 32 tiles arranged into 3 equal rows, without gaps or overlaps?

🔓 One Way Draw a model.

Think: Try to arrange the tiles into 3 equal rows to make a rectangle.

A rectangle _____ have 32 tiles arranged into 3 equal rows.

🔓 Another Way Use division.

If 3 is a factor of 32, then the unknown factor in $3 \times \blacksquare = 32$ is a whole number.

Think: Divide to see whether the unknown factor is a whole number.

> **Math Idea**
> A factor of a number divides the number evenly. This means the quotient is a whole number and the remainder is 0.

The unknown factor in $3 \times \blacksquare = 32$ _____ a whole number.

So, a rectangle _____ have 32 tiles arranged in 3 rows.

- Explain how you can tell if 4 is a factor of 30.

_____

_____

 Math Talk

Math Processes and Practices 4
Interpret a Result How does the model relate to the quotient and remainder for 32 ÷ 3?

> ▲ Mosaics are decorative patterns made with pieces of glass or other materials.

Divisibility Rules A number is **divisible** by another number if the quotient is a counting number and the remainder is 0.

Some numbers have a divisibility rule. You can use a divisibility rule to tell whether one number is a factor of another.

 Is 6 a factor of 72?

Think: If 72 is divisible by 6, then 6 is a factor of 72.

Test for divisibility by 6:

Is 72 even? _____

What is the sum of the digits of 72?

_____ + _____ = _____

Is the sum of the digits divisible by 3?

_____

72 is divisible by _____.

So, 6 is a factor of 72.

Divisibility Rules	
Number	**Divisibility Rule**
2	The number is even.
3	The sum of the digits is divisible by 3.
5	The last digit is 0 or 5.
6	The number is even and divisible by 3.
9	The sum of the digits is divisible by 9.

Try This! List all the factor pairs for 72 in the table.

Complete the table.

Factors of 72	
1 × 72 = 72	1, 72
____ × ____ = ____	____ , ____
____ × ____ = ____	____ , ____
____ × ____ = ____	____ , ____
____ × ____ = ____	____ , ____
____ × ____ = ____	____ , ____

Show your work.

Math Talk

Math Processes and Practices **7**

Identify Relationships How are divisibility and factors related? Explain.

- How did you check if 7 is a factor of 72? Explain.

_____

_____

Name _____

 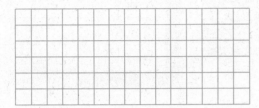
1. Is 4 a factor of 28? Draw a model to help.

Think: Can you make a rectangle with 28 squares in 4 equal rows?

[grid model]

4 _____ a factor of 28.

> **Math Talk**
> **Math Processes and Practices ❸**
> Use Counterexamples If 3 is a factor of a number, is 6 always a factor of the number? If not, give an example.

Is 5 a factor of the number? Write *yes* or *no*.

2. 27

✓ **3.** 30

4. 36

✓ **5.** 53

_____

_____

_____

_____

On Your Own

Is 9 a factor of the number? Write *yes* or *no*.

6. 54

7. 63

8. 67

9. 93

_____

_____

_____

_____

List all the factor pairs in the table.

10.

Factors of 24	
_____ × _____ = _____	_____ , _____
_____ × _____ = _____	_____ , _____
_____ × _____ = _____	_____ , _____
_____ × _____ = _____	_____ , _____

11.

Factors of 39	
_____ × _____ = _____	_____ , _____
_____ × _____ = _____	_____ , _____

Practice: Copy and Solve List all the factor pairs for the number. Make a table to help.

12. 56

13. 64

_____

_____

_____

_____

Problem Solving · Applications

Use the table to solve 14–15.

Stamps Sets	
Country	Number of stamps
Germany	90
Sweden	78
Japan	63
Canada	25

14. **THINK SMARTER** Dirk bought a set of stamps. The number of stamps in the set he bought is divisible by 2, 3, 5, 6, and 9. Which set is it?

_____

15. **GO DEEPER** Geri wants to put 6 stamps on some pages in her stamp book and 9 stamps on other pages. Explain how she could do this with the stamp set for Sweden.

_____

_____

_____

_____

16. **Math Processes and Practices ③ Use Counterexamples** George said if 2 and 4 are factors of a number, then 8 is a factor of the number. Is he correct? Explain.

_____

_____

_____

WRITE *Math*
Show Your Work

17. **THINK SMARTER** Classify the numbers. Some numbers may belong in more than one box.

| 27 | 45 | 54 | 72 | 81 | 84 |

Divisible by 5 and 9	Divisible by 3 and 9	Divisible by 2 and 6

288

Factors and Divisibility

Learning Objective You will use a list of factor pairs and divisibility rules to tell whether one number is a factor of another number for whole numbers in the range 1–100.

Is 6 a factor of the number? Write *yes* or *no*.

1. 36

   Think: $6 \times 6 = 36$

   _____ yes

2. 56

   _____

   _____

3. 42

   _____

   _____

4. 66

   _____

   _____

Is 5 a factor of the number? Write *yes* or *no*.

5. 38

   _____

6. 45

   _____

7. 60

   _____

8. 39

   _____

List all the factor pairs in the table.

9.

Factors of 12	
_____ $\times$ _____ = _____	_____ , _____
_____ $\times$ _____ = _____	_____ , _____
_____ $\times$ _____ = _____	_____ , _____

10.

Factors of 25	
_____ $\times$ _____ = _____	_____ , _____
_____ $\times$ _____ = _____	_____ , _____

11. List all the factor pairs for 48. Make a table to help.

_____

_____

Problem Solving Real World

12. Bryson buys a bag of 64 plastic miniature dinosaurs. Could he distribute them equally into six storage containers and not have any left over? **Explain**.

13. | **WRITE** ▸ *Math* Find the factors of 42. Show and explain your work, and list the factor pairs in a table.

_____

_____

Lesson Check

1. Write three numbers greater than 20 that have 9 as a factor.

   _____

   _____

2. What digit(s) can be in the ones place of a number that has 5 as a factor?

   _____

   _____

Spiral Review

3. Write an expression that can be used to find 4×275 using mental math and properties of numbers.

   _____

   _____

4. Jack broke apart 5×216 as $(5 \times 200) + (5 \times 16)$ to multiply mentally. What strategy did Jack use?

   _____

   _____

5. Jordan has $55. She earns $67 by doing chores. How much money does Jordan have now?

   _____

6. Trina has 72 collector's stamps. She puts 43 of the stamps into a stamp book. How many stamps are left?

   _____

© Houghton Mifflin Harcourt Publishing Company

**FOR MORE PRACTICE
GO TO THE
Personal Math Trainer**

Name _____

Problem Solving • Common Factors

Essential Question How can you use the *make a list* strategy to solve problems with common factors?

Learning Objective You will use the strategy *make a list* to find common factors of two or more numbers.

Unlock the Problem

Chuck has a coin collection with 30 pennies, 24 quarters, and 36 nickels. He wants to arrange the coins into rows. Each row will have the same number of coins, and all the coins in a row will be the same. How many coins can he put in each row?

The information in the graphic organizer below will help you solve the problem.

Read the Problem	Solve the Problem
What do I need to find?	I can list all the factors of each number. Then I can circle the factors that are common to all three numbers.
I need to find _____ that can go in each row so that each row has _____ _____ .	Factors of: 30 24 36
What information do I need to use?	
Chuck has _____ _____ . Each row has _____ _____ _____ .	
How will I use the information?	
I can make a list to find all the factors of _____ . Then I can use the list to find the common factors. A **common factor** is a factor of two or more numbers.	The common factors are _____ .

So, Chuck can put _____ , _____ , _____ , or _____ coins in each row.

🔓 Try Another Problem

Ryan collects animal figures. He has 45 elephants, 36 zebras, and 18 tigers. He will arrange the figures into rows. Each row will have the same number of figures, and all the figures in a row will be the same. How many figures can be in each row?

Use the graphic organizer below to help you solve the problem.

Read the Problem	Solve the Problem
What do I need to find?	
What information do I need to use?	
How will I use the information?	

So, Ryan can put _____, _____, or _____ figures in each row.

Math Talk

Math Processes and Practices ⑤

Use Appropriate Tools
How did the strategy help you solve the problem?

Name _____

Share and Show

1. Lucy has 40 bean plants, 32 tomato plants, and 16 pepper plants. She wants to put the plants in rows with only one type of plant in each row. All rows will have the same number of plants. How many plants can Lucy put in each row?

   First, read the problem and think about what you need to find. What information will you use? How will you use the information?

   _____

   _____

   Next, make a list. Find the factors for each number in the problem.

   _____

   _____

   Finally, use the list. Circle the common factors.

   So, Lucy can put _____, _____, _____, or _____ plants in each row.

2. What if Lucy has 64 bean plants instead of 40 bean plants? How many plants can Lucy put in each row?

   _____

3. **THINK SMARTER** One common factor of two numbers is 40. Another common factor is 10. If both numbers are less than 100, what are the two numbers?

   _____

4. The sum of two numbers is 136. One number is 51. What is the other number? What are the common factors of these two numbers?

   _____

WRITE ▸ Math
Show Your Work

On Your Own

5. **Math Processes and Practices ①** **Analyze** A number is called a *perfect number* if it equals the sum of all of its factors except itself. For instance, 6 is a perfect number because its factors are 1, 2, 3, and 6, and $1 + 2 + 3 = 6$. What is the next greater perfect number?

_____

6. **THINK SMARTER** Sona knits 10 squares a day for 7 days. Can she sew together the squares to make 5 equal-sized blankets? Explain.

_____

_____

7. Julianne earned $296 working at a grocery store last week. She earns $8 per hour. How many hours did Julianne work?

_____

WRITE ▸*Math* · · · · · · · · · ·
Show Your Work

8. **GO DEEPER** There are 266 students watching a play in the auditorium. There are 10 rows with 20 students in each row and 5 rows with 8 students in each row. How many students are sitting in each of the 2 remaining rows if each of those rows has an equal number of students?

_____

Personal Math Trainer

9. **THINK SMARTER +** Ben is planting a garden with 36 zinnias, 18 marigolds, and 24 petunias. Each row will have only one type of plant. Ben says he can put 9 plants in each row. He listed the common factors of 36, 18 and 24 below to support his reasoning.

36: 1, 2, 3, 4, 6, 9, 12, 18, 36
18: 1, 2, 3, 6, 8, 9, 18
24: 1, 2, 3, 4, 6, 8, 9, 12, 24

Is he correct? Explain your answer. If his reasoning is incorrect, explain how he should have found the answer.

_____

_____

Name _____

Problem Solving • Common Factors

Learning Objective You will use the strategy *make a list* to find common factors of two or more numbers.

Solve each problem.

1. Grace is preparing grab bags for her store's open house. She has 24 candles, 16 pens, and 40 figurines. Each grab bag will have the same number of items, and all the items in a bag will be the same. How many items can Grace put in each bag?

    Find the common factors of 24, 16, and 40.

    1, 2, 4, or 8 items

2. Simon is making wreaths to sell. He has 60 bows, 36 silk roses, and 48 silk carnations. He wants to put the same number of items on each wreath. All the items on a wreath will be the same type. How many items can Simon put on each wreath?

    _____

3. Justin has 20 pencils, 25 erasers, and 40 paper clips. He organizes them into groups with the same number of items in each group. All the items in a group will be the same type. How many items can he put in each group?

    _____

4. A food bank has 50 cans of vegetables, 30 loaves of bread, and 100 bottles of water. The volunteers will put the items into boxes. Each box will have the same number of food items and all the items in the box will be the same type. How many items can they put in each box?

    _____

5. **WRITE** ▸*Math* Describe how making a list can help you solve a math problem. Write a problem that could be solved by making a list.

    _____

    _____

    _____

Lesson Check

1. What are all the common factors of 24, 64, and 88?

2. What are all the common factors of 15, 45, and 90?

Spiral Review

3. Dan puts $11 of his allowance in his savings account every week. How much money will he have after 15 weeks?

4. James is reading a book that is 1,400 pages. He will read the same number of pages each day. If he reads the book in 7 days, how many pages will he read each day?

5. Emma volunteered at an animal shelter for a total of 119 hours over 6 weeks. Estimate the number of hours she volunteered each week.

6. Write an expression that can be used to multiply 6×198 mentally.

FOR MORE PRACTICE
GO TO THE
Personal Math Trainer

Name _____

Vocabulary

Choose the best term from the box.

Vocabulary
common factor
divisible
factor

1. A number that is multiplied by another number to find a product

   is called a _____. (p. 279)

2. A number is _____ by another number if the
   quotient is a counting number and the remainder is zero. (p. 286)

Concepts and Skills

List all the factors from least to greatest.

3. 8

_____

4. 14

_____

Is 6 a factor of the number? Write _yes_ or _no_.

5. 81

_____

6. 45

_____

7. 42

_____

8. 56

_____

List all the factor pairs in the table.

9.

Factors of 64	
_____ × _____ = _____	_____ , _____
_____ × _____ = _____	_____ , _____
_____ × _____ = _____	_____ , _____
_____ × _____ = _____	_____ , _____

10.

Factors of 44	
_____ × _____ = _____	_____ , _____
_____ × _____ = _____	_____ , _____
_____ × _____ = _____	_____ , _____

List the common factors of the numbers.

11. 9 and 18

12. 20 and 50

_____

_____

13. Sean places 28 tomato plants in rows. All rows contain the same number of plants. There are between 5 and 12 plants in each row. How many plants are in each row?

_____

14. [GO DEEPER] Ella bought some key chains and spent a total of $24. Each key chain cost the same whole-dollar amount. She bought between 7 and 11 key chains. How many key chains did Ella buy?

_____

15. Sandy has 16 roses, 8 daisies, and 32 tulips. She wants to arrange all the flowers in bouquets. Each bouquet has the same number of flowers and has only one type of flower. What is the greatest number of flowers that could be in each bouquet?

_____

16. Amir arranged 9 photos on a bulletin board. He put the photos in rows. Each row contains the same number of photos. How many photos could be in each row?

_____

Name _____

Factors and Multiples

Essential Question How are factors and multiples related?

Learning Objective You will describe the relationship between factors and multiples and find common multiples of two or more numbers.

🔑 Unlock the Problem

Toy animals are sold in sets of 3, 5, 10, and 12. Mason wants to make a display with 3 animals in each row. Which sets could he buy, if he wants to display all of the animals?

The product of two numbers is a multiple of each number. Factors and multiples are related.

$$3 \times 4 = 12$$

factor   factor   multiple of 3
              multiple of 4

- How many animals will be in each row?

  _____

- How many animals are sold in each set?

  _____

🔒 One Way Find factors.

Tell whether 3 is a factor of each number.

Think: If a number is divisible by 3, then 3 is a factor of the number.

Is 3 a factor of 3? _____

Is 3 a factor of 5? _____

Is 3 a factor of 10? _____

Is 3 a factor of 12? _____

3 is a factor of _____ and _____ .

🔒 Another Way Find multiples.

Multiply and make a list.   ___3___, _____, _____, _____, _____ ,...

                            1 × 3   2 × 3   3 × 3   4 × 3   5 × 3

_____ and _____ are multiples of 3.

So, Mason could buy sets of _____ and _____ toy animals.

Math Talk

Math Processes and Practices ❻

Explain how you can use what you know about factors to determine whether one number is a multiple of another number.

Chapter 5 299

Common Multiples A **common multiple** is a multiple of two or more numbers.

⓵ Example Find common multiples.

Tony works every 3 days and Amanda works every 5 days. If Tony works June 3 and Amanda works June 5, on what days in June will they work together?

Circle multiples of 3. Draw a box around multiples of 5.

June						
Sun	Mon	Tue	Wed	Thu	Fri	Sat
	1	2	3	4	5	6
7	8	9	10	11	12	13
14	15	16	17	18	19	20
21	22	23	24	25	26	27
28	29	30				

Think: The common multiples have both a circle and a box.

The common multiples are _____ and _____.

So, Tony and Amanda will work together on June _____ and June _____.

Share and Show

1. Multiply to list the next five multiples of 4.

   $\dfrac{4}{}$, _____ , _____ , _____ , _____ , _____

   1×4

Math Talk Math Processes and Practices ⑦

Identify Relationships
Discuss how factors and multiples are related. Give an example.

Is the number a factor of 6? Write *yes* or *no*.

✓ 2. 3   3. 6   4. 16   5. 18

_____   _____   _____   _____

Is the number a multiple of 6? Write *yes* or *no*.

✓ 6. 3   7. 6   8. 16   9. 18

_____   _____   _____   _____

Name _____

On Your Own

Is the number a multiple of 3? Write *yes* or *no*.

10. 4   **11.** 8   **12.** 24   **13.** 38

_____   _____   _____   _____

14. List the next nine multiples of each number. Find the common multiples.

Multiples of 2: 2, _____

Multiples of 8: 8, _____

Common multiples: _____

 Generalize **Algebra** Find the unknown number.

15. 12, 24, 36, _____   **16.** 25, 50, 75, 100, _____

Tell whether 20 is a factor or multiple of the number.
Write *factor, multiple,* or *neither*.

17. 10   **18.** 20   **19.** 30

_____   _____   _____

THINK SMARTER **Write *true* or *false*. Explain.**

20. Every whole number is a multiple of 1.   **21.** Every whole number is a factor of 1.

_____   _____

_____   _____

22. THINK SMARTER Julio wears a blue shirt every 3 days. Larry wears a blue shirt every 4 days. On April 12, both Julio and Larry wore a blue shirt. What is the next date that they will both wear a blue shirt?

_____

April						
Sun	Mon	Tue	Wed	Thu	Fri	Sat
1	2	3	4	5	6	7
8	9	10	11	12	13	14
15	16	17	18	19	20	21
22	23	24	25	26	27	28
29	30					

Problem Solving · Applications

Complete the Venn diagram. Then use it to solve 23–25.

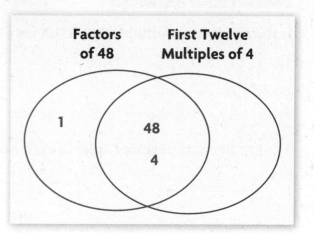

23. What multiples of 4 are not factors of 48?

_____

24. What factors of 48 are multiples of 4?

_____

25. GO DEEPER **Pose a Problem** Look back at Problem 24. Write a similar problem by changing the numbers. Then solve.

_____

_____

26. Kia paid $10 for two charms. The price of each charm was a multiple of $2. What are the possible prices of the charms?

_____

27. Math Processes and Practices 7 **Look for Structure** The answer is 9, 18, 27, 36, 45. What is the question?

_____

28. WRITE ▸Math How do you know whether a number is a multiple of another number?

_____

_____

29. THINK SMARTER   For numbers 29a–29e, select True or False for each statement.

29a.   The number 45 is a multiple of 9.   ○ True   ○ False

29b.   The number 4 is a multiple of 16.   ○ True   ○ False

29c.   The number 28 is a multiple of 4.   ○ True   ○ False

29d.   The number 4 is a factor of 28.   ○ True   ○ False

29e.   The number 32 is a factor of 8.   ○ True   ○ False

WRITE ▸Math
Show Your Work

Factors and Multiples

Learning Objective You will describe the
relationship between factors and multiples
and find common multiples of two or more
numbers.

Is the number a multiple of 8? Write *yes* or *no*.

1. 4   **2.** 8   **3.** 20   **4.** 40

Think: Since $4 \times 2 = 8$,
4 is a *factor* of 8, not a
multiple of 8.

_____ no _____   _____   _____   _____

**List the next nine multiples of each number.
Find the common multiples.**

5. Multiples of 4: 4, _____

   Multiples of 7: 7, _____

   Common multiples: _____

6. Multiples of 3: 3, _____

   Multiples of 9: 9, _____

   Common multiples: _____

**Tell whether 24 is a factor or multiple of the number.
Write *factor*, *multiple*, or *neither*.**

7. 6 _____   **8.** 36 _____   **9.** 48 _____

Problem Solving · Real World

10. Ken paid $12 for two magazines. The cost of
each magazine was a multiple of $3. What
are the possible prices of the magazines?

11. Jodie bought some shirts for $6 each.
Marge bought some shirts for $8 each.
The girls spent the same amount of money
on shirts. What is the least amount they
could have spent?

_____   _____

12. **WRITE** ▸*Math* Write a word problem that can be solved by
finding the numbers that have 4 as a factor.

_____

Lesson Check

1. Of the numbers listed below, which are NOT multiples of 4?

   2, 4, 7, 8, 12, 15, 19, 24, 34

   _____

2. What number is a common multiple of 5 and 9?

   _____

Spiral Review

3. Jenny has 50 square tiles. She arranges the tiles into a rectangular array of 4 rows. How many tiles will be left over?

   _____

4. Jerome added two numbers. The sum was 83. One of the numbers was 45. What was the other number?

   _____

5. There are 18 rows of seats in the auditorium. There are 24 seats in each row. How many seats are in the auditorium?

   _____

6. The population of Riverdale is 6,735. What is the value of the 7 in the number 6,735?

   _____

FOR MORE PRACTICE
GO TO THE
Personal Math Trainer

Name _____

Prime and Composite Numbers

Essential Question How can you tell whether a number is prime or composite?

Learning Objective You will use divisibility rules to tell whether a number is prime or composite.

 Unlock the Problem Real World

Students are arranging square tables to make one larger, rectangular table. The students want to have several ways to arrange the tables. Should they use 12 or 13 tables?

- What are the factors of 12?

_____

🔑 **Use a grid to show all the possible arrangements of 12 and 13 tables.**

Draw all of the possible arrangements of 12 tables and 13 tables. Label each drawing with the factors modeled.

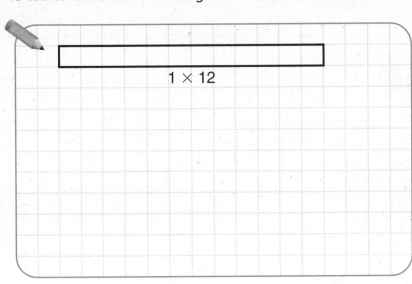

1 × 12

⚠ **ERROR Alert**

The same factors in a different order should be counted only once. For example, 3 × 4 and 4 × 3 are the same factor pair.

So, there are more ways to arrange _____ tables.

Math Talk — Math Processes and Practices ⑥

Make Connections Explain how knowing whether 12 and 13 are prime or composite could have helped you solve the problem above.

- A **prime number** is a whole number greater than 1 that has exactly two factors, 1 and itself.

- A **composite number** is a whole number greater than 1 that has more than two factors.

Factors of 12: _____ , _____ , _____ , _____ , _____ , _____

Factors of 13: _____ , _____

12 is a _____ number, and 13 is a _____ number.

© Houghton Mifflin Harcourt Publishing Company

Divisibility You can use divisibility rules to help tell whether a number is prime or composite. If a number is divisible by any number other than 1 and itself, then the number is composite.

🔑 **Tell whether 51 is *prime* or *composite*.**

Is 51 divisible by 2?

_____

Is 51 divisible by 3?

_____

Think: 51 is divisible by a number other than 1 and 51.
        51 has more than two factors.

So, 51 is _____ .

> **Math Idea**
> The number 1 is neither prime nor composite, since it has only one factor: 1.

Share and Show [MATH BOARD]

1. Use the grid to model the factors of 18. Tell whether 18 is *prime* or *composite*.

Factors of 18: _____ , _____ , _____ , _____ , _____ , _____

Think: 18 has more than two factors.

So, 18 is _____ .

Tell whether the number is *prime* or *composite*.

> **Math Talk**
> **Math Processes and Practices** ⑦
> **Look for Structure** Is the product of two prime numbers prime or composite? Explain.

2. 11
   Think: Does 11 have other factors besides 1 and itself?

   _____

3. 73

   _____

✔ 4. 69

   _____

✔ 5. 42

   _____

Name _____

Tell whether the number is *prime* or *composite*.

6. 18

_____

7. 49

_____

8. 29

_____

9. 64

_____

10. 33

_____

11. 89

_____

12. 52

_____

13. 76

_____

Write *true* or *false* for each statement. Explain or give an example to support your answer.

14. `GO DEEPER` Only odd numbers are prime numbers.

_____

_____

15. `THINK SMARTER` A composite number cannot have three factors.

_____

_____

Problem Solving • Applications

16. `GO DEEPER` I am a number between 60 and 100. My ones digit is two less than my tens digit. I am a prime number. What number am I?

17. Name a 2-digit odd number that is prime. Name a 2-digit odd number that is composite.

_____

_____

18. `THINK SMARTER` Choose the words that correctly complete the sentence.

The number 9 is
$\begin{array}{|c|} \hline \text{prime} \\ \hline \text{composite} \\ \hline \end{array}$
because it has
$\begin{array}{|c|} \hline \text{exactly} \\ \hline \text{more than} \\ \hline \end{array}$
two factors.

The Sieve of Eratosthenes

Eratosthenes was a Greek mathematician who lived more than 2,200 years ago. He invented a method of finding prime numbers, which is now called the Sieve of Eratosthenes.

19. Follow the steps below to circle all prime numbers less than 100. Then list the prime numbers.

STEP 1

Cross out 1, since 1 is not prime

STEP 2

Circle 2, since it is prime. Cross out all other multiples of 2.

STEP 3

Circle the next number that is not crossed out. This number is prime. Cross out all the multiples of this number.

STEP 4

Repeat Step 3 until every number is either circled or crossed out.

1	2	3	4	5	6	7	8	9	10
11	12	13	14	15	16	17	18	19	20
21	22	23	24	25	26	27	28	29	30
31	32	33	34	35	36	37	38	39	40
41	42	43	44	45	46	47	48	49	50
51	52	53	54	55	56	57	58	59	60
61	62	63	64	65	66	67	68	69	70
71	72	73	74	75	76	77	78	79	80
81	82	83	84	85	86	87	88	89	90
91	92	93	94	95	96	97	98	99	100

So, the prime numbers less than 100 are

_____

_____

_____

_____

_____

_____

20. **Math Processes and Practices ⑥** **Explain** why the multiples of any number other than 1 are not prime numbers.

_____

Prime and Composite Numbers

Learning Objective You will use divisibility rules to tell whether a number is prime or composite.

Tell whether the number is *prime* **or** *composite*.

1. 47

Think: Does 47 have other factors besides 1 and itself?

_____ prime _____

2. 68

_____

3. 52

_____

4. 63

_____

5. 75

_____

6. 31

_____

7. 77

_____

8. 59

_____

9. 87

_____

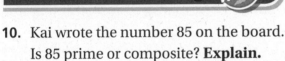

Problem Solving Real World

10. Kai wrote the number 85 on the board. Is 85 prime or composite? **Explain.**

_____

_____

11. Lisa says that 43 is a 2-digit odd number that is composite. Is she correct? **Explain.**

_____

_____

12. **WRITE** ▸*Math* Describe how to decide if 94 is a prime number or composite number.

_____

_____

Lesson Check

1. Is the number 5 prime, composite, or neither?

   _____

2. Is the number 1 prime, composite, or neither?

   _____

Spiral Review

3. A recipe for a vegetable dish contains a total of 924 calories. The dish serves 6 people. How many calories are in each serving?

   _____

4. A store clerk has 45 shirts to pack in boxes. Each box holds 6 shirts. What is the fewest boxes the clerk will need to pack all the shirts?

   _____

5. A total of 152,909 people visited a national park during one weekend. What is this number rounded to the nearest hundred thousand?

   _____

   _____

   _____

6. What is the word form of the number 602,107?

   _____

   _____

   _____

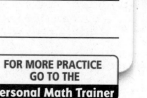

FOR MORE PRACTICE GO TO THE
Personal Math Trainer

Name _____

Number Patterns

Essential Question How can you make and describe patterns?

Learning Objective You will shade squares to find a number pattern and generate a number pattern that follows a given rule.

🔑 Unlock the Problem (Real World)

Daryl is making a pattern for a quilt. The pattern shows 40 squares. Every fourth square is blue. How many blue squares are in the pattern?

A **pattern** is an ordered set of numbers or objects. Each number or object in the pattern is called a **term**.

- Underline what you are asked to find.
- Circle what you need to use.

🔓 Activity Find a pattern.

Materials ■ color pencils

Shade the squares that are blue.

1	2	3	4	5	6	7	8	9	10
11	12	13	14	15	16	17	18	19	20
21	22	23	24	25	26	27	28	29	30
31	32	33	34	35	36	37	38	39	40

Math Talk

Math Processes and Practices ⑦

Look for a Pattern Describe another number pattern in Daryl's quilt.

Which squares are blue? _____

So, there are _____ blue squares in the pattern.

1. What patterns do you see in the arrangement of the blue squares?

   _____

   _____

2. What patterns do you see in the numbers of the blue squares?

   _____

   _____

🔒 Example Find and describe a pattern.

The rule for the pattern is *add* 5. The first term in the pattern is 5.

Ⓐ **Use the rule to write the numbers in the pattern.**

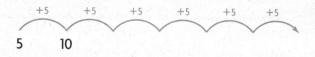

5   10   ____ ____ ____ ____

5, 10, _____, _____, _____, _____, _____, _____, _____, ...

Ⓑ **Describe other patterns in the numbers.**

What do you notice about the digits in the ones place?

_____

_____

Describe the pattern using the words *odd* and *even*.

_____

_____

Describe the pattern using the word *multiples*.

_____

_____

Try This! **Find and describe a pattern.**

The rule for the pattern is *add* 3, *subtract* 1. The first term in the pattern is 6.

Add 3.   Subtract 1.   Add 3.

6

____ ____ ____ ____ ____ ____

Describe another pattern in the numbers.

_____

_____

_____

312

Name _____

Share and Show

Math Talk Math Processes and Practices ⑤

Use Patterns How do you use the first term in a pattern to find the next term?

Use the rule to write the numbers in the pattern.

1. Rule: Subtract 10.   First term: 100

    Think: Subtract 10

    100 ____ ____ ____ ____

    100, _____, _____, _____, _____, ...

Use the rule to write the numbers in the pattern.
Describe another pattern in the numbers.

✓ 2. Rule: Multiply by 2.   First term: 4

    4, _____, _____, _____, _____, ...

    _____

✓ 3. Rule: Skip-count by 6.   First term: 12

    12, _____, _____, _____, _____, ...

    _____

On Your Own

Use the rule to write the first twelve numbers in the pattern. Describe another pattern in the numbers.

4. Rule: Add 7.   First term: 3

    _____

    _____

5. Rule: Add 2, add 1.   First term: 12

    _____

    _____

6. **Math Processes and Practices ⑤** **Use Patterns** Marcie likes to collect stickers, but she also likes to give them away. Currently, Marcie has 87 stickers in her collection. If Marcie collects 5 new stickers each week and gives away 3 stickers each week, how many stickers will Marcie have in her collection after 5 weeks?

    _____

Problem Solving • Applications Real World

7. **THINK SMARTER** John is saving
for his trip to see the Alamo.
He started with $24 in his
savings account. Every week
he earns $15 for baby-sitting.
Out of that, he spends $8
and saves the rest. John uses
the rule *add 7* to find out how much money
he has at the end of each week. What are the
first 8 numbers in the pattern?

_____

8. **THINK SMARTER +** Draw a check
under the column that describes the
number.

	Prime	Composite
81		
29		
31		
62		

Pose a Problem

9. **GO DEEPER** An activity at the Math Fair shows two charts.

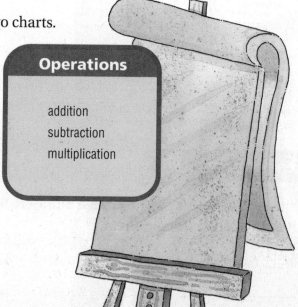

Numbers
2
3
5
6
10

Operations
addition
subtraction
multiplication

Use at least two of the numbers and an
operation from the charts to write a pattern
problem. Include the first five terms of your
pattern in the solution to your problem.

Pose a problem.	Solve your problem.

• Describe other patterns in the terms you wrote.

_____

Name _____

Number Patterns

Learning Objective You will shade squares to find a number pattern and generate a number pattern that follows a given rule.

Use the rule to write the first twelve numbers in the pattern.
Describe another pattern in the numbers.

1. Rule: *Add 8.*   First term: 5

   Think: Add 8.

   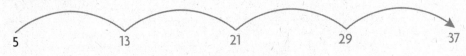

   5   13   21   29   37

   <u>5, 13, 21, 29, 37, 45, 53, 61, 69, 77, 85, 93</u>

   <u>All the terms are odd numbers.</u>

2. Rule: *Subtract 7.*   First term: 95

   _____

   _____

3. Rule: *Add 15, subtract 10.*   First term: 4

   _____

   _____

Problem Solving *Real World*

4. Barb is making a bead necklace. She strings 1 white bead, then 3 blue beads, then 1 white bead, and so on. Write the numbers for the first eight beads that are white. What is a rule for the pattern?

   _____

   _____

5. An artist is arranging tiles in rows to decorate a wall. Each new row has 2 fewer tiles than the row below it. If the first row has 23 tiles, how many tiles will be in the seventh row?

   _____

   _____

6. **WRITE** *Math* Give an example of a rule for a pattern. List a set of numbers that fit the pattern.

   _____

Chapter 5   315

Lesson Check

1. The rule for a pattern is *add 6*. The first term is 5. Write the first five terms in the pattern.

2. What are the next two terms in the pattern 3, 6, 5, 10, 9, 18, 17, . . .?

Spiral Review

3. To win a game, Roger needs to score 2,000 points. So far, he has scored 837 points. How many more points does Roger need to score?

4. Sue wants to use mental math to find 7 × 53. Write an expression she could use.

5. Pat listed all the numbers that have 15 as a multiple. Write the numbers in Pat's list.

6. Complete the following sentence using the correct term.

   14 is a _____ of 7 and 14.

FOR MORE PRACTICE
GO TO THE
Personal Math Trainer

✓ Chapter 5 Review/Test

Personal Math Trainer
Online Assessment
and Intervention

1. List all the factors of the number.

   14: _____

2. Select the numbers that have a factor of 5. Mark all that apply.

   (A) 15   (D) 5

   (B) 3   (E) 50

   (C) 45   (F) 31

3. Jackson was making a poster for his room. He arranged 50 trading cards in the shape of a rectangle on the poster. For 3a–3e, choose Yes or No to tell whether a possible arrangement of cards is shown.

   3a. 5 rows of 10 cards   ○ Yes   ○ No

   3b. 7 rows of 8 cards   ○ Yes   ○ No

   3c. 25 rows of 2 cards   ○ Yes   ○ No

   3d. 50 rows of 1 card   ○ Yes   ○ No

   3e. 45 rows of 5 cards   ○ Yes   ○ No

4. List all the factor pairs in the table.

Factors of 48	
____ × ____ = ____	____ , ____
____ × ____ = ____	____ , ____
____ × ____ = ____	____ , ____
____ × ____ = ____	____ , ____
____ × ____ = ____	____ , ____

GO DIGITAL Assessment Options
Chapter Test

5. Classify the numbers. Some numbers may belong in more than one box.

| 54 | 72 | 84 | 90 | 96 |

Divisible by 5 and 9	Divisible by 6 and 9	Divisible by 2 and 6

6. James works in a flower shop. He will put 36 tulips in vases for a wedding. He must use the same number of tulips in each vase. The number of tulips in each vase must be greater than 1 and less than 10. How many tulips could be in each vase?

_____ tulips

7. Brady has a card collection with 64 basketball cards, 32 football cards, and 24 baseball cards. He wants to arrange the cards in equal piles, with only one type of card in each pile. How many cards can he put in each pile? Mark all that apply.

Ⓐ 1 Ⓑ 2 Ⓒ 3 Ⓓ 4 Ⓔ 8 Ⓕ 32

Personal Math Trainer

8. **THINK** SMARTER **+** The Garden Club is designing a garden with 24 cosmos, 32 pansies, and 36 marigolds. Each row will have only one type of plant in each row. Ben says he can put 6 plants in each row. He listed the common factors of 24, 32, and 36 below to support his reasoning.

24: 1, 2, 3, 4, 6, 8, 12, 24

32: 1, 2, 4, 6, 9, 16, 32

36: 1, 2, 3, 4, 6, 8, 12, 18, 36

Is he correct? Explain your answer. If his reasoning is incorrect, explain how he should have found the answer.

Name _____

9. The number of pieces of art at a museum is shown in the table.

Art	
Type of Art	**Number of Pieces**
Oil paintings	30
Photographs	24
Sketches	21

Part A

The museum is hosting a show for July that features the oil paintings by different artists. All artists show the same number of paintings and each will show more than 1 painting. How many artists could be featured in the show?

_____ artists

Part B

The museum wants to display all the art pieces in rows. Each row has the same number of pieces and the same type of pieces. How many pieces could be in each row? Explain how you found your answer.

10. Charles was skip counting at the Math Club meeting. He started to count by 8s. He said 8, 16, 24, 32, 40, and 48. What number will he say next?

_____

11. Jill wrote the number 40. If her rule is *add 7*, what is the fourth number in Jill's pattern? How can you check your answer?

12. For numbers 12a–12e, select True or False for each statement.

12a. The number 36 is a
multiple of 9.   ○ True   ○ False

12b. The number 3 is a
multiple of 9.   ○ True   ○ False

12c. The number 54 is a
multiple of 9.   ○ True   ○ False

12d. The number 3 is a
factor of 9.   ○ True   ○ False

12e. The number 27 is a
factor of 9.   ○ True   ○ False

13. What multiple of 7 is also a factor of 7?

_____

14. Manny makes dinner using 1 box of pasta and 1 jar of sauce. If
pasta is sold in packages of 6 boxes and sauce is sold in packages
of 3 jars, what is the least number of dinners that Manny can make
without any supplies leftover?

_____ dinners

15. Serena has several packages of raisins. Each package contains
3 boxes of raisins. Which could be the number of boxes of raisins
Serena has? Mark all that apply.

(A) 9   (B) 18   (C) 23   (D) 27   (E) 32

16. Choose the words that make the sentence true.

The number 7 is | prime / composite | because it has | exactly / more than |
two factors.

Name _____

17. Winnie wrote the following riddle: I am a number between 60 and 100. My ones digit is two less than my tens digit. I am a prime number.

Part A

What number does Winnie's riddle describe? Explain.

```



```

Part B

Winnie's friend Marco guessed that her riddle was about the number 79. Why can't 79 be the answer to Winnie's riddle? Explain.

```



```

18. Classify the numbers as prime or composite.

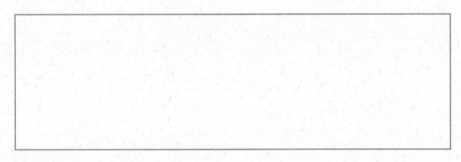

Prime	Composite

19. GO DEEPER Erica knits 18 squares on Monday. She knits 7 more squares each day from Tuesday through Thursday. How many squares did Erica knit in all by the end of the day on Thursday?

_____ squares

20. Use the rule to write the first five terms of the pattern.

Rule: Add 10, subtract 5   First term: 11

_____

21. Elina had 10 tiles to arrange in a rectangular design. She drew a model of the rectangles she could make with the ten tiles.

Part A

How does Elina's drawing show that the number 10 is a composite number?

Part B

Suppose Elina used 15 tiles to make the rectangular design. How many different rectangles could she make with the 15 tiles? Write a list or draw a picture to show the number and dimensions of the rectangles she could make.

Part C

Elina's friend Luke said that he could make more rectangles with 24 tiles than with Elina's 10 tiles. Do you agree with Luke? Explain.

Glossary

© Houghton Mifflin Harcourt Publishing Company

Pronunciation Key

a	add, map	ē	equal, tree	m	move, seem	o͞o	pool, food	u̇	pull, book
ā	ace, rate	f	fit, half	n	nice, tin	p	pit, stop	û(r)	burn, term
â(r)	care, air	g	go, log	ng	ring, song	r	run, poor	yo͞o	fuse, few
ä	palm, father	h	hope, hate	o	odd, hot	s	see, pass	v	vain, eve
b	bat, rub	i	it, give	ō	open, so	sh	sure, rush	w	win, away
ch	check, catch	ī	ice, write	ô	order, jaw	t	talk, sit	y	yet, yearn
d	dog, rod	j	joy, ledge	oi	oil, boy	th	thin, both	z	zest, muse
e	end, pet	k	cool, take	ou	pout, now	th̲	this, bathe	zh	vision, pleasure
		l	look, rule	o͝o	took, full	u	up, done		

ə the schwa, an unstressed vowel representing the sound spelled *a* in *above*, *e* in *sicken*, *i* in *possible*, *o* in *melon*, *u* in *circus*

Other symbols:
- • separates words into syllables
- ' indicates stress on a syllable

A

acute angle [ə•kyo͞ot' ang'gəl] **ángulo agudo**
An angle that measures greater than 0° and less than 90°
Example:

acute triangle [ə•kyo͞ot' trī'ang•gəl] **triángulo acutángulo** A triangle with three acute angles
Example:

addend [a'dend] **sumando** A number that is added to another in an addition problem
Example: 2 + 4 = 6;
   2 and 4 are addends.

addition [ə•di'shən] **suma** The process of finding the total number of items when two or more groups of items are joined; the opposite operation of subtraction

A.M. [ā•em'] **a.m.** The times after midnight and before noon

analog clock [anəl• ôg kläk] **reloj analógico** A tool for measuring time, in which hands move around a circle to show hours, minutes, and sometimes seconds
Example:

angle [ang'gəl] **ángulo** A shape formed by two line segments or rays that share the same endpoint
Example:

area [âr'ē•ə] **área** The measure of the number of unit squares needed to cover a surface
Example:

Area = 9 square units

array [ə•rā′] **matriz** An arrangement of objects in rows and columns
Example:

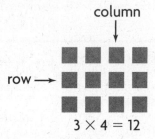

$3 \times 4 = 12$

Associative Property of Addition [ə•sō′shē•āt•iv präp′ər•tē əv ə•dish′ən] **propiedad asociativa de la suma** The property that states that you can group addends in different ways and still get the same sum
Example: $3 + (8 + 5) = (3 + 8) + 5$

Associative Property of Multiplication [ə•sō′shē•ə•tiv präp′ər•tē əv mul•tə•pli•kā′shən] **propiedad asociativa de la multiplicación** The property that states that you can group factors in different ways and still get the same product
Example: $3 \times (4 \times 2) = (3 \times 4) \times 2$

bar graph [bär graf] **gráfica de barras** A graph that uses bars to show data
Example:

base [bās] **base** A polygon's side or a two-dimensional shape, usually a polygon or circle, by which a three-dimensional shape is measured or named
Examples:

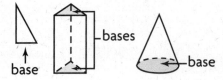

benchmark [bench′märk] **punto de referencia** A known size or amount that helps you understand a different size or amount

calendar [kal′ən•dər] **calendario** A table that shows the days, weeks, and months of a year

capacity [kə•pas′i•tē] **capacidad** The amount a container can hold when filled

Celsius (°C) [sel′sē•əs] **Celsius** A metric scale for measuring temperature

centimeter (cm) [sen′tə•mēt•ər] **centímetro (cm)** A metric unit for measuring length or distance 1 meter = 100 centimeters
Example:

1 centimeter

cent sign (¢) [sent sīn] **símbolo de centavo** A symbol that stands for *cent* or *cents*
Example: 53¢

clockwise [kläk′wīz] **en el sentido de las manecillas del reloj** In the same direction in which the hands of a clock move

closed shape [klōzd shāp] **figura cerrada** A two-dimensional shape that begins and ends at the same point
Examples:

common denominator [käm′ən dē•näm′ə•nāt•ər] **denominador común** A common multiple of two or more denominators
Example: Some common denominators for $\frac{1}{4}$ and $\frac{5}{6}$ are 12, 24, and 36.

common factor [käm′ən fak′tər] **factor común** A number that is a factor of two or more numbers

common multiple [käm′ən mul′tə•pəl] **múltiplo común** A number that is a multiple of two or more numbers

Commutative Property of Addition
[kə•myōōt′ə•tiv präp′ər•tē əv ə•dish′ən] **propiedad conmutativa de la suma** The property that states that when the order of two addends is changed, the sum is the same
Example: 4 + 5 = 5 + 4

Commutative Property of Multiplication
[kə•myōōt′ə•tiv präp′ər•tē əv mul•tə•pli•kā′shən] **propiedad conmutativa de la multiplicación** The property that states that when the order of two factors is changed, the product is the same
Example: 4 × 5 = 5 × 4

compare [kəm•pâr′] **comparar** To describe whether numbers are equal to, less than, or greater than each other

compatible numbers [kəm•pat′ə•bəl num′bərz] **números compatibles** Numbers that are easy to compute mentally

composite number [kəm•päz′it num′bər] **número compuesto** A number having more than two factors
Example: 6 is a composite number, since its factors are 1, 2, 3, and 6.

corner [kôr′nər] **esquina** See *vertex*.

counterclockwise [kount•er•kläk′wīz] **en sentido contrario a las manecillas del reloj** In the opposite direction in which the hands of a clock move

counting number [kount′ing num′bər] **número natural** A whole number that can be used to count a set of objects (1, 2, 3, 4, . . .)

cube [kyōōb] **cubo** A three-dimensional shape with six square faces of the same size
Example:

cup (c) [kup] **taza (tz)** A customary unit used to measure capacity and liquid volume
1 cup = 8 ounces

data [dāt′ə] **datos** Information collected about people or things

decagon [dek′ə•gän] **decágono** A polygon with ten sides and ten angles

decimal [des′ə•məl] **decimal** A number with one or more digits to the right of the decimal point

decimal point [des′ə•məl point] **punto decimal** A symbol used to separate dollars from cents in money amounts, and to separate the ones and the tenths places in a decimal
Example: 6.4
↑ decimal point

decimeter (dm) [des′i•mēt•ər] **decímetro (dm)** A metric unit for measuring length or distance
1 meter = 10 decimeters

degree (°) [di•grē′] **grado (°)** The unit used for measuring angles and temperatures

denominator [dē•näm′ə•nāt•ər] **denominador** The number below the bar in a fraction that tells how many equal parts are in the whole or in the group
Example: $\frac{3}{4}$ ← denominator

diagonal [dī•ag′ə•nəl] **diagonal** A line segment that connects two vertices of a polygon that are not next to each other
Example:

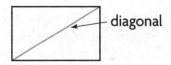
— diagonal

difference [dif′ər•əns] **diferencia** The answer to a subtraction problem

digit [dij′it] **dígito** Any one of the ten symbols 0, 1, 2, 3, 4, 5, 6, 7, 8, or 9 used to write numbers

digital clock [dij′i•təl kläk] **reloj digital** A clock that shows time to the minute, using digits
Example:

dime [dīm] **moneda de 10¢** A coin worth 10 cents and with a value equal to that of 10 pennies; 10¢
Example:

dimension [də•men'shən] **dimensión** A measure in one direction

Distributive Property [di•strib'yoo•tiv präp'ər•tē] **propiedad distributiva** The property that states that multiplying a sum by a number is the same as multiplying each addend by the number and then adding the products
Example: $5 \times (10 + 6) = (5 \times 10) + (5 \times 6)$

divide [də•vīd'] **dividir** To separate into equal groups; the opposite operation of multiplication

dividend [dəv'ə•dend] **dividendo** The number that is to be divided in a division problem
Example: $36 \div 6$; $6)\overline{36}$; the dividend is 36.

divisible [də•viz'ə•bəl] **divisible** A number is divisible by another number if the quotient is a counting number and the remainder is zero
Example: 18 is divisible by 3.

division [də•vi'zhən] **división** The process of sharing a number of items to find how many equal groups can be made or how many items will be in each equal group; the opposite operation of multiplication

divisor [də•vī'zər] **divisor** The number that divides the dividend
Example: $15 \div 3$; $3)\overline{15}$; the divisor is 3.

dollar [däl'ər] **dólar** Paper money worth 100 cents and equal to 100 pennies; $1.00
Example:

elapsed time [ē•lapst' tīm] **tiempo transcurrido** The time that passes from the start of an activity to the end of that activity

endpoint [end'point] **extremo** The point at either end of a line segment or the starting point of a ray

equal groups [ē'kwəl groopz] **grupos iguales** Groups that have the same number of objects

equal parts [ē'kwəl pärts] **partes iguales** Parts that are exactly the same size

equal sign (=) [ē'kwəl sīn] **signo de igualdad** A symbol used to show that two numbers have the same value
Example: $384 = 384$

equal to [ē'kwəl too] **igual a** Having the same value
Example: $4 + 4$ is equal to $3 + 5$.

equation [ē•kwā'zhən] **ecuación** A number sentence which shows that two quantities are equal
Example: $4 + 5 = 9$

equivalent [ē•kwiv'ə•lənt] **equivalente** Having the same value or naming the same amount

equivalent decimals [ē•kwiv'ə•lənt des'ə•məlz] **decimales equivalentes** Two or more decimals that name the same amount

equivalent fractions [ē•kwiv'ə•lənt frak'shənz] **fracciones equivalentes** Two or more fractions that name the same amount
Example: $\frac{3}{4}$ and $\frac{6}{8}$ name the same amount.

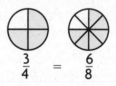

$$\frac{3}{4} = \frac{6}{8}$$

estimate [es'tə•māt] *verb* **estimar** To find an answer that is close to the exact amount

estimate [es'tə•mit] *noun* **estimación** A number that is close to the exact amount

even [ē'vən] **par** A whole number that has a 0, 2, 4, 6, or 8 in the ones place

expanded form [ek•span'did fôrm] **forma desarrollada** A way to write numbers by showing the value of each digit
Example: $253 = 200 + 50 + 3$

expression [ek•spresh'ən] **expresión** A part of a number sentence that has numbers and operation signs but does not have an equal sign

fact family [fakt fam′ə•lē] **familia de operaciones** A set of related multiplication and division equations, or addition and subtraction equations
Example: $7 \times 8 = 56$ $8 \times 7 = 56$
      $56 \div 7 = 8$ $56 \div 8 = 7$

factor [fak′tər] **factor** A number that is multiplied by another number to find a product

Fahrenheit (°F) [fâr′ən•hīt] **Fahrenheit** A customary scale for measuring temperature

fluid ounce (fl oz) [flōō′id ouns] **onza fluida (fl oz)** A customary unit used to measure liquid capacity and liquid volume
1 cup = 8 fluid ounces

foot (ft) [fŏŏt] **pie (ft)** A customary unit used for measuring length or distance
1 foot = 12 inches

formula [fôr′myōō•lə] **fórmula** A set of symbols that expresses a mathematical rule
Example: Area = base × height, or $A = b \times h$

fraction [frak′shən] **fracción** A number that names a part of a whole or part of a group
Example:

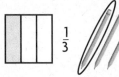

fraction greater than 1 [frak′shən grāt′ər than wun] **fracción mayor que 1** A number which has a numerator that is greater than its denominator

frequency table [frē′kwən•sē tā′bəl] **tabla de frecuencia** A table that uses numbers to record data about how often something happens
Example:

Favorite Color	
Color	**Frequency**
Blue	10
Red	7
Green	5
Other	3

gallon (gal) [gal′ən] **galón (gal)** A customary unit for measuring capacity and liquid volume
1 gallon = 4 quarts

gram (g) [gram] **gramo (g)** A metric unit for measuring mass
1 kilogram = 1,000 grams

greater than sign (>) [grāt′ər than sīn] **signo de mayor que** A symbol used to compare two quantities, with the greater quantity given first
Example: 6 > 4

grid [grid] **cuadrícula** Evenly divided and equally spaced squares on a shape or flat surface

half gallon [haf gal′ən] **medio galón** A customary unit for measuring capacity and liquid volume
1 half gallon = 2 quarts

half hour [haf our] **media hora** 30 minutes
Example: 4:00 to 4:30 is one half hour.

half-square unit [haf skwâr yōō′nit] **media unidad cuadrada** Half of a unit of area with dimensions of 1 unit × 1 unit

height [hīt] **altura** The measure of a perpendicular from the base to the top of a two-dimensional shape

hexagon [hek′sə•gän] **hexágono** A polygon with six sides and six angles
Examples:

horizontal [hôr•i•zänt′l] **horizontal** In the direction from left to right

hour (hr) [our] **hora (hr)** A unit used to measure time
1 hour = 60 minutes

hundredth [hun'drədth] **centésimo** One of one hundred equal parts
Example:

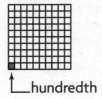
hundredth

I

Identity Property of Addition [ī•den'tə•tē präp'ər•tē əv ə•dish'ən] **propiedad de identidad de la suma** The property that states that when you add zero to any number, the sum is that number
Example: $16 + 0 = 16$

Identity Property of Multiplication [ī•den'tə•tē präp'ər•tē əv mul•tə•pli•kā'shən] **propiedad de identidad de la multiplicación** The property that states that the product of any number and 1 is that number
Example: $9 \times 1 = 9$

inch (in.) [inch] **pulgada (pulg)** A customary unit used for measuring length or distance
Example:

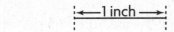
1 inch

intersecting lines [in•tər•sekt'ing līnz] **líneas secantes** Lines that cross each other at exactly one point
Example:

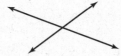

inverse operations [in'vûrs äp•ə•rā'shənz] **operaciones inversas** Operations that undo each other, such as addition and subtraction or multiplication and division
Example: $6 \times 8 = 48$ and $48 \div 6 = 8$

K

key [kē] **clave** The part of a map or graph that explains the symbols

kilogram (kg) [kil'ō•gram] **kilogramo (kg)** A metric unit for measuring mass
1 kilogram = 1,000 grams

kilometer (km) [kə•läm'ət•ər] **kilómetro (km)** A metric unit for measuring length or distance
1 kilometer = 1,000 meters

L

length [lengkth] **longitud** The measurement of the distance between two points

less than sign (<) [les <u>th</u>an sīn] **signo de menor que** A symbol used to compare two quantities, with the lesser quantity given first
Example: $3 < 7$

line [līn] **línea** A straight path of points in a plane that continues without end in both directions with no endpoints
Example:

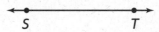
S   T

line graph [līn graf] **gráfica lineal** A graph that uses line segments to show how data change over time

line of symmetry [līn əv sim'ə•trē] **eje de simetría** An imaginary line on a shape about which the shape can be folded so that its two parts match exactly
Example:

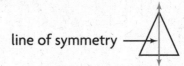
line of symmetry

line plot [līn plöt] **diagrama de puntos** A graph that records each piece of data on a number line
Example:

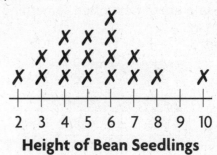
Height of Bean Seedlings

line segment [līn seg'mənt] **segmento** A part of a line that includes two points called endpoints and all the points between them
Example:

A   B

line symmetry [līn sim'ə•trē] **simetría axial** What a shape has if it can be folded about a line so that its two parts match exactly

linear units [lin'ē•ər yōo'nits] **unidades lineales** Units that measure length, width, height, or distance

liquid volume [lik'wid väl'yōom] **volumen de un líquido** The measure of the space a liquid occupies

liter (L) [lēt'ər] **litro (L)** A metric unit for measuring capacity and liquid volume
1 liter = 1,000 milliliters

mass [mas] **masa** The amount of matter in an object

meter (m) [mēt'ər] **metro (m)** A metric unit for measuring length or distance
1 meter = 100 centimeters

midnight [mid'nīt] **medianoche** 12:00 at night

mile (mi) [mīl] **milla (mi)** A customary unit for measuring length or distance
1 mile = 5,280 feet

milliliter (mL) [mil'i•lēt•ər] **mililitro (mL)** A metric unit for measuring capacity and liquid volume
1 liter = 1,000 milliliters

millimeter (mm) [mil'i•mēt•ər] **milímetro (mm)** A metric unit for measuring length or distance
1 centimeter = 10 millimeters

million [mil'yən] **millón** The counting number after 999,999; 1,000 thousands; written as 1,000,000

millions [mil'yənz] **millones** The period after thousands

minute (min) [min'it] **minuto (min)** A unit used to measure short amounts of time
1 minute = 60 seconds

mixed number [mikst num'bər] **número mixto** An amount given as a whole number and a fraction

multiple [mul'tə•pəl] **múltiplo** The product of a number and a counting number is called a multiple of the number
Example:

3	3	3	3	
× 1	× 2	× 3	× 4	← counting numbers
3	6	9	12	← multiples of 3

multiplication [mul•tə•pli•kā'shən] **multiplicación** A process to find the total number of items in equal-sized groups, or to find the total number of items in a given number of groups when each group contains the same number of items; multiplication is the inverse of division

multiply [mul'tə•plī] **multiplicar** To combine equal groups to find how many in all; the opposite operation of division

nickel [nik'əl] **moneda de 5¢** A coin worth 5 cents and with a value equal to that of 5 pennies; 5¢
Example:

noon [nōon] **mediodía** 12:00 in the day

not equal to sign (≠) [not ē'kwəl tōo sīn] **signo de no igual a** A symbol that indicates one quantity is not equal to another
Example: 12 × 3 ≠ 38

number line [num'bər līn] **recta numérica** A line on which numbers can be located
Example:

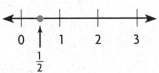

number sentence [num'bər sent'ns] **enunciado numérico** A sentence that includes numbers, operation symbols, and a greater than or less than symbol or an equal sign
Example: 5 + 3 = 8

numerator [nōō′mər•āt•ər] **numerador** The number above the bar in a fraction that tells how many parts of the whole or group are being considered

Example: $\frac{2}{3}$ ← numerator

O

obtuse angle [äb•tōōs′ ang′gəl] **ángulo obtuso** An angle that measures greater than 90° and less than 180°
Example:

Word History

The Latin prefix *ob-* means "against." When combined with *-tusus*, meaning "beaten," the Latin word *obtusus*, from which we get *obtuse*, means "beaten against." This makes sense when you look at an obtuse angle, because the angle is not sharp or acute. The angle looks as if it has been beaten against and become blunt and rounded.

---

obtuse triangle [äb•tōōs′ trī′ang•gəl] **triángulo obtusángulo** A triangle with one obtuse angle

Example:

octagon [äk′tə•gän] **octágono** A polygon with eight sides and eight angles
Examples:

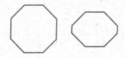

odd [od] **impar** A whole number that has a 1, 3, 5, 7, or 9 in the ones place

one-dimensional [wun də•men′shə•nəl] **unidimensional** Measured in only one direction, such as length
Examples:

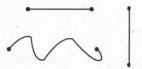

open shape [ō′pən shăp] **figura abierta** A shape that does not begin and end at the same point
Examples:

order [ôr′dər] **orden** A particular arrangement or placement of things one after the other

order of operations [ôr′dər əv äp•ə•rā′shənz] **orden de las operaciones** A special set of rules which gives the order in which calculations are done

ounce (oz) [ouns] **onza (oz)** A customary unit for measuring weight
1 pound = 16 ounces

P

parallel lines [pâr′ə•lel līnz] **líneas paralelas** Lines in the same plane that never intersect and are always the same distance apart
Example:

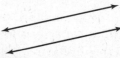

Word History

Euclid, an early Greek mathematician, was one of the first to explore the idea of parallel lines. The prefix *para-* means "beside or alongside." This prefix helps you understand the meaning of the word *parallel*.

---

parallelogram [pâr•ə•lel'ə•gram] **paralelogramo** A quadrilateral whose opposite sides are parallel and of equal length
Example:

parentheses [pə•ren'thə•sēz] **paréntesis** The symbols used to show which operation or operations in an expression should be done first

partial product [pär'shəl präd'əkt] **producto parcial** A method of multiplying in which the ones, tens, hundreds, and so on are multiplied separately and then the products are added together

partial quotient [pär'shəl kwō'shənt] **cociente parcial** A method of dividing in which multiples of the divisor are subtracted from the dividend and then the quotients are added together

pattern [pat'ərn] **patrón** An ordered set of numbers or objects; the order helps you predict what will come next
Examples: 2, 4, 6, 8, 10

pattern unit [pat'ərn yōō'nit] **unidad de patrón** The part of a pattern that repeats
Example:

pattern unit

pentagon [pen'tə•gän] **pentágono** A polygon with five sides and five angles
Examples:

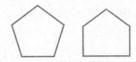

perimeter [pə•rim'ə•tər] **perímetro** The distance around a shape

period [pir'ē•əd] **período** Each group of three digits in a multi-digit number; periods are usually separated by commas or spaces.
Example: 85,643,900 has three periods.

perpendicular lines [pər•pən•dik'yōō•lər līnz] **líneas perpendiculares** Two lines that intersect to form four right angles
Example:

picture graph [pik'chər graf] **gráfica con dibujos** A graph that uses symbols to show and compare information
Example:

pint (pt) [pīnt] **pinta (pt)** A customary unit for measuring capacity and liquid volume
1 pint = 2 cups

place value [plās val'yōō] **valor posicional** The value of a digit in a number, based on the location of the digit

plane [plān] **plano** A flat surface that extends without end in all directions
Example:

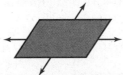

plane shape [plān shāp] **figura plana** See *two-dimensional figure.*

P.M. [pē•em] **p.m.** The times after noon and before midnight

point [point] **punto** An exact location in space

polygon [päl'i•gän] **polígono** A closed two-dimensional shape formed by three or more straight sides that are line segments
Examples:

Polygons   Not Polygons

pound (lb) [pound] **libra (lb)** A customary unit for measuring weight
1 pound = 16 ounces

prime number [prīm num'bər] **número primo** A number that has exactly two factors: 1 and itself
Examples: 2, 3, 5, 7, 11, 13, 17, and 19 are prime numbers. 1 is not a prime number.

prism [priz'əm] **prisma** A solid figure that has two same size, same polygon-shaped bases, and other faces that are all rectangles
Examples:

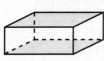

rectangular prism   triangular prism

product [präd'əkt] **producto** The answer to a multiplication problem

protractor [prō'trak•tər] **transportador** A tool for measuring the size of an angle

quadrilateral [kwä•dri•lat'ər•əl] **cuadrilátero** A polygon with four sides and four angles

quart (qt) [kwôrt] **cuarto (ct)** A customary unit for measuring capacity and liquid volume
1 quart = 2 pints

quarter hour [kwôrt'ər our] **cuarto de hora**
15 minutes
Example: 4:00 to 4:15 is one quarter hour

quotient [kwō'shənt] **cociente** The number, not including the remainder, that results from dividing
Example: 8 ÷ 4 = 2; 2 is the quotient.

ray [rā] **semirrecta** A part of a line; it has one endpoint and continues without end in one direction
Example:

rectangle [rek'tang•gəl] **rectángulo** A quadrilateral with two pairs of parallel sides, two pairs of sides of equal length, and four right angles
Example:

rectangular prism [rek•tang'gyə•lər priz'əm] **prisma rectangular** A three-dimensional shape in which all six faces are rectangles
Example:

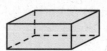

regroup [rē•grōōp'] **reagrupar** To exchange amounts of equal value to rename a number
Example: 5 + 8 = 13 ones or 1 ten 3 ones

regular polygon [reg'yə•lər päl'i•gän] **polígono regular** A polygon that has all sides that are equal in length and all angles equal in measure
Examples:

related facts [ri•lāt'id fakts] **operaciones relacionadas** A set of related addition and subtraction, or multiplication and division, number sentences
Examples: 4 × 7 = 28   28 ÷ 4 = 7
7 × 4 = 28   28 ÷ 7 = 4

remainder [ri•mān'dər] **residuo** The amount left over when a number cannot be divided equally

rhombus [räm'bəs] **rombo** A quadrilateral with two pairs of parallel sides and four sides of equal length
Example:

right angle [rīt ang'gəl] **ángulo recto** An angle that forms a square corner
Example:

right triangle [rīt trī'ang•gəl] **triángulo rectángulo**
A triangle with one right angle
Example:

round [round] **redondear** To replace a number with another number that tells about how many or how much

rule [rōōl] **regla** A procedure (usually involving arithmetic operations) to determine an output value from an input value

scale [skāl] **escala** A series of numbers placed at fixed distances on a graph to help label the graph

second (sec) [sek'ənd] **segundo (seg)** A small unit of time
1 minute = 60 seconds

simplest form [sim'pləst fôrm] **mínima expresión**
A fraction is in simplest form when the numerator and denominator have only 1 as a common factor

solid shape [sä'lid shāp] **cuerpo geométrico**
See *three-dimensional figure.*

square [skwâr] **cuadrado** A quadrilateral with two pairs of parallel sides, four sides of equal length, and four right angles
Example:

square unit [skwâr yōō'nit] **unidad cuadrada**
A unit of area with dimensions of
1 unit × 1 unit

standard form [stan'dərd fôrm] **forma normal**
A way to write numbers by using the digits 0–9, with each digit having a place value *Example:*
3,540 ← standard form

straight angle [strāt ang'gəl] **ángulo llano** An angle whose measure is 180°
Example:

subtraction [səb•trak'shən] **resta** The process of finding how many are left when a number of items are taken away from a group of items; the process of finding the difference when two groups are compared; the opposite operation of addition

sum [sum] **suma o total** The answer to an addition problem

survey [sûr'vā] **encuesta** A method of gathering information

tally table [tal'ē tā'bəl] **tabla de conteo** A table that uses tally marks to record data

> **Word History**
>
> Some people keep score in card games by making marks on paper (IIII). These marks are known as tally marks. The word *tally* is related to *tailor*, from the Latin *talea*, meaning "twig." In early times, a method of keeping count was by cutting marks into a piece of wood or bone.

temperature [tem'pər•ə•chər] **temperatura** The degree of hotness or coldness usually measured in degrees Fahrenheit or degrees Celsius

tenth [tenth] **décimo** One of ten equal parts
Example:

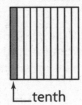

tenth

term [tûrm] **término** A number or object in a pattern

thousands [thou'zəndz] **miles** The period after the ones period in the base-ten number system

three-dimensional [thrē də•men′shə•nəl] **tridimensional** Measured in three directions, such as length, width, and height
Example:

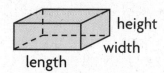

three-dimensional figure [thrē də•men′shə•nəl fig′yər] **figura tridimensional** A figure having length, width, and height

ton (T) [tun] **tonelada (t)** A customary unit used to measure weight
1 ton = 2,000 pounds

trapezoid [trap′i•zoid] **trapecio** A quadrilateral with at least one pair of parallel sides
Examples:

triangle [trī′ang•gəl] **triángulo** A polygon with three sides and three angles
Examples:

two-dimensional [tōō də•men′shə•nəl] **bidimensional** Measured in two directions, such as length and width
Example:

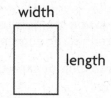

two-dimensional figure [tōō də•men′shə•nəl fig′yər] **figura bidimensional** A figure that lies in a plane; a shape having length and width

unit fraction [yōō′nit frak′shən] **fracción unitaria** A fraction that has a numerator of one

variable [vâr′ē•ə•bəl] **variable** A letter or symbol that stands for a number or numbers

Venn diagram [ven dī′ə•gram] **diagrama de Venn** A diagram that shows relationships among sets of things
Example:

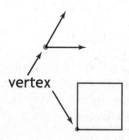

vertex [vûr′teks] **vértice** The point at which two rays of an angle meet or two (or more) line segments meet in a two-dimensional shape
Examples:

vertical [vûr′ti•kəl] **vertical** In the direction from top to bottom

weight [wāt] **peso** How heavy an object is

whole [hōl] **entero** All of the parts of a shape or group

word form [wûrd fôrm] **en palabras** A way to write numbers by using words
Example: Four hundred fifty-three thousand, two hundred twelve

yard (yd) [yärd] **yarda (yd)** A customary unit for measuring length or distance
1 yard = 3 feet

Z

Zero Property of Multiplication [zē′rō präp′ər•tē əv mul•tə•pli•kā′shən] **propiedad del cero de la multiplicación** The property that states that the product of 0 and any number is 0
Example: $0 \times 8 = 0$

Index

Clocks
    analog, 602, 685–688
    elapsed time, 691–694

Clockwise, 601–604

Combined rectangles, 729–732

Common denominators, 345–348, 365–368, 409–412, 527–530

Common factors, 291–294
    fractions in simplest form using, 340

Common multiples, 299–302, 345–348

Common numerators, 365–368

Communicate Math Ideas
    Math Talk, In every Student Edition
    lesson. Some examples are: 5, 12, 64,
    82, 114, 132, 177, 209, 228, 279, 299,
    328, 359, 386, 429, 455, 495, 520, 556,
    602, 642, 723
    Read Math, 555, 685
    Write Math, In every Student Edition
    lesson. Some examples are: 8, 40, 96,
    116, 224, 288, 348, 420, 510, 530, 682

Commutative Property
    of Addition, 39, 435–438
    of Multiplication, 63–66, 107–110, 171

Comparing
    decimals, 533–536
    fractions, 359–362, 365–368, 371–374
    measurement units, 647–650, 653–656,
      659–662, 673–676, 679–682, 685–688
    whole numbers, 17–20

Comparison problems, 49–52, 69–72, 481–484

Compatible numbers, 152, 221–223

Composite numbers, 305–307

Connect, 99, 163, 260, 435, 607, 703

Connect to Art, 400, 424

Connect to Reading, 84, 224

Connect to Science, 26, 218, 510, 616, 688, 740

Connect to Social Studies, 308

Counterclockwise, 601–604

Counters, 203–206, 235, 236

Counting numbers, 197, 455–458, 461–464

Cross-Curricular Activities and Connections
    Connect to Art, 400, 570
    Connect to Reading, 84, 224

Connect to Science, 26, 218, 510, 616, 688, 740

Connect to Social Studies, 308

Cup, 659

Customary units
    benchmarks, 641-644
    converting, 647–650, 653–656, 659–662
    of distance, 641
    of length, 641, 647–650
    of liquid volume, 641, 659–662
    of weight, 641, 653–656

D

Data
    gathering, 26
    using
      bar graphs, 116
      line plots, 665–668
      tables. *See* Tables
      tally tables, 665–668, 671
      Venn diagrams, 196, 556, 558, 568, 716

Days, 686

Decimal point, 495

Decimals
    comparing
      using models, 533–536
      using place value, 533–536
    defined, 495
    equivalent decimals
      defined, 508
      modeling, 507–510
    hundredths, 501–504, 507–510
    place value and, 495–498, 501–504,
      534–536
    relating
      to fractions, 495–498, 501–504,
        507–510, 513–516, 527–530
      to mixed numbers, 495–497, 501–503,
        509, 514–515
      to money, 513–516
    tenths, 495–498, 507–510

Decimeters, 673

Degrees
    angle measures and, 607–610

Denominators, 365–368

© Houghton Mifflin Harcourt Publishing Company

© Houghton Mifflin Harcourt Publishing Company

renaming as mixed numbers, 417–420, 476
simplest form, 339–342
subtraction
  like denominators, 409–412, 423–426
  mixed numbers, 423–426
  modeling, 385–388, 403–406, 409–412, 429–432
  with renaming, 429–432

G

Gallon, 659–662

Geometry. *See also* Two-dimensional figures
angles, 549–552
  acute, 550, 555, 608, 615
  angle equations, 622–623, 627–630, 631–632
  classify triangles by size of, 555–558
  find unknown measures, 737–740
  measure and draw, 613–616
  obtuse, 550, 555, 608, 615
  right, 550, 555, 567, 608, 723
  turns on a clock and angle measures, 602, 603, 685
hexagons, 581
lines, 549–552
  parallel, 561–564
  perpendicular, 561–564
polygons, 555–558, 567–570
quadrilaterals, 567–570
  classifying, 567–570
rays, 549–552
rectangles, 567–569
shape patterns, 587–590
squares, 567–569, 581
symmetry
  lines of symmetry, 581–584
  line symmetry, 575–578, 581–584
trapezoids, 567–569, 581
triangles, 555–558
  classifying, 555–558

Glossary, Multimedia. *See* Multimedia eGlossary

Go Deeper, In some Student Edition lessons. Some examples are: 19, 90, 229, 262, 294, 388, 444, 463, 536, 609, 687

Grams, 679–682

Graphic Organizers. *See also* Tables

Brainstorming Diagram, 640
Bubble Map, 384, 454, 600
Flow Map, 62, 278, 326, 548
H-Diagram, 144
problem solving, 49–51, 113–114, 183–184, 291–292, 351–352, 441–442, 481–482, 519–520, 587–588, 627–628, 691–692, 743–744
Semantic Map, 494
Venn diagram, 196, 556, 558, 568, 716

Graphs. *See also* Data
bar graphs, 116
line plots, 665–668
Venn diagrams, 196, 556, 558, 568, 716

Greater than (>), 17–18, 151, 153, 259

Grid, 38, 44, 87, 89, 157, 227, 229, 235, 305, 306, 729

H

Half gallon, 659

Half hour, 685–688

Height, 723–726, 737, 739

Hexagons, 581

Hours
elapsed time and, 691–694
half, 685–688
minutes after the hour, 685, 692

Hundreds, 11–14
addition, 37–40
multiply by whole numbers, 75–78, 125
place value, 5–8, 11–14, 37–40
subtraction, 43–46

Hundred thousands, 11–14
addition, 37–40
place value, 5–8, 11–14, 37–40
rounding, 23
subtraction, 43–46

Hundredths, 501–504, 507–510

I

Identity Property of Multiplication, 476

Inches, 647–650

Interpret remainders, 209–212

© Houghton Mifflin Harcourt Publishing Company

Intersecting lines, 561–564

Intervention
  Show What You Know, 3, 61, 143, 195, 277, 325, 383, 453, 493, 547, 599, 639, 715
  Introduce the Chapter, 3, 61, 143, 195, 277, 325, 383, 453, 493, 547, 599, 639, 715

Inverse operations
  addition and subtraction, 44, 50
  multiplication and division, 260

Investigate, 31, 87–88, 157–158, 203–204, 227–228, 235–236, 247–248, 327–328, 385–386, 601–602, 621–622

iTools. *See* Technology and Digital Resources

Kilograms, 679–682
Kilometers, 642, 643

Length
  area and unknown measures, 737–740
  convert customary units, 641, 647–650
  convert metric units, 673–676
  customary units for, 641, 647–650
  measuring and estimating, 641–644, 673–676
  metric units for, 642, 673–676
  perimeter and unknown measures, 737–740

Less than (<), 17–18, 151, 153, 253, 469
Line plots, 665–668
Line segment, 549–552, 723
Lines of symmetry, 581–584
Line symmetry, 575–578, 581–584
Linear models. *See* Number lines
Lines, 549–552
  draw, 562–563
  intersecting, 561–564
  parallel, 561–564
  perpendicular, 561–564, 723
Liquid volume, 641–642, 659–662, 679–682, 704
Liters, 679–682

Make a Table or List. *See* Problem-solving strategies
Make Connections, 32, 88, 158, 204, 228, 236, 248, 328, 386, 602, 622, 674
Manipulatives and materials
  base-ten blocks, 5–8, 31, 247–250
  bills and coins, 519–522
  color pencils, 87, 227, 327, 339, 385, 555
  construction paper, 621
  counters, 203–206, 235, 236
  decimal models, 513–514
  dot paper, 581
  fraction circles, 385, 601
  fraction strips, 359, 397–398, 404
  grid paper, 87, 163, 227, 235, 647, 729
  MathBoard. *See* MathBoard
  number line, 18, 23, 25
  pattern blocks, 575–576, 582
  place-value chart, 6, 11, 17, 32–33, 495–496, 501–502
  protractors, 613–616, 621–627
  rulers, centimeter, 673
  scissors, 575, 621
  square tiles, 279
  tracing paper, 575
Mass
  converting metric units, 679–682
  measuring, 679–682
  metric units for, 642, 679–682
MathBoard, In every Student Edition lesson. Some examples are: 7, 44, 100, 132, 172, 198, 222, 280, 329, 387, 457, 497, 551, 603, 643, 719
Math Idea, 24, 44, 253, 279, 285, 306, 371, 575, 607, 621, 673, 724
Math Processes and Practices
  1. Problem Solving. In many lessons. Some examples are: 43, 49, 63, 81, 113, 125, 131, 151, 163, 171, 183, 197, 227, 247, 265, 291, 351, 403, 423, 429, 441, 475, 481, 501, 567, 581, 601, 613, 621, 627, 641, 673, 685, 691, 717, 729, 737, 743

2. Abstract and Quantitative Reasoning. In many lessons. Some examples are: 11, 17, 23, 31, 63, 69, 75, 113, 119, 131, 145, 151, 157, 163, 221, 241, 247, 279, 297, 311, 333, 359, 365, 385, 391, 397, 403, 409, 417, 423, 435, 441, 461, 495, 501, 507, 513, 519, 527, 533, 567, 575, 601, 607, 641, 647, 653, 665, 723, 737

3. Use and Evaluate Logical Reasoning. In many lessons. Some examples are: 43, 87, 119, 125, 131, 209, 221, 253, 285, 365, 391, 397, 441, 575, 581, 601, 641, 647, 659, 665, 679, 697, 703

4. Mathematical Modeling. In many lessons. Some examples are: 11, 23, 49, 87, 99, 113, 145, 157, 183, 227, 247, 265, 279, 285, 327, 333, 345, 351, 385, 403, 429, 441, 455, 469, 513, 549, 561, 621, 627, 647, 659, 665, 673, 685, 691, 743

5. Use Mathematical Tools. In many lessons. Some examples are: 5, 31, 75, 197, 215, 235, 259, 265, 311, 327, 333, 365, 495, 587, 613, 685, 691

6. Use Precise Mathematical Language. In many lessons. Some examples are: 5, 23, 37, 63, 87, 99, 125, 151, 157, 177, 215, 221, 235, 241, 299, 339, 345, 351, 359, 403, 409, 417, 455, 495, 507, 513, 519, 533, 555, 561, 587, 607, 613, 653, 659, 703, 723, 729

7. See Structure. In many lessons. Some examples are: 11, 31, 75, 81, 119, 145, 171, 177, 197, 209, 215, 227, 253, 285, 299, 311, 327, 339, 345, 359, 409, 417, 429, 455, 461, 481, 501, 507, 527, 555, 561, 587, 607, 641, 659, 673, 685, 703, 717, 737

8. Generalize. In many lessons. Some examples are: 37, 43, 49, 163, 171, 177, 209, 241, 259, 299, 391, 417, 423, 435, 461, 475, 527, 673, 697, 717

Math in the Real World Activities, 3, 61, 143, 195, 277, 325, 383, 453, 493, 547, 599, 639, 715

Math on the Spot Videos, In every Student Edition lesson. Some examples are: 8, 46, 90, 116, 148, 217, 244, 281, 330, 388, 426, 458, 498, 552, 604, 649, 720

Math Talk, In every Student Edition lesson. Some examples are: 5, 12, 64, 82, 114, 132, 177, 209, 228, 279, 299, 328, 359, 386, 429, 455, 495, 520, 556, 602, 642, 723

Measurement
angles
and fractional parts of circle, 601–604
joining and separating, 621–624
measuring and drawing, 613–616
solving for unknown angle measures, 627–630
area, 723–726, 743–746
of combined rectangles, 729–732
concept of, 723–726
defined, 723
finding, 723–726, 729–732, 743–746
finding unknown measures, 737–740
formula for, 723–726
perimeter, related to, 731
of a rectangle, 723–726, 729–732
square unit, 723
units of, 723–726
benchmarks, 641–644
centimeter, 642–644
cup, 641
decimeter, 642
fluid ounce, 641
foot, 641, 643
gallon, 641, 643
gram, 642–643
inch, 641, 643
kilogram, 642–643
kilometer, 642–643
liter, 642–643
meter, 642–643
mile, 641, 643
milliliter, 642–644
millimeter, 642
ounce, 641, 643
pint, 641
pound, 641, 643
quart, 641
ton, 641, 643
yard, 641, 643
comparing, 642, 647–650, 653–656, 659–662, 685–688

concept of, 641
conversions, 641–644, 647–650, 653–656,
    659–662, 673–676, 679–682, 685–688,
    691–694, 697–700, 703–706, 717–720,
    723–726, 729–732, 737–740, 743–746
customary units
    benchmarks, 641–644
    of distance, 641
    of length, 641, 647–650
    of liquid volumes, 641, 659–662
    of weight, 641, 653–656
degrees (of a circle), 607–610
line plots, 665–668
mass, 642, 679–682
metric units
    benchmarks, 642–644
    converting, 673–676, 679–682
    of distance, 642
    of length, 642, 673–676
    of liquid volume, 679–682
    of mass, 642, 679–682
mixed measures, 697–700
money problems, 519–522
patterns in measurement units, 703–706
perimeter, 717–720
    defined, 717
    finding, 717–720
    finding unknown measures, 737–740
    formulas for, 717–720
    measuring, 737–740
    of a rectangle, 717–720
    of a square, 717–720
time
    elapsed, 691–694
    units of, 685–688

Mental Math, 81, 107–110, 151–152,
    435–438

Meters, 673–676

Metric units
    benchmarks, 642–644
    converting, 673–676, 679–682
    of distance, 642
    of length, 642, 673–676
    of liquid volume, 679–682
    of mass, 642, 679–682

Mid-Chapter Checkpoint, 29–30, 105–106,
    169–170, 233–234, 297–298, 357–358,
    415–416, 467–468, 525–526, 573–574,
    619–620, 671–672, 735–736

Miles, 641–643

Milliliters, 642–644, 679–682

Millimeters, 673–676

Millions
    place value and, 5–8

Minutes. *See also* Time
    elapsed time and, 691–694

Mixed measures, 697–700

Mixed numbers
    addition, 423–426
    decimals, related to, 496–498, 501–503,
        509, 514–515
    defined, 417
    modeling, 417–418, 429, 502
    multiply by a whole number, 475–478
    renaming as fractions, 417–420, 476
    subtraction, 423–426, 429–432
    subtraction with renaming, 429–432

Modeling
    area models
        decimals and, 495, 513–516
        fractions and, 327–330, 333–336,
            351–354, 359–362
    bar models, 49–52, 183–186, 265–268,
        481–484, 627–630, 659–662
    Distributive Property, 87–90, 99–101,
        108–109
    division
        with base-ten blocks, 247–249
        with counters, 203–206, 235
        draw a diagram, 265–268
        with quick pictures, 203–206, 209–212,
            247–250
        using inverse operations, 227–230,
            259–262
    equations, 131–134
    fractions
        addition, 385–388, 391–394, 397–400,
            409–412, 423–426, 435–438
        equivalent, 327–330, 333–336,
            339–342, 345–348, 351–354,
            507–510
        mixed numbers, 417–420, 423–426,
            429–432, 435–438, 475–478
        subtraction, 403–406, 409–411,
            429–432
    multiples of ten, hundred, and thousand,
        75–78
    multiplication, 63–66, 69–72
        facts, 61, 143, 277
        by one-digit numbers, 87–90, 93–96,
            99–102, 119–122
        with quick pictures, 75–78
        by two-digit numbers, 87–90, 119–122,
            157–160, 163–166, 171–174, 177–180

quick pictures
  to model division, 203–206, 248–250
  to model multiplication, 75–78

Money
  relating
    to decimals, 513–516
    to fractions, 513–516

Multimedia eGlossary, 4, 62, 144, 196, 278, 326, 384, 454, 494, 548, 600, 640, 716

Multiples
  common, 299–302
  defined, 197
  estimate quotients using, 197–200
  factors and, 299–302
  of fractions, 461–464
  of unit fractions, 455–458

Multiplication
  area model, 157–160
  arrays, 61
  bar models, 183–186
  comparison problems, 63–66
  draw a diagram, 183–186, 265–268
  equations, 63–66, 131–134, 470, 475–478
  estimating products, 81–83, 99–102, 151–154
  expanded form, 93–96
  expressions, 131–134
  factors, 279–282
  to find equivalent fractions, 333–336
  four-digit numbers, 126–128
  fractions and whole numbers, 461–464, 475–478
  halving-and-doubling strategy, 108, 146
  as inverse of division, 737–740
  mental math, 107–110
  modeling, 186, 203–206
    one-digit numbers, 87–90, 93–96, 99–102, 119–122
    with quick pictures, 75–78
    two-digit numbers, 87–90, 119–122
    by two-digit numbers, 157–160, 163–166, 171–174, 177–180
  multiples of unit fractions, 455–458
  by multiples of 10, 100, and 1,000, 75–78
  by one-digit numbers, 87–90, 93–96, 99–102, 119–122
  partial products, 99–102, 157–160, 163–166, 177
  products, 76–77, 81–83, 99–102, 151–154, 157–160
  properties
    Associative Property of Multiplication, 107–110, 145–148

Commutative Property of Multiplication, 63, 107–110, 171
Distributive Property, 87–90, 99–101, 108–109, 227–230, 718
Identity Property of Multiplication, 476
quotient estimation, 197–200
reasonableness of answers, 82–83
regrouping in, 119–122, 125–128, 171–174, 178–179
by tens, 145–148
three-digit numbers, 125–128
two-digit numbers, 87–90, 119–122
by two-digit numbers, 157–160, 163–166, 171–174, 177–180

Multistep word problems, 113–116, 131–134, 183–186, 265–268

Ⓝ

Not equal to sign (≠), 328
Number lines
  to compare decimals, 533
  to compare fractions, 371–373
  to compare numbers, 18
  to divide, 236–237
  to find multiples of fractions, 462
  to multiply, 76, 146
  to order fractions, 371–374, 665–668
  to order numbers, 18
  to round numbers, 23
  to show equivalent decimals, 501
  to show equivalent fractions and decimals, 501

Number patterns, 311–314, 587–590

Numbers. See also Counting numbers; Decimals; Fractions; Mixed numbers; Whole numbers
  benchmark, 359–362, 641–644
  comparing
    decimals, 533–536
    whole numbers, 17–20
  compatible, 152, 221–223
  composite, 305–307
  expanded form, whole numbers, 11–14
  factors of, 279–282, 291–294
  multiples of, 197–200, 299–302
  ordering
    fractions, 371–374
    whole numbers, 17–20
  place value, 5–8, 11–14, 17–20, 23–26
  prime, 305–307

read and write, 11–14
renaming, 31–34
rounding, 23–26
standard form, whole numbers, 11–14
word form, whole numbers, 11–14

Numbers and Operations
adding, 37–40. *See also* Addition
comparing, 17–20
decimals, 533–536
division. *See also* Division
and Distributive Property, 227–230
estimating quotients using compatible numbers, 221–224
estimating quotients using multiples, 197–200
placing first digit, 253–256
with regrouping, 247–250, 253–256, 259–262
remainders, 203–206, 209–212
tens, hundreds, and thousands, 215–218
using bar models to solve multistep problems, 265–268
using partial quotients, 241–244
using repeated subtraction, 235–238
fractions. *See also* Fractions
adding fractional parts of 10 and 100, 527–530
common denominators, 345–348
comparing, 359–362, 365–368, 371–374
using benchmarks, 359–362
comparison problems with, 481–484
equivalent, 327–330, 333–336, 351–354
and decimals, 507–510
multiples of, 461–464
unit fractions, 455–458
multiplying by whole number, 469–472, 475–478
using models, 469–472
ordering, 371–374
relating decimals, money and, 513–516
relating hundredths and decimals, 501–504
relating tenths and decimals, 495–498
simplest form, 339–342
multiplication. *See also* Multiplication
area models and partial products, 157–160
choosing method for, 177–180
estimating products, strategies for, 151–154

by tens, strategies for, 145–148
using Distributive Property, 87–90
using expanded form, 93–96
using mental math, 107–110
using partial products, 99–102, 163–166
using regrouping, 119–128, 171–174
ordering, 17–20
place value, 5–26, 31–52, 75–78. *See also* Place value
renaming, 31–34
rounding, 23–26, 81–84
subtracting, 43–46. *See also* Subtraction

O

Obtuse angles, 550–552, 555–558
Obtuse triangles, 555–558
Odd numbers, 312
One-digit numbers
multiplication
four-digit by one-digit, 94–96, 125–128
three-digit by one-digit, 93–96, 99–101, 125–128
two-digit by one-digit, 87–90, 119–122
Ones
addition, 37–40
place value, 5–8
subtraction, 43–46
On Your Own, In every Student Edition lesson. Some examples are: 7, 44, 83, 121, 153, 222, 281, 335, 431, 457, 497, 551, 609, 667, 719, 746
Operations and Algebraic Thinking, 63–66, 69–72, 113–116, 131–134
division
interpreting remainders, 209–212
multistep problems, 265–268
factors
common, solving problems with, 291–294
and divisibility, 285–288
modeling, 279–282
and multiples, 299–302
multiplication
comparison problems, 63–66, 69–72
multistep problems, 113–116
two-digit numbers, 183–186
number patterns, 311–314
prime and composite numbers, 305–308

unit squares, 723
units of, 723–726
find a pattern, 587–590
hexagons, 581
identifying, 549–552, 555–558, 561–564, 567–570, 575–578, 581–584
parallelograms, 567–570, 581
perimeter
    area, related to, 723–726
    defined, 717
    finding, 717–720
    find unknown measures and, 737–740
    formulas for, 717–720
    measuring, 737–740
    of a rectangle, 717–720
    of a square, 717–720
polygons, 555–558, 567, 581
quadrilaterals, 567–570
rectangles, 567–570, 581
rhombus, 567–570, 581
shape patterns, 587–590
squares, 567–570, 581
symmetry
    lines of symmetry, 575–584
    line symmetry, 575–584
trapezoids, 567–570, 581
triangles, 555–558. *See also* Triangles

Understand Vocabulary, 4, 62, 144, 196, 278, 326, 384, 454, 494, 548, 600, 640, 716

Unit fractions, 391–394, 455–458

Unit squares, 723

Unlock the Problem, In every Student Edition lesson. Some examples are: 11, 49–50, 93–94, 151–152, 209–210, 279, 345, 394, 429–430, 455–456, 495–496, 533, 549–550, 578, 647–648, 717–718

Unlock the Problem Tips, 51, 115, 185, 267, 293, 353, 443, 483, 521, 589, 693, 745

Venn diagrams, 556, 558, 568, 716

Vertex, 550, 555, 575, 601, 613

Visualize It, 4, 62, 144, 196, 278, 326, 384, 454, 494, 548, 600, 640, 716

Vocabulary
Chapter Vocabulary Cards, At the beginning of every chapter.
Mid-Chapter Checkpoint, 29, 105, 169, 233, 297, 357, 415, 467, 525, 573, 619, 671, 735
Multimedia eGlossary, 4, 62, 144, 196, 278, 326, 384, 454, 494, 548, 600, 640, 716
Vocabulary, 29, 105, 233, 297, 357, 415, 467, 525, 573, 619, 671, 735
Vocabulary Builder, 4, 62, 144, 196, 278, 326, 384, 454, 494, 548, 600, 640, 716
Vocabulary Games, 4A, 62A, 144A, 196A, 278A, 326A, 384A, 454A, 494A, 548A, 600A, 640A, 716A

Week, 686–687, 703

Weight, 641, 653–656

What If, 51, 115, 185, 211, 267, 339, 353, 391, 392, 398, 443, 461, 483, 521, 522, 589, 622, 629, 648, 666, 691, 693, 697, 737, 745

What's the Error?, 13, 19, 46, 96, 134, 148, 206, 330, 409, 478, 706

What's the Question?, 20, 342, 362, 478

Whole numbers
adding, 37–40
comparing, 17–20
multiply fractions and, 469–472, 475–478
ordering, 17–20
place value, 5–8, 11–14, 17–20
renaming, 31–34
rounding, 23–26
subtracting, 43–46

Word form
whole numbers, 11–14

Write Math, In every Student Edition lesson. Some examples are: 96, 116, 224, 510, 530, 682

Writing
Write Math, In every Student Edition lesson. Some examples are: 96, 116, 224, 510, 530, 682

Yards, 641, 643, 647–650, 703

Table of Measures

METRIC | CUSTOMARY

Length

METRIC

1 centimeter (cm) = 10 millimeters (mm)

1 meter (m) = 1,000 millimeters

1 meter = 100 centimeters

1 meter = 10 decimeters (dm)

1 kilometer (km) = 1,000 meters

CUSTOMARY

1 foot (ft) = 12 inches (in.)

1 yard (yd) = 3 feet, or 36 inches

1 mile (mi) = 1,760 yards, or 5,280 feet

Capacity and Liquid Volume

METRIC

1 liter (L) = 1,000 milliliters (mL)

CUSTOMARY

1 cup (c) = 8 fluid ounces (fl oz)

1 pint (pt) = 2 cups

1 quart (qt) = 2 pints, or 4 cups

1 half gallon = 2 quarts

1 gallon (gal) = 2 half gallons, or 4 quarts

Mass/Weight

METRIC

1 kilogram (kg) = 1,000 grams (g)

CUSTOMARY

1 pound (lb) = 16 ounces (oz)

1 ton (T) = 2,000 pounds

TIME

1 minute (min) = 60 seconds (sec)

1 half hour = 30 minutes

1 hour (hr) = 60 minutes

1 day (d) = 24 hours

1 week (wk) = 7 days

1 year (yr) = 12 months (mo), or about 52 weeks

1 year = 365 days

1 leap year = 366 days

1 decade = 10 years

1 century = 100 years

MONEY

1 penny = 1¢, or $0.01

1 nickel = 5¢, or $0.05

1 dime = 10¢, or $0.10

1 quarter = 25¢, or $0.25

1 half dollar = 50¢, or $0.50

1 dollar = 100¢, or $1.00

SYMBOLS

$<$	is less than	$\perp$	is perpendicular to
$>$	is greater than	$\parallel$	is parallel to
$=$	is equal to	$\overleftrightarrow{AB}$	line AB
$\neq$	is not equal to	$\overrightarrow{AB}$	ray AB
¢	cent or cents	$\overline{AB}$	line segment AB
$	dollar or dollars	$\angle ABC$	angle ABC or angle B
°	degree or degrees	$\triangle ABC$	triangle ABC

FORMULAS

	Perimeter		Area
Polygon	P = sum of the lengths of sides	Rectangle	$A = b \times h$
			$A = l \times w$
Rectangle	$P = (2 \times l) + (2 \times w)$ or $P = 2 \times (l + w)$		
Square	$P = 4 \times s$		

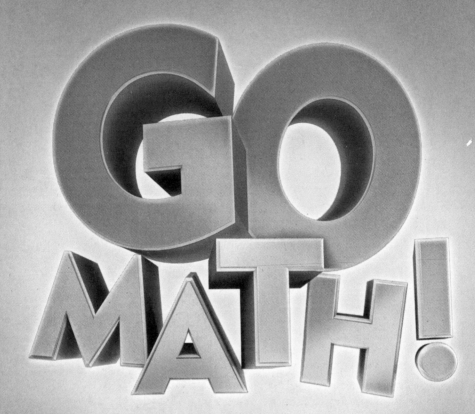

GO MATH!

Volume 2

Houghton
Mifflin
Harcourt

Made in the United States
Text printed on 100%
recycled paper

Houghton
Mifflin
Harcourt

GO MATH!

2017 Edition

Copyright © by Houghton Mifflin Harcourt Publishing Company

Printed in the U.S.A.

ISBN 978-0-544-71061-0

15 0928 24 23 22

4500842439   D E F G

Dear Students and Families,

Welcome to **Go Math!**, Grade 4! In this exciting mathematics program, there are hands-on activities to do and real-world problems to solve. Best of all, you will write your ideas and answers right in your book. In **Go Math!**, writing and drawing on the pages helps you think deeply about what you are learning, and you will really understand math!

By the way, all of the pages in your **Go Math!** book are made using recycled paper. We wanted you to know that you can Go Green with **Go Math!**

Sincerely,

The Authors

Made in the United States
Text printed on 100% recycled paper

GO MATH!

Authors

Juli K. Dixon, Ph.D.
Professor, Mathematics Education
University of Central Florida
Orlando, Florida

Edward B. Burger, Ph.D.
President, Southwestern University
Georgetown, Texas

Steven J. Leinwand
Principal Research Analyst
American Institutes for
  Research (AIR)
Washington, D.C.

Contributor

Rena Petrello
Professor, Mathematics
Moorpark College
Moorpark, CA

Matthew R. Larson, Ph.D.
K-12 Curriculum Specialist for
  Mathematics
Lincoln Public Schools
Lincoln, Nebraska

Martha E. Sandoval-Martinez
Math Instructor
El Camino College
Torrance, California

English Language Learners Consultant

Elizabeth Jiménez
CEO, GEMAS Consulting
Professional Expert on English
  Learner Education
Bilingual Education and
  Dual Language
Pomona, California

VOLUME 1
Place Value and Operations with Whole Numbers

Big Idea Develop a conceptual understanding of multi-digit multiplication, and division, including addition and subtraction to one million. Develop factors, multiples, and number patterns.

Big Idea

GO DIGITAL

Go online! Your math lessons are interactive. Use *i*Tools, Animated Math Models, the Multimedia eGlossary, and more.

Chapter 1 Overview

In this chapter, you will explore and discover answers to the following **Essential Questions**:

- How can you use place value to compare, add, subtract, and estimate with whole numbers?
- How do you compare and order whole numbers?
- What are some strategies you can use to round whole numbers?
- How is adding and subtracting 5- and 6-digit numbers similar to adding and subtracting 3-digit numbers?

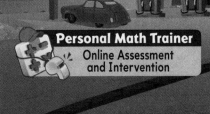

Personal Math Trainer
Online Assessment and Intervention

Practice and Homework

Lesson Check and Spiral Review in every lesson

© Houghton Mifflin Harcourt Publishing Company

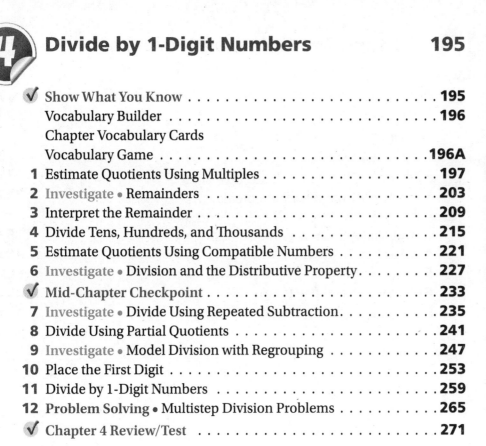

4 Divide by 1-Digit Numbers 195

Chapter 4 Overview

In this chapter, you will explore and discover answers to the following **Essential Questions**:

• How can you divide by 1-digit numbers?

• How can you use remainders in division problems?

• How can you estimate quotients?

• How can you model division with a 1-digit divisor?

Chapter 5 Overview

In this chapter, you will explore and discover answers to the following **Essential Questions**:

- How can you find factors and multiples, and how can you generate and describe number patterns?
- How can you use models or lists to find factors?
- How can you create a number pattern?

5 Factors, Multiples, and Patterns 277

GAS ST

© Houghton Mifflin Harcourt Publishing Company

VOLUME 2
Fractions and Decimals

Big Idea Develop a conceptual understanding of fraction equivalence and comparison. Use this understanding to add and subtract fractions with like denominators, to multiply fractions by whole numbers, and to relate fractions and decimals.

GO DIGITAL

Go online! Your math lessons are interactive. Use *i*Tools, Animated Math Models, the Multimedia *e*Glossary, and more.

Chapter 6 Overview

Essential Questions:
- What strategies can you use to compare fractions and write equivalent fractions?
- What models can help you compare and order fractions?
- How can you find equivalent fractions?
- How can you solve problems that involve fractions?

Chapter 7 Overview

Essential Questions:
- How do you add or subtract fractions that have the same denominator?
- Why do you add or subtract the numerators and not the denominators?
- Why do you rename mixed numbers when adding or subtracting fractions?
- How do you know that your sum or difference is reasonable?

Geometry, Measurement, and Data

Big Idea Develop a conceptual understanding that geometric figures can be analyzed and classified based on their properties, including angle measures. Develop relative sizes of measurement units and apply area and perimeter formulas for rectangles.

GO DIGITAL

Go online! Your math lessons are interactive. Use *i*Tools, Animated Math Models, the Multimedia *e*Glossary, and more.

Chapter 10 Overview

Essential Questions:
- How can you draw and identify lines and angles, and how can you classify shapes?
- What are the building blocks of geometry?
- How can you classify triangles and quadrilaterals?
- How do you recognize symmetry in a polygon?

Chapter 11 Overview

Essential Questions:
- How can you measure angles and solve problems involving angle measures?
- How can you use fractions and degrees to understand angle measures?
- How can you use a protractor to measure and classify angles?
- How can equations help you find the measurement of an angle?

© Houghton Mifflin Harcourt Publishing Company

Big Idea Fractions and Decimals

BIG IDEA Develop a conceptual understanding of fraction equivalence and comparison. Use this understanding to add and subtract fractions with like denominators, to multiply fractions by whole numbers, and to relate fractions and decimals.

A *luthier*, or guitar maker, at his workshop

Building Custom Guitars

Do you play the guitar, or would you like to learn how to play one? The guitar size you need depends on your height to the nearest inch and on *scale length*. Scale length is the distance from the *bridge* of the guitar to the *nut*.

Get Started    WRITE ▶ *Math*

Order the guitar sizes from the least size to the greatest size, and complete the table.

Important Facts

Guitar Sizes for Students

Age of Player	Height of Player (to nearest inch)	Scale Length (shortest to longest, in inches)	Size of Guitar
4–6	3 feet 3 inches to 3 feet 9 inches	19	
6–8	3 feet 10 inches to 4 feet 5 inches	20.5	
8–11	4 feet 6 inches to 4 feet 11 inches	22.75	
11–Adult	5 feet or taller	25.5	

Size of Guitar: $\frac{1}{2}$ size, $\frac{4}{4}$ size, $\frac{1}{4}$ size, $\frac{3}{4}$ size

Adults play $\frac{4}{4}$-size guitars. You can see that guitars also come in $\frac{3}{4}$, $\frac{1}{2}$, and $\frac{1}{4}$ sizes. Figure out which size guitar you would need according to your height and the scale length for each size guitar. Use the Important Facts to decide. **Explain** your thinking.

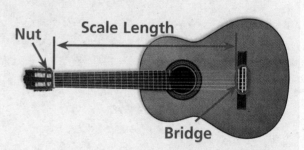

Nut   Scale Length   Bridge

Completed by _____

Fraction Equivalence and Comparison

Personal Math Trainer
Online Assessment and Intervention

✓ Show What You Know

Check your understanding of important skills.

Name _____

▶ **Part of a Whole** Write a fraction for the shaded part.

1. _____   2. _____   3. _____

▶ **Name the Shaded Part** Write a fraction for the shaded part.

4. _____   5. _____   6.

▶ **Compare Parts of a Whole** Color the fraction strips to show the fractions. Circle the greater fraction.

7. $\frac{1}{2}$

$\frac{1}{3}$

8. $\frac{1}{5}$

$\frac{1}{3}$

Math in the Real World

Earth's surface is covered by more than 57 million square miles of land. The table shows about how much of Earth's land surface each continent covers. Which continent covers the greatest part of Earth's land surface?

Continent	Part of Land Surface
Asia	$\frac{3}{10}$
Africa	$\frac{1}{5}$
Antarctica	$\frac{9}{100}$
Australia	$\frac{6}{100}$
Europe	$\frac{7}{100}$
North America	$\frac{1}{6}$
South America	$\frac{1}{8}$

Vocabulary Builder

▶ **Visualize It** •

Complete the flow map by using the words with a ✓.

Whole Numbers and Fractions

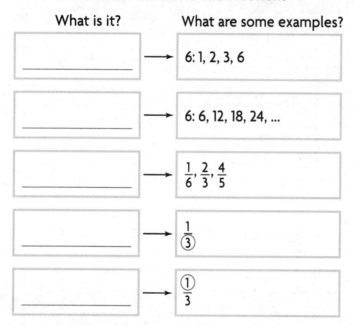

What is it?   What are some examples?

_____ →	6: 1, 2, 3, 6
_____ →	6: 6, 12, 18, 24, ...
_____ →	$\frac{1}{6}, \frac{2}{3}, \frac{4}{5}$
_____ →	$\frac{1}{3}$
_____ →	$\frac{①}{3}$

Review Words

common multiple

✓ denominator

✓ factor

✓ fraction

✓ multiple

✓ numerator

Preview Words

benchmark

common denominator

equivalent fractions

simplest form

▶ **Understand Vocabulary** •

Complete the sentences by using preview words.

1. A fraction is in _____ if the numerator and denominator have only 1 as a common factor.

2. _____ name the same amount.

3. A _____ is a common multiple of two or more denominators.

4. A _____ is a known size or amount that helps you understand a different size or amount.

GO DIGITAL
• Interactive Student Edition
• Multimedia eGlossary

Chapter 6 Vocabulary

benchmark

punto de referencia

6

common denominator

denominador común

9

denominator

denominador

22

equivalent fractions

fracciones equivalentes

29

fraction

fracción

36

multiple

múltiplo

55

numerator

numerador

56

simplest form

mínima expresión

84

A common multiple of two or more denominators

Example: Some common denominators for $\frac{1}{4}$ and $\frac{5}{6}$ are 12, 24, and 36.

A known size or amount that helps you understand a different size or amount

You can use $\frac{1}{2}$ as a benchmark to help you compare fractions.

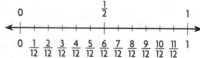

Two or more fractions that name the same amount

Example: $\frac{3}{4}$ and $\frac{6}{8}$ name the same amount.

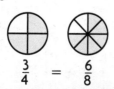

$$\frac{3}{4} = \frac{6}{8}$$

The number below the bar in a fraction that tells how many equal parts are in the whole or in the group

Example: $\frac{3}{4}$ ⟵ denominator

The product of a number and a counting number is called a multiple of the number

Example:

$$\begin{array}{cccc} 3 & 3 & 3 & 3 \\ \times\,1 & \times\,2 & \times\,3 & \times\,4 \\ \hline 3 & 6 & 9 & 12 \end{array}$$

⟵ counting numbers
⟵ multiples of 3

A number that names a part of a whole or part of a group

Example:

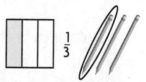

$\frac{1}{3}$

A fraction is in simplest form when the numerator and denominator have only 1 as a common factor

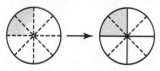

$$\frac{2}{8} = \frac{1}{4}$$

simplest form

The number above the bar in a fraction that tells how many parts of the whole or group are being considered

Example: $\frac{1}{5}$ ⟵ numerator

Going to San Francisco

For 2 to 4 players

Materials

• 3 of one color per player: red, blue, green, and yellow playing pieces
• 1 number cube

How to Play

1. Put your 3 playing pieces in the START circle of the same color.

2. To get a playing piece out of START, you must toss a 6.
   • If you toss a 6, move 1 of your playing pieces to the same-colored circle on the path.
   • If you do not toss a 6, wait until your next turn.

3. Once you have a playing piece on the path, toss the number cube to take a turn. Move the playing piece that many tan spaces. You must get all three of your playing pieces on the path.

4. If you land on a space with a question, answer it. If you are correct, move ahead 1 space.

5. To reach FINISH, you must move your playing piece up the path that is the same color as your playing piece. The first player to get all three playing pieces on FINISH wins.

Word Box

benchmark
common
  denominator
denominator
equivalent
  fractions
fraction
multiple
numerator
simplest form

CALIFORNIA

START

STRAT

What is a fraction?

What are equivalent fractions?

How can you find a fraction that is equivalent to $\frac{1}{3}$?

Why are $\frac{1}{2}$ and $\frac{2}{4}$ equivalent fractions?

Explain how you know that $\frac{2}{3}$ is in simplest form.

How do you know when a fraction is in simplest form?

FINISH

What is the difference between a multiple and common multiple?

Explain the relationship between a common multiple and a common denominator.

START

What is the meaning of common denominator?

What is the simplest form of a fraction?

How do you find the common denominator of $\frac{2}{3}$ and $\frac{3}{5}$?

What is a multiple?

FINISH

What is a benchmark?

How are benchmarks used to compare fractions?

In a fraction, what does the numerator represent?

In a fraction, what does the denominator represent?

START

FISHERMAN'S WHARF - OF SAN FRANCISCO

The Write Way

Reflect

Explain how to find the common denominator for $\frac{2}{3}$ and $\frac{1}{4}$.

• Work with a partner to explain and illustrate two ways to find equivalent fractions. Use a separate piece of paper for your drawing.

• Write about all the different ways you can show 25.

• Summarize how you would order the fractions $\frac{2}{3}$, $\frac{7}{8}$, and $\frac{4}{5}$, including any "false starts" or "dead ends."

Name _____

Equivalent Fractions

Essential Question How can you use models to show equivalent fractions?

Learning Objective You will use fraction models to write equivalent fractions and tell whether two fractions are equivalent or not equivalent.

Investigate

Materials ■ color pencils

Joe cut a pan of lasagna into third-size pieces. He kept $\frac{1}{3}$ and gave the rest away. Joe will not eat his part all at once. How can he cut his part into smaller, equal-size pieces?

A. Draw on the model to show how Joe could cut his part of the lasagna into 2 equal pieces.

You can rename these 2 equal pieces as a fraction of the original pan of lasagna.

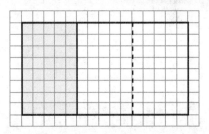

Suppose Joe had cut the original pan of lasagna into equal pieces of this size.

How many pieces would there be? _____

What fraction of the pan is 1 piece? _____

What fraction of the pan is 2 pieces? _____

You can rename $\frac{1}{3}$ as _____.

B. Now draw on the model to show how Joe could cut his part of the lasagna into 4 equal pieces.

You can rename these 4 equal pieces as a fraction of the original pan of lasagna.

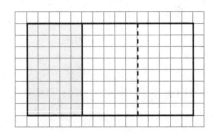

Suppose Joe had cut the original pan of lasagna into equal pieces of this size.

How many pieces would there be? _____

What fraction of the pan is 1 piece? _____

What fraction of the pan is 4 pieces? _____

You can rename $\frac{1}{3}$ as _____.

C. Fractions that name the same amount are **equivalent fractions**. Write the equivalent fractions.

$$\frac{1}{3} = \underline{} = \underline{}$$

Draw Conclusions

1. Compare the models for $\frac{1}{3}$ and $\frac{2}{6}$. How does the number of parts relate to the sizes of the parts?

   _____

   _____

2. Describe how the numerators are related and how the denominators are related in $\frac{1}{3} = \frac{2}{6}$.

   _____

   _____

   _____

3. **THINK SMARTER** Does $\frac{1}{3} = \frac{3}{9}$? Explain.

   _____

   _____

Make Connections

Savannah has $\frac{2}{4}$ yard of ribbon, and Isabel has $\frac{3}{8}$ yard of ribbon. How can you determine whether Savannah and Isabel have the same length of ribbon?

The equal sign (=) and not equal to sign (≠) show whether fractions are equivalent.

Tell whether $\frac{2}{4}$ and $\frac{3}{8}$ are equivalent. Write = or ≠.

STEP 1 Shade the amount of ribbon Savannah has.

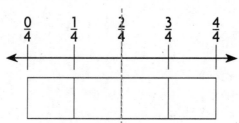

STEP 2 Shade the amount of ribbon Isabel has.

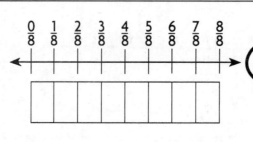

Think: $\frac{2}{4}$ yard is not the same amount as $\frac{3}{8}$ yard.

So, $\frac{2}{4}$ ◯ $\frac{3}{8}$.

Math Talk

Math Processes and Practices ④

Use Models How could you use a model to show that $\frac{4}{8} = \frac{1}{2}$?

Name _____

Use the model to write an equivalent fraction.

1.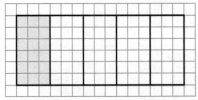

$$\frac{1}{5}$$ =   _____

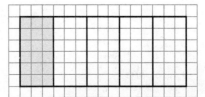

2.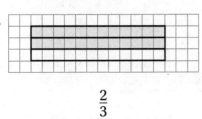

$$\frac{2}{3}$$ =   _____

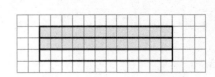

Tell whether the fractions are equivalent. Write = or ≠.

3. $\frac{1}{6}$ ◯ $\frac{2}{12}$

4. $\frac{2}{5}$ ◯ $\frac{6}{10}$

5. $\frac{4}{12}$ ◯ $\frac{1}{3}$

6. $\frac{5}{8}$ ◯ $\frac{2}{4}$

7. $\frac{5}{6}$ ◯ $\frac{10}{12}$

8. $\frac{1}{2}$ ◯ $\frac{5}{10}$

Problem Solving • Applications

9. **GO DEEPER** Manny used 8 tenth-size parts to model $\frac{8}{10}$. Ana used fewer parts to model an equivalent fraction. How does the size of a part in Ana's model compare to the size of a tenth-size part? What size part did Ana use?

_____

_____

_____

10. **Math Processes and Practices ⑤** Use a Concrete Model How many eighth-size parts do you need to model $\frac{3}{4}$? Explain.

_____

_____

_____

_____

What's the Error?

11. **THINK SMARTER** Ben brought two pizzas to a party. He says that since $\frac{1}{4}$ of each pizza is left, the same amount of each pizza is left. What is his error?

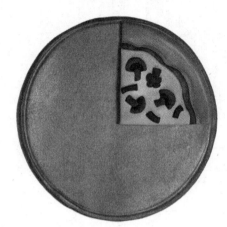

Draw models of 2 pizzas with a different number of equal pieces. Use shading to show $\frac{1}{4}$ of each pizza.

Describe Ben's error.

_____

_____

_____

_____

_____

12. **THINK SMARTER** For numbers 12a–12d, tell whether the fractions are equivalent by selecting the correct symbol.

12a. $\frac{3}{15}$ $\boxed{\begin{array}{c}=\\\neq\end{array}}$ $\frac{1}{6}$

12b. $\frac{3}{4}$ $\boxed{\begin{array}{c}=\\\neq\end{array}}$ $\frac{16}{20}$

12c. $\frac{2}{3}$ $\boxed{\begin{array}{c}=\\\neq\end{array}}$ $\frac{8}{12}$

12d. $\frac{8}{10}$ $\boxed{\begin{array}{c}=\\\neq\end{array}}$ $\frac{4}{5}$

Name _____

Equivalent Fractions

Learning Objective You will use fraction models to write equivalent fractions and tell whether two fractions are equivalent or not equivalent.

Use the model to write an equivalent fraction.

1.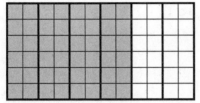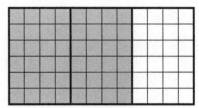

$$\frac{4}{6} \qquad = \qquad \underline{\quad \frac{2}{3} \quad}$$

2.

$$\frac{3}{4} \qquad = \qquad \underline{\qquad\qquad}$$

Tell whether the fractions are equivalent. Write = or ≠.

3. $\frac{8}{10} \bigcirc \frac{4}{5}$
4. $\frac{1}{2} \bigcirc \frac{7}{12}$
5. $\frac{3}{4} \bigcirc \frac{8}{12}$
6. $\frac{2}{3} \bigcirc \frac{4}{6}$

 Problem Solving Real World

7. Jamal finished $\frac{5}{6}$ of his homework. Margaret finished $\frac{3}{4}$ of her homework, and Steve finished $\frac{10}{12}$ of his homework. Which two students finished the same amount of homework?

8. Sophia's vegetable garden is divided into 12 equal sections. She plants carrots in 8 of the sections. Write two fractions that are equivalent to the part of Sophia's garden that is planted with carrots.

_____

9. **WRITE** ▸*Math* Draw a model to show a fraction that is equivalent to $\frac{1}{3}$ and a fraction that is not equivalent to $\frac{1}{3}$.

Lesson Check

1. A rectangle is divided into 8 equal parts. Two parts are shaded. What fraction is equivalent to the shaded area of the rectangle?

2. Jeff uses 3 fifth-size strips to model $\frac{3}{5}$. He wants to use tenth-size strips to model an equivalent fraction. How many tenth-size strips will he need?

Spiral Review

3. Cassidy places 40 stamps on each of 8 album pages. How many stamps does she place?

4. Maria and 3 friends have 1,200 soccer cards. If they share the soccer cards equally, how many will each person receive?

5. Six groups of students sell 162 balloons at the school carnival. There are 3 students in each group. If each student sells the same number of balloons, how many balloons does each student sell?

6. Four students each made a list of prime numbers.

   Eric: 5, 7, 17, 23
   Maya: 3, 5, 13, 17
   Bella: 2, 3, 17, 19
   Jordan: 7, 11, 13, 21

   Who made an error and included a composite number? Write the composite number from his or her list.

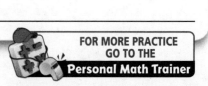

FOR MORE PRACTICE
GO TO THE
Personal Math Trainer

Name _____

Generate Equivalent Fractions

Essential Question How can you use multiplication to find equivalent fractions?

Learning Objective You will use fraction models and multiplication to write two equivalent fractions.

Unlock the Problem

Sara needs $\frac{3}{4}$ cup of dish soap to make homemade bubble solution. Her measuring cup is divided into eighths. What fraction of the measuring cup should Sara fill with dish soap?

🔑 **Find how many eighths are in $\frac{3}{4}$.**

> • Is an eighth-size part of a measuring cup bigger or smaller than a fourth-size part?
>
> _____

STEP 1 Compare fourths and eighths.

Shade to model $\frac{1}{4}$.
Use fourth-size parts.

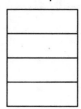

1 part

Shade to model $\frac{1}{4}$.
Use eighth-size parts.

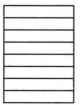

2 parts

You need _____ eighth-size parts to make 1 fourth-size part.

STEP 2 Find how many eighths you need to make 3 fourths.

Shade to model $\frac{3}{4}$.
Use fourth-size parts.

3 parts

Shade to model $\frac{3}{4}$.
Use eighth-size parts.

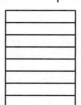

6 parts

You needed 2 eighth-size parts to make 1 fourth-size part.

So, you need _____ eighth-size parts to make 3 fourth-size parts.

So, Sara should fill $\dfrac{}{8}$ of the measuring cup with dish soap.

 Math Talk Math Processes and Practices ④

Interpret a Result Explain how you knew the number of eighth-size parts you needed to make 1 fourth-size part.

1. Explain why 6 eighth-size parts is the same amount as 3 fourth-size parts.

_____

🔑 Example · Write four fractions that are equivalent to $\frac{1}{2}$.

MODEL	WRITE EQUIVALENT FRACTIONS	RELATE EQUIVALENT FRACTIONS
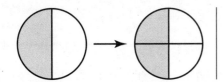	$\dfrac{1}{2} = \dfrac{2}{4}$	$\dfrac{1 \times 2}{2 \times 2} = \dfrac{2}{4}$
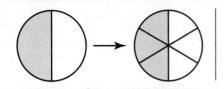	$\dfrac{1}{2} = \dfrac{}{6}$	$\dfrac{1 \times }{2 \times 3} = \dfrac{}{6}$
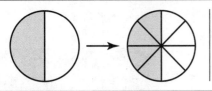	$\dfrac{1}{2} = \dfrac{}{}$	$\dfrac{1 \times }{2 \times } = \dfrac{}{}$
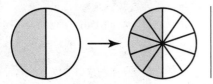	$\dfrac{1}{2} = \dfrac{}{}$	$\dfrac{1 \times }{2 \times } = \dfrac{}{}$

So, $\dfrac{1}{2} = \dfrac{2}{4} = \dfrac{}{6} = \dfrac{}{} = \dfrac{}{}$.

---

2. Look at the model that shows $\frac{1}{2} = \frac{3}{6}$. How does the number of parts in the whole affect the number of parts that are shaded? Explain.

_____

_____

3. Explain how you can use multiplication to write a fraction that is equivalent to $\frac{3}{5}$.

_____

_____

_____

4. Are $\frac{2}{3}$ and $\frac{6}{8}$ equivalent? Explain.

_____

_____

Name _____

1. Complete the table below.

MODEL	WRITE EQUIVALENT FRACTIONS	RELATE EQUIVALENT FRACTIONS
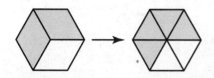	$\frac{2}{3} = \frac{4}{6}$	$\frac{2 \times \boxed{}}{3 \times \boxed{}} = \frac{\boxed{}}{\boxed{}}$
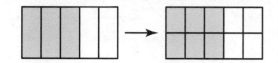	$\frac{3}{5} = \frac{6}{10}$	$\frac{3 \times \boxed{}}{5 \times \boxed{}} = \frac{\boxed{}}{\boxed{}}$
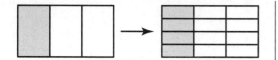	$\frac{1}{3} = \frac{4}{12}$	$\frac{1 \times \boxed{}}{3 \times \boxed{}} = \frac{\boxed{}}{\boxed{}}$

Math Talk Math Processes and Practices ②

Reason Abstractly Can you multiply the numerator and denominator of a fraction by 0? Explain.

Write two equivalent fractions.

✓ 2. $\frac{4}{5}$

$\frac{4}{5} = \frac{4 \times \boxed{}}{5 \times \boxed{}} = \frac{\boxed{}}{\boxed{}}$

$\frac{4}{5} = \frac{4 \times \boxed{}}{5 \times \boxed{}} = \frac{\boxed{}}{\boxed{}}$

$\frac{4}{5} = \frac{\boxed{}}{\boxed{}} = \frac{\boxed{}}{\boxed{}}$

✓ 3. $\frac{2}{4}$

$\frac{2}{4} = \frac{2 \times \boxed{}}{4 \times \boxed{}} = \frac{\boxed{}}{\boxed{}}$

$\frac{2}{4} = \frac{2 \times \boxed{}}{4 \times \boxed{}} = \frac{\boxed{}}{\boxed{}}$

$\frac{2}{4} = \frac{\boxed{}}{\boxed{}} = \frac{\boxed{}}{\boxed{}}$

On Your Own

Write two equivalent fractions.

4. $\frac{3}{6}$

$\frac{3}{6} = \frac{\boxed{}}{\boxed{}} = \frac{\boxed{}}{\boxed{}}$

5. $\frac{3}{10}$

$\frac{3}{10} = \frac{\boxed{}}{\boxed{}} = \frac{\boxed{}}{\boxed{}}$

6. $\frac{2}{5}$

$\frac{2}{5} = \frac{\boxed{}}{\boxed{}} = \frac{\boxed{}}{\boxed{}}$

Tell whether the fractions are equivalent. Write = or ≠.

7. $\frac{5}{6} \bigcirc \frac{10}{18}$

8. $\frac{4}{5} \bigcirc \frac{8}{10}$

9. $\frac{1}{5} \bigcirc \frac{4}{10}$

10. $\frac{1}{4} \bigcirc \frac{2}{8}$

Problem Solving · Applications Real World

Use the recipe for 11–12.

11. **THINK SMARTER** Kim says the amount of flour in the recipe can be expressed as a fraction. Is she correct? Explain.

_____

_____

_____

Face Paint Recipe

$\frac{2}{8}$ cup cornstarch

1 tablespoon flour

$\frac{9}{12}$ cup light corn syrup

$\frac{1}{4}$ cup water

$\frac{1}{2}$ teaspoon food coloring

12. **GO DEEPER** How could you use a $\frac{1}{8}$-cup measuring cup to measure the light corn syrup?

_____

_____

_____

13. **Math Processes and Practices ⑤ Communicate** Explain using words how you know a fraction is equivalent to another fraction.

_____

_____

_____

_____

WRITE ▶ Math
Show Your Work

14. **THINK SMARTER** Kyle drank $\frac{2}{3}$ cup of apple juice. Fill in each box with a number from the list to generate equivalent fractions for $\frac{2}{3}$. Not all numbers will be used.

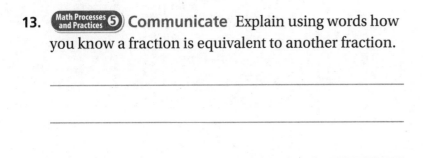

$$\frac{2}{3} = \frac{\boxed{}}{6} = \frac{12}{\boxed{}} = \frac{\boxed{}}{\boxed{}}$$

2	4	6	8
12	15	16	18

Generate Equivalent Fractions

Learning Objective You will use fraction models and multiplication to write two equivalent fractions.

Write two equivalent fractions for each.

1. $\frac{1}{3}$

$\frac{1 \times 2}{3 \times 2} = \frac{2}{6}$

$\frac{1 \times 4}{3 \times 4} = \frac{4}{12}$

2. $\frac{2}{3}$

_____

3. $\frac{1}{2}$

_____

4. $\frac{4}{5}$

_____

Tell whether the fractions are equivalent.
Write = or ≠.

5. $\frac{1}{4} \bigcirc \frac{3}{12}$

6. $\frac{4}{5} \bigcirc \frac{5}{10}$

7. $\frac{3}{8} \bigcirc \frac{2}{6}$

8. $\frac{3}{4} \bigcirc \frac{6}{8}$

9. $\frac{5}{6} \bigcirc \frac{10}{12}$

10. $\frac{6}{12} \bigcirc \frac{5}{8}$

11. $\frac{2}{5} \bigcirc \frac{4}{10}$

12. $\frac{2}{4} \bigcirc \frac{3}{12}$

Problem Solving (Real World)

13. Jan has a 12-ounce milkshake. Four ounces in the milkshake are vanilla, and the rest is chocolate. What are two equivalent fractions that represent the fraction of the milkshake that is vanilla?

14. Kareem lives $\frac{4}{10}$ of a mile from the mall. Write two equivalent fractions that show what fraction of a mile Kareem lives from the mall.

_____

_____

15. **WRITE** ▸*Math* Explain how you can determine if $\frac{1}{3}$ and $\frac{4}{12}$ are equivalent fractions.

_____

_____

Lesson Check

1. Jessie colored a poster. She colored $\frac{2}{5}$ of the poster red. Write a fraction that is equivalent to $\frac{2}{5}$.

   _____

2. Marcus makes a punch that is $\frac{1}{4}$ cranberry juice. Write two fractions that are equivalent to $\frac{1}{4}$.

   _____

Spiral Review

3. An electronics store sells a large flat screen television for $1,699. Last month, the store sold 8 of these television sets. About how much money did the televisions sell for?

   _____

   _____

4. Matthew has 18 sets of baseball cards. Each set has 12 cards. About how many baseball cards does Matthew have?

   _____

   _____

5. Diana had 41 stickers. She put them in 7 equal groups. She put as many as possible in each group. She gave the leftover stickers to her sister. How many stickers did Diana give to her sister?

   _____

6. Christopher wrote the number pattern below. The first term is 8.

   8, 6, 9, 7, 10, …

   What is a rule for the pattern?

   _____

FOR MORE PRACTICE
GO TO THE
Personal Math Trainer

Name _____

Simplest Form

Essential Question How can you write a fraction as an equivalent fraction in simplest form?

Learning Objective You will use fraction models or common factors and division to write equivalent fractions in simplest form.

Unlock the Problem

Vicki made a fruit tart and cut it into 6 equal pieces. Vicki, Silvia, and Elena each took 2 pieces of the tart home. Vicki says she and each of her friends took $\frac{1}{3}$ of the tart home. Is Vicki correct?

Activity

Materials ■ color pencils

STEP 1 Use a blue pencil to shade the pieces Vicki took home.

_____

STEP 2 Use a red pencil to shade the pieces Silvia took home.

_____

STEP 3 Use a yellow pencil to shade the pieces Elena took home.

- Into how many pieces was the tart cut?

  _____

- How many pieces did each girl take?

  _____

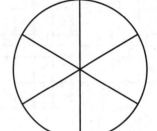

The tart is divided into _____ equal-size pieces. The 3 colors on the model show how to combine sixth-size pieces to make

_____ equal third-size pieces.

So, Vicki is correct. Vicki, Silvia, and Elena each took ——— of the tart home.

 Math Talk Math Processes and Practices ④

Interpret a Result
Compare the models for $\frac{2}{6}$ and $\frac{1}{3}$. Explain how the sizes of the parts are related.

- What if Vicki took 3 pieces of the tart home and Elena took 3 pieces of the tart home. How could you combine the pieces to write a fraction that represents the part each friend took home? Explain.

_____

_____

_____

Simplest Form A fraction is in **simplest form** when you can represent it using as few equal parts of a whole as possible. You need to describe the part you have in equal-size parts. If you can't describe the part you have using fewer parts, then you cannot simplify the fraction.

🔓 One Way Use models to write an equivalent fraction in simplest form.

MODEL	WRITE EQUIVALENT FRACTIONS	RELATE EQUIVALENT FRACTIONS
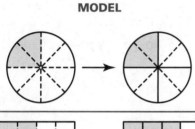	$\dfrac{2}{8} = \dfrac{1}{4}$	$\dfrac{2 \div 2}{8 \div 2} = \dfrac{1}{4}$
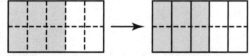	$\dfrac{6}{10} = \dfrac{\ }{5}$	$\dfrac{6 \div \ }{10 \div \ } = \dfrac{\ }{5}$
	$\dfrac{6}{12} = \dfrac{\ }{\ }$	$\dfrac{6 \div \ }{12 \div \ } = \dfrac{\ }{\ }$

To simplify $\frac{6}{10}$, you can combine tenth-size parts into equal groups with 2 parts each.

So, $\dfrac{6}{10} = \dfrac{6 \div \ }{10 \div \ } = \dfrac{\ }{\ }$.

🔓 Another Way Use common factors to write $\frac{6}{10}$ in simplest form.

A fraction is in simplest form when 1 is the only factor that the numerator and denominator have in common. The parts of the whole cannot be combined into fewer equal-size parts to show the same fraction.

STEP 1 List the factors of the numerator and denominator. Circle common factors.

Factors of 6: _____, _____, _____, _____

Factors of 10: _____, _____, _____, _____

STEP 2 Divide the numerator and denominator by a common factor greater than 1.

$\dfrac{6}{10} = \dfrac{6 \div \ }{10 \div \ } = \dfrac{\ }{\ }$

Since 1 is the only factor that 3 and 5 have in common, _____ is written in simplest form.

Name _____

1. Write $\frac{8}{10}$ in simplest form.

$$\frac{8}{10} = \frac{8 \div \boxed{}}{10 \div \boxed{}} = \frac{\boxed{}}{\boxed{}}$$

Write the fraction in simplest form.

2. $\frac{6}{12}$

3. $\frac{2}{10}$

4. $\frac{6}{8}$

5. $\frac{4}{6}$

On Your Own

Math Talk   Math Processes and Practices ⑥

Explain how you know a fraction is in simplest form.

Write the fraction in simplest form.

6. $\frac{9}{12}$

7. $\frac{4}{8}$

8. $\frac{10}{12}$

9. $\frac{20}{100}$

Tell whether the fraction is in simplest form.
Write *yes* or *no*.

10. $\frac{2}{8}$

11. $\frac{9}{12}$

12. $\frac{5}{6}$

13. $\frac{4}{10}$

14. **GO DEEPER**   There are 18 students in Jacob's homeroom. Six students bring their lunch to school. The rest eat lunch in the cafeteria. In simplest form, what fraction of students eat lunch in the cafeteria?

_____

Problem Solving · Applications

Use the map for 15–16.

15. **Math Processes and Practices ⑦** **Identify Relationships** What fraction of the states in the southwest region share a border with Mexico? Is this fraction in simplest form?

_____

16. **THINK SMARTER** **What's the Question?** $\frac{1}{3}$ of the states in this region are on the Gulf of Mexico.

_____

_____

_____

17. **GO DEEPER** Pete says that to write $\frac{4}{6}$ as $\frac{2}{3}$, you combine pieces, but to write $\frac{4}{6}$ as $\frac{8}{12}$, you break apart pieces. Does this make sense? Explain.

_____

_____

_____

WRITE ▸Math
Show Your Work

18. **THINK SMARTER +** In Michelle's homeroom, $\frac{9}{15}$ of the students ride the bus to school, $\frac{4}{12}$ get a car ride, and $\frac{2}{30}$ walk to school. For numbers 18a–18c, select True or False for each statement.

18a. In simplest form, $\frac{3}{5}$ of the students ride the bus to school.   ○ True   ○ False

18b. In simplest form, $\frac{1}{4}$ of the students get a car ride to school.   ○ True   ○ False

18c. In simplest form, $\frac{1}{15}$ of the students walk to school.   ○ True   ○ False

Simplest Form

Learning Objective You will use fraction models or common factors and division to write equivalent fractions in simplest form.

Write the fraction in simplest form.

1. $\frac{6}{10}$

2. $\frac{6}{8}$

3. $\frac{5}{5}$

4. $\frac{8}{12}$

$\frac{6}{10} = \frac{6 \div 2}{10 \div 2} = \frac{3}{5}$

_____ _____ _____

5. $\frac{100}{100}$

6. $\frac{2}{6}$

7. $\frac{2}{8}$

8. $\frac{4}{10}$

_____ _____ _____ _____

Tell whether the fractions are equivalent. Write = or ≠.

9. $\frac{6}{12} \bigcirc \frac{1}{12}$

10. $\frac{3}{4} \bigcirc \frac{5}{6}$

11. $\frac{6}{10} \bigcirc \frac{3}{5}$

12. $\frac{3}{12} \bigcirc \frac{1}{3}$

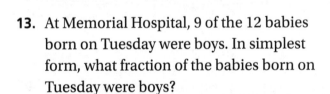

13. At Memorial Hospital, 9 of the 12 babies born on Tuesday were boys. In simplest form, what fraction of the babies born on Tuesday were boys?

14. Cristina uses a ruler to measure the length of her math textbook. She says that the book is $\frac{4}{10}$ meter long. Is her measurement in simplest form? If not, what is the length of the book in simplest form?

_____ _____

15. **WRITE** ►*Math* Explain using words or drawings how to write $\frac{6}{9}$ in simplest form.

_____

_____

_____

Lesson Check

1. Six out of the 12 members of the school choir are boys. In simplest form, what fraction of the choir is boys?

_____

2. Write $\frac{10}{12}$ in simplest form.

_____

Spiral Review

3. Each of the 23 students in Ms. Evans' class raised $45 for the school by selling coupon books. How much money did the class raise?

_____

_____

4. List two common factors of 36 and 48.

_____

_____

5. Bart uses $\frac{3}{12}$ cup milk to make muffins. Write a fraction that is equivalent to $\frac{3}{12}$.

6. Ashley bought 4 packages of juice boxes. There are 6 juice boxes in each package. She gave 2 juice boxes to each of 3 friends. How many juice boxes does Ashley have left?

_____

_____

FOR MORE PRACTICE
GO TO THE
Personal Math Trainer

Name _____

Common Denominators

Learning Objective You will use common multiples to write a pair of fractions as fractions with a common denominator.

Essential Question How can you write a pair of fractions as fractions with a common denominator?

Unlock the Problem

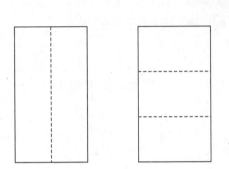

Martin has two rectangles that are the same size. One rectangle is cut into $\frac{1}{2}$-size parts. The other rectangle is cut into $\frac{1}{3}$-size parts. He wants to cut the rectangles so they have the same size parts. How can he cut each rectangle?

A **common denominator** is a common multiple of the denominators of two or more fractions. Fractions with common denominators represent wholes cut into the same number of parts.

Activity Use paper folding and shading.

Materials ■ 2 sheets of paper

Find a common denominator for $\frac{1}{2}$ and $\frac{1}{3}$.

STEP 1

Model the rectangle cut into $\frac{1}{2}$-size parts. Fold one sheet of paper in half. Draw a line on the fold.

_____

STEP 2

Model the rectangle cut into $\frac{1}{3}$-size parts. Fold the other sheet of paper into thirds. Draw lines on the folds.

_____

STEP 3

Fold each sheet of paper so that both sheets have the same number of parts. Draw lines on the folds. How many equal

parts does each sheet of paper have? _____

STEP 4

Draw a picture of your sheets of paper to show how many parts each rectangle could have.

So, each rectangle could be cut into _____ parts.

Math Talk

Math Processes and Practices ❹

Use Models How did the models help you find the common denominator for $\frac{1}{2}$ and $\frac{1}{3}$?

🔓 **Example** Write $\frac{4}{5}$ and $\frac{1}{2}$ as a pair of fractions with common denominators.

You can use common multiples to find a common denominator. List multiples of each denominator. A common multiple can be used as a common denominator.

STEP 1 List multiples of 5 and 2. Circle common multiples.

5:     5,   10,   _____, _____, _____, _____

2:     _____, _____, _____, _____, _____, _____

STEP 2 Write equivalent fractions.

$$\frac{4}{5} = \frac{4 \times \boxed{}}{5 \times \boxed{}} = \frac{\boxed{}}{10}$$

$$\frac{1}{2} = \frac{1 \times \boxed{}}{2 \times \boxed{}} = \frac{\boxed{}}{10}$$

Choose a denominator that is a common multiple of 5 and 2.

You can write $\frac{4}{5}$ and $\frac{1}{2}$ as _____ and _____ .

ERROR Alert

Remember that when you multiply the denominator by a factor, you must multiply the numerator by the same factor to write an equivalent fraction.

1. Are $\frac{4}{5}$ and $\frac{1}{2}$ equivalent? Explain.

_____

_____

_____

2. Describe another way you could tell whether $\frac{4}{5}$ and $\frac{1}{2}$ are equivalent.

_____

_____

_____

Share and Show

1. Find a common denominator for $\frac{1}{3}$ and $\frac{1}{12}$ by dividing each whole into the same number of equal parts. Use the models to help.

common denominator: _____

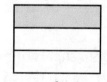

$\frac{1}{3}$

$\frac{1}{12}$

346

Name _____

**Write the pair of fractions as a pair of fractions with a
common denominator.**

2. $\frac{1}{2}$ and $\frac{1}{4}$

3. $\frac{3}{4}$ and $\frac{5}{8}$

_____

4. $\frac{1}{3}$ and $\frac{1}{4}$

5. $\frac{4}{12}$ and $\frac{5}{8}$

_____

Math Talk   Math Processes and Practices 6

Explain how using a
model or listing multiples
helps you find a common
denominator.

On Your Own

**Write the pair of fractions as a pair of fractions with a
common denominator.**

6. $\frac{1}{4}$ and $\frac{5}{6}$

7. $\frac{3}{5}$ and $\frac{4}{10}$

_____

Tell whether the fractions are equivalent. Write = or ≠.

8. $\frac{3}{4} \bigcirc \frac{1}{2}$

9. $\frac{3}{4} \bigcirc \frac{6}{8}$

10. $\frac{1}{2} \bigcirc \frac{4}{8}$

11. $\frac{6}{8} \bigcirc \frac{4}{8}$

12. **GO DEEPER**   Jerry has two same-size circles divided into the same
number of equal parts. One circle has $\frac{3}{4}$ of the parts shaded, and
the other has $\frac{2}{3}$ of the parts shaded. His sister says the least number
of pieces each circle could be divided into is 7. Is his sister correct?
Explain.

_____

_____

Problem Solving • Applications

13. **GO DEEPER** Carrie has a red streamer that is $\frac{3}{4}$ yard long and a blue streamer that is $\frac{5}{6}$ yard long. She says the streamers are the same length. Does this make sense? Explain.

_____

_____

_____

_____

14. **THINK SMARTER** Leah has two same-size rectangles divided into the same number of equal parts. One rectangle has $\frac{1}{3}$ of the parts shaded, and the other has $\frac{2}{5}$ of the parts shaded. What is the least number of parts into which both rectangles could be divided?

_____

15. **Math Processes and Practices 6** Julian says a common denominator for $\frac{3}{4}$ and $\frac{2}{5}$ is 9. What is Julian's error? **Explain.**

WRITE ▸ *Math* · · · · · · · · · ·
Show Your Work

_____

_____

_____

Personal Math Trainer

16. **THINK SMARTER +** Miguel has two same-size rectangles divided into the same number of equal parts. One rectangle has $\frac{3}{4}$ of the parts shaded, and the other has $\frac{5}{8}$ of the parts shaded.

Into how many parts could each rectangle be divided? Show your work by sketching the rectangles.

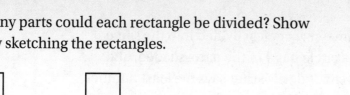

Common Denominators

Write the pair of fractions as a pair of fractions with a common denominator.

1. $\frac{2}{3}$ and $\frac{3}{4}$

Think: Find a common multiple.

3: 3, 6, 9, (12) 15
4: 4, 8, (12) 16, 20

$$\frac{8}{12}, \frac{9}{12}$$
_____

2. $\frac{1}{4}$ and $\frac{2}{3}$

_____

3. $\frac{3}{10}$ and $\frac{1}{2}$

_____

4. $\frac{3}{5}$ and $\frac{3}{4}$

_____

5. $\frac{2}{4}$ and $\frac{7}{8}$

_____

6. $\frac{2}{3}$ and $\frac{5}{12}$

_____

7. $\frac{1}{4}$ and $\frac{1}{6}$

_____

Tell whether the fractions are equivalent. Write $=$ or $\neq$.

8. $\frac{1}{2} \bigcirc \frac{2}{5}$

9. $\frac{1}{2} \bigcirc \frac{3}{6}$

10. $\frac{3}{4} \bigcirc \frac{5}{6}$

11. $\frac{6}{10} \bigcirc \frac{3}{5}$

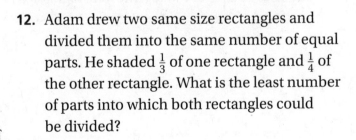

12. Adam drew two same size rectangles and divided them into the same number of equal parts. He shaded $\frac{1}{3}$ of one rectangle and $\frac{1}{4}$ of the other rectangle. What is the least number of parts into which both rectangles could be divided?

_____

13. Mera painted equal sections of her bedroom wall to make a pattern. She painted $\frac{2}{5}$ of the wall white and $\frac{1}{2}$ of the wall lavender. Write an equivalent fraction for each fraction using a common denominator.

_____

14. **WRITE** ▸*Math* How are a common denominator and a common multiple alike and different?

_____

_____

Lesson Check

1. Write a common denominator for $\frac{1}{4}$ and $\frac{5}{6}$.

   _____

   _____

2. Two fractions have a common denominator of 8. What could the two fractions be?

   _____

   _____

Spiral Review

3. What number is 100,000 more than seven hundred two thousand, eighty-three?

   _____

4. Aiden baked 8 dozen muffins. How many total muffins did he bake?

   _____

5. On a bulletin board, the principal, Ms. Gomez, put 115 photos of the fourth-grade students in her school. She put the photos in 5 equal rows. How many photos did she put in each row?

   _____

6. Judy uses 12 tiles to make a mosaic. Eight of the tiles are blue. What fraction, in simplest form, represents the tiles that are blue?

   _____

FOR MORE PRACTICE
GO TO THE
Personal Math Trainer

Name _____

Problem Solving • Find Equivalent Fractions

Essential Question How can you use the strategy *make a table* to solve problems using equivalent fractions?

🔓 Try Another Problem

Two friends are knitting scarves. Each scarf has 3 rectangles, and $\frac{2}{3}$ of the rectangles have stripes. If the friends are making 10 scarves, how many rectangles do they need? How many rectangles will have stripes?

Read the Problem

What do I need to find?	What information do I need to use?	How will I use the information?

Solve the Problem

2. Does your answer make sense? Explain how you know.

_____

_____

_____

Math Talk

Math Processes and Practices 1

Analyze What other strategy could you have used and why?

Name _____

Share and Show

Unlock the Problem

✓ Use the Problem Solving Mathboard.
✓ Underline important facts.
✓ Choose a strategy you know.

1. Keisha is helping plan a race route for a 10-kilometer charity run. The committee wants to set up the following things along the course.

> **Viewing areas:** At the end of each half of the course
>
> **Water stations:** At the end of each fifth of the course
>
> **Distance markers:** At the end of each tenth of the course

Which locations have more than one thing located there?

First, make a table to organize the information.

	Number of Locations	First Location	All the Locations
Viewing Areas	2	$\frac{1}{2}$	$\frac{1}{2}$
Water Stations	5	$\frac{1}{5}$	$\frac{1}{5}$
Distance Markers	10	$\frac{1}{10}$	$\frac{1}{10}$

Next, identify a relationship. Use a common denominator, and find equivalent fractions.

Finally, identify the locations at which more than one thing will be set up. Circle the locations.

_____

_____

2. **THINK SMARTER** What if distance markers will also be placed at the end of every fourth of the course? Will any of those markers be set up at the same location as another distance marker, a water station,

or a viewing area? Explain. _____

_____

_____

3. Fifty-six students signed up to volunteer for the race. There were 4 equal groups of students, and each group had a different task.

How many students were in each group? _____

On Your Own

4. **THINK SMARTER**   A baker cut a pie in half. He cut each half into 3 equal pieces and each piece into 2 equal slices. He sold 6 slices. What fraction of the pie did the baker sell?

_____

5. **GO DEEPER**   Andy cut a tuna sandwich and a chicken sandwich into a total of 15 same-size pieces. He cut the tuna sandwich into 9 more pieces than the chicken sandwich. Andy ate 8 pieces of the tuna sandwich. What fraction of the tuna sandwich did he eat?

WRITE *Math*
Show Your Work

_____

6. **Math Processes and Practices ⑥**   Luke threw balls into these buckets at a carnival. The number on the bucket gives the number of points for each throw. What is the least number of throws needed to score exactly 100 points? **Explain.**

_____

_____

7. **THINK SMARTER**   Victoria arranges flowers in vases at her restaurant. In each arrangement, $\frac{2}{3}$ of the flowers are yellow. What other fractions can represent the part of the flowers that are yellow? Shade the models to show your work.

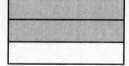 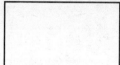 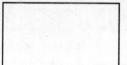

$\frac{2}{3}$ $\dfrac{}{12}$ $\dfrac{}{}$

Problem Solving • Find Equivalent Fractions

Learning Objective You will use the strategy *make a table* to find equivalent fractions by drawing models or by organizing fraction information.

Solve each problem.

1. Miranda is braiding her hair. Then she will attach beads to the braid. She wants $\frac{1}{3}$ of the beads to be red. If the greatest number of beads that will fit on the braid is 12, what other fractions could represent the part of the beads that are red?

$\dfrac{2}{6}, \dfrac{3}{9}, \dfrac{4}{12}$

2. Ms. Groves has trays of paints for students in her art class. Each tray has 5 colors. One of the colors is purple. What fraction of the colors in 20 trays is purple?

_____

3. Miguel is making an obstacle course for field day. At the end of every sixth of the course, there is a tire. At the end of every third of the course, there is a cone. At the end of every half of the course, there is a hurdle. At which locations of the course will people need to go through more than one obstacle?

_____

4. **WRITE** ▸*Math* Draw and compare models of $\frac{3}{4}$ of a pizza pie and $\frac{6}{8}$ of a same-size pie.

_____

_____

_____

Lesson Check

1. A used bookstore will trade 2 of its books for 3 of yours. If Val brings in 18 books to trade, how many books can she get from the store?

   _____

2. Every $\frac{1}{2}$ hour Naomi stretches her neck; every $\frac{1}{3}$ hour she stretches her legs; and every $\frac{1}{6}$ hour she stretches her arms. Which parts of her body will Naomi stretch when $\frac{2}{3}$ of an hour has passed?

   _____

Spiral Review

3. At the beginning of the year, the Wong family car had been driven 14,539 miles. At the end of the year, their car had been driven 21,844 miles. How many miles did the Wong family drive their car during that year?

   _____

4. Widget Company made 3,600 widgets in 4 hours. They made the same number of widgets each hour. How many widgets did the company make in one hour?

   _____

5. Tyler is thinking of a number that is divisible by 2 and by 3. Write another number by which Tyler's number must also be divisible.

   _____

6. Jessica drew a circle divided into 8 equal parts. She shaded 6 of the parts. What fraction is equivalent to the part of the circle that is shaded?

   _____

FOR MORE PRACTICE
GO TO THE
Personal Math Trainer

Name _____

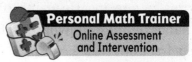

Vocabulary

Choose the best term from the box.

Vocabulary
common denominator
equivalent fractions
factor

1. _____ name the same amount. (p. 327)

2. A _____ is a common multiple of two or more denominators. (p. 345)

Concepts and Skills

Write two equivalent fractions.

3. $\frac{2}{5} =$ _____ = _____

4. $\frac{1}{3} =$ _____ = _____

5. $\frac{3}{4} =$ _____ = _____

Tell whether the fractions are equivalent. Write = or ≠.

6. $\frac{2}{3} \bigcirc \frac{4}{12}$

7. $\frac{5}{6} \bigcirc \frac{10}{12}$

8. $\frac{1}{4} \bigcirc \frac{4}{8}$

Write the fraction in simplest form.

9. $\frac{6}{8}$

10. $\frac{25}{100}$

11. $\frac{8}{10}$

Write the pair of fractions as a pair of fractions with a common denominator.

12. $\frac{3}{10}$ and $\frac{2}{5}$

13. $\frac{1}{3}$ and $\frac{3}{4}$

14. Sam needs $\frac{5}{6}$ cup mashed bananas and $\frac{3}{4}$ cup mashed strawberries for a recipe. He wants to find whether he needs more bananas or more strawberries. How can he write $\frac{5}{6}$ and $\frac{3}{4}$ as a pair of fractions with a common denominator?

_____

15. Karen will divide her garden into equal parts. She will plant corn in $\frac{8}{12}$ of the garden. What is the fewest number of parts she can divide her garden into?

_____

16. GO DEEPER   Olivia is making scarves. Each scarf will have 5 rectangles, and $\frac{2}{5}$ of the rectangles will be purple. How many purple rectangles does she need for 3 scarves?

_____

17. Paul needs to buy $\frac{5}{8}$ pound of peanuts. The scale at the store measures parts of a pound in sixteenths. What measure is equivalent to $\frac{5}{8}$ pound?

_____

Name _____

Compare Fractions Using Benchmarks

Essential Question How can you use benchmarks to compare fractions?

Learning Objective You will use fraction strips and benchmarks to compare two fractions with different numerators and different denominators.

Unlock the Problem

David made a popcorn snack. He mixed $\frac{5}{8}$ gallon of popcorn with $\frac{1}{2}$ gallon of dried apple rings. Did he use more dried apple rings or more popcorn?

Activity Compare $\frac{5}{8}$ and $\frac{1}{2}$.

Materials ■ fraction strips

Use fraction strips to compare $\frac{5}{8}$ and $\frac{1}{2}$. Record on the model below.

$\frac{1}{2}$

$\frac{1}{2}$	$\frac{1}{2}$

$\frac{5}{8}$

$\frac{1}{8}$	$\frac{1}{8}$	$\frac{1}{8}$	$\frac{1}{8}$	$\frac{1}{8}$	$\frac{1}{8}$	$\frac{1}{8}$	$\frac{1}{8}$

$\frac{5}{8} \bigcirc \frac{1}{2}$

So, David used more _____.

Math Talk

Math Processes and Practices 7

Look for Structure How are the number of eighth-size parts in $\frac{5}{8}$ related to the number of eighth-size parts you need to make $\frac{1}{2}$?

1. Write five fractions equivalent to $\frac{1}{2}$. What is the relationship between the numerator and the denominator of fractions equivalent to $\frac{1}{2}$?

   _____

   _____

2. How many eighths are equivalent to $\frac{1}{2}$?

   _____

3. How can you compare $\frac{5}{8}$ and $\frac{1}{2}$ without using a model?

   _____

   _____

Benchmarks A **benchmark** is a known size or amount that helps you understand a different size or amount. You can use $\frac{1}{2}$ as a benchmark to help you compare fractions.

🔑 Example Use benchmarks to compare fractions.

A family hiked the same mountain trail. Evie and her father hiked $\frac{5}{12}$ of the trail before they stopped for lunch. Jill and her mother hiked $\frac{9}{10}$ of the trail before they stopped for lunch. Who hiked farther before lunch?

Compare $\frac{5}{12}$ and $\frac{9}{10}$ to the benchmark $\frac{1}{2}$.

STEP 1 Compare $\frac{5}{12}$ to $\frac{1}{2}$.

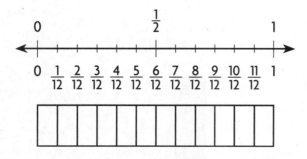

Think: Shade $\frac{5}{12}$.

$\frac{5}{12}$ ◯ $\frac{1}{2}$

STEP 2 Compare $\frac{9}{10}$ to $\frac{1}{2}$.

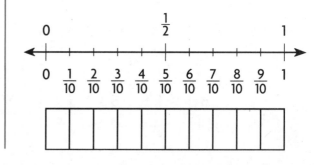

Think: Shade $\frac{9}{10}$.

$\frac{9}{10}$ ◯ $\frac{1}{2}$

Since $\frac{5}{12}$ is _____ than $\frac{1}{2}$ and $\frac{9}{10}$ is _____ than $\frac{1}{2}$, you know that $\frac{5}{12}$ ◯ $\frac{9}{10}$.

So, _____ hiked farther before lunch.

4. Explain how you can tell $\frac{5}{12}$ is less than $\frac{1}{2}$ without using a model.

   _____

   _____

5. Explain how you can tell $\frac{7}{10}$ is greater than $\frac{1}{2}$ without using a model.

   _____

   _____

Name _____

1. Compare $\frac{2}{5}$ and $\frac{1}{8}$. Write $<$ or $>$.

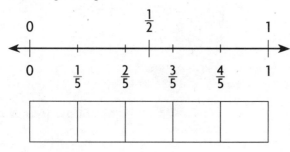

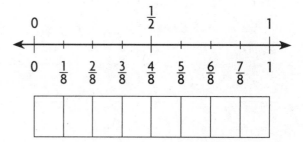

$\frac{2}{5}$ ◯ $\frac{1}{8}$

Compare. Write $<$ or $>$.

✓ **2.** $\frac{1}{2}$ ◯ $\frac{4}{6}$

3. $\frac{3}{10}$ ◯ $\frac{1}{2}$

✓ **4.** $\frac{11}{12}$ ◯ $\frac{4}{8}$

5. $\frac{5}{8}$ ◯ $\frac{2}{5}$

Math Talk Math Processes and Practices ❻

Compare How do you know $\frac{1}{3} < \frac{1}{2}$?

On Your Own

Compare. Write $<$ or $>$.

6. $\frac{8}{10}$ ◯ $\frac{3}{8}$

7. $\frac{1}{3}$ ◯ $\frac{7}{12}$

8. $\frac{2}{6}$ ◯ $\frac{7}{8}$

9. $\frac{4}{8}$ ◯ $\frac{2}{10}$

Math Processes and Practices ❷ Reason Quantitatively **Algebra** Find a numerator that makes the statement true.

10. $\frac{2}{4} < \frac{\square}{6}$

11. $\frac{8}{10} > \frac{\square}{8}$

12. $\frac{10}{12} > \frac{\square}{4}$

13. $\frac{2}{5} < \frac{\square}{10}$

14. When two fractions are between 0 and $\frac{1}{2}$, how do you know which fraction is greater? Explain.

15. GO DEEPER If you know that $\frac{2}{6} < \frac{1}{2}$ and $\frac{3}{4} > \frac{1}{2}$, what do you know about $\frac{2}{6}$ and $\frac{3}{4}$?

16. GO DEEPER Sandra has ribbons that are $\frac{3}{4}$ yard, $\frac{2}{6}$ yard, $\frac{1}{5}$ yard, and $\frac{4}{7}$ yard long. She needs to use the ribbon longer than $\frac{2}{3}$ yard to make a bow. Which length of ribbon could she use for the bow?

Problem Solving • Applications (Real World)

17. **THINK SMARTER** Saundra ran $\frac{7}{12}$ of a mile. Lamar ran $\frac{3}{4}$ of a mile. Who ran farther? Explain.

_____

_____

_____

_____

WRITE ▸ Math • **Show Your Work**

18. **What's the Question?** Selena ran farther than Manny.

_____

_____

19. **GO DEEPER** Chloe made a small pan of ziti and a small pan of lasagna. She cut the ziti into 8 equal parts and the lasagna into 9 equal parts. Her family ate $\frac{2}{3}$ of the lasagna. If her family ate more lasagna than ziti, what fraction of the ziti could have been eaten?

_____

20. **THINK SMARTER** James, Ella, and Ryan biked around Eagle Lake. James biked $\frac{2}{10}$ of the distance in an hour. Ella biked $\frac{4}{8}$ of the distance in an hour. Ryan biked $\frac{2}{5}$ of the distance in an hour. Compare the distances biked by each person by matching the statements to the correct symbol. Each symbol may be used more than once or not at all.

$\frac{2}{10}$ ● $\frac{4}{8}$ •   • =

$\frac{4}{8}$ ● $\frac{2}{5}$ •   • <

$\frac{2}{10}$ ● $\frac{2}{5}$ •   • >

Compare Fractions Using Benchmarks

Learning Objective You will use fraction strips and benchmarks to compare two fractions with different numerators and different denominators.

Compare. Write < or >.

1. $\frac{1}{8}$ $\boxed{<}$ $\frac{6}{10}$

   Think: $\frac{1}{8}$ is less than $\frac{1}{2}$.

   $\frac{6}{10}$ is more than $\frac{1}{2}$.

2. $\frac{4}{12}$ $\bigcirc$ $\frac{4}{6}$

3. $\frac{2}{8}$ $\bigcirc$ $\frac{1}{2}$

4. $\frac{3}{5}$ $\bigcirc$ $\frac{3}{3}$

5. $\frac{7}{8}$ $\bigcirc$ $\frac{5}{10}$

6. $\frac{9}{12}$ $\bigcirc$ $\frac{1}{3}$

7. $\frac{4}{6}$ $\bigcirc$ $\frac{7}{8}$

8. $\frac{2}{4}$ $\bigcirc$ $\frac{2}{3}$

9. $\frac{3}{5}$ $\bigcirc$ $\frac{1}{4}$

10. $\frac{6}{10}$ $\bigcirc$ $\frac{2}{5}$

11. $\frac{1}{8}$ $\bigcirc$ $\frac{2}{10}$

12. $\frac{2}{3}$ $\bigcirc$ $\frac{5}{12}$

Problem Solving · Real World

13. Erika ran $\frac{3}{8}$ mile. Maria ran $\frac{3}{4}$ mile. Who ran farther?

14. Carlos finished $\frac{1}{3}$ of his art project on Monday. Tyler finished $\frac{1}{2}$ of his art project on Monday. Who finished more of his art project on Monday?

_____

_____

15. **WRITE** ▸*Math* Explain a strategy you could use to compare $\frac{2}{6}$ and $\frac{5}{8}$.

_____

_____

_____

Lesson Check

1. What symbol makes the statement true?

$$\frac{4}{6} \bigcirc \frac{3}{8}$$

2. Write a fraction, less than 1, with a demoninator of 6 that is greater than $\frac{3}{4}$.

_____

Spiral Review

3. Abigail is putting tiles on a table top. She needs 48 tiles for each of 8 rows. Each row will have 6 white tiles. The rest of the tiles will be purple. How many purple tiles will she need?

_____

4. Each school bus going on the field trip holds 36 students and 4 adults. There are 6 filled buses on the field trip. How many people are going on the field trip?

_____

5. Noah wants to display his 72 collector's flags. He is going to put 6 flags in each row. How many rows of flags will he have in his display?

_____

6. Julian wrote this number pattern on the board:

3, 10, 17, 24, 31, 38.

Which of the numbers in Julian's pattern are composite numbers?

_____

© Houghton Mifflin Harcourt Publishing Company

FOR MORE PRACTICE
GO TO THE
Personal Math Trainer

Name _____

Compare Fractions

Essential Question How can you compare fractions?

Learning Objective You will compare two fractions with different numerators and different denominators by using common denominators.

Unlock the Problem (Real World)

Every year, Avery's school has a fair. This year, $\frac{3}{8}$ of the booths had face painting and $\frac{1}{4}$ of the booths had sand art. Were there more booths with face painting or sand art?

Compare $\frac{3}{8}$ and $\frac{1}{4}$.

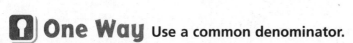

One Way Use a common denominator.

When two fractions have the same denominator, they have equal-size parts. You can compare the number of parts.

THINK	MODEL AND RECORD
Think: 8 is a multiple of both 4 and 8. Use 8 as a common denominator.	Shade the model. Then compare.

$$\frac{1}{4} = \frac{1 \times \boxed{}}{4 \times \boxed{}} = \frac{\boxed{}}{8}$$

$\frac{3}{8}$ already has 8 as a denominator.

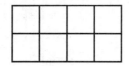   ◯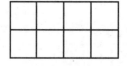

$\frac{3}{8}$ $\frac{2}{8}$

Another Way Use a common numerator.

When two fractions have the same numerator, they represent the same number of parts. You can compare the size of the parts.

THINK	MODEL AND RECORD
Think: 3 is a multiple of both 3 and 1. Use 3 as a common numerator.	Shade the model. Then compare.

$\frac{3}{8}$ already has 3 as a numerator.

$$\frac{1}{4} = \frac{1 \times \boxed{}}{4 \times \boxed{}} = \frac{3}{\boxed{}}$$

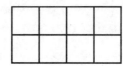   ◯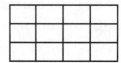

$\frac{3}{8}$ $\frac{3}{12}$

Since $\frac{3}{8}$ ◯ $\frac{1}{4}$, there were more booths with _____.

 Math Talk

Math Processes and Practices ②

Reason Abstractly Why can you not use $\frac{1}{2}$ as a benchmark to compare $\frac{3}{8}$ and $\frac{1}{4}$?

Try This! Compare the fractions. Explain your reasoning.

A $\frac{3}{4}$ ◯ $\frac{1}{3}$

_____

_____

_____

_____

B $\frac{3}{5}$ ◯ $\frac{3}{8}$

_____

_____

_____

_____

C $\frac{3}{4}$ ◯ $\frac{7}{8}$

_____

_____

_____

_____

_____

D $\frac{4}{5}$ ◯ $\frac{2}{3}$

_____

_____

_____

_____

_____

1. Which would you use to compare $\frac{11}{12}$ and $\frac{5}{6}$, a common numerator or a common denominator? Explain.

_____

_____

2. Can you use simplest form to compare $\frac{8}{10}$ and $\frac{3}{5}$? Explain.

_____

_____

Name _____

1. Compare $\frac{2}{5}$ and $\frac{1}{10}$.

Think: Use _____ as a common denominator.

$$\frac{2}{5} = \frac{\boxed{} \times \boxed{}}{\boxed{} \times \boxed{}} = \frac{\boxed{}}{\boxed{}}$$

$$\frac{1}{10}$$

Think: 4 tenth-size parts ◯ 1 tenth-size part.

$$\frac{2}{5} \bigcirc \frac{1}{10}$$

2. Compare $\frac{6}{10}$ and $\frac{3}{4}$.

Think: Use _____ as a common numerator.

$$\frac{6}{10}$$

$$\frac{3}{4} = \frac{\boxed{} \times \boxed{}}{\boxed{} \times \boxed{}} = \frac{\boxed{}}{\boxed{}}$$

Think: A tenth-size part ◯ an eighth-size part.

$$\frac{6}{10} \bigcirc \frac{3}{4}$$

Compare. Write <, >, or =.

✓ **3.** $\frac{7}{8} \bigcirc \frac{2}{8}$

✓ **4.** $\frac{5}{12} \bigcirc \frac{3}{6}$

5. $\frac{4}{10} \bigcirc \frac{4}{6}$

6. $\frac{6}{12} \bigcirc \frac{2}{4}$

Math Talk

Math Processes and Practices ②

Use Reasoning How can using a common numerator or a common denominator help you compare fractions?

On Your Own

Compare. Write <, >, or =.

7. $\frac{1}{3} \bigcirc \frac{1}{4}$

8. $\frac{4}{5} \bigcirc \frac{8}{10}$

9. $\frac{3}{4} \bigcirc \frac{2}{6}$

10. $\frac{1}{2} \bigcirc \frac{5}{8}$

Math Processes and Practices ② **Reason Quantitatively** **Algebra** Find a number that makes the statement true.

11. $\frac{1}{2} > \frac{\boxed{}}{3}$

12. $\frac{3}{10} < \frac{\boxed{}}{5}$

13. $\frac{5}{12} < \frac{\boxed{}}{3}$

14. $\frac{2}{3} > \frac{4}{\boxed{}}$

15. GO DEEPER Students cut a pepperoni pizza into 12 equal slices and ate 5 slices. They cut a veggie pizza into 6 equal slices and ate 4 slices. Use fractions to compare the amounts of each pizza that were eaten.

_____

Unlock the Problem

16. **THINK SMARTER** Jerry is making a strawberry smoothie. Which measure is greatest, the amount of milk, cottage cheese, or strawberries?

Strawberry Smoothie

3 ice cubes

$\frac{3}{4}$ cup milk

$\frac{2}{6}$ cup cottage cheese

$\frac{8}{12}$ cup strawberries

$\frac{1}{4}$ teaspoon vanilla

$\frac{1}{8}$ teaspoon sugar

a. What do you need to find?

_____

b. How will you find the answer?

_____

_____

c. Show your work.

d. Jerry needs more _____ than the other two ingredients.

---

17. **GO DEEPER** Angie, Blake, Carlos, and Daisy went running. Angie ran $\frac{1}{3}$ mile, Blake ran $\frac{3}{5}$ mile, Carlos ran $\frac{7}{10}$ mile, and Daisy ran $\frac{1}{2}$ mile. Which runner ran the shortest distance? Who ran the greatest distance?

_____

18. **THINK SMARTER** Elaine bought $\frac{5}{8}$ pound of potato salad and $\frac{4}{6}$ pound of macaroni salad for a picnic. Use the numbers to compare the amounts of potato salad and macaroni salad Elaine bought.

```
┌──────┐     ┌──────┐          ┌────┐
│      │     │      │          │ 4  │
├──────┤  <  ├──────┤          └────┘
│      │     │      │          ┌────┐
└──────┘     └──────┘          │ 5  │
                               └────┘
                               ┌────┐
                               │ 6  │
                               └────┘
                               ┌────┐
                               │ 8  │
                               └────┘
```

Compare Fractions

Learning Objective You will compare two fractions with different numerators and different denominators by using common denominators.

Compare. Write <, >, or =.

1. $\frac{3}{4}$ $\bigcirc\!\!\!\!<$ $\frac{5}{6}$

Think: 12 is a common denominator.

$\frac{3}{4} = \frac{3 \times 3}{4 \times 3} = \frac{9}{12}$

$\frac{5}{6} = \frac{5 \times 2}{6 \times 2} = \frac{10}{12}$

$\frac{9}{12} < \frac{10}{12}$

2. $\frac{1}{5}$ $\bigcirc$ $\frac{2}{10}$

3. $\frac{2}{4}$ $\bigcirc$ $\frac{2}{5}$

4. $\frac{3}{5}$ $\bigcirc$ $\frac{7}{10}$

5. $\frac{4}{12}$ $\bigcirc$ $\frac{1}{6}$

6. $\frac{2}{6}$ $\bigcirc$ $\frac{1}{3}$

7. $\frac{1}{3}$ $\bigcirc$ $\frac{2}{4}$

Problem Solving

8. A recipe uses $\frac{2}{3}$ cup of flour and $\frac{5}{8}$ cup of blueberries. Is there more flour or more blueberries in the recipe?

9. Peggy completed $\frac{5}{6}$ of the math homework and Al completed $\frac{4}{5}$ of the math homework. Did Peggy or Al complete more of the math homework?

_____

_____

10. **WRITE** ▸*Math* Give an example of fractions that you would compare by finding common denominators, and an example of fractions you would compare by finding common numerators.

_____

_____

Lesson Check

1. Pedro fills a glass $\frac{2}{4}$ full with orange juice. Write a fraction with a denominator of 6 that is greater than $\frac{2}{4}$.

_____

_____

2. Today Ian wants to run less than $\frac{7}{12}$ mile. Write a fraction with a denominator of 4 to represent a distance that is less than $\frac{7}{12}$ mile.

_____

_____

Spiral Review

3. Ms. Davis traveled 372,645 miles last year on business. What is the value of 6 in 372,645?

_____

4. One section of an auditorium has 12 rows of seats. Each row has 13 seats. What is the total number of seats in that section?

_____

5. Sam has 12 black-and-white photos and 18 color photos. He wants to put the photos in equal rows so each row has either black-and-white photos only or color photos only. In how many rows can Sam arrange the photos?

_____

6. The teacher writes $\frac{10}{12}$ on the board. Write this fraction in simplest form.

_____

FOR MORE PRACTICE
GO TO THE
Personal Math Trainer

Compare and Order Fractions

Essential Question How can you order fractions?

Learning Objective You will use number lines to compare two fractions with different numerators and different denominators and record the results of comparisons with symbols >, =, or <.

Unlock the Problem

Jody has equal-size bins for the recycling center. She filled $\frac{3}{5}$ of a bin with plastics, $\frac{1}{12}$ of a bin with paper, and $\frac{9}{10}$ of a bin with glass. Which bin is the most full?

• Underline what you need to find.

• Circle the fractions you will compare.

Example 1 Locate and label $\frac{3}{5}$, $\frac{1}{12}$, and $\frac{9}{10}$ on the number line.

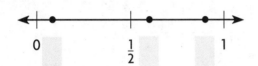

Math Idea

Sometimes it is not reasonable to find the exact location of a point on a number line. Benchmarks can help you find approximate locations.

STEP 1 Compare each fraction to $\frac{1}{2}$.

$\frac{3}{5} \bigcirc \frac{1}{2}$ $\frac{1}{12} \bigcirc \frac{1}{2}$ $\frac{9}{10} \bigcirc \frac{1}{2}$

_____ and _____ are both greater than $\frac{1}{2}$.

_____ is less than $\frac{1}{2}$.

Label $\frac{1}{12}$ on the number line above.

STEP 2 Compare $\frac{3}{5}$ and $\frac{9}{10}$.

Think: Use 10 as a common denominator.

$$\frac{3}{5} = \frac{\quad \times \quad}{\quad \times \quad} = \frac{\quad}{\quad}$$

Since $\frac{6}{10} \bigcirc \frac{9}{10}$, you know that $\frac{3}{5} \bigcirc \frac{9}{10}$.

Label $\frac{3}{5}$ and $\frac{9}{10}$ on the number line above.

The fraction the greatest distance from 0 has the greatest value.

The fraction with the greatest value is _____.

So, the bin with _____ is the most full.

Math Talk

Math Processes and Practices ④

Use Models How do you know you located $\frac{3}{5}$ on the number line correctly?

• Compare the distance between $\frac{3}{5}$ and 0 and the distance between $\frac{9}{10}$ and 0. What can you conclude about the relationship between $\frac{3}{5}$ and $\frac{9}{10}$? Explain.

_____

_____

Example 2 Write $\frac{7}{10}$, $\frac{1}{3}$, $\frac{7}{12}$, and $\frac{8}{10}$ in order from least to greatest.

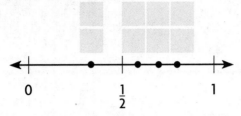

0      $\frac{1}{2}$ 1

STEP 1 Compare each fraction to $\frac{1}{2}$.

List fractions that are less than $\frac{1}{2}$: _____

List fractions that are greater than $\frac{1}{2}$: _____

The fraction with the least value is _____.

Locate and label $\frac{1}{3}$ on the number line above.

_____

STEP 2 Compare $\frac{7}{10}$ to $\frac{7}{12}$ and $\frac{8}{10}$.

Think: $\frac{7}{10}$ and $\frac{7}{12}$ have a common numerator.

$\frac{7}{10}$ ◯ $\frac{7}{12}$

Think: $\frac{7}{10}$ and $\frac{8}{10}$ have a common denominator.

$\frac{7}{10}$ ◯ $\frac{8}{10}$

Locate and label $\frac{7}{10}$, $\frac{7}{12}$, and $\frac{8}{10}$ on the number line above.

The fractions in order from least to greatest are _____.

So, _____ < _____ < _____ < _____.

Try This! Write $\frac{3}{4}$, $\frac{3}{6}$, $\frac{1}{3}$, and $\frac{2}{12}$ in order from least to greatest.

_____ < _____ < _____ < _____

Name _____

1. Locate and label points on the number line to help you write
$\frac{3}{10}$, $\frac{11}{12}$, and $\frac{5}{8}$ in order from least to greatest.

0       $\frac{1}{2}$ 1

_____

Write the fraction with the greatest value.

✓ 2. $\frac{7}{10}, \frac{1}{5}, \frac{9}{10}$

3. $\frac{5}{6}, \frac{7}{12}, \frac{7}{10}$

4. $\frac{2}{8}, \frac{1}{8}, \frac{2}{4}, \frac{2}{6}$

Write the fractions in order from least to greatest.

✓ 5. $\frac{1}{4}, \frac{3}{6}, \frac{1}{8}$

6. $\frac{3}{5}, \frac{2}{3}, \frac{3}{10}, \frac{4}{5}$

7. $\frac{3}{4}, \frac{7}{12}, \frac{5}{12}$

Math Talk

Math Processes and Practices ❷

Use Reasoning How can benchmarks help you order fractions?

On Your Own

Write the fractions in order from least to greatest.

8. $\frac{2}{5}, \frac{1}{3}, \frac{5}{6}$

9. $\frac{4}{8}, \frac{5}{12}, \frac{1}{6}$

10. $\frac{7}{100}, \frac{9}{10}, \frac{4}{5}$

Math Processes and Practices ❷ **Reason Quantitatively** **Algebra** Write a numerator that makes the statement true.

11. $\frac{1}{2} < \frac{\square}{10} < \frac{4}{5}$

12. $\frac{1}{4} < \frac{5}{12} < \frac{\square}{6}$

13. $\frac{\square}{8} < \frac{3}{4} < \frac{7}{8}$

Unlock the Problem

14. **THINK SMARTER** Nancy, Lionel, and Mavis ran in a
5-kilometer race. The table shows their finish times. In
what order did Nancy, Lionel, and Mavis finish the race?

a. What do you need to find?

_____

_____

b. What information do you need to solve the problem?

_____

_____

c. What information is not necessary?

_____

Finish line

5-Kilometer Race Results	
Name	**Time**
Nancy	$\frac{2}{3}$ hour
Lionel	$\frac{7}{12}$ hour
Mavis	$\frac{3}{4}$ hour

d. How will you solve the problem?

_____

_____

e. Show the steps to solve the problem.

f. Complete the sentences.

The runner who finished first is _____.

The runner who finished second is _____.

The runner who finished third is _____.

15. **GO DEEPER** Alma used 3 beads to make
a necklace. The lengths of the beads are
$\frac{5}{6}$ inch, $\frac{5}{12}$ inch, and $\frac{1}{3}$ inch. What are the
lengths in order from shortest to longest?

16. **THINK SMARTER** Victor has his
grandmother's recipe for making
mixed nuts.

$\frac{3}{4}$ cup pecans	$\frac{2}{12}$ cup peanuts
$\frac{1}{2}$ cup almonds	$\frac{7}{8}$ cup walnuts

Order the ingredients used in the recipe
from least to greatest.

_____

_____

Compare and Order Fractions

Learning Objective You will use number lines to compare two fractions with different numerators and different denominators and record the results of comparisons with symbols >, =, or <.

Write the fractions in order from least to greatest.

1. $\frac{5}{8}, \frac{2}{12}, \frac{8}{10}$

Use benchmarks and a number line.

Think: $\frac{5}{8}$ is close to $\frac{1}{2}$. $\frac{2}{12}$ is close to 0.

$\frac{8}{10}$ is close to 1.

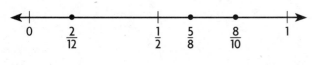

$$\frac{2}{12} < \frac{5}{8} < \frac{8}{10}$$
_____

2. $\frac{1}{5}, \frac{2}{3}, \frac{5}{8}$

_____

3. $\frac{1}{2}, \frac{2}{5}, \frac{6}{10}$

4. $\frac{4}{6}, \frac{7}{12}, \frac{5}{10}$

5. $\frac{1}{4}, \frac{5}{8}, \frac{1}{2}$

_____   _____   _____

Problem Solving · Real World

6. Amy's math notebook weighs $\frac{1}{2}$ pound, her science notebook weighs $\frac{7}{8}$ pound, and her history notebook weighs $\frac{3}{4}$ pound. What are the weights in order from lightest to heaviest?

7. Carl has three picture frames. The thicknesses of the frames are $\frac{4}{5}$ inch, $\frac{3}{12}$ inch, and $\frac{5}{6}$ inch. What are the thicknesses in order from least to greatest?

_____   _____

_____   _____

8. **WRITE** ▸Math How is ordering fractions on a number line similar to and different from ordering whole numbers on a number line?

_____

_____

Lesson Check

1. Juan's three math quizzes this week took him $\frac{1}{3}$ hour, $\frac{4}{6}$ hour, and $\frac{1}{5}$ hour to complete. List the lengths of time in order from least to greatest.

2. On three days last week, Maria ran $\frac{3}{4}$ mile, $\frac{7}{8}$ mile, and $\frac{3}{5}$ mile. List the distances in order from least to greatest.

Spiral Review

3. Santiago collects 435 cents in nickels. How many nickels does he collect?

4. Lisa has three classes that each last 50 minutes. What is the total number of minutes of the three classes?

5. Alicia wrote these numbers: 2, 9, 15, 21. Which of Alicia's numbers is NOT a composite number?

6. Mrs. Carmel serves $\frac{6}{8}$ of a loaf of bread with dinner. Write a fraction with a denominator of 4 that is equivalent to $\frac{6}{8}$.

© Houghton Mifflin Harcourt Publishing Company

FOR MORE PRACTICE
GO TO THE
Personal Math Trainer

Name _____

✓ Chapter 6 Review/Test

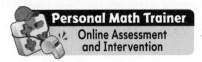

Personal Math Trainer
Online Assessment
and Intervention

1. For numbers 1a–1d, tell whether the fractions are equivalent by selecting the correct symbol.

1a. $\frac{4}{16}$ [= / ≠] $\frac{1}{4}$

1c. $\frac{5}{6}$ [= / ≠] $\frac{25}{30}$

1b. $\frac{3}{5}$ [= / ≠] $\frac{12}{15}$

1d. $\frac{6}{10}$ [= / ≠] $\frac{5}{8}$

2. Juan's mother gave him a recipe for trail mix.

$\frac{3}{4}$ cup cereal	$\frac{2}{3}$ cup almonds
$\frac{1}{4}$ cup peanuts	$\frac{1}{2}$ cup raisins

Order the ingredients used in the recipe from least to greatest.

☐ ☐ ☐ ☐

3. Taylor cuts $\frac{1}{5}$ sheet of construction paper for an arts and crafts project. Write $\frac{1}{5}$ as an equivalent fraction with the denominators shown.

$\frac{\Box}{10}$ $\frac{\Box}{15}$ $\frac{\Box}{25}$ $\frac{\Box}{40}$

4. A mechanic has sockets with the sizes shown below. Write each fraction in the correct box.

$\frac{7}{8}$ in. $\frac{3}{16}$ in. $\frac{1}{4}$ in. $\frac{3}{8}$ in. $\frac{4}{8}$ in. $\frac{11}{16}$ in.

less than $\frac{1}{2}$ in.	equal to $\frac{1}{2}$ in.	greater than $\frac{1}{2}$ in.

© Houghton Mifflin Harcourt Publishing Company

GO DIGITAL Assessment Options
Chapter Test

Chapter 6 377

5. Darcy bought $\frac{1}{2}$ pound of cheese and $\frac{3}{4}$ pound of hamburger for a barbecue. Use the numbers to compare the amounts of cheese and hamburger Darcy bought.

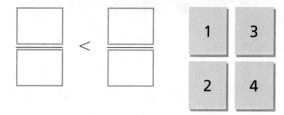

6. Brad is practicing the piano. He spends $\frac{1}{4}$ hour practicing scales and $\frac{1}{3}$ hour practicing the song for his recital. For numbers 6a–6c, select Yes or No to tell whether each of the following is a true statement.

6a.   12 is a common denominator of $\frac{1}{4}$ and $\frac{1}{3}$. ⚪ Yes   ⚪ No

6b.   The amount of time spent practicing scales can be rewritten as $\frac{3}{12}$. ⚪ Yes   ⚪ No

6c.   The amount of time spent practicing the song for the recital can be rewritten as $\frac{6}{12}$. ⚪ Yes   ⚪ No

7. In the school chorus, $\frac{4}{24}$ of the students are fourth graders. In simplest form, what fraction of the students in the school chorus are fourth graders?

_____ of the students

8. Which pairs of fractions are equivalent? Mark all that apply.

⚪ $\frac{8}{12}$ and $\frac{2}{3}$ ⚪ $\frac{4}{5}$ and $\frac{12}{16}$

⚪ $\frac{3}{4}$ and $\frac{20}{28}$ ⚪ $\frac{7}{10}$ and $\frac{21}{30}$

9. Sam worked on his science fair project for $\frac{1}{4}$ hour on Friday and $\frac{1}{2}$ hour on Saturday. What are four common denominators for the fractions? Explain your reasoning.

Name _____

10. Morita works in a florist shop and makes flower arrangements. She puts 10 flowers in each vase, and $\frac{2}{10}$ of the flowers are daisies.

Part A

If Morita makes 4 arrangements, how many daisies does she need? Show how you can check your answer.

_____ daisies

Part B

Last weekend, Morita used 10 daisies to make flower arrangements. How many flowers other than daisies did she use to make the arrangements? Explain your reasoning.

_____ other flowers

Personal Math Trainer

11. **THINK SMARTER +** In Mary's homeroom, $\frac{10}{28}$ of the students have a cat, $\frac{6}{12}$ have a dog, and $\frac{2}{14}$ have a pet bird. For numbers 11a–11c, select True or False for each statement.

11a. In simplest form, $\frac{5}{14}$ of the students have a cat. ○ True ○ False

11b. In simplest form, $\frac{2}{4}$ of the students have a dog. ○ True ○ False

11c. In simplest form, $\frac{1}{7}$ of the students have a pet bird. ○ True ○ False

12. Regina, Courtney, and Ellen hiked around Bear Pond. Regina
hiked $\frac{7}{10}$ of the distance in an hour. Courtney hiked $\frac{3}{6}$ of the
distance in an hour. Ellen hiked $\frac{3}{8}$ of the distance in an hour.
Compare the distances hiked by each person by matching the
statements to the correct symbol. Each symbol may be used more
than once or not at all.

$\frac{7}{10}$ ● $\frac{3}{6}$ ●   ● <

$\frac{3}{8}$ ● $\frac{3}{6}$ ●   ● >

$\frac{7}{10}$ ● $\frac{3}{8}$ ●   ● =

13. Ramon is having some friends over after a baseball game.
Ramon's job is to make a vegetable dip. The ingredients for the
recipe are given.

Ingredients in Vegetable Dip	
$\frac{3}{4}$ cup parsley	$\frac{5}{8}$ cup buttermilk
$\frac{1}{3}$ cup dill	$\frac{1}{2}$ cup cream cheese
$\frac{6}{8}$ cup scallions	$\frac{1}{16}$ cup lemon juice

Part A

Which ingredient does Ramon use the greater amount of,
buttermilk or cream cheese? Explain how you found your answer.

Part B

Ramon says that he needs the same amount of two different
ingredients. Is he correct? Support your answer with information
from the problem.

380

Name _____

14. Sandy is ordering bread rolls for her party. She wants $\frac{3}{5}$ of the rolls to be whole wheat. What other fractions can represent the part of the rolls that will be whole wheat? Shade the models to show your work.

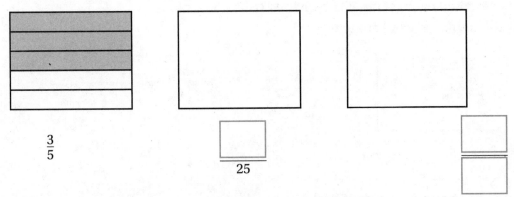

$\frac{3}{5}$ $\frac{}{25}$

15. Angel has $\frac{4}{8}$ yard of ribbon and Lynn has $\frac{3}{4}$ yard of ribbon. Do Angel and Lynn have the same amount of ribbon? Shade the model to show how you found your answer. Explain your reasoning.

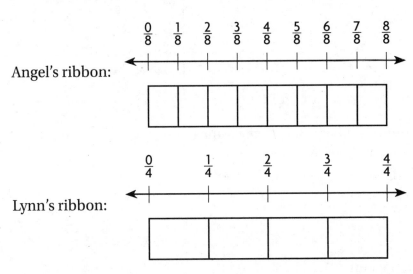

16. Ella used $\frac{1}{4}$ yard of red ribbon. Fill in each box with a number from the list to show equivalent fractions for $\frac{1}{4}$. Not all numbers will be used.

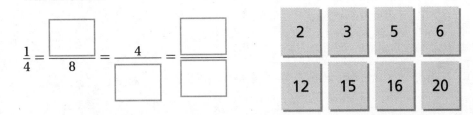

$$\frac{1}{4} = \frac{\boxed{}}{8} = \frac{4}{\boxed{}} = \frac{\boxed{}}{\boxed{}}$$

| 2 | 3 | 5 | 6 |
| 12 | 15 | 16 | 20 |

17. 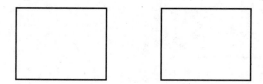 Frank has two same-size rectangles divided into the same number of equal parts. One rectangle has $\frac{3}{4}$ of the parts shaded, and the other has $\frac{1}{3}$ of the parts shaded.

Part A

Into how many parts could each rectangle be divided? Show your work by drawing the parts of each rectangle.

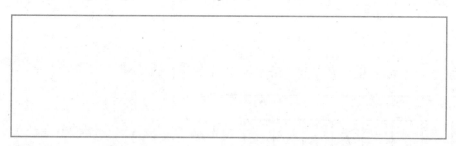

Part B

Is there more than one possible answer to Part A? If so, did you find the least number of parts into which both rectangles could be divided? Explain your reasoning.

18. Suki rode her bike $\frac{4}{5}$ mile. Claire rode her bike $\frac{1}{3}$ mile. They want to compare how far they each rode their bikes using the benchmark $\frac{1}{2}$. For numbers 18a–18c, select the correct answers to describe how to solve the problem.

18a. Compare Suki's distance to the benchmark: $\frac{4}{5}$ | $<$ $>$ $=$ | $\frac{1}{2}$.

18b. Compare Claire's distance to the benchmark: $\frac{1}{3}$ | $<$ $>$ $=$ | $\frac{1}{2}$.

18c. Suki rode her bike | a longer distance than / the same distance as / a shorter distance than | Claire.

Add and Subtract Fractions

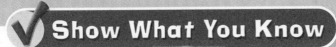

✓ Show What You Know

Personal Math Trainer
Online Assessment
and Intervention

Check your understanding of important skills.

Name _____

▶ **Fractions Equal to 1** Write the fraction that names the whole.

1.

2.

▶ **Parts of a Whole** Write a fraction that names the shaded part.

3. _____

4. _____

5. _____

▶ **Read and Write Fractions** Write a fraction for the shaded part. Write a fraction for the unshaded part.

6.

shaded: _____

unshaded: _____

7.

shaded: _____

unshaded: _____

Math in the Real World

The electricity that powers our appliances is converted from many sources of energy. About $\frac{5}{10}$ is made from coal, about $\frac{2}{10}$ from natural gas, and about $\frac{2}{10}$ from nuclear power. About how much of our electricity comes from sources other than coal, natural gas, or nuclear power?

Vocabulary Builder

▶ **Visualize It** •

Complete the bubble map using the words with a ✓.

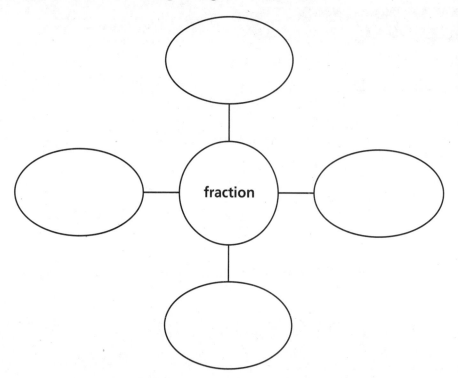

▶ **Understand Vocabulary** •

Write the word or phrase that matches the description.

1. When the numerator and denominator have only 1 as a common factor

   _____

2. A number that names a part of a whole or part of a group

   _____

3. An amount given as a whole number and a fraction

   _____

4. The number in a fraction that tells how many equal parts

   are in the whole or in the group _____

5. A fraction that has a numerator of one _____

 GO DIGITAL
• **Interactive Student Edition**
• **Multimedia eGlossary**

Chapter 7 Vocabulary

Associative Property of Addition

propiedad asociativa de la suma

3

Commutative Property of Addition

propiedad conmutativa de la suma

12

denominator

denominador

22

fraction

fracción

36

mixed number

número mixto

54

numerator

numerador

56

simplest form

mínima expresión

84

unit fraction

fracción unitaria

94

The property that states that when the order of two addends is changed, the sum is the same

Example: $4 + 5 = 5 + 4$

The property that states that you can group addends in different ways and still get the same sum

Example: $3 + (8 + 5) = (3 + 8) + 5$

A number that names a part of a whole or part of a group

Example:

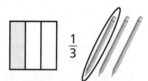

$\frac{1}{3}$

The number below the bar in a fraction that tells how many equal parts are in the whole or in the group

Example: $\frac{3}{4}$ ⟵ denominator

The number above the bar in a fraction that tells how many parts of the whole or group are being considered

Example: $\frac{1}{5}$ ⟵ numerator

An amount given as a whole number and a fraction

Example: $2\frac{3}{6}$ is a mixed number

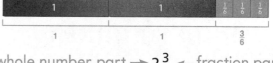

whole number part ⟶ $2\frac{3}{6}$ ⟵ fraction part

A fraction that has a numerator of one

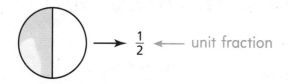

⟶ $\frac{1}{2}$ ⟵ unit fraction

A fraction is in simplest form when the numerator and denominator have only 1 as a common factor

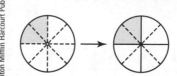

$\frac{2}{8} = \frac{1}{4}$

simplest form

Bingo

For 3 to 6 players

Materials

- 1 set of word cards
- 1 bingo board for each player
- game markers

How to Play

1. The caller chooses a card and reads the definition. Then the caller puts the card in a second pile.

2. Players put a marker on the word that matches the definition each time they find it on their bingo boards.

3. Repeat Steps 1 and 2 until a player marks 5 boxes in a line going down, across, or on a slant and calls "Bingo."

4. Check the answers. Have the player who said "Bingo" read the words aloud while the caller checks the definitions on the cards in the second pile.

Word Box
Associative Property of Addition
Commutative Property of Addition
denominator
fraction
mixed number
numerator
simplest form
unit fraction

Journal

The Write Way

Reflect

Choose one idea. Write about it.

- Is $\frac{3}{4}$ a unit fraction? Explain why or why not.
- Explain what is most important to understand about mixed numbers.
- Write a creative story that includes addition and subtraction of fractions.

Name _____

Add and Subtract Parts of a Whole

Essential Question When can you add or subtract parts of a whole?

Learning Objective You will use fraction circles to tell when you can add or subtract parts of a whole.

Investigate

Materials ■ fraction circles ■ color pencils

Ms. Clark has the following pie pieces left over from a bake sale.

She will combine the pieces so they are on the same dish.
How much pie will be on the dish?

A. Model the problem using fraction circles. Draw a picture
of your model. Then write the sum.

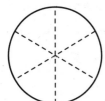 + 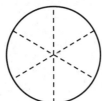 =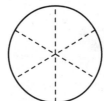

_____ + _____ = _____

So, _____ of a pie is on the dish.

B. Suppose Ms. Clark eats 2 pieces of the pie. How much pie
will be left on the dish? Model the problem using fraction circles.
Draw a picture of your model. Then write the difference.

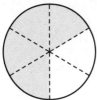

_____ − _____ = _____

So, _____ of the pie is left on the dish.

1. Kevin says that when you combine 3 pieces of pie and 1 piece of pie, you have 4 pieces of pie. Explain how Kevin's statement is related to the equation $\frac{3}{6} + \frac{1}{6} = \frac{4}{6}$.

_____

_____

_____

2. Isabel wrote the equation $\frac{1}{2} + \frac{1}{6} = \frac{4}{6}$ and Jonah wrote $\frac{3}{6} + \frac{1}{6} = \frac{4}{6}$ to represent combining the pie pieces. Explain why both equations are correct.

_____

3. **THINK SMARTER** If there is $\frac{4}{6}$ of a pie on a plate, what part of the pie is missing from the plate? Write an equation to justify your answer.

_____

_____

Make Connections

You can only join or separate parts that refer to the same whole.

Suppose Randy has $\frac{1}{4}$ of a round cake and $\frac{1}{4}$ of a square cake.

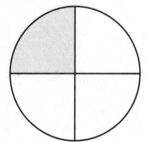 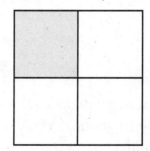

Math Talk

Math Processes and Practices ④

Interpret a Result Give an example of a situation where the equation $\frac{1}{4} + \frac{1}{4} = \frac{2}{4}$ makes sense. Explain your reasoning.

a. Are the wholes the same? Explain.

_____

b. Does the sum $\frac{1}{4} + \frac{1}{4} = \frac{2}{4}$ make sense in this situation? Explain.

_____

_____

_____

Name _____

Use the model to write an equation.

1.

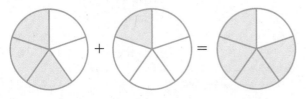

_____

2.

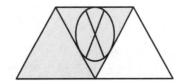

_____

3.

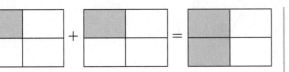

_____

4.

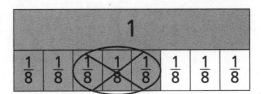

_____

Use the model to solve the equation.

5. $\frac{3}{4} - \frac{1}{4} =$ _____

1			
$\frac{1}{4}$	$\frac{1}{4}$	$\frac{1}{4}$	$\frac{1}{4}$

6. $\frac{5}{6} + \frac{1}{6} =$ _____

7. **Math Processes and Practices** ② **Reason Abstractly** Sean has $\frac{1}{5}$ of a cupcake and $\frac{1}{5}$ of a large cake.

  a. Are the wholes the same? Explain.

  _____

  b. Does the sum $\frac{1}{5} + \frac{1}{5} = \frac{2}{5}$ make sense in this situation? Explain.

  _____

8. **GO DEEPER** Carrie's dance class learned $\frac{1}{5}$ of a new dance on Monday, and $\frac{2}{5}$ of the dance on Tuesday. What fraction of the dance is left for the class to learn on Wednesday?

  _____

Sense or Nonsense?

9. **THINK SMARTER** Samantha and Kim used different models to help find $\frac{1}{3} + \frac{1}{6}$. Whose model makes sense? Whose model is nonsense? Explain your reasoning below each model.

Samantha's Model

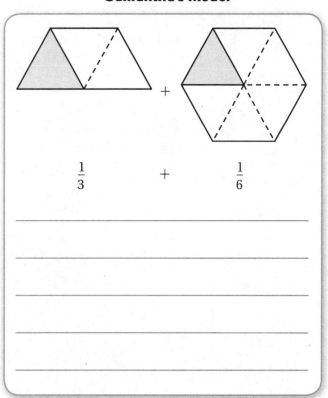

$\frac{1}{3}$ + $\frac{1}{6}$

_____

_____

_____

_____

_____

Kim's Model

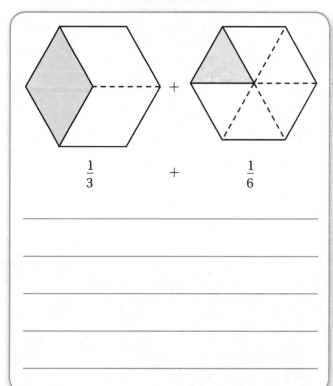

$\frac{1}{3}$ + $\frac{1}{6}$

_____

_____

_____

_____

_____

10. **GO DEEPER** Draw a model you could use to add $\frac{1}{4} + \frac{1}{2}$.

11. **THINK SMARTER +** Cindy has two jars of paint. One jar is $\frac{3}{8}$ full. The other jar is $\frac{2}{8}$ full.

Use the fractions to write an equation that shows the amount of paint Cindy has.

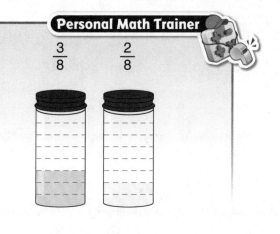

Personal Math Trainer

$\frac{3}{8}$ $\frac{2}{8}$

$\frac{1}{8}$ $\frac{2}{8}$ $\frac{3}{8}$ $\frac{5}{8}$ $\frac{7}{8}$

_____ + _____ = _____

Add and Subtract Parts of a Whole

Learning Objective You will use fraction circles to tell when you can add or subtract parts of a whole.

Use the model to write an equation.

1.

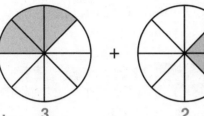

Think: $\frac{3}{8}$ + $\frac{2}{8}$ = $\frac{5}{8}$

$\frac{3}{8} + \frac{2}{8} = \frac{5}{8}$

2.

_____

3.

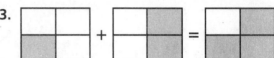

_____

Use the model to solve the equation.

4.

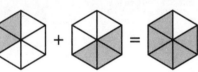

$\frac{2}{6} + \frac{3}{6} =$ _____

5.

$\frac{3}{5} - \frac{2}{5} =$ _____

Problem Solving Real World

6. Jake ate $\frac{4}{8}$ of a pizza. Millie ate $\frac{3}{8}$ of the same pizza. How much of the pizza was eaten by Jake and Millie?

_____

7. **WRITE** ▸*Math* Draw a fraction circle to model $\frac{5}{6} - \frac{1}{6}$ and write the difference.

Lesson Check

1. A whole pie is cut into 8 equal slices. Three of the slices are served. How much of the pie is left?

_____

2. An orange is divided into 6 equal wedges. Jody eats 1 wedge. Then she eats 3 more wedges. How much of the orange did Jody eat?

_____

Spiral Review

3. Put these distances in order from least to greatest: $\frac{3}{16}$ mile, $\frac{1}{8}$ mile, $\frac{3}{4}$ mile

_____

4. Jeremy walked $\frac{6}{8}$ of the way to school and ran the rest of the way. What fraction, in simplest form, shows the part of the way that Jeremy walked?

_____

5. An elevator starts on the 100th floor of a building. It descends 4 floors every 10 seconds. At what floor will the elevator be 60 seconds after it starts?

_____

6. For a school play, the teacher asked the class to set up chairs in 20 rows with 25 chairs in each row. After setting up all the chairs, they were 5 chairs short. How many chairs did the class set up?

_____

FOR MORE PRACTICE
GO TO THE
Personal Math Trainer

Name _____

Write Fractions as Sums

Essential Question How can you write a fraction as a sum of fractions with the same denominators?

Learning Objective You will write a fraction as a sum of unit fractions.

 Unlock the Problem

Emilio cut a sandwich into 8 equal pieces and ate 1 piece. He has $\frac{7}{8}$ of the sandwich left. Emilio put each remaining piece on a snack plate. How many snack plates did he use? What part of the sandwich did he put on each plate?

Each piece of the sandwich is $\frac{1}{8}$ of the whole. $\frac{1}{8}$ is called a **unit fraction** because it tells the part of the whole that 1 piece represents. A unit fraction always has a numerator of 1.

Example 1 Write $\frac{7}{8}$ as a sum of unit fractions.

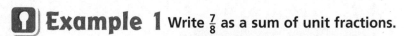

$\frac{7}{8} =$ _____ + _____ + _____ + _____ + _____ + _____ + _____

The number of addends represents the number of plates used.

The unit fractions represent the part of the sandwich on each plate.

So, Emilio used _____ plates. He put _____ of a sandwich on each plate.

1. What if Emilio ate 3 pieces of the sandwich instead of 1 piece? How many snack plates would he need? What part of the sandwich would be on each plate? Explain.

_____

_____

_____

_____

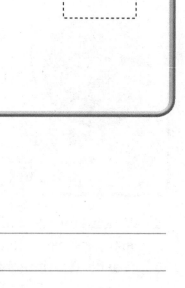

🔑 Example 2 Write a fraction as a sum.

Kevin and Isabel are going to share a whole pizza. The pizza is cut into 6 equal slices. They will put the slices on two separate dishes. What part of the whole pizza could be on each dish?

Shade the models to show three different ways Kevin and Isabel could share the pizza. Write an equation for each model.

Think: $\frac{6}{6} = 1$ whole pizza.

$$= \underline{\qquad} + \underline{\qquad}$$

$$= \underline{\qquad} + \underline{\qquad}$$

$$= \underline{\qquad} + \underline{\qquad}$$

Math Talk

Math Processes and Practices ⑧

Use Repeated Reasoning
If there were 8 dishes, could $\frac{1}{6}$ of the whole pizza be on each dish? Explain.

2. What if 3 friends share the pizza and they put the pizza slices on three separate dishes? What part of the pizza could be on each dish? Write equations to support your answer.

_____

_____

Name _____

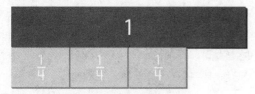

1. Write $\frac{3}{4}$ as a sum of unit fractions.

1

$\frac{1}{4}$	$\frac{1}{4}$	$\frac{1}{4}$

$\frac{3}{4} = $ _____ + _____ + _____

Write the fraction as a sum of unit fractions.

✓ **2.**

1

$\frac{1}{6}$	$\frac{1}{6}$	$\frac{1}{6}$	$\frac{1}{6}$	$\frac{1}{6}$	$\frac{1}{6}$

$\frac{5}{6} = $ _____

✓ **3.**

1

$\frac{1}{3}$	$\frac{1}{3}$	$\frac{1}{3}$

$\frac{2}{3} = $ _____

Math Talk

Math Processes and Practices ②

Use Reasoning How is the numerator in $\frac{5}{6}$ related to the number of addends in the sum of its unit fractions?

On Your Own

Write the fraction as a sum of unit fractions.

4. $\frac{4}{12} = $ _____

5. $\frac{6}{8} = $ _____

Write the fraction as a sum of fractions three different ways.

6. $\frac{8}{10}$

_____

_____

_____

7. $\frac{6}{6}$

_____

_____

_____

8. **Math Processes and Practices ③** **Compare Representations** How many different ways can you write a fraction that has a numerator of 2 as a sum of fractions? Explain.

_____

_____

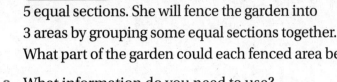

Unlock the Problem

9. **THINK SMARTER**   Holly's garden is divided into
    5 equal sections. She will fence the garden into
    3 areas by grouping some equal sections together.
    What part of the garden could each fenced area be?

    a. What information do you need to use?

    _____

    _____

    b. How can writing an equation help you solve the problem? _____

    _____

    _____

    c. How can drawing a model help you write an equation?

    _____

    _____

    d. Show how you can solve the problem.

    e. Complete the sentence.

        The garden can be fenced into _____,

        _____, and _____ parts or _____,

        _____, and _____ parts.

10. **GO DEEPER** Leena walked $\frac{2}{3}$ of a mile. What
    is $\frac{2}{3}$ written as a sum of unit fractions with a
    denominator of 9?

    _____

11. **THINK SMARTER** Ellie's mom sells toys. She
    sold $\frac{7}{10}$ of the toys. Select a way $\frac{7}{10}$ can be
    written as a sum of fractions. Mark all that
    apply.

    (A) $\frac{4}{10} + \frac{1}{10} + \frac{1}{10} + \frac{1}{10}$

    (B) $\frac{4}{10} + \frac{3}{10} + \frac{1}{10} + \frac{1}{10} + \frac{1}{10}$

    (C) $\frac{1}{10} + \frac{2}{10} + \frac{3}{10} + \frac{1}{10}$

Write Fractions as Sums

Learning Objective You will write a
fraction as a sum of unit fractions.

Write the fraction as a sum of unit fractions.

1. $\dfrac{4}{5} = \underline{\dfrac{1}{5} + \dfrac{1}{5} + \dfrac{1}{5} + \dfrac{1}{5}}$

 Think: Add $\frac{1}{5}$ four times.

2. $\dfrac{3}{8} = $ _____

3. $\dfrac{6}{12} = $ _____

4. $\dfrac{4}{4} = $ _____

Write the fraction as a sum of fractions three different ways.

5. $\dfrac{7}{10}$

_____

_____

_____

6. $\dfrac{6}{6}$

_____

_____

_____

Problem Solving · Real World

7. Petra is asked to color $\frac{6}{6}$ of her grid. She must use 3 colors: blue, red, and pink. There must be more blue sections than red sections or pink sections. What are the different ways Petra can color the sections of her grid and follow all the rules?

_____

_____

_____

8. **WRITE** ▸ *Math* Write $\frac{9}{12}$ as a sum of unit fractions.

_____

_____

_____

Lesson Check

1. Jorge wants to write $\frac{4}{5}$ as a sum of unit fractions. What should he write?

2. What fraction is equivalent to the expression $\frac{4}{8} + \frac{2}{8} + \frac{1}{8}$?

Spiral Review

3. An apple is cut into 6 equal slices. Nancy eats 2 of the slices. What fraction of the apple is left?

4. Which of these numbers is a prime number: 1, 11, 21, 51?

5. A teacher has a bag of 100 unit cubes. She gives an equal number of cubes to each of the 7 groups in her class. She gives each group as many cubes as she can. How many unit cubes are left over?

6. Jessie sorted the coins in her bank. She made 7 stacks of 6 dimes and 8 stacks of 5 nickels. She then found 1 dime and 1 nickel. How many dimes and nickels does Jessie have in all?

**FOR MORE PRACTICE
GO TO THE
Personal Math Trainer**

Add Fractions Using Models

Essential Question How can you add fractions with like denominators using models?

Learning Objective You will use fraction strips and a number line to add fractions with like denominators.

Unlock the Problem

Ms. Clark made a loaf of bread. She used $\frac{1}{8}$ of the bread for a snack and $\frac{5}{8}$ of the bread for lunch. How much did she use for a snack and lunch?

One Way Use a picture.

$\frac{1}{8}$ is _____ eighth-size piece of bread.

$\frac{5}{8}$ is _____ eighth-size pieces of bread.

Shade 1 eighth-size piece. Then shade 5 eighth-size pieces.

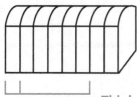

snack lunch

Think: The pieces you shaded represent the pieces Ms. Clark used.

So, Ms. Clark used _____ eighth-size

pieces, or $\frac{}{8}$ of the bread.

Another Way Use fraction strips.

The 1 strip represents the whole loaf.

Each $\frac{1}{8}$ part represents 1 eighth-size piece of bread.

Shade $\frac{1}{8}$. Then shade $\frac{5}{8}$.

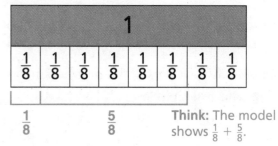

$\frac{1}{8}$ $\frac{5}{8}$

Think: The model shows $\frac{1}{8} + \frac{5}{8}$.

How many $\frac{1}{8}$-size parts are shaded? _____

Write the sum. $\frac{1}{8} + \frac{5}{8} = \frac{}{8}$

So, Ms. Clark used _____ of the bread.

1. Explain how the numerator of the sum is related to the fraction strip model.

_____

_____

Math Talk

Math Processes and Practices ②

Reason Abstractly
Explain why $\frac{1}{8} + \frac{5}{8} \neq \frac{6}{16}$.

2. Explain how the denominator of the sum is related to the fraction strip model.

_____

_____

🔑 Example

Jacob needs two strips of wood to make masts for a miniature sailboat. One mast will be $\frac{3}{6}$ foot long. The other mast will be $\frac{2}{6}$ foot long. He has a strip of wood that is $\frac{4}{6}$ foot long. Is this strip of wood long enough to make both masts?

Shade the model to show $\frac{3}{6} + \frac{2}{6}$.

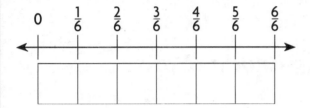

Write the sum. $\frac{3}{6} + \frac{2}{6} = \frac{}{6}$

Is the sum less than or greater than $\frac{4}{6}$? _____

So, the strip of wood _____ long enough to make both masts.

3. Explain how you used the number line to determine if the sum was less than $\frac{4}{6}$.

_____

_____

4. What if each mast was $\frac{2}{6}$ foot long? Could Jacob use the strip of wood to make both masts? Explain.

_____

Share and Show [MATH BOARD]

1. Adrian's cat ate $\frac{3}{5}$ of a bag of cat treats in September and $\frac{1}{5}$ of the same bag of cat treats in October. What part of the bag of cat treats did Adrian's cat eat in both months?

Use the model to find the sum $\frac{3}{5} + \frac{1}{5}$.

How many fifth-size pieces are shown? _____

$\frac{3}{5} + \frac{1}{5} = \frac{}{5}$ of a bag

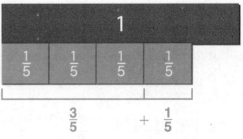

© Houghton Mifflin Harcourt Publishing Company

Name _____

Use the model to find the sum.

2.
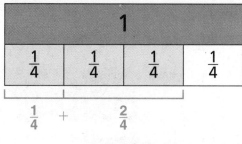

$$\frac{1}{4} + \frac{2}{4} = \underline{\hspace{2cm}}$$

3.
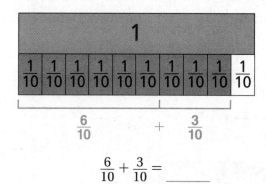

$$\frac{6}{10} + \frac{3}{10} = \underline{\hspace{2cm}}$$

Find the sum. Use models to help.

4. $\frac{3}{6} + \frac{3}{6} = \underline{\hspace{2cm}}$

5. $\frac{5}{8} + \frac{2}{8} = \underline{\hspace{2cm}}$

6. $\frac{1}{3} + \frac{1}{3} = \underline{\hspace{2cm}}$

On Your Own

 Math Talk — Math Processes and Practices ③

Apply Explain how to add $\frac{2}{6} + \frac{3}{6}$.

Find the sum. Use models or *i*Tools to help.

7. $\frac{5}{8} + \frac{2}{8} = \underline{\hspace{2cm}}$

8. $\frac{2}{5} + \frac{2}{5} = \underline{\hspace{2cm}}$

9. $\frac{4}{6} + \frac{1}{6} = \underline{\hspace{2cm}}$

10. **GO DEEPER** Jason is making a fruit drink. He mixes $\frac{2}{8}$ quart of grape juice with $\frac{3}{8}$ quart of apple juice. Then he adds $\frac{1}{8}$ quart of lemonade. How much fruit drink does Jason make?

Problem Solving • Applications (Real World)

11. **THINK SMARTER** A sum has five addends. Each addend is a unit fraction. The sum is 1. What are the addends?

_____

12. **THINK SMARTER** In a survey, $\frac{4}{12}$ of the students chose Friday and $\frac{5}{12}$ chose Saturday as their favorite day of the week. What fraction shows the students who chose Friday or Saturday as their favorite day? Shade the model to show your answer.

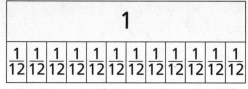

_____ of the students chose Friday or Saturday.

13. (Math Processes and Practices ④) **Model Mathematics** Jin is putting colored sand in a jar. She filled $\frac{2}{10}$ of the jar with blue sand and $\frac{4}{10}$ of the jar with pink sand. Describe one way to model the part of the jar filled with sand.

_____

_____

Connect to Art

Stained Glass Windows

Have you ever seen a stained glass window in a building or home? Artists have been designing stained glass windows for hundreds of years.

Help design the stained glass sail on the boat below.

Materials ■ color pencils

Look at the eight triangles in the sail. Use the guide below to color the triangles:

- $\frac{2}{8}$ blue
- $\frac{3}{8}$ red
- $\frac{2}{8}$ orange
- $\frac{1}{8}$ yellow

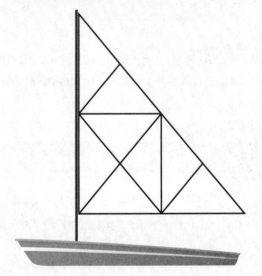

14. (Math Processes and Practices ④) **Write an Equation** Write an equation that shows the fraction of triangles that are red or blue.

15. *GO DEEPER* What color is the greatest part of the sail? Write a fraction for that color. How do you know that fraction is greater than the other fractions? Explain.

_____

_____

_____

Add Fractions Using Models

Learning Objective You will use fraction strips and a number line to add fractions with like denominators.

Find the sum. Use fraction strips to help.

1. $\dfrac{2}{6} + \dfrac{1}{6} = \underline{\quad \dfrac{3}{6} \quad}$

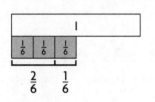

2. $\dfrac{4}{10} + \dfrac{5}{10} = \underline{\qquad\qquad}$

3. $\dfrac{1}{3} + \dfrac{2}{3} = \underline{\qquad\qquad}$

4. $\dfrac{2}{4} + \dfrac{1}{4} = \underline{\qquad\qquad}$

5. $\dfrac{2}{12} + \dfrac{4}{12} = \underline{\qquad\qquad}$

6. $\dfrac{1}{6} + \dfrac{2}{6} = \underline{\qquad\qquad}$

Problem Solving · Real World

7. Lola walks $\dfrac{4}{10}$ mile to her friend's house. Then she walks $\dfrac{5}{10}$ mile to the store. How far does she walk in all?

   _____

8. Evan eats $\dfrac{1}{8}$ of a pan of lasagna and his brother eats $\dfrac{2}{8}$ of it. What fraction of the pan of lasagna do they eat?

   _____

9. Jacqueline buys $\dfrac{2}{4}$ yard of green ribbon and $\dfrac{1}{4}$ yard of pink ribbon. How many yards of ribbon does she buy?

   _____

10. Shu mixes $\dfrac{2}{3}$ pound of peanuts with $\dfrac{1}{3}$ pound of almonds. How many pounds of nuts does Shu mix?

    _____

11. **WRITE** ▸*Math* Find a recipe in a book or online that includes the amount of salt as a fraction. Model how to find the amount of salt needed when the recipe is doubled.

Lesson Check

1. Mary Jane has $\frac{3}{8}$ of a medium pizza left. Hector has $\frac{2}{8}$ of another medium pizza left. How much pizza do they have altogether? Use models to help.

2. Jeannie ate $\frac{1}{4}$ of an apple. Kelly ate $\frac{2}{4}$ of the apple. How much did they eat together? Use models to help.

Spiral Review

3. Karen is making 14 different kinds of greeting cards. She is making 12 of each kind. How many greeting cards is she making?

4. Jefferson works part time and earns $1,520 in four weeks. How much does he earn each week?

5. By installing efficient water fixtures, the average American can reduce water use to about 45 gallons of water per day. Using such water fixtures, about how many gallons of water would the average American use in December?

6. Collin is making a bulletin board and note center. He is using square cork tiles and square dry-erase tiles. One of every 3 squares will be a cork square. If he uses 12 squares for the center, how many will be cork squares?

© Houghton Mifflin Harcourt Publishing Company

FOR MORE PRACTICE GO TO THE Personal Math Trainer

Subtract Fractions Using Models

Essential Question How can you subtract fractions with like denominators using models?

Learning Objective You will use fraction strips and a number line to subtract fractions with like denominators.

Unlock the Problem

A rover needs to travel $\frac{5}{8}$ mile to reach its destination. It has already traveled $\frac{3}{8}$ mile. How much farther does the rover need to travel?

Compare fractions to find the difference.

STEP 1 Shade the model.

Shade the model to show the total distance.

Then shade the model to show how much distance the rover has already covered.

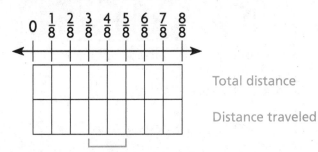

Total distance

Distance traveled

Think: The difference is _____.

STEP 2 Write the difference.

$$\frac{5}{8} - \frac{3}{8} = \frac{}{8}$$

So, the rover needs to travel _____ mile farther.

1. Explain how the model shows how much farther the rover needs to travel.

   _____

   _____

2. Explain how you can use the model to find $\frac{6}{8} - \frac{2}{8}$.

   _____

   _____

🔓 Example

Sam ordered a small pizza, which was cut into 6 equal slices. He ate $\frac{2}{6}$ of the pizza and put the rest away for later. How much of the pizza did he put away for later?

Find $1 - \frac{2}{6}$.

- How much pizza did Sam begin with?

  _____

- How many slices are in the whole? _____

- How many slices did Sam eat? _____

🔓 One Way Use a picture.

Shade 1 whole.

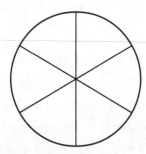

Cross out the parts Sam ate.

Think: He ate $\frac{2}{6}$ of the pizza, or 2 sixth-size parts.

How many sixth-size parts are left? _____

So, Sam put _____ of the pizza away for later.

🔓 Another Way Use fraction strips.

Use six $\frac{1}{6}$-size parts to model the whole pizza.

1					
$\frac{1}{6}$	$\frac{1}{6}$	$\frac{1}{6}$	$\frac{1}{6}$	$\frac{1}{6}$	$\frac{1}{6}$

How many $\frac{1}{6}$-size parts should you cross out to model the slices Sam ate? _____

How many $\frac{1}{6}$-size parts are left? _____

Write the difference.

$1 - \dfrac{}{} = \dfrac{}{}$

Math Talk

Math Processes and Practices ④

Use Models Explain why it makes sense to think of 1 whole as $\frac{6}{6}$ in this problem.

3. Explain how the equation $\frac{6}{6} - \frac{2}{6} = \frac{4}{6}$ is related to the problem situation.

_____

_____

4. Sam ate $\frac{2}{3}$ of the pizza and put the rest away for later. Explain how you can use the circle to find how much of the pizza Sam put away for later.

_____

_____

_____

Name _____

1. Lisa needs $\frac{4}{5}$ pound of shrimp to make shrimp salad. She has $\frac{1}{5}$ pound of shrimp. How much more shrimp does Lisa need to make the salad?

   Subtract $\frac{4}{5} - \frac{1}{5}$. Use the model to help.

   Shade the model to show how much shrimp Lisa needs.

   Then shade the model to show how much shrimp Lisa has. Compare the difference between the two shaded rows.

   $\frac{4}{5} - \frac{1}{5} = \frac{}{5}$ pound

   Lisa needs _____ pound more shrimp.

Use the model to find the difference.

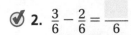

2. $\frac{3}{6} - \frac{2}{6} = \frac{}{6}$

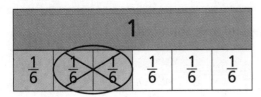

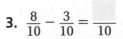

3. $\frac{8}{10} - \frac{3}{10} = \frac{}{10}$

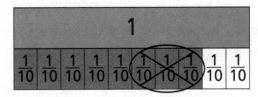

Subtract. Use models to help.

4. $\frac{5}{8} - \frac{2}{8} =$ _____

5. $\frac{7}{12} - \frac{2}{12} =$ _____

6. $\frac{3}{4} - \frac{2}{4} =$ _____

On Your Own

Subtract. Use models to help.

7. $\frac{2}{3} - \frac{1}{3} =$ _____

8. $\frac{7}{8} - \frac{5}{8} =$ _____

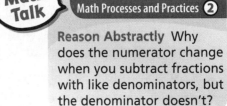

Math Talk   Math Processes and Practices ②

Reason Abstractly Why does the numerator change when you subtract fractions with like denominators, but the denominator doesn't?

9. **THINK SMARTER** Explain how you could find the unknown addend in $\frac{2}{6} +$ _____ $= 1$ without using a model.

_____

_____

_____

Unlock the Problem

10. **GO DEEPER** Mrs. Ruiz served a pie for dessert two nights in a row. The drawings below show the pie after her family ate dessert on each night. What fraction of the pie did they eat on the second night?

First night

Second night

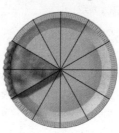

a. What do you need to know? _____

_____

b. How can you find the number of pieces eaten on the second night? _____

_____

c. Explain the steps you used to solve the problem.

_____

_____

_____

d. Complete the sentences.

After the first night, _____ pieces were left.

After the second night, _____ pieces were left.

So, _____ of the pie was eaten on the second night.

11. **Math Processes and Practices 6** **Make Connections Between Models** Judi ate $\frac{7}{8}$ of a small pizza and Jack ate $\frac{2}{8}$ of a second small pizza. How much more of a pizza did Judi eat?

_____

12. **THINK SMARTER** Keiko sewed $\frac{3}{4}$ yard of lace on her backpack. Pam sewed $\frac{1}{4}$ yard of lace on her backpack. Shade the model to show how much more lace Keiko sewed on her backpack than Pam.

1			
$\frac{1}{4}$	$\frac{1}{4}$	$\frac{1}{4}$	$\frac{1}{4}$

Keiko sewed _____ yard more lace on her backpack than Pam.

Subtract Fractions Using Models

Learning Objective You will use fraction strips and a number line to subtract fractions with like denominators.

Subtract. Use fraction strips to help.

1. $\dfrac{4}{5} - \dfrac{1}{5} = $ _____ $\dfrac{3}{5}$

2. $\dfrac{3}{4} - \dfrac{1}{4} = $ _____

$\dfrac{2}{4}$

3. $\dfrac{5}{6} - \dfrac{1}{6} = $ _____

4. $\dfrac{7}{8} - \dfrac{1}{8} = $ _____

Problem Solving Real World

Use the table for 5 and 6.

5. Ena is making trail mix. She buys the items shown in the table. How many more pounds of pretzels than raisins does she buy?

_____

6. How many more pounds of granola than banana chips does she buy?

_____

Item	Weight (in pounds)
Pretzels	$\dfrac{7}{8}$
Peanuts	$\dfrac{4}{8}$
Raisins	$\dfrac{2}{8}$
Banana Chips	$\dfrac{3}{8}$
Granola	$\dfrac{5}{8}$

7. **WRITE** ▸*Math* List and describe the steps you would use to model $\dfrac{7}{10} - \dfrac{4}{10}$.

_____

_____

Lesson Check

1. Lee reads for $\frac{3}{4}$ hour in the morning and $\frac{2}{4}$ hour in the afternoon. How much longer does Lee read in the morning than in the afternoon? Use models to help.

2. What equation does the model below represent?

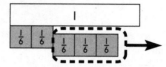

Spiral Review

3. A city received 2 inches of rain each day for 3 days. The meteorologist said that if the rain had been snow, each inch of rain would have been 10 inches of snow. How much snow would that city have received in the 3 days?

4. At a party there were four large submarine sandwiches, all the same size. During the party, $\frac{2}{3}$ of the chicken sandwich, $\frac{3}{4}$ of the tuna sandwich, $\frac{7}{12}$ of the roast beef sandwich, and $\frac{5}{6}$ of the veggie sandwich were eaten. Which sandwich had the least amount left?

5. Deena uses $\frac{3}{8}$ cup milk and $\frac{2}{8}$ cup oil in a recipe. How much liquid is this?

6. In the car lot, $\frac{4}{12}$ of the cars are white and $\frac{3}{12}$ of the cars are blue. What fraction of the cars in the lot are either white or blue?

FOR MORE PRACTICE GO TO THE
Personal Math Trainer

Name _____

Add and Subtract Fractions

Essential Question How can you add and subtract fractions with like denominators?

Learning Objective You will add and subtract fractions with common denominators.

🔑 Unlock the Problem

Julie is making a poster for a book report. The directions say to use $\frac{1}{5}$ of the poster to describe the setting, $\frac{2}{5}$ of the poster to describe the characters, and the rest of the poster to describe the plot. What part of the poster will she use to describe the plot?

🔒 Example Use a model.

Shade _____ to represent the part for the setting.

Shade _____ to represent the part for the characters.

1				
$\frac{1}{5}$	$\frac{1}{5}$	$\frac{1}{5}$	$\frac{1}{5}$	$\frac{1}{5}$

- Write an equation for the part of the poster used for

  the setting and characters. _____

- What does the part of the model that is not shaded represent?

  _____

- Write an equation for the part of the poster she will use for the plot.

  _____

So, Julie will use _____ of the poster to describe the plot.

Math Processes and Practices ⑦

Look for Structure Why should Julie divide her poster into 5 equal parts instead of 3 equal parts?

1. **What's the Error?** Luke says $\frac{1}{5} + \frac{2}{5} = \frac{3}{10}$. Describe his error.

   _____

   _____

   _____

Chapter 7 409

Common Denominators Fractions with common denominators represent wholes divided into the same number of equal-size parts. To add or subtract fractions with the same denominator, you can add or subtract the number of parts given in the numerators.

Example Complete each equation.

Words	Fractions
1 fourth-size part + 2 fourth-size parts = _____ fourth-size parts	$\frac{1}{4} + \frac{2}{4} = \frac{}{4}$
3 sixth-size parts + 2 sixth-size parts = _____	$\frac{3}{6} + \frac{2}{6} = \underline{}$
7 tenth-size parts − 4 tenth-size parts = _____	$\underline{} - \underline{} = \underline{}$

Share and Show MATH BOARD

Math Talk Math Processes and Practices ②

Reason Abstractly
Explain why $\frac{11}{12} - \frac{5}{6} \neq \frac{6}{6}$.

1. 9 twelfth-size parts − 5 twelfth-size parts = _____

   $\frac{9}{12} - \frac{5}{12} =$ _____

Find the sum or difference.

2. $\frac{3}{12} + \frac{8}{12} =$ _____

3. $\frac{1}{3} + \frac{1}{3} =$ _____

4. $\frac{3}{4} - \frac{1}{4} =$ _____

5. $\frac{2}{6} + \frac{2}{6} =$ _____

6. $\frac{3}{8} + \frac{1}{8} =$ _____

7. $\frac{6}{10} - \frac{2}{10} =$ _____

On Your Own

Find the sum or difference.

8. $\frac{1}{2} + \frac{1}{2} =$ _____

9. $\frac{5}{6} - \frac{4}{6} =$ _____

10. $\frac{4}{5} - \frac{2}{5} =$ _____

Practice: Copy and Solve Find the sum or difference.

11. $\frac{1}{4} + \frac{1}{4} =$ _____

12. $\frac{9}{10} - \frac{5}{10} =$ _____

13. $\frac{1}{12} + \frac{7}{12} =$ _____

14. **GO DEEPER** Christopher mixes $\frac{3}{8}$ gallon of red paint with $\frac{5}{8}$ gallon of blue paint to make purple paint. He uses $\frac{2}{8}$ gallon of the purple paint. How much purple paint is left?

_____

Name _____

15. (Math Processes and Practices 6) A city worker is painting a stripe down the center of Main Street. Main Street is $\frac{8}{10}$ mile long. The worker painted $\frac{4}{10}$ mile of the street. **Explain** how to find what part of a mile is left to paint.

_____

_____

_____

16. (THINK SMARTER) **Sense or Nonsense?** Brian says that when you add or subtract fractions with the same denominator, you can add or subtract the numerators and keep the same denominator. Is Brian correct? Explain.

_____

_____

_____

_____

_____

17. (GO DEEPER) The length of a rope was $\frac{6}{8}$ yard. Jeff cut the rope into 3 pieces. Each piece is a different length measured in eighths of a yard. What is the length of each piece of rope?

_____

18. (THINK SMARTER) For 18a–18d, choose Yes or No to show if the sum or difference is correct.

18a. $\frac{3}{5} + \frac{1}{5} = \frac{4}{5}$ ○ Yes   ○ No

18b. $\frac{1}{4} + \frac{2}{4} = \frac{3}{8}$ ○ Yes   ○ No

18c. $\frac{5}{8} - \frac{4}{8} = \frac{1}{8}$ ○ Yes   ○ No

18d. $\frac{4}{9} - \frac{2}{9} = \frac{6}{9}$ ○ Yes   ○ No

Sense or Nonsense?

19. Harry says that $\frac{1}{4} + \frac{1}{8} = \frac{2}{8}$. Jane says $\frac{1}{4} + \frac{1}{8} = \frac{3}{8}$.
Whose answer makes sense? Whose answer is
nonsense? Explain your reasoning. Draw a
model to help.

Harry
$$\frac{1}{4} + \frac{1}{8} = \frac{2}{8}$$

Jane
$$\frac{1}{4} + \frac{1}{8} = \frac{3}{8}$$

Model

Harry

Jane

Add and Subtract Fractions

Learning Objective You will add and subtract fractions with common denominators.

Find the sum or difference.

1. $\frac{4}{12} + \frac{8}{12} =$ _____ $\frac{12}{12}$

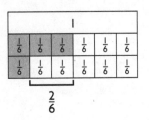

$\frac{4}{12}$ $\frac{8}{12}$

2. $\frac{3}{6} - \frac{1}{6} =$ _____

$\frac{2}{6}$

3. $\frac{4}{5} - \frac{3}{5} =$ _____

4. $\frac{6}{10} + \frac{3}{10} =$ _____

5. $1 - \frac{3}{8} =$ _____

6. $\frac{1}{4} + \frac{2}{4} =$ _____

Problem Solving Real World

Use the table for 7 and 8.

7. Guy finds how far his house is from several locations and makes the table shown. How much farther away from Guy's house is the library than the cafe?

   _____

8. If Guy walks from his house to school and back, how far does he walk?

   _____

Distance from Guy's House	
Location	Distance (in miles)
Library	$\frac{9}{10}$
School	$\frac{5}{10}$
Store	$\frac{7}{10}$
Cafe	$\frac{4}{10}$
Yogurt Shop	$\frac{6}{10}$

9. **WRITE** ▸ *Math* Compare how you would model and record finding the sum and difference of two rocks weighing $\frac{2}{8}$ pound and $\frac{3}{8}$ pound.

_____

_____

Lesson Check

1. Mr. Angulo buys $\frac{5}{8}$ pound of red grapes and $\frac{3}{8}$ pound of green grapes. How many pounds of grapes did Mr. Angulo buy?

2. What equation does the model below represent?

1							
$\frac{1}{8}$	$\frac{1}{8}$	$\frac{1}{8}$	$\frac{1}{8}$	$\frac{1}{8}$	$\frac{1}{8}$	$\frac{1}{8}$	$\frac{1}{8}$
$\frac{1}{8}$	$\frac{1}{8}$	$\frac{1}{8}$	$\frac{1}{8}$	$\frac{1}{8}$	$\frac{1}{8}$	$\frac{1}{8}$	$\frac{1}{8}$

Spiral Review

3. There are 6 muffins in a package. How many packages will be needed to feed 48 people if each person has 2 muffins?

4. Camp Oaks gets 32 boxes of orange juice and 56 boxes of apple juice. Each shelf in the cupboard can hold 8 boxes of juice. What is the least number of shelves needed for all the juice boxes?

5. A machine makes 18 parts each hour. If the machine operates 24 hours a day, how many parts can it make in one day?

6. What equation does the model below represent?

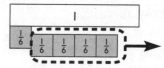

FOR MORE PRACTICE
GO TO THE
Personal Math Trainer

Name _____

 **Mid-Chapter Checkpoint**

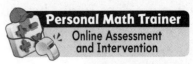
Personal Math Trainer
Online Assessment
and Intervention

Vocabulary

Choose the best term from the box.

Vocabulary
fraction
simplest form
unit fraction

1. A _____ always has a numerator of 1. (p. 391)

Concepts and Skills

Write the fraction as a sum of unit fractions.

2. $\frac{3}{10} =$ _____

3. $\frac{6}{6} =$ _____

Use the model to write an equation.

4.
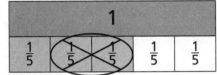

5.
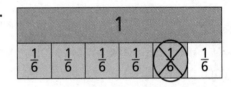

_____

Use the model to solve the equation.

6. $\frac{3}{8} + \frac{2}{8} =$ _____

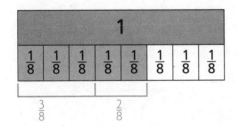

7. $\frac{4}{10} + \frac{5}{10} =$ _____

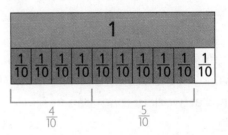

Find the sum or difference.

8. $\frac{9}{12} - \frac{7}{12} =$ _____

9. $\frac{2}{3} + \frac{1}{3} =$ _____

10. $\frac{1}{5} + \frac{3}{5} =$ _____

11. $\frac{2}{6} + \frac{2}{6} =$ _____

12. $\frac{4}{4} - \frac{2}{4} =$ _____

13. $\frac{7}{8} - \frac{4}{8} =$ _____

© Houghton Mifflin Harcourt Publishing Company

Chapter 7 **415**

14. Tyrone mixed $\frac{7}{12}$ quart of red paint with $\frac{1}{12}$ quart of yellow paint. How much paint does Tyrone have in the mixture?

_____

15. Jorge lives $\frac{6}{8}$ mile from school and $\frac{2}{8}$ mile from a ballpark. How much farther does Jorge live from school than from the ballpark?

_____

16. GO DEEPER Su Ling started an art project with 1 yard of felt. She used $\frac{2}{6}$ yard on Tuesday and $\frac{3}{6}$ yard on Wednesday. How much felt does Su Ling have left?

_____

17. Eloise hung artwork on $\frac{2}{5}$ of a bulletin board. She hung math papers on $\frac{1}{5}$ of the same bulletin board. What part of the bulletin board has artwork or math papers?

_____

Name _____

Rename Fractions and Mixed Numbers

Essential Question How can you rename mixed numbers as fractions greater than 1 and rename fractions greater than 1 as mixed numbers?

Lesson 7.6

Learning Objective You will use fraction strips and a number line to write mixed numbers as fractions and write fractions as mixed numbers.

▸ Unlock the Problem

Mr. Fox has $2\frac{3}{6}$ loaves of corn bread. Each loaf was cut into $\frac{1}{6}$-size pieces. If he has 14 people over for dinner, is there enough bread for each person to have 1 piece?

A **mixed number** is a number represented by a whole number and a fraction. You can write a mixed number as a fraction.

To find how many $\frac{1}{6}$-size pieces are in $2\frac{3}{6}$, write $2\frac{3}{6}$ as a fraction.

- What is the size of 1 piece of bread relative to the whole?

_____

- How much bread does Mr. Fox need for 14 people?

_____

_____

▸ Example Write a mixed number as a fraction.

THINK	**MODEL AND RECORD**

STEP 1 Model $2\frac{3}{6}$.

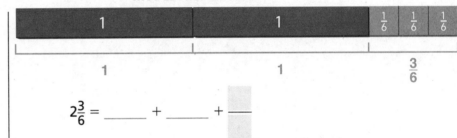

$$2\frac{3}{6} = \underline{\quad} + \underline{\quad} + \underline{\quad}$$

STEP 2 Find how many $\frac{1}{6}$-size pieces are in each whole. Model $2\frac{3}{6}$ using only $\frac{1}{6}$-size pieces.

$$2\frac{3}{6} = \frac{\quad}{\quad} + \frac{\quad}{\quad} + \frac{\quad}{\quad}$$

STEP 3 Find the total number of $\frac{1}{6}$-size pieces in $2\frac{3}{6}$.

Think: Find $\frac{6}{6} + \frac{6}{6} + \frac{3}{6}$.

$$2\frac{3}{6} = \frac{\quad}{\quad}$$

There are _____ sixth-size pieces in $2\frac{3}{6}$.

So, there is enough bread for 14 people to each have 1 piece.

Math Talk

Math Processes and Practices ➐

Look for Structure Give an example of how to write a mixed number as a fraction without using a model.

© Houghton Mifflin Harcourt Publishing Company

🔑 Example Write a fraction greater than 1 as a mixed number.

To weave a bracelet, Charlene needs 7 pieces of brown thread. Each piece of thread must be $\frac{1}{3}$ yard long. How much thread should she buy to weave the bracelet?

Write $\frac{7}{3}$ as a mixed number.

THINK	MODEL AND RECORD
STEP 1 Model $\frac{7}{3}$.	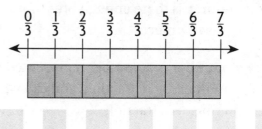$$\frac{7}{3} = \underline{\quad} + \underline{\quad} + \underline{\quad} + \underline{\quad} + \underline{\quad} + \underline{\quad} + \underline{\quad}$$
STEP 2 Find how many wholes are in $\frac{7}{3}$, and how many thirds are left over.	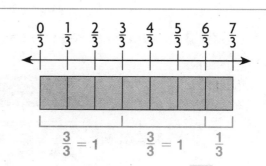$\frac{3}{3} = 1 \qquad \frac{3}{3} = 1 \qquad \frac{1}{3}$$$\frac{7}{3} = \underline{\quad} + \underline{\quad} + \dfrac{\quad}{\quad}$$
STEP 3 Write $\frac{7}{3}$ as a mixed number.	$\frac{7}{3} = \square\,\dfrac{\quad}{\quad}$

So, Charlene should buy _____ yards of thread.

Share and Show

Write the unknown numbers. Write mixed numbers above the number line and fractions greater than one below the number line.

1.

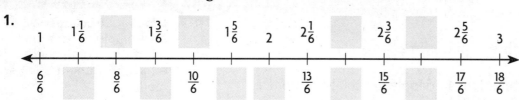

Name _____

Write the mixed number as a fraction.

2. $1\frac{1}{8}$

3. $1\frac{3}{5}$

✓ 4. $1\frac{2}{3}$

_____   _____   _____

Write the fraction as a mixed number.

5. $\frac{11}{4}$

6. $\frac{6}{5}$

✓ 7. $\frac{13}{10}$

_____   _____   _____

Math Talk Math Processes and Practices ⑥

Describe how you can compare $1\frac{3}{5}$ and $\frac{7}{5}$.

On Your Own

Write the mixed number as a fraction.

8. $2\frac{7}{10}$

9. $3\frac{2}{3}$

10. $4\frac{2}{5}$

_____   _____   _____

Math Processes and Practices ⑧ Use Repeated Reasoning **Algebra** Find the unknown numbers.

11. $\frac{13}{7} = 1\frac{\blacksquare}{7}$

12. $\blacksquare\frac{5}{6} = \frac{23}{6}$

13. $\frac{57}{11} = \blacksquare\frac{\blacksquare}{11}$

_____   _____   _____

14. **Go DEEPER** Pen has $\frac{1}{2}$-cup and $\frac{1}{8}$-cup measuring cups. What are two ways he could measure out $1\frac{3}{4}$ cups of flour?

_____

_____

15. **Go DEEPER** Juanita is making bread. She needs $3\frac{1}{2}$ cups of flour. Juanita only has a $\frac{1}{4}$-cup measuring cup. How many $\frac{1}{4}$ cups of flour will Juanita use to prepare the bread?

_____

_____

Problem Solving • Applications

Use the recipe to solve 16–18.

Energy Squares
$1\frac{1}{3}$ cups honey
$1\frac{1}{2}$ cups peanut butter
1 cup dry milk
$3\frac{1}{4}$ cups bran cereal

16. **Math Processes and Practices (2) Reason Quantitatively** Cal is making energy squares. How many $\frac{1}{2}$ cups of peanut butter are used in the recipe?

_____

17. **THINK SMARTER**   Suppose Cal wants to make 2 times as many energy squares as the recipe makes. How many cups of bran cereal should he use? Write your answer as a mixed number and as a fraction greater than 1 in simplest form.

_____

WRITE *Math* • **Show Your Work**

18. Cal added $2\frac{3}{8}$ cups of raisins. Write this mixed number as a fraction greater than 1 in simplest form.

_____

19. **GO DEEPER**   Jenn is preparing brown rice. She needs $1\frac{1}{2}$ cups of brown rice and 2 cups of water. Jenn has only a $\frac{1}{8}$-cup measuring cup. How many $\frac{1}{8}$ cups each of rice and water will Jenn use to prepare the rice?

_____

20. **THINK SMARTER**   Draw a line to show the mixed number and fraction that have the same value.

$1\frac{2}{5}$	$2\frac{3}{8}$	$4\frac{1}{3}$	$1\frac{2}{3}$
•	•	•	•
•	•	•	•
$\frac{30}{3}$	$\frac{13}{3}$	$\frac{4}{3}$	$\frac{8}{5}$

Name _____

Rename Fractions and Mixed Numbers

Learning Objective You will use fraction strips and a number line to write mixed numbers as fractions and write fractions as mixed numbers.

Write the mixed number as a fraction.

1. $2\frac{3}{5}$

Think: Find $\frac{5}{5} + \frac{5}{5} + \frac{3}{5}$.

$\frac{13}{5}$
_____

2. $4\frac{1}{3}$
_____

3. $1\frac{2}{5}$
_____

4. $3\frac{2}{3}$
_____

5. $4\frac{1}{8}$
_____

6. $1\frac{7}{10}$
_____

7. $5\frac{1}{2}$
_____

8. $2\frac{3}{8}$
_____

Write the fraction as a mixed number.

9. $\frac{31}{6}$
_____

10. $\frac{20}{10}$
_____

11. $\frac{15}{8}$
_____

12. $\frac{13}{6}$
_____

Problem Solving

13. A recipe calls for $2\frac{2}{4}$ cups of raisins, but Julie only has a $\frac{1}{4}$ cup measuring cup. How many $\frac{1}{4}$ cups does Julie need to measure out $2\frac{2}{4}$ cups of raisins?

14. If Julie needs $3\frac{1}{4}$ cups of oatmeal, how many $\frac{1}{4}$ cups of oatmeal will she use?

_____

_____

15. **WRITE** ▸ *Math* Draw and explain how you can use a number line to rename a fraction greater than 1 as a mixed number.

_____

_____

_____

Lesson Check

1. Write a mixed number that is equivalent to $\frac{16}{3}$.

2. Stacey filled her $\frac{1}{2}$ cup measuring cup seven times to have enough flour for a cake recipe. How much flour does the cake recipe call for?

_____

_____

Spiral Review

3. Becki put some stamps into her stamp collection book. She put 14 stamps on each page. If she completely filled 16 pages, how many stamps did she put in the book?

4. Brian is driving 324 miles to visit some friends. He wants to get there in 6 hours. How many miles does he need to drive each hour?

_____

_____

5. During a bike challenge, riders have to collect various colored ribbons. Each $\frac{1}{2}$ mile they collect a red ribbon, each $\frac{1}{8}$ mile they collect a green ribbon, and each $\frac{1}{4}$ mile they collect a blue ribbon. Which colors of ribbons will be collected at the $\frac{3}{4}$ mile marker?

6. Stephanie had $\frac{7}{8}$ pound of bird seed. She used $\frac{3}{8}$ pound to fill a bird feeder. How much bird seed does Stephanie have left?

_____

_____

FOR MORE PRACTICE
GO TO THE
Personal Math Trainer

Name _____

Add and Subtract Mixed Numbers

Essential Question How can you add and subtract mixed numbers with like denominators?

Learning Objective You will use fraction circles to add and subtract mixed numbers with like denominators.

 Unlock the Problem *Real World*

After a party, there were $1\frac{4}{6}$ quesadillas left on one tray and $2\frac{3}{6}$ quesadillas left on another tray. How many quesadillas were left?

- What operation will you use?

  _____

- Is the sum of the fractional parts of the mixed numbers greater than 1?

  _____

Example Add mixed numbers.

THINK	MODEL	RECORD
STEP 1 Add the fractional parts of the mixed numbers.	Think: Shade to model $\frac{4}{6} + \frac{3}{6}$.	$1\frac{4}{6}$ $+ 2\frac{3}{6}$
STEP 2 Add the whole-number parts of the mixed numbers.	Think: Shade to model $1 + 2$.	$1\frac{4}{6}$ $+ 2\frac{3}{6}$ $\frac{7}{6}$

STEP 3 Rename the sum.

Think: $\frac{7}{6}$ is greater than 1. Group the wholes together to rename the sum.

The model shows a total of ▢ wholes and ___ left over.

$3\frac{7}{6} = 3 + \frac{6}{6} +$ ___

$= 3 + 1 +$ ___ $=$ ___

So, _____ quesadillas were left.

Math Talk

Math Processes and Practices ②

Reason Abstractly When modeling sums such as $\frac{4}{6}$ and $\frac{3}{6}$, why is it helpful to combine parts into wholes when possible? Explain.

Example Subtract mixed numbers.

Alejandro had $3\frac{4}{6}$ quesadillas. His family ate $2\frac{3}{6}$ of the quesadillas. How many quesadillas are left?

Find $3\frac{4}{6} - 2\frac{3}{6}$.

MODEL

Shade the model to show $3\frac{4}{6}$.

Then cross out $2\frac{3}{6}$ to model the subtraction.

The difference is _____.

So, there are _____ quesadillas left.

RECORD

Subtract the fractional parts of the mixed numbers.

Then subtract the whole-number parts of the mixed numbers.

$$3\frac{4}{6}$$
$$-\ 2\frac{3}{6}$$
$$\overline{\qquad}$$

Share and Show

Write the sum as a mixed number with the fractional part less than 1.

1. $1\frac{1}{6}$ Add whole numbers.   Add fractions.

    $+3\frac{3}{6}$

    _____ + _____

    _____ + _____ = _____

2. $1\frac{4}{5}$

    $+7\frac{2}{5}$

✓ 3. $2\frac{1}{2}$

    $+3\frac{1}{2}$

Name _____

Find the difference.

4. $3\frac{7}{12}$

    $-2\frac{5}{12}$
    _____

5. $4\frac{2}{3}$

    $-3\frac{1}{3}$
    _____

✓ 6. $6\frac{9}{10}$

    $-3\frac{7}{10}$
    _____

Math Talk

Math Processes and Practices 8

Draw Conclusions
Explain how adding and subtracting mixed numbers is different from adding and subtracting fractions.

On Your Own

Write the sum as a mixed number with the fractional part less than 1.

7. $7\frac{4}{6}$

    $+4\frac{3}{6}$
    _____

8. $8\frac{1}{3}$

    $+3\frac{2}{3}$
    _____

9. $5\frac{4}{8}$

    $+3\frac{5}{8}$
    _____

10. $3\frac{5}{12}$

    $+4\frac{2}{12}$
    _____

Find the difference.

11. $5\frac{7}{8}$

    $-2\frac{3}{8}$
    _____

12. $5\frac{7}{12}$

    $-4\frac{1}{12}$
    _____

13. $3\frac{5}{10}$

    $-1\frac{3}{10}$
    _____

14. $7\frac{3}{4}$

    $-2\frac{2}{4}$
    _____

Practice: Copy and Solve **Find the sum or difference.**

15. $1\frac{3}{8} + 2\frac{7}{8}$

16. $6\frac{5}{8} - 4$

17. $9\frac{1}{2} + 8\frac{1}{2}$

18. $6\frac{3}{5} + 4\frac{3}{5}$

19. $8\frac{7}{10} - \frac{4}{10}$

20. $7\frac{3}{5} - 6\frac{3}{5}$

Problem Solving · Applications

Solve. Write your answer as a mixed number.

21. **Math Processes and Practices ①** **Make Sense of Problems** The driving distance from Alex's house to the museum is $6\frac{7}{10}$ miles. What is the round-trip distance?

22. **THINK SMARTER** The driving distance from the sports arena to Kristina's house is $10\frac{9}{10}$ miles. The distance from the sports arena to Luke's house is $2\frac{7}{10}$ miles. How much greater is the driving distance between the sports arena and Kristina's house than between the sports arena and Luke's house?

23. Pedro biked from his house to the nature preserve, a distance of $23\frac{4}{5}$ miles. Sandra biked from her house to the lake, a distance of $12\frac{2}{5}$ miles. How many miles less did Sandra bike than Pedro?

24. **GO DEEPER** During the Martinez family trip, they drove from home to a ski lodge, a distance of $55\frac{4}{5}$ miles, and then drove an additional $12\frac{4}{5}$ miles to visit friends. If the family drove the same route back home, what was the distance traveled during their trip?

25. **THINK SMARTER** For 25a–25d, select True or False for each statement.

   25a. $2\frac{3}{8} + 1\frac{6}{8}$ is equal to $4\frac{1}{8}$.   ○ True   ○ False

   25b. $3\frac{6}{12} + 1\frac{4}{12}$ is equal to $2\frac{2}{12}$.   ○ True   ○ False

   25c. $5\frac{5}{6} - 2\frac{4}{6}$ is equal to $1\frac{3}{6}$.   ○ True   ○ False

   25d. $5\frac{5}{8} - 3\frac{2}{8}$ is equal to $2\frac{3}{8}$.   ○ True   ○ False

Add and Subtract Mixed Numbers

Learning Objective You will use fraction circles to add and subtract mixed numbers with like denominators.

Find the sum. Write the sum as a mixed number, so the fractional part is less than 1.

1. $6\frac{4}{5}$
$+ 3\frac{3}{5}$
$\overline{9\frac{7}{5}} = 10\frac{2}{5}$

2. $4\frac{1}{2}$
$+ 2\frac{1}{2}$

3. $2\frac{2}{3}$
$+ 3\frac{2}{3}$

4. $6\frac{4}{5}$
$+ 7\frac{4}{5}$

5. $9\frac{3}{6}$
$+ 2\frac{2}{6}$

6. $8\frac{4}{12}$
$+ 3\frac{6}{12}$

7. $4\frac{3}{8}$
$+ 1\frac{5}{8}$

8. $9\frac{5}{10}$
$+ 6\frac{3}{10}$

Find the difference.

9. $6\frac{7}{8}$
$- 4\frac{3}{8}$

10. $4\frac{2}{3}$
$-3\frac{1}{3}$

11. $6\frac{4}{5}$
$-3\frac{3}{5}$

12. $7\frac{3}{4}$
$-2\frac{1}{4}$

Problem Solving Real World

13. James wants to send two gifts by mail. One package weighs $2\frac{3}{4}$ pounds. The other package weighs $1\frac{3}{4}$ pounds. What is the total weight of the packages?

_____

_____

14. **WRITE** ▸*Math* Describe how adding and subtracting mixed numbers can help you with recipes.

_____

_____

Lesson Check

1. Brad has two lengths of copper pipe to fit together. One has a length of $2\frac{5}{12}$ feet and the other has a length of $3\frac{7}{12}$ feet. How many feet of pipe does he have?

_____

2. A pattern calls for $2\frac{1}{4}$ yards of material and $1\frac{1}{4}$ yards of lining. How much total fabric is needed?

_____

Spiral Review

3. Shanice has 23 baseball trading cards of star players. She agrees to sell them for $16 each. How much money will she make from selling the cards?

_____

4. Nanci is volunteering at the animal shelter. She wants to spend an equal amount of time playing with each dog. She has 145 minutes to play with all 7 dogs. About how much time can she spend with each dog?

_____

5. Frieda has 12 red apples and 15 green apples. She is going to share the apples equally among 8 people and keep any extra apples for herself. How many apples will Frieda keep for herself?

_____

6. The Lynch family bought a house for $75,300. A few years later, they sold the house for $80,250. How much greater was the selling price than the purchase price?

_____

© Houghton Mifflin Harcourt Publishing Company

FOR MORE PRACTICE
GO TO THE
Personal Math Trainer

Subtraction with Renaming

Essential Question How can you rename a mixed number to help you subtract?

Learning Objective You will use fraction strips and a number line to rename a mixed number to subtract.

 Unlock the Problem

Ramon, Chandler, and Chase go bike riding on weekends. On one weekend, Chase rode his bike for 3 hours, Chandler rode her bike for $2\frac{1}{4}$ hours, and Ramon rode his bike for $1\frac{3}{4}$ hours. How much longer did Chandler ride her bike than Ramon did?

- Which operation will you use?

_____

- In the problem, circle the numbers that you need to use to find a solution.

Use a model. Find $2\frac{1}{4} - 1\frac{3}{4}$.

Shade the model to show how long Chandler rode her bike.
Then shade the model to show how long Ramon rode his bike.

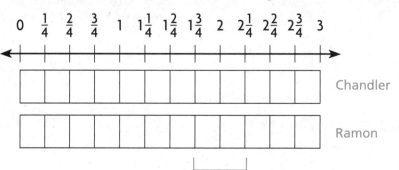

Chandler

Ramon

Think: The difference is _____.

So, Chandler rode her bike _____ hour longer than Ramon did.

---

1. If you have 1 fourth-size part, can you take away 3 fourth-size parts? Explain.

_____

_____

2. If you have 1 whole and 1 fourth-size part, can you take away 3 fourth-size parts? Explain.

_____

_____

Math Talk

Math Processes and Practices ④

Use Models How can you use models to find how much longer Chase rode his bike than Chandler did?

🔑 One Way Rename the first mixed number.

Find the difference. $5\frac{1}{8} - 3\frac{3}{8}$

STEP 1

Rename $5\frac{1}{8}$ as a mixed number with a fraction greater than 1.

Think:

$$5\frac{1}{8} = 4 + 1 + \frac{1}{8}$$

$$= 4 + \frac{\boxed{}}{8} + \frac{1}{8}$$

$$= \boxed{}$$

STEP 2

Subtract the mixed numbers.

$$5\frac{1}{8} = \boxed{}$$

$$-3\frac{3}{8} = -3\frac{3}{8}$$

$$\boxed{}$$

Math Talk

Math Processes and Practices 7

Look for Structure
Explain why you need to rename $5\frac{1}{8}$.

🔑 Another Way Rename both mixed numbers.

Find the difference. $3\frac{4}{12} - 1\frac{6}{12}$

STEP 1

Rename both mixed numbers as fractions greater than 1.

$$3\frac{4}{12} = \frac{\boxed{}}{12} \qquad 1\frac{6}{12} = \frac{\boxed{}}{12}$$

STEP 2

Subtract the fractions greater than 1.

$$\frac{\boxed{}}{12}$$

$$-\frac{\boxed{}}{12}$$

$$\boxed{}$$

- Explain how you could rename 5 to subtract $3\frac{1}{4}$.

Name _____

1. Rename both mixed numbers as fractions. Find the difference.

$$3\frac{3}{6} = \frac{}{6}$$

$$-1\frac{4}{6} = -\frac{}{6}$$

Find the difference.

2. $1\frac{1}{3}$
$-\frac{2}{3}$

3. $4\frac{7}{10}$
$-1\frac{9}{10}$

4. $3\frac{5}{12}$
$-\frac{8}{12}$

Math Talk

Math Processes and Practices ④

Model Mathematics
Describe how you would model $\frac{13}{6} - \frac{8}{6}$.

On Your Own

Find the difference.

5. $8\frac{1}{10}$
$-2\frac{9}{10}$

6. 2
$-1\frac{1}{4}$

7. $4\frac{1}{5}$
$-3\frac{2}{5}$

Practice: Copy and Solve Find the difference.

8. $4\frac{1}{6} - 2\frac{5}{6}$

9. $6\frac{9}{12} - 3\frac{10}{12}$

10. $3\frac{3}{10} - \frac{7}{10}$

11. $4 - 2\frac{3}{5}$

12. GO DEEPER Lisa mixed $4\frac{2}{6}$ cups of orange juice with $3\frac{1}{6}$ cups of pineapple juice to make fruit punch. She and her friends drank $3\frac{4}{6}$ cups of the punch. How much of the fruit punch is left?

Problem Solving · Applications

Rename the fractions to solve.

Many instruments are coiled or curved so that they are easier for the musician to play, but they would be quite long if straightened out completely.

13. **Math Processes and Practices ①** **Analyze Relationships** Trumpets and cornets are brass instruments. Fully stretched out, the length of a trumpet is $5\frac{1}{4}$ feet and the length of a cornet is $4\frac{2}{4}$ feet. The trumpet is how much longer than the cornet?

_____

14. **THINK SMARTER** Tubas, trombones, and French horns are brass instruments. Fully stretched out, the length of a tuba is 18 feet, the length of a trombone is $9\frac{11}{12}$ feet, and the length of a French horn is $17\frac{1}{12}$ feet. The tuba is how much longer than the French horn? The French horn is how much longer than the trombone?

|WRITE ▸Math · **Show Your Work**

_____

15. **GO DEEPER** The pitch of a musical instrument is related to its length. In general, the greater the length of a musical instrument, the lower its pitch. Order the brass instruments identified on this page from lowest pitch to the highest pitch.

_____

Personal Math Trainer

16. **THINK SMARTER +** Alicia had $3\frac{1}{6}$ yards of fabric. After making a tablecloth, she had $1\frac{4}{6}$ yards of fabric. Alicia said she used $2\frac{3}{6}$ yards of fabric for the tablecloth. Do you agree? Explain.

_____

_____

_____

Name _____

Subtraction with Renaming

Learning Objective You will use fraction strips and a number line to rename a mixed number to subtract.

Find the difference.

1. $5\frac{1}{3} \rightarrow 4\frac{4}{3}$
   $-3\frac{2}{3} \rightarrow 3\frac{2}{3}$
   $\overline{1\frac{2}{3}}$

2. 6
   $-3\frac{2}{5}$

3. $5\frac{1}{4}$
   $-2\frac{3}{4}$

4. $9\frac{3}{8}$
   $-8\frac{7}{8}$

5. $12\frac{3}{10}$
   $-7\frac{7}{10}$

6. $8\frac{1}{6}$
   $-3\frac{5}{6}$

7. $7\frac{3}{5}$
   $-4\frac{4}{5}$

8. $10\frac{1}{2}$
   $-8\frac{1}{2}$

9. $7\frac{1}{6}$
   $-2\frac{5}{6}$

10. $9\frac{3}{12}$
    $-4\frac{7}{12}$

11. $9\frac{1}{10}$
    $-8\frac{7}{10}$

12. $9\frac{1}{3}$
    $-\frac{2}{3}$

Problem Solving Real World

13. Alicia buys a 5-pound bag of rocks for a fish tank. She uses $1\frac{1}{8}$ pounds for a small fish bowl. How much is left?

14. Xavier made 25 pounds of roasted almonds for a fair. He has $3\frac{1}{2}$ pounds left at the end of the fair. How many pounds of roasted almonds did he sell at the fair?

15. **WRITE** ▸Math Explain when you know you need to rename a mixed number to subtract.

Lesson Check

1. Reggie is making a double-layer cake. The recipe for the first layer calls for $2\frac{1}{4}$ cups of sugar. The recipe for the second layer calls for $1\frac{1}{4}$ cups of sugar. Reggie has 5 cups of sugar. How much will he have left after making both recipes?

2. Kate has $4\frac{3}{8}$ yards of fabric and needs $2\frac{7}{8}$ yards to make a skirt. How much extra fabric will she have left after making the skirt?

Spiral Review

3. Paulo has 128 glass beads to use to decorate picture frames. He wants to use the same number of beads on each frame. If he decorates 8 picture frames, how many beads will he put on each frame?

4. Madison is making party favors. She wants to make enough favors so each guest gets the same number of favors. She knows there will be 6 or 8 guests at the party. What is the least number of party favors Madison should make?

5. A shuttle bus makes 4 round-trips between two shopping centers each day. The bus holds 24 people. If the bus is full on each one-way trip, how many passengers are carried by the bus each day?

6. To make a fruit salad, Marvin mixes $1\frac{3}{4}$ cups of diced peaches with $2\frac{1}{4}$ cups of diced pears. How many cups of peaches and pears are in the fruit salad?

© Houghton Mifflin Harcourt Publishing Company

FOR MORE PRACTICE
GO TO THE
Personal Math Trainer

Name _____

Fractions and Properties of Addition

Essential Question How can you add fractions with like denominators using the properties of addition?

Learning Objective You will use the Commutative and Associative Properties of Addition and mental math to add fractions.

CONNECT The Associative and Commutative Properties of Addition can help you group and order addends to find sums mentally. You can use mental math to combine fractions that have a sum of 1.

- The Commutative Property of Addition states that when the order of two addends is changed, the sum is the same. For example, $4 + 5 = 5 + 4$.

- The Associative Property of Addition states that when the grouping of addends is changed, the sum is the same. For example, $(5 + 8) + 4 = 5 + (8 + 4)$.

 Unlock the Problem Real World

The map shows four lighthouses in the Florida Keys and their distances apart in miles. The Dry Tortugas Lighthouse is the farthest west, and the Alligator Reef Lighthouse is the farthest east.

What is the distance from the Dry Tortugas Lighthouse to the Alligator Reef Lighthouse, traveling between the four lighthouses?

Gulf of Mexico

$70\frac{5}{10}$ $43\frac{6}{10}$ $34\frac{5}{10}$

Dry Tortugas Lighthouse

Key West Lighthouse

Sombrero Key Lighthouse

Alligator Reef Lighthouse

Use the properties to order and group.

Add. $70\frac{5}{10} + 43\frac{6}{10} + 34\frac{5}{10}$

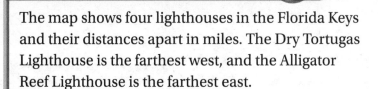

$70\frac{5}{10} + 43\frac{6}{10} + 34\frac{5}{10} =$ _____ + _____ + _____

$= ($ _____ + _____ $) +$ _____

$= ($ _____ $) +$ _____

$=$ _____

Use the Commutative Property to order the addends so that the fractions with a sum of 1 are together.

Use the Associative Property to group the addends that you can add mentally.

Add the grouped numbers, and then add the other mixed number.

Write the sum.

So, the distance from the Dry Tortugas Lighthouse to the Alligator Reef Lighthouse, traveling between the four lighthouses,

is _____ miles.

Try This! Use the properties and mental math to solve. Show each step, and name the property used.

$$1\frac{1}{3} + \left(2 + 3\frac{2}{3}\right)$$

 **Share and Show**

1. Complete. Name the property used.

$$\left(3\frac{4}{10} + 5\frac{2}{10}\right) + \frac{6}{10} = \left(5\frac{2}{10} + 3\frac{4}{10}\right) + \underline{\hspace{1cm}} \quad \underline{\hspace{3cm}}$$

$$= 5\frac{2}{10} + \left(3\frac{4}{10} + \underline{\hspace{1cm}}\right) \quad \underline{\hspace{3cm}}$$

$$= 5\frac{2}{10} + \underline{\hspace{1cm}}$$

$$= \underline{\hspace{1cm}}$$

 Math Talk

Math Processes and Practices ②

Reason Abstractly
Describe how you could use the properties to find the sum $1\frac{1}{3} + 2\frac{5}{8} + 1\frac{2}{3}$.

Use the properties and mental math to find the sum.

2. $\left(2\frac{7}{8} + 3\frac{2}{8}\right) + 1\frac{1}{8}$

3. $1\frac{2}{5} + \left(1 + \frac{3}{5}\right)$

4. $5\frac{3}{6} + \left(5\frac{5}{6} + 4\frac{3}{6}\right)$

5. $\left(1\frac{1}{4} + 1\frac{1}{4}\right) + 2\frac{3}{4}$

6. $\left(12\frac{4}{9} + 1\frac{2}{9}\right) + 3\frac{5}{9}$

7. $\frac{3}{12} + \left(1\frac{8}{12} + \frac{9}{12}\right)$

Name _____

Use the properties and mental math to find the sum.

8. $\left(45\frac{1}{3} + 6\frac{1}{3}\right) + 38\frac{2}{3}$

9. $\frac{1}{2} + \left(103\frac{1}{2} + 12\right)$

10. $\left(3\frac{5}{10} + 10\right) + 11\frac{5}{10}$

11. **GO DEEPER** Pablo is training for a marathon. He ran $5\frac{4}{8}$ miles on Friday, $6\frac{5}{8}$ miles on Saturday, and $7\frac{4}{8}$ miles on Sunday. How many miles did he run on all three days?

12. **GO DEEPER** At lunchtime, Dale's Diner served a total of $2\frac{2}{6}$ pots of vegetable soup, $3\frac{5}{6}$ pots of chicken soup, and $4\frac{3}{6}$ pots of tomato soup. How many pots of soup were served in all?

Problem Solving • Applications Real World

Use the expressions in the box for 13–14.

13. Which property of addition would you use to regroup the addends in Expression A?

   _____

14. **THINK SMARTER** Which two expressions have the same value?

   _____

A	$\frac{1}{8} + \left(\frac{7}{8} + \frac{4}{8}\right)$
B	$\frac{1}{2} + 2$
C	$\frac{3}{7} + \left(\frac{1}{2} + \frac{4}{7}\right)$
D	$\frac{1}{3} + \frac{4}{3} + \frac{2}{3}$

15. **THINK SMARTER** Match the equation with the property used.

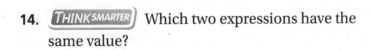

$\frac{6}{12} + \left(\frac{6}{12} + \frac{3}{12}\right) = \left(\frac{6}{12} + \frac{6}{12}\right) + \frac{3}{12}$ •

$3\frac{2}{5} + \left(5\frac{4}{5} + 2\frac{1}{5}\right) = 3\frac{2}{5} + \left(2\frac{1}{5} + 5\frac{4}{5}\right)$ •   • Commutative Property

$\left(4\frac{1}{6} + 3\frac{5}{6}\right) + 2\frac{2}{6} = \left(3\frac{5}{6} + 4\frac{1}{6}\right) + 2\frac{2}{6}$ •   • Associative Property

$\left(1\frac{1}{8} + \frac{5}{8}\right) + 3\frac{3}{8} = 1\frac{1}{8} + \left(\frac{5}{8} + 3\frac{3}{8}\right)$ •

Pose a Problem

16. **GO DEEPER** Costumes are being made for the
high school musical. The table at the right
shows the amount of fabric needed for the
costumes of the male and female leads. Alice
uses the expression $7\frac{3}{8} + 1\frac{5}{8} + 2\frac{4}{8}$ to find the total
amount of fabric needed for the costume of the
female lead.

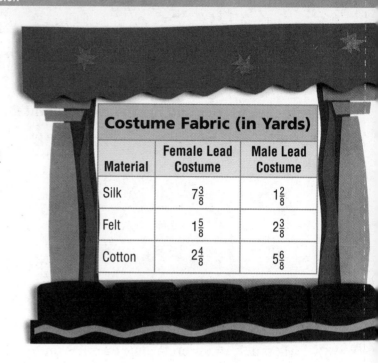

Costume Fabric (in Yards)

Material	Female Lead Costume	Male Lead Costume
Silk	$7\frac{3}{8}$	$1\frac{2}{8}$
Felt	$1\frac{5}{8}$	$2\frac{3}{8}$
Cotton	$2\frac{4}{8}$	$5\frac{6}{8}$

To find the value of the expression using mental
math, Alice used the properties of addition.

$$7\frac{3}{8} + 1\frac{5}{8} + 2\frac{4}{8} = \left(7\frac{3}{8} + 1\frac{5}{8}\right) + 2\frac{4}{8}$$

Alice added $7 + 1$ and was able to quickly add
$\frac{3}{8}$ and $\frac{5}{8}$ to the sum of 8 to get 9. She added $2\frac{4}{8}$
to 9, so her answer was $11\frac{4}{8}$.

So, the amount of fabric needed for the costume of the female lead
actor is $11\frac{4}{8}$ yards.

**Write a new problem using the information for the costume for
the male lead actor.**

Pose a Problem	Solve your problem. Check your solution.

- **Math Processes and Practices ⑦ Identify Relationships** Explain how using the properties of
addition makes both problems easier to solve.

Name _____

Fractions and Properties of Addition

Learning Objective You will use the Commutative and Associative Properties of Addition and mental math to add fractions.

Use the properties and mental math to find the sum.

1. $5\frac{1}{3} + \left(2\frac{2}{3} + 1\frac{1}{3}\right)$

   $5\frac{1}{3} + (4)$

   $\underline{\qquad 9\frac{1}{3} \qquad}$

2. $10\frac{1}{8} + \left(3\frac{5}{8} + 2\frac{7}{8}\right)$

   $\underline{\qquad\qquad}$

3. $8\frac{1}{5} + \left(3\frac{2}{5} + 5\frac{4}{5}\right)$

   $\underline{\qquad\qquad}$

4. $6\frac{3}{4} + \left(4\frac{2}{4} + 5\frac{1}{4}\right)$

   $\underline{\qquad\qquad}$

5. $\left(6\frac{3}{6} + 10\frac{4}{6}\right) + 9\frac{2}{6}$

   $\underline{\qquad\qquad}$

6. $\left(6\frac{2}{5} + 1\frac{4}{5}\right) + 3\frac{1}{5}$

   $\underline{\qquad\qquad}$

Problem Solving (Real World)

7. Nate's classroom has three tables of different lengths. One has a length of $4\frac{1}{2}$ feet, another has a length of 4 feet, and a third has a length of $2\frac{1}{2}$ feet. What is the length of all three tables when pushed end to end?

   $\underline{\qquad\qquad\qquad}$

8. Mr. Warren uses $2\frac{1}{4}$ bags of mulch for his garden and another $4\frac{1}{4}$ bags for his front yard. He also uses $\frac{3}{4}$ bag around a fountain. How many total bags of mulch does Mr. Warren use?

   $\underline{\qquad\qquad\qquad}$

9. **WRITE** ▸Math Describe how the Commutative and Associative Properties of Addition can make adding mixed numbers easier.

   $\underline{\qquad\qquad\qquad\qquad\qquad\qquad}$

   $\underline{\qquad\qquad\qquad\qquad\qquad\qquad}$

   $\underline{\qquad\qquad\qquad\qquad\qquad\qquad}$

   $\underline{\qquad\qquad\qquad\qquad\qquad\qquad}$

Lesson Check

1. A carpenter cut a board into three pieces. One piece was $2\frac{5}{6}$ feet long. The second piece was $3\frac{1}{6}$ feet long. The third piece was $1\frac{5}{6}$ feet long. How long was the board?

   _____

2. Harry works at an apple orchard. He picked $45\frac{7}{8}$ pounds of apples on Monday. He picked $42\frac{3}{8}$ pounds of apples on Wednesday. He picked $54\frac{1}{8}$ pounds of apples on Friday. How many pounds of apples did Harry pick those three days?

   _____

Spiral Review

3. There were 6 oranges in the refrigerator. Joey and his friends ate $3\frac{2}{3}$ oranges. How many oranges were left?

   _____

4. Darlene was asked to identify which of the following numbers is prime:

   $$2, 12, 21, 39$$

   Which number should she choose?

   _____

5. A teacher has 100 chairs to arrange for an assembly into equal rows. Write one way the chairs could be arranged. Include the number of rows and the number of chairs in each row.

   _____

   _____

6. Nic bought 28 folding chairs for $16 each. How much money did Nic spend on chairs?

   _____

   _____

FOR MORE PRACTICE
GO TO THE
Personal Math Trainer

Name _____

Problem Solving • Multistep Fraction Problems

Essential Question How can you use the strategy *act it out* to solve multistep problems with fractions?

Learning Objective You will use fraction circles and the strategy *act it out* to solve multistep problems with fractions.

Unlock the Problem

A gift shop sells walnuts in $\frac{3}{4}$-pound bags. Ann will buy some bags of walnuts and repackage them into 1-pound bags. What is the least number of $\frac{3}{4}$-pound bags Ann could buy, if she wants to fill each 1-pound bag, without leftovers?

Read the Problem

What do I need to find?

I need to find how many

_____ bags of walnuts Ann needs to make 1-pound bags of walnuts, without leftovers.

What information do I need to use?

The bags she will buy contain

_____ pound of walnuts. She will repackage the walnuts into

_____ -pound bags.

How will I use the information?

I can use fraction circles to

_____ the problem.

Solve the Problem

Describe how to act it out. Use fraction circles.

One $\frac{3}{4}$-pound bag   Not enough for a 1-pound bag

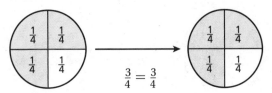

$$\frac{3}{4} = \frac{3}{4}$$

Two $\frac{3}{4}$-pound bags   One 1-pound bag with $\frac{2}{4}$ pound left over

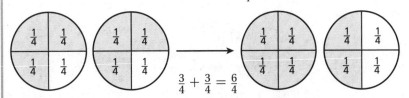

$$\frac{3}{4} + \frac{3}{4} = \frac{6}{4}$$

Three $\frac{3}{4}$-pound bags have $\frac{3}{4} + \frac{3}{4} + \frac{3}{4} = \frac{}{4}$ pounds of

walnuts. This makes _____ 1-pound bags with _____ pound left over.

Four $\frac{3}{4}$-pound bags have $\frac{3}{4} + \frac{3}{4} + \frac{3}{4} + \frac{3}{4} = \frac{}{4}$-pounds of walnuts.

This makes _____ 1-pound bags with _____ left over.

So, Ann could buy _____ $\frac{3}{4}$-pound bags of walnuts.

🔑 Try Another Problem

At the end of dinner, a restaurant had several dishes of quiche, each with 2 sixth-size pieces of quiche. The chef was able to combine these pieces to make 2 whole quiches, with no leftovers. How many dishes did the chef combine?

Read the Problem	Solve the Problem
What do I need to find?	**Describe how to act it out.**
What information do I need to use?	
How will I use the information?	

So, the chef combined _____ dishes each with $\frac{2}{6}$ quiche.

Name _____

Share and Show 📝 MATH BOARD

Unlock the Problem
√ Underline the question.
√ Circle the important facts.
√ Cross out unneeded information.

1. Last week, Sia ran $1\frac{1}{4}$ miles each day for 5 days and then took 2 days off. Did she run at least 6 miles last week?

   First, model the problem. Describe your model.

   _____

   _____

   _____

   Then, regroup the parts in the model to find the number of whole miles Sia ran.

   Sia ran _____ whole miles and _____ mile.

   Finally, compare the total number of miles she ran to 6 miles.

   $6\frac{1}{4}$ miles ◯ 6 miles

   So, Sia _____ run at least 6 miles last week.

2. What if Sia ran only $\frac{3}{4}$ mile each day? Would she have run at least 6 miles last week? Explain.

   _____

   _____

3. A quarter is $\frac{1}{4}$ dollar. Noah has 20 quarters. How much money does he have? Explain.

   _____

   _____

   _____

4. **THINK SMARTER** How many $\frac{2}{5}$ parts are in 2 wholes?

   _____

On Your Own

5. A company shipped 15,325 boxes of apples and 12,980 boxes of oranges. How many more boxes of apples than oranges did the company ship?

_____

6. **Math Processes and Practices ❶ Analyze** A fair sold a total of 3,300 tickets on Friday and Saturday. It sold 100 more on Friday than on Saturday. How many tickets did the fair sell on Friday?

_____

7. **THINK SMARTER** Emma walked $\frac{1}{4}$ mile on Monday, $\frac{2}{4}$ mile on Tuesday, and $\frac{3}{4}$ mile on Wednesday. If the pattern continues, how many miles will she walk on Friday? Explain how you found the number of miles.

_____

_____

_____

_____

_____

8. **GO DEEPER** Jared painted a mug $\frac{5}{12}$ red and $\frac{4}{12}$ blue. What part of the mug is **not** red or blue?

_____

9. **THINK SMARTER** Choose the number that correctly completes the sentence.

Each day, Mrs. Hewes knits $\frac{1}{3}$ of a scarf in the morning and $\frac{1}{3}$ of a scarf in the afternoon.

It will take Mrs. Hewes
| 2 |
| 3 |
| 4 |
days to knit 2 scarves.

WRITE ► *Math*
Show Your Work

Name _____

Problem Solving • Multistep Fraction Problems

Read each problem and solve.

1. Each child in the Smith family was given an orange cut into 8 equal sections. Each child ate $\frac{5}{8}$ of the orange. After combining the leftover sections, Mrs. Smith noted that there were exactly 3 full oranges left. How many children are in the Smith family?

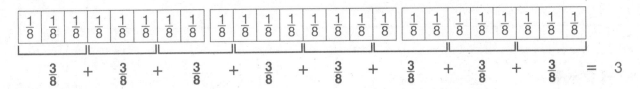

$$\frac{3}{8} + \frac{3}{8} + \frac{3}{8} + \frac{3}{8} + \frac{3}{8} + \frac{3}{8} + \frac{3}{8} + \frac{3}{8} = 3$$

There are 8 addends, so there are 8 children in the Smith family.

_____ 8 children _____

2. Val walks $2\frac{3}{5}$ miles each day. Bill runs 10 miles once every 4 days. In 4 days, who covers the greater distance?

_____

3. Chad buys peanuts in 2-pound bags. He repackages them into bags that hold $\frac{5}{6}$ pound of peanuts. How many 2-pound bags of peanuts should Chad buy so that he can fill the $\frac{5}{6}$-pound bags without having any peanuts left over?

_____

4. **WRITE** ▸ *Math* Write a word problem that involves adding or subtracting two fractions. Draw a model and describe how you would act out the problem to solve it.

_____

_____

_____

Lesson Check

1. Karyn cuts a length of ribbon into 4 equal pieces, each $1\frac{1}{4}$ feet long. How long was the ribbon?

2. Several friends each had $\frac{2}{5}$ of a bag of peanuts left over from the baseball game. They realized that they could have bought 2 fewer bags of peanuts between them. How many friends went to the game?

Spiral Review

3. A frog made three jumps. The first was $12\frac{5}{6}$ inches. The second jump was $8\frac{3}{6}$ inches. The third jump was $15\frac{1}{6}$ inches. What was the total distance the frog jumped?

4. LaDanian wants to write the fraction $\frac{4}{6}$ as a sum of unit fractions. What expression should he write?

5. Greta made a design with squares. She colored 8 out of the 12 squares blue. What fraction of the squares did she color blue?

6. The teacher gave this pattern to the class: the first term is 5 and the rule is *add* 4, *subtract* 1. Each student says one number. The first student says 5. Victor is tenth in line. What number should Victor say?

FOR MORE PRACTICE
GO TO THE
Personal Math Trainer

Name _____

1. A painter mixed $\frac{1}{4}$ quart of red paint with $\frac{3}{4}$ blue paint to make purple paint.

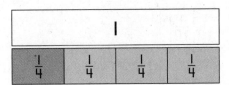

   How much purple paint did the painter make?

   [   ] quart of purple paint

2. Ivan biked $1\frac{2}{3}$ hours on Monday, $2\frac{1}{3}$ hours on Tuesday, and $2\frac{2}{3}$ hours on Wednesday. What is the total number of hours Ivan spent biking?

   Ivan spent [   ] hours biking.

Personal Math Trainer

3. **THINK SMARTER +** Tricia had $4\frac{1}{8}$ yards of fabric to make curtains. When she finished she had $2\frac{3}{8}$ yards of fabric left. She said she used $2\frac{2}{8}$ yards of fabric for the curtains. Do you agree? Explain.

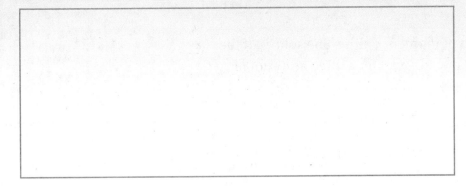

GO DIGITAL Assessment Options
Chapter Test

4. Miguel's class went to the state fair. The fairground is divided into sections. Rides are in $\frac{6}{10}$ of the fairground. Games are in $\frac{2}{10}$ of the fairground. Farm exhibits are in $\frac{1}{10}$ of the fairground.

Part A

Use the model. What fraction of the fairground is rides and games?

The fraction of the fairground with games and rides is [   ].

Part B

How much greater is the part of the fairground with rides than with farm exhibits? Explain how the model could be used to find the answer.

5. Rita is making chili. The recipe calls for $2\frac{3}{4}$ cups of tomatoes. How many cups of tomatoes, written as a fraction greater than one, are used in the recipe?

[   ] cups

6. Lamar's mom sells sports equipment online. She sold $\frac{9}{10}$ of the sports equipment. Select a way $\frac{9}{10}$ can be written as a sum of fractions. Mark all that apply.

(A) $\frac{1}{10} + \frac{1}{10} + \frac{1}{10} + \frac{1}{10} + \frac{2}{10}$ (D) $\frac{4}{10} + \frac{1}{10} + \frac{1}{10} + \frac{3}{10}$

(B) $\frac{3}{10} + \frac{2}{10} + \frac{3}{10} + \frac{1}{10}$ (E) $\frac{4}{10} + \frac{3}{10} + \frac{1}{10} + \frac{1}{10} + \frac{1}{10}$

(C) $\frac{2}{10} + \frac{2}{10} + \frac{2}{10} + \frac{2}{10}$ (F) $\frac{2}{10} + \frac{2}{10} + \frac{2}{10} + \frac{3}{10}$

7. Bella brought $\frac{8}{10}$ gallon of water on a hiking trip. She drank $\frac{6}{10}$ gallon of water. How much water is left?

gallon

8. In a survey, $\frac{6}{10}$ of the students chose Saturday and $\frac{1}{10}$ chose Monday as their favorite day of the week. What fraction shows the students who chose Saturday or Monday as their favorite day?

Part A

Shade the model to show your answer.

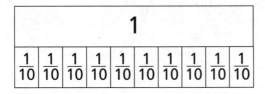

of the students chose Monday or Saturday.

Part B

How are the numerator and denominator of your answer related to the model? Explain.

9. Match the equation with the property used.

$\frac{6}{10} + \left(\frac{4}{10} + \frac{3}{10}\right) = \left(\frac{6}{10} + \frac{4}{10}\right) + \frac{3}{10}$ •

$1\frac{1}{4} + \left(3 + 2\frac{1}{4}\right) = 1\frac{1}{4} + \left(2\frac{1}{4} + 3\right)$ •   • Commutative Property

$\left(2\frac{6}{10} + \frac{1}{10}\right) + 3\frac{9}{10} = 2\frac{6}{10} + \left(\frac{1}{10} + 3\frac{9}{10}\right)$ •   • Associative Property

$\left(3\frac{4}{7} + 2\frac{1}{7}\right) + 6\frac{3}{7} = \left(2\frac{1}{7} + 3\frac{4}{7}\right) + 6\frac{3}{7}$ •

10. For numbers 10a–10e, select Yes or No to show if the sum or difference is correct.

10a. $\frac{2}{8} + \frac{1}{8} = \frac{3}{8}$ ○ Yes   ○ No

10b. $\frac{4}{5} + \frac{1}{5} = \frac{5}{5}$ ○ Yes   ○ No

10c. $\frac{4}{6} + \frac{1}{6} = \frac{5}{12}$ ○ Yes   ○ No

10d. $\frac{6}{12} - \frac{4}{12} = \frac{2}{12}$ ○ Yes   ○ No

10e. $\frac{7}{9} - \frac{2}{9} = \frac{9}{9}$ ○ Yes   ○ No

11. Gina has $5\frac{2}{6}$ feet of silver ribbon and $2\frac{4}{6}$ of gold ribbon. How much more silver ribbon does Gina have than gold ribbon?

    [____] feet more silver ribbon

12. Jill is making a long cape. She needs $4\frac{1}{3}$ yards of blue fabric for the outside of the cape. She needs $3\frac{2}{3}$ yards of purple fabric for the lining of the cape.

    Part A

    Jill incorrectly subtracted the two mixed numbers to find how much more blue fabric than purple fabric she should buy. Her work is shown below.

    $4\frac{1}{3} - 3\frac{2}{3} = \frac{12}{3} - \frac{9}{3} = \frac{3}{3}$

    Why is Jill's work incorrect?

    [ ]

    Part B

    How much more blue fabric than purple fabric should Jill buy? Show your work.

    [ ]

450

Name _____

13. Russ has two jars of glue. One jar is $\frac{1}{5}$ full. The other jar is $\frac{2}{5}$ full.

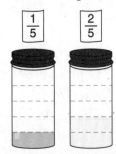

Use the fractions to write an equation to find the amount of glue Russ has.

$\boxed{\dfrac{1}{5}}$ $\boxed{\dfrac{2}{5}}$ $\boxed{\dfrac{3}{5}}$ $\boxed{\dfrac{4}{5}}$ $\boxed{}$ + $\boxed{}$ = $\boxed{}$

14. Gertie ran $\frac{3}{4}$ mile during physical education class. Sarah ran $\frac{2}{4}$ mile during the same class. How much farther did Gertie run than Sarah? Shade the model to show your answer.

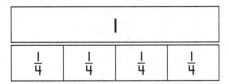

Gertie ran $\boxed{}$ mile farther than Sarah.

15. Teresa planted marigolds in $\frac{2}{8}$ of her garden and petunias in $\frac{3}{8}$ of her garden. What fraction of the garden has marigolds and petunias?

Teresa's garden has $\boxed{}$ marigolds and petunias.

16. Draw a line to show the mixed number and fraction that have the same value.

- $3\frac{2}{7}$ - $4\frac{5}{8}$ - $2\frac{3}{5}$ - $2\frac{3}{8}$

- $\frac{21}{8}$ - $\frac{37}{3}$ - $\frac{21}{7}$ - $\frac{37}{8}$

17. 𝗚𝗢 *DEEPER* Each day, Tally's baby sister eats $\frac{1}{4}$ cup of rice cereal in the morning and $\frac{1}{4}$ cup of rice cereal in the afternoon.

It will take Tally's sister $\boxed{\begin{array}{c} 2 \\ 3 \\ 4 \end{array}}$ days to eat 2 cups of rice cereal.

18. Three girls are selling cases of popcorn to earn money for a band trip. In week 1, Emily sold $2\frac{3}{4}$ cases, Brenda sold $4\frac{1}{4}$ cases, and Shannon sold $3\frac{1}{2}$ cases.

Part A

How many cases of popcorn have the girls sold in all? Explain how you found your answer.

Part B

The girls must sell a total of 35 cases in order to have enough money for the trip. Suppose they sell the same amount in week 2 and week 3 of the sale as in week 1. Will the girls have sold enough cases of popcorn to go on the trip? Explain.

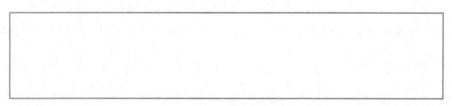

19. Henry ate $\frac{3}{8}$ of a sandwich. Keith ate $\frac{4}{8}$ of the same sandwich. How much more of the sandwich did Keith eat than Henry?

$\boxed{}$ of the sandwich

20. For numbers 20a–20d, choose True or False for each sentence.

20a. $1\frac{4}{9} + 2\frac{6}{9}$ is equal to $4\frac{1}{9}$.   ○ True   ○ False

20b. $3\frac{5}{6} + 2\frac{3}{6}$ is equal to $5\frac{2}{6}$.   ○ True   ○ False

20c. $4\frac{5}{8} - 2\frac{4}{8}$ is equal to $2\frac{3}{8}$.   ○ True   ○ False

20d. $5\frac{5}{8} - 3\frac{2}{8}$ is equal to $2\frac{3}{8}$.   ○ True   ○ False

21. Justin lives $4\frac{3}{5}$ miles from his grandfather's house. Write the mixed number as a fraction greater than one.

$$4\frac{3}{5} = \boxed{}$$

Multiply Fractions by Whole Numbers

✓ **Show What You Know**

Personal Math Trainer
Online Assessment and Intervention

Check your understanding of important skills.

Name _____

▶ **Relate Addition to Multiplication** **Complete.**

1.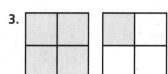

____ + ____ + ____ + ____ = ____

____ × ____ = ____

2. ●●●●●●

____ + ____ + ____ = ____

____ × ____ = ____

▶ **Read and Write Mixed Numbers** **Write a mixed number for the shaded part. Write a fraction for the unshaded part.**

3.

Shaded: _____

Unshaded: _____

4.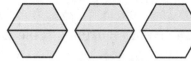

Shaded: _____

Unshaded: _____

▶ **Model Fractions and Mixed Numbers** **Write a fraction or mixed number for the model.**

5.  _____

6. _____

Math in the Real World

The budget for Carter Museum's annual party is $10,000. Food accounts for $\frac{1}{2}$ of the budget, beverages for $\frac{1}{4}$, and decorations for $\frac{1}{10}$ of the budget. The remainder is spent on staffing the party. How much money is spent on staffing the party?

Vocabulary Builder

▶ **Visualize It** ·

Complete the bubble map using the review words.

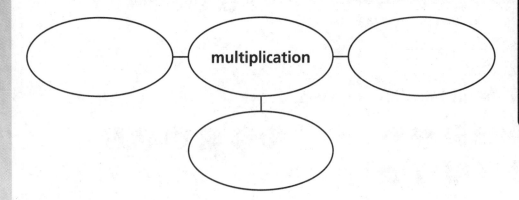

▶ **Understand Vocabulary** ·

Write the word or phrase that matches the description.

1. A _____ can name a part of a group or a whole.

2. You can write _____ of 10 such as 10, 20, 30, and so on.

3. _____ have one as the numerator.

4. The answer to a multiplication problem is called the

   _____.

5. _____ states that the product of any number and 1 is that number.

GO DIGITAL
• **Interactive Student Edition**
• **Multimedia eGlossary**

Chapter 8 Vocabulary

equation

ecuación

27

fraction

fracción

36

Identity Property of Multiplication

propiedad de identidad de la multiplicación

41

mixed number

número mixto

54

multiple

múltiplo

55

pattern

patrón

63

product

producto

72

unit fraction

fracción unitaria

94

A number that names a part of a whole or part of a group

Example:

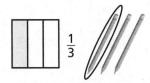

$\frac{1}{3}$

A number sentence which shows that two quantities are equal

Example: $3 + 1 = 4$

An amount given as a whole number and a fraction

Example: $2\frac{3}{6}$ is a mixed number

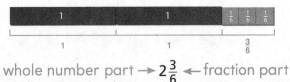

whole number part → $2\frac{3}{6}$ ← fraction part

The property that states that the product of any number and 1 is that number

Example: $9 \times 1 = 9$

An ordered set of numbers or objects; the order helps you predict what will come next

Examples: 2, 4, 6, 8, 10

The product of a number and a counting number is called a multiple of the number

Example:

$$\begin{array}{cccc} 3 & 3 & 3 & 3 \\ \times\ 1 & \times\ 2 & \times\ 3 & \times\ 4 \\ \hline 3 & 6 & 9 & 12 \end{array}$$ ← counting numbers
← multiples of 3

A fraction that has a numerator of one

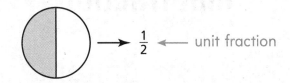

$\frac{1}{2}$ ← unit fraction

The answer to a multiplication problem

Example: $4 \times 5 = 20$

↑ product

Pick It

Word Box
equation
fraction
Identity Property of Multiplication
mixed number
multiple
pattern
product
unit fraction

For 3 players

Materials

- 4 sets of word cards

How to Play

1. Each player is dealt 5 cards. The remaining cards are a draw pile.

2. To take a turn, ask any player if he or she has a word that matches one of your word cards.

3. If the player has the word, he or she gives you the word card, and you must give the definition of the word.
   - If you are correct, keep the card and put the matching pair in front of you. Take another turn.
   - If you are wrong, return the card. Your turn is over.

4. If the player does not have the word, he or she answers, "Pick it." Then you take a card from the draw pile.

5. If the card you draw matches one of your word cards, follow the directions for Step 3 above. If it does not, your turn is over.

6. The game is over when one player has no cards left. The player with the most matches wins.

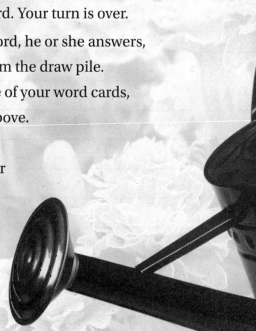

The Write Way

Reflect

Choose one idea. Write about it in the space below.

- Explain how to find multiples of a unit fraction.

- Pablo practiced piano $1\frac{1}{2}$ hours 3 times a week. Elsa practiced $\frac{3}{4}$ hour 5 times a week. Explain how you know who practiced for more time each week.

- Write two questions you have about multiplying fractions by whole numbers.

Name _____

Name _____

Name _____

Multiples The product of a number and a counting number is a multiple of the number. You have learned about multiples of whole numbers.

The products 1×4, 2×4, 3×4, and so on are multiples of 4. The numbers 4, 8, 12, and so on are multiples of 4.

You can also find multiples of unit fractions.

🔑 $1 \times \frac{1}{4}$ is $\frac{1}{4}$. **Use models to write the next four multiples of $\frac{1}{4}$. Complete the last model.**

| $\frac{1}{4}$ | $\frac{1}{4}$ | $\frac{1}{4}$ | $\frac{1}{4}$ |

$2 \times \frac{1}{4}$

| $\frac{1}{4}$ | $\frac{1}{4}$ | $\frac{1}{4}$ | $\frac{1}{4}$ |

$= \frac{2}{4}$

$\frac{1}{4}$	$\frac{1}{4}$	$\frac{1}{4}$	$\frac{1}{4}$
$\frac{1}{4}$	$\frac{1}{4}$	$\frac{1}{4}$	$\frac{1}{4}$
$\frac{1}{4}$	$\frac{1}{4}$	$\frac{1}{4}$	$\frac{1}{4}$

$3 \times \dfrac{\square}{\square}$

$= \dfrac{\square}{4}$

$\frac{1}{4}$	$\frac{1}{4}$	$\frac{1}{4}$	$\frac{1}{4}$
$\frac{1}{4}$	$\frac{1}{4}$	$\frac{1}{4}$	$\frac{1}{4}$
$\frac{1}{4}$	$\frac{1}{4}$	$\frac{1}{4}$	$\frac{1}{4}$
$\frac{1}{4}$	$\frac{1}{4}$	$\frac{1}{4}$	$\frac{1}{4}$

$4 \times \dfrac{\square}{\square}$

$= \dfrac{\square}{4}$

$\frac{1}{4}$	$\frac{1}{4}$	$\frac{1}{4}$	$\frac{1}{4}$
$\frac{1}{4}$	$\frac{1}{4}$	$\frac{1}{4}$	$\frac{1}{4}$
$\frac{1}{4}$	$\frac{1}{4}$	$\frac{1}{4}$	$\frac{1}{4}$
$\frac{1}{4}$	$\frac{1}{4}$	$\frac{1}{4}$	$\frac{1}{4}$
$\frac{1}{4}$	$\frac{1}{4}$	$\frac{1}{4}$	$\frac{1}{4}$

$\square \times \dfrac{\square}{\square}$

$= \dfrac{\square}{\square}$

Multiples of $\frac{1}{4}$ are $\frac{1}{4}$, ☐ , ☐ , ☐ , and ☐ .

🔑 **Use a number line to write multiples of $\frac{1}{5}$.**

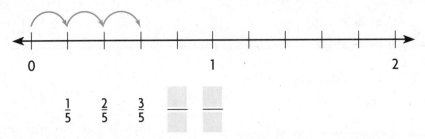

$\frac{1}{5}$ $\frac{2}{5}$ $\frac{3}{5}$ $\dfrac{\square}{\square}$ $\dfrac{\square}{\square}$

Multiples of $\frac{1}{5}$ are $\frac{1}{5}$, ☐ , ☐ , ☐ , and ☐ .

Name _____

1. Use the picture to complete the equations.

$\dfrac{3}{4} =$ _____ $+$ _____ $+$ _____

$\dfrac{3}{4} =$ _____ $\times \dfrac{1}{4}$

Write the fraction as a product of a whole number and a unit fraction.

2. $\dfrac{4}{5} =$ _____

3. $\dfrac{3}{10} =$ _____

4. $\dfrac{8}{3} =$ _____

List the next four multiples of the unit fraction.

5. $\dfrac{1}{6}$, ____, ____, ____,

6. $\dfrac{1}{3}$, ____, ____, ____,

> **Math Talk**
> Math Processes and Practices ⑥
> **Attend to Precision**
> Explain why $\dfrac{8}{5}$ is a multiple of $\dfrac{1}{5}$.

On Your Own

Write the fraction as a product of a whole number and a unit fraction.

7. $\dfrac{5}{6} =$ _____

8. $\dfrac{9}{4} =$ _____

9. $\dfrac{3}{100} =$ _____

List the next four multiples of the unit fraction.

10. $\dfrac{1}{10}$, ____, ____, ____,

11. $\dfrac{1}{8}$, ____, ____, ____,

Problem Solving • Applications

12. **Math Processes and Practices ⑥** Robyn uses $\dfrac{1}{2}$ cup of blueberries to make each loaf of blueberry bread. **Explain** how many loaves of blueberry bread she can make with $2\dfrac{1}{2}$ cups of blueberries.

13. **GO DEEPER** Nigel cut a loaf of bread into 12 equal slices. His family ate some of the bread and now $\dfrac{5}{12}$ of the loaf is left. Nigel wants to put each of the leftover slices in its own bag. How many bags does Nigel need?

14. **THINK SMARTER** Which fraction is a multiple of $\dfrac{1}{5}$? Mark all that apply.

○ $\dfrac{4}{5}$ ○ $\dfrac{5}{9}$

○ $\dfrac{5}{7}$ ○ $\dfrac{3}{5}$

Sense or Nonsense?

15. THINK SMARTER Whose statement makes sense? Whose statement is nonsense? Explain your reasoning.

There is no multiple of $\frac{1}{6}$ between $\frac{3}{6}$ and $\frac{4}{6}$.

$\frac{4}{5}$ is a multiple of $\frac{1}{4}$.

Gavin

_____
_____
_____
_____
_____
_____
_____

Abigail

_____
_____
_____
_____
_____
_____
_____

- For the statement that is nonsense, write a new statement that makes sense.

_____
_____

Name _____

Multiples of Unit Fractions

Learning Objective You will write a fraction as a product of a whole number and a unit fraction and find multiples of unit fractions.

Write the fraction as a product of a whole number and a unit fraction.

1. $\frac{5}{6}=$ _____ $5 \times \frac{1}{6}$ _____

2. $\frac{7}{8}=$ _____

3. $\frac{5}{3}=$ _____

4. $\frac{9}{10}=$ _____

5. $\frac{3}{4}=$ _____

6. $\frac{11}{12}=$ _____

List the next four multiples of the unit fraction.

7. $\frac{1}{5}$, ____, ____, ____, ____

8. $\frac{1}{8}$, ____, ____, ____, ____

Problem Solving (Real World)

9. So far, Monica has read $\frac{5}{6}$ of a book. She has read the same number of pages each day for 5 days. What fraction of the book does Monica read each day?

10. Nicholas buys $\frac{3}{8}$ pound of cheese. He puts the same amount of cheese on 3 sandwiches. How much cheese does Nicholas put on each sandwich?

_____

_____

11. **WRITE** ▸*Math* Explain how to write $\frac{5}{3}$ as a product of a whole number and a unit fraction.

_____

_____

_____

Lesson Check

1. Selena walks from home to school each morning and back home each afternoon. Altogether, she walks $\frac{2}{3}$ mile each day. How far does Selena live from school?

   _____

2. Will uses $\frac{3}{4}$ cup of olive oil to make 3 batches of salad dressing. How much oil does Will use for one batch of salad dressing?

   _____

Spiral Review

3. Liza bought $\frac{5}{8}$ pound of trail mix. She gives $\frac{2}{8}$ pound of trail mix to Michael. How much trail mix does Liza have left?

   _____

4. Leigh has a piece of rope that is $6\frac{2}{3}$ feet long. How do you write $6\frac{2}{3}$ as a fraction greater than 1?

   _____

5. A group of students have the following house numbers : 29, 39, 59, and 79. Randy's house number is a composite number. What is Randy's house number?

   _____

6. Mindy buys 12 cupcakes. Nine of the cupcakes have chocolate frosting and the rest have vanilla frosting. What fraction of the cupcakes have vanilla frosting?

   _____

FOR MORE PRACTICE
GO TO THE
Personal Math Trainer

Name _____

Multiples of Fractions

Essential Question How can you write a product of a whole number and a fraction as a product of a whole number and a unit fraction?

🔑 Unlock the Problem (Real World)

Jen is making 4 pans of baked ziti. For each pan, she needs $\frac{2}{3}$ cup cheese. Her measuring cup can scoop $\frac{1}{3}$ cup of cheese. How many scoops of cheese does she need for the 4 pans?

🔑 Example 1 Use a model to write the product of $4 \times \frac{2}{3}$ as the product of a whole number and a unit fraction.

$\frac{1}{3}$	$\frac{1}{3}$	$\frac{1}{3}$

Think: $\frac{2}{3}$ is 2 third-size parts.

$\frac{2}{3} =$ _____ + _____ or $2 \times$ _____ .

There are 4 pans of baked ziti. Each pan needs $\frac{2}{3}$ cup cheese.

$\frac{1}{3}$	$\frac{1}{3}$	$\frac{1}{3}$	← 1 pan: $2 \times \frac{1}{3} = \frac{2}{3}$
$\frac{1}{3}$	$\frac{1}{3}$	$\frac{1}{3}$	← 2 pans: $2 \times 2 \times \frac{1}{3} = 4 \times \frac{1}{3} = \frac{4}{3}$
$\frac{1}{3}$	$\frac{1}{3}$	$\frac{1}{3}$	← 3 pans: $3 \times 2 \times \frac{1}{3} = 6 \times \frac{1}{3} = \frac{6}{3}$
$\frac{1}{3}$	$\frac{1}{3}$	$\frac{1}{3}$	← 4 pans: $4 \times 2 \times \frac{1}{3} = 8 \times \frac{1}{3} = \frac{8}{3}$

$4 \times \frac{2}{3} = 4 \times$ _____ $\times \frac{1}{3} =$ _____ $\times \frac{1}{3} = \frac{}{3}$

So, Jen needs _____ third-size scoops of cheese for 4 pans of ziti.

Math Talk

Math Processes and Practices ⑦

Identify Relationships Explain how this model of $4 \times \frac{2}{3}$ is related to a model of 4×2.

1. What if Jen decides to make 10 pans of ziti? Describe a pattern you could use to find the number of scoops of cheese she would need.

_____

_____

_____

Multiples You have learned to write multiples of unit fractions. You can also write multiples of non-unit fractions.

🔑 Example 2 Use a number line to write multiples of $\frac{2}{5}$.

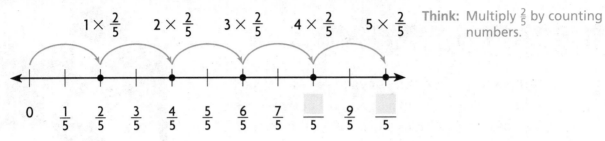

Think: Multiply $\frac{2}{5}$ by counting numbers.

Multiples of $\frac{2}{5}$ are $\frac{2}{5}$, ▢ , ▢ , ▢ , and ▢ .

$3 \times \frac{2}{5} = \frac{6}{5}$. Write $\frac{6}{5}$ as a product of a whole number and a unit fraction.

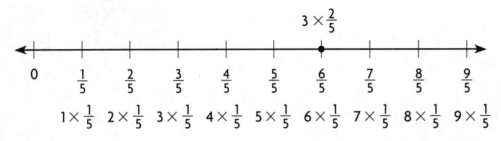

$3 \times \frac{2}{5} = \frac{6}{5} = $ _____ $\times$ _____

2. Explain how to use repeated addition to write the multiple of a fraction as the product of a whole number and a unit fraction.

_____

_____

Share and Show 🖊 MATH BOARD

1. Write three multiples of $\frac{3}{8}$.

$1 \times \frac{3}{8} = $ _____

$2 \times \frac{3}{8} = $ _____

$3 \times \frac{3}{8} = $ _____

Multiples of $\frac{3}{8}$ are _____ , _____ , and _____ .

Name _____

List the next four multiples of the fraction.

 2. $\frac{3}{6}$,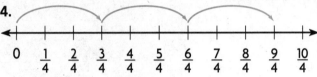

3. $\frac{2}{10}$,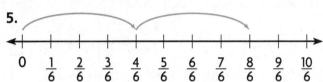

Write the product as the product of a whole number and a unit fraction.

4.

$$0 \quad \frac{1}{4} \quad \frac{2}{4} \quad \frac{3}{4} \quad \frac{4}{4} \quad \frac{5}{4} \quad \frac{6}{4} \quad \frac{7}{4} \quad \frac{8}{4} \quad \frac{9}{4} \quad \frac{10}{4}$$

$$3 \times \frac{3}{4} = \underline{\hspace{2cm}}$$

5.

$$0 \quad \frac{1}{6} \quad \frac{2}{6} \quad \frac{3}{6} \quad \frac{4}{6} \quad \frac{5}{6} \quad \frac{6}{6} \quad \frac{7}{6} \quad \frac{8}{6} \quad \frac{9}{6} \quad \frac{10}{6}$$

$$2 \times \frac{4}{6} = \underline{\hspace{2cm}}$$

Math Talk

Math Processes and Practices ②

Use Reasoning Explain how to write a product of a whole number and a fraction as a product of a whole number and a unit fraction.

On Your Own

List the next four multiples of the fraction.

6. $\frac{4}{5}$,

7. $\frac{2}{4}$,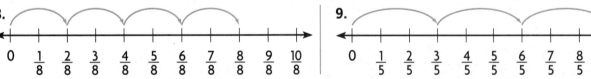

Write the product as the product of a whole number and a unit fraction.

8.

$$0 \quad \frac{1}{8} \quad \frac{2}{8} \quad \frac{3}{8} \quad \frac{4}{8} \quad \frac{5}{8} \quad \frac{6}{8} \quad \frac{7}{8} \quad \frac{8}{8} \quad \frac{9}{8} \quad \frac{10}{8}$$

$$4 \times \frac{2}{8} = \underline{\hspace{2cm}}$$

9.

$$0 \quad \frac{1}{5} \quad \frac{2}{5} \quad \frac{3}{5} \quad \frac{4}{5} \quad \frac{5}{5} \quad \frac{6}{5} \quad \frac{7}{5} \quad \frac{8}{5} \quad \frac{9}{5} \quad \frac{10}{5}$$

$$3 \times \frac{3}{5} = \underline{\hspace{2cm}}$$

10. **Math Processes and Practices ⑧** **Use Repeated Reasoning** Are $\frac{6}{10}$ and $\frac{6}{30}$ multiples of $\frac{3}{10}$? Explain.

_____

_____

11. **GO DEEPER** Which is greater, $4 \times \frac{2}{7}$ or $3 \times \frac{3}{7}$? Explain.

_____

12. **THINK SMARTER** Josh is watering his plants. He gives each of 2 plants $\frac{3}{5}$ pint of water. His watering can holds $\frac{1}{5}$ pint. How many times will he fill his watering can to water both plants?

a. What do you need to find?

_____

b. What information do you need to use?

_____

_____

c. How can drawing a model help you solve the problem?

_____

_____

_____

_____

_____

_____

_____

d. Show the steps you use to solve the problem.

e. Complete the sentence.

Josh will fill his watering can _____ times.

13. **THINK SMARTER +** Alma is making 3 batches of tortillas. She adds $\frac{3}{4}$ cup of water to each batch. The measuring cup holds $\frac{1}{4}$ cup. How many times must Alma measure $\frac{1}{4}$ cup of water to have enough for the tortillas? Shade the model to show your answer.

Alma must measure $\frac{1}{4}$ cup [ ] times.

$\frac{1}{4}$	$\frac{1}{4}$	$\frac{1}{4}$	$\frac{1}{4}$
$\frac{1}{4}$	$\frac{1}{4}$	$\frac{1}{4}$	$\frac{1}{4}$
$\frac{1}{4}$	$\frac{1}{4}$	$\frac{1}{4}$	$\frac{1}{4}$

Multiples of Fractions

Learning Objective You will write a product of a whole number and a fraction as a product of a whole number and a unit fraction and you will write multiples of non-unit fractions.

List the next four multiples of the fraction.

1. $\frac{3}{5}$, ____, ____, ____, ____

2. $\frac{2}{6}$, ____, ____, ____, ____

Write the product as the product of a whole number and a unit fraction.

3.

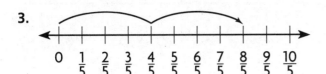

$2 \times \frac{4}{5} =$ _____

4.

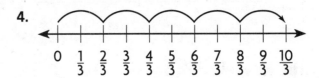

$5 \times \frac{2}{3} =$ _____

Problem Solving · Real World

5. Jessica is making 2 loaves of banana bread. She needs $\frac{3}{4}$ cup of sugar for each loaf. Her measuring cup can only hold $\frac{1}{4}$ cup of sugar. How many times will Jessica need to fill the measuring cup in order to get enough sugar for both loaves of bread?

6. A group of four students is performing an experiment with salt. Each student must add $\frac{3}{8}$ teaspoon of salt to a solution. The group only has a $\frac{1}{8}$-teaspoon measuring spoon. How many times will the group need to fill the measuring spoon in order to perform the experiment?

_____

_____

7. **WRITE** ▸ *Math* Explain how to write $3 \times \frac{3}{8}$ as the product of a whole number and a unit fraction.

_____

_____

_____

Lesson Check

1. Eloise made a list of some multiples of $\frac{8}{5}$. Write 5 fractions that could be in Eloise's list.

_____

_____

2. David is filling five $\frac{3}{4}$-quart bottles with a sports drink. His measuring cup only holds $\frac{1}{4}$ quart. How many times will David need to fill the measuring cup in order to fill the 5 bottles?

_____

_____

Spiral Review

3. Ira has 128 stamps in his stamp album. He has the same number of stamps on each of the 8 pages. How many stamps are on each page?

_____

4. Ryan is saving up for a bike that costs $198. So far, he has saved $15 per week for the last 12 weeks. How much more money does Ryan need in order to be able to buy the bike?

_____

5. Tina buys $3\frac{7}{8}$ yards of material at the fabric store. She uses it to make a skirt. Afterward, she has $1\frac{3}{8}$ yards of the fabric leftover. How many yards of material did Tina use?

_____

6. Order these fractions from **least** to **greatest:** $\frac{2}{3}$, $\frac{7}{12}$, $\frac{3}{4}$

_____

FOR MORE PRACTICE
GO TO THE
Personal Math Trainer

Name _____

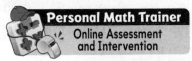

Vocabulary

Choose the best term from the box.

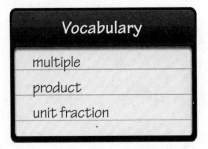

Vocabulary
multiple
product
unit fraction

1. A _____ of a number is the product of the number and a counting number. (p. 456)

2. A _____ always has a numerator of 1. (p. 455)

Concepts and Skills

List the next four multiples of the unit fraction.

3. $\frac{1}{2}$, [ ] , [ ] , [ ] , [ ]

4. $\frac{1}{5}$, [ ] , [ ] , [ ] ,

Write the fraction as a product of a whole number and a unit fraction.

5. $\frac{4}{10} =$ _____

6. $\frac{8}{12} =$ _____

7. $\frac{3}{4} =$ _____

List the next four multiples of the fraction.

8. $\frac{2}{5}$, [ ] , [ ] , [ ] , [ ]

9. $\frac{5}{6}$, [ ] , [ ] , [ ] ,

Write the product as the product of a whole number and a unit fraction.

10.
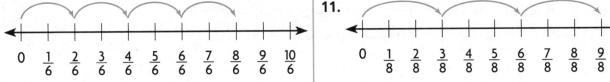

$4 \times \frac{2}{6} =$ _____

11.
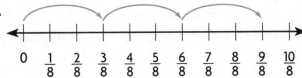

$3 \times \frac{3}{8} =$ _____

12. Pedro cut a sheet of poster board into 10 equal parts. His brother used some of the poster board and now $\frac{8}{10}$ is left. Pedro wants to make a sign from each remaining part of the poster board. How many signs can he make?

_____

13. Ella is making 3 batches of banana milkshakes. She needs $\frac{3}{4}$ gallon of milk for each batch. Her measuring cup holds $\frac{1}{4}$ gallon. How many times will she need to fill the measuring cup to make all 3 batches of milkshakes?

_____

14. Darren cut a lemon pie into 8 equal slices. His friends ate some of the pie and now $\frac{5}{8}$ is left. Darren wants to put each slice of the leftover pie on its own plate. What part of the pie will he put on each plate?

_____

15. **GO DEEPER** Beth is putting liquid fertilizer on the plants in 4 flowerpots. Her measuring spoon holds $\frac{1}{8}$ teaspoon. The directions say to put $\frac{5}{8}$ teaspoon of fertilizer in each pot. How many times will Beth need to fill the measuring spoon to fertilize the plants in the 4 pots?

_____

Name _____

Multiply a Fraction by a Whole Number Using Models

Learning Objective You will use fraction circles and patterns with fraction strips to multiply a fraction by a whole number.

Essential Question How can you use a model to multiply a fraction by a whole number?

Unlock the Problem

Rafael practices the violin for $\frac{3}{4}$ hour each day. He has a recital in 3 days. How much time will he practice in 3 days?

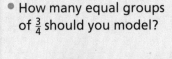

● How many equal groups of $\frac{3}{4}$ should you model?

_____

Example 1 Use a model to multiply $3 \times \frac{3}{4}$.

Think: $3 \times \frac{3}{4}$ is 3 groups of $\frac{3}{4}$ of a whole. Shade the model to show 3 groups of $\frac{3}{4}$.

$$\begin{array}{|c|c|}\hline \frac{1}{4} & \frac{1}{4} \\\hline \frac{1}{4} & \frac{1}{4} \\\hline\end{array} \quad \begin{array}{|c|c|}\hline \frac{1}{4} & \frac{1}{4} \\\hline \frac{1}{4} & \frac{1}{4} \\\hline\end{array} \quad \begin{array}{|c|c|}\hline \frac{1}{4} & \frac{1}{4} \\\hline \frac{1}{4} & \frac{1}{4} \\\hline\end{array}$$

1 group of $\frac{3}{4}$ = _____

2 groups of $\frac{3}{4}$ = _____

3 groups of $\frac{3}{4}$ = _____

$3 \times \frac{3}{4}$ = _____

So, Rafael will practice for _____ hours in all.

Math Talk

Math Processes and Practices ②

Reason Abstractly If you multiply $4 \times \frac{2}{6}$, is the product greater than or less than 4? Explain.

---

1. Explain how you can use repeated addition with the model to find the product $3 \times \frac{3}{4}$.

_____

_____

2. Rafael's daily practice of $\frac{3}{4}$ hour is in sessions that last for $\frac{1}{4}$ hour each. Describe how the model shows the number of practice sessions Rafael has in 3 days.

_____

_____

🔒 Example 2 Use a pattern to multiply.

You know how to use a model and repeated addition to multiply a fraction by a whole number. Look for a pattern in the table to discover another way to multiply a fraction by a whole number.

Multiplication Problem		Whole Number (Number of Groups)	Fraction (Size of Groups)	Product
$\frac{1}{6}$ $\frac{1}{6}$ $\frac{1}{6}$ $\frac{1}{6}$ $\frac{1}{6}$ $\frac{1}{6}$ / $\frac{1}{6}$ $\frac{1}{6}$ $\frac{1}{6}$ $\frac{1}{6}$ $\frac{1}{6}$ $\frac{1}{6}$	$2 \times \frac{1}{6}$	2	$\frac{1}{6}$ of a whole	$\frac{2}{6}$
$\frac{1}{6}$ $\frac{1}{6}$ $\frac{1}{6}$ $\frac{1}{6}$ $\frac{1}{6}$ $\frac{1}{6}$ / $\frac{1}{6}$ $\frac{1}{6}$ $\frac{1}{6}$ $\frac{1}{6}$ $\frac{1}{6}$ $\frac{1}{6}$	$2 \times \frac{2}{6}$	2	$\frac{2}{6}$ of a whole	$\frac{4}{6}$
$\frac{1}{6}$ $\frac{1}{6}$ $\frac{1}{6}$ $\frac{1}{6}$ $\frac{1}{6}$ $\frac{1}{6}$ / $\frac{1}{6}$ $\frac{1}{6}$ $\frac{1}{6}$ $\frac{1}{6}$ $\frac{1}{6}$ $\frac{1}{6}$	$2 \times \frac{3}{6}$	2	$\frac{3}{6}$ of a whole	$\frac{6}{6}$

When you multiply a fraction by a whole number, the numerator

in the product is the product of the _____ and the

_____ of the fraction. The denominator in the product

is the same as the _____ of the fraction.

3. How do you multiply a fraction by a whole number without using a model or repeated addition?

_____

_____

4. Describe two different ways to find the product $4 \times \frac{2}{3}$.

_____

_____

_____

Name _____

1. Find the product of $3 \times \frac{5}{8}$.

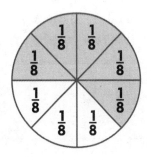
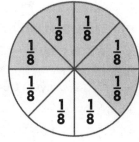

1 group of $\frac{5}{8} = \dfrac{\boxed{}}{8}$

2 groups of $\frac{5}{8} = \dfrac{\boxed{}}{8}$

3 groups of $\frac{5}{8} = \dfrac{\boxed{}}{8}$

3 groups of $\frac{5}{8}$

$3 \times \frac{5}{8} =$ _____

Multiply.

2.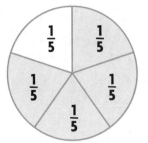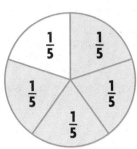

$2 \times \frac{4}{5} =$ _____

3.

$\frac{1}{3}$	$\frac{1}{3}$	$\frac{1}{3}$
$\frac{1}{3}$	$\frac{1}{3}$	$\frac{1}{3}$
$\frac{1}{3}$	$\frac{1}{3}$	$\frac{1}{3}$
$\frac{1}{3}$	$\frac{1}{3}$	$\frac{1}{3}$

$4 \times \frac{2}{3} =$ _____

4. $5 \times \frac{3}{10} =$ _____

5. $4 \times \frac{5}{6} =$ _____

Math Talk Math Processes and Practices ④

Model Mathematics
Describe how to model
Exercise 5.

On Your Own

Multiply.

6. $2 \times \frac{7}{12} =$ _____

7. $6 \times \frac{3}{8} =$ _____

8. $5 \times \frac{2}{4} =$ _____

9. $3 \times \frac{4}{6} =$ _____

10. $2 \times \frac{5}{10} =$ _____

11. $4 \times \frac{2}{8} =$ _____

Math Processes and Practices ⑦ **Look for a Pattern Algebra Write the unknown number.**

12. $\boxed{} \times \frac{2}{3} = \frac{12}{3}$

13. $5 \times \dfrac{\boxed{}}{4} = \frac{10}{4}$

14. $2 \times \dfrac{7}{\boxed{}} = \frac{14}{8}$

Unlock the Problem

15. **THINK SMARTER** Lisa makes clothes for pets. She needs $\frac{5}{6}$ yard of fabric to make 1 dog coat. How much fabric does she need to make 3 dog coats?

a. What do you need to find?

_____

b. What information do you need?

_____

c. Show the steps you use to solve the problem.

d. Complete the sentence.

Lisa needs _____ yards of fabric to make 3 dog coats.

---

16. **GO DEEPER** Manuel's small dog eats $\frac{2}{4}$ bag of dog food in 1 month. His large dog eats $\frac{3}{4}$ bag of dog food in 1 month. How many bags do both dogs eat in 6 months?

_____

17. **THINK SMARTER** Select the correct product for the equation.

| $\frac{24}{12}$ | $\frac{18}{12}$ | $\frac{24}{7}$ | $\frac{18}{7}$ |

$9 \times \frac{2}{12} = $ ⬚

$3 \times \frac{6}{7} = $ ⬚

$6 \times \frac{4}{7} = $ ⬚

$8 \times \frac{3}{12} = $ ⬚

Multiply a Fraction by a Whole Number Using Models

Learning Objective You will use fraction circles and patterns with fraction strips to multiply a fraction by a whole number.

Multiply.

1. $2 \times \dfrac{5}{6} = \underline{\dfrac{10}{6}}$

2. $3 \times \dfrac{2}{5} = \underline{\hspace{2cm}}$

3. $7 \times \dfrac{3}{10} = \underline{\hspace{2cm}}$

4. $3 \times \dfrac{5}{12} = \underline{\hspace{2cm}}$

5. $6 \times \dfrac{3}{4} = \underline{\hspace{2cm}}$

6. $4 \times \dfrac{2}{5} = \underline{\hspace{2cm}}$

Problem Solving · Real World

7. Matthew walks $\frac{5}{8}$ mile to the bus stop each morning. How far will he walk in 5 days?

8. Emily uses $\frac{2}{3}$ cup of milk to make one batch of muffins. How many cups of milk will Emily use if she makes 3 batches of muffins?

_____

_____

9. **WRITE** ▸ *Math* Explain how you can use a model to find $4 \times \frac{3}{8}$. Include a drawing and a solution.

_____

_____

_____

_____

Lesson Check

1. Aleta's puppy gained $\frac{3}{8}$ pound each week for 4 weeks. Altogether, how much weight did the puppy gain during the 4 weeks?

   _____

2. Pedro mixes $\frac{3}{4}$ teaspoon of plant food into each gallon of water. How many teaspoons of plant food should Pedro mix into 5 gallons of water?

   _____

Spiral Review

3. Ivana has $\frac{3}{4}$ pound of hamburger meat. She makes 3 hamburger patties. Each patty weighs the same amount. How much does each hamburger patty weigh?

   _____

   _____

4. Write $\frac{7}{10}$ as a sum of fractions two different ways.

   _____

   _____

5. Lance wants to find the total length of 3 boards. He uses the expression $3\frac{1}{2} + (2 + 4\frac{1}{2})$. How can Lance rewrite the expression using both the Associative and Commutative Properties of Addition?

   _____

6. Fill in the blank with a symbol that makes this statement true:

   $$\frac{5}{12} \bigcirc \frac{1}{3}$$

FOR MORE PRACTICE
GO TO THE
Personal Math Trainer

Name _____

Multiply a Fraction or Mixed Number by a Whole Number

Essential Question How can you multiply a fraction by a whole number to solve a problem?

Learning Objective You will multiply a fraction or a mixed number by a whole number and write the product as a mixed number.

Unlock the Problem

Christina is planning a dance routine. At the end of each measure of music, she will make a $1\frac{1}{4}$ turn. How many turns will she make after the first 3 measures of music?

You can multiply a mixed number by a whole number.

- Will Christina make more or less than $1\frac{1}{4}$ turns in 3 measures of music?

  _____

- What operation will you use to solve the problem?

  _____

Example

STEP 1 Write and solve an equation.

$3 \times 1\frac{1}{4} = 3 \times \underline{\quad} = \underline{\quad}$ Write $1\frac{1}{4}$ as a fraction. Multiply.

STEP 2 Write the product as a mixed number.

$$\frac{15}{4} = \underbrace{\frac{1}{4} + \frac{1}{4} + \frac{1}{4} + \frac{1}{4}}_{1} + \underbrace{\underline{\quad} + \underline{\quad} + \underline{\quad} + \underline{\quad}}_{1} + \underbrace{\underline{\quad} + \underline{\quad} + \underline{\quad} + \underline{\quad}}_{1} + \frac{1}{4} + \frac{1}{4} + \frac{1}{4}$$

$= \underline{\quad} + \underline{\quad}$ Combine the wholes. Then combine the remaining parts.

$= \underline{\quad}$ Write the mixed number.

So, Christina will make _____ turns.

Math Processes and Practices 8

Generalize How is writing the mixed number as a fraction in Step 2 related to division?

1. If you multiply $3 \times \frac{1}{4}$, is the product greater than or less than 3? Explain.

   _____

   _____

2. Explain how you can tell that $3 \times 1\frac{1}{4}$ is greater than 3 without finding the exact product.

   _____

Rename Mixed Numbers and Fractions You can use multiplication and division to rename fractions and mixed numbers.

Write $8\frac{1}{5}$ as a fraction.

$8\frac{1}{5} = 8 + \frac{1}{5}$

$\phantom{8\frac{1}{5}} = (8 \times \underline{\hspace{1cm}}) + \frac{1}{5}$ Use the Identity Property of Multiplication.

$\phantom{8\frac{1}{5}} = \left(8 \times \dfrac{}{}\right) + \frac{1}{5}$ Rename 1.

$\phantom{8\frac{1}{5}} = \dfrac{}{} + \dfrac{}{}$ Multiply.

$\phantom{8\frac{1}{5}} = \dfrac{}{}$ Add.

Write $\frac{32}{5}$ as a mixed number.

Find how many groups of $\frac{5}{5}$ are in $\frac{32}{5}$.

• Divide 32 by 5.

• The quotient is the number of wholes in $\frac{32}{5}$.

• The remainder is the number of fifths left over.

$5\overline{)32}\ r$

There are 6 groups of $\frac{5}{5}$, or 6 wholes.
There are 2 fifths, or $\frac{2}{5}$ left over.

$\dfrac{32}{5} = \dfrac{}{}$

Try This! Find $5 \times 2\frac{2}{3}$. Write the product as a mixed number.

$5 \times 2\frac{2}{3} = 5 \times \dfrac{}{}$ Write $2\frac{2}{3}$ as a fraction.

$\phantom{5 \times 2\frac{2}{3}} = \dfrac{}{}$ Multiply.

$\phantom{5 \times 2\frac{2}{3}} = \dfrac{}{}$ Divide the numerator by 3.

3. Explain why your solution to $5 \times 2\frac{2}{3} = 13\frac{1}{3}$ is reasonable.

_____

_____

4. **Sense or Nonsense?** To find $5 \times 2\frac{2}{3}$, Dylan says he can find $(5 \times 2) + \left(5 \times \frac{2}{3}\right)$. Does this make sense? Explain.

_____

_____

Name _____

1. $2 \times 3\frac{2}{3} = 2 \times$ _____

$= $ _____

$= $ _____

Multiply. Write the product as a mixed number.

2. $6 \times \frac{2}{5} = $ _____

3. $3 \times 2\frac{3}{4} = $ _____

4. $2 \times 1\frac{5}{6} = $ _____

On Your Own

Math Talk **Math Processes and Practices ❶**

Evaluate Reasonableness How do you know your answer to Exercise 3 is reasonable?

Multiply. Write the product as a mixed number.

5. $4 \times \frac{5}{8} = $ _____

6. $6 \times \frac{5}{12} = $ _____

7. $3 \times 2\frac{1}{2} = $ _____

8. $2 \times 2\frac{2}{3} = $ _____

9. $5 \times 1\frac{2}{4} = $ _____

10. $4 \times 2\frac{2}{5} = $ _____

Math Processes and Practices ❼ **Look for a Pattern** **Algebra** **Write the unknown number.**

11. ▢ $\times 2\frac{1}{3} = 9\frac{1}{3}$

12. $3 \times 2\frac{2}{▢} = 7\frac{2}{4}$

13. $3 \times ▢\frac{3}{8} = 4\frac{1}{8}$

14. Describe two different ways to write $\frac{7}{3}$ as a mixed number.

_____

_____

_____

_____

_____

© Houghton Mifflin Harcourt Publishing Company

Problem Solving • Applications

Use the recipe for 15–18.

15. Otis plans to make 3 batches of sidewalk chalk. How much plaster of Paris does he need?

   _____

16. **What's the Question?** The answer is $\frac{32}{3}$.

   _____

   _____

17. **THINK SMARTER** Patty has 2 cups of warm water. Is that enough water to make 4 batches of sidewalk chalk? Explain how you know without finding the exact product.

   _____

   _____

> **Sidewalk Chalk Recipe**
>
> $\frac{3}{4}$ cup warm water
>
> $1\frac{1}{2}$ cups plaster of Paris
>
> $2\frac{2}{3}$ tablespoons powdered paint

18. **GO DEEPER** Rita makes sidewalk chalk 2 days a week. Each of those days, she spends $1\frac{1}{4}$ hours making the chalk. How much time does Rita spend making sidewalk chalk in 3 weeks?

   _____

   Personal Math Trainer

19. **THINK SMARTER +** Oliver has music lessons Monday, Wednesday, and Friday. Each lesson is $\frac{3}{4}$ of an hour. Oliver says he will have lessons for $3\frac{1}{2}$ hours this week. Without multiplying, explain how you know Oliver is incorrect.

© Houghton Mifflin Harcourt Publishing Company • Image Credits: (cr) ©Kent Knudson/PhotoLink/Getty Images, (br), (tl) ©Houghton Mifflin Harcourt

Multiply a Fraction or Mixed Number by a Whole Number

Learning Objective You will multiply a fraction or a mixed number by a whole number and write the product as a mixed number.

Multiply. Write the product as a mixed number.

1. $5 \times \frac{3}{10} =$ ___ $1\frac{5}{10}$

2. $3 \times \frac{3}{5} =$ _____

3. $5 \times \frac{3}{4} =$ _____

4. $4 \times 1\frac{1}{5} =$ _____

5. $2 \times 2\frac{1}{3} =$ _____

6. $5 \times 1\frac{1}{6} =$ _____

Problem Solving Real World

7. Brielle exercises for $\frac{3}{4}$ hour each day for 6 days in a row. Altogether, how many hours does she exercise during the 6 days?

_____

8. A recipe for quinoa calls for $2\frac{2}{3}$ cups of milk. Conner wants to make 4 batches of quinoa. How much milk does he need?

_____

9. **WRITE** ▸*Math* Write a word problem that you can solve by multiplying a mixed number by a whole number. Include a solution.

_____

_____

_____

_____

Lesson Check

1. A mother is $1\frac{3}{4}$ times as tall as her son. Her son is 3 feet tall. How tall is the mother?

2. The cheerleaders are making a banner that is 8 feet wide. The length of the banner is $1\frac{1}{3}$ times the width of the banner. How long is the banner?

Spiral Review

3. Karleigh walks $\frac{5}{8}$ mile to school every day. How far does she walk to school in 5 days?

4. Write a fraction that is a multiple of $\frac{4}{5}$.

5. Jo cut a key lime pie into 8 equal-size slices. The next day, $\frac{7}{8}$ of the pie is left. Jo puts each slice on its own plate. How many plates does she need?

6. Over the weekend, Ed spent $1\frac{1}{4}$ hours doing his math homework and $1\frac{3}{4}$ hours doing his science project. Altogether, how much time did Ed spend doing homework over the weekend?

© Houghton Mifflin Harcourt Publishing Company

FOR MORE PRACTICE
GO TO THE
Personal Math Trainer

Name _____

Problem Solving • Comparison Problems with Fractions

Essential Question How can you use the strategy *draw a diagram* to solve comparison problems with fractions?

Learning Objective You will use the strategy *draw a diagram* to solve real-world comparison problems with fractions by drawing bar models and writing an equation.

Unlock the Problem

The deepest part of the Grand Canyon is about $1\frac{1}{6}$ miles deep. The deepest part of the ocean is located in the Mariana Trench, in the Pacific Ocean. The deepest part of the ocean is almost 6 times as deep as the deepest part of the Grand Canyon. About how deep is the deepest part of the ocean?

Read the Problem

What do I need to find?

I need to find _____

_____

_____

What information do I need to use?

The deepest part of the Grand

Canyon is about _____ miles deep.

The deepest part of the ocean is

about _____ times as deep.

How will I use the information?

I can _____ to compare the depths.

Solve the Problem

Draw a bar model. Compare the depth of the deepest part of the Grand Canyon and the deepest part of the ocean, in miles.

_____ $\boxed{1\frac{1}{6}}$

_____ (bar model with 6 sections)
$\underbrace{}_{m}$

Write an equation and solve.

m is the deepest part of _____, in miles.

$m = $ _____ _____   Write an equation.

$m = $ _____ _____   Write the mixed number as a fraction.

$m = $ _____   Multiply.

$m = $ _____   Write the fraction as a whole number.

So, the deepest part of the ocean is about _____ miles deep.

🔓 Try Another Problem

Mountains are often measured by the distance they rise above sea level. Mount Washington rises more than $1\frac{1}{10}$ miles above sea level. Mount Everest rises about 5 times as high. About how many miles above sea level does Mount Everest rise?

Read the Problem	Solve the Problem
What do I need to find?	
What information do I need to use?	
How will I use the information?	

So, Mount Everest rises about _____ miles above sea level.

- How did drawing a diagram help you solve the problem?

_____

_____

Math Talk

Math Processes and Practices ⑦

Look for Structure What strategy could you use to find the height of Mount Everest?

Name _____

Share and Show MATH BOARD

1. Komodo dragons are the heaviest lizards on Earth. A baby Komodo dragon is $1\frac{1}{4}$ feet long when it hatches. Its mother is 6 times as long. How long is the mother?

   First, draw a bar model to show the problem.

   WRITE Math
   Show Your Work

   Then, write the equation you need to solve.

   _____

   Finally, find the length of the mother Komodo dragon.

   The mother Komodo dragon is _____ feet long.

2. THINK SMARTER What if a male Komodo dragon is 7 times as long as the baby Komodo dragon? How long is the male? How much longer is the male than the mother?

   _____

3. The smallest hummingbird is the Bee hummingbird. It has a mass of about $1\frac{1}{2}$ grams. A Rufous hummingbird's mass is 3 times the mass of the Bee hummingbird. What is the mass of a Rufous hummingbird?

   _____

4. Sloane needs $\frac{3}{4}$ hour to drive to her grandmother's house. It takes her 5 times as long to drive to her cousin's house. How long does it take to drive to her cousin's house?

   _____

On Your Own

Use the table for 5 and 6.

Payton has a variety of flowers in her garden.
The table shows the average heights of the flowers.

Flower	Height
tulip	$1\frac{1}{4}$ feet
daisy	$2\frac{1}{2}$ feet
tiger lily	$3\frac{1}{3}$ feet
sunflower	$7\frac{3}{4}$ feet

5. **Math Processes and Practices ①** **Make Sense of Problems** What is the difference between the height of the tallest flower and the height of the shortest flower in Payton's garden?

_____

WRITE ▸ *Math*
Show Your Work

6. **THINK SMARTER** Payton says her average sunflower is 7 times the height of her average tulip. Do you agree or disagree with her statement? Explain your reasoning.

_____

_____

_____

7. **GO DEEPER** Miguel ran $1\frac{3}{10}$ miles on Monday. On Friday, Miguel ran 3 times as far as he did on Monday. How much farther did Miguel run on Friday than he did on Monday?

_____

_____

Personal Math Trainer

8. **THINK SMARTER +** The table shows the lengths of different types of turtles at a zoo.

Turtle Name	Type of Turtle	Length
Tuck	Common Snapping Turtle	$1\frac{1}{6}$ feet
Lolly	Leatherback Sea Turtle	$5\frac{5}{6}$ feet
Daisy	Loggerhead Sea Turtle	$3\frac{1}{2}$ feet

For numbers 8a–8d, select True or False for each statement.

8a. Daisy is 4 times as long as Tuck.   ○ True   ○ False

8b. Lolly is 5 times as long as Tuck.   ○ True   ○ False

8c. Daisy is 3 times as long as Tuck.   ○ True   ○ False

8d. Lolly is 2 times as long as Daisy.   ○ True   ○ False

Problem Solving • Comparison Problems with Fractions

Learning Objective You will use the strategy *draw a diagram* to solve real-world comparison problems with fractions by drawing bar models and writing an equation.

Read each problem and solve.

1. A shrub is $1\frac{2}{3}$ feet tall. A small tree is 3 times as tall as the shrub. How tall is the tree?

   t is the height of the tree, in feet.

   $t = 3 \times 1\frac{2}{3}$

   $t = 3 \times \frac{5}{3}$

   $t = \frac{15}{3}$

   $t = 5$

   So, the tree is 5 feet tall.

shrub	$1\frac{2}{3}$		
tree	$1\frac{2}{3}$	$1\frac{2}{3}$	$1\frac{2}{3}$

   _____ 5 feet _____

2. You run $1\frac{3}{4}$ miles each day. Your friend runs 4 times as far as you do. How far does your friend run each day?

   _____

3. At the grocery store, Ayla buys $1\frac{1}{3}$ pounds of ground turkey. Tasha buys 2 times as much ground turkey as Ayla. How much ground turkey does Tasha buy?

   _____

4. **WRITE** ▸*Math* Draw a bar model that shows a pen is 4 times as long as an eraser that is $1\frac{1}{3}$ inches long.

Lesson Check

1. A Wilson's Storm Petrel is a small bird with a wingspan of $1\frac{1}{3}$ feet. A California Condor is a larger bird with a wingspan almost 7 times as wide as the wingspan of the petrel. About how wide is the wingspan of the California Condor? (It may be helpful to draw a model.)

2. The walking distance from the Empire State Building in New York City to Times Square is about $\frac{9}{10}$ mile. The walking distance from the Empire State Building to Sue's hotel is about 8 times as far. About how far is Sue's hotel from the Empire State Building? (It may be helpful to draw a model.)

Spiral Review

3. Write an expression that is equal to $3 \times 2\frac{1}{4}$.

4. At a bake sale, Ron sells $\frac{7}{8}$ of an apple pie and $\frac{5}{8}$ of a cherry pie. Altogether, how much pie does he sell at the bake sale?

5. Write one measurement that is between $\frac{3}{16}$ inch and $\frac{7}{8}$ inch on a ruler.

6. Write a composite number that is less than 5.

FOR MORE PRACTICE
GO TO THE
Personal Math Trainer

✓ Chapter 8 Review/Test

Personal Math Trainer
Online Assessment
and Intervention

1. What are the next four multiples of $\frac{1}{8}$?

[ ]

Personal Math Trainer

2. *THINK SMARTER* + Marta is making 3 servings of fruit salad. She adds $\frac{3}{8}$ cup blueberries for each serving. Her measuring cup holds $\frac{1}{8}$ cup. How many times must Marta measure $\frac{1}{8}$ cup of blueberries to have enough for the fruit salad? Shade the models to show your answer.

$\frac{1}{8}$	$\frac{1}{8}$	$\frac{1}{8}$	$\frac{1}{8}$	$\frac{1}{8}$	$\frac{1}{8}$	$\frac{1}{8}$	$\frac{1}{8}$
$\frac{1}{8}$	$\frac{1}{8}$	$\frac{1}{8}$	$\frac{1}{8}$	$\frac{1}{8}$	$\frac{1}{8}$	$\frac{1}{8}$	$\frac{1}{8}$
$\frac{1}{8}$	$\frac{1}{8}$	$\frac{1}{8}$	$\frac{1}{8}$	$\frac{1}{8}$	$\frac{1}{8}$	$\frac{1}{8}$	$\frac{1}{8}$

Marta must measure $\frac{1}{8}$ cup _____ times.

3. Mickey exercises $\frac{3}{4}$ hour every day. How many hours does he exercise in 8 days?

_____ hours

GO DIGITAL Assessment Options
Chapter Test

4. Molly is baking for the Moms and Muffins event at her school. She will bake 4 batches of banana muffins. She needs $1\frac{3}{4}$ cups of bananas for each batch of muffins.

Part A

Molly completed the multiplication below and said she needed 8 cups of bananas for 4 batches of muffins. What is Molly's error?

$$4 \times 1\frac{3}{4} = 4 \times \frac{8}{4} = \frac{32}{4} = 8$$

Part B

What is the correct number of cups Molly needs for 4 batches of muffins? Explain how you found your answer.

5. Which fraction is a multiple of $\frac{1}{9}$? Mark all that apply.

○ $\frac{3}{9}$ ○ $\frac{9}{12}$ ○ $\frac{2}{9}$

○ $\frac{4}{9}$ ○ $\frac{9}{10}$ ○ $\frac{9}{9}$

6. Mimi recorded a soccer game that lasted $1\frac{2}{3}$ hours. She watched it 3 times over the weekend to study the plays. How many hours did Mimi spend watching the soccer game? Show your work.

7. Theo is comparing shark lengths. He learned that a horn shark is $2\frac{3}{4}$ feet long. A blue shark is 4 times as long. Complete the model. Then find the length of a blue shark.

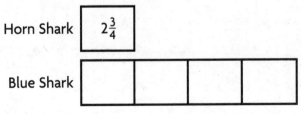

A blue shark is [ ] feet long.

Name _____

8. Joel made a number line showing the multiples of $\frac{3}{5}$.

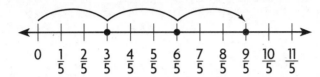

The product $2 \times \frac{3}{5}$ is shown by the fraction ☐ on the number line.

9. Bobby has baseball practice Monday, Wednesday, and Friday. Each practice is $2\frac{1}{2}$ hours. Bobby says he will have practice for 4 hours this week.

Part A

Without multiplying, explain how you know Bobby is incorrect.

☐

Part B

How long will Bobby have baseball practice this week? Write your answer as a mixed number. Show your work.

☐

10. Look at the number line. Write the missing fractions.

$\frac{1}{6}$ $\frac{2}{6}$ $\frac{3}{6}$ $\frac{4}{6}$ $\frac{5}{6}$ $\frac{6}{6}$ $\frac{7}{6}$ $\frac{8}{6}$ ___ ___ . ___ ___

11. Ana's dachshund weighed $5\frac{5}{8}$ pounds when it was born. By age 4, the dog weighed 6 times as much. Fill each box with a number or symbol from the list to show how to find the weight of Ana's dog at age 4. Not all numbers and symbols may be used.

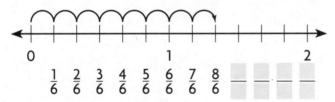

weight = ☐ ☐ ☐

12. Asta made a fraction number line to help her find $3 \times \frac{4}{5}$.

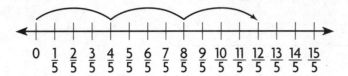

Select a way to write $3 \times \frac{4}{5}$ as the product of a whole number and a unit fraction.

$3 \times \frac{4}{5} =$

$4 \times \frac{3}{5}$
$12 \times \frac{1}{5}$
$6 \times \frac{1}{5}$

13. Yusif wants to give $\frac{1}{3}$ of his total toy car collection to each of 2 of his friends. How much of his total toy car collection will he give away?

14. Select the correct product for the equation.

$$\frac{8}{16} \qquad \frac{32}{8} \qquad \frac{16}{8} \qquad \frac{20}{8}$$

$4 \times \frac{5}{8} = \boxed{}$ $\qquad$ $4 \times \frac{4}{8} = \boxed{}$

Name _____

15. The lengths of different types of snakes at a zoo are shown in the table.

Snake's Name	Type of Snake	Length
Kenny	Kenyan Sand Boa	$1\frac{1}{2}$ feet
Bobby	Ball Python	$4\frac{1}{2}$ feet
Puck	Blood Python	$7\frac{1}{2}$ feet

For numbers 15a–15d, select True or False for the statement.

15a. Bobby is 4 times as long as Kenny. ○ True ○ False

15b. Bobby is 3 times as long as Kenny. ○ True ○ False

15c. Puck is 5 times as long as Kenny. ○ True ○ False

15d. Puck is 2 times as long as Bobby. ○ True ○ False

16. Hank used $3\frac{1}{2}$ bags of seed to plant grass in his front yard. He used 3 times as much seed to plant grass in his back yard. How much seed did Hank need for the backyard?

_____ bags

17. Jess made a big kettle of rice and beans. He used $1\frac{1}{2}$ cups of beans. He used 4 times as much rice.

Part A

Draw a model to show the problem.

Part B

Use your model to write an equation. Then solve the equation to find the amount of rice Jess needs.

18. Mrs. Burnham is making modeling clay for her class. She needs $\frac{2}{3}$ cup of warm water for each batch.

Part A

Mrs. Burnham has a 1-cup measure that has no other markings. Can she make 6 batches of modeling clay using only the 1-cup measure? Describe two ways you can find the answer.

Part B

The modeling clay recipe also calls for $\frac{1}{2}$ cup of cornstarch. Nikki says Mrs. Burnham will also need 4 cups of cornstarch. Do you agree or disagree? Explain.

19. Donna buys some fabric to make place mats. She needs $\frac{1}{5}$ yard of each type of fabric. She has 9 different types of fabrics to make her design. Use the following equation. Write the number in the box to make the statement true.

$$\frac{9}{5} = \underline{\hspace{2cm}} \times \frac{1}{5}$$

20. Mr. Tuyen uses $\frac{5}{8}$ of a tank of gas each week to drive to and from his job. How many tanks of gas does Mr. Tuyen use in 5 weeks? Write your answer two different ways.

Mr. Tuyen uses _____ or _____ tanks of gas.

21.  Rico is making 4 batches of salsa. Each batch needs $\frac{2}{3}$ cup of corn. He only has a $\frac{1}{3}$-cup measure. How many times must Rico measure $\frac{1}{3}$ cup of corn to have enough for all of the salsa?

_____ times

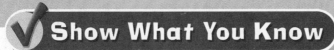

Relate Fractions and Decimals

Personal Math Trainer
Online Assessment
and Intervention

✓ Show What You Know

Check your understanding of important skills.

Name _____

▶ **Count Coins** Find the total value.

1.

Total value: _____

2.

Total value: _____

▶ **Equivalent Fractions**

Write two equivalent fractions for the picture.

3.

_____

4.

_____

▶ **Fractions with Denominators of 10**

Write a fraction for the words. You may draw a picture.

5. three tenths _____

6. six tenths _____

7. eight tenths _____

8. nine tenths _____

Math in the Real World

The Hudson River Science Barge, docked near New York City, provides a demonstration of how renewable energy can be used to produce food for large cities. Vegetables grown on the barge require _____ of the water needed by field crops. Use these clues to find the fraction and decimal for the missing amount.

• The number is less than one and has two decimal places.
• The digit in the hundredths place has a value of $\frac{5}{100}$.
• The digit in the tenths place has a value of $\frac{2}{10}$.

Vocabulary Builder

▶ **Visualize It** ....

Complete the Semantic Map by using words with a ✓.

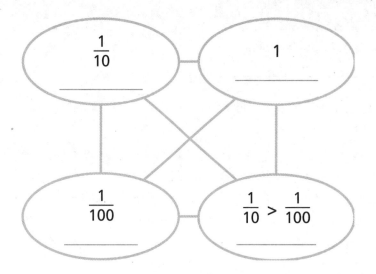

▶ **Understand Vocabulary** ....

Draw a line to match each word with its definition.

Word

1. decimal

2. decimal point

3. tenth

4. hundredth

5. equivalent decimals

Definition

• Two or more decimals that name the same amount

• One part out of one hundred equal parts

• A number with one or more digits to the right of the decimal point

• One part out of ten equal parts

• A symbol used to separate dollars from cents in money amounts and to separate the ones and the tenths places in decimals

GO DIGITAL
• Interactive Student Edition
• Multimedia eGlossary

Chapter 9 Vocabulary

compare

comparar

14

decimal

decimal

19

decimal point

punto decimal

20

equivalent decimals

decimales equivalentes

28

equivalent fractions

fracciones equivalentes

29

hundredth

centésimo

40

tenth

décimo

89

whole

entero

96

A number with one or more digits to the right of the decimal point

Examples: 0.5, 0.06, and 12.679 are decimals.

To describe whether numbers are equal to, less than, or greater than each other

Ones	.	Tenths	Hundredths
1	.	1	5
1	.	3	

1.3 > 1.15

Two or more decimals that name the same amount

Ones	.	Tenths	Hundredths
0	.	8	
0	.	8	0

Example: 0.8 and 0.80 are equivalent decimals.

A symbol used to separate dollars from cents in money amounts, and to separate the ones and the tenths places in a decimal

Example: 6.4

↑ decimal point

One of one hundred equal parts

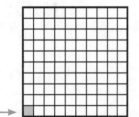

hundredth →

Two or more fractions that name the same amount

Example: $\frac{3}{4}$ and $\frac{6}{8}$ name the same amount.

$$\frac{3}{4} = \frac{6}{8}$$

All of the parts of a shape or group

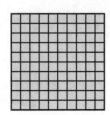

One of ten equal parts

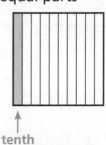

tenth

Matchup

For 2 to 3 players

Materials

• 1 set of word cards

How to Play

1. Put the cards face-down in rows. Take turns to play.

2. Choose two cards and turn them face-up.

   • If the cards show a word and its meaning, it's a match.

     Keep the pair and take another turn.

   • If the cards do not match, turn them back over.

3. The game is over when all cards have been matched. The

   players count their pairs. The player with the most pairs wins.

Word Box

compare

decimal

decimal point

equivalent

   decimals

equivalent

   fractions

hundredth

tenth

whole

Journal

The Write Way

Materials

Choose one idea. Write about it.

- Write a paragraph that uses at three of these words or phrases.
  decimal   decimal point   hundredth   tenth   whole
- Explain in your own words what equivalent decimals are.
- As the writer of a math advice column, you often hear from readers about their struggles to relate fraction and decimal forms. Write a letter explaining what those readers need to know to better understand this subject.

Name _____

Relate Tenths and Decimals

Essential Question How can you record tenths as fractions and decimals?

Learning Objective You will use a model, words, and place value understanding to write tenths in decimal and fraction notations.

Unlock the Problem

Ty is reading a book about metamorphic rocks. He has read $\frac{7}{10}$ of the book. What decimal describes the part of the book Ty has read?

A **decimal** is a number with one or more digits to the right of the **decimal point**. You can write tenths and hundredths as fractions or decimals.

One Way Use a model and a place-value chart.

Fraction

Shade $\frac{7}{10}$ of the model.

Think: The model is divided into 10 equal parts. Each part represents one **tenth**.

Decimal

$\frac{7}{10}$ is 7 tenths.

Ones	.	Tenths	Hundredths
	.		

↑ decimal point

Write: _____

Read: seven tenths

Write: _____

Read: _____

Another Way Use a number line.

Label the number line with decimals that are equivalent to the fractions. Locate the point $\frac{7}{10}$.

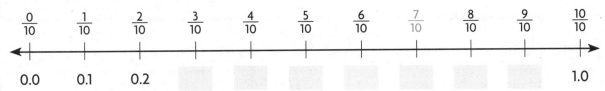

_____ names the same amount as $\frac{7}{10}$.

So, Ty read 0.7 of the book.

Math Processes and Practices ❷

Use Reasoning How is the size of one whole related to the size of one tenth?

- How can you write 0.1 as a fraction? Explain.

Chapter 9　495

Tara rode her bicycle $1\frac{6}{10}$ miles. What decimal describes how far she rode her bicycle?

You have already written a fraction as a decimal. You can also write a mixed number as a decimal.

One Way Use a model and a place-value chart.

Fraction	Decimal

Fraction

Shade $1\frac{6}{10}$ of the model.

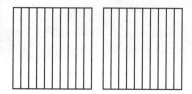

Write: _____

Read: one and six tenths

Decimal

$1\frac{6}{10}$ is 1 whole and 6 tenths.

Think: Use the ones place to record wholes.

Ones	.	Tenths	Hundredths
	.		

Write: _____

Read: _____

Another Way Use a number line.

Label the number line with equivalent mixed numbers and decimals. Locate the point $1\frac{6}{10}$.

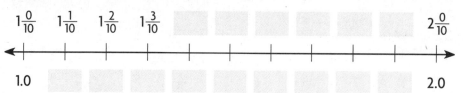

$1\frac{0}{10}$ $1\frac{1}{10}$ $1\frac{2}{10}$ $1\frac{3}{10}$ $2\frac{0}{10}$

1.0 2.0

_____ names the same amount as $1\frac{6}{10}$.

So, Tara rode her bicycle _____ miles.

Try This! Write 1 as a fraction and as a decimal.

Shade the model to show 1.

Fraction: _____

Think: 1 is 1 whole and 0 tenths.

Ones	.	Tenths	Hundredths
	.		

Decimal: _____

Name _____

Share and Show

1. Write five tenths as a fraction and as a decimal.

   Fraction: _____   Decimal: _____

Ones	.	Tenths	Hundredths
	.		

Write the fraction or mixed number and the decimal shown by the model.

2.

   _____ _____

3.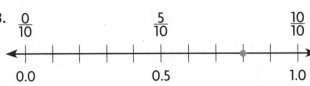

   _____ _____

Attend to Precision How can you write $1\frac{3}{10}$ as a decimal? Explain.

On Your Own

Write the fraction or mixed number and the decimal shown by the model.

4.

   _____ _____

5. $1\frac{0}{10}$ [number line 1.0 to 1.5] $1\frac{5}{10}$

   _____ _____

6.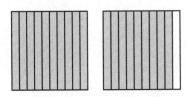

   _____ _____

7. $3\frac{0}{10}$ [number line 3.0 to 4.0] $4\frac{0}{10}$

   _____ _____

Practice: Copy and Solve Write the fraction or mixed number as a decimal.

8. $5\frac{9}{10}$ 9. $\frac{1}{10}$ 10. $\frac{7}{10}$ 11. $8\frac{9}{10}$

12. $\frac{6}{10}$ 13. $6\frac{3}{10}$ 14. $\frac{5}{10}$ 15. $9\frac{7}{10}$

Problem Solving • Applications

Use the table for 16–19.

16. What part of the rocks listed in the table are igneous? Write your answer as a decimal.

_____

17. Sedimentary rocks make up what part of Ramon's collection? Write your answer as a fraction and in word form.

_____

18. **THINK SMARTER** What part of the rocks listed in the table are metamorphic? Write your answer as a fraction and as a decimal.

19. **Math Processes and Practices ⑤ Communicate** Niki wrote the following sentence in her report: "Metamorphic rocks make up 2.0 of Ramon's rock collection." Describe her error.

_____

Ramon's Rock Collection	
Name	**Type**
Basalt	Igneous
Rhyolite	Igneous
Granite	Igneous
Peridotite	Igneous
Scoria	Igneous
Shale	Sedimentary
Limestone	Sedimentary
Sandstone	Sedimentary
Mica	Metamorphic
Slate	Metamorphic

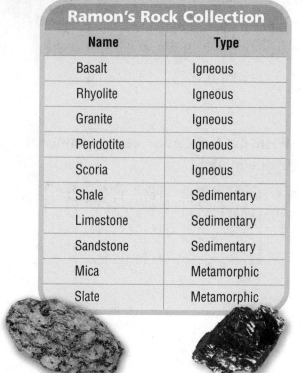

▲ Granite– Igneous    ▲ Mica–Metamorphic

▲ Sandstone– Sedimentary

20. **GO DEEPER** Josh paid for three books with two $20 bills. He received $1 in change. Each book was the same price. How much did each book cost?

_____

21. **THINK SMARTER** Select a number shown by the model. Mark all that apply.

   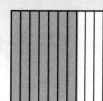

$1\frac{7}{10}$ $\frac{70}{10}$ 1.7

7 0.7 $\frac{17}{10}$

© Houghton Mifflin Harcourt Publishing Company

Relate Tenths and Decimals

Learning Objective You will use a model, words, and place value understanding to write tenths in decimal and fraction notations.

Write the fraction or mixed number and the decimal shown by the model.

1. 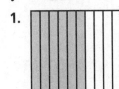 Think: The model is divided into 10 equal parts. Each part represents one tenth.

$\frac{6}{10}$; 0.6
_____

2.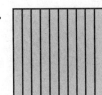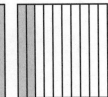

_____

3. $2\frac{0}{10}$ $2\frac{5}{10}$

2.0   2.5

_____

Write the fraction or mixed number as a decimal.

4. $\frac{4}{10}$ **5.** $3\frac{1}{10}$ **6.** $\frac{7}{10}$ **7.** $6\frac{5}{10}$ **8.** $\frac{9}{10}$

___   ___   ___   ___   ___

Problem Solving (Real World)

9. There are 10 sports balls in the equipment closet. Three are kickballs. Write the portion of the balls that are kickballs as a fraction, as a decimal, and in word form.

10. Peyton has 2 pizzas. Each pizza is cut into 10 equal slices. She and her friends eat 14 slices. What part of the pizzas did they eat? Write your answer as a decimal.

_____   _____

11. **WRITE** ▸*Math* Do 0.3 and 3.0 have the same value? Explain.

_____

_____

Lesson Check

1. Valerie has 10 CDs in her music case. Seven of the CDs are pop music CDs. What is this amount written as a decimal?

2. What decimal amount is modeled below?

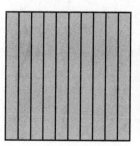 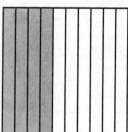

_____

_____

Spiral Review

3. Write one number that is a factor of 13.

4. An art gallery has 18 paintings and 4 photographs displayed in equal rows on a wall, with the same number of each type of art in each row. What could be the number of rows?

_____

_____

5. How do you write the mixed number shown as a fraction greater than 1?

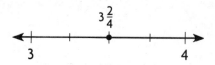

6. What fraction of this model, in simplest form, is shaded?

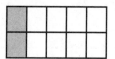

_____

_____

FOR MORE PRACTICE
GO TO THE
Personal Math Trainer

Name _____

Relate Hundredths and Decimals

Essential Question How can you record hundredths as fractions and decimals?

Learning Objective You will use a model, words, and place value understanding to write hundredths in decimal and fraction notations.

🔑 Unlock the Problem

In the 2008 Summer Olympic Games, the winning time in the men's 100-meter butterfly race was only $\frac{1}{100}$ second faster than the second-place time. What decimal represents this fraction of a second?

You can write hundredths as fractions or decimals.

● Circle the numbers you need to use.

🔓 One Way Use a model and a place-value chart.

| Fraction | Decimal |

Shade $\frac{1}{100}$ of the model.

Think: The model is divided into 100 equal parts. Each part represents one **hundredth**.

Write: _____

Read: one hundredth

Complete the place-value chart. $\frac{1}{100}$ is 1 hundredth.

Ones	.	Tenths	Hundredths
0	.	0	1

Write: _____

Read: one hundredth

🔓 Another Way Use a number line.

Label the number line with equivalent decimals. Locate the point $\frac{1}{100}$.

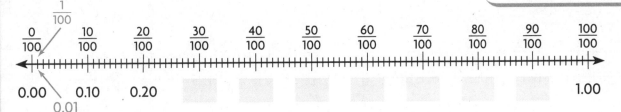

Math Talk Math Processes and Practices ②

Use Reasoning How is the size of one tenth related to the size of one hundredth?

_____ names the same amount as $\frac{1}{100}$.

So, the winning time was _____ second faster.

Alicia won her 400-meter freestyle race by $4\frac{25}{100}$ seconds. How can you write this mixed number as a decimal?

One Way Use a model and a place-value chart.

Mixed Number

Shade the model to show $4\frac{25}{100}$.

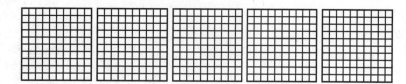

Write: _____

Read: four and twenty-five hundredths

Decimal

Complete the place-value chart.

Think: Look at the model above. $4\frac{25}{100}$ is 4 wholes and 2 tenths 5 hundredths.

Ones	.	Tenths	Hundredths
	.		

Write: _____

Read: _____

Another Way Use a number line.

Label the number line with equivalent mixed numbers and decimals. Locate the point $4\frac{25}{100}$.

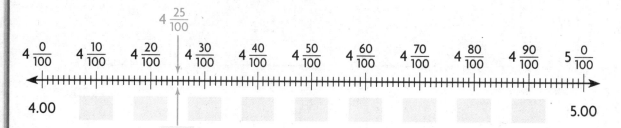

_____ names the same amount as $4\frac{25}{100}$.

So, Alicia won her race by _____ seconds.

Name _____

1. Shade the model to show $\frac{31}{100}$.

   Write the amount as a decimal. _____

Ones	.	Tenths	Hundredths
	.		

Write the fraction or mixed number and the decimal shown by the model.

✓2.   _____ _____

3.   _____ _____

✓4.

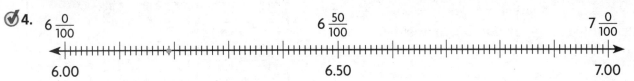

$6\frac{0}{100}$ $6\frac{50}{100}$ $7\frac{0}{100}$

6.00   6.50   7.00

_____ _____

Math Talk   Math Processes and Practices ❼

Look for Structure Are 0.5 and 0.50 equivalent? Explain.

On Your Own

Write the fraction or mixed number and the decimal shown by the model.

5.   _____ _____

6.

7.

$\frac{0}{100}$ $\frac{50}{100}$ $\frac{100}{100}$

0.00   0.50   1.00

_____ _____

Practice: Copy and Solve Write the fraction or mixed number as a decimal.

8. $\frac{9}{100}$ 9. $4\frac{55}{100}$ 10. $\frac{10}{100}$ 11. $9\frac{33}{100}$ 12. $\frac{92}{100}$ 13. $14\frac{16}{100}$

Problem Solving • Applications

14. THINK SMARTER Shade the grids to show three different ways to represent $\frac{16}{100}$ using models.

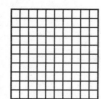

15. Math Processes and Practices ① **Describe Relationships**
Describe how one whole, one tenth, and one hundredth are related.

_____

_____

_____

16. THINK SMARTER Shade the model to show $1\frac{24}{100}$.
Then write the mixed number in decimal form.

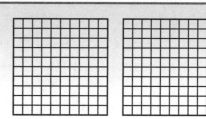

17. GO DEEPER The Memorial Library is 0.3 mile from school.
Whose statement makes sense? Whose statement is nonsense?
Explain your reasoning.

I am going to walk 3 tenths mile to the Memorial Library after school.

I am going to walk 3 miles to the Memorial Library after school.

Gabe	Tara
_____	_____
_____	_____
_____	_____
_____	_____

Relate Hundredths and Decimals

Learning Objective You will use a model, words, and place value understanding to write hundredths in decimal and fraction notations.

Write the fraction or mixed number and the decimal shown by the model.

1. 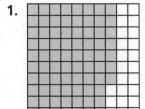 Think: The whole is divided into one hundred equal parts, so each part is one hundredth.

$\frac{77}{100}$; 0.77

2.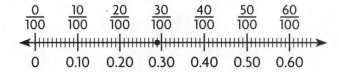

_____

3.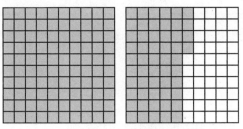

_____

4.

$4\frac{20}{100}$ $4\frac{30}{100}$ $4\frac{40}{100}$ $4\frac{50}{100}$ $4\frac{60}{100}$ $4\frac{70}{100}$ $4\frac{80}{100}$

4.20   4.30   4.40   4.50   4.60   4.70   4.80

_____

Write the fraction or mixed number as a decimal.

5. $\frac{37}{100}$

6. $8\frac{11}{100}$

7. $\frac{98}{100}$

8. $25\frac{50}{100}$

9. $\frac{6}{100}$

_____   _____   _____   _____   _____

Problem Solving · Real World

10. There are 100 pennies in a dollar. What fraction of a dollar is 61 pennies? Write it as a fraction, as a decimal, and in word form.

11. **WRITE** ▸ *Math* Describe a situation where it is easier to use decimals than fractions, and explain why.

_____

_____

_____

Lesson Check

1. What decimal represents the shaded section of the model below?

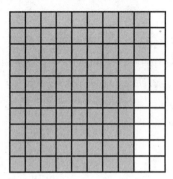

_____

2. There were 100 questions on the unit test. Alondra answered 97 of the questions correctly. What decimal represents the fraction of questions Alondra answered correctly?

_____

Spiral Review

3. Write an expression that is equivalent to $\frac{7}{8}$.

_____

4. What is $\frac{9}{10} - \frac{6}{10}$?

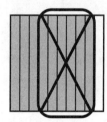

_____

5. Misha used $\frac{1}{4}$ of a carton of 12 eggs to make an omelet. How many eggs did she use?

_____

6. Kurt used the rule *add* 4, *subtract* 1 to generate a pattern. The first term in his pattern is 5. Write a number that could be in Kurt's pattern.

_____

FOR MORE PRACTICE GO TO THE
Personal Math Trainer

Name _____

Equivalent Fractions and Decimals

Essential Question How can you record tenths and hundredths as fractions and decimals?

Learning Objective You will use a model and place value understanding to write numbers as tenths or hundredths in equivalent fraction and decimal notations.

Unlock the Problem

Daniel spent a day hiking through a wildlife preserve. During the first hour of the hike, he drank $\frac{6}{10}$ liter of water. How many hundredths of a liter did he drink?

- Underline what you need to find.
- How can you represent hundredths?

_____

One Way Write $\frac{6}{10}$ as an equivalent fraction with a denominator of 100.

MODEL

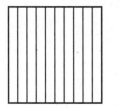 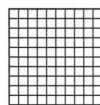

RECORD

$$\frac{6}{10} = \frac{6 \times \boxed{}}{10 \times \boxed{}} = \frac{\boxed{}}{100}$$

$$\frac{6}{10} = \frac{\boxed{}}{100}$$

Another Way Write $\frac{6}{10}$ as a decimal.

Think: 6 tenths is the same as 6 tenths 0 hundredths.

Ones	.	Tenths	Hundredths

So, Daniel drank _____, or _____ liter of water.

Math Processes and Practices ⑥

Explain how you can write 0.2 as hundredths.

- Explain why 6 tenths is equivalent to 60 hundredths.

_____

_____

Jasmine collected 0.30 liter of water in a jar during a rainstorm. How many tenths of a liter did she collect?

Equivalent decimals are decimals that name the same amount. You can write 0.30 as a decimal that names tenths.

 **One Way** Write 0.30 as an equivalent decimal.

Show 0.30 in the place-value chart.

Ones	.	Tenths	Hundredths

Think: There are no hundredths.

0.30 is equivalent to _____ tenths.

Write 0.30 as _____.

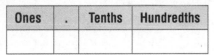 **Another Way** Write 0.30 as a fraction with a denominator of 10.

STEP 1 Write 0.30 as a fraction.

0.30 is _____ hundredths.

30 hundredths written as a fraction is _____.

STEP 2 Write $\frac{30}{100}$ as an equivalent fraction with a denominator of 10.

Think: 10 is a common factor of the numerator and the denominator.

$$\frac{30}{100} = \frac{30 \div \boxed{}}{100 \div \boxed{}} = \frac{\boxed{}}{10}$$

So, Jasmine collected _____, or _____ liter of water.

 **Share and Show**

1. Write $\frac{4}{10}$ as hundredths.

   Write $\frac{4}{10}$ as an equivalent fraction.

   $$\frac{4}{10} = \frac{4 \times \boxed{}}{10 \times \boxed{}} = \frac{\boxed{}}{100}$$

   Fraction: _____

   Write $\frac{4}{10}$ as a decimal.

Ones	.	Tenths	Hundredths
	.		

   Decimal: _____

Name _____

Write the number as hundredths in fraction form and decimal form.

✓ **2.** $\frac{7}{10}$

_____

3. 0.5

_____

4. $\frac{3}{10}$

_____

Write the number as tenths in fraction form and decimal form.

✓ **5.** 0.40

_____

6. $\frac{80}{100}$

_____

7. $\frac{20}{100}$

_____

On Your Own

Practice: Copy and Solve Write the number as hundredths in fraction form and decimal form.

8. $\frac{8}{10}$

9. $\frac{2}{10}$

10. 0.1

Math Talk

Math Processes and Practices ②

Reason Abstractly Explain whether you can write 0.25 as tenths.

Practice: Copy and Solve Write the number as tenths in fraction form and decimal form.

11. $\frac{60}{100}$

12. $\frac{90}{100}$

13. 0.70

THINK SMARTER Write the number as an equivalent mixed number with hundredths.

14. $1\frac{4}{10}$

_____

15. $3\frac{5}{10}$

_____

16. $2\frac{9}{10}$

_____

Problem Solving • Applications

17. THINK SMARTER Carter says that 0.08 is equivalent to $\frac{8}{10}$. Describe and correct Carter's error.

_____

_____

_____

18. THINK SMARTER For numbers 18a–18e, choose True or False for the statement.

18a. 0.6 is equivalent to $\frac{6}{100}$.   ○ True ○ False

18b. $\frac{3}{10}$ is equivalent to 0.30.   ○ True ○ False

18c. $\frac{40}{100}$ is equivalent to $\frac{4}{10}$.   ○ True ○ False

18d. 0.40 is equivalent to $\frac{4}{100}$.   ○ True ○ False

18e. 0.5 is equivalent to 0.50.   ○ True ○ False

Connect to Science

Inland Water

How many lakes and rivers does your state have? The U.S. Geological Survey defines inland water as water that is surrounded by land. The Atlantic Ocean, the Pacific Ocean, and the Great Lakes are not considered inland water.

19. WRITE ▸ Math Just over $\frac{2}{100}$ of the entire United States is inland water. Write $\frac{2}{100}$ as a decimal.

_____

20. Math Processes and Practices ⑥ Can you write 0.02 as tenths? **Explain.**

_____

_____

21. About 0.17 of the area of Rhode Island is inland water. Write 0.17 as a fraction.

_____

22. GO DEEPER Louisiana's lakes and rivers cover about $\frac{1}{10}$ of the state. Write $\frac{1}{10}$ as hundredths in words, fraction form, and decimal form.

_____

Name _____

Equivalent Fractions and Decimals

Learning Objective You will use a model and place value understanding to write numbers as tenths or hundredths in equivalent fraction and decimal notations.

Write the number as hundredths in fraction form and decimal form.

1. $\frac{5}{10}$

$$\frac{5}{10} = \frac{5 \times 10}{10 \times 10} = \frac{50}{100}$$

Think: 5 tenths is the same as 5 tenths and 0 hundredths. Write 0.50.

_____ $\frac{50}{100}$; 0.50 _____

2. $\frac{9}{10}$

3. 0.2

4. 0.8

_____   _____   _____

Write the number as tenths in fraction form and decimal form.

5. $\frac{40}{100}$

6. $\frac{10}{100}$

7. 0.60

_____   _____   _____

Problem Solving Real World

8. Billy walks $\frac{6}{10}$ mile to school each day. Write $\frac{6}{10}$ as hundredths in fraction form and in decimal form.

9. **WRITE** ▸ *Math* Write $\frac{5}{10}$ in three equivalent forms.

_____   _____

_____

_____

_____

Lesson Check

1. The fourth-grade students at Harvest School make up 0.3 of all students at the school. What fraction is equivalent to 0.3?

_____

2. Kyle and his brother have a marble set. Of the marbles, 12 are blue. This represents $\frac{50}{100}$ of all the marbles. What decimal is equivalent to $\frac{50}{100}$?

_____

Spiral Review

3. Jesse won his race by $3\frac{45}{100}$ seconds. What is this number written as a decimal?

_____

4. Marge cut 16 pieces of tape for mounting pictures on poster board. Each piece of tape was $\frac{3}{8}$ inch long. How much tape did Marge use?

_____

5. Of Katie's pattern blocks, $\frac{9}{12}$ are triangles. What is $\frac{9}{12}$ in simplest form?

6. A number pattern has 75 as its first term. The rule for the pattern is *subtract* 6. What is the sixth term?

_____

FOR MORE PRACTICE GO TO THE Personal Math Trainer

Name _____

Relate Fractions, Decimals, and Money

Essential Question How can you relate fractions, decimals, and money?

Learning Objective You will use models to relate fractions or mixed numbers, decimals, and money and write these numbers in their equivalent forms.

🔑 Unlock the Problem

Together, Julie and Sarah have $1.00 in quarters. They want to share the quarters equally. How many quarters should each girl get? How much money is this?

Remember
1 dollar = 100 cents
1 quarter = 25 cents
1 dime = 10 cents
1 penny = 1 cent

🔲 **Use the model to relate money, fractions, and decimals.**

4 quarters = 1 dollar = $1.00

$0.25 $0.25 $0.25 $0.25

1 quarter is $\frac{25}{100}$, or $\frac{1}{4}$ of a dollar.

2 quarters are $\frac{50}{100}$, $\frac{2}{4}$, or $\frac{1}{2}$ of a dollar.

$\frac{1}{2}$ of a dollar = $0.50, or 50 cents.

Circle the number of quarters each girl should get.

So, each girl should get 2 quarters, or $ _____ .

🔲 Examples Use money to model decimals.

1 dollar

$1.00, or

_____ cents

10 dimes = 1 dollar

1 dime = $\frac{1}{10}$, or 0.10 of a dollar

$ _____ , or 10 cents

100 pennies = 1 dollar

1 penny = $\frac{1}{100}$, or 0.01 of a dollar

$ _____ , or 1 cent

Math Talk

Math Processes and Practices ④

Model Mathematics Model 68 pennies. What part of a dollar do you have? Explain.

Chapter 9 513

Relate Money and Decimals Think of dollars as ones, dimes as tenths, and pennies as hundredths.

$1.56

Dollars	.	Dimes	Pennies
1	.	5	6

Think: $1.56 = 1 dollar and 56 pennies

There are 100 pennies in 1 dollar.
So, $1.56 = 156 pennies.

1.56 dollars

Ones	.	Tenths	Hundredths
1	.	5	6

Think: 1.56 = 1 one and 56 hundredths

There are 100 hundredths in 1 one.
So, 1.56 = 156 hundredths.

More Examples Shade the decimal model to show the money amount. Then write the money amount and a fraction in terms of dollars.

Ⓐ

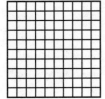

_____ , or $\frac{21}{100}$ of a dollar

Ⓑ

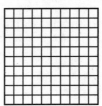

$1.46, or $1\frac{}{100}$ dollars

Try This! Complete the table to show how money, fractions, mixed numbers, and decimals are related.

$ Bills and Coins	Money Amount	Fraction or Mixed Number	Decimal
	$0.03		0.03
	$0.25	$\frac{25}{100}$, or $\frac{1}{4}$	
2 quarters 1 dime		$\frac{60}{100}$, or $\frac{6}{10}$	
2 $1 bills 5 nickels			

Math Talk

Math Processes and Practices ②

Reason Abstractly Would you rather have $0.25 or $\frac{3}{10}$ of a dollar? Explain.

Name _____

Share and Show MATH BOARD

1. Write the amount of money as a decimal in terms of dollars.

   5 pennies = $\frac{5}{100}$ of a dollar = _____ of a dollar.

Write the total money amount. Then write the amount as a fraction or a mixed number and as a decimal in terms of dollars.

2.

3.

_____ _____ _____   _____ _____

Write as a money amount and as a decimal in terms of dollars.

4. $\frac{92}{100}$ _____

5. $\frac{7}{100}$ _____

6. $\frac{16}{100}$ _____

7. $\frac{53}{100}$ _____

On Your Own

Math Talk

Math Processes and Practices ⑥

Make Connections How are $0.84 and $\frac{84}{100}$ of a dollar related?

Write the total money amount. Then write the amount as a fraction or a mixed number and as a decimal in terms of dollars.

8.

9.

_____ _____ _____   _____ _____ _____

Write as a money amount and as a decimal in terms of dollars.

10. $\frac{27}{100}$ _____

11. $\frac{4}{100}$ _____

12. $\frac{75}{100}$ _____

13. $\frac{100}{100}$ _____

Write the total money amount. Then write the amount as a fraction and as a decimal in terms of dollars.

14. 1 quarter 6 dimes 8 pennies

15. 3 dimes 5 nickels 20 pennies

_____ _____ _____   _____ _____ _____

Math Processes and Practices ⑥ **Make Connections** **Algebra** Complete to tell the value of each digit.

16. $1.05 = _____ dollar + _____ pennies,   1.05 = _____ one + _____ hundredths

17. $5.18 = _____ dollars + _____ dime + _____ pennies

    5.18 = _____ ones + _____ tenth + _____ hundredths

Problem Solving • Applications

Use the table for 18–19.

18. The table shows the coins three students have. Write Nick's total amount as a fraction in terms of dollars.

    _____

Pocket Change				
Name	Quarters	Dimes	Nickels	Pennies
Kim	1	3	2	3
Tony	0	6	1	6
Nick	2	4	0	2

19. *THINK SMARTER* Kim spent $\frac{40}{100}$ of a dollar on a snack. Write as a money amount the amount she has left.

    _____

20. *GO DEEPER* Travis has $\frac{1}{2}$ of a dollar. He has at least two different types of coins in his pocket. Draw two possible sets of coins that Travis could have.

21. *THINK SMARTER* Complete the table.

$ Bills and Coins	Money Amount	Fraction or Mixed Number	Decimal
6 pennies		$\frac{6}{100}$	0.06
	$0.50		0.50
		$\frac{70}{100}$ or $\frac{7}{10}$	0.70
3 $1 bills 9 pennies			3.09

Relate Fractions, Decimals, and Money

Learning Objective You will use models to relate fractions or mixed numbers, decimals, and money and write these numbers in their equivalent forms.

Write the total money amount. Then write the amount as a fraction or a mixed number and as a decimal in terms of dollars.

1.

    $0.18; $\frac{18}{100}$; 0.18
    _____

2.

    _____

Write as a money amount and as a decimal in terms of dollars.

3. $\frac{25}{100}$ 4. $\frac{79}{100}$ 5. $\frac{31}{100}$ 6. $\frac{8}{100}$ 7. $\frac{42}{100}$

_____   _____   _____   _____   _____

Write the money amount as a fraction in terms of dollars.

8. $0.87   9. $0.03   10. $0.66   11. $0.95   12. $1.00

_____   _____   _____   _____   _____

Write the total money amount. Then write the amount as a fraction and as a decimal in terms of dollars.

13. 2 quarters 2 dimes   14. 3 dimes 4 pennies   15. 8 nickels 12 pennies

_____   _____   _____

Problem Solving *Real World*

16. Kate has 1 dime, 4 nickels, and 8 pennies. Write Kate's total amount as a fraction in terms of a dollar.

_____

17. **WRITE** *Math* Jeffrey says he has 6.8 dollars. How do you write the decimal 6.8 when it refers to money? Explain.

_____

Lesson Check

1. Write the total amount of money shown as a fraction in terms of a dollar.

_____

_____

2. Crystal has $\frac{81}{100}$ of a dollar. What could be the coins Crystal has?

_____

_____

Spiral Review

3. Joel gives $\frac{1}{3}$ of his baseball cards to his sister. Write a fraction that is equivalent to $\frac{1}{3}$.

_____

4. Penelope bakes pretzels. She salts $\frac{3}{8}$ of the pretzels. Write a fraction that is equivalent to $\frac{3}{8}$.

_____

5. What decimal is shown by the shaded area in the model?

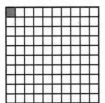

_____

6. Mr. Guzman has 100 cows on his dairy farm. Of the cows, 57 are Holstein. What decimal represents the portion of cows that are Holstein?

_____

FOR MORE PRACTICE
GO TO THE
Personal Math Trainer

Name _____

Problem Solving • Money

Essential Question How can you use the strategy *act it out* to solve problems that use money?

Learning Objective You will use the strategy *act it out* to solve problems involving money by using coins to model the problems.

Unlock the Problem

Together, Marnie and Serena have $1.20. They want to share the money equally. How much money will each girl get?

Use the graphic organizer to solve the problem.

Read the Problem

What do I need to find?

I need to find the _____

_____

What information do I need to use?

I need to use the total amount, _____, and divide

the amount into _____ equal parts.

How will I use the information?

I will use coins to model the _____ and

act out the problem.

Solve the Problem

You can make $1.20 with 4 quarters

and 2 _____.

Circle the coins to show two sets with equal value.

So, each girl gets _____ quarters and

_____ dime. Each girl gets $_____.

- Describe another way you could act out the problem with coins.

_____

_____

🔑 Try Another Problem

Josh, Tom, and Chuck each have $0.40. How much money do they have together?

Read the Problem	Solve the Problem
What do I need to find?	
What information do I need to use?	
How will I use the information?	

• How can you solve the problem using dimes and nickels?

_____

_____

Math Talk

Math Processes and Practices ❶

Describe What other strategy might you use to solve the problem? Explain.

Name _____

Unlock the Problem

✓ Circle the question.
✓ Underline the important facts.
✓ Cross out unneeded information.

Share and Show

1. Juan has $3.43. He is buying a paint brush that costs $1.21 to paint a model race car. How much will Juan have after he pays for the paint brush?

First, use bills and coins to model $3.43.

Show Your Work

Next, you need to subtract. Remove bills and coins that have a value of $1.21. Mark Xs to show what you remove.

Last, count the value of the bills and coins that are left. How much will Juan have left?

_____

2. What if Juan has $3.43, and he wants to buy a paint brush that costs $2.28? How much money will Juan have left then? Explain.

_____

_____

_____

_____

3. Sophia has $2.25. She wants to give an equal amount to each of her 3 young cousins. How much will each cousin receive?

_____

On Your Own

4. Marcus saves $13 each week. In how many weeks will he have saved at least $100?

_____

5. **Math Processes and Practices ❶** **Analyze Relationships** Hoshi has $50. Emily has $23 more than Hoshi. Karl has $16 less than Emily. How much money do they have all together?

_____

6. **THINKSMARTER** Four girls have $5.00 to share equally. How much money will each girl get? Explain.

_____

_____

_____

_____

| WRITE ▸ *Math*
Show Your Work

7. **GO DEEPER** What if four girls want to share $5.52 equally? How much money will each girl get? Explain.

_____

_____

_____

_____

Personal Math Trainer

8. **THINKSMARTER +** Aimee and three of her friends have three quarters and one nickel. If Aimee and her friends share the money equally, how much will each person get? Explain how you found your answer.

Learning Objective You will use the strategy *act it out* to solve problems involving money by using coins to model the problems.

Use the *act it out* strategy to solve.

1. Carl wants to buy a bicycle bell that costs $4.50. Carl has saved $2.75 so far. How much more money does he need to buy the bell?

   Use 4 $1 bills and 2 quarters to model $4.50. Remove bills and coins that have a value of $2.75. First, remove 2 $1 bills and 2 quarters.

   Next, exchange one $1 bill for 4 quarters and remove 1 quarter.

   Count the amount that is left.
   So, Carl needs to save $1.75 more.

   _____ $1.75

2. Together, Xavier, Yolanda, and Zachary have $4.44. If each person has the same amount, how much money does each person have?

   _____

3. Marcus, Nan, and Olive each have $1.65 in their pockets. They decide to combine the money. How much money do they have altogether?

   _____

4. Jessie saves $6 each week. In how many weeks will she have saved at least $50?

   _____

5. **WRITE** ►*Math* Write a money problem you can solve using sharing, joining, or separating.

   _____

   _____

Lesson Check

1. Four friends earned $5.20 for washing a car. They shared the money equally. How much did each friend get?

   _____

2. Write a decimal that represents the value of one $1 bill and 5 quarters.

   _____

Spiral Review

3. Bethany has 9 pennies. What fraction of a dollar is this?

   _____

4. Michael made $\frac{9}{12}$ of his free throws at practice. What is $\frac{9}{12}$ in simplest form?

   _____

5. I am a prime number between 30 and 40. What number could I be?

6. Fill in the blank with a symbol that makes this statement true:

   $$\frac{2}{5} \bigcirc \frac{1}{2}$$

   _____

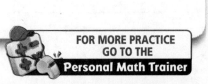

FOR MORE PRACTICE
GO TO THE
Personal Math Trainer

Name _____

Vocabulary

Choose the best term from the box to complete
the sentence.

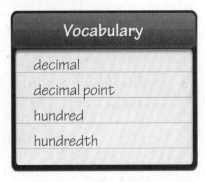

Vocabulary
decimal
decimal point
hundred
hundredth

1. A symbol used to separate the ones and the tenths place is

   called a _____. (p. 495)

2. The number 0.4 is written as a _____. (p. 495)

3. A _____ is one of one hundred equal parts of a
   whole. (p. 501)

Concepts and Skills

Write the fraction or mixed number and the decimal shown
by the model.

4.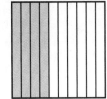

   _____

5.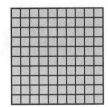

   _____

Write the number as hundredths in fraction form
and decimal form.

6. $\frac{8}{10}$

   _____

7. 0.5

   _____

8. $\frac{6}{10}$

   _____

Write the fraction or mixed number as a money amount,
and as a decimal in terms of dollars.

9. $\frac{65}{100}$

   _____

10. $1\frac{48}{100}$

    _____

11. $\frac{4}{100}$

    _____

12. Ken's turtle competed in a 0.50-meter race. His turtle had traveled $\frac{49}{100}$ meter when the winning turtle crossed the finish line. What is $\frac{49}{100}$ written as a decimal?

_____

13. Alex lives eight tenths of a mile from Sarah. What is eight tenths written as a decimal?

_____

14. 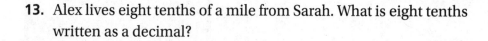 What fraction and decimal, in hundredths, is equivalent to $\frac{7}{10}$?

_____

15. Elaine found the following in her pocket. How much money was in her pocket?

_____

16. Three girls share $0.60. Each girl gets the same amount. How much money does each girl get?

_____

17. The deli scale weighs meat and cheese in hundredths of a pound. Sam put $\frac{5}{10}$ pound of pepperoni on the deli scale. What weight does the deli scale show?

_____

Name _____

Add Fractional Parts of 10 and 100

Essential Question How can you add fractions when the denominators are 10 or 100?

Learning Objective You will add fractions when the denominators are 10 or 100 by first writing the addends as fractions with a common denominator.

🔑 Unlock the Problem (Real World)

The fourth grade classes are painting designs on tile squares to make a mural. Mrs. Kirk's class painted $\frac{3}{10}$ of the mural. Mr. Becker's class painted $\frac{21}{100}$ of the mural. What part of the mural is painted?

You know how to add fractions with parts that are the same size. You can use equivalent fractions to add fractions with parts that are not the same size.

🔑 Example 1 Find $\frac{3}{10} + \frac{21}{100}$.

STEP 1 Write $\frac{3}{10}$ and $\frac{21}{100}$ as a pair of fractions with a common denominator.

Think: 100 is a multiple of 10. Use 100 as the common denominator.

$$\frac{3}{10} = \frac{3 \times \boxed{}}{10 \times \boxed{}} = \frac{\boxed{}}{100}$$

Think: $\frac{21}{100}$ already has 100 in the denominator.

So, $\frac{\boxed{}}{100}$ of the mural is painted.

STEP 2 Add.

Think: Write $\frac{3}{10} + \frac{21}{100}$ using fractions with a common denominator.

$$\frac{30}{100} + \frac{21}{100} = \frac{\boxed{}}{100}$$

Math Talk

Math Processes and Practices ⑧

Draw Conclusions When adding tenths and hundredths, can you always use 100 as a common denominator? Explain.

Try This! Find $\frac{4}{100} + \frac{1}{10}$.

Ⓐ Write $\frac{1}{10}$ as $\frac{10}{100}$.

$$\frac{1}{10} = \frac{1 \times \boxed{}}{10 \times \boxed{}} = \frac{\boxed{}}{100}$$

Ⓑ Add.

$$\frac{\boxed{}}{100} + \frac{10}{100} = \frac{\boxed{}}{100}$$

So, $\frac{4}{100} + \frac{10}{100} = \frac{14}{100}$

 **Example 2** Add decimals.

Sean lives 0.5 mile from the store. The store is 0.25 mile from his grandmother's house. Sean is going to walk to the store and then to his grandmother's house. How far will he walk?

Find 0.5 + 0.25.

STEP 1 Write 0.5 + 0.25 as a sum of fractions.

Think: 0.5 is 5 tenths.   Think: 0.25 is 25 hundredths.

$$0.5 = \frac{\quad}{\quad} \qquad 0.25 = \frac{\quad}{\quad}$$

Write 0.5 + 0.25 as $\frac{\quad}{\quad} + \frac{\quad}{\quad}$

STEP 2 Write $\frac{5}{10} + \frac{25}{100}$ as a sum of fractions with a common denominator.

Think: Use 100 as a common denominator. Rename $\frac{5}{10}$.

$$\frac{5}{10} = \frac{5 \times \quad}{10 \times \quad} = \frac{\quad}{100}$$

Write $\frac{5}{10} + \frac{25}{100}$ as $\frac{\quad}{\quad} + \frac{\quad}{\quad}$.

STEP 3 Add.

$$\frac{50}{100} + \frac{25}{100} = \frac{\quad}{\quad}$$

STEP 4 Write the sum as a decimal.

$$\frac{75}{100} = \underline{\quad}$$

So, Sean will walk _____ mile.

Math Talk

Math Processes and Practices ⑦

Identify Relationships
Explain why you can think of $0.25 as either $\frac{1}{4}$ dollar or $\frac{25}{100}$ dollar.

Try This! Find $0.25 + $0.40.

$0.25 + $0.40 = _____

Remember
A money amount less than a dollar can be written as a fraction of a dollar.

Name _____

1. Find $\frac{7}{10} + \frac{5}{100}$.

Think: Write the addends as fractions with a common denominator.

$$\frac{}{100} + \frac{}{100} = \frac{}{}$$

Find the sum.

2. $\frac{1}{10} + \frac{11}{100} = $ _____

3. $\frac{36}{100} + \frac{5}{10} = $ _____

4. $\$0.16 + \$0.45 = \$$ _____

5. $\$0.08 + \$0.88 = \$$ _____

On Your Own

6. $\frac{6}{10} + \frac{25}{100} = $ _____

7. $\frac{7}{10} + \frac{7}{100} = $ _____

8. $\$0.55 + \$0.23 = \$$ _____

9. $\$0.19 + \$0.13 = \$$ _____

Math Processes and Practices ② **Reason Quantitatively** **Algebra** Write the number that makes the equation true.

10. $\frac{20}{100} + \frac{}{10} = \frac{60}{100}$

11. $\frac{2}{10} + \frac{}{100} = \frac{90}{100}$

12. GO DEEPER Jerry had 1 gallon of ice cream. He used $\frac{3}{10}$ gallon to make chocolate milkshakes and 0.40 gallon to make vanilla milkshakes. How much ice cream does Jerry have left after making the milkshakes?

_____

Problem Solving • Applications

Use the table for 13–16.

13. **THINKSMARTER** Dean selects Teakwood stones and Buckskin stones to pave a path in front of his house. How many meters long will each set of one Teakwood stone and one Buckskin stone be?

Paving Stone Center	
Style	**Length (in meters)**
Rustic	$\frac{15}{100}$
Teakwood	$\frac{3}{10}$
Buckskin	$\frac{41}{100}$
Rainbow	$\frac{6}{10}$
Rose	$\frac{8}{100}$

14. The backyard patio at Nona's house is made from a repeating pattern of one Rose stone and one Rainbow stone. How many meters long is each pair of stones?

15. **GO DEEPER** For a stone path, Emily likes the look of a Rustic stone, then a Rainbow stone, and then another Rustic stone. How long will the three stones in a row be? Explain.

16. **WRITE** ▸ Math Which two stones can you place end-to-end to get a length of 0.38 meter? Explain how you found your answer.

17. **THINKSMARTER** Christelle is making a dollhouse. The dollhouse is $\frac{6}{10}$ meter tall without the roof. The roof is $\frac{15}{100}$ meter high. What is the height of the dollhouse with the roof? Choose a number from each column to complete an equation to solve.

$$\frac{6}{10} + \frac{15}{100} = \boxed{\begin{array}{c} \frac{6}{100} \\ \frac{60}{100} \\ \frac{61}{100} \end{array}} + \boxed{\begin{array}{c} \frac{15}{10} \\ \frac{5}{100} \\ \frac{15}{100} \end{array}} = \boxed{\begin{array}{c} \frac{65}{100} \\ \frac{7}{10} \\ \frac{75}{100} \end{array}} \text{ meter.}$$

Add Fractional Parts of 10 and 100

> **Learning Objective** You will add fractions when the denominators are 10 or 100 by first writing the addends as fractions with a common denominator.

Find the sum.

1. $\frac{2}{10} + \frac{43}{100}$

$\frac{20}{100} + \frac{43}{100} = \frac{63}{100}$

$$\frac{63}{100}$$

Think: Write $\frac{2}{10}$ as a fraction with a denominator of 100:

$$\frac{2 \times 10}{10 \times 10} = \frac{20}{100}$$

2. $\frac{17}{100} + \frac{6}{10}$

3. $\frac{9}{100} + \frac{9}{10}$

4. $\$0.25 + \$0.34$

Problem Solving (Real World)

5. Ned's frog jumped $\frac{38}{100}$ meter. Then his frog jumped $\frac{4}{10}$ meter. How far did Ned's frog jump?

6. Keiko walks $\frac{5}{10}$ kilometer from school to the park. Then she walks $\frac{19}{100}$ kilometer from the park to her home. How far does Keiko walk?

7. **WRITE** ▸*Math* Explain how you would use equivalent fractions to solve $0.5 + 0.10$.

_____

_____

_____

_____

Lesson Check

1. In a fish tank, $\frac{2}{10}$ of the fish were orange and $\frac{5}{100}$ of the fish were striped. What fraction of the fish were orange or striped?

_____

2. Greg spends $0.45 on an eraser and $0.30 on a pen. How much money does Greg spend?

_____

Spiral Review

3. Phillip saves $8 each month. How many months will it take him to save at least $60?

_____

4. Ursula and Yi share a submarine sandwich. Ursula eats $\frac{2}{8}$ of the sandwich. Yi eats $\frac{3}{8}$ of the sandwich. How much of the sandwich do the two friends eat?

_____

5. A carpenter has a board that is 8 feet long. He cuts off two pieces. One piece is $3\frac{1}{2}$ feet long and the other is $2\frac{1}{3}$ feet long. How much of the board is left?

_____

6. Jeff drinks $\frac{2}{3}$ of a glass of juice. Write a fraction that is equivalent to $\frac{2}{3}$.

_____

FOR MORE PRACTICE
GO TO THE
Personal Math Trainer

Name _____

Compare Decimals

Essential Question How can you compare decimals?

Learning Objective You will use models and place value understanding to compare two decimals to hundredths by reasoning about their size and recording using the symbols >, =, or <.

Unlock the Problem

The city park covers 0.64 square mile. About 0.18 of the park is covered by water, and about 0.2 of the park is covered by paved walkways. Is more of the park covered by water or paved walkways?

- Cross out unnecessary information.
- Circle numbers you will use.
- What do you need to find?

_____

_____

One Way Use a model.

Shade 0.18.   Shade 0.2.

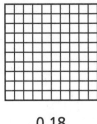   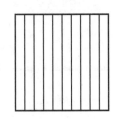

0.18   ◯   0.2

Other Ways

A Use a number line.

Locate 0.18 and 0.2 on a number line.

Think: 2 tenths is equivalent to 20 hundredths.

| 0.0 | 0.10 | 0.20 | 0.30 | 0.40 | 0.50 |

_____ is closer to 0, so 0.18 ◯ 0.2.

B Compare equal-size parts.

- 0.18 is _____ hundredths.

- 0.2 is 2 tenths, which is equivalent to _____ hundredths.

18 hundredths ◯ 20 hundredths, so 0.18 ◯ 0.2.

So, more of the park is covered by _____.

Math Talk

Math Processes and Practices 6

Compare How does the number of tenths in 0.18 compare to the number of tenths in 0.2? Explain.

Place Value You can compare numbers written as decimals by using place value. Comparing decimals is like comparing whole numbers. Always compare the digits in the greatest place-value position first.

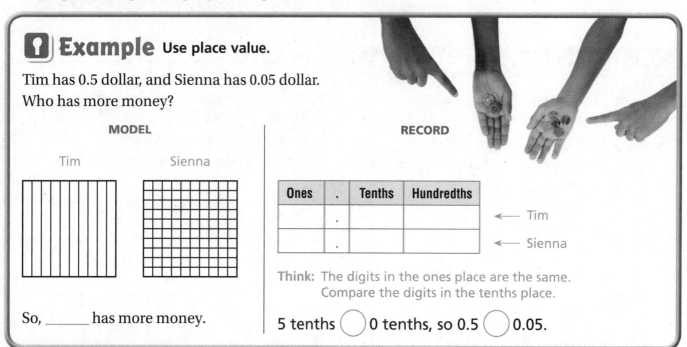

🔑 **Example** Use place value.

Tim has 0.5 dollar, and Sienna has 0.05 dollar. Who has more money?

MODEL

Tim   Sienna

RECORD

Ones	.	Tenths	Hundredths	
	.			← Tim
	.			← Sienna

Think: The digits in the ones place are the same. Compare the digits in the tenths place.

So, _____ has more money.

5 tenths ◯ 0 tenths, so 0.5 ◯ 0.05.

• Compare the size of 1 tenth to the size of 1 hundredth. How could this help you compare 0.5 and 0.05? Explain.

_____

_____

_____

Try This! Compare 1.3 and 0.6. Write <, >, or =.

1.3 ◯ 0.6

Shade to model 1.3.   Shade to model 0.6.

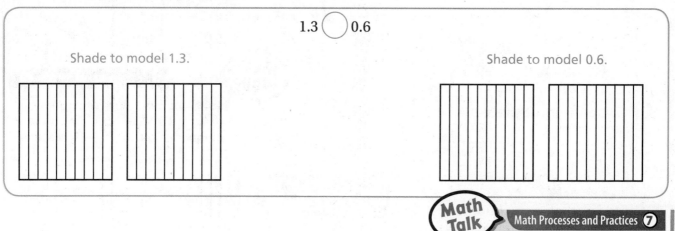

Math Talk

Math Processes and Practices ⑦

Look for Structure How could you use place value to compare 1.3 and 0.6?

Name _____

1. Compare 0.39 and 0.42. Write <, >, or =.
   Shade the model to help.

   0.39 ◯ 0.42

   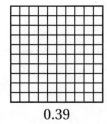   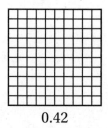

                    0.39   0.42

Compare. Write <, >, or =.

2. 0.26 ◯ 0.23

Ones	.	Tenths	Hundredths
	.		
	.		

✓ 3. 0.7 ◯ 0.54

Ones	.	Tenths	Hundredths
	.		
	.		

4. 1.15 ◯ 1.3

Ones	.	Tenths	Hundredths
	.		
	.		

✓ 5. 4.5 ◯ 2.89

Ones	.	Tenths	Hundredths
	.		
	.		

On Your Own

Math Talk

Math Processes and Practices ②

Reason Abstractly Can you compare 0.39 and 0.42 by comparing only the tenths? Explain.

Compare. Write <, >, or =.

6. 0.9 ◯ 0.81   7. 1.06 ◯ 0.6   8. 0.25 ◯ 0.3   9. 2.61 ◯ 3.29

Math Processes and Practices ② **Reason Quantitatively** **Compare. Write <, >, or =.**

10. 0.30 ◯ $\frac{3}{10}$ 11. $\frac{4}{100}$ ◯ 0.2   12. 0.15 ◯ $\frac{1}{10}$ 13. $\frac{1}{8}$ ◯ 0.8

14. **GO DEEPER** Robert had $14.53 in his pocket. Ivan had $14.25 in his pocket. Matt had $14.40 in his pocket. Who had more money, Robert or Matt? Did Ivan have more money than either Robert or Matt?

Unlock the Problem

15. **THINK SMARTER** Ricardo and Brandon ran a 1500-meter race. Ricardo finished in 4.89 minutes. Brandon finished in 4.83 minutes. What was the time of the runner who finished first?

a. What are you asked to find? _____

b. What do you need to do to find the answer? _____
_____

c. Solve the problem.

d. What was the time of the runner who finished first?
_____

e. Look back. Does your answer make sense? Explain.
_____
_____
_____
_____

16. **GO DEEPER** The Venus flytrap closes in 0.3 second and the waterwheel plant closes in 0.2 second. What decimal is halfway between 0.2 and 0.3? Explain.
_____
_____
_____
_____

Personal Math Trainer

17. **THINK SMARTER +** For numbers 17a–17c, compare then select True or False.

17a. 0.5 > 0.53   ○ True   ○ False

17b. 0.35 < 0.37   ○ True   ○ False

17c. $1.35 > $0.35   ○ True   ○ False

Compare Decimals

Learning Objective You will use models and place value understanding to compare two decimals to hundredths by reasoning about their size and recording using the symbols >, =, or <.

Compare. Write <, >, or =.

1. 0.35 $\underset{<}{\bigcirc}$ 0.53

Think: 3 tenths is less
than 5 tenths.
So, 0.35 < 0.53

2. 0.6 $\bigcirc$ 0.60

3. 0.24 $\bigcirc$ 0.31

4. 0.94 $\bigcirc$ 0.9

5. 0.3 $\bigcirc$ 0.32

6. 0.45 $\bigcirc$ 0.28

7. 0.39 $\bigcirc$ 0.93

Use the number line to compare. Write *true* **or** *false*.

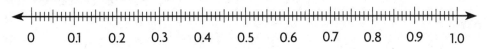

8. 0.8 > 0.78

9. 0.4 > 0.84

10. 0.7 < 0.70

11. 0.4 > 0.04

_____

_____

_____

_____

Compare. Write *true* **or** *false*.

12. 0.09 > 0.1

13. 0.24 = 0.42

14. 0.17 < 0.32

15. 0.85 > 0.82

_____

_____

_____

_____

Problem Solving · Real World

16. Kelly walks 0.7 mile to school. Mary walks 0.49 mile to school. Write an inequality using <, >, or = to compare the distances they walk to school.

_____

17. **WRITE** *Math* Show or describe two different ways to complete the comparison using <, >, or =: 0.26 $\bigcirc$ 0.4.

_____

_____

_____

Lesson Check

1. Bob, Cal, and Pete each made a stack of baseball cards. Bob's stack was 0.2 meter high. Cal's stack was 0.24 meter high. Pete's stack was 0.18 meter high. Write a number sentence that compares Cal's stack of cards to Pete's stack of cards.

_____

2. Three classmates spent money at the school supplies store. Mark spent 0.5 dollar, Andre spent 0.45 dollar, and Raquel spent 0.52 dollar. Write a number sentence that compares the money Andre spent to the money that Mark spent.

_____

Spiral Review

3. Pedro has $0.35 in his pocket. Alice has $0.40 in her pocket. How much money do Pedro and Alice have altogether?

_____

4. The measure 62 centimeters is equivalent to $\frac{62}{100}$ meter. What is this measure written as a decimal?

_____

5. Joel has 24 sports trophies. Of the trophies, $\frac{1}{8}$ are soccer trophies. How many soccer trophies does Joel have?

_____

6. Molly's jump rope is $6\frac{1}{3}$ feet long. Gail's jump rope is $4\frac{2}{3}$ feet long. How much longer is Molly's jump rope?

_____

**FOR MORE PRACTICE
GO TO THE
Personal Math Trainer**

✔ Chapter 9 Review/Test

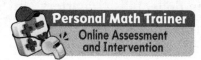

Personal Math Trainer
Online Assessment and Intervention

1. Select a number shown by the model. Mark all that apply.

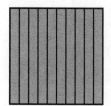 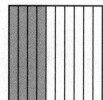

$\frac{14}{10}$ $\frac{40}{10}$ 1.4

$1\frac{4}{10}$ 14   4.1

2. Rick has one dollar and twenty-seven cents to buy a notebook. Which names this money amount in terms of dollars? Mark all that apply.

   (A) 12.7   (D) 1.27

   (B) 1.027   (E) $1\frac{27}{100}$

   (C) $1.27   (F) $\frac{127}{10}$

3. For numbers 3a–3e, select True or False for the statement.

   3a. 0.9 is equivalent to 0.90.   ○ True   ○ False

   3b. 0.20 is equivalent to $\frac{2}{100}$.   ○ True   ○ False

   3c. $\frac{80}{100}$ is equivalent to $\frac{8}{10}$.   ○ True   ○ False

   3d. $\frac{6}{10}$ is equivalent to 0.60.   ○ True   ○ False

   3e. 0.3 is equivalent to $\frac{3}{100}$.   ○ True   ○ False

4. After selling some old books and toys, Gwen and her brother Max had 5 one-dollar bills, 6 quarters, and 8 dimes. They agreed to divide the money equally.

Part A

What is the total amount of money that Gwen and Max earned? Explain.

```
┌─────────────────────────────────────────────────────┐
│                                                       │
│                                                       │
│                                                       │
│                                                       │
│                                                       │
└─────────────────────────────────────────────────────┘
```

Part B

Max said that he and Gwen cannot get equal amounts of money because 5 one-dollar bills cannot be divided evenly. Do you agree with Max? Explain.

```
┌─────────────────────────────────────────────────────┐
│                                                       │
│                                                       │
│                                                       │
│                                                       │
│                                                       │
│                                                       │
└─────────────────────────────────────────────────────┘
```

5. Harrison rode his bike $\frac{6}{10}$ of a mile to the park. Shade the model. Then write the decimal to show how far Harrison rode his bike.

Harrison rode his bike _____ mile to the park.

6. Amaldo spent $\frac{88}{100}$ of a dollar on a souvenir pencil from Zion National Park in Utah. What is $\frac{88}{100}$ written as a decimal in terms of dollars?

7. Tran has $5.82. He is saving for a video game that costs $8.95.

Tran needs _____ more to have enough money for the game.

Name _____

8. Cheyenne lives $\frac{7}{10}$ mile from school. A fraction in hundredths

   equal to $\frac{7}{10}$ is _____.

9. Write a decimal in tenths that is **less** than 2.42 but **greater**
   than 2.0.

_____

10. GO DEEPER Kylee and two of her friends are at a museum. They
    find two quarters and one dime on the ground.

    Part A

    If Kylee and her friends share the money equally, how much will
    each person get? Explain how you found your answer.

    Part B

    Kylee says that each person will receive $\frac{2}{10}$ of the money that was
    found. Do you agree? Explain.

11. Shade the model to show $1\frac{52}{100}$. Then write the mixed number in
    decimal form.

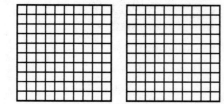

12. Henry is making a recipe for biscuits. A recipe calls for
$\frac{5}{10}$ kilogram flour and $\frac{9}{100}$ kilogram sugar.

Part A

If Henry measures correctly and combines the two amounts, how
much flour and sugar will he have? Show your work.

Part B

How can you write your answer as a decimal?

13. An orchestra has 100 musicians. $\frac{40}{100}$ of them play string
instruments—violin, viola, cello, double bass, guitar, lute, and
harp. What decimal is equivalent to $\frac{40}{100}$?

14. Complete the table.

$ Bills and Coins	Money Amount	Fraction or Mixed Number	Decimal
8 pennies		$\frac{8}{100}$	0.08
	$0.50		0.50
		$\frac{90}{100}$ or $\frac{9}{10}$	0.90
4 $1 bills 5 pennies			4.05

15. The point on the number line shows the number of seconds it
took an athlete to run the forty-yard dash. Write the decimal that
correctly names the point.

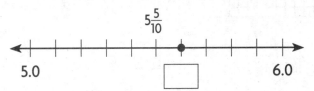

$5\frac{5}{10}$

5.0   6.0

16. Ingrid is making a toy car. The toy car is $\frac{5}{10}$ meter high without the roof. The roof is $\frac{18}{100}$ meter high. What is the height of the toy car with the roof? Choose a number from each column to complete an equation to solve.

$$\frac{5}{10} + \frac{18}{100} = \boxed{\begin{array}{c} \frac{5}{100} \\[4pt] \frac{15}{100} \\[4pt] \frac{50}{100} \end{array}} + \boxed{\begin{array}{c} \frac{18}{100} \\[4pt] \frac{81}{100} \\[4pt] \frac{18}{10} \end{array}} = \boxed{\begin{array}{c} \frac{68}{10} \\[4pt] \frac{32}{100} \\[4pt] \frac{68}{100} \end{array}}$$ meter high.

17. Callie shaded the model to represent the questions she answered correctly on a test. What decimal represents the part of the model that is shaded?

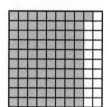

represents [ ]

18. **THINK SMARTER +** For numbers 18a–18f, compare then select True or False.

Personal Math Trainer

18a. $0.21 < 0.27$ ○ True   ○ False

18b. $0.4 > 0.45$ ○ True   ○ False

18c. $\$3.21 > \$0.2$ ○ True   ○ False

18d. $1.9 < 1.90$ ○ True   ○ False

18e. $0.41 = 0.14$ ○ True   ○ False

18f. $6.2 > 6.02$ ○ True   ○ False

19. Fill in the numbers to find the sum.

$$\frac{4}{10} + \frac{\boxed{}}{100} = \frac{8}{\boxed{}}$$

20. Steve is measuring the growth of a tree. He drew this model to show the tree's growth in meters. Which fraction, mixed number, or decimal does the model show? Mark all that apply.

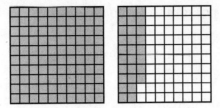

(A) 1.28

(B) 12.8

(C) 0.28

(D) $2\frac{8}{100}$

(E) $1\frac{28}{100}$

(F) $1\frac{28}{10}$

21. Luke lives 0.4 kilometer from a skating rink. Mark lives 0.25 kilometer from the skating rink.

Part A

Who lives closer to the skating rink? Explain.

Part B

How can you write each distance as a fraction? Explain.

Part C

Luke is walking to the skating rink to pick up a practice schedule. Then he is walking to Mark's house. Will he walk more than a kilometer or less than a kilometer? Explain.

544

Big Idea

Geometry, Measurement, and Data

BIG IDEA Develop a conceptual understanding that geometric figures can be analyzed and classified based on their properties, including angle measures. Develop relative sizes of measurement units and apply area and perimeter formulas for rectangles.

Landscape architects can help design and plan outdoor spaces such as botanical gardens.

Landscape Architects

When people who live and work in big cities take breaks, they leave their tall buildings to relax in patches of green. A city garden may be small, but it gives people a chance to enjoy the beauty of nature.

Get Started  WRITE Math

Design a garden that covers a whole city block. Decide on features to have in your garden and where they will be located. Mark off parts of your garden for each feature. Then find the number of square units the feature covers and record it on the design. Use the Important Facts to help you.

Important Facts

Features of a City Garden

Benches		Snack bar	
Flower garden		Spring bulb garden	
Paths		Tree garden	
Shrub garden		Waterfall and fountain	

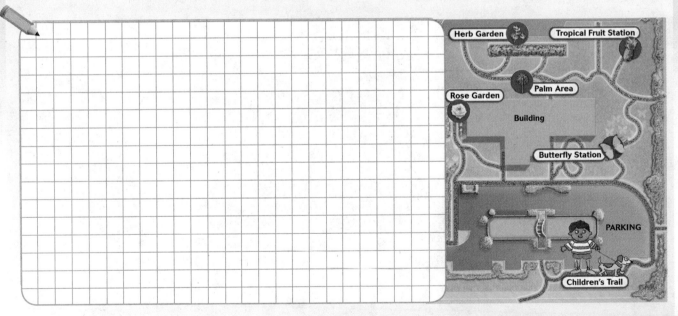

▲ This map is an example of how a city garden could be laid out.

Completed by _____

Two-Dimensional Figures

✓ Show What You Know

Personal Math Trainer
Online Assessment and Intervention

Check your understanding of important skills.

Name _____

▶ **Sides and Vertices** Write the number of vertices.

1.

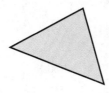

_____ vertices

2.

_____ vertices

3.

_____ vertices

▶ **Number of Sides** Write the number of sides.

4.

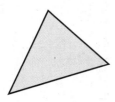

_____ sides

5.

_____ sides

6.

_____ sides

▶ **Geometric Patterns** Draw the next two shapes in the pattern.

7.

Math in the Real World

The Isle of Wight Natural History Centre, off the coast of England, has shells of every size, shape, and color. Many shells have symmetry. Investigate this shell. Describe its shape in geometric terms. Then determine whether this shell has line symmetry.

Vocabulary Builder

▶ **Visualize It** ••

Complete the flow map by using the words with a ✓.

Geometry

What is it?

What are some examples?

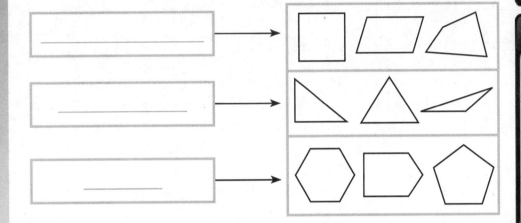

Review Words

✓ polygon

✓ triangle

✓ quadrilateral

Preview Words

acute angle

acute triangle

line

line segment

line symmetry

obtuse angle

obtuse triangle

parallel lines

parallelogram

perpendicular lines

ray

right angle

right triangle

straight angle

▶ **Understand Vocabulary** •••••••••••••••••••••••••••••••

Complete the sentences by using preview words.

1. A shape has _____ if it can be folded about a line so that its two parts match exactly.

2. A figure that has no endpoints is called a _____.

3. A figure that has two endpoints is called a _____.

4. _____ are lines that never cross.

5. When two lines cross to form a square corner, the lines are _____.

 • Interactive Student Edition
• Multimedia eGlossary

Chapter 10 Vocabulary

acute angle

ángulo agudo

1

intersecting lines

líneas secantes

42

line

línea

45

line of symmetry

eje de simetría

46

line segment

segmento

48

obtuse angle

ángulo obtuso

57

parallel lines

líneas paralelas

59

parallelogram

paralelogramo

60

Lines that cross each other at exactly one point

Example:

An angle that measures greater than 0° and less than 90°

Example:

An imaginary line on a shape about which the shape can be folded so that its two parts match exactly

Example:

line of symmetry ⟶

A straight path of points in a plane that continues without end in both directions with no endpoints

Example:

S   T

An angle that measures greater than 90° and less than 180°

Example:

A part of a line that includes two points called endpoints and all the points between them

Example:

A   B

A quadrilateral whose opposite sides are parallel and of equal length

Example:

Lines in the same plane that never intersect and are always the same distance apart

Example:

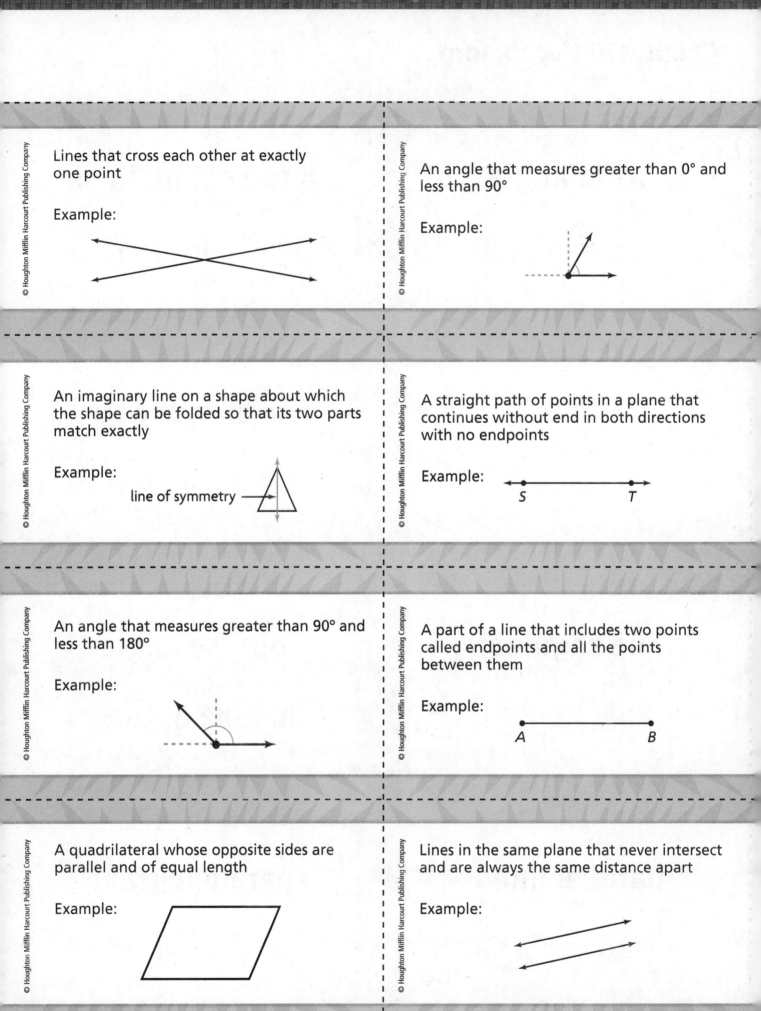

perpendicular lines

líneas perpendiculares

66

point

punto

69

rectangle

rectángulo

77

rhombus

rombo

80

right angle

ángulo recto

81

square

cuadrado

85

straight angle

ángulo llano

88

trapezoid

trapecio

93

An exact location in space

Example: *A* •

Two lines that intersect to form four right angles

Example:

A quadrilateral with two pairs of parallel sides and four sides of equal length

Example:

A quadrilateral with two pairs of parallel sides, two pairs of sides of equal length, and four right angles

Example:

A quadrilateral with two pairs of parallel sides, four sides of equal length, and four right angles

Example:

An angle that forms a square corner

Example:

A quadrilateral with at least one pair of parallel sides

Examples:

An angle whose measure is 180°

Example:

X   Y   Z

Going to a Botanical Garden

For 2 players

Materials

- 1 red playing piece
- 1 blue playing piece
- 1 number cube

How to Play

1. Each player chooses a playing piece and puts it on START.
2. Toss the number cube to take a turn. Move your playing piece that many spaces.
3. If you land on these spaces:

   White Space Tell the meaning of the math term or use it in a sentence. If your answer is correct, jump to the next space with the same term.

   Green Space Follow the directions printed in the space. If there are no directions, stay where you are.

4. The first player to reach FINISH by exact count wins.

Word Box
acute angle
intersecting lines
line
line of symmetry
line segment
obtuse angle
parallel lines
parallelogram
perpendicular lines
point
rectangle
rhombus
right angle
square
straight angle
trapezoid

Game

HOW TO PLAY

1. Put your playing piece on START.
2. Toss the number cube and move your playing piece that many spaces.
3. If you land on one of these spaces:
White Space—Explain the math word or use it in a sentence. If your answer is correct, jump ahead to the next space with that word.
Green Space—Follow the directions in the space. If there are no directions, don't move.
4. The first player to reach FINISH by exact count wins.

MATERIALS

- I red playing piece
- I blue playing piece
- I number cube

FINISH

| line | point | Go back to | acute angle |

| right angle | straight angle | acute angle | obtuse angle | intersecting lines |

| line segment | line | point | line of symmetry | Go back to |

| line | line segment | Go back to | right angle | straight angle |

| point | line of symmetry | square | rectangle | rhombus |

START

| point | line | line segment | right angle |

548B

Game

line segment | line of symmetry | square | rectangle | rhombus

parallel lines | perpendicular lines |  | trapezoid | parallelogram

square | rectangle | rhombus | parallelogram | trapezoid

acute angle | obtuse angle | intersecting lines | parallel lines | perpendicular lines

parallelogram | trapezoid | | perpendicular lines | parallel lines

straight angle | acute angle | obtuse angle | intersecting lines

548C

© Houghton Mifflin Harcourt Publishing Company • Image Credits: (flowers) ©Dynamic Graphics/Jupiterimages/Getty Images

The Write Way

Reflect

Choose one idea. Write about it.

- Summarize how you can tell if two lines are intersecting, parallel, or perpendicular.

- Write the names of as many quadrilaterals that you can think of in three minutes.

- Explain what a *line of symmetry* is so that a child will understand the idea.

Name _____

Lines, Rays, and Angles

Essential Question How can you identify and draw points, lines, line segments, rays, and angles?

Learning Objective You will draw and name points, lines, line segments, rays, and angles and classify angles based on how they compare to the measure of a right angle.

🗝 Unlock the Problem

Everyday things can model geometric figures. For example, the period at the end of this sentence models a point. A solid painted stripe in the middle of a straight road models a line.

Term and Definition	Draw It	Read It	Write It	Example
A **point** is an exact location in space.	A •	point *A*	point *A*	
A **line** is a straight path of points that continues without end in both directions.	←—•———•—→ B C	line *BC* line *CB*	$\overleftrightarrow{BC}$ $\overleftrightarrow{CB}$	
A **line segment** is part of a line between two endpoints.	•———————• D E	line segment *DE* line segment *ED*	$\overline{DE}$ $\overline{ED}$	YIELD
A **ray** is a part of a line that has one endpoint and continues without end in one direction.	•————•—→ F G	ray *FG*	$\overrightarrow{FG}$	ONE WAY

🔑 Activity 1 Draw and label $\overline{JK}$.

_____
_____

Math Talk

Math Processes and Practices ⑥

Compare Explain how lines, line segments, and rays are related.

• Is there another way to name $\overline{JK}$? Explain.

_____
_____

Angles

Term and Definition	Draw It	Read It	Write It	Example
An **angle** is formed by two rays or line segments that have the same endpoint. The shared endpoint is called the vertex.		angle *PQR* angle *RQP* angle *Q*	∠*PQR* ∠*RQP* ∠*Q*	

You can name an angle by the vertex. When you name an angle using 3 points, the vertex is always the point in the middle.

Angles are classified by the size of the opening between the rays.

A **right angle** forms a square corner.	A **straight angle** forms a line.	An **acute angle** is less than a right angle.	An **obtuse angle** is greater than a right angle and less than a straight angle.

🔓 Activity 2 Classify an angle.

Materials ■ paper

To classify an angle, you can compare it to a right angle.

Make a right angle by using a sheet of paper. Fold the paper twice evenly to model a right angle. Use the right angle to classify the angles below. Write *acute, obtuse, right,* or *straight*.

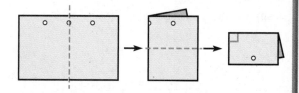

a.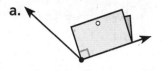

b.

c.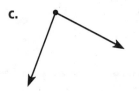

d.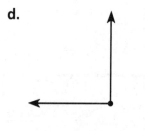

_____ _____ _____ _____

Name _____

1. Draw and label $\overline{AB}$ in the space at the right.

$\overline{AB}$ is a _____ .

Draw and label an example of the figure.

2. $\overleftrightarrow{XY}$

✓ **3.** obtuse $\angle K$

4. right $\angle CDE$

Use Figure *M* for 5 and 6.

5. Name a line segment.

✓ **6.** Name a right angle.

Figure M

On Your Own

Draw and label an example of the figure.

7. $\overrightarrow{PQ}$

8. acute $\angle RST$

9. straight $\angle WXZ$

Use Figure *F* for 10–15.

10. Name a ray.

11. Name an obtuse angle.

12. Name a line.

13. Name a line segment.

14. Name a right angle.

15. Name an acute angle.

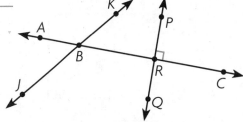

Figure F

Problem Solving • Applications

Use the picture of the bridge for 16 and 17.

16. Classify ∠A.

_____

17. **Math Processes and Practices 4** **Use Diagrams**
Which angle appears to be

obtuse? _____

18. **THINK SMARTER** How many different angles are in Figure *X*?
List them.

_____

_____

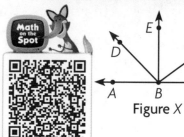

19. **GO DEEPER** Vanessa drew the angle at the right and named it
∠*TRS*. Explain why Vanessa's name for the angle is incorrect.
Write a correct name for the angle.

_____

_____

20. **THINK SMARTER** Write the word that describes
the part of Figure *A*.

 ray   line   line segment

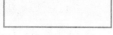 acute angle   right angle

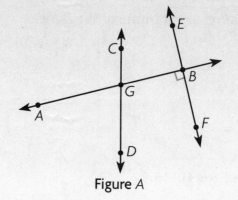
Figure A

$\overline{BG}$ [ ]

$\overleftrightarrow{CD}$ [ ]

∠*FBG* [ ]

$\overrightarrow{BE}$ [ ]

∠*AGD* [ ]

Lines, Rays, and Angles

Learning Objective You will draw and name points, lines, line segments, rays, and angles and classify angles based on how they compare to the measure of a right angle.

Draw and label an example of the figure.

1. obtuse ∠*ABC*

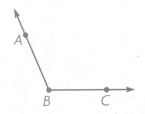

Think: An obtuse angle is greater than a right angle. The middle letter, B, names the vertex of the angle.

2. $\overrightarrow{GH}$

3. acute ∠*JKL*

4. $\overline{BC}$

Use the figure for 5–6.

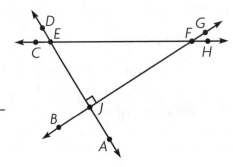

5. Name a line segment.

6. Name a right angle.

_____   _____

Problem Solving Real World

Use the figure at the right for 7–9.

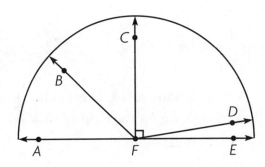

7. Classify ∠*AFD*. _____

8. Classify ∠*CFE*. _____

9. Name two acute angles.

_____

10. **WRITE** *Math* Draw and label a figure that has 4 points, 2 rays, and 1 right angle.

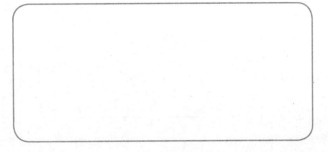

Lesson Check

1. The hands of a clock show the time 12:25.

What kind of angle exists between the hands of the clock?

_____

2. Use letters and symbols to name the figure shown below.

_____

Spiral Review

3. Jan's pencil is 8.5 cm long. Ted's pencil is longer. Write a decimal that could represent the length of Ted's pencil?

_____

4. Kayla buys a shirt for $8.19. She pays with a $10 bill. How much change should she receive?

_____

5. Sasha donated $\frac{9}{100}$ of her class's entire can collection for the food drive. What decimal is equivalent to $\frac{9}{100}$?

_____

6. Jose jumped $8\frac{1}{3}$ feet. This was $2\frac{2}{3}$ feet farther than Lila jumped. How far did Lila jump?

_____

FOR MORE PRACTICE
GO TO THE
Personal Math Trainer

Name _____

Classify Triangles by Angles

Essential Question How can you classify triangles by the size of their angles?

Learning Objective You will classify triangles based on the presence or absence of angles (right, acute, and obtuse).

⚷ Unlock the Problem

A triangle is a polygon with three sides and three angles. You can name a triangle by the vertices of its angles.

Triangle	Possible Names	
A ⟋⟍ B⎯⎯C	△ABC	△ACB
	△BCA	△BAC
	△CAB	△CBA

Read Math

When you see "△ABC," say "triangle ABC."

An angle of a triangle can be right, acute, or obtuse.

🔓 Activity 1 Identify right, acute, and obtuse angles in triangles.

Materials ■ color pencils

Use the Triangle Color Guide to color the triangles below.

Triangle Color Guide	
RED	one right angle
BLUE	one obtuse angle
ORANGE	three acute angles

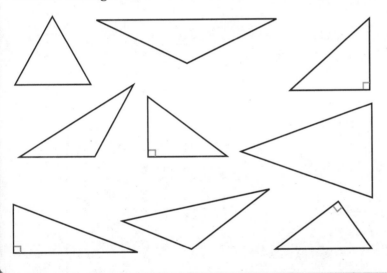

Math Talk

Math Processes and Practices ❼

Look for Structure Can a triangle have more than one obtuse angle? Explain.

Try This!

a. Name the triangle with one right angle. _____

b. Name the triangle with one obtuse angle. _____

c. Name the triangle with three acute angles. _____

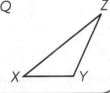

An **acute triangle** is a triangle with three acute angles.	An **obtuse triangle** is a triangle with one obtuse angle.	A **right triangle** is a triangle with one right angle.
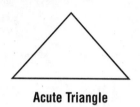 Acute Triangle	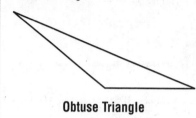 Obtuse Triangle	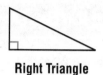 Right Triangle

🔓 Activity 2 Use a Venn diagram to classify triangles.

Write the names of the triangles in the Venn diagram.

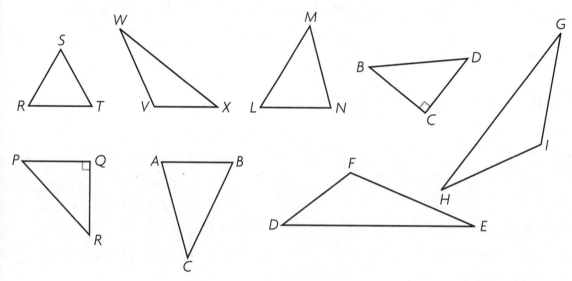

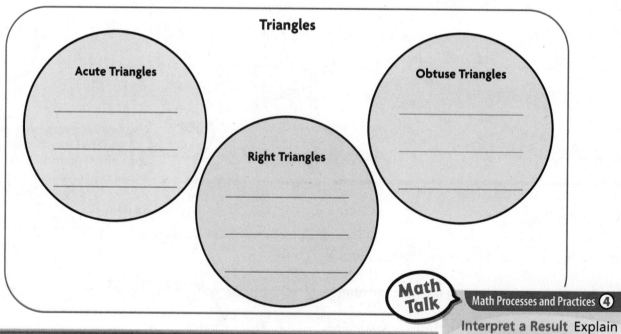

Triangles

Acute Triangles

_____

_____

_____

Right Triangles

_____

_____

_____

Obtuse Triangles

_____

_____

_____

Math Talk

Math Processes and Practices ④

Interpret a Result Explain why the three circles in this Venn diagram do not overlap.

© Houghton Mifflin Harcourt Publishing Company

556

Name _____

Share and Show

1. Name the triangle. Tell whether each angle is *acute*, *right*, or *obtuse*.

   A name for the triangle is _____.

   ∠F is _____.

   ∠G is _____.

   ∠H is _____.

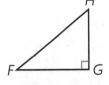

Classify each triangle. Write *acute*, *right*, or *obtuse*.

2.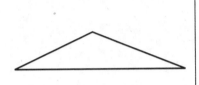

   _____

3.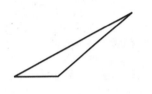

   _____

4.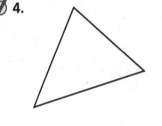

   _____

On Your Own

Classify each triangle. Write *acute*, *right*, or *obtuse*.

5.

   _____

6.

   _____

7.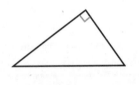

   _____

8. **THINK SMARTER** Cross out the figure that does not belong. Explain.

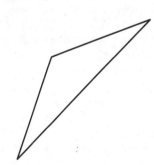 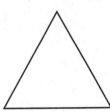 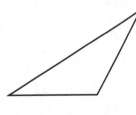 

_____

Problem Solving · Applications (Real World)

Use the Venn diagram for 9–10.

9. **THINK SMARTER** Which triangles do NOT have an obtuse angle? Explain.

_____

_____

10. **Math Processes and Practices ⑥** How many triangles have *at least* two acute angles? **Explain.**

_____

_____

_____

_____

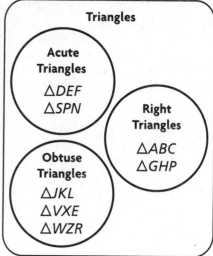

Triangles

Acute Triangles
△DEF
△SPN

Right Triangles
△ABC
△GHP

Obtuse Triangles
△JKL
△VXE
△WZR

11. **GO DEEPER** Use the square shown at the right. Draw a line segment from point *M* to point *P*. Name and classify the triangles formed by the line segment.

_____

_____

_____

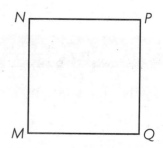

12. **THINK SMARTER** Write the letter of the triangle under its correct classification.

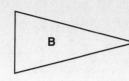
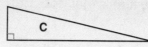

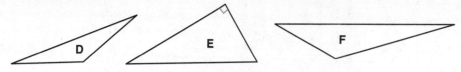

Acute Triangle	Obtuse Triangle	Right Triangle

Classify Triangles by Angles

Learning Objective You will classify triangles based on the presence or absence of angles (right, acute, and obtuse).

Classify each triangle. Write *acute*, *right*, or *obtuse*.

1.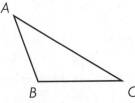

Think: Angles *A* and *C* are both acute.
Angle *B* is obtuse.

<u>obtuse</u>

2.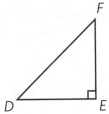

3.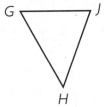

4.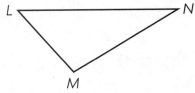

_____   _____   _____

 Problem Solving *Real World*

5. Use figure *ABCD* below. Draw a line segment from point *B* to point *D*. Name and classify the triangles formed.

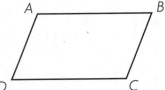

_____

_____

_____

6. **WRITE** ▸*Math* Draw and label an example of a right triangle, an acute triangle, and an obtuse triangle.

Lesson Check

1. Stephen drew this triangle. How many obtuse angles does the triangle have?

_____

2. Joan was asked to draw a right triangle. How many right angles are in a right triangle?

_____

Spiral Review

3. Oliver drew the figure below to show light traveling from the Sun to Earth. Name the figure he drew.

_____

4. Armon added $\frac{1}{10}$ and $\frac{8}{100}$. What is the sum of these fractions?

_____

5. Sam counted out loud by 6s. Jorge counted out loud by 8s. What are the first three numbers both Sam and Jorge said?

_____

6. A basketball team averaged 105 points per game. How many points did the team score in 6 games?

_____

FOR MORE PRACTICE
GO TO THE
Personal Math Trainer

Name _____

Parallel Lines and Perpendicular Lines

Essential Question How can you identify and draw parallel lines and perpendicular lines?

Learning Objective You will identify and draw parallel and perpendicular lines using appropriate tools.

🔑 Unlock the Problem

You can find models of lines in the world around you. For example, two streets that cross each other model intersecting lines. Metal rails on a train track that never cross model parallel lines.

▲ Maglev trains use magnets to lift them above the tracks while moving.

Term and Definition	Draw It	Read It	Write It
Intersecting lines are lines in a plane that cross at exactly one point. Intersecting lines form four angles.		Line *HI* intersects line *JK* at point *X*.	$\overleftrightarrow{HI}$ and $\overleftrightarrow{JK}$ intersect at point *X*
Parallel lines are lines in a plane that are always the same distance apart. Parallel lines never intersect.		Line *DE* is parallel to line *FG*.	$\overleftrightarrow{DE} \parallel \overleftrightarrow{FG}$ The symbol ∥ means "is parallel to."
Perpendicular lines are lines in a plane that intersect to form four right angles.		Line *LM* is perpendicular to line *NO*.	$\overleftrightarrow{LM} \perp \overleftrightarrow{NO}$ The symbol ⊥ means "is perpendicular to."

Try This! Tell how the streets appear to be related. Write *perpendicular*, *parallel*, or *intersecting*.

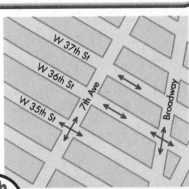

- W 36th St and Broadway _____

- W 35th St and 7th Ave _____

- W 37th St and W 36th St _____

Math Talk Math Processes and Practices 6

Use Math Vocabulary Can two rays be parallel? Explain.

Activity Draw and label $\overrightarrow{YX} \perp \overrightarrow{YZ}$ intersecting at point Y.

Materials ■ straightedge

STEP 1: Draw and label $\overrightarrow{YX}$.

STEP 2: Then draw and label $\overrightarrow{YZ}$.

STEP 3: Make sure $\overrightarrow{YX}$ and $\overrightarrow{YZ}$ intersect at point Y.

STEP 4: Make sure the rays are perpendicular.

• How can you check if two rays are perpendicular?

_____

_____

1. Name the figure you drew.

_____

2. Can you classify the figure? Explain.

_____

_____

Share and Show MATH BOARD

1. Draw and label $\overline{QR} \parallel \overline{ST}$.

Think: Parallel lines never intersect. Parallel line segments are parts of parallel lines.

Use the figure for 2 and 3.

✓ **2.** Name two line segments that appear to be parallel.

_____

✓ **3.** Name two line segments that appear to be perpendicular.

_____

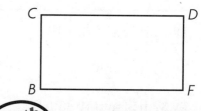

Math Talk Math Processes and Practices ④

Use Symbols How could the symbols ⊥ and ∥ help you remember which relationships they describe?

Name _____

On Your Own

Use the figure for 4–5.

4. Name a pair of lines that are perpendicular.

_____

5. Name a pair of lines that appear to be parallel.

_____

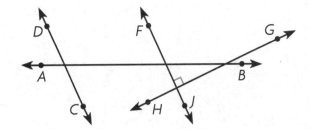

Draw and label the figure described.

6. $\overline{RS} \parallel \overline{TU}$

7. $\overrightarrow{KL}$ and $\overrightarrow{KM}$

8. $\overline{CD} \perp \overline{DE}$

9. $\overrightarrow{JK} \perp \overleftrightarrow{LM}$

10. $\overleftrightarrow{ST}$ intersecting $\overrightarrow{UV}$ at point X

11. $\overleftrightarrow{AB} \parallel \overrightarrow{FG}$

Problem Solving • Applications

Use the figure for 12–13.

12. **THINK SMARTER** Dan says that $\overleftrightarrow{HL}$ is parallel to $\overleftrightarrow{IM}$. Is Dan correct? Explain.

_____

_____

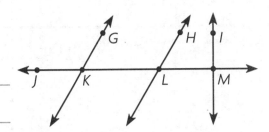

13. **GO DEEPER** Name two intersecting line segments that are not perpendicular.

_____

Use the house plan at the right for 14–16.

14. What geometric term describes a corner of the living room?

_____

_____

15. Name three parts of the plan that show line segments.

_____

_____

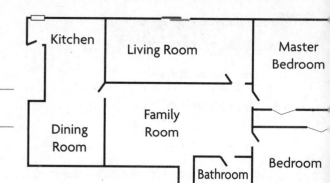

16. **THINK SMARTER** Name a pair of line segments that appear to be parallel.

_____

_____

Use the map at the right for 17–19.

17. Name a street that appears to be parallel to S 17th Street.

_____

_____

18. **Math Processes and Practices ④ Use Diagrams** Name a street that appears to be parallel to Vernon Street.

_____

19. Name a street that appears to be perpendicular to S 19th Street.

_____

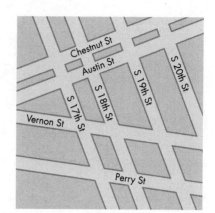

20. **THINK SMARTER** Choose the labels to make a true statement.

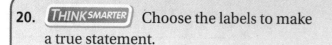

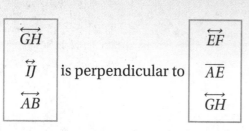

is perpendicular to

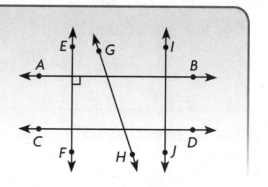

Parallel Lines and Perpendicular Lines

Learning Objective You will identify and draw parallel and perpendicular lines using appropriate tools.

Use the figure for 1–2.

1. Name a pair of lines that appear to be perpendicular.

   Think: Perpendicular lines form right angles. $\overleftrightarrow{AB}$ and $\overleftrightarrow{EF}$ appear to form right angles.

   _____$\overleftrightarrow{AB}$ and $\overleftrightarrow{EF}$_____

2. Name a pair of lines that appear to be parallel.

   _____

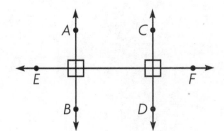

Draw and label the figure described.

3. $\overleftrightarrow{MN}$ and $\overleftrightarrow{PQ}$ intersecting at point R

4. $\overleftrightarrow{WX} \parallel \overleftrightarrow{YZ}$

5. $\overleftrightarrow{FH} \perp \overleftrightarrow{JK}$

Problem Solving · Real World

Use the street map for 6–7.

6. Name two streets that intersect but do not appear to be perpendicular.

   _____

   _____

7. Name two streets that appear to be parallel to each other.

   _____

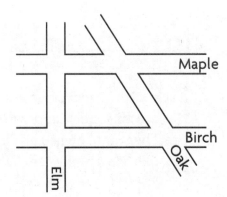

8. **WRITE** ▸*Math* Draw and label an example of two parallel lines that are perpendicular to a third line.

Lesson Check

1. Write a capital letter that appears to have perpendicular line segments?

2. In the figure, which pair of line segments appear to be parallel?

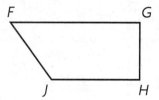

Spiral Review

3. Nolan drew a right triangle. How many acute angles did he draw?

4. Mike drank more than half the juice in his glass. What fraction of the juice could Mike have drunk?

5. A school principal ordered 1,000 pencils. He gave an equal number to each of 7 teachers until he had given out as many as possible. How many pencils were left?

6. A carton of juice contains 64 ounces. Ms. Wilson bought 6 cartons of juice. How many ounces of juice did she buy?

FOR MORE PRACTICE
GO TO THE
Personal Math Trainer

Name _____

Classify Quadrilaterals

Essential Question How can you sort and classify quadrilaterals?

Learning Objective You will classify quadrilaterals based on the presence or absence of parallel or perpendicular lines.

 Unlock the Problem *Real World*

A quadrilateral is a polygon with four sides and four angles. You can name a quadrilateral by the vertices of its angles.

Quadrilateral *ABCD* is a possible name for the figure shown at the right. Quadrilateral *ACBD* is not a possible name, since points *A* and *C* are not endpoints of the same side.

Assume that line segments that appear to be parallel are parallel.

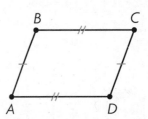

The tick marks on the line segments show that they have the same length. Sides *AD* and *BC* have the same length. Sides *AB* and *CD* have the same length.

Common Quadrilaterals

Trapezoid
- at least 1 pair of parallel sides

Parallelogram
- 2 pairs of parallel sides
- 2 pairs of sides of equal length

Rhombus
- 2 pairs of parallel sides
- 4 sides of equal length

Rectangle
- 2 pairs of parallel sides
- 2 pairs of sides of equal length
- 4 right angles

Square
- 2 pairs of parallel sides
- 4 sides of equal length
- 4 right angles

🔒 Activity 1 Identify right angles in quadrilaterals.

Materials ■ color pencils

Use the Quadrilateral Color Guide to color the quadrilaterals.

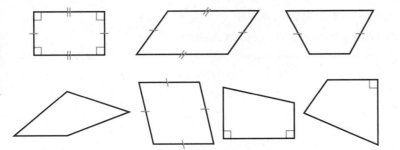

Quadrilateral Color Guide	
RED:	exactly 4 right angles
BLUE:	exactly 2 right angles
ORANGE:	exactly 1 right angle

Math Talk

Math Processes and Practices ⑥

Can a quadrilateral have exactly 3 right angles? **Explain.**

© Houghton Mifflin Harcourt Publishing Company

🔓 Activity 2 Use a Venn diagram to sort quadrilaterals.

Write the names of the quadrilaterals in the Venn diagram.

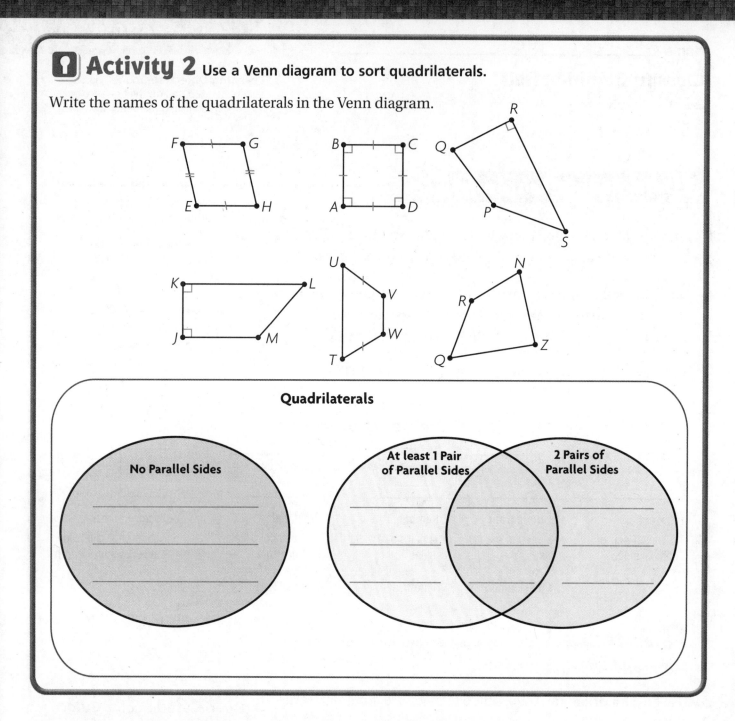

Quadrilaterals

No Parallel Sides

_____

_____

_____

At least 1 Pair
of Parallel Sides

_____

_____

_____

2 Pairs of
Parallel Sides

_____

_____

_____

Try This! Classify each figure as many ways as possible. Write
quadrilateral, trapezoid, parallelogram, rhombus, rectangle, or *square.*

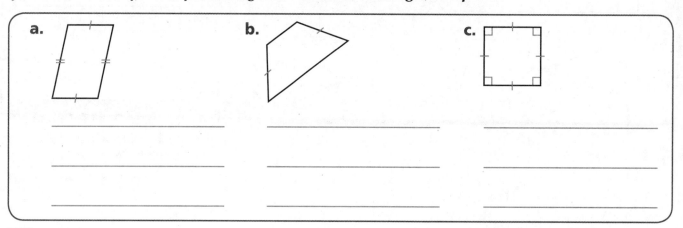

a.

_____

_____

_____

b.

_____

_____

_____

c.

_____

_____

_____

Name _____

Share and Show MATH BOARD

1. Tell whether the quadrilateral is also a trapezoid, parallelogram, rhombus, rectangle, or square.

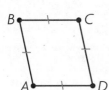

Think: _____ pairs of parallel sides

_____ sides of equal length

_____ right angles

Quadrilateral *ABCD* is also a _____

_____.

Classify each figure as many ways as possible. Write
quadrilateral, trapezoid, parallelogram, rhombus, rectangle, **or** *square.*

 2.
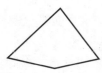

_____

_____

_____

3.

_____

_____

_____

4.

_____

_____

_____

Math Talk   Math Processes and Practices ②

Use Reasoning How would you classify a figure with 4 sides, none of which are parallel? Explain.

On Your Own

Classify each figure as many ways as possible.
Write *quadrilateral, trapezoid, parallelogram, rhombus, rectangle,* **or** *square.*

5.
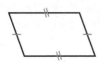

_____

_____

6.
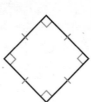

_____

_____

7.

_____

_____

© Houghton Mifflin Harcourt Publishing Company

Chapter 10 • Lesson 4   569

Problem Solving • Applications (Real World)

8. **THINK SMARTER** Explain how a rhombus and square are alike, and how they are different.

_____

_____

_____

_____

9. **THINK SMARTER** Classify the figure. Select all that apply.

- ○ quadrilateral
- ○ rectangle
- ○ trapezoid
- ○ rhombus
- ○ parallelogram
- ○ square

Connect to Art

The Louvre Museum is located in Paris, France. Architect I. M. Pei designed the glass and metal structure at the main entrance of the museum. This structure is called the Louvre Pyramid.

Below is a diagram of part of the entrance to the Louvre Pyramid.

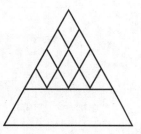

10. **Math Processes and Practices ①** Describe the quadrilaterals you see in the diagram.

_____

_____

_____

_____

11. **GO DEEPER** How many triangles do you see in the diagram? Explain.

_____

_____

_____

_____

Name _____

Classify Quadrilaterals

Learning Objective You will classify quadrilaterals based on the presence or absence of parallel or perpendicular lines.

Classify each figure as many ways as possible. Write
quadrilateral, trapezoid, parallelogram, rhombus, rectangle, or square.

1.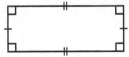

Think: 2 pairs of parallel sides
   4 sides of equal length
   0 right angles

quadrilateral, trapezoid, parallelogram, rhombus

_____

2.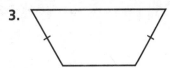

3.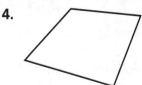

4.

_____   _____   _____

_____   _____   _____

_____   _____   _____

Problem Solving Real World

5. Alan drew a polygon with four sides and four angles. All four sides are equal. None of the angles are right angles. What figure did Alan draw?

_____

_____

6. Teresa drew a quadrilateral with 2 pairs of parallel sides and 4 right angles. What quadrilateral could she have drawn?

_____

_____

7. **WRITE** ▸*Math* Draw and label an example of each type of quadrilateral: trapezoid, parallelogram, rhombus, rectangle, and square.

Lesson Check

1. Joey is asked to name a quadrilateral that is also a rhombus and has 2 pairs of parallel sides. What should be his answer?

2. What quadrilateral has at least one pair of parallel sides, but cannot be called a parallelogram?

Spiral Review

3. Terrence has 24 eggs to divide into equal groups. What are all the possible numbers of eggs that Terence could put in each group?

4. In a line of students, Jenna is number 8. The teacher says that a rule for a number pattern is *add 4*. The first student in line says the first term, 7. What number should Jenna say?

5. Lou eats $\frac{6}{8}$ of a pizza. What fraction of the pizza , in simplest form, is left over?

6. Name a capital letter that appears to have parallel lines.

FOR MORE PRACTICE
GO TO THE
Personal Math Trainer

Name _____

 Mid-Chapter Checkpoint

 **Personal Math Trainer** Online Assessment and Intervention

Vocabulary

Choose the best term from the box to complete the sentence.

<table>
<tr><td>Vocabulary</td></tr>
<tr><td>acute angle</td></tr>
<tr><td>line segment</td></tr>
<tr><td>obtuse angle</td></tr>
<tr><td>ray</td></tr>
<tr><td>right angle</td></tr>
<tr><td>straight angle</td></tr>
</table>

1. A _____ is part of a line between two endpoints. (p. 549)

2. A _____ forms a square corner. (p. 550)

3. An _____ is greater than a right angle and less than a straight angle. (p. 550)

4. The two-dimensional figure that has one endpoint is a

   _____. (p. 549)

5. An angle that forms a line is called a _____. (p. 550)

Concepts and Skills

6. On the grid to the right, draw a polygon that has 2 pairs of parallel sides, 2 pairs of sides equal in length, and 2 acute and 2 obtuse angles. Tell all the possible names for the figure.

   _____

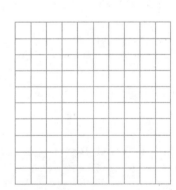

Draw the figure.

7. parallel lines	8. obtuse ∠ABC	9. intersecting lines that are not perpendicular	10. acute ∠RST

11. Which triangle has one right angle?

_____

12. A figure has 2 pairs of parallel sides, 2 pairs of sides of equal length, and 4 right angles. What quadrilateral best describes this figure?

_____

13. Which quadrilateral can have 2 pairs of parallel sides, all sides with equal length, and no right angles?

_____

14. What is the correct name of the figure shown?

_____

15. **GO DEEPER** Describe the angles of an obtuse triangle.

_____

_____

_____

Name _____

Line Symmetry

Essential Question How can you check if a shape has line symmetry?

Learning Objective You will use pattern blocks to explore symmetry and identify figures that have lines of symmetry.

Unlock the Problem

One type of symmetry found in geometric shapes is line symmetry. This sign is in the hills above Hollywood, California. Do any of the letters in the Hollywood sign show line symmetry?

A shape has **line symmetry** if it can be folded about a line so that its two parts match exactly.

A fold line, or a **line of symmetry**, divides a shape into two parts that are the same size and shape.

Activity Explore line symmetry.

Materials ▪ pattern blocks ▪ scissors

A Does the letter W have line symmetry?

STEP 1 Use pattern blocks to make the letter W.	**STEP 2** Trace the letter.

Math Idea

A vertical line goes up and down. ↕

A horizontal line goes left and right. ↔

A diagonal line goes through vertices of a polygon that are not next to each other. It can go up and down and left and right. ↗ ↘

STEP 3 Cut out the tracing.

STEP 4 Fold the tracing over a vertical line.

Think: The two parts of the folded W match exactly. The fold line is a line of symmetry.

Math Talk Math Processes and Practices ❸

Apply How can you check to see if a shape has line symmetry?

So, the letter W _____ line symmetry.

B **Does the letter L have line symmetry?**

STEP 1

Use pattern blocks or grid paper to make the letter L.

STEP 2

Trace the letter.

STEP 3

Cut out the tracing.

STEP 4

Fold the tracing over a vertical line.

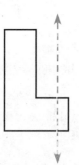

Do the two parts match exactly?

_____

STEP 5

Then open it and fold it horizontally.

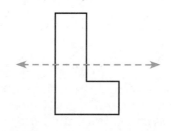

Do the two parts match exactly?

_____

STEP 6

Then open it and fold it diagonally.

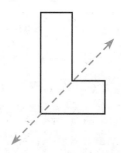

Do the two parts match exactly?

_____

So, the letter L _____ line symmetry.

---

1. Repeat Steps 1–6 for the remaining letters in HOLLYWOOD. Which letters have line symmetry?

_____

2. Do any of the letters have more than one line of symmetry? Explain.

_____

_____

Remember
You can fold horizontally, vertically, or diagonally to determine if the parts match exactly.

Name _____

**Tell whether the parts on each side of the line match.
Is the line a line of symmetry? Write *yes* or *no*.**

1.

2.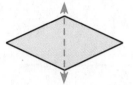

3.

✓4.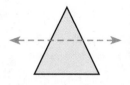

_____   _____   _____   _____

**Tell if the blue line appears to be a line of symmetry.
Write *yes* or *no*.**

5.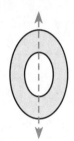

6.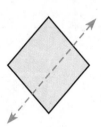

7.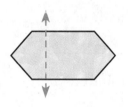

✓8.

_____   _____   _____   _____

Math Talk

Math Processes and Practices ②

Use Reasoning How can you use paper folding to check if a shape has line symmetry?

On Your Own

**Tell if the blue line appears to be a line of symmetry.
Write *yes* or *no*.**

9.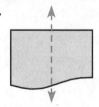

10.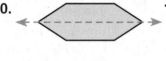

11.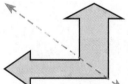

12.

_____   _____   _____   _____

13. **GO DEEPER** Which best describes the symmetry in the letter I?

I

_____

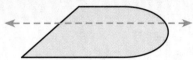 **Unlock the Problem**

14. Which shape has a correctly drawn line of symmetry?

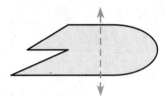

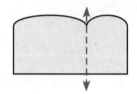

a. What do you need to find? _____

_____

b. How can you tell if the line of symmetry is correct?

_____

c. Tell how you solved the problem.

_____

_____

d. Circle the correct shape above.

15. **Math Processes and Practices ②** **Reason Abstractly** Draw a line of symmetry in the figure shown.

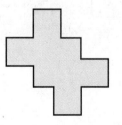

16. *THINK SMARTER +* Evie's birthday is on the 18th of May. Since May is the 5th month, Evie wrote the date as shown.

Evie says all the numbers she wrote have line symmetry. Is she correct? Explain.

_____

_____

_____

Line Symmetry

Learning Objective You will use pattern blocks to explore symmetry and identify figures that have lines of symmetry.

Tell if the dashed line appears to be a line of symmetry.
Write _yes_ or _no_.

1.

2.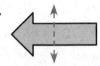

3.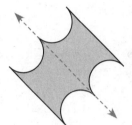

4.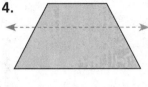

___yes___   _____   _____   _____

Complete the design by reflecting over the line of symmetry.

5.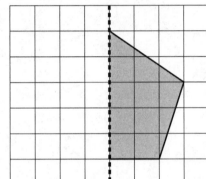

6.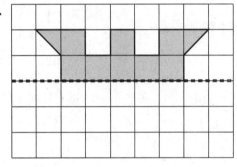

Problem Solving Real World

7. Kara uses the pattern at the right to make
   paper dolls. The dashed line represents a
   line of symmetry. A complete doll includes
   the reflection of the pattern over the line
   of symmetry. Complete the design to show
   what one of Kara's paper dolls looks like.

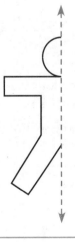

8. **WRITE** ⟩Math Write a word that has line
   symmetry, like the word OHIO. Draw the line(s)
   of symmetry for each letter.

Lesson Check

1. What word best describes the line of symmetry in the letter D?

_____

_____

2. Does the shape below show a correct line of symmetry? Explain.

_____

_____

Spiral Review

3. The class has 360 unit cubes in a bag. Johnnie divides the unit cubes equally among 8 groups. How many unit cubes will each group get?

_____

4. There are 5,280 feet in one mile. How many feet are there in 6 miles?

_____

5. Sue has 4 pieces of wood. The lengths of her pieces of wood are $\frac{1}{3}$ foot, $\frac{2}{5}$ foot, $\frac{3}{10}$ foot, and $\frac{1}{4}$ foot. Which piece of wood is the shortest?

_____

6. Alice has $\frac{1}{5}$ as many miniature cars as Sylvester has. Sylvester has 35 miniature cars. How many miniature cars does Alice have?

_____

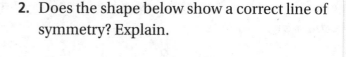

FOR MORE PRACTICE
GO TO THE
Personal Math Trainer

Find and Draw Lines of Symmetry

Essential Question How do you find lines of symmetry?

Learning Objective You will recognize and draw lines of symmetry in two-dimensional figures and tell whether a shape appears to have zero, 1, or more than 1 line of symmetry.

🔑 Unlock the Problem

How many lines of symmetry does each polygon have?

🔓 Activity 1 Find lines of symmetry.

Materials ■ isometric and square dot paper ■ straightedge

STEP 1	**STEP 2**
Draw a triangle like the one shown, so all sides have equal length.	Fold the triangle in different ways to test for line symmetry. Draw along the fold lines that are lines of symmetry.

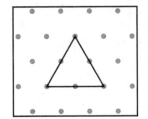

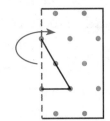

• Is there a line of symmetry if you fold the paper horizontally?

_____

STEP 3

Repeat the steps for each polygon shown. Complete the table.

Polygon	Triangle	Square	Parallelogram	Rhombus	Trapezoid	Hexagon
Number of Sides	3					
Number of Lines of Symmetry	3					

• In a regular polygon, all sides are of equal length and all angles are equal. What do you notice about the number of lines of symmetry in regular polygons?

_____

_____

Math Processes and Practices ⑧

Use Repeated Reasoning How many lines of symmetry does a circle have? Explain.

Activity 2 Make designs that have line symmetry.
Materials ■ pattern blocks

Make a design by using more than one pattern block.
Record your design. Draw the line or lines of symmetry.

Make a design with 2 lines of symmetry.

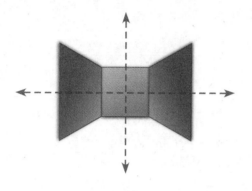

Make a design with 1 line of symmetry.

**Make a design with more than 2 lines
of symmetry.**

**Make a design with zero lines
of symmetry.**

 **Share and Show** MATH BOARD

1. The shape at the right has line symmetry.
   Draw the 2 lines of symmetry.

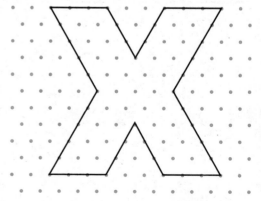

Name _____

Tell whether the shape appears to have zero lines, 1 line, or more than 1 line of symmetry. Write *zero*, *1*, or *more than 1*.

2.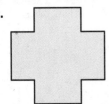

✓ 3.

4.

✓ 5.

_____

On Your Own

Math Talk

Math Processes and Practices ①

Analyze Explain how you can find lines of symmetry for a shape.

Tell whether the shape appears to have zero lines, 1 line, or more than 1 line of symmetry. Write *zero*, *1*, or *more than 1*.

6.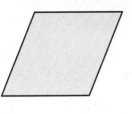

7.

8.

9.

Practice: Copy and Solve **Does the design have line symmetry? Write *yes* or *no*. If your answer is *yes*, draw all lines of symmetry.**

10.

11.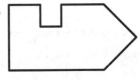

12.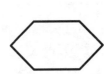

13.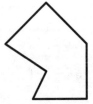

14. GO DEEPER Draw a figure that has 5 sides and exactly 1 line of symmetry.

Problem Solving • Applications

Use the chart for 15–17.

A	H	S
B	I	T
C	J	U
D	L	V
E	N	W

15. **GO DEEPER** Which letters appear to have only 1 line of symmetry?

_____

16. Which letters appear to have zero lines of symmetry?

_____

17. **THINK SMARTER** The letter C has horizontal symmetry. The letter A has vertical symmetry. Which letters appear to have both horizontal and vertical symmetry?

_____

18. **Math Processes and Practices 3** **Verify the Reasoning of Others** Jeff says that the shape has only 2 lines of symmetry.

Does his statement make sense? Explain.

_____

_____

_____

19. **THINK SMARTER +** Match each figure with the correct number of lines of symmetry it has.

   G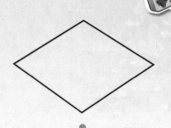

0 lines of symmetry	1 line of symmetry	2 lines of symmetry	More than 2 lines of symmetry

Name _____

Find and Draw Lines of Symmetry

Learning Objective You will recognize and draw lines of symmetry in two-dimensional figures and tell whether a shape appears to have zero, 1, or more than 1 line of symmetry.

Tell whether the shape appears to have zero lines, 1 line, or more than 1 line of symmetry. Write *zero, 1,* or *more than 1*.

1.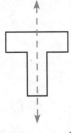

   _____1_____

2.

   _____

3.

   _____

4.

   _____

Does the design have line symmetry? Write *yes* or *no*. If your answer is yes, draw all lines of symmetry.

5.

   _____

6.

   _____

7.

   _____

8.

   _____

Draw a shape for the statement. Draw the line or lines of symmetry.

9. zero lines of symmetry

10. 1 line of symmetry

11. 2 lines of symmetry

Problem Solving · Real World

Use the chart for 12.

0 2 3 4
5 6 8 9

12. Which number or numbers appear to have 2 lines of symmetry?

   _____

13. **WRITE** ▸*Math* Draw a picture of a figure that has more than 3 lines of symmetry. Draw the lines of symmetry.

Lesson Check

1. How many lines of symmetry does this shape appear to have?

_____

2. Draw a shape that has exactly 1 line of symmetry.

Spiral Review

3. Richard practiced each of 3 piano solos for $\frac{5}{12}$ hour. Expressed in simplest form, how long did he practice in all?

_____

4. Write a decimal that is equivalent to three and ten hundredths.

_____

5. Lynne used $\frac{3}{8}$ cup of flour and $\frac{1}{3}$ cup of sugar in a recipe. What number is a common denominator for $\frac{3}{8}$ and $\frac{1}{3}$?

_____

6. Kevin draws a figure that has four sides. All sides have the same length. His figure has no right angles. What figure does Kevin draw?

_____

FOR MORE PRACTICE
GO TO THE
Personal Math Trainer

Name _____

Problem Solving • Shape Patterns

Essential Question How can you use the strategy *act it out* to solve pattern problems?

Learning Objective You will use the strategy *act it out* to solve pattern problems by using pattern blocks and drawings to find the next figures in the pattern.

Unlock the Problem

You can find patterns in fabric, pottery, rugs, and wall coverings. You can see patterns in shape, size, position, color, or number of figures.

Sofia will use the pattern below to make a wallpaper border. What might be the next three figures in the pattern?

Use the graphic organizer below to solve the problem.

Read the Problem

What do I need to find?	What information do I need to use?	How will I use the information?
I need to find the next three _____ in the pattern.	I need to use the _____ of each figure in Sofia's pattern.	I will use pattern blocks to model the _____ and act out the problem.

Solve the Problem

Math Processes and Practices 7

Look for a Pattern How can you describe the shape pattern using numbers?

Describe how you acted out the problem to solve it.

I used a trapezoid and triangle to model the first

figure in the pattern. I used a _____ and

_____ to model the second figure in the pattern. I continued to model the pattern by repeating the models of the first two figures.

These are the next three figures in the pattern.

🔓 Try Another Problem

Draw what might be the next figure in the pattern.

Figure: 1   2   3   4   5

How can you describe this pattern?

Read the Problem

What do I need to find?	What information do I need to use?	How will I use the information?

Solve the Problem

1. Use the figures to write a number pattern. Then describe the pattern in the numbers.

   _____

   _____

   _____

Math Processes and Practices ⑦

Look for Structure What other strategy could you use to solve the problem?

2. What might the tenth number in your pattern be? Explain.

   _____

   _____

Name _____

Share and Show MATH BOARD

Unlock the Problem

✓ Use the Problem Solving MathBoard.
✓ Underline the important facts.
✓ Choose a strategy you know.

1. Marisol is making a pattern with blocks.
   What might the missing shape be?

   First, look at the blocks.

   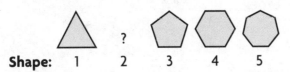

   Shape: 1   2   3   4   5

   Next, describe Marisol's pattern.

   _____

   _____

   Finally, draw the missing shape.

   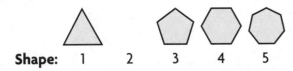

   Shape: 1   2   3   4   5

☑ 2. Use the shapes to write a number pattern. Then describe the
   pattern in the numbers.

   _____

   _____

3. **THINK SMARTER** What if the pattern continued? Write an expression
   to describe the number of sides the sixth shape has in Marisol's
   pattern.

   _____

☑ 4. Sahil made a pattern using circles. The first nine circles are shown.
   Describe Sahil's pattern. If Sahil continues the pattern, what might
   the next three circles be?

   ◯ ○ ∘ ◯ ○ ∘ ◯ ○ ∘

   _____

© Houghton Mifflin Harcourt Publishing Company

On Your Own

Use the toy quilt designs for 5–6.

5. **THINK SMARTER** Lu is making a quilt that is 20 squares wide and has 24 rows. The border of the quilt is made by using each toy design equally as often. Each square can hold one design. How many of each design does she use for the border?

_____

6. **Math Processes and Practices 5** **Communicate** Starting in the first square of her quilt, Lu lined up her toy designs in this order: plane, car, fire truck, helicopter, crane, and wagon. Using this pattern unit, which design will Lu place in the fifteenth square? Explain how you found your answer.

_____

_____

_____

7. **GO DEEPER** Missy uses 1 hexagonal, 2 rectangular, and 4 triangular pieces of fabric to make 1 bug design for a quilt. If she uses 70 pieces in all to make bug designs, how many of each shape does she use?

_____

8. **THINK SMARTER** Norris drew the pattern shown.

   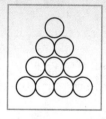 

Label the circles to show the colors in the fourth figure of the pattern.

Name ______________________

Problem Solving • Shape Patterns

Practice and Homework
Lesson 10.7

Learning Objective You will use the strategy *act it out* to solve pattern problems by using pattern blocks and drawings to find the next figures in the pattern.

Solve each problem.

1. Marta is using this pattern to decorate a picture frame. Describe Marta's pattern. Draw what might be the next three figures in her pattern.

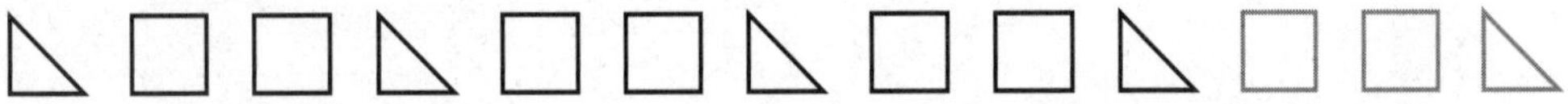

Possible answer: the pattern repeats: one triangle followed by two squares.

---

2. Describe a pattern. Draw what might be the next three figures in your pattern. How many circles are in the sixth figure in your pattern?

____

____

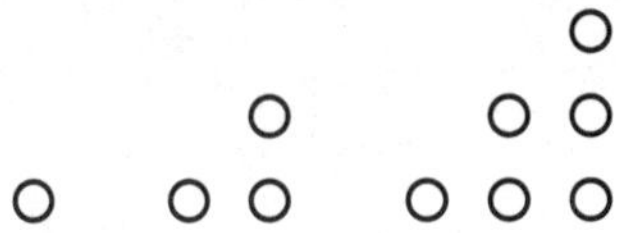

3. WRITE ▸*Math* Find a pattern in your classroom. Describe and extend the pattern.

____

____

____

Lesson Check

1. Draw what might be the next three figures in this pattern?

⇑⇓⇓⇑⇑⇑⇓⇓⇓⇓⇑⇑⇑⇑⇑⇓⇓⇓⇓

_____

2. Draw what might be the missing figure in the pattern below.

 ___

_____

Spiral Review

3. Chad has two pieces of wood. One piece is $\frac{7}{12}$ foot long. The second piece is $\frac{5}{12}$ foot longer than the first piece. How long is the second piece?

_____

4. Olivia finished a race in 40.64 seconds. Patty finished the race in 40.39 seconds. Miguel finished the race in 41.44 seconds. Chad finished the race in 40.46 seconds. Who finished the race in the least time?

_____

5. Justin bought 6 ribbons for an art project. Each ribbon is $\frac{1}{4}$ yard long. How many yards of ribbon did Justin buy?

_____

6. Kyle and Andrea were asked to make a list of prime numbers.

Kyle: 1, 3, 7, 19, 23

Andrea: 2, 3, 5, 7, 11

Whose list is correct?

_____

FOR MORE PRACTICE GO TO THE Personal Math Trainer

Name _____

☑ Chapter 10 Review/Test

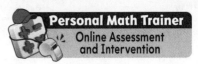

1. Gavin is designing a kite. He sketched a picture of the kite. How many right angles does the kite appear to have?

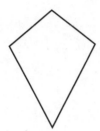

_____ right angles

2. Write the letter of the triangle under its correct classification.

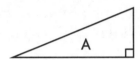 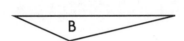

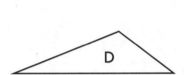

Acute Triangle	Obtuse Triangle	Right Triangle

3. Select the angles that identify an obtuse triangle. Mark all that apply.

Ⓐ acute, acute, acute

Ⓑ acute, acute, obtuse

Ⓒ right, acute, acute

Ⓓ obtuse, right, acute

GO DIGITAL Assessment Options
Chapter Test

4. Write the word that describes the part of Figure A written below.

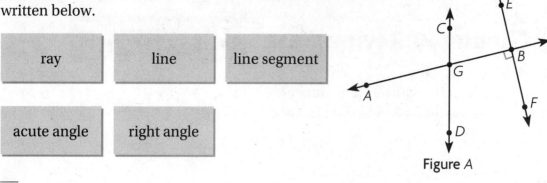

ray	line	line segment

acute angle	right angle

Figure A

$\overline{EB}$ _____ $\angle EBG$ _____

$\overleftrightarrow{AB}$ _____ $\angle CGB$ _____

$\overrightarrow{GA}$ _____

5. What term best describes the figure shown below?

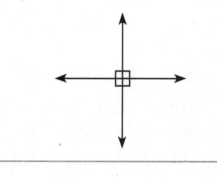

[blank box]

6. **THINK SMARTER +** Naomi leaves for her trip to Los Angeles on the 12th day of August. Since August is the 8th month, Naomi wrote the date as shown.

Naomi says all the numbers she wrote have line symmetry. Is she correct? Explain your thinking.

[blank box]

Name _____

7. Max made a pennant that looks like a triangle. How can you classify the triangle based upon its angles?

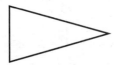

The triangle is a(n) _____ triangle.

8. Choose the labels to make a true statement.

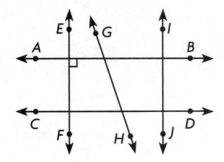

$\overleftrightarrow{GH}$		$\overleftrightarrow{EF}$
$\overleftrightarrow{CD}$	is parallel to	$\overleftrightarrow{CD}$
$\overleftrightarrow{AB}$		$\overleftrightarrow{GH}$

.

9. Classify the figure. Select all that apply.

○ quadrilateral   ○ rectangle

○ trapezoid   ○ rhombus

○ parallelogram   ○ square

10. Lily designed a deck in her backyard that looks like a quadrilateral that has only 1 pair of parallel sides. How can you classify the figure?

The quadrilateral is a _____.

11. Match each figure with the correct number of lines of symmetry it has.

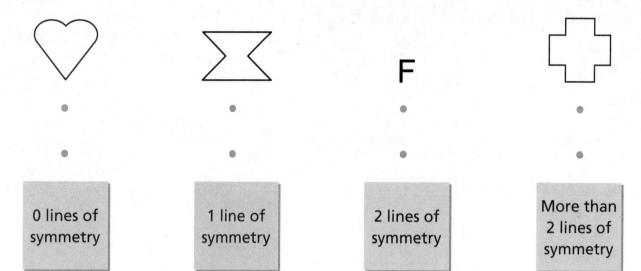

| 0 lines of symmetry | 1 line of symmetry | 2 lines of symmetry | More than 2 lines of symmetry |

12. Barb drew the pattern shown.

Use the square shown to draw the missing pattern. ☐

13. Claudia drew the figure below. Draw a line of symmetry on Claudia's figure.

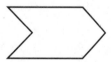

14. Write the word or words that best describe this figure.

15. How many acute angles does a right triangle have?

A right triangle has _____ acute angles.

Name _____

16. Mike drew a figure with opposite sides parallel. Write the pairs of parallel sides. What figure is it?

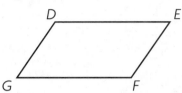

17. Circle the letter that does not have line symmetry.

DOTS

18. Joseph made a pattern using ovals and rectangles. The first four figures of his pattern are shown. Draw the next figure in the pattern.

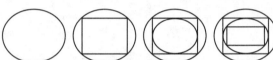

    Figure 1   **Figure 2**   **Figure 3**   **Figure 4**   **Figure 5**

19. Jeremy drew Figure 1 and Louisa drew Figure 2.

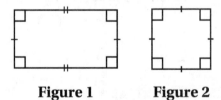

    Figure 1   **Figure 2**

Part A

Jeremy says both figures are rectangles. Do you agree with Jeremy? Support your answer.

Part B

Louisa says both figures are rhombuses. Do you agree with Louisa? Support your answer.

20. Veronica found the number of lines of symmetry for the figure below. How many lines of symmetry does it have?

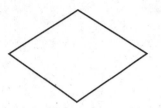

_____ lines of symmetry

21. GO DEEPER   Jordan drew the pattern below.

Figure: 1   2   3   4

Part A

Describe the pattern.

Part B

Write a rule using numbers to find the number of squares in any figure in the pattern.

Part C

Draw Figure 5.

Chapter 11 — Angles

Show What You Know

Personal Math Trainer
Online Assessment
and Intervention

Check your understanding of important skills.

Name _____

▶ **Use a Metric Ruler** Use a centimeter ruler to measure.
Find the length in centimeters.

1.

_____ centimeters

2.
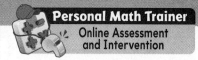

_____ centimeters

▶ **Classify Angles** Classify the angle. Write *acute, right,* or *obtuse*.

3.    _____

4. 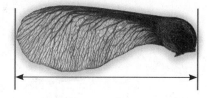   _____

5. 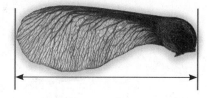   _____

▶ **Parts of a Whole** Write a fraction for each shaded part.

6. _____

7. _____

8. _____

9. _____

Math in the Real World

The Sunshine Skyway Bridge crosses over Tampa Bay, Florida. Bridges and other building structures can model geometric figures. Look at the bridge in the photo at the left. Describe the geometric figures you see. Then classify the labeled angles and triangle.

© Houghton Mifflin Harcourt Publishing Company • Image Credits: (b) ©Ilene MacDonald/Alamy; (tl) ©Photodisc/Getty Images; (tr) ©Emmanuel Lattes/Alamy

Vocabulary Builder

▶ **Visualize It** •

Complete the Bubble Map using review words.

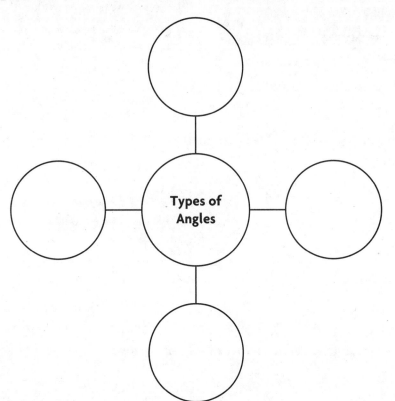

Review Words

acute

circle

obtuse

ray

right

straight

vertex

Preview Words

clockwise

counterclockwise

degree (°)

protractor

▶ **Understand Vocabulary** •

Draw a line to match each word with its definition.

1. protractor

2. degree(°)

3. clockwise

4. counterclockwise

- In the same direction in which the hands of a clock move

- In the opposite direction in which the hands of a clock move

- A tool for measuring the size of an angle

- The unit used for measuring angles

GO DIGITAL
• Interactive Student Edition
• Multimedia *eGlossary*

Chapter 11 Vocabulary

acute angle

ángulo agudo

1

clockwise

en el sentido de las manecillas del reloj

8

counterclockwise

en sentido contrario a las manecillas del reloj

17

degree (°)

grado (°)

21

protractor

transportador

73

ray

semirrecta

76

right angle

ángulo recto

81

vertex

vértice

95

In the same direction in which the hands of a clock move

An angle that measures greater than 0° and less than 90°

Example:

The unit used for measuring angles and temperatures

In the opposite direction in which the hands of a clock move

A part of a line; it has one endpoint and continues without end in one direction

K   L

A tool for measuring the size of an angle

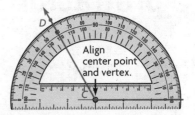

Align center point and vertex.

The point at which two rays of an angle meet or two (or more) line segments meet in a two-dimensional shape

vertex

An angle that forms a square corner

Example:

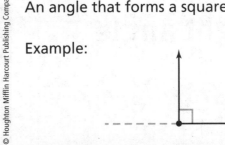

Picture It

Word Box

acute angle
clockwise
counterclockwise
degree(°)
protractor
ray
right angle
vertex

For 3 to 4 players

Materials

* timer
* sketch pad

How to Play

1. Take turns to play.
2. To take a turn, choose a word from the Word Box, but do not tell the word to the other players.
3. Set the timer for 1 minute.
4. Draw pictures and numbers on the sketch pad to give clues about the word. Do not use words.
5. The first player to guess the word before time runs out gets 1 point. If that player can use the word in a sentence, he or she gets 1 more point. Then that player gets a turn choosing a word.
6. The first player to score 10 points wins.

The Write Way

Reflect

Choose one idea. Write about it.

- Explain how to use a protractor to measure an angle or draw an angle.

- Illustrate and explain the difference between *clockwise* and *counterclockwise*. Use a separate piece of paper for your drawing.

- Write a creative story that includes a variety of angles.

Name _____

Angles and Fractional Parts of a Circle

Essential Question How can you relate angles and fractional parts of a circle?

Learning Objective You will use fraction circles to describe the relationship between the size of the fraction piece and the number of turns it takes to make a circle.

Investigate

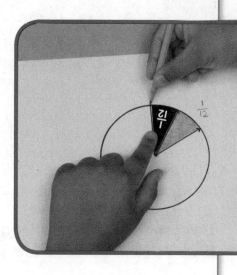

Materials ■ fraction circles

A. Place a $\frac{1}{12}$ piece on the circle. Place the tip of the fraction piece on the center of the circle. Trace the fraction piece to create an angle.

What parts of the fraction piece represent the rays

of the angle? _____

Where is the vertex of the angle?

_____

B. Shade the angle formed by the $\frac{1}{12}$ piece. Label it $\frac{1}{12}$.

C. Place the $\frac{1}{12}$ piece back on the shaded angle. Turn it counterclockwise. **Counterclockwise** is the direction opposite from the way the hands move on a clock.

Trace the fraction piece in its new position. How many twelfths have

you traced in all? _____ Label $\frac{2}{12}$.

D. Turn the fraction piece counterclockwise again and trace it. Label the total number of twelfths.

Continue until you reach the shaded angle.

How many times did you need to turn the $\frac{1}{12}$ piece to make a circle? _____

How many angles come together in the center of the circle? _____

Draw Conclusions

1. Compare the size of the angle formed by a $\frac{1}{4}$ piece and the size of the angle formed by a $\frac{1}{12}$ piece. Use a $\frac{1}{4}$ piece and your model on page 601 to help.

_____

_____

_____

2. Describe the relationship between the size of the fraction piece and the number of turns it takes to make a circle.

_____

_____

Make Connections

You can relate fractions and angles to the hands of a clock.

Let the hands of the clock represent the rays of an angle. Each 5-minute mark represents a $\frac{1}{12}$ turn **clockwise**.

15 minutes elapse.

The minute hand makes a

_____ turn clockwise.

30 minutes elapse.

The minute hand makes a

_____ turn clockwise.

45 minutes elapse.

The minute hand makes a

_____ turn clockwise.

60 minutes elapse.

The minute hand makes a

_____ turn clockwise.

Math Talk

Math Processes and Practices ❸

Compare Representations
How is an angle formed in a circle using a $\frac{1}{4}$ fraction piece like a $\frac{1}{4}$ turn and 15 minutes elapsing on a clock?

Name _____

Share and Show

Tell what fraction of the circle the shaded angle represents.

1.
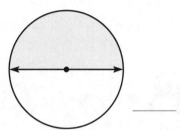
_____

2.
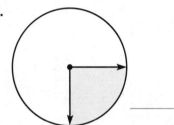
_____

3.
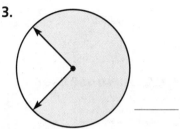
_____

4.
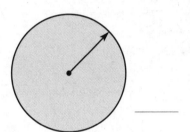
_____

5.
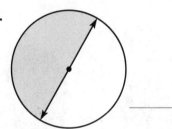
_____

6.
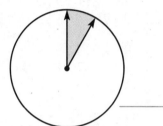
_____

Tell whether the angle on the circle shows a $\frac{1}{4}$, $\frac{1}{2}$, $\frac{3}{4}$, or 1 full turn clockwise or counterclockwise.

7.

_____

_____

8.
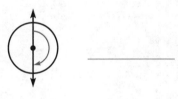
_____

_____

9.
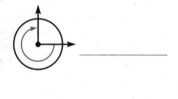
_____

_____

Problem Solving • Applications

10. **Math Processes and Practices ①** Susan watched the game from 1 P.M. to 1:30 P.M. **Describe** the turn the minute hand made.

_____

11. **GO DEEPER** Compare the angles in Exercises 1 and 5.
Does the position of the angle affect the size of the angle? Explain.

_____

_____

© Houghton Mifflin Harcourt Publishing Company

Chapter 11 • Lesson 1   603

12. **THINK SMARTER+** Malcolm drew this angle on the circle.
Which of the following describes the angle? Mark all that apply.

- ○ $\frac{3}{4}$ turn   ○ clockwise
- ○ $\frac{1}{4}$ turn   ○ counterclockwise

Sense or Nonsense?

13. **THINK SMARTER** Whose statement makes sense? Whose statement is nonsense? Explain your reasoning.

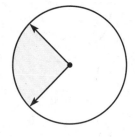

The shaded angle represents $\frac{3}{8}$ of the circle.

The shaded angle represents $\frac{1}{4}$ of the circle.

Carla's Statement	Adam's Statement

- For the statement that is nonsense, write a statement that makes sense.

_____

- What is another way to describe the size of the angle? Explain.

_____

Angles and Fractional Parts of a Circle

Learning Objective You will use fraction circles to describe the relationship between the size of the fraction piece and the number of turns it takes to make a circle.

Tell what fraction of the circle the shaded angle represents.

1.

$\dfrac{1}{4}$
_____

2.

_____

3.

_____

Tell whether the angle on the circle shows a $\frac{1}{4}$, $\frac{1}{2}$, $\frac{3}{4}$, or 1 full turn clockwise or counterclockwise.

4.

_____

_____

5.
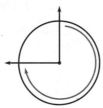

_____

_____

6.

_____

_____

Problem Solving *Real World*

7. Shelley exercised for 15 minutes. Describe the turn the minute hand made.

Start   End

_____

_____

8. **WRITE** *Math* Give a description of a $\frac{3}{4}$-turn of the minute hand on a clock face.

_____

_____

_____

_____

_____

_____

Lesson Check

1. What fraction of the circle does the shaded angle represent?

_____

_____

2. Describe the turn shown below.

_____

_____

Spiral Review

3. Write $\frac{2}{3}$ and $\frac{3}{4}$ as a pair of fractions with a common denominator.

_____

_____

4. Raymond bought $\frac{3}{4}$ of a dozen rolls. How many rolls did he buy?

_____

_____

5. List all the factors of 18.

6. Jonathan rode 1.05 miles on Friday, 1.5 miles on Saturday, 1.25 miles on Monday, and 1.1 miles on Tuesday. On which day did he ride the shortest distance?

_____

_____

FOR MORE PRACTICE
GO TO THE
Personal Math Trainer

Name _____

Degrees

Essential Question How are degrees related to fractional parts of a circle?

Learning Objective You will use fractional parts to find angle measures and relate them to turns through a circle.

CONNECT You can use what you know about angles and fractional parts of a circle to understand angle measurement. Angles are measured in units called **degrees**. Think of a circle divided into 360 equal parts. An angle that turns through $\frac{1}{360}$ of the circle measures 1 degree.

> **Math Idea**
> The symbol for degrees is °.

🔑 Unlock the Problem 🌎 Real World

The angle between two spokes on the bicycle wheel turns through $\frac{10}{360}$ of a circle. What is the measure of the angle formed between the spokes?

> • What part of an angle does a spoke represent?
>
> _____
>
> _____

🔒 Example 1 Use fractional parts to find the angle measure.

Each $\frac{1}{360}$ turn measures _____ degree.

Ten $\frac{1}{360}$ turns measure _____ degrees.

So, the measure of the angle between the spokes is _____.

 Math Talk

Math Processes and Practices ②

Reason Abstractly How many degrees is the measure of an angle that turns through 1 whole circle? Explain.

▲ The Penny Farthing bicycle was built in the 1800s.

🔓 Example 2 Find the measure of a right angle.

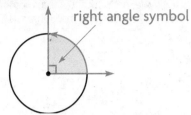

right angle symbol

Think: Through what fraction of a circle

does a right angle turn? _____

STEP 1 Write $\frac{1}{4}$ as an equivalent fraction with 360 in the denominator.

$$\frac{1}{4} = \frac{\boxed{}}{360}$$

Think: $4 \times 9 = 36$, so $4 \times$ _____ $= 360$.

Remember

To write an equivalent fraction, multiply the numerator and denominator by the same factor.

STEP 2 Write $\frac{90}{360}$ in degrees.

An angle that turns through $\frac{1}{360}$ of a circle measures _____.

An angle that turns through $\frac{90}{360}$ of a circle measures _____.

So, a right angle measures _____.

Try This! Find the measure of a straight angle.

Through what fraction of a circle does a straight angle turn? _____

Write $\frac{1}{2}$ as an equivalent fraction with 360 in the denominator.

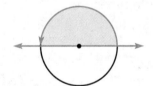

$$\frac{1}{2} = \frac{\boxed{}}{360}$$

Think: $2 \times 18 = 36$, so $2 \times$ _____ $= 360$.

So, a straight angle measures _____.

1. How can you describe the measure of an acute angle in degrees?

_____

_____

2. How can you describe the measure of an obtuse angle in degrees?

_____

Name _____

1. Find the measure of the angle.

Through what fraction of a circle does the angle turn? _____

$\dfrac{1}{3} = \dfrac{}{360}$ Think: 3 × 12 = 36, so 3 × _____ = 360.

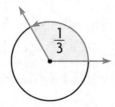

So, the measure of the angle is _____.

Tell the measure of the angle in degrees.

☑ **2.**

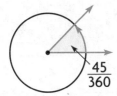

$\dfrac{45}{360}$

_____

☑ **3.**

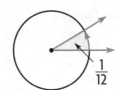

$\dfrac{1}{12}$

_____

Math Talk | Math Processes and Practices ⑥

If an angle measures 60°, through what fraction of a circle does it turn? **Explain.**

On Your Own

Tell the measure of the angle in degrees.

4.

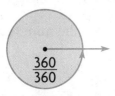

$\dfrac{360}{360}$

_____

5.

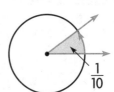

$\dfrac{1}{10}$

_____

Classify the angle. Write *acute, obtuse, right,* or *straight.*

6.

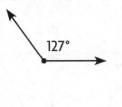

127°

_____

7.

_____

8.

37°

_____

9.

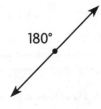

180°

_____

10. Math Processes and Practices ⑥ Is this an obtuse angle? **Explain.**

_____

_____

_____

11. GO DEEPER Alex cut a circular pizza into 8 equal slices. He removed 2 of the slices of pizza. What is the measure of the angle made by the missing slices of pizza?

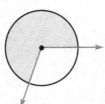

_____

Unlock the Problem (Real World)

12. **THINK SMARTER** Ava started reading at 3:30 P.M. She stopped for a snack at 4:15 P.M. During this time, through what fraction of a circle did the minute hand turn? How many degrees did the minute hand turn?

a. What are you asked to find? _____

_____

b. What information can you use to find the fraction of a circle through which the minute hand turned?

_____

_____

c. How can you use the fraction of a circle through which the minute hand turned to find how many degrees it turned?

_____

_____

d. Show the steps to solve the problem.

STEP 1 $\dfrac{3 \times \boxed{}}{4 \times } = \dfrac{?}{360}$

STEP 2 $\dfrac{3 \times 90}{4 \times 90} = \dfrac{\boxed{}}{360}$

e. Complete the sentences.

From 3:30 P.M. to 4:15 P.M., the minute hand

made a _____ turn clockwise.

The minute hand turned _____ degrees.

13. **THINK SMARTER** An angle represents $\frac{1}{15}$ of a circle. Select the number to show how to find the measure of the angle in degrees.

$\dfrac{1}{15} = \dfrac{1 \times \boxed{}}{15 \times \boxed{}} = \dfrac{\boxed{}}{360}$

| 20 |
| 24 |
| 30 |

The angle measures _____.

Degrees

Learning Objective You will use fractional parts to find angle measures and relate them to turns through a circle.

Tell the measure of the angle in degrees.

1.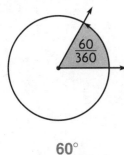

   $\dfrac{60}{360}$

   _____60°_____

2.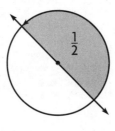

   $\dfrac{1}{2}$

   _____

3.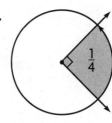

   $\dfrac{1}{4}$

   _____

Classify the angle. Write *acute, obtuse, right,* or *straight*.

4.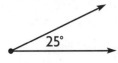

   25°

   _____

5.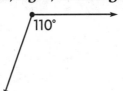

   110°

   _____

6.

   60°

   _____

7.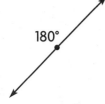

   180°

   _____

8.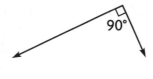

   90°

   _____

9.

   50°

   _____

Problem Solving Real World

Ann started reading at 4:00 P.M. and finished at 4:20 P.M.

10. Through what fraction of a circle did the minute hand turn?

    _____

Start

End

11. **WRITE** ▸*Math* Give an example from everyday life of an angle that measures 90 degrees.

    _____

    _____

Lesson Check

1. What kind of angle is shown?

180°

_____

2. How many degrees are in an angle that turns through $\frac{1}{4}$ of a circle?

_____

Spiral Review

3. Mae bought 15 football cards and 18 baseball cards. She separated them into 3 equal groups. How many sports cards are in each group?

_____

4. Each part of a race is $\frac{1}{10}$ mile long. Marsha finished 5 parts of the race. How far did Marsha race?

_____

5. Jeff said his city got $\frac{11}{3}$ inches of snow. Write this fraction as a mixed number.

_____

6. Amy ran $\frac{3}{4}$ mile. Write the distance Amy ran as a decimal.

_____

FOR MORE PRACTICE
GO TO THE
Personal Math Trainer

Name _____

Measure and Draw Angles

Essential Question How can you use a protractor to measure and draw angles?

Learning Objective You will measure and draw angles in whole-number degrees using appropriate tools and draw angles with a given measure.

Unlock the Problem

Emma wants to make a clay sculpture of her daughter as she appears in the photo from her dance recital. How can she measure ∠DCE, or the angle formed by her daughter's arms?

A **protractor** is a tool for measuring the size of an angle.

Activity Measure ∠DCE using a protractor.

Materials ■ protractor

STEP 1 Place the center point of the protractor on vertex C of the angle.

_____

STEP 2 Align the 0° mark on the scale of the protractor with ray CE.

_____

STEP 3 Find where ray CD intersects the same scale. Read the angle measure on that scale. Extend the ray if you need to.

m∠DCE = _____   Read m∠DCE as "the measure of angle DCE".

So, the angle formed by Emma's daughter's

arms is _____.

Align center point and vertex.

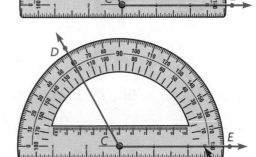

Align bottom ray and 0°.

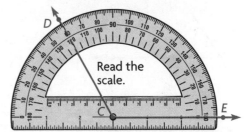

Read the scale.

Math Talk

Math Processes and Practices ⑤

Use Appropriate Tools Can you line up either ray of the angle with the protractor when measuring? Explain.

Draw Angles You can also use a protractor to draw an angle of a given measure.

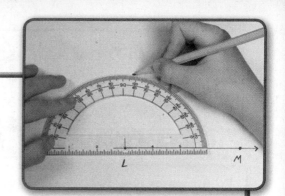

> ## 🔓 Activity Draw ∠*KLM* with a measure of 82°.
> **Materials** ■ protractor
>
> **STEP 1** Use the straight edge of the protractor to draw and label ray *LM*.
>
> ---
>
> **STEP 2** Place the center point of the protractor on point *L*. Align ray *LM* with the 0° mark on the protractor.
>
> ---
>
> **STEP 3** Using the same scale, mark a point at 82°. Label the point *K*.
>
> ---
>
> **STEP 4** Use the straight edge of the protractor to draw ray *LK*.

Share and Show MATH BOARD

1. Measure ∠*ABC*.

   Place the center of the protractor on point _____.

   Align ray *BC* with _____.

   Read where _____ intersects the same scale.

   So, m∠*ABC* is _____.

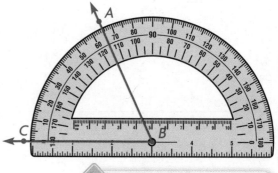

> **⚠ ERROR Alert**
>
> Be sure to use the correct scale on the protractor. Ask yourself: Is the measure reasonable?

Use a protractor to find the angle measure.

2.

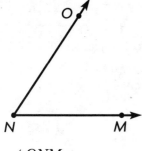

m∠*ONM* = _____

☑3.

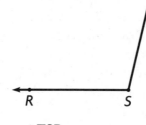

m∠*TSR* = _____

Use a protractor to draw the angle.

4. 170°

☑5. 78°

> **Math Talk** Math Processes and Practices ⑥
>
> **Describe** how drawing and measuring angles are similar.

© Houghton Mifflin Harcourt Publishing Company • Image Credits: (t) ©Houghton Mifflin Harcourt

Name _____

Use a protractor to find the angle measure.

6.

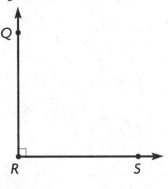

m∠QRS = _____

7.

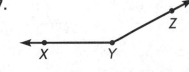

m∠XYZ = _____

Use a protractor to draw the angle.

8. 115°

9. 67°

Draw an example of each. Label the angle with its measure.

10. an acute angle

11. an obtuse angle

12. **GO DEEPER** Elizabeth is making a quilt with scraps of fabric. What is the difference between m∠ABC and m∠DEF?

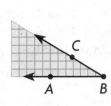
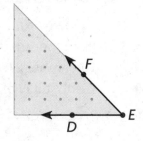

_____

13. **THINK SMARTER** Draw an angle with a measure of 0°. Describe your drawing.

_____

_____

Problem Solving • Applications

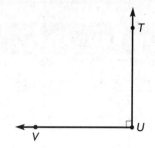

14. **GO DEEPER** Hadley wants to divide this angle into three angles with equal measure. What will the measure of each angle be?

_____

15. **Math Processes and Practices 6** Tracy measured an angle as 50° that was actually 130°. **Explain** her error.

_____

_____

16. **THINK SMARTER** Choose the word and angle measure to complete a true statement about ∠QRS.

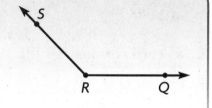

∠QRS is a(n) | acute / obtuse / right | angle that has a measure of | 45°. / 115°. / 135°.

Connect to Science

Earth's Axis

Earth revolves around the sun yearly. The Northern Hemisphere is the half of Earth that is north of the equator. The seasons of the year are due to the tilt of Earth's axis.

Use the diagrams and a protractor for 17–18.

Northern Hemisphere

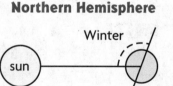

17. In the Northern Hemisphere, Earth's axis is tilted away from the sun on the first day of winter, which is often on December 21. What is the measure of the marked angle on the first day of winter, the shortest day of the year?

_____

18. Earth's axis is not tilted away from or toward the sun on the first days of spring and fall, which are often on March 20 and September 22. What is the measure of the marked angle on the first day of spring or fall?

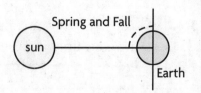

Measure and Draw Angles

Learning Objective You will measure and draw angles in whole-number degrees using appropriate tools and draw angles with a given measure.

Use a protractor to find the angle measure.

1.
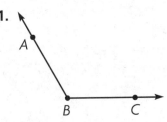

m∠ABC = _____**120°**_____

2.
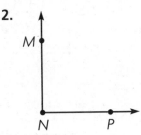

m∠MNP = _____

3.

R

S   T

m∠RST = _____

Use a protractor to draw the angle.

4. 40°

5. 170°

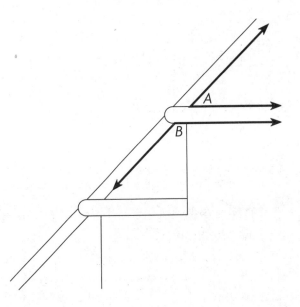

Problem Solving Real World

The drawing shows the angles a stair tread makes with a support board along a wall. Use your protractor to measure the angles.

6. What is the measure of ∠A? _____

7. What is the measure of ∠B? _____

8. **WRITE** ▸ *Math* Find an angle at home. Measure the angle. Record the measure. Classify the angle.

_____

_____

_____

Lesson Check

1. What is the measure of ∠*ABC*?

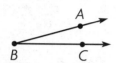

2. What is the measure of ∠*XYZ*?

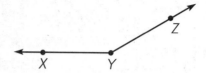

Spiral Review

3. Derrick earned $1,472 during the 4 weeks he had his summer job. If he earned the same amount each week, how much did he earn each week?

4. Arthur baked $1\frac{7}{12}$ dozen muffins. Nina baked $1\frac{1}{12}$ dozen muffins. How many dozen muffins did they bake?

5. Trisha drew the figure below. What figure did she draw?

6. Measure and describe the turn shown by the angle. Be sure to tell about the size and direction of the turn.

FOR MORE PRACTICE GO TO THE Personal Math Trainer

Name _____

 **Mid-Chapter Checkpoint**

Personal Math Trainer
Online Assessment
and Intervention

Vocabulary

Choose the best term from the box.

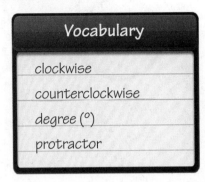

Vocabulary
clockwise
counterclockwise
degree (°)
protractor

1. The unit used to measure an angle is called

   a _____. (p. 607)

2. _____ is the opposite of the
   direction in which the hands of a clock move. (p. 601)

3. A _____ is a tool for measuring the size
   of an angle. (p. 613)

Concepts and Skills

Tell whether the angle on the circle shows a $\frac{1}{4}$, $\frac{1}{2}$, $\frac{3}{4}$, or 1 full turn
clockwise or counterclockwise.

4.

5.

6.

7.

_____ _____ _____ _____

_____ _____ _____ _____

Tell the measure of the angle in degrees.

8.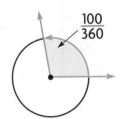

$\frac{100}{360}$

_____

9.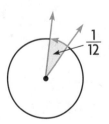

$\frac{1}{12}$

_____

Use a protractor to draw the angle.

10. 75°

11. 127°

12. Phillip watched a beach volleyball game from 1:45 P.M. to 2:00 P.M. How many degrees did the minute hand turn?

_____

13. What angle does this piece of pie form?

_____

14. What is m∠CBT? Use a protractor to help you.

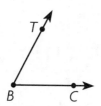

_____

_____

15. **GO DEEPER** Matt cut a circle into 8 equal sections. He drew an angle that measures the same as the total measure of 3 of the sections in the circle. What is the measure of the angle Matt drew?

_____

© Houghton Mifflin Harcourt Publishing Company

Name _____

Join and Separate Angles

Essential Question How can you determine the measure of an angle separated into parts?

Learning Objective You will draw and cut out angles to determine the measure of angles separated into parts and write the measure of the angles in a circle as a sum.

Investigate

Materials ■ construction paper ■ scissors ■ protractor

A. Use construction paper. Draw an angle that measures exactly 70°. Label it ∠ABC.

B. Cut out ∠ABC.

C. Separate ∠ABC by cutting it into two parts. Begin cutting at the vertex and cut between the rays.

What figures did you form? _____

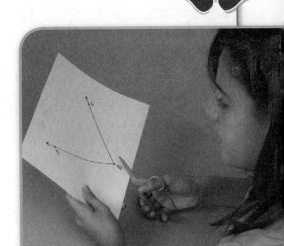

D. Use a protractor to measure the two angles you formed.

Record the measures. _____

E. Find the sum of the angles you formed.

_____ + _____ = _____
part + part = whole

Math Idea

You can think of ∠ABC as the whole and the two angles you formed as the parts of the whole.

F. Join the two angles. Compare m∠ABC to the sum of the measures of its parts. Explain how they compare.

_____

_____

_____

_____

Draw Conclusions

1. What if you cut ∠ABC into two different angles? What can you conclude about the sum of the measures of these two angles? Explain.

_____

_____

_____

2. **THINK SMARTER** Seth cut ∠ABC into 3 parts. Draw a model that shows two different ways he could have separated his angle.

3. Write a sentence that compares the measure of an angle to the sum of its parts.

_____

_____

Make Connections

Materials ■ protractor

You can write the measure of the angles shown in a circle as a sum.

STEP 1 Use a protractor to find the measure of each angle.
_____

STEP 2 Label each angle with its measure.
_____

STEP 3 Write the sum of the angle measures as an equation.

_____ + _____ + _____ = _____
 part + part + part = whole

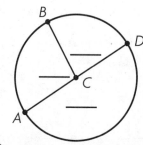

Math Talk Math Processes and Practices ⑥

Use Math Vocabulary
Describe the angles shown in the circle above using the words *whole* and *part*.

Name _____

Add to find the measure of the angle. Write an equation to record your work.

1.
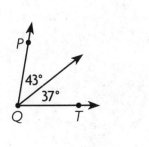

m∠PQT = _____

2.
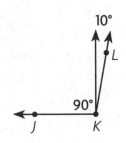

m∠JKL = _____

3.
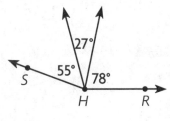

m∠RHS = _____

Use a protractor to find the measure of each angle. Label each angle with its measure.
Write the sum of the angle measures as an equation.

4.
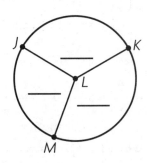

_____

5.
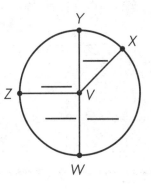

_____

6. Math Processes and Practices 4 **Use Diagrams** What is m∠QRT?

7. GO DEEPER Look back at Exercise 1. Suppose you joined an angle measuring 10° to ∠PQT. Draw the new angle, showing all three parts. What type of angle is formed?

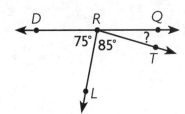

Unlock the Problem

8. **THINK SMARTER** Stephanie, Kay, and Shane each ate an equal-sized piece of a pizza. The measure of the angle of each piece was 45°. When the pieces were together, what is the measure of the angle they formed?

a. What are you asked to find? _____

_____

b. What information do you need to use? _____

_____

_____

c. Tell how you can use addition to solve the problem. _____

_____

_____

_____

d. Complete the sentence. The three pieces of pizza formed a _____ angle.

9. What is the measure of ∠XZW? Write an equation to record your work.

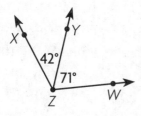

10. **THINK SMARTER** ✛ What is m∠PRS? Use equations to explain and check your answer.

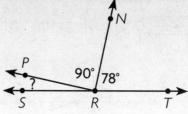

_____

_____

_____

_____

_____

Join and Separate Angles

Learning Objective You will draw and cut out angles to determine the measure of angles separated into parts and write the measure of the angles in a circle as a sum.

Add to find the measure of the angle. Write an equation to record your work.

1.
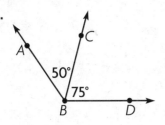

$50° + 75° = 125°$
_____

m∠ABD = ___125°___

2.
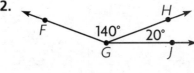

_____

m∠FGJ = _____

3.
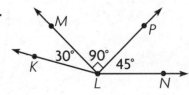

_____

m∠KLN = _____

Use a protractor to find the measure of each angle in the circle.

4. m∠ABC = _____

5. m∠DBE = _____

6. m∠CBD = _____

7. m∠EBA = _____

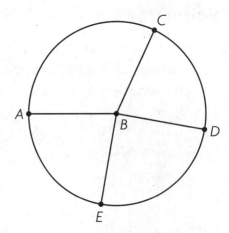

 Problem Solving (Real World)

8. Ned made the design at the right. Use a protractor. Find and write the measure of each of the 3 angles.

_____

9. Write an equation to find the measure of the total angle.

_____

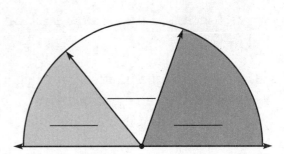

10. **WRITE** ▸ Math How can you use addition and subtraction to put together and separate measures of an angle and its parts?

_____

_____

Lesson Check

1. What is the measure of ∠*WXZ*?

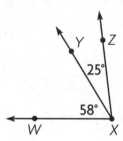

_____

2. Write an equation that you can use to find the m∠*MNQ*.

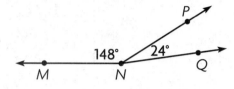

_____

Spiral Review

3. Joe bought 6 packages of envelopes. Each package contains 125 envelopes. How many envelopes did he buy?

_____

4. Bill hiked $\frac{3}{10}$ mile on the Lake Trail. Then he hiked $\frac{5}{10}$ mile on the Rock Trail to get back to where he started. How many miles did he hike?

_____

5. Ron drew a quadrilateral with 4 right angles and 4 sides with the same length. What figure best describes his quadrilateral?

_____

6. How many degrees are in an angle that turns through $\frac{3}{4}$ of a circle?

_____

FOR MORE PRACTICE
GO TO THE
Personal Math Trainer

Name _____

Problem Solving • Unknown Angle Measures

Essential Question How can you use the strategy *draw a diagram* to solve angle measurement problems?

Learning Objective You will use the strategy *draw a diagram* to solve angle measurement problems by drawing a bar model and writing an equation.

 Unlock the Problem Real World

Mr. Tran is cutting a piece of kitchen tile as shown at the right. He needs tiles with 45° angles to make a design. After the cut, what is the angle measure of the part left over? Can Mr. Tran use both pieces in the design?

Use the graphic organizer below to solve the problem.

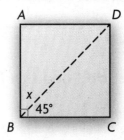

Read the Problem

What do I need to find?	**What information do I need to use?**	**How will I use the information?**
I need to find _____ _____	I can use the measures of the angles I know. _____ _____	I can draw a bar model and use the information to _____ _____

Solve the Problem

I can draw a bar model to represent the problem.
Then I can write an equation to solve the problem.

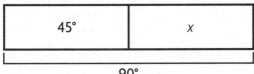

$$m\angle ABD + m\angle CBD = m\angle ABC$$

$$x + \underline{\quad\quad} = \underline{\quad\quad}$$

$$x = \underline{\quad\quad}$$

The $m\angle ABD =$ _____.

Since both tiles measure _____, Mr. Tran can use both pieces in the design.

 Math Talk Math Processes and Practices ④

Write an Equation What other equation can you write to solve the problem? Explain.

© Houghton Mifflin Harcourt Publishing Company

Chapter 11 627

🔑 Try Another Problem

Marisol is building a frame for a sandbox, but the boards she has are too short. She must join two boards together to build a side as shown. At what angle did she cut the first board?

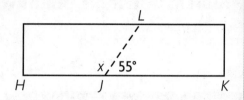

Read the Problem

What do I need to find?	What information do I need to use?	How will I use the information?

Solve the Problem

- Explain how you can check the answer to the problem.

_____

_____

Name _____

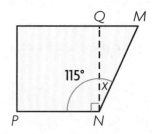

1. Laura cuts a square out of scrap paper as shown. What is the angle measure of the piece left over?

First, draw a bar model to represent the problem.

Next, write the equation you need to solve.

_____

_____

Last, find the angle measure of the piece left over.

m∠MNQ = _____

So, the angle measure of the piece left over is _____.

2. Jackie trimmed a piece of scrap metal to make a straight edge as shown. What is the measure of the piece she trimmed off?

_____

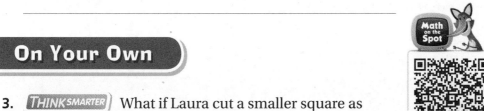

On Your Own

3. **THINK SMARTER** What if Laura cut a smaller square as shown? Would m∠MNQ be different? Explain.

_____

_____

_____

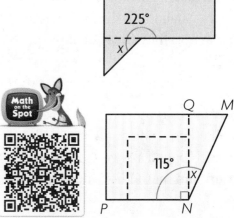

4. **GO DEEPER** The map shows Marco's paper route. When Marco turns right onto Center Street from Main Street, what degree turn does he make? **Hint:** Draw a dashed line to extend Oak Street to form a 180° angle.

_____

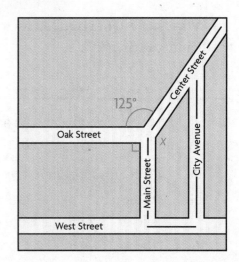

Problem Solving • Applications

5. **Math Processes and Practices ④ Write an Equation** Two angles form a straight angle. One angle measures 89°. What is the measure of the other angle? Explain.

_____

_____

_____

6. **Pose a Problem** Look back at Problem 5. Write a similar problem about two angles that form a right angle.

_____

_____

_____

WRITE ▸*Math* • **Show Your Work**

7. **GO DEEPER** Sam paid $20 for two T-shirts. The price of each T-shirt was a multiple of 5. What are the possible prices of the T-shirts?

_____

8. **GO DEEPER** Zayna has 3 boxes with 15 art books in each box. She has 2 bags with 11 math books in each bag. If she gives 30 books away, how many art and math books does she have left?

_____

9. **What's the Question?** It measures greater than 0° and less than 90°.

_____

10. **THINK SMARTER** Two angles, $\angle A$ and $\angle B$, form a straight angle. $\angle A$ measures 65°. For numbers 10a–10c, select True or False for the statement.

10a. $\angle B$ is an acute angle. ○ True ○ False

10b. The equation $180° - 65° = x°$ can be used to find the measure of $\angle B$. ○ True ○ False

10c. The measure of $\angle B$ is 125°. ○ True ○ False

Problem Solving • Unknown
Angle Measures

Learning Objective You will use the strategy *draw a diagram* to solve angle measurement problems by drawing a bar model and writing an equation.

Solve each problem. Draw a diagram to help.

1. Wayne is building a birdhouse. He is cutting a board as shown. What is the angle measure of the piece left over?

   Draw a bar model to represent the problem.

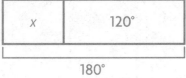

   $$x + 120° = 180°$$
   $$x = 180° - 120°$$
   $$x = 60°$$

   180°

   _____ 60° _____

2. An artist is cutting a piece of metal as shown. What is the angle measure of the piece left over?

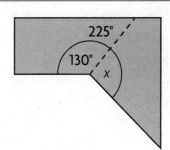

   _____

3. **WRITE** ▸*Math* Give one example of when you would draw a diagram to solve an angle measurement problem.

   _____

   _____

   _____

   _____

Lesson Check

1. Angelo cuts a triangle from a sheet of paper as shown. What is the measure of ∠x in the triangle?

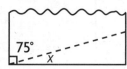

75°
x

2. Cindy cuts a piece of wood as shown. What is the angle measure of the piece left over?

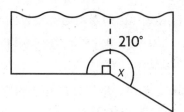

210°
x

Spiral Review

3. Tyronne worked 21 days last month. He earned $79 each day. How much did Tyronne earn last month?

4. Meg inline skated for $\frac{7}{10}$ mile. Write this distance as a decimal.

5. Kerry ran $\frac{3}{4}$ mile. Sherrie ran $\frac{1}{2}$ mile. Marcie ran $\frac{2}{3}$ mile. List the friends in order from who ran the least distance to who ran the greatest distance.

6. What is the measure of ∠ABC?

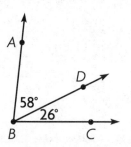

A
D
58°
26°
B
C

FOR MORE PRACTICE
GO TO THE
Personal Math Trainer

Name _____

1. An angle represents $\frac{1}{12}$ of a circle. Use the numbers to show how to find the measure of the angle in degrees.

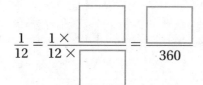

$$\frac{1}{12} = \frac{1 \times \boxed{}}{12 \times \boxed{}} = \frac{\boxed{}}{360}$$

The angle measure is _____.

| 24 |

| 30 |

| 36 |

2. Match the measure of each ∠C with the measure of ∠D that forms a straight angle.

∠C   ∠D

                   ●145°

122° ●   ● 75°

35° ●   ●148°

62° ●   ● 58°

105° ●   ● 55°

                 ●118°

3. Katie drew an obtuse angle. Which could be the measure of the angle she drew? Mark all that apply.

  (A) 35°   (C) 180°

  (B) 157°   (D) 92°

4. Draw an angle that represents a $\frac{1}{4}$ turn counterclockwise on the circle.

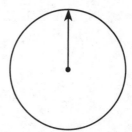

GO DIGITAL   Assessment Options
Chapter Test

5. Renee drew the figure shown. For 5a–5c, select Yes or No to tell whether the statement is true.

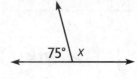

5a. The measure of a straight angle is 180°.　　　○ Yes　　　○ No

5b. To find the measure of x, Renee can subtract 75° from 180°.　　　○ Yes　　　○ No

5c. The measure of x is 115°.　　　○ Yes　　　○ No

6. **THINK SMARTER +** Trey drew this figure with a protractor.

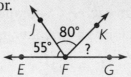

Part A

Write an equation that can be used to find m∠KFG.

Part B

What is the measure of ∠KFG? Describe how you solved the equation and how you can check your answer.

7. Use a protractor to find the measure of the angle.

The angle measures _____.

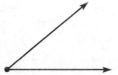

Name _____

8. Alex drew this angle on the circle.
   Which describes the angle?
   Mark all that apply.

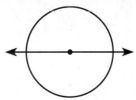

   (A) $\frac{1}{4}$ turn

   (B) $\frac{1}{2}$ turn

   (C) clockwise

   (D) counterclockwise

9. Miles has a piece of paper that is $\frac{1}{4}$ of a large circle.
   He cuts the paper into three equal parts from the
   center point of the circle. What is the angle
   measure of each part?

   The angle measures _____.

10. Use a protractor to find the measure of each
    angle. Write each angle and its measure in
    a box ordered by the measure of the angles
    from least to greatest.

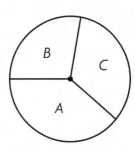

Angle:	Angle:	Angle:
Measure:	Measure:	Measure:

11. Use the numbers and symbols to write an equation that can be
    used to find the measure of the unknown angle.

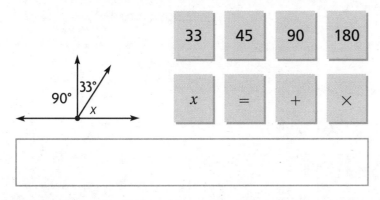

33	45	90	180
x	=	+	×

   _____

   What is the measure of the unknown angle? _____

12. Choose the word and angle measure to complete a true statement about ∠JKL.

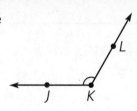

∠JKL is a(n)

| acute |
| obtuse |
| right |

angle that has a measure of

| 60°. |
| 120°. |
| 135°. |

13. Vince began practicing piano at 5:15 P.M. He stopped at 5:35 P.M. How many degrees did the minute hand turn during Vince's practice time? Explain how you found your answer.

Start

Stop

14. An angle measures 125°. Through what fraction of a circle does the angle turn?

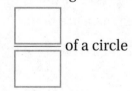 of a circle

15. Write the letter for each angle measure in the correct box.

Ⓐ 125°   Ⓑ 90°   Ⓒ 180°   Ⓓ 30°   Ⓔ 45°   Ⓕ 95°

| acute | obtuse | right | straight |
| | | | |

Name _____

16. For numbers 16a–16b, select the fraction
that makes a true statement about the figure.

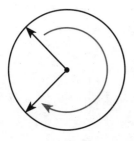

Figure 1   Figure 2

16a.   The angle in Figure 1 represents a

| $\frac{1}{4}$ |
| $\frac{1}{2}$ |
| $\frac{3}{4}$ |

turn.

16b.   The angle in Figure 2 represents a

| $\frac{1}{4}$ |
| $\frac{1}{2}$ |
| $\frac{3}{4}$ |

turn.

17. **GO DEEPER**   Melanie cuts a rectangle out of a piece of
scrap paper as shown. She wants to calculate the angle
measure of the piece that is left over.

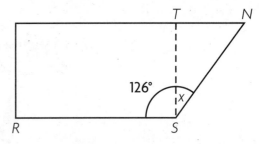

Part A

Draw a bar model to represent the problem.

Part B

Write and solve an equation to find x.

The angle measures _____.

18. Two angles, $\angle A$ and $\angle B$, form a right angle. $\angle A$ measures 32°. For numbers 18a–18c, select True or False for the statement.

18a.　$\angle B$ is an acute angle.　　　　○ True　　○ False

18b.　The equation $180° - 32° = x°$　　○ True　　○ False
　　　　can be used to find the
　　　　measure of $\angle B$.

18c.　The measure of $\angle B$ is 58°.　　○ True　　○ False

19. A circle is divided into parts. Which sum could represent the angle measures that make up the circle? Mark all that apply.

Ⓐ　$120° + 120° + 120° + 120°$

Ⓑ　$25° + 40° + 80° + 105° + 110°$

Ⓒ　$33° + 82° + 111° + 50° + 84°$

Ⓓ　$40° + 53° + 72° + 81° + 90° + 34°$

20. Use a protractor to find the measures of the unknown angles.

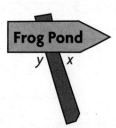

m$\angle x =$ _____　　　　　　　m$\angle y =$ _____

What do you notice about the measures of the unknown angles? Is this what you would have expected? Explain your reasoning.

Chapter 12 Relative Sizes of Measurement Units

 Show What You Know

Personal Math Trainer
Online Assessment
and Intervention

Check your understanding of important skills.

Name _____

▶ **Time to the Half Hour** **Read the clock. Write the time.**

1.
_____

2.
_____

3.
_____

▶ **Multiply by 1-Digit Numbers** **Find the product.**

4. 84
$\times$ 7

5. 536
$\times$ 8

6. 748
$\times$ 5

7. 2,524
$\times$ 2

8. 360
$\times$ 9

9. 296
$\times$ 3

10. $1,428
$\times$ 4

11. 64
$\times$ 5

Math in the Real World

A team was given a bucket of water and a sponge. The team had 1 minute to fill an empty half-gallon bucket with water using only the sponge. The line plot shows the amount of water squeezed into the bucket. Did the team squeeze enough water to fill the half-gallon bucket?

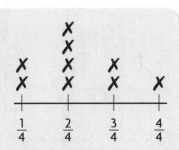

Amount of Water Squeezed into the Bucket (in cups)

Vocabulary Builder

▶ **Visualize It** •

Complete the Brain Storming diagram by using words with a ✓.

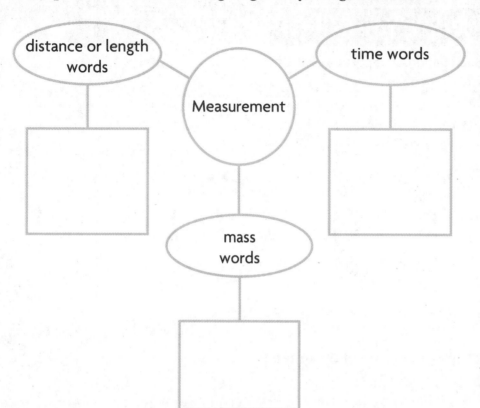

distance or length words

time words

Measurement

mass words

▶ **Understand Vocabulary** •

Draw a line to match each word with its definition.

1. decimeter

2. second

3. fluid ounce

4. ton

5. line plot

• A customary unit for measuring liquid volume

• A graph that shows the frequency of data along a number line

• A customary unit used to measure weight

• A small unit of time

• A metric unit for measuring length or distance

GO DIGITAL

• Interactive Student Edition
• Multimedia eGlossary

Chapter 12 Vocabulary

cup (c)

taza (tz)

18

fluid ounce (fl oz)

onza fluida (fl oz)

34

gallon (gal)

galón (gal)

37

half gallon

medio galón

38

kilometer (km)

kilómetro (km)

44

line plot

diagrama de puntos

47

liquid volume

volumen de un líquido

49

mile (mi)

milla (mi)

51

A customary unit used to measure liquid capacity and liquid volume

1 cup = 8 fluid ounces

A customary unit used to measure capacity and liquid volume
1 cup = 8 ounces

A customary unit for measuring capacity and liquid volume
1 half gallon = 2 quarts

 1 half gallon

A customary unit for measuring capacity and liquid volume
1 gallon = 4 quarts

 1 gallon

A graph that records each piece of data on a number line

Example:

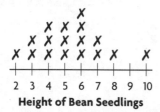

Height of Bean Seedlings

A metric unit for measuring length or distance
1 kilometer = 1,000 meters

A customary unit for measuring length or distance
1 mile = 5,280 feet

The measure of the space a liquid occupies

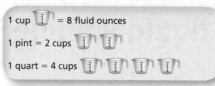

1 cup = 8 fluid ounces
1 pint = 2 cups
1 quart = 4 cups

Metric Units of Liquid Volume
1 liter (L) = 1,000 milliliters (mL)

milliliter (mL)

mililitro (mL)

52

millimeter (mm)

milímetro (mm)

53

ounce (oz)

onza (oz)

58

pint (pt)

pinta (pt)

67

pound (lb)

libra (lb)

70

quart (qt)

cuarto (ct)

74

second (sec)

segundo (seg)

83

ton (T)

tonelada (t)

92

A metric unit for measuring length or distance
1 centimeter = 10 millimeters

A metric unit for measuring capacity and liquid volume
1 liter = 1,000 milliliters

1 milliliter

A customary unit for measuring capacity and liquid volume
1 pint = 2 cups

1 pint

A customary unit for measuring weight
1 pound = 16 ounces

about 1 ounce

A customary unit for measuring capacity and liquid volume
1 quart = 2 pints

A customary unit for measuring weight
1 pound = 16 ounces

about 1 pound

A customary unit used to measure weight
1 ton = 2,000 pounds

about 1 ton

A small unit of time
1 minute = 60 seconds

1 second

Bingo

For 3 to 6 players

Materials

- 1 set of word cards
- 1 Bingo board for each player
- game markers

How to Play

1. The caller chooses a card and reads the definition. Then the caller puts the card in a second pile.

2. Players put a marker on the word that matches the definition each time they find it on their Bingo boards.

3. Repeat Steps 1 and 2 until a player marks 5 boxes in a line going down, across, or on a slant and calls "Bingo."

4. Check the answers. Have the player who said "Bingo" read the words aloud while the caller checks the definitions on the cards in the second pile.

Word Box
cup
fluid ounce
gallon
half gallon
kilometer
line plot
liquid volume
mile
milliliter
millimeter
ounce
pint
pound
quart
second
ton

The Write Way

Reflect

Choose one idea. Write about it.

- Do 50 milliliters and 50 millimeters represent the same amount? Explain why or why not.
- Write a paragraph that uses at least three of these words.

  cup   mile   pound   second   ton
- Explain what is most important to understand about line plots.

Name _____

Measurement Benchmarks

Essential Question How can you use benchmarks to understand the relative sizes of measurement units?

Learning Objective You will use benchmark customary and metric units to understand the relative sizes of measurement units.

⚷ Unlock the Problem (Real World)

Jake says the length of his bike is about four yards. Use the benchmark units below to determine if Jake's statement is reasonable.

Customary Units of Length			
1 in. about 1 inch	E45 4PM ⌐ 1 ft ⌐ about 1 foot	⌐ 1 yd ⌐ about 1 yard	1 mile in about 20 minutes

A **mile** is a customary unit for measuring length or distance. The benchmark shows the distance you can walk in about 20 minutes.

A baseball bat is about one yard long. Since Jake's bike is shorter than four times the length of a baseball bat, his bike is shorter than four yards long.

So, Jake's statement _____ reasonable.

Jake's bike is about _____ baseball bats long.

⚷ Example 1 Use the benchmark customary units.

Customary Units of Liquid Volume				
1 cup = 8 fluid ounces	1 pint	1 quart	1 half gallon	1 gallon

- About how much liquid is in a mug of hot chocolate? _____

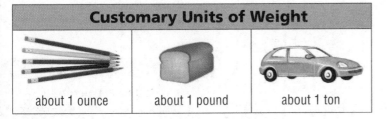

Customary Units of Weight		
about 1 ounce	about 1 pound	about 1 ton

Math Talk Math Processes and Practices ②

Use Reasoning Use benchmarks to explain how you would order the units of weight from heaviest to lightest.

- About how much does a grapefruit weigh? _____

© Houghton Mifflin Harcourt Publishing Company • Image Credits: (tr) ©hamurishi/Shutterstock

Benchmarks for Metric Units Like place value, the metric system is based on multiples of ten. Each unit is 10 times as large as the next smaller unit. Below are some common metric benchmarks.

🔑 **Example 2** Use the benchmark metric units.

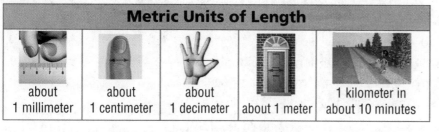

Metric Units of Length				
about 1 millimeter	about 1 centimeter	about 1 decimeter	about 1 meter	1 kilometer in about 10 minutes

A **kilometer** is a metric unit for measuring length or distance. The benchmark shows the distance you can walk in about 10 minutes.

- Is the length of your classroom greater than or less than one kilometer?

_____

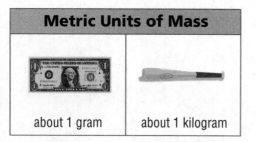

Metric Units of Liquid Volume	
1 milliliter	1 liter

- About how much medicine is usually in a medicine bottle?

about 120 _____

Metric Units of Mass	
about 1 gram	about 1 kilogram

- About how much is the mass of a paper clip?

_____

Math Talk

Math Processes and Practices ⑦

Look for Structure
Explain how benchmark measurements can help you decide which unit to use when measuring.

642

Name _____

Use benchmarks to choose the metric unit you would use to measure each.

1. mass of a strawberry

✓ 2. length of a cell phone

_____

_____

Circle the better estimate.

3. width of a teacher's desk

   10 meters or 1 meter

4. the amount of liquid a
   punch bowl holds

   2 liters or 20 liters

✓ 5. distance between Seattle
   and San Francisco

   6 miles or 680 miles

Math Processes and Practices ❸

Apply Which metric unit
would you use to measure
the distance across the
United States? Explain.

Metric Units
centimeter
meter
kilometer
gram
kilogram
milliliter
liter

On Your Own

Use benchmarks to choose the customary unit you would use to measure each.

6. length of a football field

7. weight of a pumpkin

_____

_____

Circle the better estimate.

8. weight of a watermelon

   4 pounds or 4 ounces

9. the amount of liquid a fish
   tank holds

   10 cups or 10 gallons

Customary Units
inch
foot
yard
ounce
pound
cup
gallon

Complete the sentence. Write *more* or *less*.

10. Matthew's large dog weighs _____ than one ton.

11. The amount of liquid a sink can hold is _____ than one cup of water.

12. A paper clip has a mass of _____ than one kilogram.

Problem Solving · Applications

For 13–15, use benchmarks to explain your answer.

13. **THINK SMARTER** Cristina is making macaroni and cheese for her family. Would Cristina use 1 pound of macaroni or 1 ounce of macaroni?

_____

_____

14. Which is the better estimate for the length of a kitchen table, 200 centimeters or 200 meters?

_____

_____

15. **GO DEEPER** Jodi wants to weigh her cat and measure its standing height. Which two units should she use?

_____

16. **Math Processes and Practices ①** **Evaluate Reasonableness** Dalton used benchmarks to estimate that there are more cups than quarts in one gallon. Is Dalton's estimate reasonable? Explain.

_____

_____

17. **THINK SMARTER** Select the correct word to complete the sentence.

Justine is thirsty after running two miles.

She should drink

1 pint
1 meter
10 pounds

of water.

Name _____

Measurement Benchmarks

Learning Objective You will use benchmark customary and metric units to understand the relative sizes of measurement units.

Use benchmarks to choose the customary unit you would use to measure each.

1. height of a computer

   _____foot_____

2. weight of a table

   _____

3. length of a semi-truck

   _____

4. the amount of liquid a bathtub holds

   _____

Customary Units	
ounce	yard
pound	mile
inch	gallon
foot	cup

Use benchmarks to choose the metric unit you would use to measure each.

5. mass of a grasshopper

   _____

6. the amount of liquid a water bottle holds

   _____

7. length of a soccer field

   _____

8. length of a pencil

   _____

Metric Units	
milliliter	centimeter
liter	meter
gram	kilometer
kilogram	

Circle the better estimate.

9. mass of a chicken egg

   50 grams   50 kilograms

10. length of a car

    12 miles   12 feet

11. amount of liquid a drinking glass holds

    8 ounces   8 quarts

Problem Solving · Real World

12. What is the better estimate for the mass of a textbook, 1 gram or 1 kilogram?

    _____

13. What is the better estimate for the height of a desk, 1 meter or 1 kilometer?

    _____

14. **WRITE** ▸Math Use benchmarks to determine the customary and metric units you would use to measure the height of your house. Explain your answer.

    _____

    _____

Lesson Check

1. What unit would be best to use for measuring the weight of a stapler?

   _____

   _____

2. Which is the best estimate for the length of a car?

   _____

   _____

Spiral Review

3. Bart practices his trumpet $1\frac{1}{4}$ hours each day. How many hours will he practice in 6 days?

   _____

   _____

4. Millie collected 100 stamps from different countries. Thirty-two of the stamps are from countries in Africa. What is $\frac{32}{100}$ written as a decimal?

   _____

   _____

5. Diedre drew a quadrilateral with 4 right angles and opposite sides of the same length. Name all the kinds of polygons that could be Diedre's quadrilateral.

   _____

   _____

6. How many degrees are in an angle that turns through $\frac{1}{2}$ of a circle?

   _____

   _____

FOR MORE PRACTICE
GO TO THE
Personal Math Trainer

Name _____

Customary Units of Length

Essential Question How can you use models to compare customary units of length?

Learning Objective You will use models to compare the relative sizes of customary units of length and record the measurement equivalents in a two-column table.

 Unlock the Problem

You can use a ruler to measure length. A ruler that is 1 foot long shows 12 inches in 1 foot. A ruler that is 3 feet long is called a yardstick. There are 3 feet in 1 yard.

How does the size of a foot compare to the size of an inch?

Activity

Materials ■ 1-inch grid paper ■ scissors ■ tape

STEP 1 Cut out the paper inch tiles. Label each tile 1 inch.

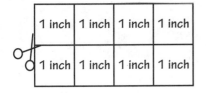

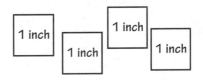

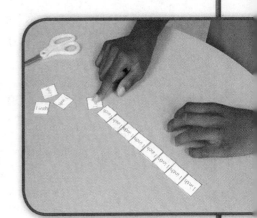

STEP 2 Place 12 tiles end-to-end to build 1 foot. Tape the tiles together.

1 foot

| 1 inch | 1 inch | 1 inch | 1 inch | 1 inch | 1 inch | 1 inch | 1 inch | 1 inch | 1 inch | 1 inch | 1 inch |

STEP 3 Compare the size of 1 foot to the size of 1 inch.

1 foot

| 1 inch | 1 inch | 1 inch | 1 inch | 1 inch | 1 inch | 1 inch | 1 inch | 1 inch | 1 inch | 1 inch | 1 inch |

| 1 inch |

1 inch

Think: You need 12 inches to make 1 foot.

So, 1 foot is _____ times as long as 1 inch.

 Math Talk

Math Processes and Practices ②

Use Reasoning Explain how you know the number of inches you need to make a yard.

① Example Compare measures.

Emma has 4 feet of thread. She needs 50 inches of thread to make some bracelets. How can she determine if she has enough thread to make the bracelets?

Since 1 foot is 12 times as long as 1 inch, you can write feet as inches by multiplying the number of feet by 12.

STEP 1 Make a table that relates feet and inches.

Feet	Inches
1	12
2	
3	
4	
5	

Think:

1 foot × 12 = 12 inches

2 feet × 12 = _____

3 feet × _____ = _____

4 feet × _____ = _____

5 feet × _____ = _____

STEP 2 Compare 4 feet and 50 inches.

4 feet   50 inches

Think: Write each measure in inches and compare using <, >, or =.

_____ ◯ _____

Emma has 4 feet of thread. She needs 50 inches of thread.

4 feet is _____ than 50 inches.

So, Emma _____ enough thread to make the bracelets.

Math Talk

Math Processes and Practices ②

Represent a Problem
Explain how making a table helped you solve the problem.

• What if Emma had 5 feet of thread? Would she have enough thread to make the bracelets? Explain.

_____

_____

_____

Name _____

1. Compare the size of a yard to the size of a foot.
   Use a model to help.

1 yard

___	___	___

Customary Units of Length
1 foot (ft) = 12 inches (in.)
1 yard (yd) = 3 feet
1 yard (yd) = 36 inches

1 yard is _____ times as long as _____ foot.

Complete.

✓ 2. 2 feet = _____ inches   3. 3 yards = _____ feet   ✓ 4. 7 yards = _____ feet

Math Processes and Practices ④

Interpret a Result If you measured the length of your classroom in yards and then in feet, which unit would have a greater number of units? Explain.

On Your Own

Complete.

5. 4 yards = _____ feet   6. 10 yards = _____ feet   7. 7 feet = _____ inches

Math Processes and Practices ④ Use Symbols **Algebra** Compare using <, >, or =.

8. 1 foot ◯ 13 inches   9. 2 yards ◯ 6 feet   10. 6 feet ◯ 60 inches

Problem Solving • Applications

11. **THINK SMARTER** Joanna has 3 yards of fabric. She needs 100 inches of fabric to make curtains. Does she have enough fabric to make curtains? Explain. Make a table to help.

Yards	Inches
1	
2	
3	

_____

_____

_____

12. **THINK SMARTER** Select the measures that are equal. Mark all that apply.

Ⓐ 4 feet   Ⓒ 36 feet   Ⓔ 15 feet

Ⓑ 12 yards   Ⓓ 480 inches   Ⓕ 432 inches

13. **GO DEEPER** Jasmine and Luke used fraction strips to compare
the size of a foot to the size of an inch using fractions. They
drew models to show their answers. Whose answer makes
sense? Whose answer is nonsense? Explain your reasoning.

Jasmine's Work

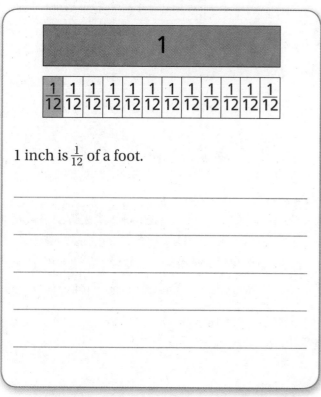

1 inch is $\frac{1}{12}$ of a foot.

_____

_____

_____

_____

Luke's Work

1 inch is $\frac{1}{3}$ of a foot.

_____

_____

_____

_____

a. **Math Processes and Practices 3** **Apply** For the answer that is nonsense, write an answer
that makes sense.

_____

_____

b. Look back at Luke's model. Which two units could you compare
using his model? Explain.

_____

_____

_____

650

Customary Units of Length

Learning Objective You will use models to compare the relative sizes of customary units of length and record the measurement equivalents in a two-column table.

Complete.

1. 3 feet = ___36___ inches   Think: 1 foot = 12 inches,
   so 3 feet = 3 × 12 inches, or 36 inches

2. 2 yards = _____ feet

3. 8 feet = _____ inches

4. 7 yards = _____ feet

5. 4 feet = _____ inches

6. 15 yards = _____ feet

7. 10 feet = _____ inches

Compare using <, >, or =.

8. 3 yards ◯ 10 feet

9. 5 feet ◯ 60 inches

10. 8 yards ◯ 20 feet

Problem Solving Real World

11. Carla has two lengths of ribbon. One ribbon is 2 feet long. The other ribbon is 30 inches long. Which length of ribbon is longer? **Explain.**

    _____

    _____

    _____

12. A football player gained 2 yards on one play. On the next play, he gained 5 feet. Was his gain greater on the first play or the second play? **Explain.**

    _____

    _____

    _____

13. **WRITE** ▸*Math* Write a problem that can be solved by comparing feet and inches using a model. Include a solution. Explain why you are changing from a larger unit to a smaller unit.

    _____

    _____

Lesson Check

1. Marta has 14 feet of wire to use to make necklaces. She needs to know the length in inches so she can determine how many necklaces to make. How many inches of wire does Marta have?

2. Jarod bought 8 yards of ribbon. He needs 200 inches to use to make curtains. How many inches of ribbon does he have?

Spiral Review

3. Describe the turn shown below. (Be sure to include both the size and direction of the turn in your answer.)

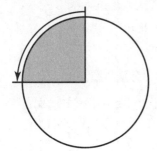

4. What decimal represents the shaded part of the model below?

5. Three sisters shared $3.60 equally. How much did each sister get?

6. Which is the best estimate for the width of your index finger?

FOR MORE PRACTICE
GO TO THE
Personal Math Trainer

Name _____

Customary Units of Weight

Essential Question How can you use models to compare customary units of weight?

Learning Objective You will use a number line to compare the relative sizes of customary units of weight and record the measurement equivalents in a two-column table.

 Unlock the Problem *Real World*

Ounces and **pounds** are customary units of weight. How does the size of a pound compare to the size of an ounce?

Activity

Materials ■ color pencils

The number line below shows the relationship between pounds and ounces.

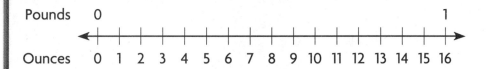

Pounds   0   1

Ounces   0 1 2 3 4 5 6 7 8 9 10 11 12 13 14 15 16

▲ You can use a spring scale to measure weight.

STEP 1 Use a color pencil to shade 1 pound on the number line.

STEP 2 Use a different color pencil to shade 1 ounce on the number line.

STEP 3 Compare the size of 1 pound to the size of 1 ounce.

You need _____ ounces to make _____ pound.

So, 1 pound is _____ times as heavy as 1 ounce.

 Math Talk

Math Processes and Practices ❻

Attend to Precision How can you compare the size of 9 pounds to the size of 9 ounces?

- *Math Processes and Practices* ❻ **Explain** how the number line helped you to compare the sizes of the units.

_____

_____

_____

© Houghton Mifflin Harcourt Publishing Company

Chapter 12   **653**

🔒 Example Compare measures.

Nancy needs 5 pounds of flour to bake pies for a festival. She has 90 ounces of flour. How can she determine if she has enough flour to bake the pies?

STEP 1 Make a table that relates pounds and ounces.

Pounds	Ounces
1	16
2	
3	
4	
5	

Think:

1 pound × 16 = 16 ounces

2 pounds × 16 = _____

3 pounds × _____ = _____

4 pounds × _____ = _____

5 pounds × _____ = _____

STEP 2 Compare 90 ounces and 5 pounds.

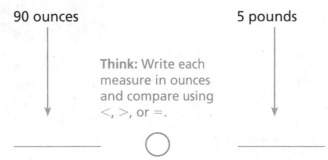

90 ounces   5 pounds

Think: Write each measure in ounces and compare using <, >, or =.

_____ ◯ _____

Nancy has 90 ounces of flour. She needs 5 pounds of flour.

90 ounces is _____ than 5 pounds.

So, Nancy _____ enough flour to make the pies.

Try This! There are 2,000 pounds in 1 **ton**.
Make a table that relates tons and pounds.

Tons	Pounds
1	2,000
2	
3	

1 ton is _____ times as heavy as 1 pound.

654

© Houghton Mifflin Harcourt Publishing Company

Name _____

Share and Show

1. 4 tons = _____ pounds

Think: 4 tons × _____ = _____

Complete.

2. 5 tons = _____ pounds

3. 6 pounds = _____ ounces

Customary Units of Weight
1 pound (lb) = 16 ounces (oz)
1 ton (T) = 2,000 pounds

 Math Talk **Math Processes and Practices ④**

Write an Equation What equation can you use to solve Exercise 4? Explain.

On Your Own

Complete.

4. 7 pounds = _____ ounces

5. 6 tons = _____ pounds

Math Processes and Practices ④ Use Symbols **Algebra** Compare using >, <, or =.

6. 1 pound ◯ 15 ounces

7. 2 tons ◯ 2 pounds

Problem Solving • Applications

8. A landscaping company ordered 8 tons of gravel. It sells the gravel in 50-pound bags. How many pounds of gravel did the company order?

_____

9. **THINK SMARTER** If you could draw a number line that shows the relationship between tons and pounds, what would it look like? Explain.

_____

_____

_____

10. **THINK SMARTER** Write the symbol that compares the weights correctly.

<	=	>

160 ounces _____ 10 pounds   600 pounds _____ 3 tons

11. 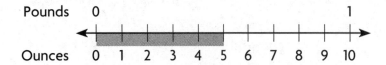 Alexis bought $\frac{1}{2}$ pound of grapes. How many ounces of grapes did she buy?

Dan drew the number line below to solve the problem. He says his model shows that there are 5 ounces in $\frac{1}{2}$ pound. What is his error?

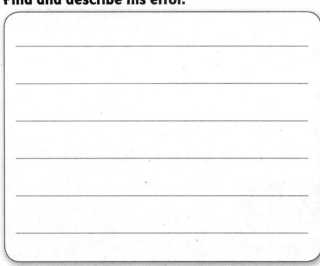

Look at the way Dan solved the problem. Find and describe his error.

Draw a correct number line and solve the problem.

So, Alexis bought _____ ounces of grapes.

• **Math Processes and Practices 6** Look back at the number line you drew. How many ounces are in $\frac{1}{4}$ pound? **Explain.**

_____

_____

_____

Customary Units of Weight

Learning Objective You will use a number line to compare the relative sizes of customary units of weight and record the measurement equivalents in a two-column table.

Complete.

1. 5 pounds = _____80_____ ounces

Think: 1 pound = 16 ounces, so
5 pounds = 5 × 16 ounces, or 80 ounces

2. 7 tons = _____ pounds

3. 2 pounds = _____ ounces

4. 3 tons = _____ pounds

5. 10 pounds = _____ ounces

Compare using <, >, or =.

6. 8 pounds ◯ 80 ounces

7. 1 ton ◯ 100 pounds

8. 3 pounds ◯ 50 ounces

9. 5 tons ◯ 1,000 pounds

Problem Solving Real World

10. A company that makes steel girders can produce 6 tons of girders in one day. How many pounds is this?

11. Larry's baby sister weighed 6 pounds at birth. How many ounces did the baby weigh?

_____

_____

12. **WRITE** ▸ *Math* Write a problem that can be solved by comparing pounds and ounces using a model. Include a solution. Explain why you are changing from a larger unit to a smaller unit.

_____

_____

Lesson Check

1. Ann bought 2 pounds of cheese to make lasagna. The recipe gives the amount of cheese needed in ounces. How many ounces of cheese did she buy?

2. A school bus weighs 7 tons. The weight limit for a bridge is given in pounds. What is this weight of the bus in pounds?

Spiral Review

3. What is the measure of ∠EHG?

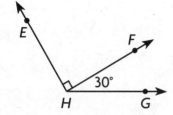

4. How many lines of symmetry does the square below have?

5. To make dough, Reba needs $2\frac{1}{2}$ cups of flour. How much flour does she need to make 5 batches of dough?

6. Judi's father is 6 feet tall. The minimum height to ride a rollercoaster is given in inches. How many inches tall is Judi's father?

**FOR MORE PRACTICE
GO TO THE
Personal Math Trainer**

Name _____

Customary Units of Liquid Volume

Essential Question How can you use models to compare customary units of liquid volume?

Learning Objective You will use models to compare the relative sizes of customary units of liquid volume and record the measurement equivalents in a two-column table.

🗝 Unlock the Problem

Liquid volume is the measure of the space a liquid occupies. Some basic units for measuring liquid volume are **gallons**, **half gallons**, **quarts**, **pints**, and **cups**.

The bars below model the relationships among some units of liquid volume. The largest units are gallons. The smallest units are **fluid ounces**.

1 cup [🥛] = 8 fluid ounces
1 pint = 2 cups [🥛] [🥛]
1 quart = 4 cups [🥛] [🥛] [🥛] [🥛]

1 gallon

1 gallon															
1 half gallon								1 half gallon							
1 quart				1 quart				1 quart				1 quart			
1 pint		1 pint		1 pint		1 pint		1 pint		1 pint		1 pint		1 pint	
1 cup	1 cup	1 cup	1 cup	1 cup	1 cup	1 cup	1 cup	1 cup	1 cup	1 cup	1 cup	1 cup	1 cup	1 cup	1 cup
8 fluid ounces	8 fluid ounces	8 fluid ounces	8 fluid ounces	8 fluid ounces	8 fluid ounces	8 fluid ounces	8 fluid ounces	8 fluid ounces	8 fluid ounces	8 fluid ounces	8 fluid ounces	8 fluid ounces	8 fluid ounces	8 fluid ounces	8 fluid ounces

🗝 Example How does the size of a gallon compare to the size of a quart?

Math Talk

Math Processes and Practices ⑦

Look for a Pattern
Describe the pattern in the units of liquid volume.

STEP 1 Draw two bars that represent this relationship. One bar should show gallons and the other bar should show quarts.

STEP 2 Shade 1 gallon on one bar and shade 1 quart on the other bar.

STEP 3 Compare the size of 1 gallon to the size of 1 quart.

So, 1 gallon is _____ times as much as 1 quart.

🔒 Example Compare measures.

Serena needs to make 3 gallons of lemonade for the lemonade sale. She has a powder mix that makes 350 fluid ounces of lemonade. How can she decide if she has enough powder mix?

STEP 1 Use the model on page 659. Find the relationship between gallons and fluid ounces.

1 gallon = _____ cups

1 cup = _____ fluid ounces

1 gallon = _____ cups × _____ fluid ounces

1 gallon = _____ fluid ounces

STEP 2 Make a table that relates gallons and fluid ounces.

Gallons	Fluid Ounces
1	128
2	
3	

Think:

1 gallon = 128 fluid ounces

2 gallons × 128 = _____ fluid ounces

3 gallons × 128 = _____ fluid ounces

STEP 3 Compare 350 fluid ounces and 3 gallons.

350 fluid ounces   3 gallons

Think: Write each measure in fluid ounces and compare using <, >, or =.

_____   ◯   _____

Serena has enough mix to make 350 fluid ounces. She needs to make 3 gallons of lemonade.

350 fluid ounces is _____ than 3 gallons.

So, Serena _____ enough mix to make 3 gallons of lemonade.

Name _____

1. Compare the size of a quart to the size of a pint. Use a model to help.

1 quart

_____	_____

Customary Units of Liquid Volume
1 cup (c) = 8 fluid ounces (fl oz)
1 pint (pt) = 2 cups
1 quart (qt) = 2 pints
1 quart (qt) = 4 cups
1 gallon (gal) = 4 quarts
1 gallon (gal) = 8 pints
1 gallon (gal) = 16 cups

1 quart is _____ times as much as _____ pint.

Complete.

 2. 2 pints = _____ cups

3. 3 gallons = _____ quarts

4. 6 quarts = _____ cups

On Your Own

 Math Talk

Math Processes and Practices ⑥

Make Connections Explain how the conversion chart above relates to the bar model in Exercise 1.

Use a model or *iTools* to complete.

5. 4 gallons = _____ pints

6. 5 cups = _____ fluid ounces

Use Symbols **Algebra** Compare using >, <, or =.

7. 2 gallons ◯ 32 cups

8. 4 pints ◯ 6 cups

9. 5 quarts ◯ 11 pints

Problem Solving • Applications

10. *THINK SMARTER* A soccer team has 25 players. The team's thermos holds 4 gallons of water. If the thermos is full, is there enough water for each player to have 2 cups? Explain. Make a table to help.

_____

_____

_____

Gallons	Cups
1	
2	
3	
4	

11. **Math Processes and Practices 3** **Verify the Reasoning of Others** Whose statement makes sense? Whose statement is nonsense? Explain your reasoning.

1 pint is $\frac{1}{4}$ of a gallon.

1 pint is $\frac{1}{8}$ of a gallon.

Zach's Statement

_____

_____

_____

Angela's Statement

_____

_____

_____

12. **GO DEEPER** Peter's glasses each hold 8 fluid ounces. How many glasses of juice can Peter pour from a bottle that holds 2 quarts?

_____

13. **THINK SMARTER** A pitcher contains 5 quarts of water. Josy says the pitcher contains 10 cups of water. Explain Josy's error. Then find the correct number of cups the pitcher contains.

_____

_____

_____

_____

Customary Units of Liquid Volume

Learning Objective You will use models to compare the relative sizes of customary units of liquid volume and record the measurement equivalents in a two-column table.

Complete.

1. 6 gallons = ___24___ quarts

    Think: 1 gallon = 4 quarts,
    so 6 gallons = 6 × 4 quarts, or 24 quarts

2. 12 quarts = _____ pints

3. 6 cups = _____ fluid ounces

4. 9 pints = _____ cups

5. 10 quarts = _____ cups

6. 5 gallons = _____ pints

7. 3 gallons = _____ cups

Compare using <, >, or =.

8. 6 pints ◯ 60 fluid ounces

9. 3 gallons ◯ 30 quarts

10. 5 quarts ◯ 20 cups

11. 12 pints ◯ 6 cups

Problem Solving (Real World)

12. A chef makes $1\frac{1}{2}$ gallons of soup in a large pot. How many 1-cup servings can the chef get from this large pot of soup?

13. Kendra's water bottle contains 2 quarts of water. She wants to add drink mix to it, but the directions for the drink mix give the amount of water in fluid ounces. How many fluid ounces are in her bottle?

_____

_____

14. **WRITE** ▸Math Write a problem that can be solved by comparing quarts and cups using a model. Include a solution. Explain why you are changing from a larger unit to a smaller unit.

_____

_____

Lesson Check

1. Joshua drinks 8 cups of water a day. The recommended daily amount is given in fluid ounces. How many fluid ounces of water does he drink each day?

_____

2. A cafeteria used 5 gallons of milk in preparing lunch. How many 1-quart containers of milk did the cafeteria use?

_____

Spiral Review

3. Roy uses $\frac{1}{4}$ cup of batter for each muffin. Make a list to show the amounts of batter he will use depending on the number of muffins he makes.

_____

_____

4. Beth has $\frac{7}{100}$ of a dollar. What is the amount of money Beth has?

_____

_____

5. Name the figure that Enrico drew below.

_____

6. A hippopotamus weighs 4 tons. Feeding instructions are given for weights in pounds. How many pounds does the hippopotamus weigh?

_____

FOR MORE PRACTICE
GO TO THE
Personal Math Trainer

Name _____

Line Plots

Essential Question How can you make and interpret line plots with fractional data?

Learning Objective You will make and interpret line plots with fractional data.

🔑 Unlock the Problem

The data show the lengths of the buttons in Jen's collection. For an art project, she wants to know how many buttons are longer than $\frac{1}{4}$ inch.

You can use a line plot to solve the problem. A **line plot** is a graph that shows the frequency of data along a number line.

Length of Buttons in Jen's Collection (in inches)
$\frac{1}{4}, \frac{3}{4}, \frac{1}{4}, \frac{4}{4}, \frac{1}{4}, \frac{4}{4}$

Make a line plot to show the data.

🔒 Example 1

STEP 1 Order the data from least to greatest length and complete the tally table.

_____

_____

STEP 2 Label the fraction lengths on the number line below from the least value of the data to the greatest.

STEP 3 Plot an *X* above the number line for each data point. Write a title for the line plot.

Buttons in Jen's Collection	
Length (in inches)	Tally
$\frac{1}{4}$	
$\frac{3}{4}$	
$\frac{4}{4}$	

So, _____ buttons are longer than $\frac{1}{4}$ inch.

Math Talk

Math Processes and Practices ④

Use Models Explain how you labeled the numbers on the number line in Step 2.

1. How many buttons are in Jen's collection? _____

2. What is the difference in length between the longest button and the shortest button in Jen's collection? _____

Think: To find the difference, subtract the numerators. The denominators stay the same.

© Houghton Mifflin Harcourt Publishing Company

Chapter 12   665

🔒 Example 2

Some of the students in Ms. Lee's class walk to school. The data show the distances these students walk. What distance do most students walk?

Distance Students Walk to School (in miles)
$\frac{1}{2}$, $\frac{1}{2}$, $\frac{1}{4}$, $\frac{3}{4}$, $\frac{1}{4}$, $\frac{1}{2}$, $\frac{1}{2}$

Make a line plot to show the data.

STEP 1 Order the data from least to greatest distance and complete the tally table.

_____

STEP 2 Label the fraction lengths on the number line below from the least value of the data to the greatest.

STEP 3 Plot an X above the number line for each data point. Write a title for the line plot.

Distance Students Walk to School	
Distance (in miles)	Tally

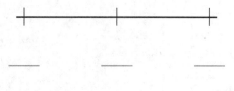

So, most students walk _____.

3. How many more students walk $\frac{1}{2}$ mile than $\frac{1}{4}$ mile to school?

_____

4. What is the difference between the longest distance and the shortest distance that students walk?

_____

5. What if a new student joins Ms. Lee's class who walks $\frac{3}{4}$ mile to school? How would the line plot change? Explain.

_____

Name _____

1. A food critic collected data on the lengths of time customers waited for their food. Order the data from least to greatest time. Make a tally table and a line plot to show the data.

Time Customers Waited for Food (in hours)
$\frac{1}{2}$, $\frac{1}{4}$, $\frac{3}{4}$, $\frac{1}{4}$, $\frac{1}{4}$, $\frac{1}{2}$, 1

Time Customers Waited for Food	
Time (in hours)	Tally

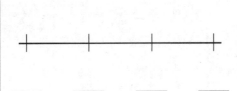

Math Talk

Math Processes and Practices ④

Use Graphs Explain how the line plot helped you answer the question for Exercise 2.

Use your line plot for 2 and 3.

2. On how many customers did the food critic collect data? _____

3. What is the difference between the longest time and the shortest time that customers waited? _____

On Your Own

4. Math Processes and Practices ④ Use Models The data show the lengths of the ribbons Mia used to wrap packages. Make a tally table and a line plot to show the data.

Ribbon Used to Wrap Packages	
Length (in yards)	Tally

Ribbon Length Used to Wrap Packages (in yards)
$\frac{1}{6}$, $\frac{2}{6}$, $\frac{5}{6}$, $\frac{3}{6}$, $\frac{2}{6}$, $\frac{6}{6}$, $\frac{3}{6}$, $\frac{2}{6}$

5. What is the difference in length between the longest ribbon and the shortest ribbon Mia used? _____

Unlock the Problem

6. **GO DEEPER** The line plot shows the distances the students in Mr. Boren's class ran at the track in miles. Altogether, did the students run more or less than 5 miles?

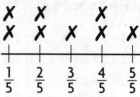

Distance Students Ran at the Track (in miles)

a. What are you asked to find? _____

_____

b. What information do you need to use? _____

_____

c. How will the line plot help you solve the problem? _____

_____

d. What operation will you use to solve the problem? _____

e. Show the steps to solve the problem.

_____

_____

f. Complete the sentences.

The students ran a total of _____ miles.

The distance is _____ than 5 miles. Altogether the students ran _____ than 5 miles.

7. **THINK SMARTER** Lena collects antique spoons. The line plot shows the lengths of the spoons in her collection. If she lines up all of her spoons in order of size, what is the size of the middle spoon? Explain.

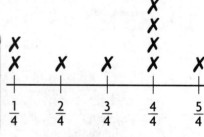

Length of Spoons (in feet)

_____

_____

Personal Math Trainer

8. **THINK SMARTER +** A hiking group recorded the distances they hiked. Complete the line plot to show the data.

Distance Hiked (in miles)
$\frac{4}{8}, \frac{5}{8}, \frac{7}{8}, \frac{7}{8}, \frac{5}{8}, \frac{6}{8}, \frac{7}{8}, \frac{7}{8}, \frac{6}{8}$

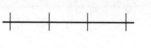

Distance Hiked

Name _____

Line Plots

Learning Objective You will make and
interpret line plots with fractional data.

1. Some students compared the time they spend
   riding the school bus. Complete the tally table
   and line plot to show the data.

Time Spent on School Bus	
Time (in hours)	**Tally**
$\frac{1}{6}$	| |
$\frac{2}{6}$	
$\frac{3}{6}$	
$\frac{4}{6}$	

Time Spent on School Bus (in hours)
$\frac{1}{6}$, $\frac{3}{6}$, $\frac{4}{6}$, $\frac{2}{6}$, $\frac{3}{6}$, $\frac{1}{6}$, $\frac{3}{6}$, $\frac{3}{6}$

**Time Spent on
School Bus (in hours)**

Use your line plot for 2 and 3.

2. How many students compared times? _____

3. What is the difference between the longest time and shortest

   time students spent riding the bus? _____

Problem Solving Real World

**For 4, make a tally table on a separate sheet of paper.
Make a line plot in the space below the problem.**

4.
Milk Drunk at Lunch (in quarts)
$\frac{1}{8}$, $\frac{2}{8}$, $\frac{2}{8}$, $\frac{4}{8}$, $\frac{1}{8}$, $\frac{3}{8}$, $\frac{4}{8}$, $\frac{2}{8}$, $\frac{3}{8}$, $\frac{2}{8}$

5. **WRITE** ▸*Math* Write a problem that can be
   solved using a line plot. Draw and label the
   line plot and solve the problem.

   _____

   _____

   _____

$\frac{1}{8}$ $\frac{2}{8}$ $\frac{3}{8}$ $\frac{4}{8}$

**Milk Drunk at Lunch
(in quarts)**

Lesson Check

Use the line plot for 1 and 2.

1. How many students were reading during study time?

   _____

2. What is the difference between the longest time and shortest time spent reading?

   _____

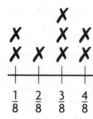

Time Spent Reading During Study Time (in hours)

Spiral Review

3. Bridget is allowed to play on-line games for $\frac{75}{100}$ of an hour each day. Write this fraction as a decimal.

   _____

4. Bobby's collection of sports cards has $\frac{3}{10}$ baseball cards and $\frac{39}{100}$ football cards. The rest are soccer cards. What fraction of Bobby's sports cards are baseball or football cards?

   _____

5. Jeremy gives his horse 12 gallons of water each day. How many 1-quart pails of water is that?

   _____

6. An iguana at a pet store is 5 feet long. Measurements for iguana cages are given in inches. How many inches long is the iguana?

   _____

**FOR MORE PRACTICE
GO TO THE
Personal Math Trainer**

Name _____

✓ Mid-Chapter Checkpoint

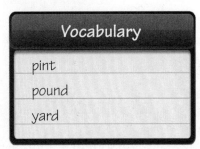

Vocabulary

Choose the best term from the box to complete the sentence.

Vocabulary
pint
pound
yard

1. A _____ is a customary unit used to measure weight. (p. 653)

2. The cup and the _____ are both customary units for measuring liquid volume. (p. 659)

Concepts and Skills

Complete the sentence. Write *more* or *less*.

3. A cat weighs _____ than one ounce.

4. Serena's shoe is _____ than one yard long.

Complete.

5. 5 feet = _____ inches

6. 4 tons = _____ pounds

7. 4 cups = _____ pints

8. Mrs. Byrne's class went raspberry picking. The data show the weights of the cartons of raspberries the students picked. Make a tally table and a line plot to show the data.

Weight of Cartons of Raspberries Picked (in pounds)
$\frac{3}{4}, \frac{1}{4}, \frac{2}{4}, \frac{4}{4}, \frac{1}{4}, \frac{1}{4}, \frac{2}{4}, \frac{3}{4}, \frac{3}{4}$

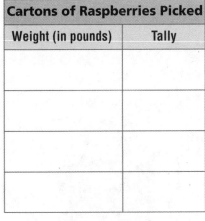

Cartons of Raspberries Picked	
Weight (in pounds)	Tally

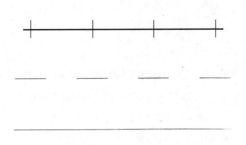

Use your line plot for 9 and 10.

9. What is the difference in weight between the heaviest carton and lightest carton of raspberries? _____

10. How many pounds of raspberries did Mrs. Byrne's class pick in all? _____

11. A jug contains 2 gallons of water. How many quarts of water does the jug contain?

_____

12. Serena bought 4 pounds of dough to make pizzas. The recipe gives the amount of dough needed for a pizza in ounces. How many ounces of dough did she buy?

_____

13. GO DEEPER   Vicki has a 50 inch roll of ribbon. She used 3 feet of the ribbon to wrap a gift. How many inches of ribbon does she have left?

_____

14. The watering can that Carlos uses in his vegetable garden holds 5 of a certain unit of liquid volume. When full, what is the best estimate for how much water is in the watering can, 5 quarts, 5 yards, or 5 ounces?

_____

Name _____

Metric Units of Length

Essential Question How can you use models to compare metric units of length?

Learning Objective You will build a 1-meter meterstick to show how the units are related, then compare the relative sizes of metric units of length.

Investigate

Materials ■ ruler (meter) ■ scissors ■ tape

Meters (m), **decimeters** (dm), centimeters (cm), and **millimeters** (mm) are all metric units of length.

Build a meterstick to show how these units are related.

A. Cut out the meterstick strips.

B. Place the strips end-to-end to build 1 meter. Tape the strips together.

C. Look at your meter strip. What patterns do you notice about the sizes of the units?

1 meter is _____ times as long as 1 decimeter.

1 decimeter is _____ times as long as 1 centimeter.

1 centimeter is _____ times as long as 1 millimeter.

Describe the pattern you see.

_____

_____

> **Math Idea**
> If you lined up 1,000 metersticks end-to-end, the length of the metersticks would be 1 kilometer.

Draw Conclusions

1. Compare the size of 1 meter to the size of 1 centimeter. Use your meterstick to help.

_____

2. Compare the size of 1 meter to the size of 1 millimeter. Use your meterstick to help.

_____

_____

3. [THINK SMARTER] What operation could you use to find how many centimeters are in 3 meters? Explain.

_____

_____

_____

Make Connections

You can use different metric units to describe the same length. For example, you can measure the length of a book as 3 decimeters or as 30 centimeters. Since the metric system is based on the number 10, decimals or fractions can be used to describe metric lengths as equivalent units.

Think of 1 meter as one whole. Use your meter strip to write equivalent units as fractions and decimals.

1 meter = 10 decimeters	1 meter = 100 centimeters
Each decimeter is	Each centimeter is
_____ or _____ of a meter.	_____ or _____ of a meter.

Complete the sentence.

- A length of 51 centimeters is _____ or _____ of a meter.

- A length of 8 decimeters is _____ or _____ of a meter.

- A length of 82 centimeters is _____ or _____ of a meter.

Math Talk

Math Processes and Practices ⑦

Look for Structure Explain how you are able to locate and write decimeters and centimeters as parts of a meter on the meterstick.

Name _____

Share and Show MATH BOARD

Metric Units of Length
1 centimeter (cm) = 10 millimeters (mm)
1 decimeter (dm) = 10 centimeters
1 meter (m) = 10 decimeters
1 meter (m) = 100 centimeters
1 meter (m) = 1,000 millimeters

Complete.

☑ **1.** 2 meters = _____ centimeters

2. 3 centimeters = _____ millimeters

3. 5 decimeters = _____ centimeters

Math Processes and Practices ④ **Use Symbols Algebra** Compare using <, >, or =.

4. 4 meters ◯ 40 decimeters

5. 5 centimeters ◯ 5 millimeters

6. 6 decimeters ◯ 65 centimeters

7. 7 meters ◯ 700 millimeters

Describe the length in meters. Write your answer as a fraction and as a decimal.

☑ **8.** 65 centimeters = _____ or _____ meter

9. 47 centimeters = _____ or _____ meter

10. 9 decimeters = _____ or _____ meter

11. 2 decimeters = _____ or _____ meter

Problem Solving • Applications Real World

12. A new building is 25 meters tall. How many decimeters tall is the building?

_____

13. **GO DEEPER** Alexis is knitting a blanket 2 meters long. Every 2 decimeters, she changes the color of the yarn to make stripes. How many stripes will the blanket have? Explain.

_____

_____

_____

© Houghton Mifflin Harcourt Publishing Company

Chapter 12 • Lesson 6 675

14. **THINK SMARTER** Julianne's desk is 75 centimeters long. She says her desk is 7.5 meters long. Describe her error.

_____

_____

15. **THINK SMARTER** Write the equivalent measurements in each column.

5,000 millimeters

$\frac{55}{100}$ meter

$\frac{500}{1,000}$ meter

500 centimeters

0.500 meter

550 millimeters

50 centimeters

0.55 meter

50 decimeters

5 meters	55 centimeters	500 millimeters

16. **THINK SMARTER** Aruna was writing a report on pecan trees. She made the table of information to the right.

Write a problem that can be solved by using the data.

Pecan Tree	
Average Measurements	
Length of nuts	3 cm to 5 cm
Height	21 m to 30 m
Width of trunk	18 dm
Width of leaf	10 cm to 20 cm

Pose a problem.

_____

_____

_____

_____

_____

Solve your problem.

• **Math Processes and Practices ❶** **Describe** how you could change the problem by changing a unit in the problem. Then solve the problem.

_____

_____

Metric Units of Length

Learning Objective You will build a 1-meter meterstick to show how the units are related, then compare the relative sizes of metric units of length.

Complete.

1. 4 meters = _____400_____ centimeters

Think: 1 meter = 100 centimeters, so 4 meters = 4 × 100 centimeters, or 400 centimeters

2. 8 centimeters = _____ millimeters

3. 5 meters = _____ decimeters

4. 9 meters = _____ millimeters

5. 7 meters = _____ centimeters

Compare using <, >, or =.

6. 8 meters ◯ 80 centimeters

7. 3 decimeters ◯ 30 centimeters

8. 4 meters ◯ 450 centimeters

9. 90 centimeters ◯ 9 millimeters

Describe the length in meters. Write your answer as a fraction and as a decimal.

10. 43 centimeters = _____ or

_____ meter

11. 6 decimeters = _____ **or**

_____ meter

Problem Solving Real World

12. A flagpole is 4 meters tall. How many centimeters tall is the flagpole?

13. Lucille runs the 50-meter dash in her track meet. How many decimeters long is the race?

_____

_____

14. **WRITE** ▸*Math* Find a measurement, in centimeters, of an object. Look through books, magazines, or the Internet. Then write the measurement as parts of a meter.

_____

_____

Lesson Check

1. A pencil is 15 centimeters long. How many millimeters long is that pencil?

2. John's father is 2 meters tall. How many centimeters tall is John's father?

Spiral Review

3. Bruce reads for $\frac{3}{4}$ hour each night. How long will he read in 4 nights?

4. Mark jogged 0.6 mile. Caroline jogged 0.49 mile. Write an inequality to compare the distances they jogged.

Use the line plot for 5 and 6.

5. How many lawns were mowed?

6. What is the difference between the greatest amount and least amount of gasoline used to mow lawns?

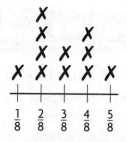

Gasoline Used to Mow Lawns in May (in Gallons)

FOR MORE PRACTICE
GO TO THE
Personal Math Trainer

Name _____

Metric Units of Mass and Liquid Volume

Essential Question How can you compare metric units of mass and liquid volume?

Learning Objective You will use models to compare the relative sizes of metric units of mass and liquid volume and record the measurement equivalents in a two-column table.

🔑 Unlock the Problem

Mass is the amount of matter in an object. Metric units of mass include kilograms (kg) and grams (g). Liters (L) and **milliliters** (mL) are metric units of liquid volume.

The charts show the relationship between these units.

Metric Units of Mass
1 kilogram (kg) = 1,000 grams (g)

Metric Units of Liquid Volume
1 liter (L) = 1,000 milliliters (mL)

🔑 Example 1 Compare kilograms and grams.

Becky planted a flower garden full of bluebonnets. She used 9 kilograms of soil. How many grams of soil is that?

number of kilograms		grams in 1 kilogram		total grams
9	×	1,000	=	_____

So, Becky used _____ grams of soil to plant her bluebonnets.

- Are kilograms heavier or lighter than grams?

_____

- Will the number of grams be greater than or less than the number of kilograms?

_____

- What operation will you use to solve the problem?

_____

🔑 Example 2 Compare liters and milliliters.

Becky used 5 liters of water to water her bluebonnet garden. How many milliliters of water is that?

number of liters		milliliters in 1 liter		total milliliters
5	×	1,000	=	_____

So, Becky used _____ milliliters of water.

Math Talk

Math Processes and Practices ⑦

Identify Relationships Compare the size of a kilogram to the size of a gram. Then compare the size of a liter to the size of a milliliter.

1. There are 3 liters of water in a pitcher. How many milliliters of water are in the pitcher?

   There are _____ milliliters in 1 liter. Since I am changing

   from a larger unit to a smaller unit, I can _____
   3 by 1,000 to find the number of milliliters in 3 liters.

   So, there are _____ milliliters of water in the pitcher.

Complete.

 2. 4 liters = _____ milliliters

 3. 6 kilograms = _____ grams

> **Math Talk**
>
> **Math Processes and Practices 7**
>
> **Look for Structure** Explain how you can find the number of grams in 8 kilograms.

On Your Own

Complete.

4. 8 kilograms = _____ grams

5. 7 liters = _____ milliliters

Math Processes and Practices 4 **Use Symbols** **Algebra** Compare using <, >, or =.

6. 1 kilogram ◯ 900 grams

7. 2 liters ◯ 2,000 milliliters

Math Processes and Practices 7 **Look for a Pattern** **Algebra** Complete.

8.

Liters	Milliliters
1	1,000
2	
3	
	4,000
5	
6	
	7,000
8	
9	
10	

9.

Kilograms	Grams
1	1,000
2	
	3,000
4	
5	
6	
7	
	8,000
9	
10	

Name _____

10. Frank wants to fill a fish tank with 8 liters of water. How many milliliters is that?

_____

11. GO DEEPER Kim has 3 water bottles. She fills each bottle with 1 liter of water. How many milliliters of water does she have?

_____

12. GO DEEPER Jared's empty backpack has a mass of 3 kilograms. He doesn't want to carry more than 7 kilograms on a trip. How many grams of equipment can Jared pack?

_____

WRITE ▸ Math
Show Your Work

13. GO DEEPER A large cooler contains 20 liters of iced tea and a small cooler contains 5 liters of iced tea. How many more milliliters of iced tea does the large cooler contain than the small cooler?

_____

14. THINK SMARTER A 500-gram bag of granola costs $4, and a 2-kilogram bag of granola costs $15. What is the least expensive way to buy 2,000 grams of granola? Explain.

_____

_____

_____

_____

15. Math Processes and Practices ❸ **Verify the Reasoning of Others** The world's largest apple had a mass of 1,849 grams. Sue said the mass was greater than 2 kilograms. Does Sue's statement make sense? Explain.

_____

_____

_____

_____

Unlock the Problem

16. **THINK SMARTER** Lori bought 600 grams of cayenne pepper and 2 kilograms of black pepper. How many grams of pepper did she buy in all?

black pepper   cayenne pepper

a. What are you asked to find?

_____

b. What information will you use?

_____

c. Tell how you might solve the problem.

_____

_____

_____

d. Show how you solved the problem.

_____

_____

_____

_____

e. Complete the sentences.

Lori bought _____ grams of cayenne pepper.

She bought _____ grams of black pepper.

_____ + _____ = _____ grams

So, Lori bought _____ grams of pepper in all.

17. **WRITE** ▸Math Jill has two rocks. One has a mass of 20 grams and the other has a mass of 20 kilograms. Which rock has the greater mass? Explain.

18. **THINK SMARTER** For numbers 18a–18c, choose Yes or No to tell whether the measurements are equivalent.

18a. 5,000 grams and 5 kilograms   ○ Yes   ○ No

18b. 300 milliliters and 3 liters   ○ Yes   ○ No

18c. 8 grams and 8,000 kilograms   ○ Yes   ○ No

Metric Units of Mass and Liquid Volume

Learning Objective You will use models to compare the relative sizes of metric units of mass and liquid volume and record the measurement equivalents in a two-column table.

Complete.

1. 5 liters = ___**5,000**___ milliliters

Think: 1 liter = 1,000 milliliters,
so 5 liters = 5 × 1,000 milliliters, or 5,000 milliliters

2. 3 kilograms = _____ grams

3. 8 liters = _____ milliliters

4. 7 kilograms = _____ grams

5. 9 liters = _____ milliliters

Compare using <, >, or =.

6. 8 kilograms $\bigcirc$ 850 grams

7. 3 liters $\bigcirc$ 3,500 milliliters

Problem Solving · Real World

8. Kenny buys four 1-liter bottles of water. How many milliliters of water does Kenny buy?

_____

9. Mrs. Jones bought three 2-kilogram packages of flour. How many grams of flour did she buy?

_____

10. Colleen bought 8 kilograms of apples and 2.5 kilograms of pears. How many more grams of apples than pears did she buy?

_____

11. Dave uses 500 milliliters of juice for a punch recipe. He mixes it with 2 liters of ginger ale. How many milliliters of punch does he make?

_____

12. **WRITE** ▸ Math Write a problem that involves changing kilograms to grams. Explain how to find the solution.

_____

_____

_____

Lesson Check

1. During his hike, Milt drank 1 liter of water and 1 liter of sports drink. How many milliliters of liquid did he drink?

   _____

2. Larinda cooked a 4-kilogram roast. The roast left over after the meal weighed 3 kilograms. How many grams of roast were eaten during that meal?

   _____

Spiral Review

3. Use a protractor to find the angle measure.

   _____

4. Draw a pair of parallel lines.

5. Carly bought 3 pounds of birdseed. How many ounces of birdseed did she buy?

   _____

6. A door is 8 decimeters wide. How wide is the door in centimeters?

   _____

FOR MORE PRACTICE
GO TO THE
Personal Math Trainer

Units of Time

Essential Question How can you use models to compare units of time?

Learning Objective You will use analog clocks and number lines to compare the relative sizes of units of time.

Unlock the Problem

The analog clock below has an hour hand, a minute hand, and a **second** hand to measure time. The time is 4:30:12.

> **Read Math**
>
> Read 4:30:12 as 4:30 and 12 seconds, or 30 minutes and 12 seconds after 4.

• Are there more minutes or seconds in one hour?

_____

There are 60 seconds in a minute and 60 minutes in an hour. The clocks show how far the hands move for each length of time.

Start Time: 3:00:00

1 second elapses.

The time is now 3:00:01.

1 minute, or 60 seconds, elapses. The second hand has made a full turn clockwise.

The time is now 3:01:00.

1 hour, or 60 minutes, elapses. The minute hand has made a full turn clockwise.

The time is now 4:00:00.

Example 1 How does the size of an hour compare to the size of a second?

There are _____ minutes in an hour.

There are _____ seconds in a minute.

60 minutes × _____ = _____ seconds

There are _____ seconds in a hour.

So, 1 hour is _____ times as long as 1 second.

Think: Multiply the number of minutes in an hour by the number of seconds in a minute.

Math Talk

Math Processes and Practices ❶

Analyze How many full turns clockwise does a minute hand make in 3 hours? Explain.

🔓 Example 2 Compare measures.

Larissa spent 2 hours on her science project.
Cliff spent 200 minutes on his science project.
Who spent more time?

STEP 1 Make a table that relates hours and
minutes.

Hours	Minutes
1	60
2	
3	

STEP 2 Compare 2 hours and 200 minutes.

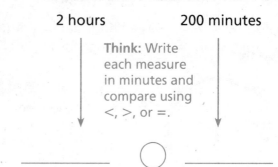

2 hours   200 minutes

Think: Write
each measure
in minutes and
compare using
<, >, or =.

2 hours is _____ than 200 minutes.

So, _____ spent more time than _____ on the
science project.

🔓 Activity Compare the length of a week to the length of a day.

Materials ■ color pencils

The number line below shows the relationship between
days and weeks.

STEP 1 Use a color pencil to shade 1 week on the number line.

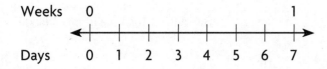

Weeks   0   1

Days   0   1   2   3   4   5   6   7

_____

STEP 2 Use a different color pencil to shade 1 day on the
number line.

_____

STEP 3 Compare the size of 1 week to the size of 1 day.

There are _____ days in _____ week.

So, 1 week is _____ times as long as 1 day.

Name _____

Units of Time
1 minute (min) = 60 seconds (s)
1 hour (hr) = 60 minutes
1 day (d) = 24 hours
1 week (wk) = 7 days
1 year (yr) = 12 months (mo)
1 year (yr) = 52 weeks

1. Compare the length of a year to the length of a month. Use a model to help.

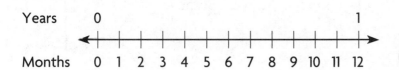

Years   0   1

Months   0   1   2   3   4   5   6   7   8   9   10   11   12

Math Talk   Math Processes and Practices ④

Use Models Explain how the number line helped you compare the length of a year and the length of a month.

1 year is _____ times as long as _____ month.

Complete.

✓ 2. 2 minutes = _____ seconds

✓ 3. 4 years = _____ months

Complete.

4. 3 minutes = _____ seconds

5. 4 hours = _____ minutes

Math Processes and Practices ④ **Use Symbols** **Algebra** Compare using >, <, or =.

6. 3 years ◯ 35 months

7. 2 days ◯ 40 hours

8. **GO DEEPER** Damien has lived in the apartment building for 5 years. Ken has lived there for 250 weeks. Who has lived in the building longer? Explain. Make a table to help.

_____

_____

Years	Weeks
1	
2	
3	
4	
5	

9. **THINK SMARTER** How many hours are in a week? Explain.

_____

_____

10. **Math Processes and Practices ⑤ Communicate** Explain how you know that 9 minutes is less than 600 seconds.

_____

_____

11. **THINK SMARTER** Draw lines to match equivalent time intervals. Some intervals might not have a match.

1 hour	2 hours	5 hours	12 hours	48 hours
•	•	•	•	•

•	•	•	•	•
2 days	120 minutes	4 days	3,600 seconds	300 minutes

Connect to Science

One day is the length of time it takes Earth to make one complete rotation. One year is the time it takes Earth to revolve around the sun. To make the calendar match Earth's orbit time, there are leap years. Leap years add one extra day to the year. A leap day, February 29, is added to the calendar every four years.

| 1 year = 365 days |
| 1 leap year = 366 days |

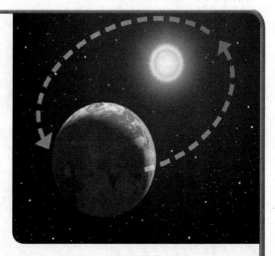

12. How many days are there in 4 years, if the fourth year is a leap year? Explain. Make a table to help.

_____

_____

Years	Days
1	
2	
3	
4	

13. Parker was born on February 29, 2008. The second time he is able to celebrate on his actual birthday is in 2016. How many days old will Parker be on February 29, 2016?

_____

Learning Objective You will use analog clocks and number lines to compare the relative sizes of units of time.

Complete.

1. 6 minutes = ___360___ seconds

   Think: 1 minute = 60 seconds,
   so 6 minutes = 6 × 60 seconds, or 360 seconds

2. 5 weeks = _____ days

3. 3 years = _____ weeks

4. 9 hours = _____ minutes

5. 9 minutes = _____ seconds

Compare using <, >, or =.

6. 2 years ◯ 14 months

7. 3 hours ◯ 300 minutes

8. 2 days ◯ 48 hours

9. 6 years ◯ 300 weeks

Problem Solving Real World

10. Jody practiced a piano piece for 500 seconds. Bill practiced a piano piece for 8 minutes. Who practiced longer? **Explain.**

    _____
    _____
    _____
    _____

11. Yvette's younger brother just turned 3 years old. Fred's brother is now 30 months old. Whose brother is older? **Explain.**

    _____
    _____
    _____
    _____

12. **WRITE** ▸ *Math* Explain how you can prove that 3 weeks is less than 24 days.

    _____
    _____
    _____

Lesson Check

1. Glen rode his bike for 2 hours. For how many minutes did Glen ride his bike?

2. Tina says that vacation starts in exactly 4 weeks. In how many days does vacation start?

Spiral Review

3. Kayla bought $\frac{9}{4}$ pounds of apples. What is that weight as a mixed number?

4. Judy, Jeff, and Jim each earned $5.40 raking leaves. How much did they earn together?

5. Melinda rode her bike $\frac{54}{100}$ mile to the library. Then she rode $\frac{4}{10}$ mile to the store. How far did Melinda ride her bike in all? Write your answer as a decimal.

6. One day, the students drank 60 quarts of milk at lunch. How many pints of milk did the students drink?

FOR MORE PRACTICE
GO TO THE
Personal Math Trainer

Name _____

Problem Solving • Elapsed Time

Essential Question How can you use the strategy *draw a diagram* to solve elapsed time problems?

Learning Objective You will use the stragey *draw a diagram* to solve elapsed time problems by drawing time lines to count elapsed time to find start and end times.

Unlock the Problem

Dora and her brother Kyle spent 1 hour and 35 minutes doing yard work. Then they stopped for lunch at 1:20 P.M. At what time did they start doing yard work?

Use the graphic organizer to help you solve the problem.

Read the Problem

What do I need to find?	**What information do I need to use?**	**How will I use the information?**
I need to find the time that Dora and Kyle _____.	I need to use the _____ and the time that they _____.	I can draw a time line to help me count backward and find the _____.

Solve the Problem

I draw a time line that shows the end time 1:20 P.M. Next, I count backward 1 hour and then 5 minutes at a time until I have 35 minutes.

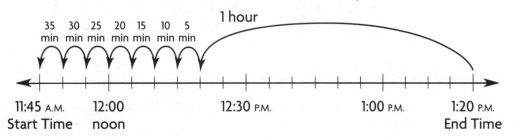

So, Dora and her brother Kyle started doing yard work at _____.

1. What if Dora and Kyle spent 50 minutes doing yard work and they stopped for lunch at 12:30 P.M.? What time would they have started doing yard work?

_____

🔒 Try Another Problem

Ben started riding his bike at 10:05 A.M. He stopped
23 minutes later when his friend Robbie asked him
to play kickball. At what time did Ben stop riding
his bike?

Read the Problem

What do I need to find?	What information do I need to use?	How will I use the information?

Solve the Problem

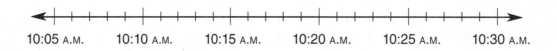

10:05 A.M.   10:10 A.M.   10:15 A.M.   10:20 A.M.   10:25 A.M.   10:30 A.M.

2. How did your diagram help you solve the problem?

_____

_____

_____

Math Talk

Math Processes and Practices ❶

Describe another way you could
find the time an activity started
or ended given the elapsed time
and either the start or end time.

Name _____

Unlock the Problem

√ Use the Problem Solving MathBoard.
√ Choose a strategy you know.
√ Underline important facts.

Share and Show

1. Evelyn has dance class every Saturday. It lasts 1 hour and 15 minutes and is over at 12:45 P.M. At what time does Evelyn's dance class begin?

   First, write the problem you need to solve.

   _____

   Next, draw a time line to show the end time and the elapsed time.

11:00 A.M.   12:00
noon   1:00 P.M.

   Finally, find the start time.

   Evelyn's dance class begins at _____ .

2. **THINK SMARTER** What if Evelyn's dance class started at 11:00 A.M. and lasted 1 hour and 25 minutes? At what time would her class end? Describe how this problem is different from Problem 1.

   _____

   _____

3. Beth got on the bus at 8:06 A.M. Thirty-five minutes later, she arrived at school. At what time did Beth arrive at school?

   _____

   _____

4. Lyle went fishing for 1 hour and 30 minutes until he ran out of bait at 6:40 P.M. At what time did Lyle start fishing?

   _____

   _____

On Your Own

5. Mike and Jed went skiing at 10:30 A.M. They skied for 1 hour and 55 minutes before stopping for lunch. At what time did Mike and Jed stop for lunch?

_____

6. GO DEEPER Mike can run a mile in 12 minutes. He starts his run at 11:30 AM. and runs 4 miles. What time does Mike finish his run?

_____

7. Math Processes and Practices ⑤ **Communicate** Explain how you can use a diagram to determine the start time when the end time is 9:00 A.M. and the elapsed time is 26 minutes. What is the start time?

WRITE ▸ Math
Show Your Work

_____

_____

_____

8. THINK SMARTER Bethany finished her math homework at 4:20 P.M. She did 25 multiplication problems in all. If each problem took her 3 minutes to do, at what time did Bethany start her math homework?

_____

9. THINK SMARTER Vincent began his weekly chores on Saturday morning at 11:20 A.M. He finished 1 hour and 10 minutes later. Draw a time line to show the end time.

11:00 A.M.   12:00   1:00 P.M.
                          noon

Vincent finished his chores at _____ P.M.

Problem Solving • Elapsed Time

Learning Objective You will use the stragey *draw a diagram* to solve elapsed time problems by drawing time lines to count elapsed time to find start and end times.

Read each problem and solve.

1. Molly started her piano lesson at 3:45 P.M. The lesson lasted 20 minutes. What time did the piano lesson end?

   Think: What do I need to find? How can I draw a diagram to help?

   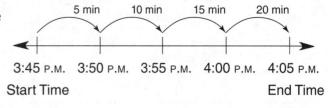

   _____ 4:05 P.M. _____

2. Brendan spent 24 minutes playing a computer game. He stopped playing at 3:55 P.M and went outside to ride his bike. What time did he start playing the computer game?

   _____

3. Aimee's karate class lasts 1 hour and 15 minutes and is over at 5:00 P.M. What time does Aimee's karate class start?

   _____

4. Mr. Giarmo left for work at 7:15 A.M. Twenty-five minutes later, he arrived at his work. What time did Mr. Giarmo arrive at his work?

   _____

5. **WRITE** ▸*Math* Explain why it is important to know if a time is in the A.M. or in the P.M. when figuring out how much time has elapsed.

   _____

   _____

Lesson Check

1. Bobbie went snowboarding with friends at 10:10 A.M. They snowboarded for 1 hour and 43 minutes, and then stopped to eat lunch. What time did they stop for lunch?

2. The Cain family drove for 1 hour and 15 minutes and arrived at their camping spot at 3:44 P.M. What time did the Cain family start driving?

Spiral Review

3. A praying mantis can grow up to 15 centimeters long. How long is this in millimeters?

4. Thom's minestrone soup recipe makes 3 liters of soup. How many milliliters of soup is this?

5. Stewart walks $\frac{2}{3}$ mile each day. List three multiples of $\frac{2}{3}$.

6. Angelica colored in 0.60 of the squares on her grid. Write 0.60 as tenths in fraction form.

FOR MORE PRACTICE
GO TO THE
Personal Math Trainer

Name _____

Mixed Measures

Essential Question How can you solve problems involving mixed measures?

Learning Objective You will solve problems involving mixed measures by first rewriting a mixed measure then adding or subtracting with regrouping as needed.

 Unlock the Problem

Herman is building a picnic table for a new campground. The picnic table is 5 feet 10 inches long. How long is the picnic table in inches?

🔑 **Change a mixed measure.**

Think of 5 feet 10 inches as 5 feet + 10 inches.

Write feet as inches.

$$\begin{array}{r} 5\ feet \\ +\ 10\ inches \end{array}$$

Think: 5 feet × 12 = ⟶ 60 inches

$$\begin{array}{r} \underline{}\ inches \\ +\ \underline{}\ inches \\ \hline \underline{}\ inches \end{array}$$

- Is the mixed measure greater than or less than 6 feet?

  _____

- How many inches are in 1 foot?

  _____

So, the picnic table is _____ inches long.

🔑 **Example 1** Add mixed measures.

Herman built the picnic table in 2 days. The first day he worked for 3 hours 45 minutes. The second day he worked for 2 hours 10 minutes. How long did it take him to build the table?

STEP 1 Add the minutes.

$$\begin{array}{r} 3\ hr\ 45\ min \\ +\ 2\ hr\ 10\ min \\ \hline min \end{array}$$

STEP 2 Add the hours.

$$\begin{array}{r} 3\ hr\ 45\ min \\ +\ 2\ hr\ 10\ min \\ \hline hr\ 55\ min \end{array}$$

So, it took Herman _____ to build the table.

 Math Talk

Math Processes and Practices ⑧

Use Repeated Reasoning How is adding mixed measures similar to adding tens and ones? How is it different? Explain.

- What if Herman worked an extra 5 minutes on the picnic table? How long would he have worked on the table then? Explain.

_____

_____

🔒 Example 2 Subtract mixed measures.

Alicia is building a fence around the picnic area. She has a pole that is 6 feet 6 inches long. She cuts off 1 foot 7 inches from one end. How long is the pole now?

STEP 1 Subtract the inches.

Think: 7 inches is greater than 6 inches. You need to regroup to subtract.

6 ft 6 in. = 5 ft 6 in. + 12 in.

        = 5 ft _____ in.

$$
\begin{array}{r}
\overset{5}{\cancel{6}}\text{ft }\overset{18}{\cancel{6}}\text{ in.}\\
-\ 1\text{ ft }7\text{ in.}\\
\hline
\text{in.}
\end{array}
$$

 ERROR Alert
Be sure to check that you are regrouping correctly. There are 12 inches in 1 foot.

STEP 2 Subtract the feet.

$$
\begin{array}{r}
\overset{5}{\cancel{6}}\text{ft }\overset{18}{\cancel{6}}\text{ in.}\\
-\ 1\text{ ft }7\text{ in.}\\
\hline
\text{ft }11\text{ in.}
\end{array}
$$

So, the pole is now _____ long.

Try This! Subtract.

3 pounds 5 ounces − 1 pound 2 ounces

Share and Show

1. A truck is carrying 2 tons 500 pounds of steel. How many pounds of steel is the truck carrying?

Think of 2 tons 500 pounds as 2 tons + 500 pounds.
Write tons as pounds.

2 tons   **Think:** 2 tons × 2,000 = ⟶   pounds

+ 500 pounds   _____ pounds   + _____ pounds

                                                                 pounds

So, the truck is carrying _____ pounds of steel.

Name _____

Rewrite each measure in the given unit.

2. 1 yard 2 feet

_____ feet

3. 3 pints 1 cup

_____ cups

 4. 3 weeks 1 day

_____ days

Add or subtract.

5.   2 lb 4 oz
     + 1 lb 6 oz

 6.   3 gal 2 qt
      − 1 gal 3 qt

7.   5 hr 20 min
      − 3 hr 15 min

Math Talk   **Math Processes and Practices ②**

Reason Quantitatively
How do you know when you need to regroup to subtract? Explain.

On Your Own

Rewrite each measure in the given unit.

8. 1 hour 15 minutes

_____ minutes

9. 4 quarts 2 pints

_____ pints

10. 10 feet 10 inches

_____ inches

Add or subtract.

11.   2 tons 300 lb
      − 1 ton   300 lb

12.   10 gal 8 c
       + 8 gal 9 c

13.   7 lb 6 oz
       − 2 lb 12 oz

Problem Solving • Applications

14. **Math Processes and Practices ③** **Apply** Ahmed fills 6 pitchers with juice. Each pitcher contains 2 quarts 1 pint. How many pints of juice does he have in all?

_____

15. **Sense or Nonsense?** Sam and Dave each solve the problem at the right. Sam says the sum is 4 feet 18 inches. Dave says the sum is 5 feet 6 inches. Whose answer makes sense? Whose answer is nonsense? Explain.

       2 ft 10 in.
     + 2 ft   8 in.

_____

_____

16. **THINK SMARTER** Jackson has a rope 1 foot 8 inches long. He cuts it into 4 equal pieces. How many inches long is each piece?

_____

🔑 Unlock the Problem

17. Theo is practicing for a 5-kilometer race. He runs 5 kilometers every day and records his time. His normal time is 25 minutes 15 seconds. Yesterday it took him only 23 minutes 49 seconds. How much faster was his time yesterday than his normal time?

a. What are you asked to find?

_____

_____

b. What information do you know?

_____

_____

c. How will you solve the problem?

_____

d. Solve the problem.

e. Fill in the sentence.

   Yesterday, Theo ran 5 kilometers in a time

   that was _____ faster than his

   normal time.

   _____

18. **GO DEEPER** Don has 5 pieces of pipe. Each piece is 3 feet 6 inches long. If Don joins the pieces end to end to make one long pipe, how long will the new pipe be?

Personal Math Trainer

19. **THINK SMARTER +** Ana mixes 2 quarts 1 pint of apple juice and 1 quart 3 cups of cranberry juice. Will her mixture be able to fit in a 1 gallon pitcher? Explain.

_____

_____

_____

_____

Mixed Measures

Learning Objective You will solve
problems involving mixed measures by first
rewriting a mixed measure then adding or
subtracting with regrouping as needed.

Complete.

1. 8 pounds 4 ounces = _____132_____ ounces

> Think: 8 pounds = 8 × 16 ounces, or 128 ounces.
>
> 128 ounces + 4 ounces = 132 ounces

2. 5 weeks 3 days = _____ days

3. 4 minutes 45 seconds = _____ seconds

4. 4 hours 30 minutes = _____ minutes

5. 3 tons 600 pounds = _____ pounds

Add or subtract.

6.   9 gal 1 qt
   + 6 gal 1 qt

7.   12 lb 5 oz
   − 7 lb 10 oz

8.   8 hr 3 min
   + 4 hr 12 min

Problem Solving Real World

9. Michael's basketball team practiced for
2 hours 40 minutes yesterday and 3 hours
15 minutes today. How much longer did the
team practice today than yesterday?

10. Rhonda had a piece of ribbon that was
5 feet 3 inches long. She removed a 5-inch
piece to use in her art project. What is the
length of the piece of ribbon now?

_____

_____

11. **WRITE** ▸ *Math* Write a subtraction problem involving
pounds and ounces. Solve the problem and show your work.

_____

_____

_____

Lesson Check

1. Marsha bought 1 pound 11 ounces of roast beef and 2 pounds 5 ounces of corned beef. How much more corned beef did she buy than roast beef?

   _____

2. Theodore says there are 2 weeks 5 days left in the year. How many days are left in the year?

   _____

Spiral Review

3. On one grid, 0.5 of the squares are shaded. On another grid, 0.05 of the squares are shaded. Compare the shaded parts of the grids using <, =, or >.

   _____

   _____

4. Classify the triangle by the size of its angles.

   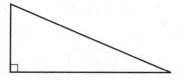

   _____

   _____

5. Sahil's brother is 3 years old. How many weeks old is his brother?

6. Sierra's swimming lessons last 1 hour 20 minutes. She finished her lesson at 10:50 A.M. At what time did her lesson start?

**FOR MORE PRACTICE
GO TO THE
Personal Math Trainer**

Name _____

Patterns in Measurement Units

Essential Question How can you use patterns to write number pairs for measurement units?

Learning Objective You will use the relationship between number pairs to determine the measurement units to use in measurement data.

CONNECT The table at the right relates yards and feet. You can think of the numbers in the table as number pairs. 1 and 3, 2 and 6, 3 and 9, 4 and 12, and 5 and 15 are number pairs.

Yards	Feet
1	3
2	6
3	9
4	12
5	15

The number pairs show the relationship between yards and feet. 1 yard is equal to 3 feet, 2 yards is equal to 6 feet, 3 yards is equal to 9 feet, and so on.

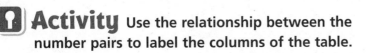

Unlock the Problem

Lillian made the table below to relate two units of time. What units of time does the pattern in the table show?

Activity Use the relationship between the number pairs to label the columns of the table.

_____	_____
1	7
2	14
3	21
4	28
5	35

- List the number pairs.

  _____

- Describe the relationship between the numbers in each pair.

  _____

  _____

- Label the columns of the table.   **Think:** What unit of time is 7 times as great as another unit?

Math Talk

Math Processes and Practices 7

Identify Relationships
Look at each number pair in the table. Could you change the order of the numbers in the number pairs? Explain why or why not.

Try This! Jasper made the table below to relate two customary units of liquid volume. What customary units of liquid volume does the pattern in the table show?

- List the number pairs.

  _____

- Describe the relationship between the numbers in each pair.

  _____

  _____

  _____

_____	_____
1	4
2	8
3	12
4	16
5	20

- Label the columns of the table.

Think: What customary unit of liquid volume is 4 times as great as another unit?

- What other units could you have used to label the columns of the table above? Explain.

  _____

  _____

  _____

Share and Show

1. The table shows a pattern for two units of time. Label the columns of the table with the units of time.

   Think: What unit of time is 24 times as great as another unit?

_____	_____
1	24
2	48
3	72
4	96
5	120

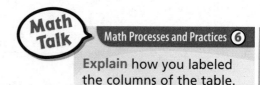

Math Talk

Math Processes and Practices ⑥

Explain how you labeled the columns of the table.

Each table shows a pattern for two customary units. Label the columns of the table.

2.

_____	_____
1	2
2	4
3	6
4	8
5	10

3.

_____	_____
1	16
2	32
3	48
4	64
5	80

On Your Own

Each table shows a pattern for two customary units. Label the columns of the table.

4.

_____	_____
1	36
2	72
3	108
4	144
5	180

5.

_____	_____
1	12
2	24
3	36
4	48
5	60

Each table shows a pattern for two metric units of length. Label the columns of the table.

6.

_____	_____
1	10
2	20
3	30
4	40
5	50

7.

_____	_____
1	100
2	200
3	300
4	400
5	500

8. **GO DEEPER** List the number pairs for the table in Exercise 6.
Describe the relationship between the numbers in each pair.

_____

_____

_____

Problem Solving • Applications

9. What's the Error? Maria wrote *Weeks* as the label for the first column of the table and *Years* as the label for the second column. Describe her error.

_____

_____

_____

?	?
1	52
2	104
3	156
4	208
5	260

10. **Math Processes and Practices ❸** **Verify the Reasoning of Others** The table shows a pattern for two metric units. Lou labels the columns *Meters* and *Millimeters*. Zayna labels them *Liters* and *Milliliters*. Whose answer makes sense? Whose answer is nonsense? Explain.

_____

_____

_____

_____

?	?
1	1,000
2	2,000
3	3,000
4	4,000
5	5,000

11. *THINK SMARTER* Look at the following number pairs: 1 and 365, 2 and 730, 3 and 1,095. The number pairs describe the relationship between which two units of time? Explain.

_____

_____

12. *THINK SMARTER* The tables show patterns for some units of measurement. Write the correct labels in each table.

Ounces	Days	Feet	Gallons	Hours	Inches	Pounds	Quarts

___	___
1	12
2	24
3	36
4	48

___	___
1	24
2	48
3	72
4	96

___	___
1	4
2	8
3	12
4	16

Name _____

Patterns in Measurement Units

Learning Objective You will use the relationship between number pairs to determine the measurement units to use in measurement data.

Each table shows a pattern for two customary units of time, liquid volume, or weight. Label the columns of the table.

1.

Gallons	Quarts
1	4
2	8
3	12
4	16
5	20

2.

_____	_____
1	2,000
2	4,000
3	6,000
4	8,000
5	10,000

3.

_____	_____
1	2
2	4
3	6
4	8
5	10

4.

_____	_____
1	60
2	120
3	180
4	240
5	300

Problem Solving ·Real· ·World·

Use the table for 5.

5. Marguerite made the table to compare two metric measures of length. Name a pair of units Marguerite could be comparing.

?	?
1	10
2	20
3	30
4	40
5	50

_____

6. **WRITE** ▸*Math* Draw a table to represent months and years. Explain how you labeled each column.

_____

_____

Lesson Check

1. Joanne made a table to relate two units of measure. The number pairs in her table are 1 and 16, 2 and 32, 3 and 48, 4 and 64. What are the best labels for Joanne's table?

2. Cade made a table to relate two units of time. The number pairs in his table are 1 and 24, 2 and 48, 3 and 72, 4 and 96. What are the best labels for Cade's table?

Spiral Review

3. Anita has 2 quarters, 1 nickel, and 4 pennies. Write Anita's total amount as a fraction of a dollar.

4. The minute hand of a clock moves from 12 to 6. What describes the turn the minute hand makes?

5. Roderick has a dog that has a mass of 9 kilograms. What is the mass of the dog in grams?

6. Kari mixed 3 gallons 2 quarts of lemon-lime drink with 2 gallons 3 quarts of pink lemonade to make punch. How much more lemon-lime drink did Kari use than pink lemonade?

FOR MORE PRACTICE
GO TO THE
Personal Math Trainer

Name _____

1. Mrs. Miller wants to estimate the width of the steps in front of her house. Select the best benchmark for her to use.

   (A) her fingertip

   (B) the thickness of a dime

   (C) the width of a license plate

   (D) how far she can walk in 20 minutes

2. **GO DEEPER** Franco played computer chess for 3 hours. Lian played computer chess for 150 minutes. Compare the times spent playing computer chess. Complete the sentence.

   _____ played for _____ longer than _____.

3. Select the measures that are equal. Mark all that apply.

   (A) 6 feet   (D) 600 inches

   (B) 15 yards   (E) 12 feet

   (C) 45 feet   (F) 540 inches

4. Jackie made 6 quarts of lemonade. Jackie says she made 3 pints of lemonade. Explain Jackie's error. Then find the correct number of pints of lemonade.

5. Josh practices gymnastics each day after school. The data show the lengths of time Josh practiced gymnastics for 2 weeks.

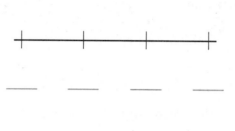

Time Practicing Gymnastics (in hours)
$\frac{1}{4}, \frac{1}{4}, \frac{3}{4}, \frac{3}{4}, \frac{1}{2}$, 1, 1, 1, $\frac{3}{4}$, 1

Part A

Make a tally table and line plot to show the data.

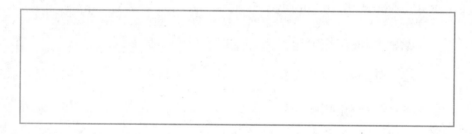

Time Practicing Gymnastics	
Time (in hours)	Tally

Part B

Explain how you used the tally table to label the numbers and plot the Xs.

Part C

What is the difference between the longest time and shortest time Josh spent practicing gymnastics?

_____ hour

6. Select the correct word to complete the sentence.

Juan brings a water bottle with him to soccer practice.

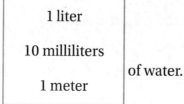

A full water bottle holds | 1 liter / 10 milliliters / 1 meter | of water.

Name _____

7. Write the symbol that compares the weights correctly.

| < | = | > |

128 ounces _____ 8 pounds

8,000 pounds _____ 3 tons

8. Dwayne bought 5 yards of wrapping paper. How many inches of wrapping paper did he buy?

_____ inches

9. A sack of potatoes weighs 14 pounds 9 ounces. After Wendy makes potato salad for a picnic, the sack weighs 9 pounds 14 ounces. What is the weight of the potatoes Wendy used for the potato salad? Write the numbers to show the correct subtraction.

| 4 | 5 | 11 | 13 | 19 | 25 | 39 |

```
    [ ]              [ ]
  14 pounds        9 ounces
 − 9 pounds       14 ounces
 _____    _____
  [ ] pounds      [ ] ounces
```

10. Sabita made this table to relate two customary units of liquid volume.

Part A

List the number pairs for the table. Then describe the relationship between the numbers in each pair.

_____	_____
1	2
2	4
3	6
4	8
5	10

Part B

Label the columns of the table. Explain your answer.

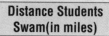
11. **THINK SMARTER +** The table shows the distances some students swam in miles. Complete the line plot to show the data.

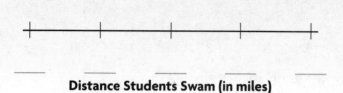

Distance Students Swam(in miles)
$\frac{1}{8}, \frac{2}{8}, \frac{3}{8}, \frac{3}{8}, \frac{5}{8}, \frac{3}{8}, \frac{2}{8}, \frac{4}{8}, \frac{3}{8}, \frac{1}{8}, \frac{4}{8}, \frac{4}{8}$

┼———————┼———————┼———————┼———————┼

____   ____   ____   ____   ____

Distance Students Swam (in miles)

What is the difference between the longest distance and the shortest distance the students swam?

☐ mile

12. An elephant living in a wildlife park weighs 4 tons. How many pounds does the elephant weigh?

_____ pounds

13. Katia bought two melons. She says the difference in mass between the melons is 5,000 grams. Which two melons did Katia buy?

(A) watermelon: 8 kilograms

(B) cantaloupe: 5 kilograms

(C) honeydew: 3 kilograms

(D) casaba melon: 2 kilograms

(E) crenshaw melon: 1 kilogram

14. Write the equivalent measurements in each column.

3,000 millimeters   300 centimeters   30 centimeters

$\frac{35}{100}$ meter   0.300 meter   0.35 meter

$\frac{300}{1,000}$ meter   350 millimeters   30 decimeters

3 meters	35 centimeters	300 millimeters

15. Cheryl is making a mixed fruit drink for a party. She mixes 7 pints each of apple juice and cranberry juice. How many fluid ounces of mixed fruit drink does Cheryl make?

_____ fluid ounces

16. Hamid's soccer game will start at 11:00 A.M., but the players must arrive at the field three-quarters of an hour early to warm up. The game must end by 1:15 P.M.

Part A

Hamid says he has to be at the field at 9:45 A.M. is Hamid correct? Explain your answer.

```
┌─────────────────────────────────────────────────────────┐
│                                                           │
│                                                           │
│                                                           │
│                                                           │
│                                                           │
└─────────────────────────────────────────────────────────┘
```

Part B

The park closes at 6:30 P.M. There is a 15-minute break between each game played at the park, and each game takes the same amount of time as Hamid's soccer game. How many more games can be played before the park closes? Explain your answer.

```
┌─────────────────────────────────────────────────────────┐
│                                                           │
│                                                           │
│                                                           │
└─────────────────────────────────────────────────────────┘
```

17. For numbers 17a–17e, select Yes or No to tell whether the measurements are equivalent.

17a.   7,000 grams and 7 kilograms   ○ Yes   ○ No

17b.   200 milliliters and 2 liters   ○ Yes   ○ No

17c.   6 grams and 6,000 kilograms   ○ Yes   ○ No

17d.   5 liters and 5,000 milliliters   ○ Yes   ○ No

17e.   2 milliliters and 2,000 liters   ○ Yes   ○ No

18. Draw lines to match equivalent time intervals.

$\frac{1}{2}$ hour   2 hours   3 hours   8 hours   72 hours

   •   •   •   •   •

   •   •   •   •   •

3 days   180 minutes   1,800 seconds   480 minutes   7,200 seconds

19. Anya arrived at the library on Saturday morning at 11:10 A.M. She left the library 1 hour 20 minutes later. Draw a time line to show the end time.

11:00 A.M.   12:00 noon   1:00 P.M.

Anya left the library at _____ P.M.

20. The tables show patterns for some units of measurement. Write the correct labels in each table.

Pints	Days	Feet	Cups	Week	Yards	Inches	Quarts

1	3	1	7	1	4
2	6	2	14	2	8
3	9	3	21	3	12
4	12	4	28	4	16

21. An Olympic swimming pool is 25 meters wide. How many decimeters wide is an Olympic swimming pool?

_____ decimeters wide

22. Frankie is practicing for a 5-kilometer race. His normal time is 31 minutes 21 seconds. Yesterday it took him only 29 minutes 38 seconds.

How much faster was Frankie yesterday than his normal time?

_____

714

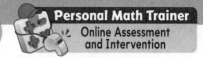

✓ Show What You Know

Check your understanding of important skills.

Name _____

▶ **Missing Factors** **Find the missing factor.**

1.

   _____ × 6 = 24

2.

   3 × _____ = 27

▶ **Add Whole Numbers** **Find the sum.**

3. 17 + 153 + 67 = _____

4. 8 + 78 + 455 = _____

5. 211 + 52 + 129 + 48 = _____

6. 42 + 9 + 336 + 782 = _____

▶ **Multiply Whole Numbers** **Find the product.**

7. 78
   × 6

8. 29
   × 7

9. 42
   × 5

10. 57
    × 9

Math in the Real World

Native Americans once lived near Cartersville, Georgia, in an area that is now a state park. They constructed burial mounds that often contained artifacts, such as beads, feathers, and copper ear ornaments. One of the park's mounds is 63 feet in height. If the top of the mound is rectangular in shape with a perimeter of 322 yards, what could be the side lengths of the rectangle?

Vocabulary Builder

▶ Visualize It

Sort words with a ✓ using the Venn diagram.

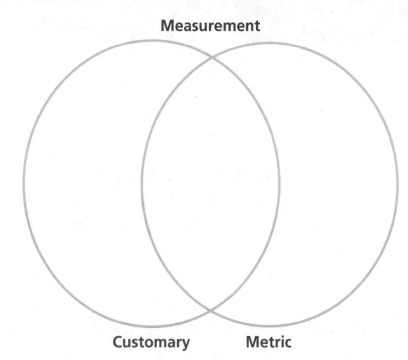

Measurement

Customary　　**Metric**

▶ Understand Vocabulary

Write the word or term that answers the riddle.

1. I am the measure of the number of unit squares needed to cover a surface.

   _____

2. I am the distance around a shape.

   _____

3. I am a unit of area that measures 1 unit by 1 unit.

   _____

4. I am a set of symbols that expresses a mathematical rule.

   _____

GO DIGITAL
• Interactive Student Edition
• Multimedia eGlossary

Chapter 13 Vocabulary

area

área

2

base

base

5

centimeter (cm)

centímetro (cm)

7

formula

fórmula

35

height

altura

39

meter (m)

metro (m)

50

perimeter

perímetro

64

square unit

unidad cuadrada

86

A polygon's side or a two-dimensional shape, usually a polygon or circle, by which a three-dimensional shape is measured or named

Examples:

base

bases

base

The measure of the number of unit squares needed to cover a surface

Example:

Area = 9 square units

A set of symbols that expresses a mathematical rule

Example: Area = base × height, or $A = b \times h$

A metric unit used for measuring length or distance
1 meter = 100 centimeters

Example:

1 centimeter

A metric unit for measuring length or distance
1 meter = 100 centimeters

Example:

about 1 meter

The measure of a perpendicular from the base to the top of a two-dimensional shape

Example:

height

base

A unit of area with dimensions of
1 unit × 1 unit

Example:

1 unit

1 unit

The distance around a shape

4 cm

2 cm

2 cm

4 cm

Perimeter = 2 cm + 4 cm + 2 cm + 4 cm = 12 cm

Game

Guess the Word

For 3 to 4 players

Materials

- timer

How to Play

1. Take turns to play.

2. Choose a math term, but do not say it aloud.

3. Set the timer for 1 minute.

4. Give a one-word clue about your term. Give each player one chance to guess the term.

5. If nobody guesses correctly, repeat Step 4 with a different clue. Repeat until a player guesses the term or time runs out.

6. The player who guesses gets 1 point. If the player can use the word in a sentence, he or she gets 1 more point. Then that player gets a turn choosing a word.

7. The first player to score 10 points wins.

© Houghton Mifflin Harcourt Publishing Company • Image Credits: ©Perry Mastrovito/Corbis

The Write Way

Reflect

Choose one idea. Write about it in the space below.

• Define *perimeter* and *area* in your own words.

• Explain how to use a formula to find the area of a rectangle.

• Write an area word problem so that the solution is 36 square units.

Perimeter

Essential Question How can you use a formula to find the perimeter of a rectangle?

Learning Objective You will apply the perimeter formula to find the perimeter of rectangles and squares.

 Unlock the Problem Real World

Julio is putting a stone border around his rectangular garden. The length of the garden is 7 feet. The width of the garden is 5 feet. How many feet of stone border does Julio need?

Perimeter is the distance around a shape.

To find how many feet of stone border Julio needs, find the perimeter of the garden.

- Circle the numbers you will use.
- What are you asked to find?

_____

_____

Use addition.

Perimeter of a Rectangle = length + width + length + width

    7 + 5 + 7 + 5 = _____

    The perimeter is _____ feet.

So, Julio needs _____ feet of stone border.

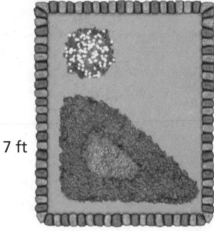

7 ft

5 ft

Use multiplication.

A Find Perimeter of a Rectangle

Perimeter = (2 × length) + (2 × width)

8 cm

12 cm   12 cm

8 cm

Perimeter = (2 × 12) + (2 × 8)

        = 24 + 16

        = _____

So, the perimeter is _____ centimeters.

B Find Perimeter of a Square

Perimeter = 4 × one side

16 in.

16 in.   16 in.

16 in.

Perimeter = 4 × 16

        = _____

So, the perimeter is _____ inches.

 Math Talk

Math Processes and Practices ⑦

Identify Relationships How is using addition and using multiplication to find the perimeter of a rectangle related?

Use a Formula A **formula** is a mathematical rule. You can use a formula to find perimeter.

$$P = (2 \times l) + (2 \times w)$$
↑   ↑   ↑
perimeter   length   width

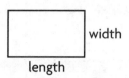
width
length

Example **Find the perimeter of the rectangle.**

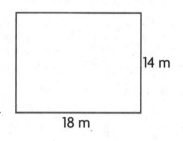
14 m
18 m

$P = (2 \times l) + (2 \times w)$

$= (2 \times \underline{\hspace{1cm}}) + (2 \times \underline{\hspace{1cm}})$ Think: Write the measures you know.

$= \underline{\hspace{1cm}} + \underline{\hspace{1cm}}$ Think: Do what is in parentheses first.

$= \underline{\hspace{1cm}}$

The perimeter of the rectangle is _____.

1. Can you use the Distributive Property to write the formula
$P = (2 \times l) + (2 \times w)$ another way? Explain.

_____

_____

_____

_____

Try This! **Write a formula for the perimeter of a square.**

Use the letter _____ for perimeter.

Use the letter _____ for the length of a side.

Formula: _____

2. Justify the formula you wrote for the perimeter of a square.

_____

_____

_____

_____

Name _____

Formulas for Perimeter

Rectangle:
$P = (2 \times l) + (2 \times w)$ or
$P = 2 \times (l + w)$

Square:
$P = 4 \times s$

1. Find the perimeter of the rectangle.

$P = (\underline{\hspace{1cm}} \times \underline{\hspace{1cm}}) + (\underline{\hspace{1cm}} \times \underline{\hspace{1cm}})$

$= (\underline{\hspace{1cm}} \times \underline{\hspace{1cm}}) + (\underline{\hspace{1cm}} \times \underline{\hspace{1cm}})$

$= \underline{\hspace{1cm}} + \underline{\hspace{1cm}}$

$= \underline{\hspace{1cm}}$

The perimeter is _____ feet.

8 ft

4 ft

Find the perimeter of the rectangle or square.

2.
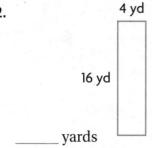
4 yd

16 yd

_____ yards

☑3.
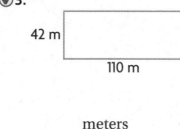
42 m

110 m

_____ meters

☑4.
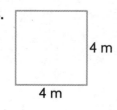
4 m

4 m

_____ meters

Math Talk   Math Processes and Practices ⑧

Draw Conclusions Can you use the formula $P = (2 \times l) + (2 \times w)$ to find the perimeter of a square? Explain.

On Your Own

Find the perimeter of the rectangle or square.

5.
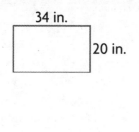
34 in.

20 in.

_____ inches

6.
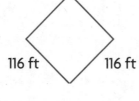
116 ft   116 ft

_____ feet

7.
21 m

42 m

_____ meters

8. **GO DEEPER**   Robert wants to put lights around the front of his house. The house is 12 yards long and 7 yards high. How many feet of lights does he need?

9. **Math Processes and Practices ①** **Analyze** What is the side length of a square with a perimeter of 60 meters?

🔑 Unlock the Problem

10. **THINK SMARTER** Alejandra plans to sew fringe on a scarf. The scarf is shaped like a rectangle. The length of the scarf is 48 inches. The width is one half the length. How much fringe does Alejandra need?

a. Draw a picture of the scarf, and label the given measurements on your drawing.

b. What do you need to find?

_____

d. Show the steps you use to solve the problem.

c. What formula will you use?

_____

e. Complete.

The length of the scarf is _____ inches.

The width is one half the length,

or _____ ÷ 2 = _____ inches.

So, the perimeter is (_____ × _____) +

(_____ × _____) = _____ inches.

f. Alejandra needs _____ of fringe.

11. **GO DEEPER** Marcia will make a frame for her picture. The picture frame will be three times as long as it is wide. The width of the frame will be 5 inches. How much wood does Marcia need for the frame?

_____

12. **THINK SMARTER** Maya is building a sandbox that is 36 inches wide. The length is four times the width. What is the perimeter of the sandbox? Show your work. Explain.

Perimeter

Learning Objective You will apply the
perimeter formula to find the perimeter of
rectangles and squares.

Find the perimeter of the rectangle or square.

1.

3 in.

9 in.

$9 + 3 + 9 + 3 = 24$

___24___ inches

2.

8 m

8 m

_____ meters

3.

12 ft

10 ft

_____ feet

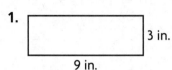
Problem Solving Real World

4. Troy is making a flag shaped like a square.
Each side measures 12 inches. He wants
to add ribbon along the edges. He has
36 inches of ribbon. Does he have enough
ribbon? **Explain.**

_____

5. The width of the Ochoa Community Pool
is 20 feet. The length is twice as long as its
width. What is the perimeter of the pool?

_____

6. **WRITE** ▸*Math* Imagine you want to put a border around a
rectangular room. Summarize the steps you would use to find
the length of border needed.

_____

_____

_____

_____

Lesson Check

1. What is the perimeter of a square window with sides 36 inches long?

2. What is the perimeter of the rectangle below?

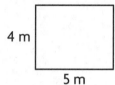

4 m

5 m

_____

_____

Spiral Review

3. Natalie drew the angle below.

What is the most reasonable estimate for the measure of the angle Natalie drew?

4. Ethan has 3 pounds of mixed nuts. How many ounces of mixed nuts does Ethan have?

_____

_____

5. How many lines of symmetry does the shape below appear to have?

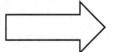

6. Janna drank 0.7 liter of water before soccer practice and 0.70 liter of water after practice. Compare the two decimals using <, =, or >.

_____

_____

FOR MORE PRACTICE
GO TO THE
Personal Math Trainer

Name _____

Area

Essential Question How can you use a formula to find the area of a rectangle?

Learning Objective You will apply the area formula to find the area of rectangles and squares.

Unlock the Problem

The **base, *b*,** of a two-dimensional figure can be any side. The **height, *h*,** is the measure of a perpendicular line segment from the base to the top of the figure.

Area is the measure of the number of unit squares needed to cover a flat surface without gaps or overlaps. A **square unit** is a square that is 1 unit long and 1 unit wide. To find the area of a figure, count the number of unit squares inside the figure.

How are the base, height, and area of a rectangle related?

Remember

Perpendicular lines and perpendicular line segments form right angles.

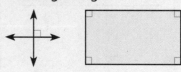

🔑 **Complete the table to find the area.**

Figure	Base	Height	Area
	5 units		

1. What relationship do you see among the base, height, and area?

_____

_____

2. Write a formula for the area of a rectangle. Use the letter *A* for area. Use the letter *b* for base. Use the letter *h* for height.

Formula: _____

Math Talk

Math Processes and Practices ⑦

Look for Structure How do you decide which side of a rectangle to use as the base?

Use a Formula You can use a formula to find the area.

$$A = b \times h$$

↑   ↑   ↑
area   base   height

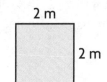
height

base

🔑 **Examples** Use a formula to find the area of a rectangle and a square.

A

6 ft

2 ft

$A = \quad b \quad \times \quad h$

= _____ × _____

= _____

The area is _____.

B

2 m

2 m

$A = \quad b \quad \times \quad h$

= _____ × _____

= _____

The area is _____.

Try This! Write a formula for the area of a square.

Use the letter _____ for area.

Use the letter _____ for the length of a side.

Formula: _____

Share and Show **MATH BOARD**

1. Find the area of the rectangle.

$A = b \times$ _____

= _____ × _____

= _____

11 cm

13 cm

724

© Houghton Mifflin Harcourt Publishing Company

Name _____

Find the area of the rectangle or square.

2.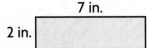
7 in.
2 in.

✓ 3.
9 m   9 m

✓ 4.
8 ft
14 ft
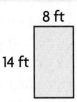

Math Talk

Math Processes and Practices ⑥

Explain how to find the area of a square if you only know the length of one side is 23 feet.

On Your Own

Find the area of the rectangle or square.

5.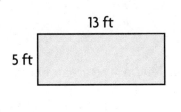
13 ft
5 ft

6.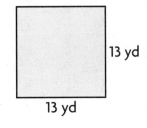
13 yd
13 yd

7.
2 cm
20 cm
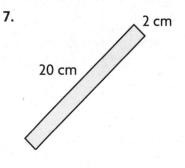

Practice: Copy and Solve Find the area of the rectangle.

8. base: 16 feet

   height: 6 feet

9. base: 9 yards

   height: 17 yards

10. base: 14 centimeters

    height: 11 centimeters

11. **GO DEEPER** Terry's rectangular yard is 15 meters by 18 meters. Todd's rectangular yard is 20 meters by 9 meters. How much greater is the area of Terry's yard than Todd's yard?

12. **Math Processes and Practices ②** Reason Quantitatively
Carmen sewed a square baby quilt that measures 36 inches on each side. What is the area of the quilt?

Unlock the Problem

13. **THINK SMARTER** Nancy and Luke are drawing plans for rectangular flower gardens. In Nancy's plan, the garden is 18 feet by 12 feet. In Luke's plan, the garden is 15 feet by 15 feet. Who drew the garden plan with the greater area? What is the area?

a. What do you need to find? _____

_____

b. What formula will you use? _____

c. What units will you use to write the answer? _____

d. Show the steps to solve the problem.

e. Complete the sentences.

The area of Nancy's garden is

_____.

The area of Luke's garden is

_____.

_____ garden has the greater area.

14. **GO DEEPER** Victor wants to buy fertilizer for his yard. The yard is 35 feet by 55 feet. The directions on the bag of fertilizer say that one bag will cover 1,250 square feet. How many bags of fertilizer should Victor buy to be sure that he covers the entire yard?

15. **THINK SMARTER** Tuan is an artist. He is painting on a large canvas that is 45 inches wide. The height of the canvas is 9 inches less than the width. What is the area of Tuan's canvas?

_____

_____ square inches

Area

Find the area of the rectangle or square.

1.
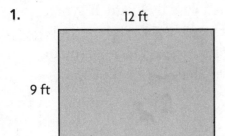
12 ft

9 ft

$A = b \times h$

$= 12 \times 9$

108 square feet

2.
8 yd

8 yd

_____

3.
15 m

3 m

_____

Problem Solving · Real World

4. Meghan is putting wallpaper on a wall that measures 8 feet by 12 feet. How much wallpaper does Meghan need to cover the wall?

   _____

5. Bryson is laying down sod in his yard to grow a new lawn. Each piece of sod is a 1-foot by 1-foot square. How many pieces of sod will Bryson need to cover his yard if his yard measures 30 feet by 14 feet?

   _____

6. **WRITE** ▸ *Math* Think about what you know about perimeter and area. Describe how to find the perimeter and area of your classroom.

_____

_____

_____

_____

Lesson Check

1. Ellie and Heather drew floor models of their living rooms. Ellie's model represented 20 feet by 15 feet. Heather's model represented 18 feet by 18 feet. Whose floor model represents the greater area? How much greater?

   _____

   _____

2. Tyra is laying down square carpet pieces in her photography studio. Each square carpet piece is 1 yard by 1 yard. If Tyra's photography studio is 7 yards long and 4 yards wide, how many pieces of square carpet will Tyra need?

   _____

   _____

Spiral Review

3. Typically, blood fully circulates through the human body 8 times each minute. How many times does blood circulate through the body in 1 hour?

   _____

4. Each of the 28 students in Romi's class raised at least $25 during the jump-a-thon. What is the least amount of money the class raised?

   _____

5. What is the perimeter of the shape below if each unit is 1 foot?

   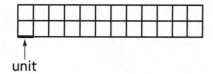

   unit

6. Ryan is making small meat loaves. Each small meat loaf uses $\frac{3}{4}$ pound of meat. How much meat does Ryan need to make 8 small meat loaves?

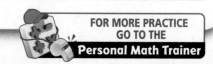

Name _____

Area of Combined Rectangles

Essential Question How can you find the area of combined rectangles?

Learning Objective You will find the area of complex shapes composed of rectangles by decomposing them into non-overlapping rectangles and adding the areas of the non-overlapping parts.

Unlock the Problem

Jan is visiting a botanical garden with her family. The diagram shows two rectangular sections of the garden. What is the total area of the two sections?

There are different ways to find the area of combined rectangles.

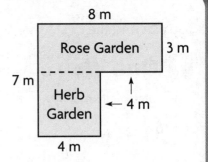

One Way Count unit squares.

Materials ■ grid paper

- Draw the garden on grid paper. Then find the area of each section by counting unit squares inside the shape.

Rose Garden	Herb Garden
Area = _____ square meters	Area = _____ square meters

- Add the areas.

_____ + _____ = _____ square meters

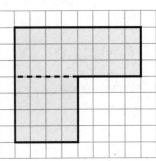

1 square = 1 square meter

Another Way Use the area formula for a rectangle.

Ⓐ Rose Garden

$A = b \times h$

= _____ × _____

= _____ square meters

Ⓑ Herb Garden

$A = b \times h$

= _____ × _____

= _____ square meters

- Add the areas.

_____ + _____ = _____ square meters

So, the total area is _____ square meters.

Math Talk

Math Processes and Practices ①

Analyze Is there another way you could divide the figure to find the total area? Explain.

🔑 Example

Greg is laying carpet in the space outside his laundry room. The diagram shows where the carpet will be installed. The space is made of combined rectangles. What is the area of the carpeted space?

You can find the area using addition or subtraction.

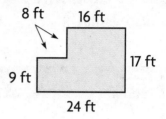

🔑 One Way Use addition.

Rectangle A	**Rectangle B**
$A = b \times h$	$A = b \times h$
$= 8 \times$ _____	$=$ _____ $\times\ 17$
$=$ _____	$=$ _____

Sum of the areas:

_____ + _____ = _____ square feet

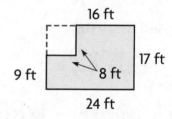

🔑 Another Way Use subtraction.

Area of whole space	**Area of missing section**
$A = b \times h$	$A = b \times h$
$= 24 \times$ _____	$=$ _____ $\times$ _____
$=$ _____	$=$ _____

Difference between the areas:

_____ − _____ = _____ square feet

So, the area of the carpeted space is _____ square feet.

- Is there another way you could divide the figure to find the total area? Explain.

_____

_____

_____

Name _____

1. Explain how to find the total area of the figure.

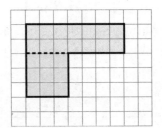

_____

_____

_____

Find the area of the combined rectangles.

2.

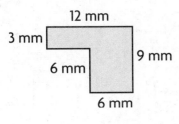

_____

☑ 3.

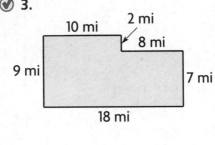

_____

☑ 4.

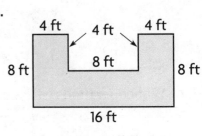

_____

Math Talk Math Processes and Practices ⑥

Describe the characteristics of combined rectangles.

On Your Own

Find the area of the combined rectangles.

5. **Math Processes and Practices ⑥** **Attend to Precision** Jamie's mom wants to enlarge her rectangular garden by adding a new rectangular section. The garden is now 96 square yards. What will the total area of the garden be after she adds the new section?

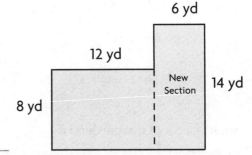

_____

6. **GO DEEPER** Explain how to find the perimeter and area of the combined rectangles at the right.

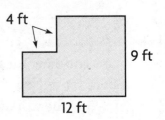

_____

_____

_____

_____

Unlock the Problem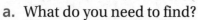

7. **THINK SMARTER** The diagram shows the layout of Mandy's garden. The garden is the shape of combined rectangles. What is the area of the garden?

a. What do you need to find?

_____

b. How can you divide the figure to help you find the total area?

_____

_____

c. What operations will you use to find the answer?

_____

d. Draw a diagram to show how you divided the figure. Then show the steps to solve the problem.

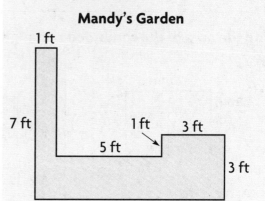

Mandy's Garden

So, the area of the garden is _____ .

Personal Math Trainer

8. **THINK SMARTER +** Workers are painting a large letter L for an outdoor sign. The diagram shows the dimensions of the L. For numbers 8a–8c, select Yes or No to tell whether you can add the products to find the area that the workers will paint.

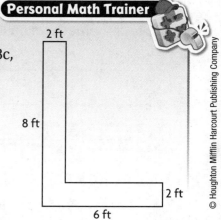

8a.	2×8 and 2×4	○ Yes ○ No
8b.	2×6 and 2×8	○ Yes ○ No
8c.	2×6 and 6×2	○ Yes ○ No

Area of Combined Rectangles

Find the area of the combined rectangles.

1.

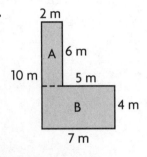

Area A = 2 × 6,

Area B = 7 × 4

12 + 28 = 40

_____ **40 square meters**

2.

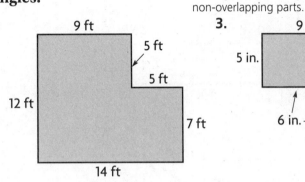

_____

3.

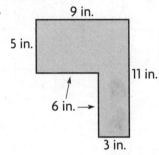

_____

Problem Solving Real World

Use the diagram for 4–5.

Nadia makes the diagram below to represent the counter space she wants to build in her craft room.

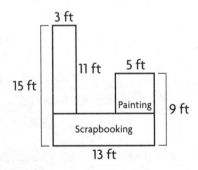

4. What is the area of the space that Nadia has shown for scrapbooking?

_____

5. What is the area of the space she has shown for painting?

_____

6. **WRITE** ▸*Math* Write a word problem that involves combined rectangles. Include a diagram and the solution.

_____

_____

_____

Lesson Check

1. What is the area of the combined rectangles below?

   20 yd

   5 yd

   3 yd

   12 yd

   _____

2. Marquis is redecorating his bedroom. What could Marquis use the area formula to find?

   _____

Spiral Review

3. Giraffes are the tallest land animals. A male giraffe can grow as tall as 6 yards. How tall would the giraffe be in feet?

   _____

4. Drew purchased 3 books each with a different price, for $24. The cost of each book was a multiple of 4. What could be the prices of the 3 books?

   _____

5. Esmeralda has a magnet in the shape of a square. Each side of the magnet is 3 inches long. What is the perimeter of her magnet?

6. What is the area of the rectangle below?

   9 feet

   7 feet

   _____

FOR MORE PRACTICE
GO TO THE
Personal Math Trainer

Name _____

✓ Mid-Chapter Checkpoint

▶ **Vocabulary**

Choose the best term from the box.

Vocabulary
area
base
formula
perimeter
square unit (sq un)

1. A square that is 1 unit wide and 1 unit long is a

   _____. (p. 723)

2. The _____ of a two-dimensional figure can be
   any side. (p. 723)

3. A set of symbols that expresses a mathematical rule is

   called a _____. (p. 718)

4. The _____ is the distance around a shape. (p. 717)

▶ **Concepts and Skills**

Find the perimeter and area of the rectangle or square.

5.
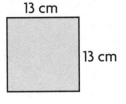
13 cm
13 cm

_____

6.
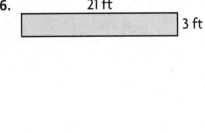
21 ft
3 ft

_____

7.
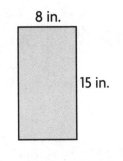
8 in.
15 in.

_____

Find the area of the combined rectangles.

8.
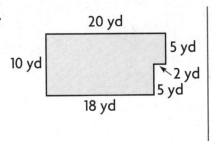
20 yd
10 yd
5 yd
2 yd
5 yd
18 yd

_____

9.
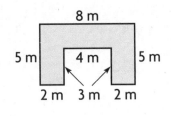
8 m
5 m
4 m
5 m
2 m 3 m 2 m

_____

10.
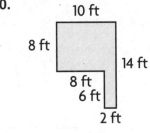
10 ft
8 ft
14 ft
8 ft
6 ft
2 ft

_____

11. Which figure has the greatest perimeter?

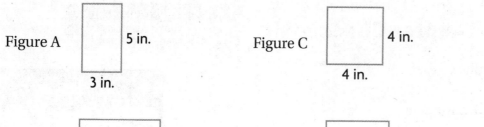

Figure A   5 in.   3 in.

Figure C   4 in.   4 in.

Figure B   3 in.   6 in.

Figure D   3 in.   4 in.

_____

12. Which figure has an area of 108 square centimeters?

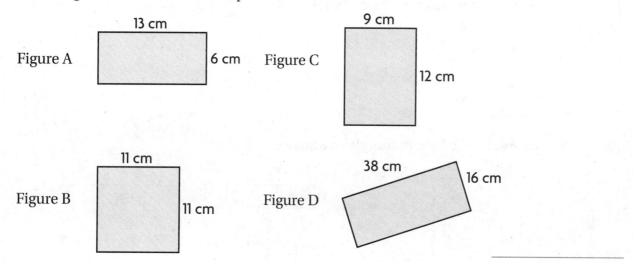

Figure A   13 cm   6 cm

Figure C   9 cm   12 cm

Figure B   11 cm   11 cm

Figure D   38 cm   16 cm

_____

13. **GO DEEPER** Which of the combined rectangles has an area of 40 square feet?

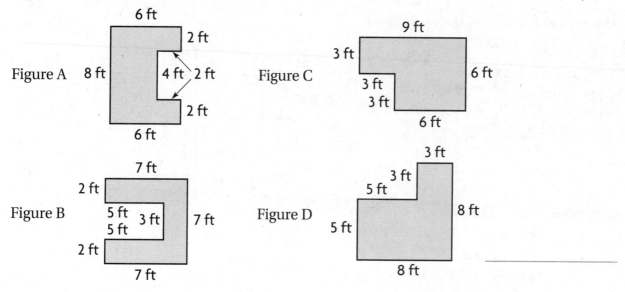

Figure A   6 ft   2 ft   8 ft   4 ft   2 ft   2 ft   6 ft

Figure C   9 ft   3 ft   3 ft   3 ft   6 ft   6 ft

Figure B   7 ft   2 ft   5 ft   3 ft   5 ft   7 ft   2 ft   7 ft

Figure D   3 ft   3 ft   5 ft   8 ft   5 ft   8 ft

_____

Name _____

Find Unknown Measures

Essential Question How can you find an unknown measure of a rectangle given its area or perimeter?

Learning Objective You will use a formula to find the unknown measure of a side of a rectangle when given its perimeter or area.

Unlock the Problem

Tanisha is painting a mural that is in the shape of a rectangle. The mural covers an area of 54 square feet. The base of the mural measures 9 feet. What is its height?

Use a formula for area.

- **What do you need to find?**

  _____

- **What information do you know?**

  _____

🔑 Example 1 Find an unknown measure given the area.

MODEL	RECORD

MODEL

Think: Label the measures you know. Use *n* for the unknown.

A = _____   *h* = _____

b = _____

So, the height of the mural is _____ feet.

RECORD

Use the model to write an equation and solve.

_____ = _____ _____   Write the formula for area.

_____ = _____ _____   Use the model to write an equation.

54 = 9 × _____   What times 9 equals 54?

The value of *n* is _____.

Think: *n* is the height of the mural.

Math Talk

Math Processes and Practices ②

Reason Abstractly How can you use division to find an unknown factor?

1. What if the mural were in the shape of a square with an area of 81 square feet? What would the height of the mural be? Explain.

   _____

   _____

2. Explain how you can find an unknown side length of any square, when given only the area of the square.

   _____

   _____

   _____

Example 2 Find an unknown measure given the perimeter.

Gary is building an outdoor pen in the shape of a rectangle for his dog. He will use 24 meters of fencing. The pen will be 3 meters wide. How long will the pen be?

Use a formula for perimeter.

MODEL

Think: Label the measures you know. Use n for the unknown.

$w =$ _____

$l =$ _____

$P =$ _____

RECORD

Use the model to write an equation and solve.

$$P = (2 \times l) + (2 \times w)$$

_____ = (_____ _____) + (_____ _____)

_____ = (_____ _____) + _____

Think: $(2 \times n)$ is an unknown addend.

$24 =$ _____ $+ 6$ Think: What is $24 - 6$?

The value of $(2 \times n)$ is 18.

To find the value of n, find the unknown factor.

$2 \times$ _____ $= 18$

The value of n is _____.

Think: n is the length of the pen.

So, the pen will be _____ long.

ERROR Alert

Check that you are using the correct formula. Are you given the area or the perimeter?

Try This! The perimeter of a square is 24 feet. Find the side length.

Draw a model.	Write an equation.
	$P = 4 \times s$

Name _____

1. Find the unknown measure. The area of the rectangle is 36 square feet.

$A = b \times h$

_____ $= b \times$ _____

The base of the rectangle is _____ .

3 ft [rectangle]
?

Find the unknown measure of the rectangle.

2.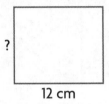
?
12 cm

Perimeter = 44 centimeters

width = _____

3. 9 in
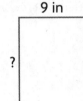
?

Area = 108 square inches

height = _____

4.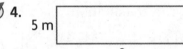
5 m
?

Area = 90 square meters

base = _____

Math Talk

Math Processes and Practices ②

Represent a Problem Explain how using the area formula helps you find the base of a rectangle when you know its area and height.

On Your Own

5.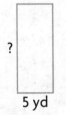
?
5 yd

Perimeter = 34 yards

length = _____

6.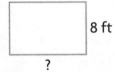
8 ft
?

Area = 96 square feet

base = _____

7.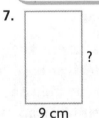
?
9 cm

Area = 126 square centimeters

height = _____

8. **GO DEEPER** A square has an area of 49 square inches. Explain how to find the perimeter of the square.

_____

_____

_____

_____

Problem Solving • Applications

9. **Math Processes and Practices 7** **Identify Relationships** The area of a swimming pool is 120 square meters. The width of the pool is 8 meters. What is the length of the pool in centimeters?

_____

Personal Math Trainer

10. **THINK SMARTER +** An outdoor deck is 7 feet wide. The perimeter of the deck is 64 feet. What is the length of the deck? Use the numbers to write an equation and solve. A number may be used more than once.

| 7 | 9 | 5 | 14 | 25 | 50 | 64 |

$P = (2 \times l) + (2 \times w)$

$\boxed{} = (2 \times l) + (2 \times \boxed{})$

$\boxed{} = 2 \times l + \boxed{}$

$\boxed{} = 2 \times l$

$\boxed{} = l$

So, the length of the deck is _____ feet.

Connect to Science

Mountain Lions

Mountain lions are also known as cougars, panthers, or pumas. Their range once was from coast to coast in North America and from Argentina to Alaska. Hunting and habitat destruction now restricts their range to mostly mountainous, unpopulated areas.

Mountain lions are solitary animals. A male's territory often overlaps two females' territories but never overlaps another male's. The average size of a male's territory is 108 square miles, but it may be smaller or larger depending on how plentiful food is.

11. **THINK SMARTER** A male mountain lion has a rectangular territory with an area of 96 square miles. If his territory is 8 miles wide, what is the length of his territory? _____

Name _____

Find Unknown Measures

Learning Objective You will use a formula to find the unknown measure of a side of a rectangle when given its perimeter or area.

Find the unknown measure of the rectangle.

1.

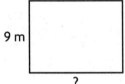

20 ft

Perimeter = 54 feet

width = __7 feet__

Think: $P = (2 \times l) + (2 \times w)$
$54 = (2 \times 20) + (2 \times w)$
$54 = 40 + (2 \times w)$
Since $54 = 40 + 14$, $2 \times w = 14$, and $w = 7$.

2.

9 m

?

3.

?

4 cm

4.

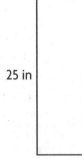

25 in

Perimeter = 42 meters

length = _____

Area = 28 square centimeters

height = _____

Area = 200 square inches

base = _____

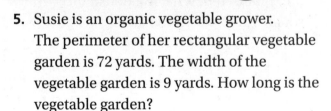

Problem Solving *Real World*

5. Susie is an organic vegetable grower. The perimeter of her rectangular vegetable garden is 72 yards. The width of the vegetable garden is 9 yards. How long is the vegetable garden?

_____

6. **WRITE** *Math* Write a problem that involves finding the unknown measure of a side of a rectangle. Include the solution.

_____

_____

_____

Lesson Check

1. The area of a rectangular photograph is 35 square inches. If the width of the photo is 5 inches, how tall is the photo?

2. Natalie used 112 inches of blue yarn as a border around her rectangular bulletin board. If the bulletin board is 36 inches wide, how long is it?

Spiral Review

3. A professional basketball court is in the shape of a rectangle. It is 50 feet wide and 94 feet long. A player runs one time around the edge of the court. How far does the player run?

4. On a compass, due east is a $\frac{1}{4}$ turn clockwise from due north. How many degrees are in a $\frac{1}{4}$ turn?

5. Hakeem's frog made three quick jumps. The first was 1 meter. The second jump was 85 centimeters. The third jump was 400 millimeters. What was the total length in centimeters of the frog's three jumps?

6. Karen colors in squares on a grid. She colored $\frac{1}{8}$ of the squares blue and $\frac{5}{8}$ of the squares red. What fraction of the squares are not colored in?

FOR MORE PRACTICE
GO TO THE
Personal Math Trainer

Name _____

Problem Solving • Find the Area

Essential Question How can you use the strategy *solve a simpler problem* to solve area problems?

Learning Objective You will use the strategy *solve a simpler problem* to solve area problems by breaking apart the problem into simpler steps.

Unlock the Problem

A landscaper is laying grass for a rectangular playground. The grass will cover the whole playground except for a square sandbox. The diagram shows the playground and sandbox. How many square yards of grass will the landscaper use?

Use the graphic organizer below to solve the problem.

25 yd

Playground

Sandbox →

15 yd

6 yd

Read the Problem

What do I need to find?

I need to find how many _____ the landscaper will use.

What information do I need to use?

The grass will cover the _____.

The grass will not cover the _____.

The length and width of the playground are

_____ and _____.

The side length of the square sandbox is

_____.

How will I use the information?

I can solve simpler problems.

Find the area of the _____.

Find the area of the _____.

Then _____ the area of the _____

from the area of the _____.

Solve the Problem

First, find the area of the playground.

$A = b \times h$

= _____ × _____

= _____ square yards

Next, find the area of the sandbox.

$A = s \times s$

= _____ × _____

= _____ square yards

Last, subtract the area of the sandbox from the area of the playground.

$$\begin{array}{r} 375 \\ -\ 36 \\ \hline \end{array}$$ square yards

So, the landscaper will use _____

_____ of grass to cover the playground.

 Math Processes and Practices ❶

Make Sense of Problems
How did the strategy help you solve the problem?

🔓 Try Another Problem

Zach is laying a rectangular brick patio for a new museum. Brick will cover the whole patio except for a rectangular fountain, as shown in the diagram. How many square meters of brick does Zach need?

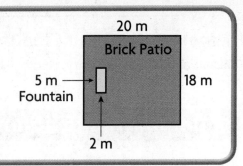

Read the Problem	Solve the Problem
What do I need to find?	
What information do I need to use?	
How will I use this information?	

- How many square meters of brick does Zach need? Explain.

_____

_____

_____

Name _____

Share and Show MATH BOARD

1. Lila is wallpapering one wall of her bedroom, as shown in the diagram. She will cover the whole wall except for the doorway. How many square feet of wall does Lila need to cover?

First, find the area of the wall.

$A = b \times h$

= _____ × _____

= _____ square feet

Next, find the area of the door.

$A = b \times h$

= _____ × _____

= _____ square feet

Last, subtract the area of the door from the area of the wall.

_____ − _____ = _____ square feet

So, Lila needs to cover _____ of wall.

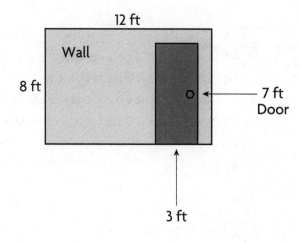

12 ft

Wall

8 ft

7 ft
Door

3 ft

2. What if there was a square window on the wall with a side length of 2 feet? How much wall would Lila need to cover then? Explain.

_____

_____

_____

3. Ed is building a model of a house with a flat roof, as shown in the diagram. There is a chimney through the roof. Ed will cover the roof with square tiles. If the area of each tile is 1 square inch, how many tiles will he need? Explain.

_____

_____

_____

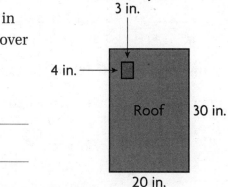

Chimney
3 in.

4 in.

Roof

30 in.

20 in.

© Houghton Mifflin Harcourt Publishing Company

On Your Own

4. **Math Processes and Practices ❶** **Make Sense of Problems** Lia has a dog and a cat. Together, the pets weigh 28 pounds. The dog weighs 3 times as much as the cat. How much does each pet weigh?

_____

5. **THINK SMARTER** Mr. Foster is covering two rectangular pictures with glass. One is 6 inches by 4 inches and the other one is 5 inches by 5 inches. Does he need the same number of square inches of glass for each picture? Explain.

_____

6. **GO DEEPER** Claire says the area of a square with a side length of 100 centimeters is greater than the area of a square with a side length of 1 meter. Is she correct? Explain.

WRITE ▸ Math
Show Your Work

_____

_____

_____

7. **THINK SMARTER** A rectangular floor is 12 feet long and 11 feet wide. Janine places a rug that is 9 feet long and 7 feet wide and covers part of the floor in the room. Select the word(s) to complete the sentence.

To find the number of square feet of the floor that is NOT covered by the rug,

add		area of the rug		from	
subtract	the	length of the rug		by	the area of the floor.
multiply		area of the floor		to	

Name _____

Problem Solving • Find the Area

Learning Objective You will use the strategy *solve a simpler problem* to solve area problems by breaking apart the problem into simpler steps.

Solve each problem.

1. A room has a wooden floor. There is a rug in the center of the floor. The diagram shows the room and the rug. How many square feet of the wood floor still show?

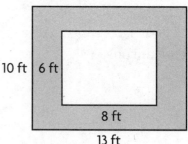

_____ **82 square feet** _____

Area of the floor: 13 × 10 = 130 square feet
Area of the rug: 8 × 6 = 48 square feet
Subtract to find the area of the floor still showing: 130 − 48 = 82 square feet

2. A rectangular wall has a square window, as shown in the diagram.

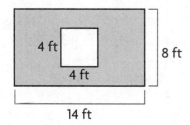

What is the area of the wall NOT including the window?

_____

_____

3. Bob wants to put down new sod in his backyard, except for the part set aside for his flower garden. The diagram shows Bob's backyard and the flower garden.

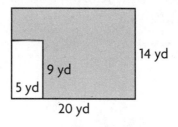

How much sod will Bob need?

_____

_____

4. A rectangular painting is 24 inches wide and 20 inches tall without the frame. With the frame, it is 28 inches wide and 24 inches tall. What is the area of the frame not covered by the painting?

5. **WRITE** ▸*Math* Suppose you painted the walls of your classroom. Describe how to find the area of the walls that are painted.

_____

_____

_____

Lesson Check

1. One wall in Zoe's bedroom is 5 feet wide and 8 feet tall. Zoe puts up a poster of her favorite athlete. The poster is 2 feet wide and 3 feet tall. How much of the wall is not covered by the poster?

_____

2. A garage door is 15 feet wide and 6 feet high. It is painted white, except for a rectangular panel 1 foot high and 9 feet wide that is brown. How much of the garage door is white?

_____

Spiral Review

3. Kate made a box to hold her jewelry collection. She used 42 inches of wood to build the sides of the box. If the box was 9 inches wide, how long was the box?

_____

4. Larry, Mary, and Terry each had a full glass of juice. Larry drank $\frac{3}{4}$ of his. Mary drank $\frac{3}{8}$ of hers. Terry drank $\frac{7}{10}$ of his. Who drank less than $\frac{1}{2}$ of their juice?

_____

5. List all of the numbers between 20 and 30 that are prime.

_____

6. Tom and some friends went to a movie. The show started at 2:30 P.M. and ended at 4:15 P.M. How long did the movie last?

_____

FOR MORE PRACTICE
GO TO THE
Personal Math Trainer

Name _____

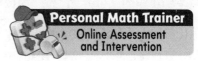
1. For numbers 1a–1e, select Yes or No to indicate if a rectangle with the given dimensions would have a perimeter of 50 inches.

    1a. length: 25 inches   width: 2 inches   ○ Yes   ○ No

    1b. length: 20 inches   width: 5 inches   ○ Yes   ○ No

    1c. length: 17 inches   width: 8 inches   ○ Yes   ○ No

    1d. length: 15 inches   width: 5 inches   ○ Yes   ○ No

    1e. length: 15 inches   width: 10 inches   ○ Yes   ○ No

2. The swimming club's indoor pool is in a rectangular building. Marco is laying tile around the rectangular pool.

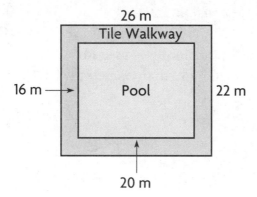

Part A

What is the area of the pool and the area of the pool and the walkway? Show your work.

Part B

How many square meters of tile will Marco need for the walkway? Explain how you found your answer.

Assessment Options
Chapter Test

3. Match the dimensions of the rectangles in the top row with the correct area or perimeter in the bottom row.

length: 5 cm width: 9 cm	length: 6 cm width: 6 cm	length: 6 cm width: 5 cm	length: 9 cm width: 6 cm

•   •   •   •

•   •   •   •

area = 36 sq cm	perimeter = 22 cm	perimeter = 30 cm	area = 45 sq cm

4. Kyleigh put a large rectangular sticker on her notebook. The height of the sticker measures 18 centimeters. The base is half as long as the height. What area of the notebook does the sticker cover?

_____ square centimeters

Personal Math Trainer

5. THINK SMARTER＋ A rectangular flower garden in Samantha's backyard has 100 feet around its edge. The width of the garden is 20 feet. What is the length of the garden? Use the numbers to write an equation and solve. A number may be used more than once.

10	20	50	30	40	60	100

$P = (2 \times l) + (2 \times w)$

$\boxed{} = (2 \times l) + (2 \times \boxed{})$

$\boxed{} = 2 \times l + \boxed{}$

$\boxed{} = 2 \times l$

$\boxed{} = l$

So, the length of the garden is $\boxed{}$ feet.

6. Gary drew a rectangle with a perimeter of 20 inches. Then he tried to draw a square with a perimeter of 20 inches.

Draw 3 different rectangles that Gary could have drawn. Then draw the square, if possible.

© Houghton Mifflin Harcourt Publishing Company

Name _____

7. Ami and Bert are drawing plans for rectangular vegetable gardens. In Ami's plan, the garden is 13 feet by 10 feet. In Bert's plan the garden is 12 feet by 12 feet. For numbers 7a–7d, select True or False for each statement.

    7a.   The area of Ami's garden is 130 square feet.   ○ True   ○ False

    7b.   The area of Bert's garden is 48 square feet.   ○ True   ○ False

    7c.   Ami's garden has a greater area than Bert's garden.   ○ True   ○ False

    7d.   The area of Bert's garden is 14 square feet greater than Ami's.   ○ True   ○ False

8. A farmer planted corn in a square field. One side of the field measures 32 yards. What is the area of the cornfield? Show your work.

9.  Harvey bought a frame in which he put his family's picture.

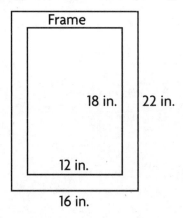

Frame

18 in.   22 in.

12 in.

16 in.

What is the area of the frame?

_____ square inches

10. Kelly has 236 feet of fence to use to enclose a rectangular space for her dog. She wants the width to be 23 feet. Draw a rectangle that could be the space for Kelly's dog. Label the length and the width.

11. The diagram shows the dimensions of a new parking lot at Helen's Health Food store.

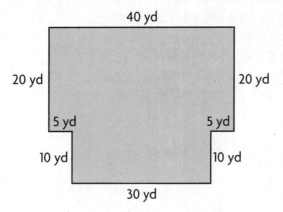

Use either addition or subtraction to find the area of the parking lot. Show your work.

12. Chad's bedroom floor is 12 feet long and 10 feet wide. He has an area rug on his floor that is 7 feet long and 5 feet wide. Which statement tells how to find the amount of the floor that is not covered by the rug? Mark all that apply.

(A) Add 12×10 and 7×5.

(B) Subtract 35 from 12×10

(C) Subtract 10×5 from 12×7.

(D) Add $12 + 10 + 7 + 5$.

(E) Subtract 7×5 from 12×10.

(F) Subtract 12×10 from 7×5.

13. A row of plaques covers 120 square feet of space along a wall. If the plaques are 3 feet tall, what length of the wall do they cover?

_____ feet

Name _____

14. Ms. Bennett wants to buy carpeting for her living room and dining room.

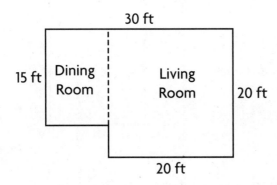

Explain how she can find the amount of carpet she needs to cover the floor in both rooms. Then find the amount of carpet she will need.

15. Lorenzo built a rectangular brick patio. He is putting a stone border around the edge of the patio. The width of the patio is 12 feet. The length of the patio is two feet longer than the width.

How many feet of stone will Lorenzo need? Explain how you found your answer.

16. Which rectangle has a perimeter of 10 feet? Mark all that apply.

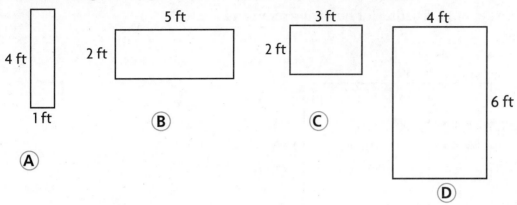

17. A folder is 11 inches long and 8 inches wide. Alyssa places a sticker that is 2 inches long and 1 inch wide on the notebook. Choose the words that correctly complete the sentence.

To find the number of square inches of the folder that is NOT covered by the sticker,

add		width of the sticker	from		width of the sticker.
subtract	the	area of the sticker	by	the	area of the sticker.
multiply		area of the notebook	to		area of the notebook.

18. Tricia is cutting her initial from a piece of felt.

For numbers 18a–18c, select Yes or No to tell whether you can add the products to find the number of square centimeters Tricia needs.

8 cm
1 cm   1 cm
3 cm   3 cm
5 cm

18a. 1×8 and 5×2 ○ Yes   ○ No

18b. 3×5 and 1×8 ○ Yes   ○ No

18c. 2×5 and 1×3 and 1×3 ○ Yes   ○ No

19. Mr. Butler posts his students' artwork on a bulletin board.

The width and length of the bulletin board are whole numbers. What could be the dimensions of the bulletin board Mr. Butler uses?

Area = 15 square feet

Math and Science Skills

Use with *ScienceFusion* pages 22–23.

Develop Concepts

1. Suppose you are a space scientist who wants to send a robot to Mars to test soil samples. How might you use math?

_____

_____

_____

2. Suppose you are a weather scientist. How would you use numbers in your investigations?

_____

_____

_____

Develop Inquiry Skills

3. Which estimated whale populations are the smallest and the largest?

_____

_____

_____

4. How can you tell that these numbers are all estimates?

_____

_____

_____

Do the Math!

5. Complete the table with the data from the whale populations table. List the whales in order from least population to greatest population. Then find how much less the whale population for one kind of whale is compared to the whale with the next greatest population.

Kind of Whale	Population	Amount Greater than Previous Whale Population
Blue whale	14,000	N/A
Humpback whale	40,000	26,000

6. Which two kinds of whales have a population that is the closest to one another? Explain your answer.

_____

_____

7. How much greater is the greatest population than the least population? How did you find it?

_____

_____

Summarize

8. What skills do you use in math and science?

_____

_____

_____

Name _____

Heat Proofing a Home

Use with *ScienceFusion*
pages 210–211.

Develop Concepts

1. Why do you think a specific gas is used instead of air?

_____

_____

_____

2. What are some ways that we keep heat from coming into our homes when the weather is hot and leaving our homes when the weather is cold?

_____

_____

_____

Develop Inquiry Skills

3. Why are basements usually cool year-round?

_____

_____

_____

4. How might you eliminate the need to air-condition your house, even in the hottest weather?

_____

_____

_____

Do the Math!

5. Complete the table with the data on the Ogburn family's plan to heat proof their house.

Action	Savings per year	Cost
Adding insulation	$	$400
Wrapping pipes	$	$100
Buying new windows	$	$10,500
Total	$	$

6. About how much more money will replacing the windows save each year than wrapping the water pipes? Justify your answer mathematically.

_____

_____

7. In how many years will the savings pay for the cost of these home improvements? Explain your answer.

_____

_____

Summarize

8. What causes heat transfer, and how can you reduce it?

_____

_____

_____

_____

The Food Eaters

Develop Inquiry Skills

1. How does the amount of food that the animal eats relate to how much it weighs? Is anything surprising?

_____

_____

_____

2. Which animal is most likely to have more changes in its diet during the year? Explain.

_____

_____

_____

Develop Vocabulary

3. Define the following terms in your own words.

Consumer: _____

_____

_____

Producer: _____

_____

_____

Do the Math!

4. Complete the table to find the fraction of an animal's body weight that it eats each day. The numerator is how much the animal eats and the denominator is how much the animal weighs.

Animal	How Much It Eats a Day	How Much It Weighs	Fraction of Its Body Weight	Rank (1 is greatest fraction)
Giant panda	20 kg	160 kg		
Giraffe	25 kg	1,250 kg		
Blue whale	7 metric tons	180 metric tons		

5. Which animal eats the highest fraction of its body weight of food every day? Least?

_____

_____

_____

6. How many kilograms of food would 18 giraffes eat? Show your work.

_____

_____

_____

Summarize

7. What is a consumer? Give some examples.

_____

_____

_____

Fast or Slow?

Use with *ScienceFusion* pages 268–269.

Develop Vocabulary

1. Define the following terms in your own words.

Speed: _____

_____

_____

Velocity: _____

_____

_____

Develop Concepts

2. What does the number line show? Which animal traveled the farthest?

_____

_____

_____

3. Which animal was the fastest? Which animal was the slowest? How do you know?

_____

_____

_____

Do the Math!

4. Complete the table with the data on the distance traveled for the turtle, cat, and rabbit. Divide the distance traveled by the time to calculate the speed of the animal.

Animal	Distance Traveled (meters)	Time (seconds)	Speed (meters per second)
Rabbit		10	
Turtle		10	
Cat		10	

5. Which animal was the fastest? List the animals in order from the slowest to the fastest.

_____

_____

_____

6. A chicken joins the race and runs at 4 meters per second. How far would the chicken run in 10 seconds?

_____

_____

Summarize

7. Compare speed and velocity.

_____

_____

_____

Name _____

Flash and Boom!

Use with *ScienceFusion* pages 176–177.

Develop Concepts

1. The sun is Earth's main source of light energy. How else do we get light energy?

_____

_____

_____

2. How is sound made? How can you describe sound?

_____

_____

_____

Develop Inquiry Skills

3. Which instruments are most alike? Explain.

_____

_____

_____

4. How are the drum and saxophone alike?

_____

_____

_____

Do the Math!

5. Complete the table to show how far away lightning is based on the time between seeing the lightning and hearing the thunder.

Time (sec)	35	20	40		15	
Distance (mi)				10		6

6. There are 15 seconds from the time you see lightning to the time you hear thunder. How far away is the lightning? Explain how you found your answer.

_____

_____

_____

7. Lightning is 60 miles away. How many seconds will there be between seeing the lightning and hearing the thunder? Explain how you found your answer.

_____

_____

Summarize

8. How are light and sound alike? How are they different?

_____

_____

_____

Name _____

What Goes Up Must Come Down

Use with *ScienceFusion* pages 348–349.

Develop Vocabulary

1. Define the following terms in your own words.

Condensation: _____

_____

_____

Precipitation: _____

_____

_____

Develop Concepts

2. What happens to all water on Earth?

_____

_____

_____

3. Imagine you are a raindrop falling to Earth's surface. Describe your path through the water cycle.

_____

_____

_____

_____

Do the Math!

4. Complete the table with the sizes of droplets and dust particles compared to a raindrop. Then, rank their sizes from 1–4 with 1 being the smallest.

Object	Fraction of a Raindrop	Rank
Average droplet		
Raindrop		
Dust particle		
Large droplet		

5. How do you know which fraction is the smallest? The largest?

_____

_____

_____

6. Another droplet is $\frac{1}{50}$ the size of a raindrop. Write all of the fractions, including this one, from largest to smallest.

_____

_____

_____

Summarize

7. What are the stages of the water cycle?

_____

_____

_____

Bringing Up Baby

Use with *ScienceFusion* pages 502–505.

Develop Inquiry Skills

1. What visual clues in the picture tell you that an alligator's eggs are soft and leathery instead of hard and brittle?

_____

_____

_____

2. Compare and contrast the life cycle of a penguin and a kangaroo.

_____

_____

_____

Develop Concepts

3. Animals that feed their young are called mammals. What other animals do you know that feed they young milk?

_____

_____

_____

4. How do young animals that are not mammals get fed?

_____

_____

_____

Do the Math!

5. Raccoons usually give birth to 3 to 5 young at a time. Raccoons give birth only once a year. Suppose a female raccoon lives 10 years. She is able to give birth for 9 of those years. Complete the table to show possible numbers of offspring that a female raccoon can have in her lifetime.

	Year 1	Year 2	Year 3	Year 4	Year 5	Year 6	Year 7	Year 8	Year 9	Total
3 babies										
5 babies										

6. How many offspring will she have? Explain how you found the answer.

_____

_____

_____

7. Why is there not an exact answer?

_____

_____

_____

Summarize

8. Compare the life cycles of the following groups of organisms: turtles and penguins, cats and kangaroos, or bluebirds and deer?

_____

_____

_____

Generating Electricity

Use with *ScienceFusion* pages 250–251.

Develop Concepts

1. What might happen if people don't conserve electricity?

_____

_____

_____

2. What are some ways that you, personally, can conserve electricity?

_____

_____

_____

Develop Vocabulary

3. Define the following terms in your own words.

Generator: _____

_____

_____

Do the Math!

4. Complete the table with the data on Sam's electricity bill.

Animal	Fraction of Bill	Amount (in dollars)
Air Conditioner	$\frac{1}{2}$	
Water Heater	$\frac{1}{5}$	
Other		

5. How much did it cost to run everything besides the air conditioner and the water heater? Explain how you found your answer.

_____

_____

_____

6. What might be included in "other"?

_____

_____

_____

Summarize

7. Why is it important to conserve electricity?

_____

_____

_____

The Good and the Bad of It

Use with *ScienceFusion* pages 92–93.

Develop Concepts

1. Why do people want different kinds of light bulbs?

_____

_____

_____

2. Do all light bulbs serve a practical purpose?

_____

_____

_____

Develop Inquiry Skills

3. Before airplanes were invented, in what other ways did people travel long distances? Were these ways better or worse than flying?

_____

_____

_____

4. What are some examples of new problems caused by the invention of airplanes?

_____

_____

_____

Do the Math!

Complete the table using the Light Bulb Cost Comparison chart. Then use the data in the table to answer the questions below.

Light Bulb Cost Comparisons		
	25-Watt CFL	**100-Watt Incandescent**
Cost of bulb	$3.40	
Bulb life	1,667 days (4.5 years)	
Energy cost per year	$6.00	
Total cost over 4.5 years	$27.00	

5. How much more is the total cost of an incandescent bulb than a CFL? How much would your yearly energy cost be if you had 20 CFL bulbs in your home? Which bulb lasts longer?

_____

_____

6. How can you tell which bulb is better for the bulb life? For the total cost over 4.5 years? Explain your answer.

_____

_____

7. Costs are usually written as decimals. Write the following costs from the table using fractions instead of decimals: 3.40, 0.60, 118.50.

_____

_____

Summarize

8. What is the connection between technology growth, new problems, and further technology growth?

_____

_____

_____

Name _____

You Have a Solution

Develop Vocabulary

1. Define the following terms in your own words.

Solution: _____

_____

_____

Solvent: _____

_____

_____

Develop Concepts

2. Do the pepper and water make a solution? Explain your answer.

_____

_____

_____

_____

3. Do the salt and water make a solution? Explain your answer.

_____

_____

_____

_____

Do the Math!

4. Complete the table. Find the amount of sugar or water needed for each solution.

Substance	Ratio	Solution 1	Solution 2	Solution 3
Sugar	210 g	g	g	1,050 g
Water	100 ml	200 ml	700 ml	ml

5. Explain how you found the number of grams of sugar when you knew the number of milliliters of water.

_____

_____

_____

6. How much water will it take to dissolve 1,050 g of sugar? Explain your answer.

_____

_____

_____

Summarize

7. How are solutions and mixtures alike? How are they different?

_____

_____

_____

© Houghton Mifflin Harcourt Publishing Company

Other Models Scientists Use

Develop Concepts

1. What kinds of toys are used to build three-dimensional models?

_____

_____

_____

_____

2. Why might you choose to use a computer model instead of a physical model?

_____

_____

_____

_____

Develop Vocabulary

3 . Define the following terms in your own words.

Three-dimensional model: _____

_____

_____

Computer model: _____

_____

_____

Do the Math!

4. Complete the table with the data for the model of the solar system. Use whole numbers, fractions, or mixed numbers to estimate the size of Earth compared to each object.

Planet	Diameter (mm)	Diameter compared to Earth
Sun	1,100	
Mercury	4	
Venus	9	$\frac{9}{10}$
Earth	10	$\frac{1}{1}$
Mars	5	
Jupiter	110	
Saturn	92	
Uranus	37	
Neptune	36	

5. Which fractions tell the sizes of Mars, Venus, and Mercury compared to Earth?

_____

_____

6. Which object is 11 times the diameter of Earth? Which object is about 9 times the diameter of Earth?

_____

Summarize

7. What are some different kinds of models, and why do we use them?

_____

_____

Name _____

Night and Day

Use with *ScienceFusion*
pages 398–399.

Develop Concepts

1. Why do you see different things at different times?

_____

_____

_____

2. How does facing different directions model day and night?

_____

_____

_____

Develop Vocabulary

3. Define the following terms in your own words.

Rotates: _____

_____

_____

Axis: _____

_____

_____

Do the Math!

4. Complete the table with the data to find the difference between a day on Earth and a day on other planets.

Planet	Day	Day on Earth	Difference	Shorter/ Longer than Earth Day
Mercury	59 Earth days			
Jupiter	9 Earth hours, 55 minutes			
Neptune	16 Earth hours, 6 minutes			

5. How did you know which value to use for an Earth day: 1 day or 24 hours?

_____

_____

_____

6. A new planet is discovered. Its day is 4 Earth days, 17 hours, 43 minutes long. What is the difference between its day and an Earth day? Is it longer or shorter than an Earth day?

_____

_____

_____

Summarize

7. What causes day and night?

_____

_____

_____

Name _____

Pump Up the Volume!

Use with *ScienceFusion*
pages 116–117.

Develop Vocabulary

1. Define the following term in your own words.

Volume: _____

_____

Develop Concepts

2. What causes the difference in the two volume measurements, with and without your object?

_____

_____

3. How can you use the two measurements to find the volume of the object?

_____

_____

Interpret Visuals

4. How much water pushed out of the tub when the dog is put in it?

_____

_____

5. Would more or less water be pushed out by a smaller dog? Why?

_____

_____

Do the Math!

5. The surface area is the sum of the areas of each face of a rectangular prism. Complete the table with the data about the surface area and volume of a rectangular solid.

Rectangular Prism	5 cm × 4 cm × 2 cm	3 cm × 3 cm × 3 cm
Area of top (square cm)		
Area of bottom (square cm)		
Area of left (square cm)		
Area of right (square cm)		
Area of front (square cm)		
Area of back (square cm)		

6. What patterns do you see when finding the areas of each face of a rectangular prism?

_____

_____

7. Complete the table to find the volume.

Rectangular Prism	5 cm × 4 cm × 2 cm	3 cm × 3 cm × 3 cm
Volume (cubic cm)		

8. Compare finding the area of a face of a rectangular prism and the prism's volume.

_____

_____

Summarize

8. What is volume? How can you find the volume of an irregularly-shaped object?

_____

_____

_____

Glossary

© Houghton Mifflin Harcourt Publishing Company

Pronunciation Key

a	add, map	ē	equal, tree	m	move, seem	o͞o	pool, food	u̇	pull, book
ā	ace, rate	f	fit, half	n	nice, tin	p	pit, stop	û(r)	burn, term
â(r)	care, air	g	go, log	ng	ring, song	r	run, poor	yo͞o	fuse, few
ä	palm, father	h	hope, hate	o	odd, hot	s	see, pass	v	vain, eve
b	bat, rub	i	it, give	ō	open, so	sh	sure, rush	w	win, away
ch	check, catch	ī	ice, write	ô	order, jaw	t	talk, sit	y	yet, yearn
d	dog, rod	j	joy, ledge	oi	oil, boy	th	thin, both	z	zest, muse
e	end, pet	k	cool, take	ou	pout, now	th	this, bathe	zh	vision, pleasure
		l	look, rule	o͝o	took, full	u	up, done		

ə   the schwa, an unstressed vowel representing the sound spelled *a* in *above*, *e* in *sicken*, *i* in *possible*, *o* in *melon*, *u* in *circus*

Other symbols:
- • separates words into syllables
- ′ indicates stress on a syllable

acute angle [ə•kyo͞ot′ ang′gəl] **ángulo agudo**
An angle that measures greater than 0° and less than 90°
Example:

acute triangle [ə•kyo͞ot′ trī′ang•gəl]
triángulo acutángulo A triangle with three acute angles
Example:

addend [a′dend] **sumando** A number that is added to another in an addition problem
Example: 2 + 4 = 6;
         2 and 4 are addends.

addition [ə•di′shən] **suma** The process of finding the total number of items when two or more groups of items are joined; the opposite operation of subtraction

A.M. [ā•em′] **a.m.** The times after midnight and before noon

analog clock [anəl• ôg kläk] **reloj analógico**
A tool for measuring time, in which hands move around a circle to show hours, minutes, and sometimes seconds
Example:

angle [ang′gəl] **ángulo** A shape formed by two line segments or rays that share the same endpoint
Example:

area [âr′ē•ə] **área** The measure of the number of unit squares needed to cover a surface
Example:

Area = 9 square units

array [ə•rā′] **matriz** An arrangement of objects in rows and columns
Example:

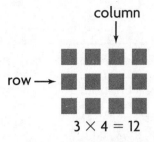

$3 \times 4 = 12$

Associative Property of Addition [ə•sō′shē•āt•iv präp′ər•tē əv ə•dish′ən] **propiedad asociativa de la suma** The property that states that you can group addends in different ways and still get the same sum
Example: $3 + (8 + 5) = (3 + 8) + 5$

Associative Property of Multiplication [ə•sō′shē•ə•tiv präp′ər•tē əv mul•tə•pli•kā′shən] **propiedad asociativa de la multiplicación** The property that states that you can group factors in different ways and still get the same product
Example: $3 \times (4 \times 2) = (3 \times 4) \times 2$

bar graph [bär graf] **gráfica de barras** A graph that uses bars to show data
Example:

base [bās] **base** A polygon's side or a two-dimensional shape, usually a polygon or circle, by which a three-dimensional shape is measured or named
Examples:

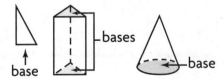

benchmark [bench′märk] **punto de referencia** A known size or amount that helps you understand a different size or amount

calendar [kal′ən•dər] **calendario** A table that shows the days, weeks, and months of a year

capacity [kə•pas′i•tē] **capacidad** The amount a container can hold when filled

Celsius (°C) [sel′sē•əs] **Celsius** A metric scale for measuring temperature

centimeter (cm) [sen′tə•mēt•ər] **centímetro (cm)** A metric unit for measuring length or distance
1 meter = 100 centimeters
Example:

1 centimeter

cent sign (¢) [sent sīn] **símbolo de centavo** A symbol that stands for *cent* or *cents*
Example: 53¢

clockwise [kläk′wīz] **en el sentido de las manecillas del reloj** In the same direction in which the hands of a clock move

closed shape [klōzd shāp] **figura cerrada** A two-dimensional shape that begins and ends at the same point
Examples:

common denominator [käm′ən dē•näm′ə•nāt•ər] **denominador común** A common multiple of two or more denominators
Example: Some common denominators for $\frac{1}{4}$ and $\frac{5}{6}$ are 12, 24, and 36.

common factor [käm′ən fak′tər] **factor común** A number that is a factor of two or more numbers

common multiple [käm′ən mul′tə•pəl] **múltiplo común** A number that is a multiple of two or more numbers

Commutative Property of Addition
[kə•myo͞ot′ə•tiv präp′ər•tē əv ə•dish′ən] **propiedad conmutativa de la suma** The property that states that when the order of two addends is changed, the sum is the same
Example: 4 + 5 = 5 + 4

Commutative Property of Multiplication
[kə•myo͞ot′ə•tiv präp′ər•tē əv mul•tə•pli•kā′shən] **propiedad conmutativa de la multiplicación** The property that states that when the order of two factors is changed, the product is the same
Example: 4 × 5 = 5 × 4

compare [kəm•pâr′] **comparar** To describe whether numbers are equal to, less than, or greater than each other

compatible numbers [kəm•pat′ə•bəl num′bərz] **números compatibles** Numbers that are easy to compute mentally

composite number [kəm•päz′it num′bər] **número compuesto** A number having more than two factors
Example: 6 is a composite number, since its factors are 1, 2, 3, and 6.

corner [kôr′nər] **esquina** See *vertex*.

counterclockwise [kount•er•kläk′wīz] **en sentido contrario a las manecillas del reloj** In the opposite direction in which the hands of a clock move

counting number [kount′ing num′bər] **número natural** A whole number that can be used to count a set of objects (1, 2, 3, 4, . . .)

cube [kyo͞ob] **cubo** A three-dimensional shape with six square faces of the same size
Example:

cup (c) [kup] **taza (tz)** A customary unit used to measure capacity and liquid volume
1 cup = 8 ounces

data [dāt′ə] **datos** Information collected about people or things

decagon [dek′ə•gän] **decágono** A polygon with ten sides and ten angles

decimal [des′ə•məl] **decimal** A number with one or more digits to the right of the decimal point

decimal point [des′ə•məl point] **punto decimal** A symbol used to separate dollars from cents in money amounts, and to separate the ones and the tenths places in a decimal
Example: 6.4
↑ decimal point

decimeter (dm) [des′i•mēt•ər] **decímetro (dm)** A metric unit for measuring length or distance
1 meter = 10 decimeters

degree (°) [di•grē′] **grado (°)** The unit used for measuring angles and temperatures

denominator [dē•näm′ə•nāt•ər] **denominador** The number below the bar in a fraction that tells how many equal parts are in the whole or in the group
Example: $\frac{3}{4}$ ← denominator

diagonal [dī•ag′ə•nəl] **diagonal** A line segment that connects two vertices of a polygon that are not next to each other
Example:

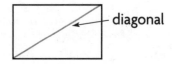

difference [dif′ər•əns] **diferencia** The answer to a subtraction problem

digit [dij′it] **dígito** Any one of the ten symbols 0, 1, 2, 3, 4, 5, 6, 7, 8, or 9 used to write numbers

digital clock [dij′i•təl kläk] **reloj digital** A clock that shows time to the minute, using digits
Example:

dime [dīm] **moneda de 10¢** A coin worth 10 cents and with a value equal to that of 10 pennies; 10¢
Example:

dimension [də•men'shən] **dimensión** A measure in one direction

Distributive Property [di•strib'yoo•tiv präp'ər•tē] **propiedad distributiva** The property that states that multiplying a sum by a number is the same as multiplying each addend by the number and then adding the products
Example: $5 \times (10 + 6) = (5 \times 10) + (5 \times 6)$

divide [də•vīd'] **dividir** To separate into equal groups; the opposite operation of multiplication

dividend [dəv'ə•dend] **dividendo** The number that is to be divided in a division problem
Example: $36 \div 6$; $6\overline{)36}$; the dividend is 36.

divisible [də•viz'ə•bəl] **divisible** A number is divisible by another number if the quotient is a counting number and the remainder is zero
Example: 18 is divisible by 3.

division [də•vi'zhən] **división** The process of sharing a number of items to find how many equal groups can be made or how many items will be in each equal group; the opposite operation of multiplication

divisor [də•vī'zər] **divisor** The number that divides the dividend
Example: $15 \div 3$; $3\overline{)15}$; the divisor is 3.

dollar [däl'ər] **dólar** Paper money worth 100 cents and equal to 100 pennies; $1.00
Example:

elapsed time [ē•lapst' tīm] **tiempo transcurrido** The time that passes from the start of an activity to the end of that activity

endpoint [end'point] **extremo** The point at either end of a line segment or the starting point of a ray

equal groups [ē'kwəl groopz] **grupos iguales** Groups that have the same number of objects

equal parts [ē'kwəl pärts] **partes iguales** Parts that are exactly the same size

equal sign (=) [ē'kwəl sīn] **signo de igualdad** A symbol used to show that two numbers have the same value
Example: 384 = 384

equal to [ē'kwəl too] **igual a** Having the same value
Example: 4 + 4 is equal to 3 + 5.

equation [ē•kwā'zhən] **ecuación** A number sentence which shows that two quantities are equal
Example: 4 + 5 = 9

equivalent [ē•kwiv'ə•lənt] **equivalente** Having the same value or naming the same amount

equivalent decimals [ē•kwiv'ə•lənt des'ə•məlz] **decimales equivalentes** Two or more decimals that name the same amount

equivalent fractions [ē•kwiv'ə•lənt frak'shənz] **fracciones equivalentes** Two or more fractions that name the same amount
Example: $\frac{3}{4}$ and $\frac{6}{8}$ name the same amount.

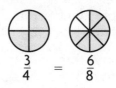

$$\frac{3}{4} = \frac{6}{8}$$

estimate [es'tə•māt] *verb* **estimar** To find an answer that is close to the exact amount

estimate [es'tə•mit] *noun* **estimación** A number that is close to the exact amount

even [ē'vən] **par** A whole number that has a 0, 2, 4, 6, or 8 in the ones place

expanded form [ek•span'did fôrm] **forma desarrollada** A way to write numbers by showing the value of each digit
Example: 253 = 200 + 50 + 3

expression [ek•spresh'ən] **expresión** A part of a number sentence that has numbers and operation signs but does not have an equal sign

H4 Glossary

fact family [fakt fam'ə•lē] **familia de operaciones**
A set of related multiplication and division
equations, or addition and subtraction
equations
Example: $7 \times 8 = 56$ $8 \times 7 = 56$
          $56 \div 7 = 8$ $56 \div 8 = 7$

factor [fak'tər] **factor** A number that is multiplied
by another number to find a product

Fahrenheit (°F) [fâr'ən•hīt] **Fahrenheit** A customary
scale for measuring temperature

fluid ounce (fl oz) [floo'id ouns] **onza fluida (fl oz)**
A customary unit used to measure liquid
capacity and liquid volume
1 cup = 8 fluid ounces

foot (ft) [foot] **pie (ft)** A customary unit used for
measuring length or distance
1 foot = 12 inches

formula [fôr'myoo•lə] **fórmula** A set of symbols that
expresses a mathematical rule
Example: Area = base × height, or $A = b \times h$

fraction [frak'shən] **fracción** A number that names
a part of a whole or part of a group
Example:

fraction greater than 1 [frak'shən grāt'ər than wun]
fracción mayor que 1 A number which has a
numerator that is greater than its denominator

frequency table [frē'kwən•sē tā'bəl] **tabla de
frecuencia** A table that uses numbers to
record data about how often something
happens
Example:

Favorite Color	
Color	**Frequency**
Blue	10
Red	7
Green	5
Other	3

gallon (gal) [gal'ən] **galón (gal)** A customary unit
for measuring capacity and liquid volume
1 gallon = 4 quarts

gram (g) [gram] **gramo (g)** A metric unit for
measuring mass
1 kilogram = 1,000 grams

greater than sign (>) [grāt'ər than sīn] **signo de
mayor que** A symbol used to compare two
quantities, with the greater quantity given first
Example: $6 > 4$

grid [grid] **cuadrícula** Evenly divided and equally
spaced squares on a shape or flat surface

half gallon [haf gal'ən] **medio galón** A customary
unit for measuring capacity and liquid volume
1 half gallon = 2 quarts

half hour [haf our] **media hora** 30 minutes
Example: 4:00 to 4:30 is one half hour.

half-square unit [haf skwâr yoo'nit] **media unidad
cuadrada** Half of a unit of area with dimensions
of 1 unit × 1 unit

height [hīt] **altura** The measure of a perpendicular
from the base to the top of a two-dimensional
shape

hexagon [hek'sə•gän] **hexágono** A polygon with six
sides and six angles
Examples:

horizontal [hôr•i•zänt'l] **horizontal** In the direction
from left to right

hour (hr) [our] **hora (hr)** A unit used to measure
time
1 hour = 60 minutes

hundredth [hun'drədth] **centésimo** One of one hundred equal parts
Example:

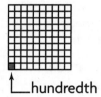
hundredth

I

Identity Property of Addition [ī•den'tə•tē präp'ər•tē əv ə•dish'ən] **propiedad de identidad de la suma** The property that states that when you add zero to any number, the sum is that number
Example: $16 + 0 = 16$

Identity Property of Multiplication [ī•den'tə•tē präp'ər•tē əv mul•tə•pli•kā'shən] **propiedad de identidad de la multiplicación** The property that states that the product of any number and 1 is that number
Example: $9 \times 1 = 9$

inch (in.) [inch] **pulgada (pulg)** A customary unit used for measuring length or distance
Example:

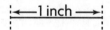
1 inch

intersecting lines [in•tər•sekt'ing līnz] **líneas secantes** Lines that cross each other at exactly one point
Example:

inverse operations [in'vûrs äp•ə•rā'shənz] **operaciones inversas** Operations that undo each other, such as addition and subtraction or multiplication and division
Example: $6 \times 8 = 48$ and $48 \div 6 = 8$

K

key [kē] **clave** The part of a map or graph that explains the symbols

kilogram (kg) [kil'ō•gram] **kilogramo (kg)** A metric unit for measuring mass
1 kilogram = 1,000 grams

kilometer (km) [kə•läm'ət•ər] **kilómetro (km)** A metric unit for measuring length or distance
1 kilometer = 1,000 meters

L

length [lengkth] **longitud** The measurement of the distance between two points

less than sign (<) [les than sīn] **signo de menor que** A symbol used to compare two quantities, with the lesser quantity given first
Example: $3 < 7$

line [līn] **línea** A straight path of points in a plane that continues without end in both directions with no endpoints
Example:

S   T

line graph [līn graf] **gráfica lineal** A graph that uses line segments to show how data change over time

line of symmetry [līn əv sim'ə•trē] **eje de simetría** An imaginary line on a shape about which the shape can be folded so that its two parts match exactly
Example:

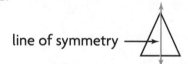
line of symmetry

line plot [līn plöt] **diagrama de puntos** A graph that records each piece of data on a number line
Example:

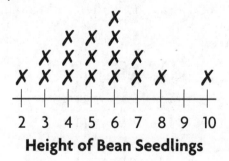
Height of Bean Seedlings

line segment [līn seg'mənt] **segmento** A part of a line that includes two points called endpoints and all the points between them
Example:

A   B

line symmetry [līn sim'ə•trē] **simetría axial** What a shape has if it can be folded about a line so that its two parts match exactly

linear units [lin'ē•ər yoo'nits] **unidades lineales** Units that measure length, width, height, or distance

liquid volume [lik'wid väl'yoom] **volumen de un líquido** The measure of the space a liquid occupies

liter (L) [lēt'ər] **litro (L)** A metric unit for measuring capacity and liquid volume
1 liter = 1,000 milliliters

mass [mas] **masa** The amount of matter in an object

meter (m) [mēt'ər] **metro (m)** A metric unit for measuring length or distance
1 meter = 100 centimeters

midnight [mid'nīt] **medianoche** 12:00 at night

mile (mi) [mīl] **milla (mi)** A customary unit for measuring length or distance
1 mile = 5,280 feet

milliliter (mL) [mil'i•lēt•ər] **mililitro (mL)** A metric unit for measuring capacity and liquid volume
1 liter = 1,000 milliliters

millimeter (mm) [mil'i•mēt•ər] **milímetro (mm)** A metric unit for measuring length or distance
1 centimeter = 10 millimeters

million [mil'yən] **millón** The counting number after 999,999; 1,000 thousands; written as 1,000,000

millions [mil'yənz] **millones** The period after thousands

minute (min) [min'it] **minuto (min)** A unit used to measure short amounts of time
1 minute = 60 seconds

mixed number [mikst num'bər] **número mixto** An amount given as a whole number and a fraction

multiple [mul'tə•pəl] **múltiplo** The product of a number and a counting number is called a multiple of the number
Example:

3	3	3	3	
× 1	× 2	× 3	× 4	← counting numbers
3	6	9	12	← multiples of 3

multiplication [mul•tə•pli•kā'shən] **multiplicación** A process to find the total number of items in equal-sized groups, or to find the total number of items in a given number of groups when each group contains the same number of items; multiplication is the inverse of division

multiply [mul'tə•plī] **multiplicar** To combine equal groups to find how many in all; the opposite operation of division

nickel [nik'əl] **moneda de 5¢** A coin worth 5 cents and with a value equal to that of 5 pennies; 5¢
Example:

noon [noon] **mediodía** 12:00 in the day

not equal to sign (≠) [not ē'kwəl too sīn] **signo de no igual a** A symbol that indicates one quantity is not equal to another
Example: 12 × 3 ≠ 38

number line [num'bər līn] **recta numérica** A line on which numbers can be located
Example:

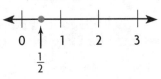

number sentence [num'bər sent'ns] **enunciado numérico** A sentence that includes numbers, operation symbols, and a greater than or less than symbol or an equal sign
Example: 5 + 3 = 8

numerator [nōō′mər·āt·ər] **numerador** The number above the bar in a fraction that tells how many parts of the whole or group are being considered

Example: $\frac{2}{3}$ ← numerator

obtuse angle [äb·tōōs′ ang′gəl] **ángulo obtuso** An angle that measures greater than 90° and less than 180°
Example:

obtuse triangle [äb·tōōs′ trī′ang·gəl] **triángulo obtusángulo** A triangle with one obtuse angle

Example:

octagon [äk′tə·gän] **octágono** A polygon with eight sides and eight angles
Examples:

odd [od] **impar** A whole number that has a 1, 3, 5, 7, or 9 in the ones place

one-dimensional [wun də·men′shə·nəl] **unidimensional** Measured in only one direction, such as length
Examples:

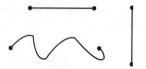

open shape [ō′pən shāp] **figura abierta** A shape that does not begin and end at the same point
Examples:

order [ôr′dər] **orden** A particular arrangement or placement of things one after the other

order of operations [ôr′dər əv äp·ə·rā′shənz] **orden de las operaciones** A special set of rules which gives the order in which calculations are done

ounce (oz) [ouns] **onza (oz)** A customary unit for measuring weight
1 pound = 16 ounces

parallel lines [pâr′ə·lel līnz] **líneas paralelas** Lines in the same plane that never intersect and are always the same distance apart
Example:

parallelogram [pär•ə•lel′ə•gram] **paralelogramo** A quadrilateral whose opposite sides are parallel and of equal length
Example:

parentheses [pə•ren′thə•sēz] **paréntesis** The symbols used to show which operation or operations in an expression should be done first

partial product [pär′shəl präd′əkt] **producto parcial** A method of multiplying in which the ones, tens, hundreds, and so on are multiplied separately and then the products are added together

partial quotient [pär′shəl kwō′shənt] **cociente parcial** A method of dividing in which multiples of the divisor are subtracted from the dividend and then the quotients are added together

pattern [pat′ərn] **patrón** An ordered set of numbers or objects; the order helps you predict what will come next
Examples: 2, 4, 6, 8, 10

pattern unit [pat′ərn yoo′nit] **unidad de patrón** The part of a pattern that repeats
Example:

pattern unit

pentagon [pen′tə•gän] **pentágono** A polygon with five sides and five angles
Examples:

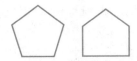

perimeter [pə•rim′ə•tər] **perímetro** The distance around a shape

period [pir′ē•əd] **período** Each group of three digits in a multi-digit number; periods are usually separated by commas or spaces.
Example: 85,643,900 has three periods.

perpendicular lines [pər•pən•dik′yoo•lər līnz] **líneas perpendiculares** Two lines that intersect to form four right angles
Example:

picture graph [pik′chər graf] **gráfica con dibujos** A graph that uses symbols to show and compare information
Example:

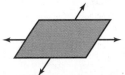

pint (pt) [pīnt] **pinta (pt)** A customary unit for measuring capacity and liquid volume
1 pint = 2 cups

place value [plās val′yoo] **valor posicional** The value of a digit in a number, based on the location of the digit

plane [plān] **plano** A flat surface that extends without end in all directions
Example:

plane shape [plān shāp] **figura plana** See *two-dimensional figure.*

P.M. [pē′em] **p.m.** The times after noon and before midnight

point [point] **punto** An exact location in space

polygon [päl′i•gän] **polígono** A closed two-dimensional shape formed by three or more straight sides that are line segments
Examples:

Polygons   Not Polygons

pound (lb) [pound] **libra (lb)** A customary unit for measuring weight
1 pound = 16 ounces

prime number [prīm num′bər] **número primo** A number that has exactly two factors: 1 and itself
Examples: 2, 3, 5, 7, 11, 13, 17, and 19 are prime numbers. 1 is not a prime number.

prism [priz′əm] **prisma** A solid figure that has two same size, same polygon-shaped bases, and other faces that are all rectangles
Examples:

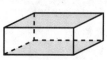

rectangular prism   triangular prism

product [präd′əkt] **producto** The answer to a multiplication problem

protractor [prō′trak•tər] **transportador** A tool for measuring the size of an angle

 Q

quadrilateral [kwä•dri•lat′ər•əl] **cuadrilátero** A polygon with four sides and four angles

quart (qt) [kwôrt] **cuarto (ct)** A customary unit for measuring capacity and liquid volume
1 quart = 2 pints

quarter hour [kwôrt′ər our] **cuarto de hora** 15 minutes
Example: 4:00 to 4:15 is one quarter hour

quotient [kwō′shənt] **cociente** The number, not including the remainder, that results from dividing
Example: 8 ÷ 4 = 2; 2 is the quotient.

 R

ray [rā] **semirrecta** A part of a line; it has one endpoint and continues without end in one direction
Example:

K   L

rectangle [rek′tang•gəl] **rectángulo** A quadrilateral with two pairs of parallel sides, two pairs of sides of equal length, and four right angles
Example:

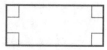

rectangular prism [rek•tang′gyə•lər priz′əm] **prisma rectangular** A three-dimensional shape in which all six faces are rectangles
Example:

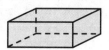

regroup [rē•grōōp′] **reagrupar** To exchange amounts of equal value to rename a number
Example: 5 + 8 = 13 ones or 1 ten 3 ones

regular polygon [reg′yə•lər päl′i•gän] **polígono regular** A polygon that has all sides that are equal in length and all angles equal in measure
Examples:

related facts [ri•lāt′id fakts] **operaciones relacionadas** A set of related addition and subtraction, or multiplication and division, number sentences
Examples: 4 × 7 = 28   28 ÷ 4 = 7
                7 × 4 = 28   28 ÷ 7 = 4

remainder [ri•mān′dər] **residuo** The amount left over when a number cannot be divided equally

rhombus [räm′bəs] **rombo** A quadrilateral with two pairs of parallel sides and four sides of equal length
Example:

right angle [rīt ang′gəl] **ángulo recto** An angle that forms a square corner
Example:

H10   Glossary

right triangle [rīt trī′ang•gəl] **triángulo rectángulo** A triangle with one right angle
Example:

round [round] **redondear** To replace a number with another number that tells about how many or how much

rule [rool] **regla** A procedure (usually involving arithmetic operations) to determine an output value from an input value

scale [skāl] **escala** A series of numbers placed at fixed distances on a graph to help label the graph

second (sec) [sek′ənd] **segundo (seg)** A small unit of time
1 minute = 60 seconds

simplest form [sim′pləst fôrm] **mínima expresión** A fraction is in simplest form when the numerator and denominator have only 1 as a common factor

solid shape [sä′lid shāp] **cuerpo geométrico** See *three-dimensional figure.*

square [skwâr] **cuadrado** A quadrilateral with two pairs of parallel sides, four sides of equal length, and four right angles
Example:

square unit [skwâr yoo′nit] **unidad cuadrada** A unit of area with dimensions of 1 unit × 1 unit

standard form [stan′dərd fôrm] **forma normal** A way to write numbers by using the digits 0–9, with each digit having a place value *Example:* 3,540 ← standard form

straight angle [strāt ang′gəl] **ángulo llano** An angle whose measure is 180°
Example:

subtraction [səb•trak′shən] **resta** The process of finding how many are left when a number of items are taken away from a group of items; the process of finding the difference when two groups are compared; the opposite operation of addition

sum [sum] **suma o total** The answer to an addition problem

survey [sûr′vā] **encuesta** A method of gathering information

tally table [tal′ē tā′bəl] **tabla de conteo** A table that uses tally marks to record data

Word History

Some people keep score in card games by making marks on paper (IIII). These marks are known as tally marks. The word *tally* is related to *tailor*, from the Latin *talea*, meaning "twig." In early times, a method of keeping count was by cutting marks into a piece of wood or bone.

temperature [tem′pər•ə•chər] **temperatura** The degree of hotness or coldness usually measured in degrees Fahrenheit or degrees Celsius

tenth [tenth] **décimo** One of ten equal parts
Example:

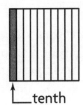

tenth

term [tûrm] **término** A number or object in a pattern

thousands [thou′zəndz] **miles** The period after the ones period in the base-ten number system

three-dimensional [thrē də•men'shə•nəl]
tridimensional Measured in three directions,
such as length, width, and height
Example:

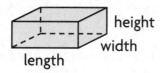

height
width
length

three-dimensional figure [thrē də•men'shə•nəl
fig'yər] **figura tridimensional** A figure having
length, width, and height

ton (T) [tun] **tonelada (t)** A customary unit used to
measure weight
1 ton = 2,000 pounds

trapezoid [trap'i•zoid] **trapecio** A quadrilateral
with at least one pair of parallel sides
Examples:

triangle [trī'ang•gəl] **triángulo** A polygon with
three sides and three angles
Examples:

two-dimensional [tōō də•men'shə•nəl]
bidimensional Measured in two directions,
such as length and width
Example:

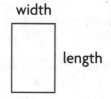

width
length

two-dimensional figure [tōō də•men'shə•nəl fig'yər]
figura bidimensional A figure that lies in a
plane; a shape having length and width

unit fraction [yōō'nit frak'shən] **fracción unitaria**
A fraction that has a numerator of one

variable [vâr'ē•ə•bəl] **variable** A letter or symbol
that stands for a number or numbers

Venn diagram [ven dī'ə•gram] **diagrama de Venn**
A diagram that shows relationships among
sets of things
Example:

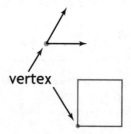

2-Digit
Numbers   Even
               Numbers
35   12   8
17   6
29   10   4

vertex [vûr'teks] **vértice** The point at which two
rays of an angle meet or two (or more) line
segments meet in a two-dimensional shape
Examples:

vertex

vertical [vûr'ti•kəl] **vertical** In the direction from
top to bottom

weight [wāt] **peso** How heavy an object is

whole [hōl] **entero** All of the parts of a shape or
group

word form [wûrd fôrm] **en palabras** A way to
write numbers by using words
Example: Four hundred
fifty-three thousand, two
hundred twelve

yard (yd) [yärd] **yarda (yd)** A customary unit for
measuring length or distance
1 yard = 3 feet

Z

Zero Property of Multiplication [zē′rō präp′ər•tē əv mul•tə•pli•kā′shən] **propiedad del cero de la multiplicación** The property that states that the product of 0 and any number is 0
Example: $0 \times 8 = 0$

Index

© Houghton Mifflin Harcourt Publishing Company

Clocks
    analog, 602, 685–688
    elapsed time, 691–694
Clockwise, 601–604
Combined rectangles, 729–732
Common denominators, 345–348, 365–368, 409–412, 527–530
Common factors, 291–294
    fractions in simplest form using, 340
Common multiples, 299–302, 345–348
Common numerators, 365–368
Communicate Math Ideas
    Math Talk, In every Student Edition lesson. Some examples are: 5, 12, 64, 82, 114, 132, 177, 209, 228, 279, 299, 328, 359, 386, 429, 455, 495, 520, 556, 602, 642, 723
    Read Math, 555, 685
    Write Math, In every Student Edition lesson. Some examples are: 8, 40, 96, 116, 224, 288, 348, 420, 510, 530, 682
Commutative Property
    of Addition, 39, 435–438
    of Multiplication, 63–66, 107–110, 171
Comparing
    decimals, 533–536
    fractions, 359–362, 365–368, 371–374
    measurement units, 647–650, 653–656, 659–662, 673–676, 679–682, 685–688
    whole numbers, 17–20
Comparison problems, 49–52, 69–72, 481–484
Compatible numbers, 152, 221–223
Composite numbers, 305–307
Connect, 99, 163, 260, 435, 607, 703
Connect to Art, 400, 424
Connect to Reading, 84, 224
Connect to Science, 26, 218, 510, 616, 688, 740
Connect to Social Studies, 308
Counterclockwise, 601–604
Counters, 203–206, 235, 236
Counting numbers, 197, 455–458, 461–464
Cross-Curricular Activities and Connections
    Connect to Art, 400, 570
    Connect to Reading, 84, 224

Connect to Science, 26, 218, 510, 616, 688, 740
Connect to Social Studies, 308
Cup, 659
Customary units
    benchmarks, 641-644
    converting, 647–650, 653–656, 659–662
    of distance, 641
    of length, 641, 647–650
    of liquid volume, 641, 659–662
    of weight, 641, 653–656

D

Data
    gathering, 26
    using
        bar graphs, 116
        line plots, 665–668
        tables. See Tables
        tally tables, 665–668, 671
        Venn diagrams, 196, 556, 558, 568, 716
Days, 686
Decimal point, 495
Decimals
    comparing
        using models, 533–536
        using place value, 533–536
    defined, 495
    equivalent decimals
        defined, 508
        modeling, 507–510
    hundredths, 501–504, 507–510
    place value and, 495–498, 501–504, 534–536
    relating
        to fractions, 495–498, 501–504, 507–510, 513–516, 527–530
        to mixed numbers, 495–497, 501–503, 509, 514–515
        to money, 513–516
    tenths, 495–498, 507–510
Decimeters, 673
Degrees
    angle measures and, 607–610
Denominators, 365–368

Diagrams. *See also* Graphic Organizers
  Draw a Diagram, 49–52, 72, 113–116, 183–186, 265–268, 481–484, 627–630, 691–694
  using, 49–52, 72, 113–116, 158, 183–186, 265–268, 481–484, 627–630, 691–694, 729–732
  Venn diagrams, 196, 556, 558, 568, 716

Difference, 43–44, 195, 403–405, 410–411, 423–425, 430–431

Differentiated Instruction
  Show What You Know, 3, 61, 143, 195, 277, 325, 383, 453, 493, 547, 599, 639, 715

Digit, 6
  value of, 5–8

Distance, 641–642

Distributive Property, 87–90, 99–100, 227–230, 718
  division using, 227–230
  models, 87–90, 99–101
  multiplication using, 87–90, 99–101

Dividend, 209. *See also* Division

Divisibility, 285–288, 306

Division
  basic facts, 215–216, 221–222, 259–262
  Distributive Property, 227–230
  dividend, 209
  divisor, 209
  equations, 210–212, 215–218, 222–223
  estimating quotients
      using compatible numbers, 221–224
      using multiples, 197–200
  to find equivalent fractions, 340–341
  inverse relationship to multiplication, 260
  modeling
      with bar models, 265–268
      with base-ten blocks, 247–249
      with counters, 203–205, 235
      draw a diagram, 265–268
      with fraction circles, 404–406
      with fraction strips, 404–405, 409
      with quick pictures, 203–206, 209–212
  of multidigit numbers, 253–256, 259–262
  partial quotients, 241–244
  patterns, 216–217, 285–287
  placing the first digit of the quotient, 253–256
  quotient, 209

  regrouping, 247–250, 253–256, 259–262
  remainders, 203–206
      defined, 204
      interpreting, 209–212
  tens, hundreds, thousands, 215–218
  types of problems, 197–200
  using repeated subtraction, 235–238
  with zero, 215
  zero in the quotient, 260

Divisor, 209. *See also* Division

Dollar, 513–514

Draw a Diagram. *See* Problem-solving strategies

Draw Conclusions, 31–32, 88, 158, 204, 228, 236, 247, 328, 386, 602, 622, 673–674

E

Elapsed time
  draw a diagram, 691–694
  find, 691–694

Equal sign, 17–18, 328

Equations
  addition, 50, 385–388, 409–412
  angle equations, 623, 630, 633
  division, 209–223, 738
  inverse operations and, 260
  multiplication, 63–66, 131–134, 470, 475–478
  multistep problems and, 131–134
  representing, 69–72, 131–134, 157–159, 203–204, 391, 394
      using mental math, 107–110
  subtraction, 49–52, 132, 409–412
  writing, 49–51, 63–66, 69–72, 386–387, 391–394

Equivalent decimals
  defined, 508
  model, 507–510

Equivalent fractions
  defined, 327
  modeling, 327–330, 333–336, 339–342, 351–354
  multiplication and division to find, 333–336, 340

Error Alert, 38, 260, 305, 346, 582, 614, 698, 738

renaming as mixed numbers, 417–420, 476
simplest form, 339–342
subtraction
    like denominators, 409–412, 423–426
    mixed numbers, 423–426
    modeling, 385–388, 403–406, 409–412, 429–432
    with renaming, 429–432

Gallon, 659–662

Geometry. *See also* Two-dimensional figures
angles, 549–552
    acute, 550, 555, 608, 615
    angle equations, 622–623, 627–630, 631–632
    classify triangles by size of, 555–558
    find unknown measures, 737–740
    measure and draw, 613–616
    obtuse, 550, 555, 608, 615
    right, 550, 555, 567, 608, 723
    turns on a clock and angle measures, 602, 603, 685
hexagons, 581
lines, 549–552
    parallel, 561–564
    perpendicular, 561–564
polygons, 555–558, 567–570
quadrilaterals, 567–570
    classifying, 567–570
rays, 549–552
rectangles, 567–569
shape patterns, 587–590
squares, 567–569, 581
symmetry
    lines of symmetry, 581–584
    line symmetry, 575–578, 581–584
trapezoids, 567–569, 581
triangles, 555–558
    classifying, 555–558

Glossary, Multimedia. *See* Multimedia eGlossary

Go Deeper, In some Student Edition lessons. Some examples are: 19, 90, 229, 262, 294, 388, 444, 463, 536, 609, 687

Grams, 679–682

Graphic Organizers. *See also* Tables

Brainstorming Diagram, 640
Bubble Map, 384, 454, 600
Flow Map, 62, 278, 326, 548
H-Diagram, 144
problem solving, 49–51, 113–114, 183–184, 291–292, 351–352, 441–442, 481–482, 519–520, 587–588, 627–628, 691–692, 743–744
Semantic Map, 494
Venn diagram, 196, 556, 558, 568, 716

Graphs. *See also* Data
bar graphs, 116
line plots, 665–668
Venn diagrams, 196, 556, 558, 568, 716

Greater than (>), 17–18, 151, 153, 259

Grid, 38, 44, 87, 89, 157, 227, 229, 235, 305, 306, 729

Half gallon, 659

Half hour, 685–688

Height, 723–726, 737, 739

Hexagons, 581

Hours
elapsed time and, 691–694
half, 685–688
minutes after the hour, 685, 692

Hundreds, 11–14
addition, 37–40
multiply by whole numbers, 75–78, 125
place value, 5–8, 11–14, 37–40
subtraction, 43–46

Hundred thousands, 11–14
addition, 37–40
place value, 5–8, 11–14, 37–40
rounding, 23
subtraction, 43–46

Hundredths, 501–504, 507–510

Identity Property of Multiplication, 476

Inches, 647–650

Interpret remainders, 209–212

2. Abstract and Quantitative Reasoning. In many lessons. Some examples are: 11, 17, 23, 31, 63, 69, 75, 113, 119, 131, 145, 151, 157, 163, 221, 241, 247, 279, 297, 311, 333, 359, 365, 385, 391, 397, 403, 409, 417, 423, 435, 441, 461, 495, 501, 507, 513, 519, 527, 533, 567, 575, 601, 607, 641, 647, 653, 665, 723, 737

3. Use and Evaluate Logical Reasoning. In many lessons. Some examples are: 43, 87, 119, 125, 131, 209, 221, 253, 285, 365, 391, 397, 441, 575, 581, 601, 641, 647, 659, 665, 679, 697, 703

4. Mathematical Modeling. In many lessons. Some examples are: 11, 23, 49, 87, 99, 113, 145, 157, 183, 227, 247, 265, 279, 285, 327, 333, 345, 351, 385, 403, 429, 441, 455, 469, 513, 549, 561, 621, 627, 647, 659, 665, 673, 685, 691, 743

5. Use Mathematical Tools. In many lessons. Some examples are: 5, 31, 75, 197, 215, 235, 259, 265, 311, 327, 333, 365, 495, 587, 613, 685, 691

6. Use Precise Mathematical Language. In many lessons. Some examples are: 5, 23, 37, 63, 87, 99, 125, 151, 157, 177, 215, 221, 235, 241, 299, 339, 345, 351, 359, 403, 409, 417, 455, 495, 507, 513, 519, 533, 555, 561, 587, 607, 613, 653, 659, 703, 723, 729

7. See Structure. In many lessons. Some examples are: 11, 31, 75, 81, 119, 145, 171, 177, 197, 209, 215, 227, 253, 285, 299, 311, 327, 339, 345, 359, 409, 417, 429, 455, 461, 481, 501, 507, 527, 555, 561, 587, 607, 641, 659, 673, 685, 703, 717, 737

8. Generalize. In many lessons. Some examples are: 37, 43, 49, 163, 171, 177, 209, 241, 259, 299, 391, 417, 423, 435, 461, 475, 527, 673, 697, 717

Math in the Real World Activities, 3, 61, 143, 195, 277, 325, 383, 453, 493, 547, 599, 639, 715

Math on the Spot Videos, In every Student Edition lesson. Some examples are: 8, 46, 90, 116, 148, 217, 244, 281, 330, 388, 426, 458, 498, 552, 604, 649, 720

Math Talk, In every Student Edition lesson. Some examples are: 5, 12, 64, 82, 114, 132, 177, 209, 228, 279, 299, 328, 359, 386, 429, 455, 495, 520, 556, 602, 642, 723

Measurement
angles
and fractional parts of circle, 601–604
joining and separating, 621–624
measuring and drawing, 613–616
solving for unknown angle measures, 627–630
area, 723–726, 743–746
of combined rectangles, 729–732
concept of, 723–726
defined, 723
finding, 723–726, 729–732, 743–746
finding unknown measures, 737–740
formula for, 723–726
perimeter, related to, 731
of a rectangle, 723–726, 729–732
square unit, 723
units of, 723–726
benchmarks, 641–644
centimeter, 642–644
cup, 641
decimeter, 642
fluid ounce, 641
foot, 641, 643
gallon, 641, 643
gram, 642–643
inch, 641, 643
kilogram, 642–643
kilometer, 642–643
liter, 642–643
meter, 642–643
mile, 641, 643
milliliter, 642–644
millimeter, 642
ounce, 641, 643
pint, 641
pound, 641, 643
quart, 641
ton, 641, 643
yard, 641, 643
comparing, 642, 647–650, 653–656, 659–662, 685–688

quick pictures
    to model division, 203–206, 248–250
    to model multiplication, 75–78

Money
    relating
        to decimals, 513–516
        to fractions, 513–516

Multimedia *eGlossary*, 4, 62, 144, 196, 278, 326, 384, 454, 494, 548, 600, 640, 716

Multiples
    common, 299–302
    defined, 197
    estimate quotients using, 197–200
    factors and, 299–302
    of fractions, 461–464
    of unit fractions, 455–458

Multiplication
    area model, 157–160
    arrays, 61
    bar models, 183–186
    comparison problems, 63–66
    draw a diagram, 183–186, 265–268
    equations, 63–66, 131–134, 470, 475–478
    estimating products, 81–83, 99–102, 151–154
    expanded form, 93–96
    expressions, 131–134
    factors, 279–282
    to find equivalent fractions, 333–336
    four-digit numbers, 126–128
    fractions and whole numbers, 461–464, 475–478
    halving-and-doubling strategy, 108, 146
    as inverse of division, 737–740
    mental math, 107–110
    modeling, 186, 203–206
        one-digit numbers, 87–90, 93–96, 99–102, 119–122
        with quick pictures, 75–78
        two-digit numbers, 87–90, 119–122
        by two-digit numbers, 157–160, 163–166, 171–174, 177–180
    multiples of unit fractions, 455–458
    by multiples of 10, 100, and 1,000, 75–78
    by one-digit numbers, 87–90, 93–96, 99–102, 119–122
    partial products, 99–102, 157–160, 163–166, 177
    products, 76–77, 81–83, 99–102, 151–154, 157–160
    properties
        Associative Property of Multiplication, 107–110, 145–148

Commutative Property of Multiplication, 63, 107–110, 171
    Distributive Property, 87–90, 99–101, 108–109, 227–230, 718
    Identity Property of Multiplication, 476
    quotient estimation, 197–200
    reasonableness of answers, 82–83
    regrouping in, 119–122, 125–128, 171–174, 178–179
    by tens, 145–148
    three-digit numbers, 125–128
    two-digit numbers, 87–90, 119–122
    by two-digit numbers, 157–160, 163–166, 171–174, 177–180

Multistep word problems, 113–116, 131–134, 183–186, 265–268

N

Not equal to sign (≠), 328
Number lines
    to compare decimals, 533
    to compare fractions, 371–373
    to compare numbers, 18
    to divide, 236–237
    to find multiples of fractions, 462
    to multiply, 76, 146
    to order fractions, 371–374, 665–668
    to order numbers, 18
    to round numbers, 23
    to show equivalent decimals, 501
    to show equivalent fractions and decimals, 501

Number patterns, 311–314, 587–590

Numbers. *See also* Counting numbers; Decimals; Fractions; Mixed numbers; Whole numbers
    benchmark, 359–362, 641–644
    comparing
        decimals, 533–536
        whole numbers, 17–20
    compatible, 152, 221–223
    composite, 305–307
    expanded form, whole numbers, 11–14
    factors of, 279–282, 291–294
    multiples of, 197–200, 299–302
    ordering
        fractions, 371–374
        whole numbers, 17–20
    place value, 5–8, 11–14, 17–20, 23–26
    prime, 305–307

solving multistep problems using
equations, 131–134

Ordering
fractions, 371–374
whole numbers, 17–20

Order of Operations, 132

Ounces, 641, 643, 653–656

P

P.M., 691, 693

Parallel lines, 561–564

Parallelograms, 567–570

Parentheses, 107, 145

Partial products, 93–96, 99–102
defined, 88
four-digit by one-digit, 100–102
three-digit by one-digit, 99–102
two-digit by two-digit, 157–160, 163–166

Partial quotients, 241–244

Patterns
factor patterns, 285–287
finding, 311
in measurement units, 703–706
multiplication, 76–77, 470
number, 311–314
shape, 587–590

Perimeter
area, related to, 723–726
defined, 717
finding, 717–720
find unknown measures, 737–740
formulas for, 717–720
measuring, 737–740
of a rectangle, 717–720
of a square, 717–720

Period
place value, 11

Perpendicular lines, 561–564

Personal Math Trainer, In some Student
Edition lessons. Some examples are: 277,
294, 314, 325, 383

Pint, 641, 659–662

Place value
addition and, 37–40
chart, 6, 11, 17, 32–33, 495–497,
501–502, 508
to compare and order numbers, 17–20

decimals and, 495–498, 534–536
estimate using, 24
hundreds, 5–8, 11–14
hundred thousands, 5–8, 11–14
millions, 5–8
number line and, 18
ones, 5–8, 11–14
period and, 11
relationships, 5–8
renaming, 31–34
rounding and, 23–26
tens, 5–8, 11–14, 100, 221
ten thousands, 5–8, 11–14
thousands, 5–8, 11–14, 75–78

Polygons, 555–558, 567–570
regular, 581

Pose a Problem, 90, 212, 230, 302, 314, 438

Pounds, 641, 653–656

Practice and Homework
In every Student Edition lesson. Some
examples are: 9–10, 79–80, 231–232,
337–338, 407–408, 523–524, 605–606,
645–646, 727–728

Predictions, making, 84

Prerequisite Skills
Show What You Know, 3, 61, 143, 195,
277, 325, 383, 453, 493, 547, 599, 639,
715

Prime numbers, 305–307

Problem solving
addition and subtraction, 49–52

Problem-Solving Applications
Mental Math, 81, 107–110, 146, 151–152,
435–438
Pose a Problem, 90, 230, 302, 314, 438
Real-World Problem Solving, 8, 13, 20, 25,
40, 45, 72, 89, 90, 96, 102, 110, 122,
128, 133, 148, 154, 159, 166, 200, 205,
212, 217, 223, 229, 230, 237, 244, 249,
262, 281, 288, 302, 307, 314, 336, 342,
348, 362, 387, 411, 420, 426, 432, 457,
478, 498, 504, 510, 516, 530, 564, 570,
603, 616, 629, 644, 649, 655, 661, 675,
681, 687, 699, 706
Real-World Unlock the Problem, 11, 14,
17, 23–24, 34, 37, 43, 49–50, 63, 66,
69–70, 75–76, 78, 81, 93–94, 99–100,
107, 113–114, 119–120, 125, 131–132,
145–146, 151–152, 163–164, 171, 174,
177–178, 180, 183–184, 197–198,
209–210, 215, 221, 238, 241, 253, 256,

© Houghton Mifflin Harcourt Publishing Company

259–260, 265–266, 279, 282, 285,
291–292, 299, 305, 311, 333–334,
339–340, 345, 351–352, 359–360, 365,
368, 371, 374, 391–392, 394, 397–398,
403–404, 406, 409, 417–418, 423–424,
429–430, 435–436, 455–456, 461–462,
464, 469, 472, 475–476, 481–482,
495–496, 501–502, 507–508, 513,
519–520, 527–528, 533, 536, 549–550,
555–556, 561–562, 567–568, 575–576,
578, 581–582, 587–588, 607–608, 610,
613, 626, 627, 641–642, 647–648,
653–654, 659–660, 665–666, 668, 679,
682, 685–686, 691–692, 697–698, 700,
703, 717–718, 720, 723–724, 726,
729–730, 732, 737–738, 743–744
Reason Abstractly, 387
Sense or Nonsense?, 160, 250, 388, 411,
412, 458, 476, 604, 699
Think Smarter Problems, In every Student
Edition lesson. Some examples are: 8,
25, 63, 88, 122, 154, 211, 228, 262,
281, 328, 386, 426, 457, 498, 552, 610,
644, 720
Try This!, 11, 24, 44, 64, 107, 120, 146,
152, 178, 209, 210, 286, 312, 366,
372, 436, 476, 496, 514, 527, 528,
534, 555, 561, 568, 608, 654, 698,
704, 718, 724, 738
What's the Error?, 13, 46, 96, 134, 330,
409, 706
What's the Question?, 20, 342, 362, 478
Problem-solving strategies
Act It Out, 441–444, 519–522, 587–590
Draw a Diagram, 49–52, 113–116,
183–186, 265–268, 481–484, 627–630,
691–694
Make a List, 291–294
Make a Table, 351–354
Solve a Simpler Problem, 743–746
Products. *See also* Multiplication
estimating, 81–83, 99–102, 151–154
partial, 88, 99–101, 157–160, 163–166
Project, 2, 324, 546
Properties
Associative Property
of Addition, 39, 435–438
of Multiplication, 107–110, 145–148
Commutative Property
of Addition, 39, 435–438
of Multiplication, 63, 107–110, 171

Distributive Property, 87–90, 99–101,
108–109, 227–230, 718
Identity Property of Multiplication, 476

Quadrilaterals, 567–570
defined, 567
parallelogram, 567–570
rectangle, 567–570
rhombus, 567–570
square, 567–570
trapezoid, 567–570
Quart, 641, 659–662
Quarters, 513–516, 519–520
Quick pictures
to model division, 203–206, 248–250
to model multiplication, 75–78
Quotients, 210, 235–238. *See also* Division
estimating, 197–200, 221–224
partial, 241–244
placing the first digit, 253–256

Rays, 549–552
Reading
Connect to Reading, 84, 224
Read Math, 555, 685
Read/Solve the Problem, 49–50, 113–114,
183–184, 265–266, 291–292, 351–352,
441–442, 481–482, 519–520, 587–588,
627–628, 691–692, 743–744
Visualize It, 4, 62, 144, 196, 278, 326, 384,
454, 494, 548, 600, 640, 716
Real World
Problem Solving, In every Student Edition
lesson. Some examples are: 8, 45, 96,
148, 200, 237, 302, 348, 411, 437, 457,
498, 552, 603, 649, 699
Unlock the Problem, In every Student
Edition lesson. Some examples are: 11,
49–50, 93–94, 151–152, 209–210, 279,
345, 394, 429–430, 435–436, 441–442,
455–456, 495–496, 533, 549–550, 578,
647–648, 717–718
Reasonableness of an answer, 23, 43, 82, 93,
99, 119, 151–154, 163, 171, 221, 641

Table of Measures

METRIC

CUSTOMARY

Length

1 centimeter (cm) = 10 millimeters (mm)

1 meter (m) = 1,000 millimeters

1 meter = 100 centimeters

1 meter = 10 decimeters (dm)

1 kilometer (km) = 1,000 meters

1 foot (ft) = 12 inches (in.)

1 yard (yd) = 3 feet, or 36 inches

1 mile (mi) = 1,760 yards, or 5,280 feet

Capacity and Liquid Volume

1 liter (L) = 1,000 milliliters (mL)

1 cup (c) = 8 fluid ounces (fl oz)

1 pint (pt) = 2 cups

1 quart (qt) = 2 pints, or 4 cups

1 half gallon = 2 quarts

1 gallon (gal) = 2 half gallons, or 4 quarts

Mass/Weight

1 kilogram (kg) = 1,000 grams (g)

1 pound (lb) = 16 ounces (oz)

1 ton (T) = 2,000 pounds

TIME

1 minute (min) = 60 seconds (sec)

1 half hour = 30 minutes

1 hour (hr) = 60 minutes

1 day (d) = 24 hours

1 week (wk) = 7 days

1 year (yr) = 12 months (mo), or about 52 weeks

1 year = 365 days

1 leap year = 366 days

1 decade = 10 years

1 century = 100 years

MONEY

1 penny = 1¢, or $0.01

1 nickel = 5¢, or $0.05

1 dime = 10¢, or $0.10

1 quarter = 25¢, or $0.25

1 half dollar = 50¢, or $0.50

1 dollar = 100¢, or $1.00

SYMBOLS

$<$	is less than	$\perp$	is perpendicular to
$>$	is greater than	$\parallel$	is parallel to
$=$	is equal to	$\overleftrightarrow{AB}$	line AB
$\neq$	is not equal to	$\overrightarrow{AB}$	ray AB
¢	cent or cents	$\overline{AB}$	line segment AB
$	dollar or dollars	$\angle ABC$	angle ABC or angle B
°	degree or degrees	$\triangle ABC$	triangle ABC

FORMULAS

	Perimeter		Area
Polygon	$P = $ sum of the lengths of sides	Rectangle	$A = b \times h$
			$A = l \times w$
Rectangle	$P = (2 \times l) + (2 \times w)$ or $P = 2 \times (l + w)$		
Square	$P = 4 \times s$		